# Short Stories for Students

# Short Stories for Students

Presenting Analysis, Context and Criticism on Commonly Studied Short Stories

## Volume 2

Kathleen Wilson, *Editor*

Daphne Grabovoi, Silverado High School, *Advisor*
Katherine Nyberg, Farmington Hills School District, *Advisor*
Nancy Rosenberger, Conestoga High School, *Advisor*

Foreword by Nancy Rosenberger, Conestoga High School

DETROIT · NEW YORK · TORONTO · LONDON

# STAFF

Kathleen Wilson, *Editor*

Tim Akers, Pamela S. Dear, David M. Galens, Jeffrey W. Hunter, Dan Jones, John D. Jorgenson, Marie Lazzari, Jerry Moore, Deborah A. Stanley, Diane Telgen, Polly Vedder, Thomas Wiloch, *Contributing Editors*

Jeff Chapman, *Programmer/Analyst*

Greg Barnhisel, Stephan Dziemianowicz, Tim Engles, Mary Beth Folia, Christopher Giroux, Cynthia Hallett, Karen Holleran, Jennifer Hicks, Logan Hill, Heidi Johnson, Tamara Kendig, David Kippen, Maryanne Kocis, Rena Korb, Kim Long, Harvey Lynch, Thomas March, Carl Mowery, Robert Peltier, Elisabeth Piedmont-Marton, Trudy Ring, Judy Sobeloff, Michael Sonkowsky, Anne Trubek, Julianne White, Janet Witalec, *Contributing Writers*

Susan Trosky, *Permissions Manager*
Kim Smilay, *Permissions Specialist*
Sarah Chesney, *Permissions Associate*
Steve Cusack, Kelly A. Quin, *Permissions Assistants*

Victoria Cariappa, *Research Team Leader*
Michele LaMeau, Barbara McNeil, Maureen Richards, *Research Specialists*
Laura C. Bissey, Julia C. Daniel, Tamara C. Nott, Tracie Richardson,
Norma Sawaya, Cheryl L. Warnock, *Research Associates*

Mary Beth Trimper, *Production Director*
Shanna Heilveil, *Production Assistant*

Cynthia Baldwin, *Production Design Manager*
Pamela A. E. Galbreath, *Senior Art Director*

Barbara J. Yarrow, *Graphic Services Manager*
Pamela Reed, *Photography Coordinator*
Randy Bassett, *Image Database Supervisor*

---

Since this page cannot legibly accommodate all copyright notices, the acknowledgments constitute an extension of the copyright notice.

While every effort has been made to ensure the reliability of the information presented in this publication, Gale Research neither guarantees the accuracy of the data contained herein nor assumes any responsibility for errors, omissions or discrepancies. Gale accepts no payment for listing, and inclusion in the publication of any organization, agency, institution, publication, service, or individual does not imply endorsement of the editors or publisher. Errors brought to the attention of the publisher and verified to the satisfaction of the publisher will be corrected in future editions.

This publication is a creative work fully protected by all applicable copyright laws, as well as by misappropriation, trade secret, unfair competition, and other applicable laws. The authors and editors of this work have added value to the underlying factual material herein through one or more of the following: unique and original selection, coordination, expressions, arrangement, and classification of the information.

All rights to this publication will be vigorously defended.

Copyright © 1997
Gale Research
835 Penobscot Building
Detroit, MI 48226-4094

All rights reserved including the right of reproduction in whole or in part in any form.

---

This book is printed on acid-free paper that meets the minimum requirements
of American National Standard for Information Sciences-
Permanence Paper for Printed Library Materials, ANSI Z39.48-1984.

ISBN 0-7876-1691-5
ISSN 1092-7735

Printed in the United States of America.

10 9 8 7 6 5 4 3 2

# Table of Contents

**Guest Foreword**
"An Adventure in Reading"
by Nancy Rosenberger . . . . . . vii

**Introduction** . . . . . . . . . . ix

**Literary Chronology** . . . . . . xiii

**Acknowledgments** . . . . . . . xvii

**The Bear**
by William Faulkner . . . . . . . 1

**A Christmas Memory**
by Truman Capote . . . . . . . . 20

**Everyday Use**
by Alice Walker . . . . . . . . 36

**The Fall of the House of Usher**
by Edgar Allan Poe . . . . . . . 51

**The Gift of the Magi**
by O. Henry . . . . . . . . . . 67

**Gimpel the Fool**
by Isaac Bashevis Singer . . . . . 83

**A Good Man Is Hard to Find**
by Flannery O'Connor . . . . . . 97

**In the Cemetery Where Al Jolson Is Buried**
by Amy Hempel . . . . . . . . 115

## Table of Contents

**Miss Brill**
by Katherine Mansfield . . . . . . 132

**The Monkey's Paw**
by W. W. Jacobs . . . . . . . 146

**An Occurrence at Owl Creek Bridge**
by Ambrose Bierce . . . . . . 160

**The Ones Who Walk Away from Omelas**
by Ursula K. Le Guin . . . . . . 174

**Paul's Case**
by Willa Cather . . . . . . . . 192

**The Red-Headed League**
by Arthur Conan Doyle . . . . . 210

**The Rocking-Horse Winner**
by D. H. Lawrence . . . . . . . 230

**Sonny's Blues**
by James Baldwin . . . . . . . 245

**The Story of an Hour**
by Kate Chopin . . . . . . . . 263

**The Swimmer**
by John Cheever . . . . . . . 278

**The Train from Rhodesia**
by Nadine Gordimer . . . . . . 295

**A Worn Path**
by Eudora Welty . . . . . . . 312

**Glossary of Literary Terms** . . . 329
**Cumulative Author/Title Index** . 341
**Nationality/Ethnicity Index** . . 343
**Subject/Theme Index** . . . . . . 345

# An Adventure in Reading

Sitting on top of my desk is a Pueblo storytelling doll. Her legs stick straight out before her and around her neck and flowing down into her lap are wide-eyed children. Her mouth is open as though she were telling the Zuni tale of the young husband who followed his wife to the Land of the Dead, a story strangely like the Greek myth of Orpheus and Euridice, as both teach the dangers of youthful impatience.

Although the Pueblo doll was created in New Mexico, she symbolizes a universal human activity. The pharaohs listened intently to tales of the goddess Isis, who traveled to foreign lands to rescue the dismembered body of her husband Osiris. Biblical narratives thrill the reader with stories like that of mortal combat between David and the giant Goliath. Greek and Roman myths immortalize the struggles of the wandering warriors Odysseus and Aeneas. In the Middle Ages, kings, queens and courtiers sat spellbound in drafty halls as troubadours sang of tragic lovers and pious pilgrims.

Around the world and down through the ages, myths, folktales, and legends have spoken to us about the human condition and our place in the world of nature and of spirit. Despite its ancient beginnings, however, there is no rigid criteria to which a story must adhere. It is one of the most protean literary forms. Though many scholars credit the nineteenth-century Romantic writers Edgar Allan Poe and Nathaniel Hawthorne with creating the modern short story, the form refuses to be frozen by a list of essential characteristics. Perhaps this is one of the reasons William Faulkner called it the "most demanding form after poetry." Jack London felt it should be "concrete, to the point, with snap and go and life, crisp and crackling and interesting." Eudora Welty wrote that each story should reveal something new yet also contain something "as old as time."

Below are some of the qualities you may observe as you explore the works discussed in *Short Stories for Students*. These characteristics also demonstrate some of the ways the short story differs from the novel:

1. Because time is compressed or accelerated, **unity** in plot, character development, tone, or mood is essential.

2. The author has chosen to **focus** on one character, event, or conflict within a limited time.

3. Poe wrote that **careful craftsmanship** serves unity by ensuring that every word must contribute to the story's design.

4. Poe also believed that reading should take place in **one sitting** so that the story's unity is not lost.

5. A character is **revealed** through a series of incidents or a conflict. The short story generally stops when it has achieved this purpose. A novel **develops** a character throughout its many chapters.

Now that we have briefly explored the history of the short story and heard from a few of its creators, let us consider the role of the reader. Readers are not empty vessels that wait, lids raised, to receive a teacher's or a critic's interpretation. They bring their unique life experiences to the story. With these associations, the best readers also bring their attention (a word that means "leaning towards"), their reading skills, and, most importantly, their imagination to a reading of a story.

My students always challenged me to discuss, analyze, interpret, and evaluate the stories we read without destroying the thrill of being beamed up into another world. For years I grappled with one response after the other to this challenge. Then one day I read an article by a botanist who had explored the beauty of flowers by x-raying them. His illustrations showed the rose and the lily in their external beauty, and his x-rays presented the wonders of their construction. I brought the article to class, where we discussed the benefits of examining the internal design of flowers, relationships, current events, and short stories.

A short story, however, is not a fossil to admire. Readers must ask questions, guess at the answers, predict what will happen next, then read to discover. They and the author form a partnership that brings the story to life. Awareness of this partnership keeps the original excitement alive through discussion, analysis, interpretation, and evaluation. Literary explorations allow the reader to admire the authors' craftsmanship as well as their artistry. In fact, original appreciation may be enhanced by this x-ray vision. The final step is to appreciate once again the story in its entirety—to put the pieces back together.

Now it is your turn. Form a partnership with your author. During or following your adventure in reading, enter into a dialogue with the published scholars featured in *Short Stories for Students*. Through this dialogue with experts you will revise, enrich, and/or confirm your original observations and interpretations.

During this adventure, I hope you will feel the same awe that illuminates the faces of the listeners that surround the neck of my Pueblo storyteller.

*Nancy Rosenberger*
*Conestoga High School*
*Berwyn, Pennsylvania*

# Introduction

## Purpose of the Book

The purpose of *Short Stories for Students* (*SSfS*) is to provide readers with a guide to understanding, enjoying, and studying short stories by giving them easy access to information about the work. Part of Gale's "For Students" Literature line, *SSfS* is specifically designed to meet the curricular needs of high school and undergraduate college students and their teachers, as well as the interests of general readers and researchers considering specific short fiction. While each volume contains entries on "classic" stories frequently studied in classrooms, there are also entries containing hard-to-find information on contemporary stories, including works by multicultural, international, and women writers.

The information covered in each entry includes an introduction to the story and the story's author; a plot summary, to help readers unravel and understand the events in the work; descriptions of important characters, including explanation of a given character's role in the narrative as well as discussion about that character's relationship to other characters in the story; analysis of important themes in the story; and an explanation of important literary techniques and movements as they are demonstrated in the work.

In addition to this material, which helps the readers analyze the story itself, students are also provided with important information on the literary and historical background informing each work. This includes a historical context essay, a box comparing the time or place the story was written to modern Western culture, a critical overview essay, and excerpts from critical essays on the story or author. A unique feature of *SSfS* is a specially commissioned overview essay on each story by an academic expert, targeted toward the student reader.

To further aid the student in studying and enjoying each story, information on media adaptations is provided, as well as reading suggestions for works of fiction and nonfiction on similar themes and topics. Classroom aids include ideas for research papers and lists of critical sources that provide additional material on the work.

## Selection Criteria

The titles for each volume of *SSfS* were selected by surveying numerous sources on teaching literature and analyzing course curricula for various school districts. Some of the sources surveyed include: literature anthologies, *Reading Lists for College-Bound Students: The Books Most Recommended by America's Top Colleges; Teaching the Short Story: A Guide to Using Stories from Around the World*, by the National Council of Teachers of English (NTCE); and "A Study of High School Literature Anthologies," conducted by Arthur Applebee at the Center for the Learning and Teaching of Literature and sponsored by the National Endowment for the Arts and the Office of Educational Research and Improvement.

Input was also solicited from our expert advisory board, as well as educators from various areas. From these discussions, it was determined that each volume should have a mix of "classic" stories (those works commonly taught in literature classes) and contemporary stories for which information is often hard to find. Because of the interest in expanding the canon of literature, an emphasis was also placed on including works by international, multicultural, and women authors. Our advisory board members—current high-school teachers— helped pare down the list for each volume. Works not selected for the present volume were noted as possibilities for future volumes. As always, the editor welcomes suggestions for titles to be included in future volumes.

## How Each Entry Is Organized

Each entry, or chapter, in *SSfS* focuses on one story. Each entry heading lists the title of the story, the author's name, and the date of the story's publication. The following elements are contained in each entry:

- **Introduction:** a brief overview of the story which provides information about its first appearance, its literary standing, any controversies surrounding the work, and major conflicts or themes within the work.

- **Author Biography:** this section includes basic facts about the author's life, and focuses on events and times in the author's life that may have inspired the story in question.

- **Plot Summary:** a description of the events in the story, with interpretation of how these events help articulate the story's themes.

- **Characters:** an alphabetical listing of the characters who appear in the story. Each character name is followed by a brief to an extensive description of the character's role in the story, as well as discussion of the character's actions, relationships, and possible motivation.

  Characters are listed alphabetically by last name. If a character is unnamed—for instance, the narrator in "The Eatonville Anthology"—the character is listed as "The Narrator" and alphabetized as "Narrator." If a character's first name is the only one given, the name will appear alphabetically by that name.

- **Themes:** a thorough overview of how the topics, themes, and issues are addressed within the story. Each theme discussed appears in a separate subhead, and is easily accessed through the boldface entries in the Subject/Theme Index.

- **Style:** this section addresses important style elements of the story, such as setting, point of view, and narration; important literary devices used, such as imagery, foreshadowing, symbolism; and, if applicable, genres to which the work might have belonged, such as Gothicism or Romanticism. Literary terms are explained within the entry, but can also be found in the Glossary of Literary Terms.

- **Historical and Cultural Context:** This section outlines the social, political, and cultural climate *in which the author lived and the work was created*. This section may include descriptions of related historical events, pertinent aspects of daily life in the culture, and the artistic and literary sensibilities of the time in which the work was written. If the story is historical in nature, information regarding the time in which the story is set is also included. Long sections are broken down with helpful subheads.

- **Critical Overview:** this section provides background on the critical reputation of the author and the story, including bannings or any other public controversies surrounding the work. For older works, this section may include a history of how story was first received and how perceptions of it may have changed over the years; for more recent works, direct quotes from early reviews may also be included.

- **Sources:** an alphabetical list of critical material quoted in the entry, with bibliographical information.

- **For Further Study:** an alphabetical list of other critical sources which may prove useful for the student. Includes full bibliographical information and a brief annotation.

- **Criticism:** an essay commissioned by *SSfS* which specifically deals with the story and is written specifically for the student audience, as well as excerpts from previously published criticism on the work.

In addition, each entry contains the following highlighted sections, if applicable, set separate from the main text:

- **Media Adaptations:** where applicable, a list of film and television adaptations of the story, including source information. The list also includes stage adaptations, audio recordings, musical adaptations, etc.

- **Compare and Contrast Box:** an "at-a-glance" comparison of the cultural and historical differences between the author's time and culture and late twentieth-century Western culture. This box includes pertinent parallels between the major scientific, political, and cultural movements of the time or place the story was written, the time or place the story was set (if a historical work), and modern Western culture. Works written after the mid-1970s may not have this box.
- **What Do I Read Next?:** a list of works that might complement the featured story or serve as a contrast to it. This includes works by the same author and others, works of fiction and nonfiction, and works from various genres, cultures, and eras.
- **Study Questions:** a list of potential study questions or research topics dealing with the story. This section includes questions related to other disciplines the student may be studying, such as American history, world history, science, math, government, business, geography, economics, psychology, etc.

## *Other Features*

*SSfS* includes "An Adventure in Reading," a foreword by Nancy Rosenberger, chair of the English department at Conestoga High School in Berwyn, Pennsylvania. This essay provides an enlightening look at how readers interact with literature and how *Short Stories for Students* can help students enrich their own reading experiences.

A Cumulative Author/Title Index lists the authors and titles covered in each volume of the *SSfS* series.

A Cumulative Nationality/Ethnicity Index breaks down the authors and titles covered in each volume of the *SSfS* series by nationality and ethnicity.

A Subject/Theme Index, specific to each volume, provides easy reference for users who may be studying a particular subject or theme rather than a single work. Significant subjects from events to broad themes are included, and the entries pointing to the specific theme discussions in each entry are indicated in **boldface.**

Entries may include illustrations, including an author portrait, stills from film adaptations (when available), maps, and/or photos of key historical events.

## *Citing Short Stories for Students*

When writing papers, students who quote directly from any volume of *SSfS* may use the following general forms to document their source. These examples are based on MLA style; teachers may request that students adhere to a different style, thus, the following examples may be adapted as needed.

When citing text from *SSfS* that is not attributed to a particular author (for example, the Themes, Style, Historical Context sections, etc.) the following format may be used:

> "The Celebrated Jumping Frog of Calaveras County." *Short Stories for Students.* Ed. Kathleen Wilson. Vol. 1. Detroit: Gale, 1997. 19-20.

When quoting the specially commissioned essay from *SSfS* (usually the first essay under the Criticism subhead), the following format may be used:

> Korb, Rena. Essay on "Children of the Sea." *Short Stories for Students.* Ed. Kathleen Wilson. Vol. 1. Detroit: Gale, 1997. 42.

When quoting a journal essay that is reprinted in a volume of *Short Stories for Students,* the following form may be used:

> Schmidt, Paul. "The Deadpan on Simon Wheeler." *The Southwest Review* XLI, No. 3 (Summer, 1956), 270-77; excerpted and reprinted in *Short Stories for Students,* Vol. 1, ed. Kathleen Wilson (Detroit: Gale, 1997), pp. 29-31.

When quoting material from a book that is reprinted in a volume of *SSfS,* the following form may be used:

> Bell-Villada, Gene H. "The Master of Short Forms," in *Garcia Marquez: The Man and His Work* (University of North Caroline Press, 1990); excerpted and reprinted in *Short Stories for Students,* Vol. 1, ed. Kathleen Wilson (Detroit: Gale, 1997), pp. 90-1.

## *We Welcome Your Suggestions*

The editor of *Short Stories for Students* welcomes your comments and ideas. Readers who wish to suggest short stories to appear in future volumes, or who have other suggestions, are cordially invited to contact the editor. You may write to the editor at:

> Editor, *Short Stories for Students*
> Gale Research
> 835 Penobscot Bldg.
> 645 Griswold St.
> Detroit, MI 48226-4094

# Literary Chronology

**1776:** The signing of the Declaration of Independence signals the end of the American Revolution.

**1789:** The French Revolution, marked by the violent Reign of Terror, shifts the balance of power in France.

**1809:** Edgar Allan Poe is born in Boston, Massachusetts, on January 19.

**1839:** ''The Fall of the House of Usher'' by Edgar Allan Poe is published.

**1842:** Ambrose Bierce is born in Horse Cave Creek, Meigs County, Ohio, on June 24.

**1845:** *The Raven and Other Poems* by Edgar Allan Poe is published.

**1849:** Edgar Allan Poe dies under mysterious circumstances on October 7.

**1851:** Kate Chopin is born Katherine O'Flaherty, in St. Louis, Missouri, on February 8.

**1859:** Arthur Conan Doyle is born in Edinburgh, Scotland, on May, 22.

**1861:** The U.S. Civil War begins when Confederate forces capture Fort Sumter in South Carolina.

**1862:** O. Henry is born William Sydney Porter in Greensboro, North Carolina, on September 11.

**1863:** William Wymark Jacobs is born in London, England, on September 8.

**1865:** The U.S. Civil War ends; Abraham Lincoln is assassinated.

**1873:** Willa Cather is born December 7, in the village of Back Creek (now Gore), near Winchester, Virginia.

**1885:** D(avid) H(erbert) Lawrence is born in Nottinghamshire, England, on September 11.

**1888:** Katherine Mansfield is born Kathleen Mansfield Beauchamp in Wellington, New Zealand, on October 14.

**1891:** ''Occurrence at Owl Creek Bridge'' by Ambrose Bierce is published.

**1891:** ''The Red-Headed League'' by Arthur Conan Doyle is published.

**1894:** ''A Story of an Hour'' by Kate Chopin is published.

**1897:** William Faulkner is born in New Albany, Mississippi, on September 25.

**1899:** *The Awakening* by Kate Chopin is published.

**1902:** ''The Monkey's Paw'' by W. W. Jacobs is published.

**1904:** Isaac Bashevis Singer is born Icek-Hersz Zynger in Leoncin, Poland, on July 14.

**1904:** Kate Chopin dies on August, 22.

**1905:** ''Paul's Case'' by Willa Cather is published.

# Literary Chronology

**1906:** "The Gift of the Magi" by O. Henry is published.

**1909:** Eudora Welty is born in Jackson, Mississippi, on April 13.

**1910:** O. Henry dies on June 5.

**1912:** The *Titanic* sinks on her maiden voyage.

**1912:** John Cheever is born in Quincy, Massachusetts, on May, 27.

**1913:** *Sons and Lovers* by D. H. Lawrence is published, which becomes one of the author's most notorious works.

**1914:** With the assassination of Archduke Ferdinand of Austria, long-festering tensions in Europe erupt into the what becomes known as the Great War.

**1914:** Ambrose Bierce disappears in Mexico and is presumed dead.

**1918:** World War I, the most deadly war in history, ends with the signing of the Treaty of Versailles.

**1918:** Willa Cather's *My Antonia*, her novel about prairie life, is published.

**1920:** The 18th Amendment, outlawing the sale, manufacture, or transportation of alcohol—known as Prohibition—goes into effect. This law led to the creation of "speakeasies"—illegal bars—and an increase in organized crime, both reflected in F. Scott Fitzgerald's novel *The Great Gatsby*. Prohibition is eventually repealed in 1933.

**1922:** "Miss Brill" by Katherine Mansfield is published.

**1923:** Katherine Mansfield dies in France of tuberculosis on January 9.

**1923:** Nadine Gordimer is born in Springs, Transvaal, South Africa, on November 20.

**1924:** James Baldwin is born in New York City on August 2.

**1924:** Truman Capote is born Truman Streckfus Persons in New Orleans, Louisiana, on September 30.

**1925:** Flannery O'Connor is born Mary Flannery O'Connor in Savannah, Georgia, on March 25.

**1926:** "The Rocking-Horse Winner" by D. H. Lawrence is published.

**1929:** The stock market crash in October signals the beginning of a worldwide economic depression.

**1929:** Ursula K. Le Guin is born in Berkeley, California, on October 21.

**1929:** *The Sound and the Fury*, one of William Faulkner's most acclaimed novels, is published.

**1930:** D. H. Lawrence dies in France on March 2.

**1930:** Arthur Conan Doyle dies in England on July 7.

**1939:** World War II begins when Nazi Germany, led by Adolf Hitler, invades Poland; England and France declare war in response.

**1941:** "A Worn Path" by Eudora Welty is published.

**1942:** The longer version of "The Bear" by William Faulkner is published.

**1943:** W. W. Jacobs dies on September 1.

**1944:** Alice Walker is born in Eatonton, Georgia, on February 9.

**1945:** World War II ends in August with the atomic bombing of Hiroshima and Nagasaki, Japan.

**1947:** Willa Cather dies of a cerebral hemorrhage on April 24.

**1950:** Sen. Joseph McCarthy of Wisconsin sets off the "Red Scare" that leads to government hearings and blacklisting of suspected communists.

**1951:** Amy Hempel is born in Chicago, Illinois, on December 14.

**1952:** "The Train from Rhodesia" by Nadine Gordimer is published.

**1952:** *Wise Blood*, Flannery O'Connor's acclaimed novel of sin and redemption is published.

**1953:** "Gimpel the Fool," originally written in Yiddish by Isaac Bashevis Singer, is published in English.

**1953:** *Go Tell It on the Mountain*, James Baldwin's most celebrated novel, is published.

**1955:** "A Good Man Is Hard to Find" by Flannery O'Connor is published.

**1956:** "A Christmas Memory" by Truman Capote is first published.

**1957:** "Sonny's Blues" by James Baldwin is published.

**1962:** William Faulkner dies on July 6.

**1963:** President John F. Kennedy is assassinated in Dallas, Texas, on November 22.

**1964:** "The Swimmer" by John Cheever is published.

**1964:** Flannery O'Connor dies from complications of lupus in Georgia on August 3.

**1966:** *In Cold Blood,* Truman Capote's true-crime novel is published.

**1969:** Neil Armstrong becomes the first person to walk on the moon on July 21.

**1969:** *The Left Hand of Darkness* is published by Ursula K. Le Guin.

**1972:** President Nixon resigns following the Watergate scandal.

**1973:** "The Ones Who Walk Away from Omelas" by Ursula K. Le Guin is published.

**1973:** "Everyday Use" by Alice Walker is published.

**1982:** John Cheever dies of cancer on June 18.

**1982:** *The Color Purple* by Alice Walker, her most acclaimed work, is published.

**1983:** "In the Cemetery Where Al Jolson Is Buried" by Amy Hempel is published.

**1984:** Truman Capote dies in Los Angeles, California, on August 25.

**1987:** James Baldwin dies of stomach cancer November 30.

**1990:** Soviet leader Mikhail Gorbachev's policy of *glasnost* results in the fracturing of the Iron Curtain. By December the Soviet flag is lowered from the Kremlin.

**1991:** Isaac Bashevis Singer dies on July 24.

# Acknowledgments

The editors wish to thank the copyright holders of the excerpted criticism included in this volume and the permissions managers of many book and magazine publishing companies for assisting us in securing reproduction rights. We are also grateful to the staffs of the Detroit Public Library, the Library of Congress, the University of Detroit Mercy Library, Wayne State University Purdy/Kresge Library Complex, and the University of Michigan Libraries for making their resources available to us. Following is a list of the copyright holders who have granted us permission to reproduce material in this volume of *SSFS*. Every effort has been made to trace copyright, but if omissions have been made, please let us know.

**COPYRIGHTED EXCERPTS IN *SSFS*, VOLUME 2, WERE REPRODUCED FROM THE FOLLOWING PERIODICALS:**

*American Literature,* v. XXXV, January, 1964. Copyright © 1964 Duke University Press, Durham, NC. Reproduced with permission.—*The Baker Street Journal,* n. s. v. 29, September, 1969 for "Sherlock Holmes: Victorian Archetype" by Gordon L. Iseminger. © copyright 1969 by The Baker Street Irregulars. All rights reserved. Reproduced by permission of the author.—*The CEA Critic,* v. XXIX, March, 1967. Copyright © 1967 by the College English Association, Inc. Reproduced by permission.—*Classical and Modern Literature,* v. 10, Summer, 1990. © 1990 CML, Inc. Reproduced by permission.—*College English,* v. 27, December, 1965 for Faulkner's Poetic Prose: Style and Meaning in 'The Bear' " by Richard Lehan. Copyright © 1965 by the National Council of Teachers of English. Reproduced by permission of the publisher and the author.—*College Literature,* v. VII, Spring, 1980. Copyright © 1980 by West Chester University. Reproduced by permission.—*Commonweal,* v. CXII, September 20, 1985. Copyright © 1985 Commonweal Foundation. Reproduced by permission of Commonweal Foundation.—*Critical Inquiry,* v. 1, September, 1974 for "Artist's on Criticism of Their Art: 'Is Phoenix Jackson's Grandson Really Dead?'"by Eudora Welty. Copyright © 1974 by The University of Chicago. Copyright © 1974 Eudora Welty. Reproduced by permission of Russell & Volkening as agents for the author. British Commonwealth text rights by Little Brown & Company (UK) Ltd.—*English Journal,* v. 62, April, 1973 for "'A Worn Path': Immortality of Stereotype" by Dan Donlan. Copyright © 1973 by the National Council of Teachers of English. Reproduced by permission of the publisher and the author.—*English Language Notes,* v. XXVI, December, 1991. Copyright © 1991, Regents of the University of Colorado. Reproduced by permission.—*The Explicator,* v. 43, Fall, 1984 for "Bierce's 'An Occurrence at Owl Creek Bridge'" by George Cheatham and Judy Cheatham. Copyright 1984 by Helen Dwight Reid Educational Foundation. Reproduced by permission of the authors./

v. 45, Fall, 1986; v. 51, Winter, 1993. Copyright 1986, 1993 by the Helen Dwight Reid Educational Foundation. Both reproduced with permission of the Helen Dwight Reid Educational Foundation, published by Heldref Publications, 1319 18th Street, NW, Washington, DC 20036-1802.—*The Markham Review,* n.11, Winter, 1982. © Wagner College 1982. Reproduced by permission.—*The Missouri Review,* v. 16, 1993. Copyright © 1991 by The Curators of the University of Missouri. Reprinted by permission of the publisher and the American Audio Prose Library, Inc. Copyright © 1992 by The American Audio Prose Library, Inc. This is a print version of an interview which is available on audio cassette. For a free catalog write AAPL, P.O. Box 842, Columbia, MO 65205 or call (800) 447-2275.—*Modern Fiction Studies,* v. 36, Spring, 1990. Copyright © 1990 by The Johns Hopkins University Press. All rights reserved. Reproduced by permission of The Johns Hopkins University Press.—*Negro American Literature Forum,* v. 8, Fall, 1974 for "James Baldwin's Sonny Blues: A Message in Music" by Suzy Berstein Goldman. Copyright © Indiana State University 1974. Reproduced with the permission of *Black American Literature Forum* and the author.—*The New York Times Book Review,* April 28, 1985. Copyright © 1985 by The New York Times Company. Reproduced by permission.—*The Sewanee Review,* v. LXXI, 1963. © 1963, renewed 1991 by The University of the South. Reproduced with the permission of the editor of *The Sewanee Review* and the author.—*Southern Humanities Review,* v. VII, Summer, 1973. Copyright 1973 by Auburn University. Reproduced by permission.—*The Southern Review,* Louisiana State University, v. 21, July, 1985 for "Patches: Quilts and Community in Alice Walker's 'Everyday Use' " by Houston A. Baker, Jr. and Charlotte Pierce-Baker. Copyright, 1985, by the author. Reproduced by permission of the authors.—*Studies in American Fiction,* v. 18, Spring, 1990. Copyright © 1990 Northeastern University. Reproduced by permission.—*Studies in Short Fiction,* v. V, Fall, 1967; v. VI, Fall, 1969; v. 20, Spring-Summer, 1983; v. 23, Summer, 1986; v. 24, Fall, 1987; v. 27, Fall, 1990; v. 30, Summer, 1993. Copyright 1967, 1969, 1983, 1986, 1987, 1990, 1993 by Newberry College. All reproduced by permission. / v. II, Fall, 1964. Copyright 1964, renewed 1992 by Newberry College. Reproduced by permission.—*The University of Mississippi Studies in English,* n.s. v. IX, 1991. Copyright © 1991 The University of Mississippi. Reproduced by permission.

**COPYRIGHTED EXCERPTS IN *SSFS,* VOLUME 2, WERE REPRODUCED FROM THE FOLLOWING BOOKS:**

Blansfield, Karen Charmaine. From *Cheap Rooms and Restless Hearts: A Study of Formula in the Urban Tales of William Sydney Porter.* Bowling Green State University Popular Press, 1988. Copyright © 1988 by Bowling Green State University Popular Press. Reproduced by permission.—Carroll, David.—Ewell, Barbara C. From *Kate Chopin.* Ungar, 1986. Copyright © 1986 by The Ungar Publishing Company. Reproduced by permission.—Garson, Helen S. From *Truman Capote.* Ungar, 1980. Copyright © 1980 by Frederick Ungar Publishing Co., Inc. Reproduced by permission.—Gordimer, Nadine. From *Selected Stories.* J. Cape, 1975; The Viking Press, 1976. Copyright 1952, © 1956, 1957, 1959, 1960, 1961, 1964, 1965, 1968, 1969, 1971, 1975 by Nadine Gordimer. All rights reserved. Reproduced by permission by Nadine Gordimer. In North America and the Philippines by permission of Viking Penguin, a division of Penguin Books USA Inc. In the British Commonwealth by Random House UK Limited.—Hanson, Clare, and Andrew Gurr. From *Katherine Mansfield.* St. Martin's Press, 1981. Copyright © Clare Hanson and Andrew Gurr 1981. All rights reserved. Reproduced by permission of Macmillan Administration (Basingstoke) Ltd. In North America with the permission of St. Martin's Press, Incorporated.—Kazin, Alfred. From *Contemporaries.* Little, Brown and Company, 1962. Copyright © 1962 by Alfred Kazin. Reproduced by permission of the author.—Nance, William L. From *The Worlds of Truman Capote.* Stein and Day, 1970. Copyright © 1970 by William L. Nance. All rights reserved. Reproduced with permission of Stein and Day Publishers.—Papke, Mary E. From *Verging on the Abyss: The Social Fiction of Kate Chopin and Edith Wharton.* Contribution to Women's Studies, No. 119. Greenwood Press, 1990. Copyright © 1990 by Mary E. Papke. All rights reserved. Reproduced by permission of Greenwood Publishing Group, Inc., Westport, CT.—Perluck, Herbert A. From " 'The Bear': An Unromantic Reading," in *Religious Perspectives in Faulkner's Fiction: Yoknapatawpha and Beyond.* Edited by J. Robert Barth, S. J. University of Notre Dame Press, 1972. Copyright © 1972 by University of Notre Dame Press; Notre Dame, IN 46556. Reproduced by permission of the publisher.—Siegel, Paul N. From "Gimpel and the Archetype of the Wise Fool," in *The Achievement of Isaac Bashevis Singer.* Edited by Marcia Allentuck. Southern Illinois University Press, 1969. Copyright © 1969, Southern Illinois University Press. All rights reserved. Reproduced by permission.

**PHOTOGRAPHS AND ILLUSTRATIONS APPEARING IN *SSFS*, VOLUME 2, WERE RECEIVED FROM THE FOLLOWING SOURCES:**

An illustration by Beth Peck in *A Christmas Memory.* By Truman Capote. Knopf, 1986. Illustrations copyright © 1989 by Beth Peck. All rights reserved. Reproduced by permission of Alfred A. Knopf, Inc. From the cover of *A Good Man Is Hard to Find.* By Flannery O'Connor. New American Library, 1956. Copyright © 1956 by Flannery O'Connor. Used by permission of Dutton Signet, a division of Penguin Books USA Inc. Engraving by Fritz Eichenberg. From *Tales of Edgar Allan Poe.* By Edgar Allan Poe. Random House, 1944. Copyright, 1944, by Random House, Inc. Reproduced by permission. Al Jolson's memorial shrine, photograph. UPI/Corbis-Bettmann. Reproduced by permission. *An Occurrence at Owl Creek Bridge,* 1961, movie still. The Kobal Collection. Reproduced by permission. Apollo Theater, photograph. Corbis-Bettmann. Reproduced by permission. Baldwin, James, photograph. The Granger Collection, New York. Reproduced by permission. Bierce, Ambrose, photograph. Corbis-Bettmann. Reproduced by permission. Brooks, Clive, in his role as Sherlock Holmes, photograph. Corbis-Bettmann. Reproduced by permission. Capote, Truman, photograph by Carl Van Vechten. The Library of Congress. Cather, Willa, photograph by Carl Van Vechten. The Library of Congress. Cheever, John, photograph. © Jerry Bauer. Reproduced by permission. Chopin, Kate, photograph. Missouri Historical Society. Reproduced by permission. New Orleans courtyard, photograph. Corbis-Bettmann. Reproduced by permission. *O. Henry's Full House,* movie still. 20th Century Fox. Courtesy of the Kobal Collection. Reproduced by permission. Doyle, Arthur Conan, photograph. UPI/Corbis-Bettmann. Reproduced by permission. *The Rocking-Horse Winner,* movie still. Corbis-Bettmann. Reproduced by permission.

Faulkner, William, photograph by Carl Van Vechten. The Library of Congress. Gordimer, Nadine, photograph. © Jerry Bauer. Reproduced by permission. Hempel, Amy, photograph. © Thomas Victor 1986. All rights reserved. Reproduced by permission of the estate of Thomas Victor. Henry, O., photograph. AP/Wide World Photos. Reproduced by permission. Jacobs, W. W., painting. The Granger Collection, New York. Reproduced by permission. *The Swimmer,* movie still. Corbis-Bettmann. Reproduced by permission. Lawrence, D. H., photograph. AP/Wide World Photos. Reproduced by permission. LeGuin, Ursula K, photograph. UPI/Corbis-Bettmann. Reproduced by permission. Mansfield, Katherine, photograph. Corbis-Bettmann. Reproduced by permission. Mano Tribe Mask, photograph. Corbis-Bettmann. Reproduced by permission. *The Monkey's Paw,* photograph. Corbis-Bettmann. Reproduced by permission. *The Nightmare,* painting. Corbis-Bettmann. Reproduced by permission. O'Connor, Flannery, photograph. Corbis-Bettmann. Reproduced by permission. Owens, Catherine Dale, photograph. Corbis-Bettmann. Reproduced by permission. Porter, Katherine Anne, photograph. AP/Wide World Photos. Reproduced by permission. *The House of Usher,* photograph. Corbis-Bettmann. Reproduced by permission. Singer, Isaac Bashevis, photograph. Corbis-Bettmann. Reproduced by permission. Waldorf-Astoria, photograph. Corbis-Bettmann. Reproduced by permission. Walker, Alice, photograph. AP/Wide World Photos. Reproduced by permission. Welty, Eudora, photograph. AP/Wide World Photos. Reproduced by permission.

# The Bear

**William Faulkner**
**1942**

Although several versions of "The Bear" exist, the one most commonly read comes from William Faulkner's 1942 novel, *Go Down, Moses*. Isaac (Ike) McCaslin, the young hero of "The Bear," remains a central figure throughout the novel as well. The story of a young man's development against a background of vanishing wilderness was well received by readers and critics alike. Today it appears in many anthologies. Faulkner did not add the long fourth section of the story until it appeared in *Go Down, Moses,* and he argued that its primary role was to connect the story to the rest of the novel. If read alone, the fourth section of "The Bear" should be omitted. Yet the fourth section puts into context the relationships and events that contributed to young Ike's upbringing in the woods. It is learned that Major deSpain and Colonel Compson received their commissions in the Civil War, an historical event of resounding importance. In addition, Ike's decisions in the fourth section are primarily due to the lessons he has learned in the wilderness. Thus the fourth section shows how he translates the morality of the woods into social responsibility. Whether read alone or as part of the longer novel in which it eventually appeared, "The Bear" provides a unique glimpse into the Mississippi region where Faulkner, himself an avid hunter, was born and raised. As Ike McCaslin learns about his family's past, Faulkner portrays a varied cast of characters in a tale about the wilderness destroyed by human greed and a man who refuses to further this destructive trend.

## Author Biography

Born on September 25, 1897, William Faulkner belonged to a once-wealthy family of former plantation owners. Raised among a circle of acquaintances similar to General Compson and Major deSpain, Faulkner knew first-hand about life in the South after the Civil War. His fictional Yoknapatawpha County, and its county seat, Jefferson, represent the actual Lafayette County and the city of Oxford, Mississippi, where Faulkner lived most of his life. Although Faulkner dropped out of high school and never finished college, he was a passionate fan of poetry and originally planned to become a poet. He worked for a brief period as a bank clerk before being accepted into the Royal Canadian Air Force during World War I, although he never saw combat action.

After working in a New York bookstore and as the university postmaster at the University of Mississippi, Faulkner began publishing stories and poems. His novel *The Sound and the Fury* brought him to the attention of several critics. Once he realized his talent for fiction writing, Faulkner became a prolific writer, publishing almost twenty novels and several short stories in addition to two volumes of poetry. He also wrote screenplays, essays, and newspaper articles. In his later years, Faulkner traveled widely, giving lectures at American colleges as well as in other countries. He won two Pulitzer Prizes for fiction and a National Book Award. He died on July 6, 1962.

Much of Faulkner's work concerns the decline of Southern life in the aftermath of the Civil War. Once perceived to be a gracious, genteel society, the South as portrayed by Faulkner consists largely of impoverished descendants of former plantation families eking out a living alongside sharecroppers of African-American descent as well as those farmers who had never been affluent. Although these rural areas may seem isolated from world events such as wars and economic depression, Faulkner's works often mirror outside struggle within his fictional county. "The Bear," for example, creates a sense of disillusionment and grief at the decline of natural man in the face of man-made "progress." The story examines how modern society, with its advanced warfare techniques and increasingly mechanized workforce, threatens to destroy man and nature for good.

Another issue of great concern for Faulkner was the ongoing racism that continued to plague the South. Faulkner hated slavery and the social problems that remained in spite of emancipation, and his works often reflect his ongoing concern. Ike McCaslin shares Faulkner's horror at the idea of slavery. He rejects his inheritance in an attempt to escape his connection to this history.

As a writer of the early part of the twentieth century, Faulkner became an influential figure during the modernist period, a movement characterized by experimental forms of fiction such as interior monologue, multiple narrators, and shifts in narrative time. Each of these characteristics can be found in "The Bear," particularly in section four, which Faulkner labored over for several years after completing the first portion of the hunting story.

## Plot Summary

"The Bear" immediately introduces readers to numerous time periods simultaneously. "There was a man and a dog too this time," Faulkner writes, and readers are alerted that at least two time periods are being described in the narrative. The story follows sixteen-year-old Ike McCaslin as he embarks upon his sixth year of an annual hunting trip and the experiences he undergoes during his two weeks in the hunting camp. The narrative weaves between a number of years in Ike's life, from his first hunting trip at age ten to the current year. As Ike ages, the elements of the trip that remain constant are the men he travels with—Major de Spain (owner of the land on which they hunt), General Compson, McCaslin Edmonds, Uncle Ash, Sam Fathers, Boon Hogganbeck, and Walter Ewell—and Old Ben, the "big old bear with one trap-ruined foot" whom the hunters track. After this initial setting of scene, the narration returns to Ike's first hunting trip, where Sam Fathers teaches Ike the code of the wilderness. In one exercise, Sam forces Ike to watch game animals pass in front of him without shooting. Ike gradually learns more about the wilderness in the rest of the first section. One day when he ranges through the woods without a gun, a watch, or a compass, he finally catches a glimpse of Old Ben.

The second section of this story begins three years later. Ike is thirteen and has now killed his first buck and his first bear. "By now, he was a better woodsman than most grown men," according to the narrative. During the hunting trip described in this section, the hunters lose one of their colts to a wild animal. General Compson is sure that the predator is a panther, but Sam Fathers—acknowledged as the most skilled woodsman of the group—is unsure of this. The party traps the animal only to find that it is a "fyce," a wild mongrel dog. Sam decides to keep the dog, whom he names "Lion," in order to help the party corner and kill Old Ben. In November of the next year, Lion tracks the bear down. General Compson shoots the bear and draws blood, but Ben escapes.

The third section of the story takes place the following year, in December of 1883. The weather is too unforgiving to hunt, so the men spend their time in the cabin drinking and gambling. When the whisky runs low, the men send Boon and Ike to Memphis to get more. While in Memphis, Boon and Ike stand out among the city folk because of their dirty hunting clothes. Boon, especially, looks like a wild man, and in the space of fourteen hours he gets drunk twice. The next morning, General Compson decides that Ike will ride the mule the next day because of Ike's superior skill—the mule, unlike the horses, will not bolt at the sight of the bear. Lion tracks the bear and corners him; the bear fights back, and Boon leaps upon its back and stabs it to death. As the hunting party surveys the aftermath of the battle, they find that not only Lion, but Sam as well, are in grave condition, and both soon die. As the chapter closes, Edmonds confronts Boon about Sam, wondering if Boon has had some part in Sam's death.

The fourth section recounts Ike's learning about his family's history. He and Edmonds, who has raised Ike since his father died, discuss their common ancestor Carothers McCaslin. Studying the family's business documents in their commissary, Ike discovers that Carothers not only was his own grandfather, but also fathered a daughter, Tomasina, with his slave Eunice. Unacknowledged in the documents but obvious by context is the fact that Carothers also fathered another son, Terrell, by his own daughter Tomasina. Moving backwards and forwards in time, the narrative describes Ike's efforts to track down Terrell's children—his own second cousins, as closely related to him as Edmonds—and give them the thousand-dollar legacy left to them by Carothers' will. He fails to find one of them (Tennie's Jim) in Tennessee, but does find another, Fonsiba, in Midnight, Arkansas, where she has settled with her black Union Army veteran husband. Ike sets up a three-dollar-a-month pension for Fonsiba out of the legacy and returns to Mississippi. Thinking about the history bequeathed to him by his planta-

*William Faulkner*

tion-owner grandfather, and disgusted by what he sees as his grandfather's crimes, Ike finally, at age twenty-one, declines to inherit the land left to him in his father's will. He thinks about the degraded life of the plantation owner and the pure life of the hunter and chooses the latter. As the section ends, Ike finds out that he does not even have the silver cup full of gold pieces that had been promised him; his uncle Hubert Beauchamp borrowed all of the pieces from the cup and then substituted the cup itself for a coffee-pot, leaving Ike with nothing but I.O.U.'s. His wife, introduced at the very close of the chapter, hopes for Ike to reclaim his inheritance. When Ike refuses to do so, she turns her back to him, symbolic of the chaste marriage which they will then have.

In the final section, Ike returns to Major de Spain's land one more time. The Major has leased a section of the land to a lumber company, and the primeval wilderness that gave Ike his most important education will soon be gone. As the story ends, Ike meets Boon, the killer of Old Ben and the symbol of man's disrupted relationship with nature, under a gum tree. Boon is "hammering furiously at something in his lap" that turns out to be the disassembled components of his gun.

# Characters

### Ash

Ash is an African-American servant to Major deSpain. He is described in womanly terms and is relegated to tending to camp. After Ike kills his first buck, Ash airs his resentment at not being allowed to hunt. When Major deSpain allows him to go out the next day, Ash shows himself to be an untrained and inept hunter.

### Hub Beauchamp

*See* Hubert Beauchamp

### Hubert Beauchamp

Hubert Beauchamp is Ike's uncle. Hubert promised Ike a silver cup full of gold coins as an inheritance; however, he gradually replaced the coins and then the cup with IOU's. Ike rejects his own inheritance on the assumption that the gift from Uncle Hubert would be enough to live on. The worthless inheritance epitomizes the fruitless expectations of many Southern plantation families, most of whom lost their family fortunes in the Civil War.

### Uncle Buck

*See* Theophilus McCaslin

### Uncle Buddy

*See* Amodeus McCaslin

### Cass

*See* McCaslin Edmonds

### General Compson

General Compson is a close friend of the McCaslin's and Major deSpain. Compson respects Ike for his woodsmanship and gives him his compass and his silver hunting horn. He also offers to house Ike after Ike leaves the family farm.

### Major deSpain

Major deSpain owns the land on which the men hunt. A former officer in the Civil War, Major deSpain now works in a bank and eventually sells off most of the hunting grounds to a logging company.

### McCaslin Edmonds

Cousin and guardian of Ike McCaslin, Cass attempts to convince his ward to accept his inheritance. Their complex dialog in part four of the story indicates that he and Ike do share a special bond that allows them to anticipate each other's thoughts, though he is nowhere as near to Ike as is Sam Fathers. While he understands Ike's position in regard to the family's history, Cass views events with a more practical eye. He acknowledges the scandalous role his family has played in Southern history, but is content to let go the burdens of his past.

### Sam Fathers

Sam Fathers is part Native American and part African American. Descendant of a Chickasaw chief named Ikkemotubbe, Sam teaches Isaac McCaslin to hunt the former lands of his ancestors. He is struck down mysteriously when Old Ben dies and shortly thereafter asks Boon to kill him and bury him according to Chickasaw tradition. It is Sam Fathers's love of the land and respect for the hunt that make him an important role model for young Ike. Because he is the descendent of both chiefs and slaves, Sam represents a unique aspect of the human condition; his nobility is checked by the servile role he is given in society.

### Fonsiba

A descendant of Carothers McCaslin through her father, Terrel, Fonsiba is entitled to a one-thousand dollar inheritance. She is also a product of his incest with her grandmother, Tomey.

### Boon Hogganbeck

Like Sam Fathers in that he is part Native American, Boon possesses none of Sam' nobility, intelligence or hunting skill. Instead, Boon relies on brute strength to kill Old Ben.

### Uncle Hubert

*See* Hubert Beauchamp

### Ike

*See* Isaac McCaslin

### Uncle Ike

*See* Isaac McCaslin

### Lion

First captured and subdued by Sam Fathers, Lion is a fearless mongrel hunting dog. Ike and the others know that only Lion is capable of baying an animal as strong and as smart as Old Ben. In finally doing so, Lion inadvertently ends the hunting trips.

### Amodeus McCaslin

Ike first learns of his grandfather's sins through a farm ledger in which Uncle Buddy insists that the slave Eunice drowned herself. Uncle Buddy, a lifelong bachelor, cooked and did the housekeeping for himself and his brother Buck until Buck's marriage to Sophonsiba and their subsequent move back into the big house.

### Carothers McCaslin

Ike's grandfather, Carothers McCaslin, owned a plantation and several slaves. His most important actions as they affect Ike are his adulterous relationship with his slave, Eunice, and his incestuous relationship with their daughter, Tomasina. It is Carothers's role in the family's history, and in the history of the South, to which Ike objects.

### Isaac McCaslin

Isaac McCaslin, also known as Ike and Uncle Ike, is the central figure of "The Bear" as well as the larger work, *Go Down, Moses*. The son of Uncle Buck McCaslin and Sophonsiba Beauchamp McCaslin, Ike is the sole heir to the McCaslin plantation. Orphaned at an early age, Ike is raised primarily by his cousin, McCaslin "Cass" Edmonds. Nevertheless, he considers the part Native-American, part African-American Sam Fathers his "spiritual father." Ike identifies strongly with Sam, whose woodsmanship and hunting skill he eagerly learns. Because of the lessons he learns from Sam Fathers in the woods, Ike chooses to reject his tainted inheritance and live instead the purer life of a carpenter. His business-minded cousin, McCaslin, tries to dissuade him, but Ike will not change his mind. His stubbornness, however, accomplishes little in the way of social progress; his own material deprivation is his longest-lasting achievement. For Ike, that is enough.

### Sophonsiba Beauchamp McCaslin

As Buck's wife and Ike's mother, Sophonsiba tries valiantly to maintain her brother's estate as well as restore her husband's plantation. Her at-

## Media Adaptations

- "The Bear" was made into a motion picture by Frank Stokes in 1972, although the adaptation does not include section four of the story. It can be found on videocassette, distributed by AIMS Media.

- A 1980 motion picture of "The Bear" was filmed by Encyclopaedia Britannica Educational Corporation. This version does not include section four of the story. Available on videocassette.

- Barr Films published a similar video in 1981, again focusing on the work as a hunting story.

- A reel-to-reel version was written and produced by Bernard Wilets in 1980 and distributed by BFA Educational Media.

- There is a cassette tape of many of Faulkner's stories. The cassette is published as *The Stories of William Faulkner, Parts I and II,* read by Wolfram Kandinsky and Michael Kramer, Books on Tape, 1994.

tempts to preserve delusions of grandeur contrast with the McCaslins' lack of concern for elegant appearances.

### Theophilus McCaslin

Ike's father, Uncle Buck, lost a card game to Hubert Beauchamp and as a result had to marry Hubert's spinster sister, Sophonsiba. Ike is their only child. Along with his twin brother, Uncle Buddy, Uncle Buck lives in a log cabin on the family's plantation and allows his slaves to live in the plantation house. After their marriage, Sophonsiba urges him to restore the house for their own use.

### Old Ben

Old Ben, a bear who has eluded pursuers for years, is hunted every year by the hunting club on the final day of their trip. Boon Hogganbeck, with the help of Lion, finally kills him. His death symbolizes the death of the wilderness itself due to the encroachment of civilization and progress. Once he is dead, the group of hunters stop returning to the area.

### Tomasina

Daughter of the slave Eunice and Carothers McCaslin, Tomey also bears her father a child, the son named Turl (Terrel).

### Tomey

See Tomasina

### Tomy

See Tomasina

# Themes

### Rites of Passage

"The Bear" describes several important rites of passage for Ike McCaslin. The first rites of passage that readers encounter are the hunting rituals marking the various stages of his growth as a hunter. His first hunting trip at age ten, killing his first deer at age twelve, and other important landmarks in his hunting experience are described in the narrative. Ike is well acquainted with the normal progression of the hunter's apprenticeship, and is able to anticipate his experiences before they occur: "It seemed to him that at the age of ten he was witnessing his own birth. It was not even strange to him. He had experienced it all before, and not merely in dreams." Ike is prepared to follow the procedures of his apprenticeship: taking the worst hunting stand on his first trip; Sam marking his face and hands with blood after he kills his first deer; and the long evenings of storytelling. Camping and hunting with the men is itself an important right of passage, an ancient tradition of teaching and camaraderie that links men through stories of great hunters and legendary kills. Rites of passage preserve cultures for the next generation, and Ike's experiences place him at the end of a long line of skillful woodsmen. Much of Ike's apprenticeship seems to come from nature itself. The bear teaches the boy about the woods as much as Sam Fathers does. The death of Old Ben becomes a sort of graduation ceremony for Ike, indicating the end of this important period of learning in Ike's life. After he returns home, Ike tries to apply his respect for the land and the life it upholds to the world in which he lives. He discovers that his training in the woods does not help him function in society; those lessons prove useless when it comes to dealing with his family history. Rather than forsake his mentors, Sam Fathers and Old Ben, Ike chooses to distance himself from the role his family has left for him in an attempt to emulate the "purer" life of a woodsman.

### Race and Slavery

Like many of Faulkner's works, "The Bear" confronts issues of race and slavery directly. Ike's sense of personal responsibility forces him to evaluate not only his own actions but also those of his family. More than anything, the chronicle of slavery found in the commissary ledgers convinces Ike that he must make amends for his family's past. Yet Faulkner does not leave readers with the impression that the social evils of slavery and racism can be righted in any simple way. Ike's attempts to find Eunice's descendants indicates that the struggle is lengthy and complicated. Even the restitution Ike offers is tainted by slavery. Furthermore, Ike makes no attempt to claim them as his kin, suggesting the preservation of racial divisions. Race remains an important part of Sam Fathers's identity as well. Although Sam is highly respected as a hunter and a woodsman, his plight is that of any other freed slave: "For seventy years he had had to be a negro." Sam's situation indicates the degree to which being even part African American determines one's role on the bottom rung of society. The irony of Sam's situation is mentioned throughout the story, and perhaps most notably in the fourth section, where Ike tells McCaslin that Sam's teachings are what enable him to reject his birthright—the land that is also Sam's birthright. In this section Ike's past runs together in a fragmented narrative style that serves to represent his thoughts as they occur in his mind. Ike's thoughts focus on Sam's mixed bloodlines and on his prior ownership of the land. The stream-of-consciousness narrative presented here reflects the complicated relationships between the native Indian race, the Arican—American slaves, and the white race. In this moment of self-examination Ike feels that the land is no longer rightfully his. His feelings about both the taking of land from the Indians and about slavery cause him to ultimately reject his birthright.

## Style

### Point of View

While "The Bear" is a third-person narrative, it is told from the point of view of Ike McCaslin. Yet not all that Ike knows is told. For example, neither Ike nor the narrator ever actually confirms that Boon killed Sam. McCaslin makes this assumption, and Ike, the only witness, lets his statement remain uncontested. Even more complicated are the conjectures of Ike and McCaslin about Eunice's suicide. It is here that the narrator is demonstrated to be not omniscient (all-knowing), but a more limited, and experimental, version of the traditional third-person narrator.

### Setting

Set in Faulkner's fictitious Yoknapatawpha County, Mississippi, "The Bear" covers different time periods during Ike McCaslin's youth. Although the first section begins while Ike is age sixteen, most of the section covers Ike's first hunting trips during the fall of 1877 and the summer of 1878. The second section details events of 1879 (Lion's capture) and then two years later (when he nearly bayed Old Ben). Old Ben's death the following year is the subject of the third section. Section four moves from the pre-war days of Carothers McCaslin and forward, through Ike's relinquishing of his estate, to his childless marriage and austere life. The narrative of this fourth section is molded into a fairly understandable order by the events of Eunice's life. A slave bought in 1807, Eunice gives birth to Tomey in 1810 and commits suicide in 1832. Chapter five moves backward in time to Ike's final trip to the hunting camp in 1882.

### Symbolism

The most prominent symbol in "The Bear" is, of course, Old Ben. Symbolizing the natural world of which he is a part, Old Ben, by dying, also

## Topics for Further Study

- Investigate the Native American Chickasaw tribe to determine their original tribal grounds. What happened to the Chickasaws? Is there a tribal community still in the area today?

- Find out what was on the site of your town or city before the present community was established. Was it a wilderness area? Were there any aboriginal tribes living there? Who first settled the area?

- Research the wildlife of Mississippi to find out what species of bear Old Ben is. Compare the typical characteristics of bears in this area of the country with Old Ben's behavior. Is Faulkner's portrayal realistic?

- Do some reading on the lives of slaves who were freed during the Civil War. What sorts of problems did they have to face in their new lives? What did being "free" mean for them?

symbolizes the destruction of nature that the railroad and the foresters bring. Ben's killer, Boon Hogganbeck, represents modern man seeking to wrest nature to his advantage with blind brute strength. Though Boon does succeed in killing Ben, he is finally defeated by a tree full of frantic squirrels, suggesting that the blind destruction of modern man must eventually end in frustration and misery.

### Allusion

As with much of Faulkner's work, Biblical allusions in "The Bear" are numerous. Sam Fathers, for example, has been viewed as a Christ figure whose teachings provide a set of absolute truths that Ike must follow. Buck and Sophonsiba are a modern Abraham and Sarah, and Ike functions as the unlikely child born during their old age. This allusion heightens the irony of Isaac's choosing to reject their inherited truths for the teachings of Sam Fathers. Some references are only subtly presented.

The woods full of snakes that Ash warns Ike of in section five depicts an Eden no longer innocent, but only partially pure. The snake, an important symbol in Chickasaw myth, is also hailed as "Grandfather" by Ike. A familiarity with the Bible may help readers understand certain allusions, but the combined effect of these references creates the sense that "The Bear" discusses issues that are not particular to a time and place.

## Foreshadowing

The phrase "And so he should have feared and hated Lion" recurs several times in section two of "The Bear," and serves as a foreshadowing of Lion's role in the hunt for Old Ben. The frequent repetition of the phrase is a constant reminder of how the story will end. To read that Lion is to be hated and feared each time readers are told of his strength, competence, and courage is slightly misleading, but it is not Ike or humans who need to fear the dog. Why should Ike hate and fear Lion if he is the best possible dog for helping Ike and the others achieve their goal? The answer is not within the foreshadowing itself, but within the later knowledge of how the story actually does end. Though the men hunt Ben for several years, his actual death signals the beginning of the end of many things. With Ben's death comes the end of the hunting club and the hunting grounds, the end of a wilderness untainted by development and civilization, the end of traditions and rituals carried on by Sam Fathers and others. "And so he should have feared and hated Lion" presents readers with a "20–20 hindsight" perspective in which knowledge of the future influences looking back at the past.

## Modernism

Faulkner's works fulfill several expectations for modernist literature. Modernism is a term used to describe an international artistic movement that began near the start of World War I and continued through World War II. Modernism broke with the traditional narrative forms of realism and naturalism. The modernists played with narrative form and dialogue, attempting to approximate subjective thought and experience. The movement experimented with new ways of seeing things and new ways of communicating. In the art world, this movement was appropriated by painters like Pablo Picasso and Henri Matisse. One of the most striking characteristics of Faulkner's works, and of modernism in general, is the experimentation with narrative time. While the first three sections of "The Bear" seem fairly straightforward, section four moves back and forth in time with little indication of where the story is going next. Section four also presents a shift in technique. Instead of the fairly simple sentences used in the other sections, section four uses long confusing sentences that may span several paragraphs as well as different time periods. In fact, the whole section takes up almost half the story and yet contains only one hundred sentences. These passages approximate interior monologues, as if the narrator and the characters were talking to themselves without bothering to make sense to any listener. Because of these experiments, some find Faulkner's work frequently difficult to read and understand. Many readers have concluded this confusing technique represents Faulkner's views on the complexity of modern life.

# Historical Context

## Emancipation

Though the 1862 Emancipation Proclamation freed the slaves, their economic conditions were dire, as inequalities kept them from many jobs and educational opportunities. Southern states, bitter upon losing their bid for secession, attempted to deal with emancipated slaves by passing laws known as the "Black Codes." These laws, effectively perpetuating the racial segregation and degradation formerly applied to slaves, kept the ex-slaves from achieving economic opportunity and fair judicial process almost as thoroughly as before Emancipation. Congress, however, refused re-admittance to the Union to those states who would not ratify the Thirteenth Amendment, which abolished slavery, and the Fourteenth Amendment, which guaranteed civil liberties to all citizens. By 1877, the plans for Reconstruction were completed. Rather than integrate African Americans into society, however, the South erected a system of segregation that supposedly provided separate but equal opportunity for freed slaves and their descendants. "White supremacy" undercut any sense of fairness as the South began to rejoin the Union. Conditions had improved very little by Faulkner's day. Segregation

# Compare & Contrast

- **1880s:** The Thirteenth Amendment, abolishing slavery, and the Fourteenth Amendment, guaranteeing civil liberty, are ratified by all states.

  **1942:** The Georgia Contract Labor Act is overturned by the Supreme Court, which declares that the act of "peonage" it sanctions is a violation of the anti-slavery amendment.

  **Today:** All peoples are protected under the law from slavery, though immigrants and people of color are often the victim of civil liberty infringements.

- **1882:** Standard Oil forms a trust to secure its monopoly of the industry and eliminate competition. Other industries soon follow, causing the loss of many jobs.

  **1941:** Ford Motor Company signs its first contract with a labor union. A wage increase is awarded by General Motors in an effort to avoid strikes.

  **Today:** Big business continues to battle against government intervention and labor unions in order to maximize profits and reduce any external regulations that interfere with those profits.

- **1883:** Theodore Roosevelt begins buying up ranches in the Dakota Territory. In 1887, his interest in hunting and the outdoors leads him to form the Boone-Crockett Club, named after two legendary woodsmen.

  **1933:** The first U.S. textbook on game management is published by Aldo Leopold, reflecting society's growing concern with the wise and effective management of America's land, animals, and resources.

  **Today:** Lumber companies in the Pacific Northwest seek legal protection allowing them to cut old-growth forests, even though their actions may cause the extinction of the spotted owl.

- **1887:** The Dawes General Allotment Act is enacted, allowing two-thirds of Indian reservation lands to fall into the hands of whites.

  **1934:** The Wheeler-Howard Act, also known as the Indian Reorganization Act, attempts to rectify deplorable conditions on many reservations that are blamed on the earlier Dawes General Allotment Act of 1887.

  **Today:** The Chickasaw tribe, which had approximately 4,000 members when it was forced to move to Oklahoma in the 1830s, boasts 25,000 descendants today.

---

still kept African Americans from entering the better schools and from securing jobs, and they were still in frequent danger of violence and humiliation.

## Big Industry

The United States was a very different place at the conclusion of the Civil War. The agricultural South was virtually destroyed, while the industrial Northeast had grown strong. The railroad industry exploded as opportunists in the Midwest and the West sought ways to get their products—primarily beef and grain—to market. Owned largely by New Yorkers, the railroad received free land and millions of dollars in loans. The bankers, led by financier J. P. Morgan, could not get rich fast enough; nor could the railroad-owning families of Vanderbilts, Goulds, and others. Soon the nation's wealth was controlled by fewer and fewer businessmen who sought to protect their riches through trusts. Big business had been born, and its foremost goal was to protect itself. Railroad companies manipulated rates to favor the business of associates while extracting huge fees from unknown independent companies. They were represented in government by the Republican Party, while the South and poorer northerners, including immigrants, sought leadership in the Democratic Party. The Republicans usually won, but Democrat Grover Cleveland did serve an eight year term, and it is during his presidency that "The Bear" is set. These big business families also controlled the stock market, and their efforts to manipulate the market are blamed by many for the stock market crash of 1929. It is Faulkner's perspective in the early twentieth century, a period when industrialization began to seem overwhelming, that gives the destruction of deSpain's hunting grounds a certain urgency.

## Economic Depression

Although "The Bear" is set in the late nineteenth century, Faulkner initially began writing the story during the Depression. Economic conditions in the post-war South were similar to those during the Depression. People in both eras lost land and family possessions, suffering an identity crisis in the process. The post-war South was ripe for "carpetbaggers," those who moved from the North seeking opportunities in business and land ownership. Many desperate Southerners felt they had no choice but to sell out, as Major deSpain does when he sells the land to the forestry company. The Great Depression uprooted families in many parts of the country, as people were forced to migrate to other cities in their search for work. Similarly, slaves freed during the Civil War soon began migrating, some to the industrialized north and others to land promised to them by the Union before Emancipation. Some slaves were skilled craftsman, and a few, like Fonsiba's intellectual husband, could read. Most freed slaves, however, had no education, no money, no work skills, and no understanding of how to manage for themselves. They were often the victims of fast-talking carpetbaggers, sometimes joining them in their quest for power and money. Some even opted to stay on the plantation, seeking a certain amount of security from their former owners in exchange for their loyalty. Tennie and her son Jim are among those of the McCaslin slaves who opt to stay with the McCaslin family.

## Critical Overview

Faulkner's reputation has been largely based on his novels, rather than his short stories. Critics have found that Faulkner's novels are often more experimental and include a larger narrative sweep than his short stories. "The Bear," however, stands in contrast to this general rule. In the fourth section of the story, Faulkner employs a stream-of-consciousness narration to represent Isaac McCaslin's thought patterns. This fragmented narration is an example of the modernist approach Faulkner was using in his writing to portray modern existence in a new way. The story's unusual juxtaposition of episodes from very different points in time is another technique that Faulkner developed. These juxtapositions account for a large time period during which the saga of the McCaslin family unfolds. Finally, it is important to remember that the story is part of a larger work that Faulkner insisted should be read as an integrated novel. Thus, the attributes of Faulkner's fiction that steer admirers toward his novels rather than his short stories can all be found in "The Bear."

Early readers claimed "The Bear" was a simple hunting story, partly because the versions of the story published in 1935 and 1942 did not include the fourth section on McCaslin Edmonds and his descendants. When read with the fourth section, the tale remains an excellent example of the hunting story genre. Cleanth Brooks points out in his book *William Faulkner: The Yoknapatawpha Country* that today's urban citizens may not understand the depth of the work. Brooks asserts that "The Bear" portrays a hunter who "loves the game that he pursues, and that his code of sportsmanship embodies—however inadequately and however crudely—a regard for his prey which is probably much deeper than that of those citizens who have no first-hand concern for the animals of the wilderness." "The Bear" is much more than a hunting story in many ways, and criticism tends to focus not on the peculiar relationship of the hunter to his prey, but on Isaac's moral struggle to deal with his ancestors' sins of slavery and incest. In general, critics have found Isaac incapable of his task of making restitution for his family's violations of human conduct. His efforts to find Tomey's grandchildren are only partially successful, and his refusal to accept the McCaslin farm as his rightful inheritance appears to many critics like more of an attempt to evade responsibility than to embrace it. Early critics generally were sympathetic to Isaac, noting most often the Biblical symbolism of his decision to follow the career path of the Nazarene. More recent articles seem to react against this initial viewpoint to find Isaac a weak and ineffective protester against the long-lasting effects of slavery and racism. Various explanations for Isaac's unwillingness—or inability—to act have been made, including the notion that his lack of a stable father figure has created his psychological inability to attain fully the manhood for which Sam Fathers and Cass have trained him.

Many critics have focused on part four of "The Bear." One aspect that consistently receives critical attention is the stance toward writing and narration that Faulkner takes in this section. Much of section four concerns the information Isaac finds in the books kept by Uncle Buck and Uncle Buddy, and later, Cass Edmonds. In his essay in *Faulkner and Race*, Michael Grimwood discusses Faulkner's writing technique in section four of the story. Grimwood notes Isaac's aversion to book learning, including his cavalier attitude toward homework missed while hunting and his wary approach to the farm's ledgers. Ike's attitude is in contrast with Cass's upkeep of the ledgers and his insistence that Isaac keep up with his schoolwork. Books are found inadequate in comparison to the real-life learning that takes place in the woods. Even the Bible, Ike argues, is fallible, as it is the result of people's self-serving words. Thus Faulkner's story becomes a commentary on the shortcomings of the written word.

As with most of Faulkner's work, attempts to relate "The Bear" to Faulkner's own life in Mississippi can be found. A compelling argument is made by Charles Aiken to relate the story to the author's life in his essay "A Geographical Approach to William Faulkner's 'The Bear'." Aiken compares the maps of Yoknapatawpha County that Faulkner provides to those areas where Faulkner himself learned to hunt. Faulkner's lifelong interest in hunting and his genuine concern for endangered wildlife areas have led critics to speculate on his attitude toward conservation of the land in the story. Aiken, for example, believes that Faulkner is arguing for acceptance of the inevitability of man's development of the land: "The theme in 'The Bear' [is] that landscape change cannot be halted or even arrested when a landuse is outmoded and the altering forces set in motion." Others, such as Norman Rudich, disagree. In his essay "Faulkner and the Sin of Private Property," Rudich argues that the chronicle of land ownership and the related crimes of inhumanity in "The Bear" are a comment on the evils of private property. Faulkner's view of the land is a "mythopoeic, arcadian Biblical vision of a world which at creation belonged to none and belonged to all." Rudich continues: "private property had its origin in an original sin of expropriation of the primal wilderness, which sin and land were then transmitted from generation to generation as a cumulative curse, ripening gradually for retribution."

## Criticism

### Greg Barnhisel

*Greg Barnhisel is an educator and Assistant Director of the Undergraduate Writing Center at the University of Austin, Texas. In the following essay, Barnhisel discusses the themes, narrative structure, and character development in Faulkner's story "The Bear."*

William Faulkner is generally regarded as the most important writer to be produced by the American South. A native of Mississippi, Faulkner wrote about the land where he lived for most of his life. The great majority of Faulkner's work is set in the fictional Mississippi county of Yoknapatawpha (which, in turn, is based on the actual Lafayette County, home to the city of Oxford and the University of Mississippi). The influence of the past, the relationships between men, and the difficulties brought about by change are all recurrent themes in Faulkner's novels and stories. "The Bear" is a good example of a story that embodies all of these themes.

"The Bear" was originally published in 1935. In 1942, Faulkner revised it and included it in his book *Go Down, Moses*. Later, he insisted that "The Bear" could not be fully understood unless it was read with the other stories in *Go Down, Moses* as a segment of a novel. In its seven stories, *Go Down, Moses* recounts many of the events in the life of Isaac (Ike) McCaslin, a member of one of Yoknapatawpha's three most important families. (The other families, representatives of which appear in "The Bear," are the Compsons and the Sutpens).

The complex narrative of "The Bear" makes it difficult to sort out the family relations of the characters in the story. This is, of course, part of Faulkner's objective: through the tangled narration, he illustrates the often tangled genealogies of South-

> The complex narrative of 'The Bear' makes it difficult to sort out the family relations of the characters in the story."

ern families, especially those involving illegitimate children who were the offspring of white men and slave women. Ike McCaslin, the main character, is the grandson of one of Yoknapatawpha's settlers and founders, Carothers McCaslin. Carothers' sons include Uncle Buck and Uncle Buddy, who, upon the death of their father in 1837, move into a log cabin on their plantation grounds and moved the plantation's slaves into the "big house." Late in his life, Uncle Buck marries Sophonsiba Beauchamp and they produce Ike in 1867. Carothers also has a daughter married to an Edmonds, who is either the father or the grandfather (Faulkner does not say) of McCaslin "Cass" Edmonds. Cass, seventeen years older than Ike, in effect becomes Ike's father after Uncle Buck's death. In "The Bear," we see Ike and Cass together through much of the story, and in the fourth section Cass teaches Ike many of the family's secrets and much of its history. The other characters in "The Bear" include General Compson and Major de Spain, two of Yoknapatawpha's leading citizens; Sam Fathers, a hunting guide of Chickasaw descent, and Boon, another part-Chickasaw member of the hunting party; and Ash, the black cook for the hunting party.

The story recounts the efforts of Major de Spain's annual hunting party to track down Old Ben, an old and wily bear who is "ravaging the countryside." We see the hunt through Ike's eyes, and the first section of the story shifts in time through Ike's first expedition with the hunting party, in 1877, to the 1883 trip in which Old Ben is finally killed. Although the slaying of Old Ben is the climax of the story's action, it is not the story's focus. Instead, in the first half of the story we are confronted by the story of a boy's growing into manhood through learning the ancient ways of the hunter. On his first trip, the boy is not allowed to shoot his gun. On his second hunt, Sam Fathers teaches Ike that he must become a part of the wilderness before he earns the right to kill anything. That year, Ike discards his gun and goes off into the wilderness in search of Ben. Unable to lure the bear out of hiding, Ike leaves behind the trappings of civilization—his watch and compass—and is rewarded with a glimpse of the old bear. Subsequent trips bring the party closer to killing the bear, and in 1881 Sam captures a wild dog, whom he names "Lion," in hopes that he will help them corner the bear. Finally, in 1883 Lion and the hunters corner the bear. Ben kills the dog, but at the same time Boon jumps up on the bear's back and fatally stabs it. As the party prepares to return to town, Sam dies, and Ike suspects that Boon has "helped" in this.

The story of the hunt, although exciting, only takes up the first half (the first three sections) of "The Bear." After Sam dies, the narrative shifts. The sentences become extremely long, a characteristic Faulkner technique, and the narrator begins to discuss the early history of the county. This fourth section, stylistically the most difficult of the five, recounts Ike's investigation into his family's history and leads up to his decision to renounce his inheritance. The majority of the chapter takes place in the McCaslin family commissary, where Ike and McCaslin Edmonds discuss many topics. Their discussions include the Chickasaws, who sold Ike's grandfather the land for his plantation, the legacy of slavery in the McCaslin family, and their convoluted family history. In addition, we see Ike working through his confusion about his own father: he cannot decide whether Cass, his grandfather Carothers, his spiritual father Sam, or Uncle Buck is his legitimate father.

Here, Faulkner is at his most ambitious. In this section, the past and the present co-exist almost without differentiation. In the same sentence, the actions of such figures as the Chickasaw chief Ikkemotubbe, Ike's Uncle Buddy, and Buddy's slave Tennie exert almost equal force on Ike. Similarly, Ike is ten, sixteen, and twenty-one, all in the space of a few lines. Faulkner uses this strategy to examine Ike's reaction to the pressure of the legacy that has been left to him. Ike, at age twenty-one, is finally legally able to inherit the McCaslin plantation, but he refuses. He is haunted by his abhorrence of slavery and the fields he now owns "whose laborers it still held in thrall '65 or no." Similarly, he is disgusted by his family's refusal to acknowledge that old Carothers not only fathered a daugh-

## What Do I Read Next?

- *Go Down, Moses* is the 1942 novel by William Faulkner in which "The Bear" first appeared in its entirety. Each of the stories within the novel center around the McCaslin clan, starting with Uncle Buck and Uncle Buddy and ending when "Uncle Ike" is an old man.

- Jack London's 1910 novel *White Fang* tells the story of a boy coming of age in the wilderness of Alaska near the turn of the century. The enduring lessons of the wilderness are taught by a very special dog who is also part wolf.

- Published in 1845, the autobiographical *Narrative of the Life of Frederick Douglass* is a good starting point for investigating slavery from the slaves' point of view. Douglass's account is relevant to the plight of all slaves in any time period.

- Faulkner was an influential figure for Nobel prize-winner Toni Morrison. Her 1977 novel, *Song of Solomon,* is the account of a youth named Milkman Dead, whose investigations into his family tree take him, among other places, on a hunting trip.

- *Winesburg, Ohio*, published in 1919 by Faulkner's friend Sherwood Anderson, is the coming-of-age story of young George Willard, whose upbringing in a small Midwest town is told in a collection of short stories. George's neighbors all confide their personal stories to this budding young journalist, an act that unifies the disparate members of the town into a cohesive whole.

- Ernest Hemingway's short story "Big Two-Hearted River" was first published in his 1925 collection *In Our Time*. The story details the return of Nick Adams to a familiar fishing camp of his youth, where he goes to heal after surviving injuries sustained in World War I.

- Margaret Mitchell's 1939 novel *Gone with the Wind*, written about the time that Faulkner was reworking "The Bear," makes an interesting contrast to the stark portrayal of the South that Faulkner provides. Mitchell's plantations are magnificent, gracious icons of genteel Southern living. Her portrayal of slaves reduces them to picturesque stereotypes of ignorant but faithful servantry.

---

ter, Tomey, by his slave Eunice, but also incestuously fathered a son by Tomey. Finally he is deeply disturbed by the single-minded search for profit which the ownership of the plantation has fostered. Thus Ike refuses to take over the farm. By doing this, he hopes to cleanse himself of the stains that history has placed upon him.

The story is rich with meaning and resonance. Critics have drawn parallels of "The Bear" with ancient fertility myths, with the story of Christianity, and with Marxist critiques of modern consumer society. The connection of the hunt story to various myths is certainly an appealing one; many cultures have some type of a rite in which boys "come of age" by going off by themselves and hunting an animal. Ike learns not only how to "be a man" but also what man's "proper place" is within nature when Sam requires that he go without his gun before he can actually begin hunting. Major de Spain and General Compson also believe in the inherent value of the hunt as a learning tool. For both of them, killing Old Ben is not really the ultimate goal; until Boon kills the bear, they view the stalking of Ben (which always takes place on the last day of the hunting trip) almost as a ritual. When Boon kills Old Ben, Sam—who symbolizes the old ways and the ideal relation of man to nature—also dies. Boon here represents the predations of the modern world, his act symbolizing the severed relationship between man and nature. At the end, as he smashes his gun, he seems to have reached the impasse which Faulkner suggests all men will reach without an understanding of the proper role of man in nature.

The fact that Boon, the agent of the modern world, is sitting in the middle of a forest that is soon to be "harvested" by a Memphis lumber company demonstrates how the modern world, according to Faulkner, is willfully destroying itself.

To read "The Bear" as a Christian allegory requires us to view Sam Fathers as the Christ-figure. He shows Ike the way, "the code of the hunter as an alternative to the planation world." Two critics, R. W. B. Lewis and Lewis P. Simpson, discuss whether Ike McCaslin's choice is the "key to salvation" for a fallen man. Lewis sees Ike's renunciation of his tainted family estate as a cleansing act in his essay in the *Kenyon Review,* but Simpson holds the contrary. According to Simpson's article in *Nine Essays in Modern Literature,* Faulkner believes that man's sins of slavery and of unquestioning faith in science and technology are of different moral types. He asserts that slavery, although a "curse," is rooted in man's inherent sinfulness, and is therefore less preventable. He further contends that our contemporary reliance on technology and belief in its power "separates man from both his sense of involvement with his fellow man and with nature and dehumanizes him." Ike repudiates the first sin, but simply by virtue of his being a member of modern society he cannot fully repudiate the second. The destruction of the land for the sake of profit is such an integral part of his own existence that we cannot see him as a savior figure.

Faulkner's treatment of race is extremely complex. There are as many explanations for his attitude towards the racial situation in the South as there are critics. We can attribute at least two solid beliefs to him: he abhors slavery, which he feels is an enduring curse not only upon the three races of the South (he here includes the Native Americans) but also upon the very land of Mississippi. He feels that the white race bears some responsibility for the black race's welfare (and this is epitomized by Ike's need to make sure his black cousins obtain the legacy which Carothers set aside for them). Faulkner's other belief is that he feels that the black race "endures." Ike tells McCaslin that "they [African Americans] are better than we are. Stronger than we are." "The Bear," in many ways, is the story of Ike McCaslin's coming to terms with the racial inequity that his family helped to construct.

Although rooted in the particular historical conditions of post-Civil War Mississippi, Faulkner's story reaches beyond the limitations of historical fiction. In "The Bear," we have not only one of the greatest hunting stories in literature, but also a dissection of the condition of man in the fallen world. It is not necessary to agree with Faulkner on the pitiable condition of modern man to enjoy the story. However, the image of Boon ineffectually battering his own tools as he sits in a condemned wilderness speaks even more powerfully today than it did when Faulkner first created the scene.

**Source:** Greg Barnhisel, for *Short Stories for Students,* Gale Research, 1997.

## Herbert A. Perluck

*In the following excerpt, Perluck explains that he does not believe that Isaac McCaslin acted honorably in rejecting his inheritance. Rather, he believes that McCaslin failed to accept responsibility.*

The usual reading of "The Bear" makes of Isaac McCaslin a kind of saint who, by repudiating his inheritance—the desecrated land upon which a whole people has been violated— performs an act of expiation and atonement which is a model for those acts that must follow before the curse upon the land is lifted. Ike's repudiation of the land, at twenty-one, with which the tortuous inner section of "The Bear" opens, and over which he and his cousin, McCaslin Edmonds, debate in the commissary, is seen in terms of what the reader understands Ike to have learned and attained under the influence of Sam Fathers in the untainted Wilderness: the "freedom and humility and pride." The story is of one man's repudiation of the forces of greed and materialism that have all but extinguished God's hope for man of freedom and generosity.

The whole sequence of the commissary, the Beauchamp legacy, and the later life of Isaac McCaslin, is thus ordinarily taken as a sort of complementary sequel to what may be called the hunt-narrative; Part IV in the total structure and intention of the work is a filling-out, past and future, of the "story proper," as it is sometimes regarded: the hunt-narrative and especially the episode of the fyce, in which the later renunciation, at twenty-one, is prefigured.

There is much, however, in this difficult portion of the work that suggests a contrary view. Instead of a romantic Christian pastoral of redemption, in which the repudiation of the land and earlier the apparently selfless rescue of the fyce from under the erect bear are seen as almost sanctifying gestures of renunciation, a searing tragedy of human desire and human limitation evolves, chiefly through ironic means. From McCaslin's scornful skepticism as he listens to Ike's account of God's circuitous providence, and the "lip-lift" of contempt when he realizes that even Ike does not wholly believe in his "freedom," to the almost hysterical laughter with which Part IV concludes, the principal effects are ironic.

The central thematic irony, however, upon which these effects are grounded, is slowly constructed of larger elements. The repudiation in the commissary *is* prefigured in the hunt-narrative; something of a parallel does develop between the selfless non-possession of Ike's gesture at twenty-one and the repudiation of passion earlier—that effort to preserve the idyll of the Big Woods, in the reluctance of both Ike and Sam Fathers to slay Old Ben. But the point of the parallel is not merely to provide background and extension to the "story-proper"; it is drawn and pressed home by McCaslin Edmonds on Ike because in both gestures there is weakness and something even sinister which cannot become clear to McCaslin, or to the reader, until the dense and complex drama of the debate in the commissary is enacted.

The terrible irony of Part IV develops in the growing awareness in the reader, as well as in the characters, of the discrepancy between what we and Ike supposed him to have achieved, to have attained to, and what in fact his repudiations actually represent. The whole inner section of "The Bear" reflects back on the hunt-narrative and forward into the last sequence: Ike's return at eighteen to the woods, which are being destroyed by the lumber company; his vague, troubled guilt at the sight of the nearly demented, grieving Boon. Coming where it does in the story structure, Part IV has the effect of making the reader, as it makes Ike and McCaslin, remember and painfully reinterpret the earlier events as of some dream-idyll of human perfection, of perhaps a kind of angelic pre-existence, now dissipated in the wakeful glare of the human reality. Slowly and relentlessly, Faulkner's intention takes hold in Part IV, in the tragic incompleteness of man, as the gulf is drawn between action, life as lived, and the memory of action and events, in which our dreams of life, our poems, are created.

"The Bear" is no Saint's Life; on the contrary, what it expresses is that there is no "freedom" in renunciation, no sanctity through repudiation—that actually there is no such thing as human sainthood as we have conceived it. If Isaac McCaslin is a saint at all, it is not in the traditional ascetic sense of a

> "'The Bear' is no Saint's Life; on the contrary, what it expresses is that there is no 'freedom' in renunciation, no sanctity through repudiation—that actually there is no such thing as human sainthood as we have conceived it."

successful renunciation of the world and the flesh in atonement and expiation; it is rather a "sainthood" of *un*success, an unwitting, unwilled elevation produced in the tragic *defeat* of spirit and soul in the "uncontrollable mystery" of the world which men and "saints" must live in perforce. In much the same way that [Franz] Kafka's Bucketrider is unaccountably (to him) "upraised" into the "regions of the icy mountains and [is] lost forever," Isaac McCaslin ascends without comprehending wherein that only "sainthood" man is allowed resides: in the anguished complex heart. "The Bear" is a story of a renunciation that fails, as they all must. It is also the story of man's ineluctable fate of being only man. And on another level, it is a parable of man's pride, in his trying to be more than man, and of the evil this pride accomplishes in its condescending ascription of all that man does not want to see in himself to a certain few untouchables, the Boons of the world....

McCaslin tried to explain to Ike, by quoting the "Ode [on a Grecian Urn]," why Ike saved the fyce instead of killing Old Ben, or at least what McCaslin had thought then—that the humility and pride Ike had wanted to learn in order to become worthy of the Wilderness and of a manhood in which the Bear was hunted by men like Sam Fathers, Major de Spain, Walter Ewell, and McCaslin, that these he had just learned, had come to possess, through forbearance and selfless courage, through, in short, a kind of renunciation, *non* possession. McCaslin's purpose in quoting Keats had been to show Ike how we may pursue bravely and fiercely and yet not kill, out of pity and love; how we may love by not loving;

how we may be proud and humble, fierce and gentle, at the same time; how by not possessing in the heart we may possess all. . . .

Ike's failure to kill Old Ben was a way out, an escape from himself; . . . Keats had only helped him to repudiate, and so think he had *freed* himself from, what being human and alive in time imposes on a man. McCaslin hadn't told him that what we may know in the heart is not what we are allowed to live. The non-possession, the renunciations, and thus the "freedom" which may be realized in the heart—this Ike has tried to *live*. "Sam Fathers set me free," he protests to McCaslin. . . But the freedom he had indeed obtained was only "freedom of the heart," which Sam Fathers showed him how to achieve by virtue of giving himself up to the Wilderness, as he does when he "relinquishes" his gun and compass and goes alone to see and be seen by Old Ben— much as Henry Fleming, in that other story of a boy's initiation into manhood, comes to touch the great god Death and discovers it is only death after all. He momentarily relinquishes self and pride, in effect—the way they are relinquished provisionally in a poem—the better to confront that naked red heart of the world, the Wilderness of the human heart, which is "free" only when it is so confronted and acknowledged. This "freedom" is from the blind, uncomprehending *fear* of the "Wilderness" and its creatures, but is not, as Ike would desire it— a confusion that leads to his agony in the commissary—a freedom from the necessary human commitment in acts and time. The moral freedom to choose *not* to act does not exist, except in the heart, where it is not a moral but a spiritual or aesthetic freedom. Sam Fathers set Ike free only in the sense of his enabling him to look at *all* that a man can feel and do, *all* that the "Wilderness" contains; he could not free him from himself. So it was not the fyce that had kept him from shooting—out of love and forbearance; he had, in fact, blanched from that full sight of himself as a man, who at the same time he was humble and loved the thing he pursued, was a slayer and ravener.

The "poem," as it were, that Ike has tried to live is one in which his hunting of Old Ben but his not having to kill him is the chief symbol—as it is even now in the commissary. And it *was* very much like the girl and the youth on the Urn, although Ike had not quite been able to see the analogy. He has wished, Hamlet-like, to kill and yet not kill, to realize fully a state of "being" out of time, which is realized only in a play, in art, and in the complex heart. But the Prince must slay, the hunter must slay; they cannot, if they would be princes and hunters, preserve that moment of excruciated sensibility in the timeless drama of the heart. The "Old Free Fathers" were aware of this painful human paradox of action, in which man commits himself in the irrevocable, and they celebrated it in the sacramental gesture of grief and responsibility (but there was also pride) for the life they spilled: a consecrating gesture—the smearing the warm blood of a youth's first kill on his forehead—which absolved a man from *regret* but not from *grief*. . . .

Faulkner's meaning in "The Bear" is that if man would live, he must be prepared for the dying too; if he would love, he must also grieve for the spilled life that loving and living require. Simply to repudiate the spilling, to relinquish the grief, by relinquishing the passion, is to remove oneself from life, and from love, which, like the hunt, necessarily involves us in blood. There is no renunciation of life and the world which we can choose to make, and there can be no "acceptance" of the inevitabilities; we may only choose life. What we may renounce is only renunciation itself, and what we may attain to is not a regenerate state, sainthood, being, but our humanity. We gain life by "losing" it only in the sense of having it *taken away,* of trying to live what is in the heart, and failing. Renunciation, "acceptance," is to surrender life to live in the "pretty rooms" of sonnets ("and Isaac McCaslin, not yet Uncle Ike . . . living in one small cramped fireless rented room in a Jefferson boarding-house . . . with his kit of brand-new carpenter's tools . . . the shotgun McCaslin had given him with his name engraved in silver . . . and the bright tin coffee-pot."

We prefer to think the Boons of this world do the slaying, and our renunciations are our way of *allowing* them to. We construct our "pretty rooms" right in the Wilderness where we play at virtue and perform our purification rites, just as Major de Spain, Walter Ewell, McCaslin Edmonds and the rest did each year. The Negroes and their white masters, at the camp site, lived under an entirely different dispensation from the one which ordinarily prevailed in town, in real life, where they were virtually slaves. In the Big Woods they could play at being untainted, guiltless—there one felt free. The pursuit of Old Ben over the years is unsuccessful, not merely because he is a wily old beast, almost supernatural, but because they didn't want to kill him, and not killing him is the ritual of purification; by this, and by the altered relationship of Negro and white master, they could free themselves, for a while at least. Sam Fathers had begun, long before, to live at the camp site all year round, but when they approach him after he has collapsed, he murmurs, "Let me out, master," knowing that only death can really free him, that he hasn't been free at all in the white man's lodge and woods. The Boons, with the hard button eyes—the insensitive, un-human destroyers and raveners, as we conceive them—are there at the last, almost by design, to shatter the pretty glass room of this dream of redemption: we create them and then sacrifice them in our condescensions and our renunciations in this last act of the ritual. . . .

**Source:** Herbert A. Perluck, "'The Bear': An Unromantic Reading," in *Religious Perspectives in Faulkner's Fiction: Yoknapatawpha and Beyond,* edited by J. Robert Barth, S.J, University of Notre Dame Press, 1972, pp. 173–201.

## Richard Lehan

*In the portion of the review excerpted below, Lehan, an assistant professor at UCLA, interprets "The Bear" in much the same way as a poem would be analyzed. He also focuses on the relationships between several characters, especially Lion and Boon, Sam Fathers and the bear.*

Faulkner's "The Bear," published in *The Saturday Evening Post* and in *Go Down, Moses,* has received its share of critical explication, and the pattern and meaning of the novel seems to have been thoroughly discussed. Certainly there is much that can be taken for granted: the bear is a symbol of nature; its death symbolizes the loss of the wilderness and all the wilderness represents, and the wilderness seems to represent a kind of Emersonian realm where man and nature are spiritually and emotionally at one, an Edenic world before the Fall where time does not exist and where, like Keats's Grecian urn, one is not subject to the exigencies of time. Ike McCaslin, in fact, has to divest himself of watch and compass before he can see the bear, because these man-made instruments impose a mechanical and unnatural order upon nature; and Ike sees the bear at the same spot where he left the watch and compass, as if time and space begin with the bear because he encompassed both.

The critics have so focused on the larger and more engrossing matters of the story—the ritual aspect of the hunt, the symbolic meaning of the bear's death, the moral connection between the "sins" of Carothers McCaslin and the loss of the wilderness—that matters of technique, the "telling" of the story, have received little attention and, as a result, much of the meaning of the novel has

> "The death of the bear and the loss of the wilderness are thus thematically spliced through descriptive detail."

gone unnoticed or is still subject to argument. Meaning in "The Bear" stems, at least in part, from Faulkner's use of descriptive detail, from verbal associations, which interrelate characters and extend the theme of the novel imagistically, as if "The Bear" were a poem.

Critics, for example, have failed to notice that Faulkner makes a verbal connection between Lion, the dog, and Boon Hogganbeck. When we first see Lion, trapped in the emptied corn-crib which has been baited with the colt's carcass, he is smashing with tremendous power against the deadfall door. His force is that of nature itself, a cold and malignant element of nature, diametrically removed from what the bear represents. When Lion is slowly and painfully tamed, it seems as if nature has been turned back upon itself. If the bear is a pristine and uncorrupted part of nature, Lion stands for the forces of nature which have been harnessed by man. A vicious, wild dog, he is finally tamed by man and, like a machine subject to its maker, he is turned against the wilderness.

It is for this reason that Lion is described as if he *were* a man-made object; the men peering between the logs into the cage see an animal almost the color of a gun or pistol barrel." The dog "stood, and they could see it now—part mastiff, something of Airedale and something of a dozen other strains probably, better than thirty inches at the shoulders and weighing as they guessed almost ninety pounds, with cold yellow eyes and a tremendous chest and over all that strange color like a blued gun-barrel."

It is these descriptive details that link Lion and Boon in the novel. Unlike Ike or Sam Fathers, Boon is not really a woodsman, a member of the initiate, not a high priest in the annual ritual hunt. Like Lion, Boon is once removed from both the pristine wilderness and civilization. He is completely out of place in Memphis, where he gets drunk and suffers from a severe cold, and yet he lacks the capacity to relate spiritually with the wilderness. He is in a kind of no-man's land, and it is significant that at the end of the novel, when the wilderness has been destroyed by the lumber company, Boon becomes a deputy sheriff. Like Lion, in other words, he eventually becomes the tool of men, a corruptible part of nature, "tamed" by society, and turned against nature. Lion and Boon thus come to represent nature turned back upon itself in an act of destruction. It is thematically appropriate that Boon and Lion have a kind of "love affair." Ike watches when Boon touches Lion "as if Lion were a woman—or perhaps Boon was the woman. That was more like it—the big, brave sleepy-seeming dog which, as Sam Fathers said, cared about no man and no thing; and the violent, insensitive, hard-faced man with his touch of remote Indian blood and the mind almost of a child." And it is further appropriate that Faulkner describes Boon in exactly the same way that he describes Lion. Where Lion's coat has "that strange color like a blued gun-barrel," Boon has a "blue stubble on his face like the filings from a new gun-barrel." This is not mere rhetoric, mere accidental detail. In his imagination, Faulkner reconciled Boon and Lion; the two serve the same thematic purpose in the novel, and Faulkner bridged this connection and extended meaning in "The Bear" through such descriptive detail—detail that the reader must first interrelate, just as one has to go through the imagery of a [John] Donne poem before he can come to its final meaning.

When Boon and Lion kill the bear, the forces of nature corrupted by a mechanized civilization have been turned against an elemental and pristine nature. Sam Fathers, who like the bear is also uncorrupted, dies when the bear dies, and it is once again significant that Boon is the agent of his death, that Boon kills him at Sam's own request.

The death of both the bear and of Sam Fathers represents the passing of an old order. Their death occurs simultaneously with the loss of the wilderness as it is ruthlessly raped by the timber company. The novel, in fact, opens on this theme, Faulkner describing "that doomed wilderness whose edges were being constantly and punily gnawed at by men with plows and axes who feared it because it was wilderness." The death of the bear parallels, to be more exact, what happened to the South after the Civil War when the older agrarian order was disrupted, when an industrialized North tried to make it over in its own image. Boon and Lion destroy the bear, just as the timber company, the spirit of industry, destroys the wilderness—and again Faulkner makes this point through descriptive detail. In the passage describing the death of the bear, perhaps one of the most moving passages in contemporary fiction, he describes Boon and Lion, both astride the bear, Boon with his knife probing for the bear's heart, the knife rising and falling once:

> It fell just once. For an instant they almost resembled a piece of statuary [cf. Keats's Grecian urn]: the clinging dog, the bear, the man astride its back, working and probing the buried blade. Then they went down, pulled over backward, by Boon's weight, Boon underneath. It was the bear's back which reappeared first but at once Boon was astride it again. He had never released the knife and again the boy saw the almost infinitesimal movement of his arm and shoulder as he probed and sought; then the bear surged erect, raising with it the man and the dog too, and turned and still carrying the man and the dog it took two or three steps toward the woods on its hind feet as a man would have walked and *crashed down*. It didn't collapse, crumple. It fell all of a piece, *as a tree falls,* so that all three of them, man dog and bear, seemed to bounce once. (italics mine)

The death of the bear and the loss of the wilderness are thus thematically spliced through descriptive detail. The bear did not fall, it "crashed down," as a "tree falls," and the death of the bear and the loss of the forest become one.

**Source:** Richard Lehan, "Faulkner's Poetic Prose: Style and Meaning in 'The Bear'," *College English,* Vol. 27, No. 3, December, 1965, pp. 243–47.

# Sources

Aiken, Charles. "A Geographical Approach to William Faulkner's 'The Bear'," in *Geographical Review,* Vol. 71, no. 4, October, 1981, pp. 446-459.

Brooks, Cleanth. *William Faulkner: The Yoknapatawpha Country,* Louisiana State University Press, 1963.

Grimwood, Michael. "Faulkner and the Vocational Liabilities of Black Characterization," in *Faulkner and Race,* edited by Doreen Fowler and Ann J. Abadie, University Press of Mississippi, 1987, pp. 255-271.

Lewis, R. W. B. "The Hero in the New World: William Faulkner's 'The Bear'," in *Kenyon Review,* Vol. XIII, no. 4, Autumn, 1951, pp. 641–660.

Rudich, Norman. "Faulkner and the Sin of Private Property," in *The Minnesota Review,* Vol. 17, 1981, pp. 55-57.

Simpson, Lewis. An essay in *Nine Essays in Modern Literature,* edited by Donald E. Stanford, Louisiana University Press, 1965, 194 p.

# Further Reading

Adams, Richard P. "Focus on William Faulkner's 'The Bear': Moses and the Wilderness," in *American Dreams, American Nightmares,* edited by David Madden, Southern Illinois University Press, 1970, pp. 129-135.

   This article finds Ike unable to set anyone free, in spite of his own belief that it is his responsibility to do so.

*Bear, Man and God: Eight Approaches to William Faulkner's "The Bear,"* edited by Francis Lee Utley, Lynn Z. Bloom, and Arthur F. Kinney, Random House, 1971.

   Includes the text of the story, source material, excerpts from other Faulkner works, and several critical essays on the story.

Claridge, Laura P. "Isaac McCaslin's Failed Bid for Adulthood," *American Literature,* Vol. 55, no. 2, May, 1983, pp. 241-251.

   Claridge argues that Isaac "relinquishes," rather than "repudiates," his inheritance, suggesting his lifelong inability to act and, by acting, to become a man.

Hoffman, Daniel. "William Faulkner: 'The Bear'," in *Landmarks of American Writing,* edited by Hennig Cohen, Basic Books, Inc. 1969, pp. 341-352.

   Hoffman's chapter on "The Bear" focuses on several critical themes, including Ike as a hero on a quest similar to the Grail Knight of the Round Table, the image of the Native American as instinctual in contrast to the Christian understanding of sin, and the contrast of primeval forest with the tangled world of plantation society.

Kern, Alexander C. "Myth and Symbol in Criticism of Faulkner's 'The Bear'," in *Myth and Symbol,* edited by Bernice Slote, University of Nebraska Press, 1963, pp. 252-262.

   Kern's paper discusses the various symbols in the story, in particular, the bear, the deer and the snake.

Sundquist, Eric J. "The True Inheritance of Ike McCaslin," in *Critical Essays on William Faulkner: The McCaslin Family,* edited by Arthur F. Kinney, G. K. Hall, 1990.

   Sundquist places "The Bear" in the context of the McCaslin family story and discusses the mythic archetypes of hunting contained within the narrative.

Willis, Susan. "Aesthetics of the Rural Slum: Contradiction and Dependency in 'The Bear'," in *Faulkner: New Perspectives,* edited by Richard H. Broadhead, Prentice-Hall, 1983.

   Willis examines "The Bear" as the story of the economic development of the South, and proposes the commissary and the wilderness as the opposite poles of this development.

# A Christmas Memory

Truman Capote

1956

"A Christmas Memory" was issued by Random House in 1966 during the holiday season in order to capitalize on Truman Capote's growing popularity following the release of his true-crime novel, *In Cold Blood.* Though "A Christmas Memory" had initially appeared in *Mademoiselle* magazine in December, 1956, and was reprinted in *The Selected Writings of Truman Capote* in 1963, it was the 1966 edition that established the story's enduring popularity. The story of a seven-year-old boy and his aging cousin's holiday traditions was made into an Emmy Award-winning television movie starring Geraldine Page in 1968 and continues to be produced by high-school and regional theaters throughout the United States.

The story is a prime example of what William L. Nance in *The Worlds of Truman Capote* calls Capote's "fiction of nostalgia," in which the author looks back fondly upon his Southern childhood. These nostalgic stories evoke a gentle, simple, and secure childhood uncorrupted by the complications of adulthood. Autobiographical elements in "A Christmas Memory" are apparent: Capote lived with relatives in the South as a child, and during this time his older female cousin, the childlike Sook Faulk, was his closest companion. The nostalgic mood has prompted some critics to dismiss the story as "saccharine." However, the story also contains darker elements such as loneliness, poverty, social isolation, and death, which demonstrate that the innocence of childhood may protect young people from the elements of the human condition, but not remove them from it. The story is also an example of a common theme in Capote's writings: the friendship forged among social outcasts, many of which are eccentric women.

## Author Biography

Truman Capote drew on his own youthful experience in rural Alabama to write "A Christmas Memory." This story, which he called his personal favorite, is an idealized recollection of one of the few relatively secure periods of his unstable early childhood.

Capote was born Truman Streckfus Persons on September 30, 1924, in New Orleans, Louisiana. Although his parents did not formally divorce until he was seven years old, they never created a stable home for young Truman, and some of his earliest memories are of accompanying his mother, Lillie Mae, on job-hunting excursions to St. Louis, Missouri, and Louisville, Kentucky. At other times he was shuttled between the homes of various relatives in Alabama. One of these households of his mother's relatives provided the settings for much of his early fiction, including "A Christmas Memory."

In 1930, Capote was sent to live in Monroeville, Alabama, while his mother went to New York City to seek work. His new "family" consisted of the three middle-aged Faulk sisters and their older brother. One of the sisters, Sook, is the model for Buddy's friend in "A Christmas Memory." While in Monroeville, Truman became friends with Harper Lee, a young girl who lived next door and later gained recognition for writing the critically acclaimed novel *To Kill a Mockingbird*. Lee allegedly based the character of Dill, a wildly imaginative young boy, on Capote. The two writers remained lifelong friends, and she later traveled to Kansas to help research his most famous work, *In Cold Blood*, the true story of the murder of a wealthy farm family. His mother remarried in 1932, and later that year he joined her and his new stepfather, Joseph Capote, in New York; in 1934 Truman became Truman Garcia Capote when Joseph formally adopted him.

In New York, Lillie Mae (who now called herself Nina) became alarmed by her son's effeminate tendencies and sent him to St. John's Military Academy. The other cadets made his life miserable by mocking his Southern accent and ridiculing his mannerisms. Eventually his mother withdrew him from St. John's, and he returned to New York, where he developed his flair for storytelling and became quite popular as a *raconteur*—a teller of stories—at parties. Around 1943 he landed a job as a copyboy at the prestigious magazine *The New Yorker*, where he saw firsthand the ins and outs of the New York publishing world. His first story, "Miriam," was published in *Mademoiselle* in June, 1945, and at the tender age of 21, Capote became the darling of the New York literary establishment.

*Other Voices, Other Rooms* appeared in 1948 and another novel, *The Grass Harp*, in 1951. In 1958 he wrote the short novel *Breakfast at Tiffany's*, which was made into a movie starring Audrey Hepburn, and he also wrote two screenplays. But it is *In Cold Blood*, in which he claimed to have invented a new genre, the nonfiction novel, which ensured his reputation and made him a social celebrity. Toward the end of his life, problems with alcohol and drugs sapped his creativity, and he never completed his final project, *Answered Prayers*, which was published posthumously in 1987. In his later years, Capote was known more as a social gadfly, one who hosted celebrated parties, like the infamous Black and White Ball held at the Plaza Hotel in New York in 1966. During the 1970s, he could frequently be found at the notorious Manhattan discotheque Studio 54. Capote died in Los Angeles, California, on August 25, 1984.

## Plot Summary

The narrator of the story tells the reader to "imagine a morning in late November" more than twenty years ago. The scene is a kitchen of a rambling house in a small rural town in the 1930s. An elderly woman stands at the kitchen window and proclaims that "it's fruitcake weather!" This is delightful news to her seven-year-old cousin and best friend, Buddy. "Fruitcake weather" signals the beginning of the holiday season for the unconventional cousins, who bake the loaves for the people in their lives who have been kind to them through the year. The two proceed with their tradition more or less oblivious to the other relatives who live in the house: "they have power over us, and frequently make us cry, [but] we are not, on the whole, too much aware of them."

*Truman Capote*

They begin the routine by gathering pecans for the fruitcakes. The unnamed woman and the little boy, accompanied by their dog Queenie, spend three hours filling an old baby carriage with the nuts that have fallen on the ground in the neighbor's orchard. Then they return to the kitchen to shell the nuts by firelight and plan the next day's work— buying the other ingredients for the fruitcakes. Later, they go up to the woman's bedroom, where she keeps a change purse hidden under her bed. The purse is filled with the money they have accumulated all year from their various enterprises: selling fruit and flowers, and once even charging neighbors to see a deformed chicken. At this time the narrator, grown now and relating the story in flashback, reveals more facts about his cousin. She has never seen a movie or eaten in a restaurant, but she knows how to tame hummingbirds, tell chilling ghost stories, and create elixirs to cure a variety of ills.

The next day, they go on their shopping trip. During their most unusual errand they visit a man named Haha Jones, the local whiskey bootlegger. Jones is large and frightening-looking, but he is kind to the cousins, giving them a bottle of whiskey in exchange for the promise of a fruitcake. Over the next four days they bake thirty-one cakes, most of which they send to people they know only slightly or not at all; people who have passed through their town once, or famous people such as President Franklin D. Roosevelt. The woman, the narrator points out, "is shy with everyone *except* strangers." After the cakes are baked and sent, they split the leftover whiskey and give a spoonful to the dog. A little drunk, they sing and dance around the kitchen, but soon two relatives come in and scold the woman for giving whiskey to the boy. Sobbing, she retreats to her room. Buddy comforts her by reminding her that they will cut down a Christmas tree the next day.

In the morning, they find the perfect Christmas tree, twice as tall as Buddy. They drag it home themselves along with other holiday greenery. They make decorations from colored paper and tinfoil to supplement the few store-bought ornaments they own and sprinkle the tree with shredded cotton. They finish their decorating tasks by creating holly wreaths for the house's front windows. Gifts are created for the rest of the family; Buddy makes his cousin a kite, and he suspects she is making him one as well. His suspicions are confirmed on Christmas Eve when they are too excited to sleep and they reveal their presents to one another. After they open their presents on Christmas Day, they go out to fly the kites. They have such a good time that the old woman feels as if she has seen God.

The narrator reveals that this is the last Christmas he shared with his cousin. Buddy is sent to military school, and spends his summers at camp. For a while, his cousin writes him and continues her holiday fruitcake tradition, sending him "the best of the batch." Eventually, though, she becomes mentally and physically frail, unable to keep up her routine. When she dies, Buddy knows before he is told: "A message saying so merely confirms a piece of news some secret vein had already received." The story closes with him walking over the grounds of his school and looking at the sky: "As if I expected to see, rather like hearts, a lost pair of kites hurrying toward heaven."

## Characters

### Buddy

Throughout "A Christmas Memory" the narrator refers to himself only in the first person (I, me, myself), but his friend calls him Buddy "in memory of a boy who was formerly her best friend" and who had died when she was a child. Truman Capote said that Buddy is based on himself; as a boy, Capote indeed lived with an elderly, somewhat eccentric cousin in a country house full of relatives. At the time the story takes place Buddy is seven years old, and his age influences the way he perceives the events going on around him. Despite his youth, he proves perceptive. Buddy understands that even though his friend is in her sixties, "She is still a child." He lives with relatives in "a spreading old house in a country town," but he and his cousin manage to remain somewhat separate from them. "We are not, on the whole, too much aware of them. We are each other's best friend," he says. By recognizing this, Buddy reveals his compassion for society's outsiders, as his cousin is considered. Every Saturday she gives him a dime and he goes to the movies, which influences his decision to be a tap dancer when he grows up. Because his friend never goes to movies, Buddy tells her about them, thus honing his storytelling skills. Later, when he recounts that he has been sent to military school, the sensitive narrator breaks the nostalgic mood of the story and provides its bittersweet resolution: "home is where my friend is, and there I never go."

### Mr. Haha Jones

Described as a "giant with razor scars across his cheeks," Haha Jones is proprietor of a "sinful" fish-fry and dancing cafe. The name "Haha" is ironic, because he is purportedly a gloomy man who never smiles. Buddy and his friend purchase whiskey for their fruitcakes from Haha, and when he gives them their money back he demonstrates that there is good in all people.

### My friend

Although she remains unnamed throughout the story, this "sixty-something" distant cousin is the narrator's best friend. Capote said in interviews that he based this character on Miss Sook Faulk, an elderly cousin with whom he spent much of his childhood. Buddy's friend is described as "still a child," and it is her innocence which allows their friendship to occur. The narrator reveals her to be a very idiosyncratic person—one who possesses unusual characteristics—by stating the things she has never done: "eaten in a restaurant, traveled more than five miles from home, received or sent a telegram, read anything except the funny papers and the Bible." She is also very wise, however, and it is she who teaches Buddy to value each individual object because "there are never two of anything."

## Media Adaptations

- "A Christmas Memory" was adapted for television in 1967 with Geraldine Page and Donnie Melvin; Truman Capote was the narrator. It is available on video under such titles as *ABC Playhouse 67: A Christmas Memory* or *Truman Capote's "A Christmas Memory"*; the latter version was also released by Allied Artists in 1969 as part of *Truman Capote's Trilogy*.

- The story has been adapted as part of *Short Story Anthology*, a sixteen-part series available from Children's Television International; "A Christmas Memory" comprises episodes 11 and 12 of the series.

- An audio adaptation of the story read by Capote is available from Knopf Book & Cassette Classics; a version read by Celeste Holm which includes "The Thanksgiving Visitor" is available from Random House Audiobooks.

- *Holiday Memories* is a musical stageplay adaptation by Malcolm Ruhl and Russell Vandenbroucke combining both "A Christmas Memory" and "The Thanksgiving Visitor"; it was published by Berwyn Press in 1991.

She also helps Buddy to appreciate nature as the place where God reveals Himself every day.

### Queenie

Queenie is a dog, described as a "tough little orange and white rat terrier who has survived distemper and two rattlesnake bites." Her resilience symbolizes the main characters' friendship, for though each is small and physically insignificant, their spirits are united by a strong bond. Queenie's death symbolizes the friends' forced separation and foreshadows the eventual death of the narrator's friend.

### Those Who Know Best

*See* Two Relatives

### Two Relatives

Buddy never refers to the other people who live with him and his friend by name, and by doing so he demonstrates his emotional distance from them. The irony in the term "Those Who Know Best" signifies that he believes they really do not know what is best for him. The relatives are shown to be harsh and scolding. He admits that "they have power over us, and frequently make us cry." Buddy also does not think much of their pious religious attitudes. When he receives a subscription to a religious magazine for children as a Christmas present, he says, "It makes me boil. It really does."

## Themes

"A Christmas Memory" is an evocation of an idealized early childhood, a memory clouded by the innocence of a seven-year-old. The narrator, who is now an adult, remembers making fruitcakes with his elderly cousin, an annual event which marked the coming of Christmas.

### Memory and Reminiscence

From the beginning of the story, the narrator's memory is linked to the act of storytelling and creativity. "Imagine a morning in late November. A coming of winter morning more than twenty years ago." Though the narrator sets the scene, he depends on the reader's own experiences to bring it into focus so he can tell the story. This technique plays upon the questionable nature of memory, in which personal experience is combined with images from other stories, books, and pictures to form a mind's-eye view. Thus, the veracity, or truthfulness, of memory is cast into doubt.

The story also illustrates the power of specific objects to evoke a particular memory. Just as in the beginning of the story "a great black stove" is the object around which the remembered kitchen is constructed, so at the end does the image of kites help the narrator to remember his cousin and their friendship. Likewise, the "hateful heap of bitter-odored pennies" which comprises the bulk of the two friends' fortune recalls "the carnage of August" when they were paid one penny for every twenty-five flies they killed. This image exemplifies the nature of memory in which one sense (in this case the smell of the pennies) leads to the remembrance of another sensory experience (the sight of the dead flies).

Another trait of personal reminiscence is the listing of objects, such as what the narrator eats for dinner ("cold biscuits, bacon, blackberry jam"), the fruitcake ingredients ("Cherries and citron, ginger and vanilla and canned Hawaiian pineapple," etc.) and the Christmas tree decoration ("a shoe box of ermine tails . . . , coils of frazzled tinsel . . . , one silver star," etc.). These lists not only aid the reader in conjuring an image of the scene being described, they also establish the authority of the narrator, as though he were saying, "I can prove that I was there because this is what I saw."

Memory also acts as a retreat from reality, as evidenced by the narrator's elderly friend calling him Buddy "in memory of a boy who was formerly her best friend" and who died. Her later inability to distinguish him from "the other Buddy" signals the increasing confusion of her mind and also her death, when she herself becomes a memory of the narrator.

### Friendship

Friendship among social outcasts is a common theme in Capote's work, and in "A Christmas Memory" the friendship between Buddy and his friend provide strength for the narrator. Buddy and his friend are outsiders within their household; the other members of the family "have power over [them], and frequently make [them] cry," but on the whole they "are not too much aware of them" because the friendship is their refuge. This friendship is made possible because even though his cousin is "sixty-something," she is "still a child" and shares his innocent view of the world. The strength of their friendship is further underscored by the statement that the narrator's real name is not Buddy; it is the name his friend has given him, and it is the only name the reader learns. From his cousin, Buddy learns how the beauty of nature signifies God's presence and that money is not the only measure of value. When the "rich mill owner's lazy wife" tries to buy their Christmas tree, his friend exclaims "We wouldn't take a dollar," underscoring the intrinsic value of nature by stating: "There's never two of anything." The friendship helps the narrator survive once he is separated from her, though he recognizes the irreversible loss of his childhood innocence: "Home is where my friend is, and there I never go." Even twenty years later, he likens their friendship to a "lost pair of kites hurrying toward heaven."

### Coming of Age

"A Christmas Memory" shows how children pass into adulthood not only by growing older, but also by learning the ways of the world. Two conflicting worldviews confront Buddy in the story, and it is his ability to synthesize the two that leads to his increased wisdom. His friend's childlike qualities exemplify her refusal to leave childhood and assume an adult role. The narrator states: "She is still a child." Though seven-year-old Buddy respects this quality, it is the basis for her ostracism from the rest of the family, who treat her as a subordinate. Her inability or refusal to properly distinguish between what is socially acceptable behavior and what is not is demonstrated in her allowing Buddy to become drunk on the leftover whiskey. She does understand that society might have good reason for refusing to allow children to drink alcohol. Told in flashback, the narrator relates the bittersweet nature of coming of age. Once removed from his best friend and sent to military school, he states that "Home is where my friend is, and there I never go." He recognizes the symbolic innocence of his younger days when he "[expects] to see, rather like hearts, a lost pair of kites hurrying toward heaven."

## Style

"A Christmas Memory" is a personal reminiscence which depends on first-person narration and the nostalgia of a rural Southern setting to evoke its mood. Its realism is supported by its straightforward, linear structure, while its use of lyrical language evokes the idea of a mythical past.

### Point of View

The story employs a first-person narrator who is called Buddy, though we are also told that this is not his real name, but a name given to him by his friend. By telling us this, the narrator suggests that

## Topics for Further Study

- What role does money play in "A Christmas Memory"? In what ways does the story suggest the economic hardship of the Great Depression, and how do the characters compensate for their lack of money?

- Write a brief story about a memory of your own. Now rewrite it from the viewpoint of someone who is not a central character in the story. How has your story changed? How would "A Christmas Memory" have been different if it had been told from the perspective of one of the other relatives in the household? How might the "rich mill owner's lazy wife" have recounted the story of trying to buy the Christmas tree to her husband that night over dinner?

- Does the Southern setting of "A Christmas Memory" enhance or detract from the nostalgic quality of the story? What images come to mind when you think of the South, and how do these images compare to your experience of reading the story?

---

the story is not his alone, but also belongs to his friend, the other major character in the story. The advantage of the first-person point of view lies in its allowing us to experience the story as Buddy himself did. The description of Mr. Haha is not an objective view; rather it is the view of a seven-year-old boy: "he *is* a giant; he *does* have scars; he *doesn't* smile." The italicized words demonstrate the amazement and fear felt by seven-year-old Buddy. Likewise, what the narrator thinks of the others in the household comes through in his references to them. "Other people inhabit the house," and his emotional distance is underscored by his using the generic term "people" and his refusal to give them personalities. His later reference to "those who Know Best" suggests his belief that they really do not know best. The fact that the narrator is an adult while he is telling the story is also significant, because it allows him to put his earlier memories into perspective and to understand events in ways which a seven-year-old boy could not: The adult narrator recognizes that his friend was "still a child." The main disadvantage of first-person narration is its limited ability to portray others. The reader must rely on Buddy's description of the woman, since her thoughts are never shown. Likewise, the reader cannot form valid judgments about the other family members because the point of view does not allow their perspective to be heard.

### Setting

"A Christmas Memory" is set in the rural South during the early 1930s. This can be deduced from the fact that the story first appeared in 1956, and the narrator tells us it took place during the winter "more than twenty years ago." This places the story during the Great Depression, a time of great poverty, which may explain why so many relatives are living in a house together, including a young boy without his parents. In reality, Capote spent several years with relatives while his mother sought work in other parts of the country. Furthermore, placing a nostalgic, "coming-of-age" story during the Christmas season, a time many people remember fondly, further emphasizes the story's goal of evoking a warm, bittersweet reminiscence.

### Structure

Partly because "A Christmas Memory" is a reminiscence, time is its dominant structural element. There are two time periods in the story: the present, in which the narrator relates the story, and the distant past, when the narrator was a boy. The narrator quickly moves the reader into the distant past by issuing a series of commands: "Imagine a morning in late November.... Consider the kitchen of a spreading old house." At the climax of the story, as Buddy and his cousin fly kites on Christmas day, the narrator brings the reader back to the present: "This is our last Christmas together." This sudden shift in time abruptly ends the story's nostalgic mood, and in the several subsequent paragraphs that recount events leading up to the narrator's present life, Capote quickly establishes a tone of bittersweet melancholy. By placing the main action of the story nearly twenty years before, that time is made to seem distant and remote. That Buddy's cousin is no longer living by the end of the story further serves to emphasize the passing of time and the inability for people to return to the past.

## Historical Context

### Growing up in the Depression

Capote's "A Christmas Memory" takes place in the South during the Depression. Though a larger historical framework is not apparent in the story, the traditions of the era are well represented by Buddy's adventures with his cousin. Living in a house with many relatives was common in times of great poverty, and Buddy was most likely there because his parents' economic situation prevented them from providing him with a stable life. In addition, the activities he pursues with his cousin—baking fruitcakes, cutting down a tree in the woods, making homemade decorations and Christmas presents together—not only evoke a nostalgia for a simpler time but also represent common amusements in a rural community when money was scarce. One of Buddy's favorite pastimes is going to the movies, which costs only a dime. During the Depression, millions attended the country's elaborate movie palaces every week; it was the cheapest, most common form of entertainment in a world not yet captivated by radio and television. That Buddy's cousin has never been to a movie herself may not seem so strange when one considers that she grew up in an era before the film industry had captured the public's attention.

### An Intolerant Era

Less apparent in the writing of "A Christmas Memory" are the cultural attitudes that fostered what Thomas Dukes has called "the quintessential homosexual writing style" of the 1950s. In an era of considerable sexual repression, addressing homosexual themes overtly in literature was uncommon. Instead, authors, especially Capote, created situations in a type of "code" that were often interpreted in a homosexual context. One aspect of this "code" in Capote's story is the sensitivity of the central male character, particularly his preference for emphasizing his feelings and emotions over action. Another aspect of this "code" is the emphasis on female characters and domestic concerns. Note also the joke that Mr. Haha Jones makes when he asks Buddy and his cousin, "Which of you is a drinking man?" That Haha finds this funny suggests that he equates Buddy's gender identity more with his female friend rather than with his status as a young male. Outside of his writing, Capote defined himself as homosexual in the often homophobic culture of the 1950s and 1960s through the way in which he chose to be photographed and the effeminate manner he assumed during television interviews.

## Critical Overview

"A Christmas Memory" was first published in *Mademoiselle* in 1956 and then reprinted in *Selected Writings of Truman Capote* in 1963, but it received little attention until it was reprinted as a gift-boxed set for Christmas in 1966. Reviews at the time were generally favorable, with a writer for *Harper's* calling it "an enchanting little book destined ... to become a classic." Nancy McKenzie noted in *The New York Times* that the story "seesaws slowly and nostalgically in time." However, other critics, including playwright Tennessee Williams, characterized the story as saccharine, overly sentimental, or even repulsive. Capote himself described the story as a catharsis which helped him to deal with his experiences as a child in the South: "The moment I wrote that short story I knew I would never write another word about the South. I am not going to be haunted by it any more, so I see no reason to deal with those people or those settings," he said in an interview with Roy Newquist in *Counterpoint* in 1964.

William Nance sees the story in *The Worlds of Truman Capote* as important for understanding Capote's work because of the character of Buddy's elderly friend. "Asexual admiration of a childlike dreamer heroine is the usual attitude of the Capote narrator," Nance explains, linking Buddy's friend to Dolly Talbo in *The Grass Harp* and Holly Golightly in *Breakfast at Tiffany's*. Nance further notes that in "A Christmas Memory" Capote displays his typical "hostility toward those outside the magic circle," the magic circle being the closed environment manufactured by those who are alienated in some way from society.

Many critics have noted the similarity between Buddy himself and Capote's other male characters. Often lonely, thirsting for love, and in search of an identity, these characters represent Capote himself. In "A Christmas Memory," these emotional quests end on a sad note when the narrator says "Home is where my friend is, and there I never go." Other critics comment on Capote's presentation of male characters as forcing the reader to rethink gender roles. Buddy revises the traditional coming-of-age narrative, in which the male protagonist demonstrates his masculinity and self-worth by moving

*Original illustration from "A Christmas Story."*

ever westward and exploring new frontiers. Instead, Buddy remembers with fondness baking fruitcakes on a cast-iron stove, thereby romanticizing the traditionally female sphere of domesticity. During the years in which he is supposed to "come of age," he rejects the traditionally masculinizing influence of military schools, which he characterizes as "a miserable succession of bugle-blowing prisons."

## Criticism

### *Trudy Ring*

*Trudy Ring is a frequent writer, editor, and reporter on literary subjects. In the following essay, she gives an overview of Capote's "A Christmas Memory," concentrating on the portrayal of the character of Buddy's cousin.*

Truman Capote often drew on his Southern childhood in finding material for his fiction. He also frequently focused his stories on unconventional, strangely appealing women. "A Christmas Memo-

## Compare & Contrast

- **1930s:** Schools and most other public facilities across the South are segregated by race.

  **1956:** The University of Alabama expels its first black student in defiance of a federal court order; Southern congressmen issue a manifesto pledging to use "all lawful means" to defy desegregation.

  **Today:** Schools and public facilities are open to all regardless of race, but economic inequality is still seen by some as a barrier to full integration.

- **1930s:** The first "talkie" was produced in 1928; a few years later all films have sound. Elaborately staged musicals become one of the movie industry's most popular genres.

  **1956:** As a result of the country's rising prosperity following World War II, television is introduced to many homes, providing cheap, nearly endless entertainment. Movie attendance falls by millions, and many theaters close. The industry fights back by developing thousands of drive-in movie theaters.

  **Today:** New forms of mass media include cable television and the Internet.

- **1930s:** At the height of the Depression unemployment is nearly 25%. President Franklin Roosevelt attempts to stimulate economic growth through his New Deal programs.

  **1956:** Post-war prosperity makes the United States a dominant world power. President Eisenhower warns of the "military-industrial complex" at the heart of the country's economy, but government continues to expand.

  **1990s:** Both Democrats and Republicans proclaim an end to the era of big government, but true economic and social reforms are slow to impact people's lives.

- **1930s:** Fascist dictatorships and militant nationalists gain power in Europe as the Great Depression throws countries into economic and social turmoil.

  **1956:** The fear of communism fuels the Cold War. The arms race escalates, and Soviet Premier Nikita Khruschev tells the U.S. government, "History is on our side. We will bury you!"

  **1990s:** Communist regimes in Eastern Europe and the former Soviet Union have been replaced by democratic-style governments. China, the last significant communist power, enacts many capitalist reforms.

---

ry" is possibly the best example of a Capote story that exhibits both of these features. Capote described it as his favorite among his stories, and it showed his writing shifting from a preoccupation with the darker aspects of life to warmer and more sentimental subject matter. (He would return to darker subjects later, with *In Cold Blood,* his account of the murder of a family in rural Kansas.) Capote said he liked "A Christmas Memory" because of the truth in it, but the story is actually an idealized and embellished portrait of his childhood and of his elderly cousin, Sook, who provided much of the warmth and companionship he knew as a youngster.

Capote's parents were divorced when he was four years old, and his mother placed him with relatives in Monroeville, Alabama, while she went to New York City to look for a job. Young Truman lived most of the time with four cousins, all much older than he. The one with whom he formed the closest relationship was Nanny Rumbley Faulk, nicknamed Sook. She was reclusive and many people considered her peculiar. Relatives later pointed out after characterizations of her began showing up in Capote's work, however, that she was more intelligent and less naive than she appeared. At any rate, she was able to relate to Truman almost as if they were both children. Later, like Buddy in "A

## What Do I Read Next?

- "The Thanksgiving Visitor," a 1968 story also by Capote, is a companion piece to "A Christmas Memory" and recounts further adventures of Buddy and his friend Sook, as well as Buddy's run-in with Odd Henderson, the town bully.

- Capote's novel *The Grass Harp* (1951) tells the story of a band of social outcasts, including a young boy and his older female relative, who disrupt their complacent community when they retreat to the woods and begin living in a treehouse.

- Carson McCullers's *Ballad of the Sad Cafe* (1936) is the story of Cousin Lyman, a traveling hunchback dwarf who brings excitement to a lonely Southern town when Miss Amelia falls in love with him and follows his suggestion to open a cafe.

- *Black Boy* is Richard Wright's 1941 autobiographical novel, which vividly describes his harsh, hardscrabble boyhood and youth in rural Mississippi and Memphis, Tennessee. The book is a coming-of-age story that details how Wright worked to realize his dream of being a writer despite the constraints placed upon him by a racist society.

- *Let Us Now Praise Famous Men* (1941) is a nonfiction chronicle of the daily lives of Depression-era tenant farmers in rural Alabama with black-and-white photographs by Walker Evans and accompanying text by James Agee.

- *Paper Moon,* is a novel by Joe David Brown about a Depression-era traveling Bible salesman and the hassles he experiences when he is saddled with caring for his precocious daughter. Also filmed in 1973 under the same title; directed by Peter Bogdanovich and starring Ryan and Tatum O'Neal.

- John Dufresne's 1994 novel *Louisiana Power and Light* is a comical send-up of the Southern Gothic tradition and revolves around the adventures of Moon Pie Fontana, a physically disabled child-star radio evangelist, and his family down in the Delta.

---

Christmas Memory,'' Truman was sent away to boarding school. Unlike his fictional counterpart, he went through an emotional break with his cousin. Capote's family members, including Sook, were unable to accept his homosexuality or deal with his alcoholism and drug abuse.

Capote modeled several of his characters on Sook. In addition to the kindly and eccentric woman of "A Christmas Memory," she is represented in Dolly Talbo in his novel *The Grass Harp*. Some other Capote heroines are based less directly on Sook, but are closely related to her. One of them is the character who is perhaps Capote's most famous creation, Holly Golightly of *Breakfast at Tiffany's*. William L. Nance, a literary scholar who has written extensively about Capote, referred to Holly as "a dreamer-heroine whose prototype is the elderly friend of 'A Christmas Memory.'" Nance also noted that these characters are evidence of Capote's nonsexual yet strong attachment to women, especially women who do not quite fit into mainstream society.

The elderly woman of "A Christmas Memory" certainly is out of the mainstream. Buddy says that his cousin, although in her sixties, "is still a child." She is not stupid, but she does not live her life according to an adult idea of what is sensible or practical. She has a sense of fun that appeals to the boy. Buddy is tolerant of his cousin's eccentricities, which Capote describes in detail and with affection. Her appearance, described in the story's second paragraph, marks her as an unorthodox person. She wears tennis shoes and a baggy sweater with a lightweight calico dress; her "remarkable" face is craggy yet delicate. Later, the narrator, the boy grown up, relates more facts about her. "She has

> "Over the years, some critics have pronounced 'A Christmas Memory' overly sentimental, but most of them, along with the reading public, have found it genuinely moving."

never: eaten in a restaurant, traveled more than five miles from home, received or sent a telegram, read anything except funny papers and the Bible, worn cosmetics, cursed, wished someone harm, told a lie on purpose, let a hungry dog go hungry,'' Capote writes. Then he tells us the things she does: ''tame hummingbirds . . . tell ghost stories . . . so tingling they chill you in July, talk to herself, take walks in the rain, grow the prettiest japonicas [a flowering shrub] in town, know the recipe for every sort of old-time Indian cure.'' The story provides fewer details about the little boy, but it is obvious he is a precocious child, something that inspires admiration in his cousin. She loves to have Buddy tell her the stories of the movies he sees; she will never go to a movie because she wants to save her vision for when she sees God.

Buddy and his cousin create a happy world of their own. They ''are not, on the whole, too much aware'' of the other relatives who live with them; instead, they find joy in each other's company. Incidents throughout the story underline their attachment to each other and their distance from the rest of their family. Because Buddy and his cousin have little money, most of their pleasures are improvised, from gathering pecans left on the ground after the harvest to making their own Christmas gifts and ornaments. They are enthusiastic about their various moneymaking schemes, from entering contests advertised on the radio to setting up their homemade museum, even though these schemes are more often failures than successes. They enjoy interacting with people outside of the world of their conventional relatives and neighbors—such as the bootlegger Haha Jones or the strangers and near-strangers to whom they send their Christmas fruitcakes. The old woman lets Buddy drink whiskey, which gets her in trouble with the rest of the family. And while the other family members give him disappointingly practical Christmas gifts, she gives him a kite. That's what he gives her, too, in an exchange of gifts that, as critic Stanley Edgar Hyman once pointed out, is as corny and as emotionally effective as the exchange in O. Henry's ''The Gift of the Magi.''

Over the years, some critics have pronounced ''A Christmas Memory'' overly sentimental, but most of them, along with the reading public, have found it genuinely moving. It is particularly heart-rending when Capote moves from the idyllic Christmas Day that Buddy and his cousin spend flying their kites to Buddy's separation from his friend—a separation created first by distance when Buddy goes away to school, then by the old woman's death. It is indicative of their bond that Buddy feels her death before he is told of it. In life, Capote's bond with Sook was so strong, and so painful to break off, that he was driven to recreate it along with similar relationships in his fiction for many years afterward. ''A Christmas Memory,'' according to Nance, ''has a unique importance'' among Capote's works because it is so much a model for his later stories, often centering on unusual women who live in a world of their own and who inspire love that has little to do with sex. ''The pastness of the experience is also essential; Capote's is a fiction of nostalgia,'' Nance observed. '' 'A Christmas Memory' is one of his best and most satisfying works because it places the feelings he can dramatize most powerfully in the setting which is best suited to them.''

**Source:** Trudy Ring, for *Short Stories for Students,* Gale Research, 1997.

### Helen S. Garson

*Garson is a professor of English and a frequent contributor to literary journals. In the following excerpt from a longer chapter in a book, she discusses ''A Christmas Memory'' in terms of its autobiographical elements and its similarities to Capote's novel* A Grass Harp, *which also fictionalizes the author's youth.*

. . .Capote's ability to combine comedy, nostalgia, and a child's sense of tragedy is nowhere more evident than in the story ''A Christmas Memory.'' Declared by Capote to be his most cherished piece, it is more overtly autobiographical than anything else he has written. The author has said that the child in the story is himself and the elderly relative, his cousin, Miss Sook Faulk. He further emphasized the reality behind the fiction in "A Christmas Memory" by having a childhood picture of himself and Miss Faulk reproduced for a reprinting of the story in 1966, ten years after its original publication.

In addition to seeing the autobiographical connection between the story and the author, the reader can discern immediately similarities to Capote's novel, *The Grass Harp*. In both works, the major figures are a young boy and his older female relative; the scenes take place primarily in the kitchen and in the woods; the story is set in the past and the tone is nostalgic; and an event of great significance takes place in both the story and the novel, that is, the parting of the child and his cousin. In *The Grass Harp* the woman dies and the young man goes north to school, whereas in "A Christmas Memory" the boy is sent away to a military school, never to see his cousin again; her death occurs after his leaving.

"A Christmas Memory" opens as the narrator evokes memories of late November mornings spent in a warm country kitchen. Looking backwards the speaker becomes a seven-year-old who has lived for a long time with his distant cousin. Although it is not her house, in his child's world the other inhabitants don't matter unless they cause difficulties. The old woman and the boy, whom she has named Buddy, after a childhood friend of hers who died in the 1880s, are best friends. It is possible because the white-haired, small, sprightly, craggy yet delicate-faced woman with sherry-colored, timid eyes has never outgrown the sunny world of childhood. Buddy stresses the great difference between her and others, saying, "She is still a child."

On a particular morning every November, a special ritual is repeated. His cousin looks out the window, notes the chill of the season, thinks of Christmas, and makes the pronouncement: "It's fruitcake weather." The two of them find her hat—worn more for propriety than for warmth, a straw cartwheel decorated with roses of velvet—and get Buddy's old baby carriage, which serves as a cart for carrying the load of pecans that will go into the fruitcake. Along with their dog, Queenie, they walk to a pecan grove, where, on their hands and knees, for hours they will search out nuts.

Their expeditions are like those in *The Grass Harp*. Dolly, Catherine, and Collin go to the woods to gather ingredients for Dolly's dropsy medicine or to picnic. Buddy and his cousin collect flowers, herbs, and ferns in the spring, firewood in the winter, and fish the creek in the summer. The lives of the two families resemble each other in their

> "Capote's ability to combine comedy, nostalgia, and a child's sense of tragedy is nowhere more evident than in the story 'A Christmas Memory.'"

patterns. And another similarity exists in their attitudes toward money. It is intended to bring pleasure. However, where Dolly, Catherine, and Collin have Dolly's earnings to purchase magazines and games, Buddy and his cousin enter contests to try to win money to support their activities; they also sell jars of jams, jellies, and preserves they've made, berries they've gathered, and flowers they've picked for important occasions.

They need money for the buying of the items that go into the fruitcake, the candied fruits, the spices, the whiskey, the flour, the butter, the eggs. All year long they save in their "Fruitcake Fund;" most of it is in pennies, which they count out for the thirty or more cakes they send to people they like, such as President Roosevelt, a bus driver who waves at them every day, and a couple who once took a picture of them. And afterwards there are the thank-you letters for their scrapbooks.

The fun and excitement of shopping is followed by the pleasure of preparing the cakes: the glowing of the stove, the sounds of the mixing, the smells of the spices delight Buddy. However, in four days it is all over and he feels let down afterwards. His cousin has a remedy though for depression, the whiskey left from the baking. After Queenie gets a spoonful mixed in coffee, the two of them drink the remainder. Then the sour taste of the liquor is soon replaced by happy feelings. They begin to giggle, to sing, and to dance. Queenie rolls in drunken joy as the cousin waltzes around in her squeaky tennis shoes.

The delightful comedy of the drinking scene is produced by the deft touch of the writer, not only here but elsewhere in the work as well. The description of the meeting with Haha Jones—so named for his somber disposition—proprietor of the shop where they buy the whiskey for the cakes, is another episode enlivened by the lightness of the humor.

Looking at the odd pair, Haha asks, "Which one of you is a drinking man?" The appearance of Haha and the tongue-in-cheek designation of the "sinful" café he runs all add to the comic note.

There are also other kinds of humor in the story. A line here and there suggests the eighteenth-century satirist Alexander Pope. When the narrator tells of earning pennies by killing house flies, he says in mockheroic style, "Oh the carnage of August: the flies that flew to heaven!" Superstition further provides the opportunity for comedy; the number thirteen has several possibilities. Fear of having thirteen dollars causes Buddy and his cousin to throw a penny out of the window to avoid the multiple catastrophes that could occur from the unlucky sum. Twelve ninety-nine is safer. The importance of hoarding the money of the "Fund" provides another chance for verbal and visual humor. Buddy makes the following statement, creating an expanding comic effect by the use of detail and the repetition of the word "under": "These moneys we keep hidden in an ancient purse under a loose board under the floor under a chamber pot under my friend's bed."

The only money ever withdrawn from their savings is the ten cents Buddy is given each week for the movies, to which he goes alone. Although his elderly cousin enjoys hearing him tell the film story, she has never been to a movie. Her life, like that of Dolly Talbo, is that of a recluse. One thinks of Dolly's nunlike, pink room when Buddy describes his cousin's bedroom containing an iron bed painted in her favorite rose pink. Further, his cousin has never been far from home, has had very limited experiences, and is ignorant of the world outside the little town in which she lives. Yet she knows all kinds of wonderful things a small boy admires: how to tame hummingbirds, how to tell terrifying ghost stories, and how to treat ailments by using old Indian cures.

Buddy's cousin, who reads only the funny papers and the Bible, is a religious Christian who fully expects to come face to face with God at the end of her life. However, she also understands the natural world, loves and respects it. Once someone chides her for refusing to sell a beautiful fragrant pine she has cut for a Christmas tree and she is told she can get another one. But she responds like a nineteenth-century Romantic philosopher in tune with nature: "There's never two of anything."

Decorating the Christmas tree they have dragged home from the woods and making presents consumes much of their time. As early as August they pick cotton to sprinkle on the tree in December. Later, old treasures are brought down from the attic; cutouts of fruits and animals are made from colored paper and tinfoil angels from candy wrappers. They make holly wreaths and family gifts together. But then they separate to make the most important items, the things they will exchange with each other. Both want to give something special, but they have no money for bought presents. Because of that, every year they design colorful handmade kites.

When the holidays are over and the wind is right, they go out of doors to the nearby pastures to fly their kites. Thus the seasons pass, from fruitcake time to tree cutting and decorating, to kite-flying weather. And during the last kite-flying days they have together, Buddy's cousin speaks of a sudden vision she has. She tells him that God shows Himself in many guises, but only at the end of life do we realize that He "has already shown Himself." And as she says that to Buddy, she moves her hand in an encompassing gesture "that gathers clouds and kites and grass and Queenie pawing earth over her bone."

It is not long after his cousin has described to him her sense of a godlike indwelling that Buddy is parted from her. He is forced to take up a new life in military schools, camps, and another home. However, because of his love for his cousin and his great sense of loss in the separation, he never feels that he belongs anywhere. He always identifies home with his cousin.

Remaining alone, his cousin writes him of her activities and sorrows, of the death of Queenie. Each November she sends him the best of the fruitcakes. But she lives only a few years more. Soon her memory fails and she can no longer distinguish the narrator from the Buddy who was her childhood friend.

In the winter season when she dies, Buddy intuits her death before he is told of it. He describes his feeling of loss as an "irreplaceable part" of himself, "loose like a kite on a broken string." He looks up to the December sky as if to see that lost self of his joining with his other self, the spirit of his cousin, "rather like hearts, a lost pair of kites hurrying toward heaven." . . .

**Source:** Helen S. Garson, "Surprised by Joy: Stories of the Fifties and Sixties," in *Truman Capote*, Frederick Ungar, 1980, pp. 97–102.

## William L. Nance

*In the following essay about Truman Capote's short stories, Nance analyzes "A Christmas Memory" as a "fiction of nostalgia."*

"A Christmas Memory" is Truman Capote's nonfiction short story. In 1956, the year it was published, Capote was in the midst of a major change in literary direction. Five years had passed since his short fiction had drifted into the shallows of "House of Flowers," and his vital fictional development had shifted to the short novel. During the next three years he made disappointing experiments with drama (*The Grass Harp*) and musical comedy (*House of Flowers*), and went on a cinematic lark (*Beat the Devil*) in Italy. Then, deciding that he had been wasting his time, he began preparing seriously for the nonfiction novel with some "finger exercises," the most important of which was *The Muses Are Heard* (1956), his report on the Russian tour of an all-Negro production of *Porgy and Bess*.

In the same year he returned to the very roots of his own experience in "A Christmas Memory," a frank memoir which, while generally accepted as one of his finest and most charming short stories, has become his own avowed favorite among his shorter works because it is "true." In 1966, riding the tidal wave of popularity whipped up by *In Cold Blood*, Capote arranged for a pre-Christmas publication of the story in a slim, boxed volume bearing a reproduction of an actual snapshot of himself, a smiling little boy, with the elderly cousin with whom he spent much of his childhood.

The story is his idealized recollection of his relationship with this woman. As such it has a unique importance among his works, for it embodies the archetype of an emotional pattern which underlies all his later fiction and even exerts a subtle influence on *In Cold Blood*. Asexual admiration of a childlike dreamer-heroine is the usual attitude of the Capote narrator. The pastness of the experience is also essential; Capote's is a fiction of nostalgia. "A Christmas Memory" is one of his best and most satisfying works because it places the feelings he can dramatize most powerfully in the setting which is best suited to them—which, as Henry James would say, artistically does most for them.

Capote begins by asking the reader to remember a November morning more than twenty years ago and the kitchen of a country house. A little old woman with a craggy but delicate face and eyes "sherry-colored and timid" is standing at the window. Suddenly she exclaims, "Oh my, it's fruitcake weather!" The narrator explains:

> The person to whom she is speaking is myself. I am seven; she is sixty-something. We are cousins, very distant ones, and we have lived together—well, as long as I can remember. Other people inhabit the house, relatives; and though they have power over us, and frequently make us cry, we are not, on the whole, too much aware of them. We are each other's best friend. She calls me Buddy, in memory of a boy who was formerly her best friend. The other Buddy died in the 1880's when she was still a child. She is still a child.

Their annual ritual, the baking of thirty fruitcakes, begins with a trip to gather pecans, followed by an evening spent cracking them: "Caarackle! A cheery crunch, scraps of miniature thunder sound as the shells collapse and the golden mound of sweet oily ivory meat mounts in the milk-glass bowl." The second day is to be spent buying the many ingredients, but first there is the problem of money. During the year, they have supplemented the "skin-flint sums" given them by the family by selling handpicked fruit and preserves, holding rummage sales and backyard entertainments—once by winning seventy-ninth prize in a national football contest. The slowly accumulated Fruitcake Fund is tapped only for a weekly dime to permit Buddy to go to the picture show. His friend has never seen one and doesn't intend to. Her life has, in fact, been extremely circumscribed; yet she has numerous accomplishments, among them the ability to tame hummingbirds, tell ghost stories, and concoct old time Indian cures. She is superstitious and always spends the thirteenth of the month in her bed, which is painted rose pink, her favorite color.

To get whiskey, the most expensive of the fruitcake ingredients, the two friends pay an apprehensive visit to Mr. Haha Jones, proprietor of "a 'sinful' (to quote public opinion) fish-fry and dancing cafe down by the river." Mr. Jones, a sort of benevolent bogeyman with razor scars across his face, decides to charge them one fruitcake rather than the usual two dollars. Buddy's friend later remarks, "Well, there's a lovely man. We'll put an extra cup of raisins in *his* cake."

Then comes the baking. "The black stove, stoked with coal and firewood, glows like a lighted pumpkin. Eggbeaters whirl, spoons spin round in bowls of butter and sugar, vanilla sweetens the air, ginger spices it; melting, nose-tingling odors saturate the kitchen, suffuse the house, drift out to the world on puffs of chimney smoke."

> "'A Christmas Memory' is one of Capote's best and most satisfying works because it places the feelings he can dramatize most powerfully in the setting which is best suited to them."

In four days the cakes are finished. They are intended for "friends," most of them met only once or not at all—people who have struck their fancy. Among them are President Roosevelt, a Baptist missionary couple, a knife grinder, the driver of the six-o'clock bus from Mobile (perhaps the same who unwittingly ended the life of Miss Bobbit), and a young couple who chatted with them one day and took the only snapshot they ever had taken. Buddy decides it is because his friend is shy with everyone *except* strangers that these acquaintances seem their truest friends. Besides, the thank-you notes make them feel "connected to eventful worlds beyond the kitchen with its view of a sky that stops."

Mailing the cakes takes the last of their money, and they return home to celebrate by drinking up the last two inches of whiskey in Mr. Jones's bottle. After a while they begin singing two songs at once and dancing, she with "the hem of her poor calico skirt pinched between her fingers as though it were a party dress: *Show me the way to go home,* she sings, her tennis shoes squeaking on the floor."

Suddenly two relatives enter, very angry. They tell Buddy's friend she "must be a loony" to give whiskey to a child of seven, and exhort her to "kneel, pray, beg the Lord!" She runs to her room and cries into her pillow because she is "old and funny," but Buddy insists that she is fun—"More fun than anybody."

The next day they go to the woods for a Christmas tree. Decorations, made from colored paper and Hershey-bar tin foil, are attached to the tree with safety pins. The two friends make gifts for the family, then separate to prepare each other's. Unable to buy the bicycle and the chocolate-covered cherries which each knows to be the other's true heart's desire, they make each other kites, as they did last year and the year before.

On Christmas morning they are awake long before dawn and rouse the rest of the family by dropping a kettle and tap-dancing in the hall. The others finally appear, "looking as though they'd like to kill us both," and after breakfast the presents are opened. Except for the kite, Buddy is disappointed. "Who wouldn't be? With socks, a Sunday school shirt, some handkerchiefs, a hand-me-down sweater and a year's subscription to a religious magazine for children. *The Little Shepherd.* It makes me boil. It really does."

This hostility toward those outside the magic circle is another reminder of the social alienation of Capote's dream world. Always inclined toward this kind of exclusiveness, he has tried to counteract it in various ways, especially in the non-fiction novel. Here, at a distance of over twenty years, he allows it free rein.

Buddy and his friend spend Christmas day not with their relatives but out in the fields flying their kites. She, growing meditative, tells Buddy she has always believed that the Lord's coming would be "like looking at the Baptist window: pretty as colored glass with the sun pouring through, such a shine you don't know it's getting dark. And it's been a comfort: to think of that shine taking away all the spooky feeling." Now, however, she decides that probably the Lord shows himself even in this world: "'That things as they are'—her hand circles in a gesture that gathers clouds and kites and grass and Queenie pawing earth over her bone—'just what they've always been, was seeing Him. As for me, I could leave the world with today in my eyes'." This dreamer, because she is a Bible-reading Christian, thinks not of children on their birthdays but of a more conventional heaven. In this Christmas meditation she almost succeeds in grasping it immediately, transcending death.

And here Capote, through memory, comes closer to sharing it than anywhere else in his fiction. Buddy's own particular dream of starring in the movies links him to Miss Bobbit and Appleseed, reminding us that they and he and his elderly friend are all essentially the same dreamer.

Death intrudes, however: Buddy is sent to military school and moves to a new home. "But it doesn't count. Home is where my friend is, and there I never go." For several years she writes, but gradually she begins to confuse him with the Buddy who died in the 1880's. One November morning she cannot rouse herself to welcome fruitcake weather.

> And when that happens, I know it. A message saying so merely confirms a piece of news some secret vein had already received, severing from me an irreplaceable part of myself, letting it loose like a kite on a broken string. That is why, walking across a school campus on this particular December morning, I keep searching the sky. As if I expected to see, rather like hearts, a lost pair of kites hurrying toward heaven.

The part of himself that Capote identifies with his childhood friend did not escape him at her death. Or, if something was cut away, it has continued to pulse like a severed arm. Repeatedly he has felt a need to project the emotional pattern of this early friendship into other relationships, in most respects very unlike that first one, and to build stories around them. "A Christmas Memory" is in a sense continued in *The Grass Harp,* which was published five years earlier. There the boy is about ten years older, and it is the death of his friend, there named Dolly Talbo, and his own entry into the adult world that bring the story to a close. *Breakfast at Tiffany's* picks up his career in New York a few years later and presents, in Holly Golightly, another version of his childhood friend. In "Among the Paths to Eden," Capote's last short story to date, he portrays another of her counterparts.

**Source:** William L. Nance, in *The Worlds of Truman Capote,* Stein and Day, 1970, pp. 78–83.

## Sources

Hyman, Stanley Edgar. "Fruitcake at Tiffany's," in his *Standards: A Chronicle of Books for Our Time,* Horizon Press, 1966.

McKenzie, Nancy. A review of "A Christmas Memory," in *The New York Times,* November 17, 1966.

Newquist, Roy. An interview with Truman Capote in *Counterpoint,* Rand McNally, 1964.

A review of "A Christmas Memory," in *Harper's Magazine,* Vol. 233, December, 1966, p. 132.

## Further Reading

Clarke, Gerald. *Capote: A Biography,* Simon & Schuster, 1988.
A very readable and thorough biography of Capote. While it is not an authorized biography, Capote cooperated with Clarke up until his death.

Inge, M. Thomas. *Truman Capote: Conversations,* University Press of Mississippi, 1987.
A compilation of interviews with Truman Capote spanning 1948 to 1980. Provides insight into what Capote thought about the craft of writing and his childhood in the South.

Moates, Marianne M. "Truman Capote's Southern Years," in her *A Bridge of Childhood,* Holt, 1989, 240 p.
Moates provides background on Capote's childhood and family, including the cousin he fictionalized in "A Christmas Memory."

# Everyday Use

Alice Walker

1973

"Everyday Use" was published early in Alice Walker's writing career, appearing in her collection *In Love and Trouble: Stories of Black Women* in 1973. The work was enthusiastically reviewed upon publication, and "Everyday Use" has since been called by some critics the best of Walker's short stories. In letting a rural black woman with little education tell a story that affirms the value of her heritage, Walker articulates what has since become, as critic Barbara Christian notes, two central themes in her writing: "the importance of the quilt in her work . . . [and] the creation of African American Southern women as subjects in their own right." When Mrs. Johnson snatches her ancestors' quilts from her daughter Dee, who wants to hang them on a wall, and gives them to Maggie, Walker illuminates her life-long celebration of rural Southern black womanhood. The motif of quilting has since become central to Walker's concerns, because it suggests the strength to be found in connecting with one's roots and one's past. As with many other stories by Walker, "Everyday Use" is narrated by the unrefined voice of a rural black woman, in the author's attempt to give a voice to a traditionally disenfranchised segment of the population.

## Author Biography

Walker's short story "Everyday Use" contains several important parallels to the author's own life.

Born in 1944 in Eatonton, Georgia, Walker grew up in an environment much like that described in the story. Her parents were both sharecroppers, her family lived in a rundown shack, and racial segregation was legally enforced, prompting the author to describe the times as America's own era of apartheid. Like Maggie Johnson, Walker was disfigured as a child. A gunshot wound left her blind in one eye; she became shy and withdrew into her own world of reading and writing. Like Dee Johnson, Walker's abilities garnered her a scholarship to Spelman College, which led her away from her poverty-stricken background to Atlanta, Georgia, in 1961. These were especially turbulent times for African Americans, and Walker soon became involved in efforts to improve conditions for blacks. In 1964, she travelled to Uganda as an exchange student. She returned to the United States for graduation, and upon receiving a writing fellowship she made plans to return to Africa. However, her job as a case worker in New York City's welfare department reconfirmed her commitment to the American black community, and she soon traveled to Mississippi to work on a voter registration drive.

Walker also continued writing, and she began to achieve national attention by publishing her first book of poetry in 1968 and her first novel, *The Third Life of Grange Copeland,* in 1970. Further novels, poetry, essays, and children's books followed, and Walker's popularity grew enormously in 1983 when her novel *The Color Purple* garnered the Pulitzer Prize, making her the first black woman writer to receive the award. Her prominence as a major voice in American literature was further solidified when Steven Spielberg made the novel into a major motion picture in 1985. Throughout her career, Walker's art has shed new light on various aspects of African American experience, particularly the trials and tribulations of black women. Her feminist standpoint has led to some criticism for her often unflattering portrayals of black men.

## Plot Summary

Alice Walker's modern classic "Everyday Use" tells the story of a mother and her two daughters' conflicting ideas about their identities and ancestry. The mother narrates the story of the day one daughter, Dee, visits from college and clashes with the other daughter, Maggie, over the possession of some heirloom quilts.

*Alice Walker*

The story begins with the narrator, a "big-boned woman with rough, man-working hands" awaiting the homecoming of her daughter Dee, an educated woman who now lives in the city. Accompanying her is her younger daughter, Maggie, a shy girl who regards her sister with a "mixture of envy and awe." As they wait, the narrator reveals details of the family history, specifically the relationship between her two girls. A fire when they were children destroyed their first house and left Maggie badly scarred on her arms and legs. The mother's memory of the night the house burned defines her two daughters: Maggie "with her hair smoking and her dress falling off her in little peppery flakes" and Dee "standing off under the sweet gum tree...[with] a look of concentration on her face as she watched the last dingy gray board of the house fall in toward the red-hot chimney."

Since the fire the two daughters have taken diverging paths. Maggie has a little education, but according to her mother, "she is not bright. Like good looks and money, quickness passed her by." She is, however, engaged to marry and will soon leave her mother's house. Dee, on the other hand, has been ambitious and determined since girlhood to rise above her humble beginnings. Thanks to her mother's and the church's fundraising efforts, she has gone off to school in Augusta.

When Dee arrives, Maggie and her mother are waiting in the front yard, which serves the family as "an extended living room." She emerges from the car dressed in bright clothing and gold jewelry; her boyfriend, Hakim-a-barber, has wild-looking hair. After greeting her mother and Maggie in a language they do not understand, Dee starts taking pictures, posing Maggie and her mother in front of the house as though she were a tourist. Dee tells her mother that "Dee is dead," and her new name is "Wangero Leewanika Kemanjo." She claims she could not stand being "named after the people who oppress me." Her mother's complaints that "Dee" is an old family name do not register.

During the meal Dee reveals her true intentions in visiting: to collect objects for her home that she can use to display her heritage. First she takes the butter churn, which she plans to use "as a centerpiece for the alcove table." After dinner Dee continues to search for objects for her collection and latches on to the quilts that had been made by her mother, grandmother, and great-grandmother. The quilts contain pieces of family history, scraps from old dresses and shirts that family members have worn. One patch is constructed of the girls' great grandfather's Civil War uniform.

The quilts, however, have already been promised to Maggie for her wedding. Dee contends that she has a right to them because she understands their value as folk art, declaring them "priceless." Maggie, on the other hand, is prepared to relinquish her rights to them rather than argue with her sister. When Maggie tells her she can have the quilts, because she "can 'member Grandma Dee" without them, the mother knows instantly who is the most deserving. She hugs Maggie, who was "used to never winning anything, or having anything reserved for her," and "snatched the quilts out of Miss Wangero's hands and dumped them into Maggie's lap." After Dee departs without the quilts, Maggie smiles a "real smile" for the first time.

## Characters

### *Asalamalakim*
See Hakim-a-barber

### *Grandma Dee*
Although Grandma Dee, as the Johnson women call her, does not appear in the story, she is a significant presence. Maggie is attached to the quilts because they make her think of Grandma Dee. Thus, although the woman is dead, she represents the cherished family presence that lives on in Maggie's and her mother's connection to the past.

### *Hakim-a-barber*
Hakim-a-barber is Dee's boyfriend who accompanies her on her visit back home. Though he has grown his hair long in an African style that identifies him with the black power movement, he refuses to eat collard greens and pork at dinner—traditional African-American foods. This minor character's name is perhaps his most significant feature. Mrs. Johnson confusedly accepts his black Muslim greeting, "Asalamalakim," as his name, and "Hakim-a-barber" is her guess at the pronunciation of what he tells her to call him. This confusion signals the gap between black nationalist ideas and rural African-American life.

### *Wangero Leewanika Kemanjo*
See Dee Johnson

### *Dee Johnson*
Dee is Mrs. Johnson's oldest daughter; the one who has always been determined, popular, and successful. Upon returning home after escaping her impoverished home life and forging a new identity at college, one which ostensibly celebrates her African heritage, Dee tells her mother that "Dee is dead," and her name is now Wangero Leewanika Kemanjo. Thus, Dee denies her real heritage, in which she was named for her aunt. Dee's other attempts to appreciate her cultural heritage miss the mark: she wants to display her mother's possessions in her home as examples of folk art but refuses to recognize their greater value to her mother and sister as objects of "everyday use" that they still use.

### *Maggie Johnson*
Burned severely in a house fire as a child, the shy, stammering Maggie Johnson cowers in the overwhelming presence of her sister. While Dee has moved on to an entirely new life, Maggie still lives in poverty with her mother, putting "priceless" objects to "everyday use." At the end of the story, the quiet, self-conscious Maggie smiles, "a real

smile, not scared,'' because her mother has finally recognized that she, not Dee, is the daughter who understands her heritage and the importance of connecting with one's ancestors.

### Mrs. Johnson

Mrs. Johnson is the narrator of this story, overseeing its events and interpreting, more through her actions than her words, their significance. As she waits for her daughter Dee to return home for a visit, she demonstrates her lack of self-esteem by imagining a much thinner, prettier version of herself meeting her daughter on a television show. Near the end of the story, Mrs. Johnson demonstrates a shift in her maternal sympathies by taking the quilts from Dee and giving them to Maggie, signaling for the reader where the author's own sympathies also lie.

## Themes

In ''Everyday Use,'' the contrast between Dee's beliefs and those of her mother and sister is emphasized by the different values the characters place on some old quilts and other objects in the home.

### Heritage

The main theme in the story concerns the characters' connections to their ancestral roots. Dee Johnson believes that she is affirming her African heritage by changing her name, her mannerisms, and her appearance, even though her family has lived in the United States for several generations. Maggie and Mrs. Johnson are confused and intimidated by her new image as ''Wangero.'' Their own connections to their heritage rest on their memories of their mothers and grandmothers; they prefer to remember them for who they were as individuals, not as members of a particular race. Because of their differing viewpoints, each values the Johnson's possessions for different reasons. Dee digs around the house for objects she can display in her own home as examples of African-American folk art. Maggie and her mother value the same objects not for their artistic value, but because they remind them of their loved ones. Dee admires a butterchurn, and when Maggie says it was carved by their aunt's first husband—''His name was Henry, but they called him Stash''—Dee responds condescendingly

## Topics for Further Study

- Walker has often been considered a black feminist writer. Does this story have a feminist message? If so, is the message any different than a similar message would be if written by a white feminist writer?

- Dee and Maggie seem as different as night and day. Do either of them have any character traits in common with their mother? If so, what are these traits? What traits don't they share with their mother?

- Consider Walker's portrayal of poverty in the story. Are there areas of the country where people live in similar conditions today? Where are they, and who lives there?

that her sister's memory is like an elephant's. But the story suggests that Maggie's elephant-like memory for her loved ones and her appreciation for their handiwork is a more genuine way to celebrate their heritage than Dee's ''artistic'' interests in removing these ordinary objects and exalting them as examples of their African roots.

### Materialism

Dee's materialism is demonstrated at a young age when she watches her modest home burn with ''a look of concentration on her face.'' Later, ''Dee wanted nice things''—particularly clothes—and was interested in maintaining a style that belied her humble roots. Her mother states that when she sees the new house, a three-room shack with no ''real'' windows and a tin roof, ''she will want to tear it down.'' Her appearance confirms this trend: she is dressed in elaborate clothes and gold jewelry. Dee's interest in the butterchurn and the quilts is raised because they are ''priceless'' objects. She wants to possess them as relics and would not think of employing them for ''everyday use.'' In contrast to Dee's materialism is Maggie's and her mother's pride in their home and their contentedness with life. They have made the front yard ''clean and wavy" in anticipation of her arrival, and the yard is "more comfortable than most people know."

### Community vs. Isolation

The quilts represent the Johnsons' connection to their community. They are formed by patches of clothing from many peoples' clothes, forming a mosaic that represents the past, their loved ones' lives, and their family history. Dee's lack of interest in the people with whom Maggie associates the quilt underscores the story's emphasis on the importance of community. Furthermore, while Dee cannot wait to escape her family's poverty so she can go to college and have nice things, her mother and sister have a clean yard in which "anyone can come and sit and look up into the elm tree." Maggie, despite her shyness, is engaged to be married, showing her ability to connect with another person. Dee, who Maggie suggests has never had real friends, has been jilted by a man who "flew to marry a cheap city girl." By showing the different paths the sisters have taken, Walker suggests that black nationalists such as Dee and Hakim-a-barber, who identify with their African ancestry by rejecting white ways, have cut themselves off from connecting with their backgrounds, which often have not been steeped in African tradition. Dee's apparent embarrassment about her rural roots contrasts sharply with Maggie's heartfelt connection through the quilts to her grandmother.

## Style

Walker uses several literary devices to examine the themes in the story and to give a voice to the poor and the uneducated.

### Point of View

"Everyday Use" is told in first-person point of view. Mrs. Johnson, an uneducated woman, tells the story herself. The reader learns what she thinks about her two daughters, and her observations reveal her astute observations about life. This technique seeks to validate the experiences of an often oppressed group of people: lower-class, black women. By putting Mrs. Johnson at center stage, Walker confirms her value and importance in society. Mrs. Johnson has mixed emotions about her daughters. She likens Maggie's demeanor to "a dog run over by some careless person rich enough to own a car," and says that Dee's reading "burned us with a lot of knowledge we didn't necessarily need to know." These conflicting feelings show the reader the complex nature of her thoughts and her ability to size up people when necessary. Her thoughts are compounded further by her fantasy of reuniting with Dee on a television talk show where "Johnny Carson has much to do to keep up with my quick and witty tongue."

### Symbolism

The story is not only rich in symbolism, it is also about symbolism. The quilts are the central symbol of the story, representing the connectedness of history and the intergenerational ties of the family. Other symbols include Maggie's burned skin, which can be interpreted as depicting how she has been "burned" by the circumstances of her life. Mrs. Johnson's "man-working" hands symbolize the rough life she has hand to forge from the land on which they live. Names become symbolic in the story as well. Dee thinks her name represents "the people who oppress me," and substitutes an African name that has no relation to her family roots. When Hakim-a-barber says that he does not eat collard greens and pork—traditional African-American foods—he symbolically denies his heritage despite his complicated African name. Clothing also represents the characters. Mrs. Johnson wears utilitarian clothing: overalls and flannel nightgowns, representing her no-frills approach to life. Dee wears a "yellow organdy dress" to her graduation and other wild, colorful clothing. These outfits represent her colorful, vibrant nature as well as her unwillingness to fit in to her surroundings, a harsh land more suited to farm clothing. Maggie's character is symbolized by the dress that "[falls] off her in little black papery flakes" during the house fire: fragile and burned.

### Irony

The central contradiction in this story emerges when readers understand Walker's point about Dee's efforts to appreciate her heritage. While Dee has acquired an education and understands her African past, she mistakenly looks to this history in order to affirm her heritage, forgetting her real origins and the people who raised her. She admires the quilts, particularly because her grandmother has sewed them by hand. She is more entranced by the thought of someone sewing by hand than by the person who did the sewing.

## *Diction and Dialect*

In relating the story in first-person, Walker gives Mrs. Johnson a pattern of speech that helps define her character. An uneducated woman, Mrs. Johnson nonetheless is able to express herself well. She waits in a yard that has been made "clean and wavy," meaning that she has taken pride in her house and fixed it up in anticipation of her daughter's arrival. Walker's subtle rendering of Mrs. Johnson's voice reveals that this older rural woman can also speak with efficient, lyrical clarity, as in her account of having "knocked a bull calf straight in the brain between the eyes with a sledge hammer and [having] had the meat hung up to chill before nightfall," or in her description of Hakim-a-barber's real name, which is "twice as long and three times as hard" to pronounce. Walker artfully suggests, then, that a "good" education does not necessarily result in a "better" form of speech.

# Historical Context

## *The Black Power Movement*

Even before their emancipation from slavery, African Americans struggled to define their collective identity within the framework of American society. Even after slavery was outlawed, blacks gained the right to vote, and legal decisions dismantled formal segregation, true equality was far from reality. By the 1960s, following the success of civil rights leaders like Martin Luther King, Jr. and Malcolm X, some African Americans began to take pride in their heritage as a way of bolstering their esteem, forging a group identity, and creating a platform for greater political power. Known as "black pride" or Black Nationalism, these ideas encouraged many young African Americans to learn about their cultural ancestry, grow their hair into "Afros," dress in traditional African clothing, and reject their "slave names" (as Malcolm X called most blacks' given names). Many of these tendencies are exhibited by Dee and Hakim-a-barber in "Everyday Use." The Black Panthers, led by former Student Nonviolent Coordinating Committee president Stokely Carmichael, embodied these ideas in their "black power" slogan as they fought for civil rights and voter registration. However, by the early 1970s, many of these organizations were accused of discrimination against women in the way they were organized and run, and writers like Walker sought to portray the voice of the black woman apart from a larger political context.

## *The Nation of Islam*

Another form of African American self-assertion that gained popularity in the early 1970s was the Nation of Islam, a religious and political organization founded in the 1930s and known popularly as the Black Muslims. This movement, which since Malcolm X's death in 1965 has been led by Louis Farrakhan, asserts that white society is not capable of being nonracist. Furthermore, instead of seeking integration, the organization encourages blacks to separate themselves into an independent community within the United States (a rejection of the back-to-Africa beliefs of earlier African American separatists). Like Dee Johnson, a.k.a. Wangero Leewanika Kemanjo, Black Muslim followers usually change their names, symbolically rejecting white society by rejecting their "slave names." The Nation of Islam also espouses the home as the center of community life, with a male-led family and a helpful, supportive wife and mother.

## *The Black Arts Movement*

The cultural extension of the Black Power movement was the Black Arts movement, a conscious effort by many artists and critics to celebrate African-American culture for its own forms, ideas, and styles, rather than seeing it as derivative of European-American culture. This movement focused on the works of black artists and writers, and on the validity of various forms of black folk art, including quilts and other items normally put to "everyday use." Some artists, such as Alice Walker, questioned what they saw as three particular deficits of the Black Arts movement: its tendency to speak for all blacks in a subtle assumption that all blacks' experiences were the same; its conception of blackness in almost entirely masculine terms; and

## Compare & Contrast

- **1971:** The Supreme Court upholds busing students to various schools in order for them to achieve greater racial integration.

  **1995:** Louis Farrakhan of the Nation of Islam leads the Million Man March in Washington, DC, as a show of solidarity and an opportunity for black men to publicly declare their support for family values.

- **1974:** A black militant organization called the Symbionese Liberation Army kidnaps heiress Patty Hearst, forces her to rob a bank, and commits several other crimes.

  **1996:** Drive-by shootings spurred by gang rivalries claim the lives of African-American musicians Tupac Shakur and Notorious B.I.G.

- **1973:** Census bureau statistics place the poverty rate for a family of two at $2,984 per year.

  **1995:** The poverty threshold for a family of two is $10,259 per year.

---

its implication that urban black experience is somehow more "real" than rural black experience. Walker addressed all three of these concerns in "Everyday Use," articulating most eloquently an early assertion of Black Feminism.

### Black Feminism

As the women's movement gained momentum in the early 1970s, many African-American women began to consider themselves excluded from it because it appeared to advocate rights important mostly to white women. They pointed out, for instance, that when suburban housewives spoke of wanting to do more than take care of their homes, they were ignoring the experiences of African American women, most of whom already worked outside the home, as their mothers and grandmothers before them had. By the mid-1970s, many black women, including Walker, articulated a distinctly African-American form of feminism that heralded the efforts of one's immediate matriarchal ancestors. Some of these concerns are addressed in "Everyday Use."

### Critical Overview

When "Everyday Use" appeared in a 1973 collection of short stories, *In Love and Trouble: Stories of Black Women,* reviewers of the book recognized the uniqueness of Alice Walker's portrayals of African-American women's experiences. Jerry H. Bryant, for instance, described Walker in *The Nation* as a writer "probing for the hitherto undisclosed alpha and beta rays of black existence." Critics also enthused over Walker's artistic abilities, most agreeing with Barbara Smith, who wrote in *Ms.* magazine that "Walker's perceptions, style, and artistry . . . consistently . . . make her work a treasure, particularly for those of us whom her work describes." While "Everyday Use" was singled out for praise by several critics, it has since achieved great prominence within the opus of Walker's work. Several admiring articles have been written about it, and in 1994, Barbara Christian published *Everyday Use,* an entire book of essays built around this one story. As Christian wrote in the book's introduction, the story has come to be recognized as an exemplary, foundational piece for several of Walker's primary interests as a writer. She noted, for instance, that like many other works by Walker, it "placed African American women's voices at the center of the narrative, an unusual position at the time."

Telling African-American women's stories with honesty, and placing such previously unrecognized women on center stage to tell and act out their own stories, was a method Walker used to great success and acclaim in her 1982 novel, *The Color*

*Purple.* Thanks in large part to Walker (who in turn gives much of the credit to Zora Neale Hurston), this narrative method, exemplified in "Everyday Use," has since become a standard technique for many black women writers, including Gloria Naylor, Toni Morrison, Terry McMillan, and Toni Cade Bambara. The story's central symbol of quilting also resonates beyond the story itself. Gathering loose bits of material into beautiful, meaningful quilts has long been a form of African-American art, but as Walker realized, this and other forms of women's art have often been overlooked by the establishment. This short, rich story also announces Walker's response to her contemporaries' wish to speak for all blacks in African-nationalist terms: a viewpoint extremely popular in the early 1970s. As a writer with black feminist insight, Walker gives voice in this story "to an entire maternal ancestry often silenced by the political rhetoric of the period," quoted Christian. Finally, this story also stands out as an example of Walker's answer to many black intellectuals who have stressed the need to leave old, rural ways behind in order to improve their economic and political standing. Walker's depiction of the quiet dignity of Maggie and Mrs. Johnson has been recognized as an appreciation for what rural Southern black folk are, not what they should become. Much of Walker's critical acclaim focuses on the integrity she imparts to her characters, no matter what their circumstances.

## Criticism

### Elisabeth Piedmont-Marton

*Piedmont-Marton is a professor of English and the coordinator of the writing center at the University of Texas at Austin. In the following essay, she discusses the quilting metaphor in "Everyday Use."*

Alice Walker's early story "Everyday Use" is clustered around a central image: quilting and quilts. Her use of this metaphor is important to critics because she went on to develop the theme more fully in her later work, especially the novel *The Color Purple.* Simply put, the quilt is a metaphor for the ways in which discarded scraps and fragments may be made into a unified, even beautiful, whole.

Quilting symbolizes the process out of which the unimportant and meaningless may be transformed into the valued and useful. Walker finds this metaphor especially useful for describing African-American women's lives, which traditional history and literature have often ignored and misrepresented.

Alice Walker is not the first to turn her attention to the importance of cloth making in women's culture. Women have been associated with textiles since the days of recorded history. Although weaving and sewing has often been mandatory labor, women have historically endowed their work with special meanings and significance. In classical mythology the fates were portrayed as women, but nearly all mythologies bear traces of the Triple Goddess as the three fates, rulers of past, present, and future. One type of goddesses spin time, another group measure it and weave events together, and yet another group cut off lengths of cloth. In Homer's *Odyssey,* for example, Odysseus's wife Penelope uses her skill at the loom to keep suitors at bay until her husband returns.

Walker herself explained the significance of quilting (and gardening) to the collective lives of women, especially those of African-American women, in an essay written the year after "Everyday Use" was first published. In the essay titled "In Search of Our Mother's Gardens," Walker asks us to consider what would have become of black women artists who lived in slavery and oppression. Would they have been "driven to a numb and bleeding madness by the springs of creativity in them for which there was no release"? Walker explains how she discovered her mothers' gardens, by which she means her creative female ancestors. Having looked "high when she should have been looking low," Walker discovers that "the answer is so simple that many of us have spent years discovering it." When she sees a stunning quilt of the crucifixion hanging in the Smithsonian Museum in Washington, DC, and sees that it is credited only to "anonymous Black woman in Alabama," she knows she is in the presence of "an artist who left her mark in the only materials she could afford, and in the only medium her position in society allowed her to use."

Critic Barbara Christian reads Walker's "Everyday Use" as a sort of fictional conclusion to the essay "In Search of Our Mothers' Gardens." Christian notes that Walker's major insight in the essay is

## What Do I Read Next?

- *The Color Purple,* Walker's novel about black women who persevere despite oppression by society and abuse by the men in their lives, established the author as a voice of 1970s black feminist ideals.

- *Song of Solomon* (1977) by Toni Morrison offers a counterpart to "Everyday Use" but with a male point of view. Through a series of encounters with friends and relatives, Macon ("Milkman") Dead III learns the value of the past and the importance of human connections.

- *The Women of Brewster Place* (1982) by Gloria Naylor tells the story of seven African-American women who live on a dead-end urban street. Though their lives are often painful, they maintain their spiritual strength and use it to strengthen their community.

- *The Autobiography of Malcolm X* (1965, co-written with Alex Haley) was a cornerstone of the Black Power Movement, whose ideals Dee Johnson and Hakim-a-barber espouse. Malcolm X examines his early life as a hustler, defends his controversial social and political ideals, and explains his conversion to the Islamic faith.

- *Their Eyes Were Watching God* (1937) by Zora Neale Hurston, a writer of the Harlem Renaissance who was rediscovered and popularized by Walker, is the story of one black woman's effort to claim her own sense of independence.

---

her "illumination of the creative legacy of 'ordinary' black women of the South." Walker, according to Christian, does more than acknowledge that the quilts these women produced can be regarded as art; she is impressed "with their functional beauty and by the process that produced them." In other words, Walker is asking us to reconsider whether quilts can be counted as art. But more than that, Christian claims, she is also suggesting that they truly artistic objects may be those that have and everyday use. In "Everyday Use," Walker dramatizes the "use and misuse of the concept of heritage" using the quilt as unifying object and metaphor, and at the same time challenges our definitions of what counts as art in our culture.

The conflict between Maggie and Dee (or, Wangero, as she prefers to be called) is about whether heritage exists in *things* or in *spirit,* or process. Dee, who "at sixteen had a style of her own: and knew what style was," has recently returned to her black roots because they are fashionable. As Maggie and her mother watch warily, she goes around the house collecting objects from her heritage that she now sees as valuable. When she gets to the quilts a conflict arises. Her mother recalls that Dee had been offered a quilt when she went away to college, but had then declared it "old fashioned, out of style." Now however, her experience with the larger culture, with "words, lies, other folks' habits," gives her a frame within which to take possession of her own heritage. Walker dramatizes this when Dee declares that she plans to hang, or frame, the quilts, "as though, the mother comments to herself, 'that was the only thing you *could* do with quilts.'" Dee seems to think that art is always something that comes in a frame.

Dee views her heritage as an artifact which she can possess and appreciate from a distance instead of as a process in which she is always intimately involved. Dee's notion of framing a quilt is in stark contrast to the frame on which the quilts had been made, according to the mother: "First they had been pieced by Grandma Dee and then Big Dee and me had hung them on the quilt frames on the front porch and quilted them." For Dee's mother and her mother and sister, the value of the quilt has to do at least in part with the communal nature of its making. For the women who are, in Houston Baker's and Charlotte Pierce-Baker's words, "accustomed to living and working with fragments," the scraps and patches handed down through the generations and stitched into a meaningful and beautiful whole have a value all their own that Dee cannot even approximate when she declares them "priceless."

According to Dee, Maggie's problem is that she does not understand her "heritage," and as a consequence she will never make anything of herself. Maggie may not understand what Dee means by "heritage," but she "knows how to quilt," and furthermore she "can 'member Grandma Dee without the quilts." Unlike her sister who is dressed in an outfit made out of whole cloth that is so loud it hurts her mother's eyes, Maggie's own scarred body resembles the faded patches of the quilt, where stitching resembles healing. She is literally making something of herself every day, just as she and her mother make *things* every day. Baker and Pierce-Baker call Maggie "the arisen goddess of Walker's story . . . the sacred figure who bears the scarifications of experience and knows how to convert patches into robustly patterned and beautifully quilted wholes." Dee's final dismissal of her sister—"She'll probably be backward enough to put them to everyday use"—is meant to sway the mother to her side. Instead, her mother suddenly sees through Dee's artistic frames, and contemptuously calling her "Miss Wangero," snatches the quilts from her hands. She recognizes that like Maggie and herself, "quilts are designed for everyday use, pieced wholes defying symmetry and pattern, . . . signs of the sacred generations of women who have always been alien to a world of literate words and stylish fancy" (Baker and Pierce-Baker). Dee's final gesture is to put on a pair of sunglasses "that hid everything above the tip of her nose and her chin," which suggests that despite this lesson in what heritage really means, she will continue to see the world through the frames she chooses.

For Barbara Christian as well as Houston Baker and Charlotte Pierce-Baker, the mother's recognition of Maggie's connection to quilts and to quilting is crucial to the story. The mother's choice of Maggie over "Miss Wangero" signifies Walker's discovery of her own literary ancestor, thus writing in fiction a conclusion to the essay "In Search of Our Mothers' Gardens." Baker and Pierce-Baker argue that when Maggie finally smiles "a real smile" at the end of the story as she and her mother watch Dee's car disappear in a cloud of dust, it is because she knows her "mother's holy recognition of the scarred daughter's sacred status as quilter is the best gift of a hard-pressed womankind to the fragmented goddess of the present."

> "In 'Everyday Use,' Walker dramatizes the 'use and misuse of the concept of heritage' using the quilt as unifying object and metaphor, and at the same time challenges our definitions of what counts as art in our culture."

**Source:** Elisabeth Piedmont-Marton, for *Short Stories for Students,* Gale Research, 1997.

## Nancy Tuten

*In the following essay, Tuten concentrates on analyzing the language of "Everyday Use" and relates how the characters' words reveal their personalities.*

Commentaries on Alice Walker's "Everyday Use" typically center on Mama's awakening to one daughter's superficiality and to the other's deep-seated understanding of heritage. Most readers agree that when Mama takes the quilts from Dee and gives them to Maggie, she confirms her younger daughter's self-worth: metaphorically, she gives Maggie her voice. Elaine Hedges, for example, refers to the "reconciliation scene" in which "Mama's gift of the family quilts to Maggie empowers the previously silenced and victimized daughter." The text underscores such a reading by stating that immediately after the incident Maggie sits with her "mouth open."

This story is distinctive, however, in that Walker stresses not only the importance of language but also the destructive effects of its misuse. Clearly, Dee privileges language over silence, as she demonstrates in her determination to be educated and in the importance she places on her name. Rather than providing a medium for newfound awareness and for community, however, verbal skill equips Dee to oppress and manipulate others and to isolate herself; when she lived at home, she read to her sister and mother "without pity; forcing words, lies, other folks' habits, whole lives upon us, sitting trapped and ignorant underneath her voice." Mama recalls that Dee "washed us in a river of make-believe, burned us with a lot of knowledge we didn't necessarily need to know. Pressed us to her with the serious way she read, to shove us away at just the moment, like dimwits, we seemed about to understand." Dee uses words to *wash, burn, press,* and *shove.* We are told that the "nervous girls" and "furtive boys" whom she regarded as her friends "worshiped the well-turned phrase" and her "scalding humor that erupted like bubbles in lye."

It is not surprising, then, that Mama, mistrustful of language, expresses herself in the climactic scene of the story not through words but through deeds: she *hugs* Maggie to her, *drags* her in the room where Dee sits holding the quilts, *snatches* the quilts from Dee, and *dumps* them into Maggie's lap. Only as an afterthought does she speak at all, telling Dee to "take one or two of the others." Mama's actions, not her words, silence the daughter who has, up to this point, used language to control others and separate herself from the community: Mama tells us that Dee turns and leaves the room "without a word."

In much of Walker's work, a character's dawning sense of self is represented not only by the acquisition of an individual voice but also through integration into a community. Mama's new appreciation of Maggie is significant because it represents the establishment of a sisterhood between mother and daughter. Just before taking the quilts out of Dee's hands, Mama tells us, "I did something I never had done before." The "something" to which she refers is essentially two actions: Mama embraces Maggie and says "no" to Dee for the first time. Since we are told that she held Maggie when she was burned in the fire, and since Mama's personality suggests that she would most likely hug her daughter often. She is of course referring not merely to the literal hug but to the first spiritual embrace, representing her decision no longer to judge her younger daughter by the shallow standards Dee embodies—criteria that Mama has been using to measure both Maggie and herself up until the climax of the story. When Mama acts on Maggie's behalf, she is responding to the largely nonverbal message that her younger daughter has been sending for some time, but which Mama herself has been unable fully to accept. Now Maggie and Mama are allied in their rejection of Dee's attempts to devalue their lifestyle, and their new sense of community enables Maggie to smile "a real smile, not scared." Significantly, the story ends with the two of them sitting in silence, "just enjoying, until it was time to go in the house and go to bed."

Ultimately, however, Mama has the last word; it is she, after all, who tells the story. Yet her control over the text is won gradually. Walker employs an unusual narrative structure to parallel Mama's development as she strengthens her voice and moves toward community with Maggie. Rather than reporting the entire event in retrospect, Mama relates the first half of the story *as it occurs,* using present and future tenses up until the moment Dee announces her new name. The commentary that Mama makes about herself and Maggie in the first portion of the story is therefore made before the awakening that she undergoes during the quilt episode—before she is able to reject completely Dee's desire that she and Maggie be something that they are not. Prior to the encounter with Dee over the quilts, although Mama at times speaks sarcastically about Dee's selfish attitude, she nonetheless dreams repeatedly of appearing on a television program "the way my daughter would want me to be: a hundred pounds lighter, my skin like an uncooked barley pancake," wielding a "quick and witty tongue." Mama's distaste for Dee's egotism is tempered by her desire to be respected by her daughter. In part, then, Mama has come to define herself in terms of her failure to meet the standards of what Lindsey Tucker calls a "basically white middle-class identity"—the white-male-dominated system portrayed in the television show. When Mama holds up her own strengths next to those valued by Dee and the white Johnny Carson society, she sees herself as one poised always in a position of fear, "with one foot raised in flight.". . .

The subsequent action of the story, however, in no way supports Mama's reading of her younger daughter. Instead, Maggie's behavior—even her limited use of language—conveys disgust with her sister rather than envy and awe. She responds to Hakim-a-barber, to Dee's hair, and to the discussion over the name "Dee" with the guttural "uhnnnh," a sound of revulsion. Even prior to

Dee's arrival, when Mama recalls [Dee's] vow never to bring any friends home with her lest she be embarrassed, Maggie questions, "Mama, when did Dee ever *have* any friends?" She further reveals her distaste for Dee not by standing hopelessly, as her mother had predicted, but by acting decisively: she pulls away when Hakim-a-barber tries to hug her; she acts uninterested, her hand "limp as a fish," when he tries to teach her an unfamiliar handshake; and when she hears Dee asking for the quilts that are hers by right, she drops something noisily in the kitchen and slams the door. Whereas her mother describes Maggie as "cowering behind me," Maggie's first remarks are unsolicited, direct, and informed: "Aunt Dee's first husband whittled the dash.... His name was Henry, but they called him Stash." Her mother's observation that Maggie's voice was "so low you almost couldn't hear her" merely amplifies the vast difference between Dee's aggressive, oppressive, self-seeking use of words and Maggie's calm, selective, community-building use of language.

The story shifts abruptly to the past tense immediately after Dee declares that she has changed her name. Up until now, Mama has been caught in the tension between her annoyance with Dee and her instinctive desire to be "the way my daughter would want me to be." Yet when Dee goes so far as to disown her family identity, Mama reaches a watershed. As Hirsch explains, Mama has previously been unable to express her anger at Dee, but now her older daughter has pushed her too far; now she is able to objectify the situation, to distance herself from it. The use of present-tense verbs in the first half of the story suggests less narrative authority: if Mama is telling the events as they happen, she is merely reacting. By shifting to the past tense, Walker strengthens Mama's voice, giving her more control. That the tense shift is subtle—it is buried in the very center of the story, in the middle of a conversation—underscores the fact that although Mama has crossed an important line, she is as yet unable fully to recognize or articulate her new position. As the story moves toward the turning point, however, she gains increasing emotional distance from Dee and is ultimately able to tell her "no."

Until midway through the story, Dee's abuse of language appears to have successfully undermined the hierarchy privileging language over silence in most of Walker's works. Walker, however, cleverly derails Dee's efforts to subvert language by giving Mama more narrative control as the story unfolds—authority that she uses to affirm her allegiance to Maggie and to assert her emotional freedom from Dee. In the final paragraph of the story, Dee is not mentioned by name at all. Instead, Mama mentions only "the sunglasses," which she and Maggie find amusing, and the "car dust," which settles as Dee rides away. Maggie, on the other hand, is mentioned twice by name and is referred to a third time when Mama describes the two of them sitting together on the porch. Dee's absence in the final lines contrasts with her overbearing presence in the beginning of Mama's story, when she says, "I will wait for her" and "Maggie will be nervous." Indeed, in the end, Dee's oppressive voice is mute, for Mama has narrated her out of the story altogether.

**Source:** Nancy Tuten, "Alice Walker's 'Everyday Use'," in *Explicator,* Volume 51, No. 2, Winter, 1993, pp. 125–28.

## Houston A. Baker Jr. and Charlotte Pierce-Baker

*In the following essay, Baker and Pierce-Baker talk about the tradition of quilting in the African-American community, a ritual of creating something out of scraps, an often overlooked indigenous American art form.*

A patch is a fragment. It is a vestige of wholeness that stands as a sign of loss and a challenge to creative design. As a remainder or remnant, the patch may symbolize rupture and impoverishment; it may be defined by the faded glory of the already gone. But as a fragment, it is also rife with explosive potential of the yet-to-be-discovered. Like woman, it is a liminal element between wholes.

Weaving, shaping, sculpting, or quilting in order to create a kaleidoscopic and momentary array is tantamount to providing an improvisational response to chaos. Such activity represents a nonce response to ceaseless scattering; it constitutes survival strategy and motion in the face of dispersal. A patchwork quilt, laboriously and affectionately crafted from bits of worn overalls, shredded uniforms, tattered petticoats, and outgrown dresses stands as a signal instance of a patterned wholeness in the African diaspora.

Traditional African cultures were scattered by the European slave trade throughout the commercial time and space of the New World. The transmutation of quilting, a European, feminine tradition, into a black women's folk art, represents an innovative fusion of African cloth manufacture, piecing, and appliqué with awesome New World experiences—and expediencies. The product that resulted was, in many ways, a double patch. The hands that pieced the master's rigidly patterned quilts by day were often the hands that crafted a more functional design in slave cabins by night. The quilts of Afro-America offer a *sui generis* context (a weaving together) of experiences and a storied, vernacular representation of lives conducted in the margins, ever beyond an easy and acceptable wholeness. In many ways, the quilts of Afro-America resemble the work of all those dismembered gods who transmute fragments and remainders into the light and breath of a new creation. And the sorority of quiltmakers, fragment weavers, holy patchers, possesses a sacred wisdom that it hands down from generation to generation of those who refuse the center for the ludic and unconfined spaces of the margins. . . .

The Johnson women, who populate the generations represented in Walker's short story "Everyday Use," are inhabitants of southern cabins who have always worked with "scraps" and seen what they could make of them. The result of their labor has been a succession of mothers and daughters surviving the ignominies of Jim Crow life and passing on ancestral blessings to descendants. The guardians of the Johnson homestead when the story commences are the mother—"a large, big-boned woman with rough, man-working hands"—and her daughter Maggie, who has remained with her "chin on chest, eyes on ground, feet in shuffle, ever since the fire that burned the other house to the ground" ten or twelve years ago. The mood at the story's beginning is one of ritualistic "waiting": "I will wait for her in the yard that Maggie and I made so clean and wavy yesterday afternoon." The subject awaited is the other daughter, Dee. Not only has the yard (as ritual ground) been prepared for the arrival of a goddess, but the sensibilities and costumes of Maggie and her mother have been appropriately attuned for the occasion. The mother daydreams of television shows where parents and children are suddenly—and pleasantly—reunited, banal shows where chatty hosts oversee tearful reunions. In her fantasy, she weighs a hundred pounds less, is several shades brighter in complexion, and possesses a devastatingly quick tongue.

She returns abruptly to real life meditation, reflecting on her own heroic, agrarian accomplishments in slaughtering hogs and cattle and preparing their meat for winter nourishment. She is a robust provider who has gone to the people of her church and raised money to send her light-complexioned, lithe-figured, and ever-dissatisfied daughter Dee to college. Today, as she waits in the purified yard, she notes the stark differences between Maggie and Dee and recalls how the "last dingy gray board of the house [fell] in toward the red-hot brick chimney" when her former domicile burned. Maggie was scarred horribly by the fire, but Dee, who had hated the house with an intense fury, stood "off under the sweet gum tree . . . a look of concentration on her face." A scarred and dull Maggie, who has been kept at home and confined to everyday offices, has but one reaction to the fiery and vivacious arrival of her sister: "I hear Maggie suck in her breath. 'Uhnnnh,' is what it sounds like. Like when you see the wriggling end of a snake just in front of your foot on the road. 'Uhnnnh'.". . .

The dramatic conflict of the story surrounds the definition of holiness. The ritual purification of earth and expectant atmosphere akin to that of Beckett's famous drama ("I will wait for her in the yard that Maggie and I made so clean and wavy yesterday afternoon.") prepare us for the narrator's epiphanic experience at the story's conclusion.

Near the end of "Everyday Use," the mother (who is the tale's narrator) realizes that Dee (a.k.a., Wangero) is a *fantasy* child, a perpetrator and victim of: "words, lies, other folks's habits." The energetic daughter is as frivolously careless of other peoples' lives as the fiery conflagration that she had watched ten years previously. Assured by the makers of American fashion that "black" is currently "beautiful," she has conformed her own "style" to that notion. Hers is a trendy "blackness" cultivated as "art" and costume. She wears "a dress down to the ground. . .bracelets dangling and making noises when she moves her arm up to shake the folds of the dress out of her armpits." And she says of quilts she has removed from a trunk at the foot of her mother's bed: "Maggie can't appreciate these quilts! She'd probably be backward enough to put them to everyday use." "Art" is, thus, juxtaposed with "everyday use" in Walker's short story, and the fire goddess Dee, who has achieved literacy only to burn "us with a lot of knowledge we didn't necessarily need to know," is revealed as a perpetuator of institutional theories of aesthetics. (Such theories hold that "art" is, in fact, defined by social institutions such as museums, book reviews, and art dealers.) Of the two quilts that she has extracted from the trunk, she exclaims: "But they're 'priceless.'" And so the quilts are by "fashionable" standards of artistic value, standards that motivate the answer that Dee provides to her mother's question: "'Well,' I said, stumped. 'What would *you* do with them?'" Dee's answer: "Hang them." The stylish daughter's entire life has been one of "framed" experience; she has always sought a fashionably "aesthetic" distance from southern expediencies. (And how unlike quilt frames that signal social activity and a coming to completeness are her *frames*.) Her concentrated detachment from the fire, which so nearly symbolizes her role vis-à-vis the Afro-American community (her black friends "worshipped . . . the scalding humor that erupted like bubbles in lye") is characteristic of her attitude. Her goals include the appropriation of exactly what *she* needs to remain fashionable in the eyes of a world of pretended wholeness, a world of banal television shows, framed and institutionalized art, and Polaroid cameras—devices that instantly process and record experience as "framed" photograph. Ultimately, the framed Polaroid photograph represents the limits of Dee's vision. . . .

What is at stake in the world of Walker's short story, then, is not the prerogatives of Afro-American women as "wayward artists." Individualism and a flouting of convention in order to achieve "artistic" success constitute acts of treachery in "Everyday Use." For Dee, if she is anything, *is* a fashionable denizen of America's art/fantasy world. She is removed from the "everyday uses" of a black community that she scorns, misunderstands, burns. Certainly, she is "unconventionally" black. As such, however, she is an object of holy contempt from the archetypal weaver of black wholeness from tattered fragments. Maggie's "Uhnnnh" and her mother's designation "Miss Wangero" are gestures of utter contempt. Dee's sellout to fashion and fantasy in a television-manipulated world of "artistic" frames is a representation of the *complicity of the clerks*. Not "art," then, but use or function is the signal in Walker's fiction of sacred creation.

Quilts designed for everyday use, pieced wholes defying symmetry and pattern, are signs of the scarred generations of women who have always been alien to a world of literate words and stylish

> The crafted fabric of Walker's story is the very weave of blues and jazz traditions in the Afro-American community, daringly improvisational modes that confront breaks in the continuity of melody (or theme) by riffing."

fantasies. The crafted fabric of Walker's story is the very weave of blues and jazz traditions in the Afro-American community, daringly improvisational modes that confront breaks in the continuity of melody (or theme) by riffing. The asymmetrical quilts of southern black women are like the off-centered stomping of the jazz solo or the innovative musical showmanship of the blues interlude. They speak a world in which the deceptively shuffling Maggie is capable of a quick change into goddess, an unlikely holy figure whose dues are paid in full. Dee's anger at her mother is occasioned principally by the mother's insistence that paid dues make Maggie a more likely bearer of sacredness, tradition, and true value than the "brighter" sister. "You just don't understand," she says to her mother. Her assessment is surely correct where institutional theories and systems of "art" are concerned. The mother's cognition contains no categories for framed art. The mother works according to an entirely different scale of use and value, finally assigning proper weight to the virtues of Maggie and to the ancestral importance of the pieced quilts that she has kept out of use for so many years. Smarting, perhaps, from Dee's designation of the quilts as "old-fashioned," the mother has buried the covers away in a trunk. At the end of Walker's story, however, she has become aware of her own mistaken value judgments, and she pays homage that is due to Maggie. The unlikely daughter is a *griot* of the vernacular who remembers actors and events in a distinctively black "historical" drama. . . .

But the larger appeal of "Everyday Use" is its privileging of a distinctively woman's craft as *the* signal mode of confronting chaos through a skillful blending of patches. In *The Color Purple*, Celie's skill as a fabric worker completely transmutes the order of Afro-American existence. Not only do her talents with a needle enable her to wear the pants in the family, they also allow her to become the maker of pants par excellence. Hence, she becomes a kind of unifying goddess of patch and stitch, an instructress of mankind who bestows the gift of consolidating fragments. Her abusive husband Albert says: "When I was growing up . . . I use to try to sew along with mama cause that's what she was always doing. But everybody laughed at me. But you know, I liked it." "Well," says Celie, "nobody gon laugh at you now. . . . Here, help me stitch in these pockets."

A formerly "patched" separateness of woman is transformed through fabric craft into a new unity. Quilting, sewing, stitching are bonding activities that begin with the godlike authority and daring of women, but that are given (as a gift toward community) to men. The old disparities are transmuted into a vision best captured by the scene that Shug suggests to Celie: "But, Celie, try to imagine a city full of these shining, blueblack people wearing brilliant blue robes with designs like fancy quilt patterns." The heavenly city of quilted design is a form of unity wrested by the sheer force of the woman quiltmaker's will from chaos. As a community, it stands as both a sign of the potential effects of black women's creativity in America, and as an emblem of the effectiveness of women's skillful confrontation of patches. Walker's achievement as a southern, black, woman novelist is her own successful application of the holy patching that was a staple of her grandmother's and great-grandmother's hours of everyday ritual. "Everyday Use" is, not surprisingly, dedicated to "your grandmama": to those who began the line of converting patches into works of southern genius.

**Source:** Houston A. Baker, Jr. and Charlotte Pierce-Baker, "Patches: Quilts and Community in Alice Walker's 'Everyday Use'," in *The Southern Review,* Vol. 21, No. 3, July, 1985, pp. 706–20.

## Sources

Bryant, Jerry H. A review of *In Love and Trouble,* in *The Nation,* Vol. 217, November 12, 1973, pp. 503–5.

Christian, Barbara. "Alice Walker: The Black Woman Artist as Wayward," in *Black Feminist Criticism,* Pergamon Press, 1985, pp. 81-87.

Christian, Barbara. *Everyday Use.* Rutgers University Press, 1994.

Smith, Barbara. "The Souls of Black Women," *Ms.,* no. 2, February, 1974, p. 42.

Walker, Alice. "In Search of Our Mothers' Gardens," in *In Search of Our Mothers' Gardens: Womanist Prose by Alice Walker,* Harcourt, 1983, pp. 231-243.

## Further Reading

O'Brien, John. "Alice Walker," *Interviews with Black Writers,* Liveright, 1973, pp. 185-211.
　　An interview with Walker conducted near the time in which she wrote "Everyday Use."

*Short Story Criticism,* Vol. 5, Gale Research, 1990, pp. 400–24.
　　Excerpted criticism of Walker's short fiction.

Winchell, Donna Haisty. *Alice Walker,* Twayne, 1992.
　　This book offers an overview of Walker's life and career, including explanatory chapters on each of her works. The third chapter contains analysis of the stories in the collection in which "Everyday Use" first appeared.

# The Fall of the House of Usher

**Edgar Allan Poe**

**1839**

"The Fall of the House of Usher," written by Edgar Allan Poe in 1839, is regarded as an early and supreme example of the Gothic horror story, though Poe ascribed the term "arabesque" to this and other similar works, a term that he felt best described its flowery, ornate prose. Featuring supernatural theatrics, which critics have interpreted a number of ways, the story exhibits Poe's concept of "art for art's sake," the idea that a story should be devoid of social, political, or moral teaching. In place of a moral, Poe creates a mood—terror, in this case—through his use of language. This philosophy of "art for art's sake" later evolved into the literary movement of Aestheticism which eschewed the symbolic and preachy literature of the day—especially in England—in an attempt to overcome strict Victorian conventions. Because of his emphasis on style and language, Poe proclaimed his writing a reaction to typical literature of the day, which he called "the heresy of the Didactic" for its tendency to preach. Condemned by some critics for its tendencies toward Romanticism, a literary movement marked by melodramatic and maudlin exaggerations, "The Fall of the House of Usher" was nevertheless typical of Poe's short stories in that it presents a narrator thrust into a psychologically intense situation in which otherworldly forces conspire to drive at least one of the characters insane.

## Author Biography

Poe was born January 19, 1809, in Boston, Massachusetts. His father and mother were professional

actors who at the time of his birth were members of a repertory theater company in Boston. Before he was three years old both of his parents had died, and he was raised in the home of John Allan, a prosperous exporter from Richmond, Virginia. In 1915 Allan took his wife and foster son, whom he never formally adopted, to visit Scotland and England, where they lived for the next five years. While in England, Poe spent two years at the school he later described in the story "William Wilson."

Returning with his foster parents to Richmond in 1820, Poe attended the best schools available, wrote his first poetry, and, when he was sixteen years old, became involved in a romance which ended when Allan sent him to the University of Virginia at Charlottesville. There Poe distinguished himself academically, but as a result of bad debts and inadequate financial support from Allan he was forced to leave after less than a year. An established discord with his foster father deepened on Poe's return to Richmond in 1827, and soon afterward Poe left for Boston, where he enlisted in the army for lack of other means of supporting himself and where he also published his first poetry collection, *Tamerlane and Other Poems,* which the cover stated was "By a Bostonian." The book went unnoticed by readers and reviewers, and a second collection received only slightly more attention when it appeared in 1829.

That same year Poe was honorably discharged from the army, having attained the rank of regimental sergeant-major, and, after further conflict with Allan, he entered the West Point military academy. However, because Allan would neither provide his foster son with sufficient funds to maintain himself as a cadet nor give the consent necessary to resign from the academy, Poe gained a dismissal by ignoring his duties and violating regulations. He subsequently went to New York City, where his book *Poems* was published in 1831, and then to Baltimore, where he lived at the home of his aunt, Mrs. Clemm.

Over the next few years, Poe's first stories appeared in the Philadelphia *Saturday Courier,* and his "MS. Found in a Bottle" won a cash prize for best story in the Baltimore *Saturday Visitor.* Nevertheless, Poe was still not earning enough to live independently, nor did Allan's death in 1834 provide him with a legacy. The following year, however, his financial problems were temporarily alleviated when he went back to Richmond to become editor of the *Southern Literary Messenger,* bringing with him his aunt and his cousin Virginia, whom he married in 1836. The *Southern Literary Messenger* was the first of several magazines Poe would direct over the next ten years and through which he rose to prominence as one of the leading men of letters in America. Poe made himself known not only as a superlative author of fiction and poetry but also as a literary critic whose level of imagination and insight had been unapproached in American literature until that time.

While Poe's writings gained attention in the late 1830s and 1840s, the profits from his work remained meager. He was forced to move several times in order to secure employment that he hoped would improve his situation, editing *Burton's Gentleman's Magazine* and *Graham's Magazine* in Philadelphia and the *Broadway Journal* in New York. In addition, the royalties for *The Narrative of Arthur Gordon Pym, Tales of the Grotesque and Arabesque,* and other titles were always nominal or nonexistent. After his wife's death from tuberculosis in 1847, Poe became involved in a number of romances, including the one that had been interrupted in his youth with Elmira Royster, now the widowed Mrs. Shelton. It was during the time they were preparing for their marriage that Poe, for reasons unknown, arrived in Baltimore in late September of 1849. On October 3, he was discovered in a state of semiconsciousness. He died on October 7 without regaining the necessary lucidity to explain what had happened during the last days of his life.

## Plot Summary

The story begins with an unnamed narrator approaching a large and dreary-looking estate. As he approaches on horseback, he muses on the images before him, the darkness of the house, the oppressiveness of the clouds above, the eye-like windows, the ragged fissure in the side of the house, the fungi on the walls, and the reflection of it all in a nearby lake. He notes that some parts of the house are crumbling and other parts are not.

He sits astride his horse, thinking about the letter he received that initiated his trip and feeling uneasy about the upcoming visit. He remembers happier times he has had with his friend, Roderick, but now, in the face of the present gloomy surroundings, these seem a distant past. Looking at the house, he makes the connection between the family mansion and the family line, both called The House of Usher (a pun on the word "house" having two different meanings). Roderick and his twin sister, Madeline, are the last members of the family line.

The narrator feels as though he is dreaming, as though these visions were "the after-dream of a reveller upon opium." This foreshadows Roderick's behavior later, when the two men meet. He is puzzled by questions about the impending visit that have no answer. "What was it—I paused to think—what was it that so unnerved me in the contemplation of the House of Usher? It was a mystery all insoluable."

He enters the house and a valet shows him to Roderick's reading room. Roderick is lying on a sofa, but arises to greet him. He looks pale and cadaverous. They exchange greetings, but Roderick's voice is unsteady and feeble. His demeanor seems more that of one suffering from drunkenness or from the use of opium. Roderick wants his friend to comfort him and share his last days with him. He says he has "suffered much from a morbid acuteness of the senses." Only the most gentle stimulus could be endured, no hard food, loud music, strong odors, or bright lights. Only "peculiar sounds, and those from stringed instruments, which did not inspire him with horror" are tolerable. Roderick says he will perish from "this deplorable folly."

During this conversation Madeline is seen as she passes through a nearby corridor. She takes no notice of them. Roderick explains that she suffers from a malady even more baffling than his own. The physicians have said she would die of "a gradual wasting away of the person, and frequent although transient affectation of a partially cataleptical character."

After this sighting, her name is not mentioned and she is not seen alive again. The men talk together and engage in artistic endeavors, painting and writing poetry. Roderick composes some ballads, some of which he sings as he accompanies himself on the guitar. One titled "The Haunted Palace," which Poe published apart from this story, offers a poetic rendition of the life and times of the House of Usher, including a foreshadowing of Roderick's own death. They pass some additional time together reading fantastic novels and discussing topics of a wild and horrifying nature. One such topic is Roderick's notion that the stones in his house are alive.

*Edgar Allan Poe*

After a week, Roderick announces that Madeline is dead and that he needs assistance in burying her. The narrator agrees to help and they take her body, in a coffin, into a tomb that lies beneath the room in which the narrator has been sleeping. They view Madeline's body, noting the slight smile on her face and the blush on her cheeks, "Usual in all maladies of a strictly cataleptical character." They screw the lid tightly onto the coffin and close and seal a large iron door to the tomb.

During the next several days, Roderick's demeanor changes. He becomes more restless and his visage becomes more pallid. His voice grows more tremulous and he seems to be hiding some deep secret by his peculiar speech.

About the eighth day, the narrator experiences an intense fear and dread. He rationalizes it away by believing that it is just a consequence of staying in drab and dreary surroundings. He cannot sleep, so he dresses and paces about in his apartment. He notices a light under the door and soon Roderick knocks on the door. He enters looking "cadaverously wan" and possessed of "an evidently restrained hysteria in his whole demeanor." Roderick opens a window to a storm, letting the wind blow violently into the room.

In an attempt to calm Roderick, the narrator takes up a copy of *Mad Trist* and begins to read. At this point, the narrator hears noises coming from below, in the tomb, but he continues to read. Each of the passages from the novel foreshadows the events of that evening. As the noises get louder, Roderick says, "we have put her living in the tomb." He springs to his feet and shrieks, "Madman! I tell you that she now stands without the door!"

The passageway in the room comes open from a strong gust of wind, and Madeline appears, bloodied and trembling. She lunges forward onto her brother, and they both fall to the floor, dead.

At this, the narrator flees quickly. As he passes over the bridge leading from the house there is a flash, the fissure in the face of the house widens, and the house crumbles "and the deep dank tarn at my feet closed sullenly over the fragments of the House of Usher."

## Characters

### Narrator

The unnamed narrator of the story is described as a childhood friend of Roderick Usher's. However, the narrator notes that he does not know Roderick very well because Roderick's "reserve had always been excessive and habitual." The narrator visits the Usher family house after Roderick sends him an emotional letter begging him to come. While he seems skeptical of the supernatural and tries to find rational explanations for the disconcerting things happening around him, the narrator finds himself growing increasingly disturbed by the house and the Ushers. At the end of the story, when both Roderick and Madeline die, he flees and watches the house crumble and fall into a small lake. The narrator has been described as an objective witness to the events in the story, with some suggesting he represents rationality. Others, however, have concluded that he is unreliable and that he may, in fact, have helped Roderick Usher murder his sister, or that the ending of the story is merely his hallucination.

### Madeline Usher

Madeline is the twin sister of Roderick Usher and, along with her brother, is one of the only two surviving members of the Usher family. She is terminally ill and suffers fits of catalepsy, meaning she appears rigid and does not move for long periods of time. The narrator of the story, who sees her only briefly before she dies, regards her with "an utter astonishment not unmingled with dread." When Madeline dies, her brother and the narrator temporarily bury her in a vault on the first floor with "a faint blush upon the bosom and the face" and a "suspiciously lingering smile upon the lip." At the end of the story, she mysteriously emerges from her tomb, only to die with her brother. Madeline's fleeting appearance in the story serves to heighten the horror and suspense of the situation. Some critics have suggested that Madeline's illness is the result of a long history of incestual breeding in the Usher family; others believe that she possesses evil powers and is, in fact, a vampire.

### Roderick Usher

Roderick Usher is the last surviving male of the Usher family. Like many of his ancestors, he has an artistic temperament, engaging in such activities as writing and playing music and painting. Described as extremely pale, with weblike hair and dark eyes, he is also a hypochondriac and is unable to tolerate such physical stimulation as bright light, the scent of flowers, and peculiar sounds. Believing that the Usher family estate is evil and that the Usher family is cursed, Roderick lives in a state of constant fear and agitation. When his twin sister Madeline dies, Roderick falls into even deeper despair and, according to the narrator, seems to be "laboring with some oppressive secret." At the end of the story, Madeline emerges from her tomb, and they both die. Roderick's anguished mental state and odd behavior have been interpreted in numerous ways. Some have speculated that he is agonizing over the Usher family secret of incest while others have suggested that Roderick represents the troubled artistic temperament. Finally, those who read "The Fall of the House of Usher" as purely a supernatural horror story state that Roderick represents evil.

## Themes

"The Fall of the House of Usher," told from the point of view of an unnamed narrator, is the story of twin siblings Roderick and Madeline Usher, the last surviving members of the Usher family.

### Evil

"The Fall of the House of Usher" addresses the nature and causes of evil. Poe creates an atmosphere of evil in the story through the unnamed narrator's descriptions of the Usher family home, and of Roderick and Madeline. For example, the house is called a "mansion of gloom"; Roderick is described as having "a ghastly pallor of the skin" and hair of "wild gossamer texture"; and Madeline, who the narrator sees only briefly before she dies, stirs up feelings of dread. Although the narrator is unsettled, shocked, and taken aback by his surroundings from the very beginning of the story, it is not clear what is causing such trepidation. When Roderick attempts to explain the cause of his "nervous agitation," he states that it is "a constitutional and family evil," suggesting that he and Madeline are somehow cursed. Some have speculated that the evil behind this "curse" is a long history of incest or family inbreeding within the Usher line and that both Roderick and Madeline are suffering the physical and emotional consequences of behavior almost universally condemned as immoral. Others, however, have stated that the evil permeating the story is of purely supernatural origin and that Roderick's hysteria is not imagined but is a justifiable reaction to otherworldly forces.

The atmosphere of terror in the story is heightened by the ambiguity of Madeline's character—she can be viewed with sympathy, because of her illness, or with suspicion. Some critics have even suggested that she is a vampire attempting to sap the life force from Roderick. The narrator also heightens the aura of evil in "The Fall of the House of Usher" because while he tries to view the situation objectively and rationally, despite his increasing feelings of foreboding, he ultimately succumbs to the evil pervading the Usher home. Some critics have, in fact, stated that the narrator himself is evil and that he, along with Roderick, knowingly buried Madeline alive and that he is deliberately trying to deceive the reader about what happened.

### *Madness and Insanity*

The themes of madness and insanity grow from Poe's depiction of Roderick's increasingly unstable mental and emotional breakdown. Roderick is afflicted with numerous mysterious maladies. He suffers, as the narrator states, from "a morbid acuteness of the senses," and he is overwhelmed by feelings of fear and anxiety. Roderick's agitated mental state is also due, in part, to Madeline's fatal illness, which causes her to become cataleptic—a state of extreme muscle rigidity and apparent unconsciousness. As the story progresses, Roderick attempts to relate his fear to the narrator and engages in numerous activities—including playing the guitar, creating a disturbing painting, and composing a lyric entitled "The Haunted Palace"—in an attempt to calm himself. He also reads books on the supernatural and the occult. As Roderick becomes increasingly hysterical, both the narrator and the reader are left to speculate on the causes of such strange behavior. It remains unclear, however, if Roderick's malady is a psychological reaction to an incestual relationship with his sister or if he is, indeed, being possessed by evil forces. Nevertheless, Poe's portrayal of Roderick's deterioration raises important questions about the causes, stages, and effects of insanity.

## Style

"The Fall of the House of Usher" centers on Roderick Usher and his twin sister Madeline, the last surviving members of the Usher family.

### *Setting*

The setting of "The Fall of the House of Usher" plays an integral part in the story because it establishes an atmosphere of dreariness, melancholy, and decay. The story takes place in the Usher family mansion, which is isolated and located in a "singularly dreary tract of country." The house immediately stirs up in the narrator "a sense of insufferable gloom," and it is described as having "bleak walls," "vacant eye-like windows," and "minute *fungi* overspread [on] the whole exterior." The interior of the house is equally dreary, with "vaulted and fretted" ceilings, "dark draperies hung upon the walls," and furniture that is "comfortless, antique, and tattered." Roderick is also disturbed by the setting, believing that the house is one of the causes of his nervous agitation. The narrator notes that Roderick "was enchained by certain superstitious impressions in regard to the dwelling which he tenanted, and whence, for many years, he had never ventured forth."

### *Point of View*

"The Fall of the House of Usher" is told from the point of view of the unnamed narrator, who, being skeptical and rational, doesn't want to believe that there are supernatural causes to what is happening around him. Although he tries to tell the reader that Roderick's anxiety and nervousness are simply symptoms of the latter's mental anguish, the narrator, and therefore the reader, becomes increasingly

# Media Adaptations

- "The Fall of the House of Usher" was adapted to film in 1952. Directed and produced by Ivan Barnett, this black and white, 70-minute film starred Kay Tendeter as Roderick Usher and Gwen Watford as Madeline Usher and is available from Vigilant distributors. It is generally considered to be a poor adaptation of Poe's story.

- Considered one of the best film adaptations of "The Fall of the House of Usher," the 1960 version starred Vincent Price, Myrna Fahey, and Mark Damon and was directed by Mark Corman. It runs 65 minutes and is in color.

- The story was also adapted to film in 1980. Starring Martin Landau as Roderick Usher and Dimitra Arliss as Madeline Usher, this 101-minute color film was produced by Charles E. Sellier, Jr. and directed by James L. Conway. It is available from Sunn Classic.

- A dramatization of "The Fall of the House of Usher" was taped in 1965 as part of the "American Story Classics" series. Available from Film Video Library, this adaptation runs 29 minutes and is in black and white.

- Another dramatization of the story was taped in 1976 by Encyclopaedia Britannica Educational Corporation. Also produced by Britannica in 1976, *The Fall of the House of Usher: A Discussion* features science fiction writer Ray Bradbury discussing the Gothic traditions of "The Fall of the House of Usher" as well as Poe's influence on contemporary science fiction.

---

disturbed as the story progresses. By telling the story from the point of view of a skeptic rather than a believer, Poe increases the suspense as well as the emotional impact of the story's ending.

## *Symbolism*

Poe uses symbolism—a literary technique where an object, person, or concept represents something else—throughout "The Fall of the House of Usher." The Usher mansion is the most important symbol in the story; isolated, decayed and full of the atmosphere of death, the house represents the dying Usher family itself. The narrator emphasizes this when he notes that "about the whole mansion and domain there hung an atmosphere peculiar to themselves and their immediate vicinity—an atmosphere which had no affinity with the air of heaven, but which had reeked up from the decayed trees, and the grey wall, and the silent tarn." The fissure in the house is also an important symbol. Although it is, at first, barely visible to the narrator, it suggests a fundamental split or fault in the twin personalities of the last surviving Ushers and foretells the final ruin of the house and family. Other notable symbols of death and madness are Roderick's lyric, "The Haunted Palace"; his abstract painting, which is described as a "phantasmagoric" conception by the narrator; and the "fantastic character" of his guitar playing.

## *Imagery*

Poe uses imagery to create a foreboding atmosphere and to advance his themes in the story. An image is a concrete representation of an object or sensory experience; images help evoke the feelings associated with the object or the experience itself. For example, when the narrator briefly sees Madeline, he states: "The lady Madeline passed slowly through the remote portion of the apartment, and, without having noticed my presence, disappeared.... A sensation of stupor oppressed me, and my eyes followed her retreating steps." Such images contribute to the perception that Madeline is ghostlike and mysterious. When the narrator sees the physician on the stair at the beginning of the story, he notes: "His countenance, I thought, wore a mingled expression of low cunning and perplexity. He accosted me with trepidation and passed on." This image of the doctor is much more effective than a mere literal description; it underscores the fear and anxiety pervading the Usher home.

## *Gothicism*

"The Fall of the House of Usher" is considered a preeminent example of Gothic short fiction with its focus on such topics as incest, terminal illness, mental breakdown, and death. Gothic fiction generally includes elements of horror, the supernatural, gloom, and violence and creates in the reader feelings of terror and dread. Gothic fiction also frequently takes place in medieval-like settings; the desolate, ancient, and decaying Usher mansion is ideally suited for this story. In addition to creating an atmosphere of dread, Poe, some critics have suggested, incorporated into his story aspects of the vampire tale. J. O. Bailey, for example, contended in *American Literature* that Madeline is a vampire and that Roderick is fighting her powers ''with all he has.''

## Historical Context

''The Fall of the House of Usher'' was first published in 1839 in *Burton's Gentleman's Magazine*. At a time when most popular literature was highly moralistic, Poe's stories were concerned only with creating emotional effects. Poe charged that most of his contemporaries were ''didactic,'' that is, they were preoccupied with making religious or political statements in their writings to the detriment of the fiction itself. His own tales of terror, in which he often depicted the psychological disintegration of unstable or emotionally overwrought characters, were in sharp contrast to the works of more highly praised writers of the time. Because of Poe's disdain for didactic writing, he was little regarded by the literary establishment in his day.

But despite being dismissed by literary critics, Poe's tales were instrumental in establishing the short story as a viable literary form. Before his time, such short works were not regarded as serious literature. Poe's examples of what the short story could accomplish, and his own nonfiction writings about the form, were instrumental in establishing the short story as a legitimate form of serious literature. Poe had a strong influence in popular fiction as well. His tales of terror are considered among the finest ever produced in the horror genre. He also pioneered, some critics say invented, the genre of detective fiction with his story ''The Murders in the Rue Morgue.''

During the time Poe was writing, a distinct and mature body of American literature was beginning to develop with the contributions of such authors as Poe, Nathaniel Hawthorne, John Greenleaf Whittier, Harriet Beecher Stowe, Henry Wadsworth Longfellow, and James Fenimore Cooper. Before this time, American readers considered British literature the only serious literature available. American writers wrote imitations derived from British models. But with the advent of a new group of American writers who were writing about specifically American subjects, settings, and characters, a distinctly American literature began to emerge. Poe was one of the American writers of the time who helped to formulate this national literature.

## Topics for Further Study

- Examine the lyric ''The Haunted Palace'' written by Roderick Usher in ''The Fall of the House of Usher'' and discuss how it reflects Roderick's mental and emotional state.

- Read the short story ''The Yellow Wallpaper'' (1892) by Charlotte Perkins Gilman and compare and contrast the portrayal of mental breakdown in each story.

- Poe's fictional works and critical theories greatly impacted nineteenth-century literature, particularly the French symbolist movement. Research and discuss Poe's influence on such French writers as Charles Baudelaire and Paul Valery.

## Critical Overview

While Poe's works were not widely acclaimed during his lifetime, he did earn respect as a gifted fiction writer and poet, especially after the publication of his poem ''The Raven.'' After his death, however, the history of his critical reception becomes one of dramatically uneven judgements and interpretations. This was, in part, the fault of Poe's one-time friend and literary executor R. W. Griswold, who, in an obituary notice bearing the byline ''Ludwig,'' attributed the depravity and psychological peculiarities of many of the characters in Poe's fiction to Poe himself. In retrospect, Griswold's insults seem to have elicited as much sympathy as

*Fritz Eichenberg's illustration from* Tales of Edgar Allan Poe.

lations and commentaries of French poet Charles Baudelaire in the 1850s, Poe's works were received with high esteem by French writers, especially those associated with the late nineteenth-century symbolist movement, who admired Poe's transcendent aspirations as a poet. In other countries, Poe enjoyed similar regard, and numerous studies have been written tracing the influence of the American author on international literature.

Today, Poe is regarded as one of the foremost progenitors of modern literature, both in its popular forms, such as horror and detective fiction, and in its more complex and self-conscious forms, such as poetry and criticism. In contrast to earlier critics who viewed the man and his works as one, recent criticism has developed a view of Poe as a detached artist who was more concerned with displaying his writing talents than with expressing his feelings. While at one time critics wished to remove Poe from literary history, his works remain integral to any conception of modernism in world literature.

censure, leading subsequent biographers of the late nineteenth century to defend, sometimes avidly, Poe's name.

It was not until the 1941 biography by A. H. Quinn, *Edgar Allan Poe: A Critical Autobiography*, that a balanced view was provided of Poe, his work, and the relationship between the author's life and his imagination. Nevertheless, the identification of Poe with the murderers and madmen of his works survived and flourished in the twentieth century, most notably in the form of psychoanalytical studies by such critics as Marie Bonaparte and Joseph Wood Krutch. Added to the controversy over Poe's sanity was the question of the value of Poe's works as serious literature. Among Poe's detractors were such eminent literary figures as Henry James, Aldous Huxley, and T. S. Eliot, who dismissed Poe's works as juvenile, vulgar, and artistically debased; in contrast, these same works were judged to be of the highest literary merit by such writers as George Bernard Shaw and William Carlos Williams. Complementing Poe's erratic reputation among American and English critics was the generally more elevated opinion of critics elsewhere in the world, particularly in France. Following the extensive trans-

## Criticism

### Carl Mowery

*Carl Mowery hold a doctoral degree in rhetoric and composition and has taught at Southern Illinois University and Murray State University. In the following essay, he calls ''The Fall of the House of Usher'' a cerebral story with little physical action and emphasizes the many interpretations the story inspires.*

Of the many short stories Edgar Allan Poe wrote, ''The Fall of the House of Usher'' is likely the most cerebral. There is little action to carry the plot, no trips into a catacomb, no descent into a whirlpool, no crimes to be solved. Everything that occurs is told by the narrator. Despite this lack of physical action, this gothic story has remained one of Poe's most popular.

In ''The Philosophy of Composition'' Poe says, ''If any literary work is too long to be read at one sitting, we must be content to dispense with the immensely important effect derivable from unity of impression.'' Furthermore, he says, ''It appears evident, then, that there is a distinct limit, as regards length, to all works of literary art—the limit of a

# Compare & Contrast

- **1830s:** Common belief dictates that odors from water—such as the tarn outside the Usher house—could cause mental illness of the type suffered by Roderick Usher. Few, if any, effective treatments were available for mental illness.

  **Today:** Better understanding of the physiological causes of mental illness and a variety of medical therapies result in a vast improvement in the way the mentally ill are treated.

- **1830s:** The deceased are commonly laid in-state at home for several days. Funeral homes are rare; families prepare and bury their loved ones themselves.

  **Today:** Most people die in hospitals and wakes are most often held in churches or funeral homes.

- **1830s:** Travel is difficult, slow, and sometimes dangerous. Railroads are in their infancy and most long distance travel is in horse-drawn wagons. It was not unusual for guests to stay several weeks or for an entire season when invited to a relative's or friend's house.

  **Today:** Improved transportation—including railroads, airplanes, and automobiles—makes long-distance travel easier, while advanced communications technology like telephones and e-mail makes long visits with family and friends less popular than in previous eras.

---

single sitting—and that, (except in certain cases), it can never be properly overpassed.'' Poe developed and refined the genre of the short story based on this philosophy. His effort was so successful that this genre was taken up by authors from France as well as from the United States. This type of fiction is still popular among writers of today.

But if brevity is the rule, then intensity of presentation must accompany it. It is important to note that a short story is more a ''style'' than a ''length,'' although most will have less than thirty pages of text. Short stories have few characters and the development of those characters will be limited and sharply focused.

When discussing a short story, or any piece of literature, several options may be considered. These include discussions of plot (the order of the events in the story), theme (what the story means), imagery (descriptions), dialogue (how and what characters say), historical context (its relation to events that occurred when it was written), characterization (who the characters are and how they got that way), literary techniques (the use of puns or binary opposites), and even the reliability of the narrator (is he or she telling the truth?), especially one who is a part of the story itself. In the following discussion two of these options will be examined: the reliability of the narrator and the use of binary opposites.

Since this story is a first person narrative (it is told by a narrator from his, and only his, point of view), we have to make a decision about his reliability. (Remember, the narrator of a story is a creation of the author, NOT the author himself.) During the first passages of the story, the narrator gives us clues to his reliability. As he looks at the house he says that what he sees is more like ''the after-dream of a reveller upon opium.'' Later, still looking at the house, he says, ''Shaking off from my spirit what *must* have been a dream, I scanned . . . the building.'' Taking these two statements together, the narrator seems to be dreaming more than dealing with the reality before him. By his own admission, then, his narration must be scrutinized with great care.

Additionally, as the narrator contemplates the purpose of his trip and the mystery that is before him, he says, ''What was it—I paused to think—what was it that so unnerved me in the contempla-

*Henry Fuseli's painting "The Nightmare," which may have inspired Poe.*

tion of the House of Usher? It was a mystery all insoluable.'' Later he says, ''. . .the analysis of this power lies among considerations beyond our depth.'' Now, despite his admission that the mystery is beyond solution, he enters the house and attempts to solve it for the reader.

Another aspect of the narrator's character which is cause for our concern is his shift from telling about Roderick's madness to revealing his own madness. During their first meeting, he describes Roderick's manner with the following words: incoherence, inconsistency, excessive nervous agitation, and ''lost drunkard, or the irreclaimable eater of opium.'' Alone, these would not describe madness, but together they create the image of madness. Add to this Roderick's inability to endure harsh sensations of any kind, and we have a more convincing picture of a madman.

The most compelling discussion of this madness comes in the final scene when Roderick comes to the narrator's room. He enters the room, very agitated, and opens a window to the raging storm. As the narrator reads from the novel *Mad Trist* Roderick sits sullenly in a chair looking at the door. They both hear noises outside the door and Roderick speaks, ''Said I not that my senses were acute?''

Roderick explains that he has heard noises from the tomb for several days because of his acute hearing, and, like the narrator in ''The Tell-tale Heart,'' claims to hear Madeline's heart beating. In one final cry, he screams, ''Madman! I tell you she now stands without the door!'' Madeline appears when the door is blown open. She lunges toward him and they fall to the floor, dead.

In these last scenes some of Roderick's madness is transferred to the narrator. In the beginning the narrator thinks that what he sees is a dream, yet for the first several days he is at the house, he seems sane and in control of his senses. But after Madeline is entombed, the narrator becomes more agitated, just as Roderick does, and on the evening of the ''seventh or eighth day'' he is so uneasy that he cannot sleep. He is nervous and bewildered but he rationalizes that this is the result of sleeping in a room with drab and gloomy furniture. As the night progresses, he loses more and more control. ''An irrepressible tremor gradually pervaded my frame.'' The madness ascribed to Roderick is now afflicting the narrator.

As the final scene unfolds, the narrator also claims to hear the noises from the tomb. He dismisses this since the window was still open and there

*Vincent Price in* The Fall of the House of Usher, *1960.*

was a great deal of noise coming from the storm. As he reads more of the novel, *Mad Trist,* he stops abruptly and says, "I did actually hear . . . a low and apparently distant . . . sound." By his own admission, the narrator reveals his own acuteness of hearing, an aspect that he uses to define madness in Roderick. Now, the narrator himself has succumbed to the same madness.

Binary opposition is the literary technique of setting two situations, persons, or objects in opposition to one another. Some examples are good and evil, light and dark, open and closed, near and far, or any set of items or concepts that can be reduced to two aspects. Of course, in most situations, things are more involved and complicated than this. But for our purposes, as well as for use in analysis of other literature, the use of binary opposites provides a focal point for discussion. But what is more important than just listing binary oppositions is determining the sense of conflict that the opposites create in the story. (Remember, if there is no conflict in a tale, there is no interest generated by it.)

In "The Fall of the House of Usher" one such binary opposition is the male/female opposition of Roderick and Madeline. This is especially intense knowing that they are twins. To demonstrate how this simple opposition works, imagine how different this story would be if Roderick's twin had been another male character. The tension of Madeline's passage through the corner of the apartment (possibly wearing a flowing gown, making her seem ghostlike), of her untimely death, and especially of her return from the tomb, would be lost. Additionally, since the two lived alone in the house, some critics believe that there was an incestuous relationship between them. If they had been brothers, this kind of sexual innuendo would have to include a homosexual relationship. For Poe, writing about that sort of relationship in the early 19th century would have been almost impossible. Therefore, the binary opposition of male/female served Poe well in creating tension and conflict.

Regarding the male/female conflict, we see certain aspects of Roderick that can be called "feminine." His delicate features, his aptitude for the arts, and his frailty, all add up to a feminine character. Madeline, on the other hand, summons up strength to break the bonds of the tomb and to slay her brother in the final scene. These qualities might be seen as masculine. It is in the subtle shifts in our expectations of the character that tension and conflict are developed. (The aspects of feminine and

## What Do I Read Next?

- Poe's epic poem "The Raven," published in 1845, centers on a young scholar who is emotionally tormented by a raven's ominous repetition of the word "nevermore" in answer to his question about the probability of an afterlife with his deceased lover.

- Poe's "Ligeia" is a long poem in which a husband narrates the story of his beautiful dead wife who returns from the grave and assumes the identity of his second wife.

- "Young Goodman Brown" is a story by Nathaniel Hawthorne, a contemporary of Poe. Written in 1835, it concerns a newly married Puritan in New England who ventures forth one night against the wishes of his wife, Faith, and encounters several of his neighbors conducting satanic rituals in the woods.

- Stephen King's novel *The Shining* (1977) tells how the evil forces in a remote resort hotel manipulate the alcoholic caretaker into attempting to murder his wife and child.

- The short story "The Shunned House" by H. P. Lovecraft centers on a house possessed by evil powers. The somewhat Gothic horror story was inspired by "The Fall of the House of Usher" and Nathaniel Hawthorne's *House of the Seven Gables,* in which a haunted house inflicts terror upon its inhabitants.

---

masculine should not be misunderstood in sexist or sexual ways. Rather, the broadest stereotypical definition of these terms is desired.)

Another important binary opposition is the difference between sanity and madness. At first the narrator seems to be a sane person going to visit a friend who (he believes) is going mad. During the first meetings he describes Roderick's personal and psychological weaknesses. Roderick is feeble, shaking, and his voice is unstable. He looks ashen and cadaverous. He is also described as "alternately vivacious and sullen" which is a description of manic depression, a mental illness.

In contrast, the narrator tells of his own calmness and control of the situation. He says that he tried to calm his friend as they painted, wrote poetry and read novels together. Even in the final scene, when Roderick appears to have lost all sanity, the narrator reads to him in a vain attempt to calm the storm in Roderick as well as the storm outside the window. (It is ironic that the narrator tries to soothe his "mad" friend by reading from a novel entitled *Mad Trist.*)

It is the binary opposition of sanity/insanity that is the main focus of this tale. Many critics and students have wrestled with the issue of who is or is not insane in the story. This question rests upon the reliability of the narrator. If the narrator is fully reliable, then it is relatively easy to come to the conclusion that Roderick is mad. But if the narrator is not telling us the truth, or if the narrator is mad himself, then our conclusion will be somewhat less certain. The reader must grapple with the uncertainty along with the narrator. The issue of madness vs. sanity provided Poe with the grist for many of his stories, including "The Tell-tale Heart" and "The Black Cat."

As we can see, there are a variety of approaches to short story interpretation. None is exclusive of another; they may all contribute to our understanding. We cannot see binary oppositions in Roderick and the narrator without also seeing their characters and character development. We cannot examine the narrator alone without looking at his surroundings. The most important thing in any analysis is to trust the text itself. Two different interpretations may arise from one passage, as long as both derive from the text. We canot make up things, but we may interpret them.

**Source:** Carl Mowery, for *Short Stories for Students,* Gale Research, 1997.

### J.O. Bailey

*In the following essay, Bailey raises several theories about "The Fall of the House of Usher," one of which is that it is a vampire story, citing as evidence the strange behavior of Madeline and Roderick and how their actions fit the conventions of other vampire tales.*

What happens in "The Fall of the House of Usher"? This story contains many suggestions of psychic and supernatural influences upon the feelings of the narrator and the nerves of Roderick Usher. But the influences are not defined. No ghosts appear. Surely, Poe as craftsman intended the story to do what it does, to arouse a sense of unearthly terror that springs from a vague source, hinted and mysterious. Poe stated that his aim in tales of terror was to create "terror . . . not of Germany but of the soul," or not of the charnel but of the mind. He wrote to Thomas W. White, owner of the *Southern Literary Messenger,* that tales of terror are made into excellent stories by "the singular heightened into the strange and mystical." The influences that seem to drive Roderick Usher to madness, to kill him and Madeline, and even to destroy the House are certainly strange and mysterious. They seem rooted in some postulate of the supernatural, but the postulate is concealed. . . .

Roderick seems engaged in a struggle against a power that he feels to be supernatural. Apparently, as in the strange books he reads, he seeks knowledge of this power and how to combat it. He has found some explanations in a quasi-scientific theory about the sentience of vegetable matter. He seeks the help of objective reason by calling upon the narrator, to whom he repeatedly attempts to explain the nature of his invisible foe. But the narrator refuses to believe that the threatening power exists outside Roderick's imagination. . . .

Hints that may suggest a vampire appear in the first view of the House. The vegetation around the House is dead; though water is usually a symbol of life, the "black and lurid tarn" seems dead. It amplifies the House, reflecting it in "remodelled and inverted images." The narrator feels "an iciness" and "a sickening of the heart." He sees "about the whole mansion . . . a pestilent and mystic vapor, dull, sluggish, faintly discernible and leaden-hued." On entering the House, the narrator meets the family physician, whose countenance wears "a mingled expression of low cunning and perplexity." The physician accosts him "with trepidation."

Certain details about Roderick Usher seem significant. As a boy in school he displayed a hereditary "peculiar sensibility of temperament." This sensibility would make Roderick an easy prey to psychic or supernatural influence. His present illness has developed since he has lived in the House, "whence, for many years, he had never ventured forth." Thus, some influence in the House is suggested. It may be vampiric. Montague Summers's study of vampire lore states that when a

> In these last scenes some of Roderick's madness is transferred to the narrator."

person psychically sensitive even "visits a house which is powerfully haunted by malefic influences . . . a vampirish entity may . . . utilize his vitality," causing "debility and enervation" in the victim. . . .

Let us turn to the events of the story to discover what [Roderick] possibly knew. As the narrator approaches the House, he observes that the windows are "eye-like." Roderick's poem later gives the palace the features of a human head. These suggestions seem to mean that the House itself has some evil, destructive life, manifest in a spirit faintly visible as a vapor. Can it be regarded as a kind of vampire? In vampire lore, places or houses may be possessed: "Even to-day there are places and there are properties in England which owing to deeds of blood and violence . . . entail some dire misfortune upon all who seek to enjoy . . . them." . . .

Roderick's symptoms include "a morbid acuteness of the senses; the most insipid food was alone endurable; he could wear only garments of certain texture; the odors of all flowers were oppressive; his eyes were tortured by even a faint light; and there were but peculiar sounds, and these from stringed instruments, which did not inspire him with horror." These are specific symptoms of vampiric attack. Vampires, if not always their polluted victims, seldom touch ordinary food. Though some vampires, for instance Ruthven in Polidori's *The Vampyre,* wear ordinary clothing, most vampires appear in the garments of the grave. If Poe had vampire lore in mind, why did he say "the odors of all flowers"? We may look first at odors. Disgusting odors are associated with vampires. A vampire's breath is "unbearably fetid and rank with corruption, the stench of the charnel." This is the very material Poe rejected. The House draws vitality instead of blood; flowers seem a similar substitute for heightening the gory into the strange and mysterious. Poe's "all flowers" had to be left vague. If Poe had mentioned garlic and its whitish flower, universally accepted specifics against vampirism, he would have given away the secret he sought to suggest, but conceal. It seems significant that Poe mentions flowers at all. No garden can grow near the House; no flowers would be ordered from a tenant or a market if Roderick finds them oppressive. The mention seems Poe's tauntingly deliberate effort to be faithful to the lore he was using, without defining it. Perhaps the odors of flowers were "oppressive," rather than welcome to ward off attack, because Roderick was already polluted to the extent that he shared the aversions of the vampire. Most vampires cannot endure daylight; they must return to the tomb at the first hint of dawn. Roderick's horror of all sounds except those of stringed instruments seems natural for anyone who senses the presence of a demon. Poe often associates stringed instruments with angelic forces.

After detailing his symptoms, Roderick cries out: "I *must* perish in this deplorable folly." What folly? for none is mentioned. Perhaps his folly is that, through living as a recluse in the House and through curious reading, Roderick had laid himself open to attack. A "Vampire was often a person who during his life had read deeply in poetic lore and practised black magic." Roderick says, "I dread the events of the future, not in themselves, but in their results." Perhaps he does not dread death, but fears becoming a vampire if killed by a vampire.

At this point Roderick states—specifies—that the attack upon his vitality comes from the House. The narrator, reporting with scorn, says: "He was enchained by certain superstitious impressions in regard to the dwelling which he tenanted . . . in regard to an influence . . . which some peculiarities in the mere form and substance of his family mansion had . . . obtained over his spirit—an effect which the *physique* of the gray walls and turrets, and of the dim tarn into which they looked down, had . . . brought about upon the *morale* of his existence."

Madeline seems a victim of the same attack, and she dies. When? On the evening of the first day Roderick tells the narrator "with inexpressible agitation" that Madeline had "succumbed . . . to the prostrating power of the destroyer." But she is not declared dead, that she "was no more" and is ready for burial, until several days later. Perhaps in the interval she is undead, "living" as a vampire. All definitions say that a person killed by a vampire becomes a vampire with a craving to pass on the pollution. . . .

During the entombment, the narrator notices a "striking similitude between the brother and sister." Roderick explains that he and Madeline "had been twins" and that "sympathies of a scarcely intelligible nature had always existed between them." What were these sympathies? T. O. Mabbott has stated, I think rightly, that "Poe's twins share their family soul with the house, and Roderick knew it." If Madeline was destroyed by the House, she is now a vampire; a vampire attacks first its closest blood-kin. A French writer on vampire lore, Augustin Calmet, says: "Cette persécution ne s'arrête pas à une seule personne; elle s'étend jusqu'à la dernière personne de la famille." This feature of vampirism is presented in Lord Byron's "The Giaour." A curse dooms an Infidel to become a vampire and to

> . . . suck the blood of all thy race;
> There from thy daughter, sister, wife
> At midnight drain the stream of life?

Thus, just because he is a twin, Roderick has reason to be terrified of Madeline. . . .

If Madeline were an ordinary vampire buried in a cemetery, she could dematerialize, escape through crevices, and rematerialize. But how could she escape from a sealed coffin in an airtight vault closed and secured by an iron door? I suggest that Poe established these seemingly impossible conditions because he had in mind a supernatural agency in Madeline's escape. If she is now a vampire killed by the House and therefore the agent of the House, the House might help set her free. To do so, it seems, required the total vitality of the House, with added draughts from Roderick's life, all redoubled in power by the full moon, and engaged in the violent effort manifested in the storm. How could the House help set her free? Let us observe below how it opened heavy doors for her to reach Roderick.

Roderick hears her approach and asks, "Is she not hurrying to upbraid me for my haste?" He may mean his haste in sealing her in the vault before his own death. Perhaps Roderick knows that when he dies—if he can die before Madeline sucks his blood—the House and Madeline must also die in "final death-agonies."

As Madeline approaches with a "heavy and horrible beating of her heart," typical of the vampire, Roderick speaks in his "gibbering murmur, as if unconscious of [the narrator's] presence." What is he saying? Perhaps part of his monologue is an incantation from the *Vigilia*. When Madeline reaches the "huge antique panels" of the chamber, she simply stands there waiting. The doors open. The narrator says, "It was the work of the rushing gust." How can this be? These doors face the interior of the House, not the storm outside. The casement has been closed. This gust may be the spirit of the vampire House, rooted in Madeline's vault, and manifest in the forces of the storm. When the doors of the chamber throw "slowly back ... their ponderous and ebony jaws," between these jaws stands the "lofty and enshrouded figure of the lady Madeline of Usher," with "blood upon her white robes." Are these images a symbolist painting: between the jaws of the vampire House stands its white and blood-stained tooth poised to plunge into Roderick's life-stream?

For a moment, Madeline "remained trembling and reeling to and fro upon the threshold." Perhaps she wavered between remnants of human compassion aided by Roderick's incantations, and the evil power driving her onward. But she "then, with a low moaning cry, fell heavily inward upon the person of her brother, and in her violent and now final death-agonies, bore him to the floor a corpse, and a victim to the terrors he had anticipated." Was Roderick's death heart failure? The narrator does not stop to observe: he "fled aghast." But the somewhat erotic embrace of its victim, the prone position for the kill, and the moan of pleasure are commonplaces of vampire lore. In terms of this lore, Madeline reached the jugular vein. But as Roderick dies, Madeline and the House die, for their source of vitality is cut off. Does Roderick continue undead, a vampire by pollution, as "he had anticipated"? When a vampire is destroyed, it squeals or screams horribly. As the fragments of the House sink into the tarn, there is a "shouting sound like the voice of a thousand waters." Perhaps, as both Madeline and the House die in the instant of Roderick's death, the curse is fulfilled, and Roderick's soul is, after all, saved by the finally innocuous water. The narrator observes no more except the "full, setting, and blood-red moon."...

**Source:** J.O. Bailey, "What Happens in 'The Fall of the House of Usher,'" in *American Literature,* Vol. XXXV, No. 4, January, 1964, pp. 445–66.

## Lynne P. Shackelford

*In the following brief essay, Shackelford comments on the relationship between Henri Fuseli's painting,* The Nightmare, *and Poe's story.*

In "The Fall of the House of Usher," Edgar Allan Poe entices his readers to view the narrator's experiences as a dream. Many critics have noted the tale's iterative images of water, mist, sleep, and descent, connoting the subconscious, as well as the explicit verbal clues Poe provides in such passages as "I looked upon the scene before me ... with an utter depression of soul which I can compare to no earthly sensation more properly than to the afterdream of the reveller upon opium ... , " "Shaking off from my spirit what *must* have been a dream ... ," and "... I listened, as if in a dream, to the wild improvisations of his speaking guitar." No critical attention, however, has yet been given to the significance of Poe's allusion to the eighteenth-century artist John Henry Fuseli.

Describing the paintings of Roderick Usher, Poe's narrator observes:

> If ever mortal painted an idea, that mortal was Roderick Usher. For me at least—in the circumstances then surrounding me—there arose out of the pure abstractions which the hypochondriac contrived to throw upon his canvas, an intensity of intolerable awe, no shadow of which felt I ever yet in the contemplations of the certainly glowing yet too concrete reveries of Fuseli.

Why did Poe choose Fuseli as the one artist with whom to compare Usher? The answer is that Fuseli shared Poe's preoccupation with the realm of the subconscious. Indeed, he based his career upon his oft-cited aphorism: "One of the most unexplored regions of art are dreams...."

The work upon which Fuseli's fame rests and the work which Poe evokes in his tale is *The Nightmare,* which the artist painted in 1781 and exhibited at the Royal Academy in London. *The Nightmare* is an unforgettable, to many viewers even shocking, canvas composed of three key elements: a beautiful woman, dressed in virginal white, lying prostrate upon a bed; an incubus, or demon, crouched maliciously upon the woman's breast; and a horse's head with fiery eyes emerging from a shadowy background. Intending to depict a general rather than an individual experience of the bad dream, Fuseli combines evil spirits from Germanic folklore with an Enlightenment medical belief that the nightmare is caused by sleeping on one's back. This position creates a difficulty in circulation that induces frightful visions and a feeling of weight upon the chest.

That Poe knew Fuseli's painting is highly likely. The exhibition of *The Nightmare* became a *cause célèbre.* Soon engravers disseminated prints of it throughout Europe and then America, while cartoonists amused the public with their vulgarized burlesques of Fuseli's demon-tormented sleeper. However, it is the text of "The Fall of the House of Usher" that provides the most compelling evidence of Poe's familiarity with Fuseli's composition; for shortly before the appearance of the specter-like

> "Why did Poe choose Fuseli as the one artist with whom to compare Usher? The answer is that Fuseli shared Poe's preoccupation with the realm of the subconscious."

Madeline, arisen from the crypt, Poe's narrator assumes the exact position of Fuseli's dreaming damsel. Retiring to his sleeping apartment—a chamber directly above the vault in which Madeline has been buried, the narrator rests fitfully. He then reveals, "An irrepressible tremor gradually pervaded my frame; and, at length, there sat upon my heart an incubus of utterly causeless alarm." This description of a demon upon the narrator's breast and his subsequent feeling of "an intense sentiment of horror" suggest strongly that his final vision of Madeline and Roderick's embrace of death is, in fact, a nightmare.

**Source:** Lynne P. Shackelford, "Poe's 'The Fall of the House of Usher'," in *Explicator,* Vol. 45, No. 1, Fall, 1986, pp. 18–9.

## Further Reading

Abel, Darrel. "A Key to the House of Usher," in *University of Toronto Quarterly,* Vol. XVII, No. 2, January, 1949, pp. 176-85.

> Abel talks about the setting of "The Fall of the House of Usher," and how the themes of isolation and self-destructive concentration are symbolized by the character of Roderick Usher.

Baym, Nina. "'The Fall of the House of Usher,' Character Analysis," in *The Norton Anthology of American Literature,* W. W. Norton, 1995, p. 664.

> Baym offers a brief analysis of the three characters and their mental disorders.

Bieganowski, Ronald. "The Self-consuming Narrator in Poe's 'Ligeia' and 'Usher'," in *American Literature,* Volume 60, No. 2, May, 1988, pp. 175-87.

> Bieganowski shows how the narrators in these two tales become enamored of their own rhetoric and therefore fail to tell the tale in the complete manner they intend. They fail because their desire to tell their story in the most ideal manner possible overwhelms the story itself.

Brennan, Matthew C. "Turnerian Topography: The Paintings of Roderick Usher," in *Studies in Short Fiction,* Volume 27, Fall, 1990, pp. 605-8.

> Brennan argues that Poe's descriptions of Roderick's paintings show a strong similarity to the paintings of Englishman Joseph Turner. He believes that both Poe and Turner reject the realist's approach to their art in favor of a more vague, expressionist approach called the "sublime style."

Brooks, Cleanth, Jr. and Robert Penn Warren. "The Fall of the House of Usher," in their *Understanding Fiction,* New York, F.S. Crofts & Co., 1943, pp. 202-5.

> Reduces "The Fall of the House of Usher" to a "relatively meaningless" horror story which serves principally as a case study in morbid psychology and lacks any quality of pathos or tragedy.

Evans, Walter. "'The Fall of the House of Usher' and Poe's Theory of the Tale," in *Studies in Short Fiction,* Volume 14, No. 2, Spring, 1977, pp. 137-44.

> Evans contends that there are significant discrepancies between Poe's theory of the tale and his literary practice as exemplified by "The Fall of the House of Usher."

May, Leila S. "Sympathies of Scarcely Intelligible Nature: The Brother-Sister Bond in Poe's 'Fall of the House of Usher'," in *Studies in Short Fiction,* Volume 30, Summer, 1993, pp. 387-96.

> May makes the relationship of the Ushers and their fall a symbolic representation of the fall of the family in the 19th century.

Poe, Edgar Allan. "The Philosophy of Composition" in *Selected Writings of Edgar Allan Poe,* edited by Edward H. Davidson, Houghton, 1956, pp. 452-61.

> Poe outlines his philosophy of literary composition, discussing the proper length and content of literary works.

Rout, Kay Kinsella. "The Unreliable and Unbalanced Narrator," in *Studies in Short Fiction,* Volume 19, Winter, 1982, pp. 27-33.

> While this article is more about John Gardner's story, "The Ravages of Spring," Rout compares the narrator in it to the narrator of "Usher." She sees both as unreliable and emotionally unbalanced.

Voloshin, Beverly R. "Explanation in 'The Fall of the House of Usher'," in *Studies in Short Fiction,* Volume 23, Fall, 1986, pp. 419-28.

> Voloshin argues that the story is a turning point in the development of the Gothic tale in the hands of Poe. She says it contains all the necessary ingredients: romance, mystery, darkness, supernatural, decay, a corpse, and even vampirism.

# The Gift of the Magi

**O. Henry**
**1906**

"The Gift of the Magi" is one of O. Henry's most famous stories. Included in *The Four Million*, his first collection of short stories, in 1906, it has been anthologized many times since then. The story contains many of the elements for which O. Henry is widely known, including poor, working-class characters, a humorous tone, realistic detail, and a surprise ending. A major reason given for its enduring appeal is its affirmation of unselfish love. Such love, the story and its title suggest, is like the gifts given by the wise men, called magi, who brought gold, frankincense, and myrrh to the newborn Jesus.

## Author Biography

O. Henry was born William Sydney Porter on September 11, 1862, in Greensboro, North Carolina. Though his father, Algernon Porter, was a doctor, the young boy did not receive much formal education. As a teenager, he worked as a pharmacist's assistant in his uncle's drugstore to help support his family. At 19, worried that he might be susceptible to the pneumonia that had killed his mother at a young age, he moved to Texas to take advantage of its warm, dry climate. There he worked on a cattle ranch owned by friends of his family. These early jobs—pharmacist, ranch hand, and bank teller—gave him plenty of material for his stories about poor, working-class people.

When he was twenty-two, Porter moved to Austin, where he landed a job as a bank teller. He also met Athol Estes, who soon became his wife; together they had a daughter, Margaret. For about a year, he owned and wrote a weekly humor paper; when this folded, he continued to submit articles and humorous stories to other newspapers under the pseudonym O. Henry.

In 1894 he was dismissed from the bank because of shortages in his accounts. When the case was reinvestigated in 1895, and it became apparent that he would be charged with embezzlement, O. Henry fled Austin and sailed for Honduras. He gathered material and wrote stories set in Central America while he was there. These stories were collected under the title *Cabbages and Kings* in 1904. In 1897, however, he learned that his wife was seriously ill, so he returned to the United States and turned himself in.

Athol died in July of that year, and O. Henry was convicted of embezzlement and sentenced to five years in the Federal Penitentiary in Ohio, where he worked in the prison pharmacy. He had sold his first professional story to a magazine just before he was convicted, and he continued to write and sell stories during his time in prison. He used his in-laws' address in Pittsburgh to hide his actual circumstances.

After his release, O. Henry moved to New York City, at the encouragement of the editors of *Ainslee's Magazine,* who had been printing his stories and believed he could make a living writing for the many New York-based magazines that existed in the early 1900s. He soon signed a contract with the New York *Sunday World* to provide weekly short stories, and he continued to sell stories to other magazines as well. For once, O. Henry seemed headed for financial security. As it turned out, he proved rather reckless and irresponsible with his income—he could perhaps be called generous to a fault. He left big tips in bars and restaurants and gave large handouts to the panhandlers and prostitutes who, he said, inspired many of his stories.

In 1906 O. Henry's second collection, *The Four Million,* was published, which included "The Gift of the Magi." An anthology of his work came out every year after that, continuing for several years after his death.

O. Henry suffered from a variety of health problems, including diabetes and cirrhosis of the liver, which were made worse by his alcoholism. In 1910 he died at the age of 47, widowing his second wife, Sarah Lindsay Coleman, whom he had married three years earlier. During the last ten years of his short life, and for the next decade, O. Henry was considered by many to be the country's best-known, most widely read short story writer.

## Plot Summary

Della and Jim Young, the main characters in "The Gift of the Magi," are a young married couple with very little money. Jim has suffered a thirty-percent pay cut, and the two must scrimp for everything. On the day before Christmas, Della counts the money she has painstakingly saved for months. She is dismayed to find she has less than two dollars, hardly enough to buy anything at all. After a good long cry, Della determines to find a way to buy Jim the present he deserves. As she looks into a mirror, an idea comes to her.

Jim and Della have two possessions of which they are both proud. One is Jim's gold watch, which has been handed down from his grandfather. The other is Della's hair, lustrous, shining, and falling past her knees. Before she can lose her nerve, Della races out of the apartment to a wigmaker, Mme. Sofronie, to whom she sells her hair for twenty dollars. With the money in her hand, Della goes to the stores, trying to find something worthy of Jim. At last she finds it: a platinum watch chain.

Once home, Della attempts to fix her shorn hair. She heats a frying pan for dinner and waits nervously by the front door for Jim. When he comes in and sees Della's hair, he says nothing. His face shows no anger, surprise, disapproval, or horror—none of the sentiments Della was expecting. Instead, he only stares.

Della goes to him, explaining that she sold her hair to buy his gift. Jim has a difficult time understanding, but suddenly he snaps out of his daze. He draws from his pocket Della's Christmas present. She opens it and finds a set of combs for her hair, which she had been admiring in a store window for a long time. She now understands why Jim was so stunned. Della gives Jim his present, but he does not pull out his watch to fit to the chain, for he has sold his watch to buy Della's combs.

The narrator explains that the wise men, or magi, brought gifts to the baby Jesus and so invented the giving of Christmas gifts. Because these men were wise, they no doubt gave wise gifts. Della and Jim, the narrator asserts, have unwisely sacrificed their most precious possessions. Yet, because they gave from the heart, they are wise: "They are the magi."

## Characters

### Dell
*See* Della Young

### Jim
*See* James Dillingham Young

### Madame
*See* Mme Sofronie

### Mme Sofronie

Madame Sofronie, the only character in the story other than the Youngs, owns the local hair-goods shop; in the early 1900s, when this story was written, wigs were made of real human hair. She has a small role in the story, but O. Henry provides a rich characterization with only one sentence: "Madame, large, too white, chilly, hardly looked the 'Sofronie.'" She is blunt: when Della asks whether she would buy her hair, she says, "I buy hair" and brusquely tells Della to take her hat off so she can see it. She offers Della twenty dollars for her hair.

### Della Young

Della is the wife of Jim Young. As the story opens, she is counting the money that she has saved to buy her husband his Christmas present, and she is reduced to tears when she realizes how little she has. Della and Jim are poor; she has only managed to scrape together $1.87, despite saving carefully for months. But O. Henry makes Della's happiness in her love for Jim quite clear: "Many a happy hour she had spent planning for something nice for him. Something fine and rare and sterling—something just a little bit near to being worthy of the honour of being owned by Jim."

She is a pretty, slender young woman. Her long brown hair, when she lets it down, cascades past her knees. In one of several biblical allusions, O. Henry

*O. Henry*

notes that Della's beautiful hair would be envied by the Queen of Sheba herself. In a moment of resourcefulness and courage, Della decides to sell her hair so that she can buy a present for her beloved Jim. With the money from her hair, she buys Jim a beautiful watch chain elegant enough to complement his gold heirloom watch—their only other material possession of any worth.

Later that day, while waiting for Jim to return home from work, Della experiences a moment of insecurity. Though she has curled what is left of her hair as attractively as she can, she worries that Jim might no longer find her beautiful. When he arrives and appears stunned by her appearance, Della again shows unselfishness, courage, and resilience, reminding him that her hair grows quickly and that she loves him. She entreats him to be happy, for it is Christmas eve, and she has sold her hair because she could not face Christmas without a gift for him.

### James Dillingham Young

Della's husband, Jim, is a thin, serious young man, twenty-two years old. O. Henry tells the reader what Jim is like, and also indicates Della's feelings for him, when he compares Jim to the platinum watch chain: "[the watch fob] was like

## Media Adaptations

- "The Gift of the Magi" was adapted for film as a 21-minute segment of *O. Henry's Full House,* produced by Andre Hakim, starring Jeanne Crain and Farley Granger, narrated by John Steinbeck, and with music by Alfred Newman, Twentieth Century-Fox, 1952.

- It also appeared in a 15-minute segment of the four-part *Short Story Classics Series,* produced in 1980 and distributed by Britannica Films.

- It was also one of several O. Henry stories adapted for the musical *Gifts of the Magi,* produced in New York City at the Lamb's Theater, 1985.

- This famous story has also been recorded on audiocassette by Miller-Brody Productions.

- "The Gift of the Magi" was adapted as a stage play by Anne Coulter Martens.

---

him. Quietness and value—the description applied to both." He works hard, not returning home until seven o'clock, and is reliable: "Jim was never late."

Jim's most prized possession is the gold watch that has been handed down to him from his grandfather and his father. Continuing the biblical allusion begun with the Queen of Sheba, O. Henry claims that King Solomon himself would have envied Jim's watch. But Jim clearly values his young wife more than his gold watch, because he sells it in order to buy her a set of beautiful, jewel-edged tortoiseshell combs for her long hair.

When the couple discover that both have sold their treasures to buy a wonderful present—and in the process, made those presents useless—Jim reacts with gentle humor and the same kind of resilience Della has shown. First he affirms his love, telling her, "I don't think there's anything in the way of a haircut or a shave or a shampoo that could make me like my girl any less." In the end, rather than bemoaning their situation, he smiles and suggests, "Let's put our presents away and keep 'em awhile. They're too nice to use just at present."

## Themes

### Love

Love, generosity, and the various definitions of wealth and poverty are central themes in "The Gift of the Magi," in which a poor, loving young husband and wife sell the only valuable things they own to give each other special Christmas gifts. Della Young sells her beautiful hair to buy Jim a platinum watch chain, and Jim sells his heirloom watch to buy Della some tortoiseshell hair combs. These gifts are useless, in one sense; Della cannot wear her combs without her hair, and Jim, without his watch, cannot use his watch chain.

But the narrator of the story points out that the Youngs possess a gift greater than any object: the gift of love. He compares them to the magi (the wise men who brought gifts to the baby Jesus in Bethlehem), saying: "let it be said that of all who give gifts these two were the wisest.... They are the magi."

### Generosity

Growing out of the Youngs' love is their deep generosity. Della and Jim are very poor, and yet Della decides to sell her only treasure: her hair. O. Henry shows that this is not an easy sacrifice for Della to make. He contrasts Della's gorgeous hair with the Youngs' impoverished apartment. The Queen of Sheba herself would have been jealous of this treasure, he asserts, and he gives his readers a vivid image of it: "Della's beautiful hair fell about her, rippling and shining like a cascade of brown waters. It reached below her knee and made itself almost a garment for her." The color drains from Della's face when she makes her decision, and she urges Mme. Sofronie to hurry—perhaps so she will not change her mind.

O. Henry does not show the decision-making process when Jim sells his watch, but he does describe how important the watch is to him. Handed down from his grandfather to his father to Jim, the watch is lauded as a treasure that even wealthy King Solomon would covet. Jim, too, sells his only valuable possession, so that he may buy his wife a special Christmas gift. Della has never asked for the combs that Jim buys her, but clearly he has seen her face when she has passed the combs in the shop window and has decided that his wife, and his love for her, are more important than his precious keepsake.

### *Wealth and Poverty*

The themes of love and generosity work hand in hand with the story's examination of what it means to be rich or poor. O. Henry provides many details to illustrate Jim and Della's poverty. The furniture in their apartment is shabby; the apartment's doorbell does not work, and it is not possible even to put a letter in their mail slot. They do not own a proper mirror. When Della goes out, she puts on "her old brown jacket" and "her old brown hat," and Jim needs gloves and a new overcoat. Their rent is $8 per week, and Jim makes only $20 per week.

In contrast, the narrator of the story makes biblical allusions concerning the great value of Della's hair and Jim's watch; even King Solomon and the Queen of Sheba would be jealous of such fine things. And yet Jim and Della each sacrifice their only good material possessions out of love for the other.

O. Henry makes the point that while Jim and Della are terribly poor by material standards, they are wealthy beyond compare in their love for each other. "The Gift of the Magi" is often held up as a story about true love and about the true spirit of Christmas and of giving.

## Style

### *Point of View*

In "The Gift of the Magi," O. Henry uses a folksy narrator to tell the story of Jim and Della Young, a poor young couple who buy each other special Christmas gifts, which ironically cancel each other out because Della sells her hair to buy Jim a chain for his watch, which he in turn has sold to buy her a fine set of combs for her hair. Despite the fact that these gifts are now useless, Jim and Della have given each other the greatest gift of all, which the narrator compares to the gifts given to the Christ child by the wise men, or magi: selfless love.

O. Henry employs several techniques, or literary devices, in "The Gift of the Magi" that are typical of most of his short stories. The first of these is a narrator with personality and presence. Although the story focuses on Della's point of view—the reader sees primarily what Della sees—the

## Topics for Further Study

- Compare the typical living and working conditions in New York in the early 1900s with today. What does a "normal" working person make per week today in New York City, and what would his or her rent be? How much did food and clothing cost at the time "The Gift of the Magi" takes place?

- Where, exactly, in New York did O. Henry live? Research what his life was like when he lived there.

- Find the places in the Bible that O. Henry alludes to in "The Gift of the Magi." Also, do some historical research on King Solomon, the Queen of Sheba, and the magi. What do these references bring to the story?

story is told in another narrative voice that directly addresses the reader as "you." It is almost as if the narrator is an additional character that is heard, but never seen, engaging the reader as a friend and sharing his insights into the Youngs' situation. The narrator tells the story in a joking, neighborly way, with several funny asides directed at the reader. He uses casual expressions such as "took a mighty pride" and interrupts his tale with humorous phrases like "forget the hashed metaphor." Another writer who often uses this technique, sometimes called authorial intrusion, is Charles Dickens.

### *Setting*

Although "The Gift of the Magi" is a famous story, O. Henry is mainly known for the *type* of story he wrote, rather than for individual pieces. All of the stories follow certain patterns of character, plot, structure, and setting. The settings of O. Henry's stories are often grouped into five categories: the American South, the West, Central America, prison, and New York.

"The Gift of the Magi" is a New York story. Although almost half of his stories are set in New York, O. Henry establishes the particular settings of each story with great attention to detail. In "The Gift of the Magi," the writer uses details of the setting to show that Jim and Della are poor. As soon as the story opens, he describes "the shabby little couch," the dismal view ("she...looked out dully at a grey cat walking a grey fence in a grey backyard"), "the letter box into which no letter would go, and an electric button from which no mortal finger could coax a ring." The writer's careful rendering of setting—and mood—help the reader understand just how big are the sacrifices Della and Jim are making when they sell their most prized possessions. The details of place also help make the story seem realistic on one level, although on another level it becomes an allegory.

### Structure

"The Gift of the Magi" is also a good example of the kind of story structure, or organization, for which O. Henry became famous. One of the most widely recognized elements of his fiction is the surprise ending; in fact, many critics refer to the sudden, unexpected turn of events at the very end of a story as "the O. Henry twist."

O. Henry was an economical writer. As in this story, he often began by introducing a character and giving telling details about setting that hint at plot. The first paragraph, primarily made up of short phrases and sentence fragments, introduces Della and her money problem. Using very little space, O. Henry gives readers an accurate sense of her character, her predicament, and her surroundings. He outlines her decision and its aftermath in a tightly constructed plot, moving quickly from introduction to action and on to the surprise ending.

### Allusion

Another element of "The Gift of the Magi" is allusion, or references to well-known people, places, events, or artistic works. When the narrator in this story describes Della's hair and Jim's watch, he alludes to the Bible: "Had the Queen of Sheba lived in the flat across the airshaft, Della would have let her hair hang out of the window some day to dry just to depreciate Her Majesty's jewels and gifts. Had King Solomon been the janitor, with all his treasures piled up in the basement, Jim would have pulled out his watch every time he passed, just to see him pluck at his beard from envy."

O. Henry's use of allusion here accomplishes three things. First, it is funny. The thought of the Queen of Sheba living in the apartment across the airshaft from Della and Jim Young, and the thought of King Solomon as a janitor—these are silly images, designed not just to make readers laugh but also, perhaps, to remind them that Della and Jim do not take their circumstances too seriously. Second, by comparing Della's hair and Jim's watch to royal treasures, O. Henry lets his readers know how special these items are. Finally, this lighthearted allusion to the Bible prepares the way for the more serious allusion which appears at the end of the story, when Della and Jim are compared to the Magi.

## Historical Context

O. Henry does not specify where or when "The Gift of the Magi" takes place. The reader may assume that "the city" he refers to is New York City and that the story occurs around the time he wrote it—in the early 1900s. Details from the story, such as the clothes the characters wear, the physical descriptions of the apartment and of the city, and the language in the story (both the slang used by the characters and the vocabulary of the narrator) help support this assumption. For instance, the Youngs' flat has an electric buzzer (even though it is broken), but Della must use the gas to heat her curling irons, showing that the story takes place before electricity was as widely used as it is today. Wigs are made with real human hair, and watches are commonly carried in a pocket rather than worn on the wrist.

When this story was first published, in 1906, the roles of American men and women were fairly clearly defined. Jim and Della show several signs of meeting conventional expectations: he works outside the home, while she shops and cooks and takes care of the household; he is emotionally secure, comforting her during her crying spells. Women did not yet have the right to vote, although the suffrage movement had begun.

In the United States, an economic crisis was building, made worse by the tremendous amount of federal aid needed to help the people of San Francisco, California, after the infamous 1906 earthquake, the worst ever to hit an American city. The quake was calculated to register 8.3 on the Richter scale, cracking water and gas mains and igniting a 3-day-long fire that burned two thirds of the city. Twenty-five hundred people died, 250,000 were left homeless, and over $400 million in property was destroyed.

# Compare & Contrast

- **Early 1900s:** In most married couples, the husband works and the wife stays home. Only one-third of the workforce is women.

  **Today:** Women represent 40 percent of the workforce, and two-income families are common.

- **Early 1900s:** Fewer than half of the families in America–46 percent–own their own homes.

  **Today:** Home ownership extends to 64 percent of all families.

- **Early 1900s:** Average annual income is $700, with an average work week of 53 hours.

  **Today:** Average annual income is $31,000, with an average work week of 40 hours.

---

O. Henry did not allude to the current events of his day in "The Gift of the Magi" or in many of his other stories. This may have been because his characters were mainly working-class people, too involved with getting along in their day-to-day lives to pay much attention to international or even national events that did not affect them directly and immediately.

## Critical Overview

When O. Henry published "The Gift of the Magi," his stories were popular with the reading public and critics alike. For the last ten years of his life, and for ten years or so after that, he was hailed as a master of the short story. Critics ranked him with Edgar Allan Poe, Nathaniel Hawthorne, and Bret Harte, and his techniques were taught in creative writing courses.

Although O. Henry's characters are often regarded more as types than as unique individuals—vagabonds, shop girls, criminals, cowboys—critics find them likeable, and the writer's use of detail creates a sense that they are "real people." Della and Jim fit this pattern in that the reader knows little about the details of their personalities or backgrounds—just enough to sympathize with their circumstances. Reviewers also find the story typical of O. Henry in its tight structure, humorous tone, and signature surprise ending. These qualities have kept his stories popular with the reading public, even during times when his work has been out of favor with critics.

Ironically, just when his popularity was at its height, and C. Alphonso Smith published *O. Henry Biography* in 1916, critics began to question the value of his work. Some—in particular, Fred Lewis Pattee—dismissed his stories as superficial, false and predictable. The craftsmanship that made tales such as "The Gift of the Magi" compact and pointed fables began to seem mere trickery. His reputation continued to fall throughout the 1920s and 1930s, when Gertrude Stein, James Joyce, Virginia Woolf and other Modernists began to experiment with literary form.

O. Henry's work remained popular among readers, however, and in the 1960s, literary critics began to reassess his work. Today, most critics agree that his short, funny, inventive stories have earned him a permanent place in American literature. "The Gift of the Magi" has earned a niche as one of his masterpieces.

## Criticism

### Rena Korb

*Rena Korb has a master's degree in English literature and creative writing and has written for a wide variety of educational publishers. In the following essay, she discusses the varying critical opinions expressed about O. Henry's work, main-*

*Jeanne Crain as Della in* Gift of the Magi, *1952.*

*taining that stories such as "The Gift of the Magi" are carefully crafted, achieve the author's intentions, and successfully speak to the audience for which they were written.*

It would be difficult to find a reader of short American fiction who does not have at least an acquaintance with O. Henry's story "The Gift of the Magi." This story, penned for the Christmas edition of a weekly magazine, is essential O. Henry. It is as synonymous with his name as its technique of the surprise ending.

O. Henry, pseudonym for William Sydney Porter, reached great fame in the first decade of the twentieth century as a writer of some 300 short stories. They are known for their pervasive sense of humor, their quick, chatty beginnings, their confidential narrator, and, of course, their inclusion of one of several types of surprise endings. O. Henry's fame traveled beyond the borders of the United States; his short story collections have been translated into many foreign languages and can be found throughout the world. Some stories have also been adapted for television, screen, and stage. Such exposure has led O. Henry biographer Eugene Current-Garcia to maintain that "the pseudonym O.

Henry has become a symbol representing, especially to foreigners, a particular kind of 'All-American' short story, as well as a touchstone for evaluating the art of short fiction writing in general." An annual award for a volume of the best short stories was named for him in 1819, and *The O. Henry Awards* is still published each year.

Though the decade following his death in 1910 saw critics comparing his short stories to those of such greats as Nathaniel Hawthorne and Edgar Allan Poe, O. Henry's star began to decline in the 1930s, particularly as new, "experimental" writers, such as Ernest Hemingway and F. Scott Fitzgerald, rose to prominence. The majority of critics then dubbed O. Henry's stories facile, anecdotal, superficial, and flippant. His work was discredited for its convenient endings, its sentimentality, and what Katherine Fullerton Gerrould in a 1916 assessment called its "pernicious influence" on the genre of the short story because his stories lacked intellectual content. Over the years, some critics have continued to fight against the mainstream, and with the help of a loyal reading public they have reinstated O. Henry among important American writers. Though his work is constantly being reassessed, it is now generally agreed that O. Henry's stories are the

# What Do I Read Next?

- *Whirligigs*, a collection of O. Henry's short stories published in 1910, features the popular story "The Ransom of Red Chief," about two men who kidnap a boy so impossible that soon they are offering to pay his parents to take him back. This story has been made into films and is often anthologized.

- *O. Henry: A Biography of William Sydney Porter.* Written by David Stuart and published by Doubleday in 1987, this biography offers a recent look at O. Henry's life.

- "The Open Window," from Saki's collection *Beasts and Super-Beasts* (1914), is a short story that features many of the characteristics common to O. Henry's work, including brevity and a surprise ending.

- Ambrose Bierce's story "Occurrence at Owl Creek Bridge," included in his collection *Tales of Soldiers and Civilians* (1891), is a suspenseful tale of a man's last moments before his hanging, ending with a dark surprise.

- The play *Our Town* (1938), by Thornton Wilder, features a narrator who comments on and draws a moral from the lives of the play's ordinary, small-town characters, who are largely symbolic.

- Damon Knight's science fiction story "To Serve Man"—published in *Galaxy* magazine in 1950, adapted as an episode of television's *Twilight Zone,* and anthologized numerous times—makes effective use of the surprise ending.

---

work of a skilled and inventive writer; it is recognized that part of his gift is the ability to write of people and situations with which the American public could identify. His place as a major player in the development of a truly American literature is perhaps finally assured. But the question remains, however, of why readers throughout the twentieth century, in comparison to critics, have little quarrel with the stories of O. Henry.

There are many possibilities. One might suggest that readers are not averse to the surprise ending, even when it is so much a part of a writer's repertoire that it is no longer a surprise. Guy de Maupassant, one of the masters of the short story, uses a surprise ending tragically in "The Necklace"; this ending assuredly does not detract from the skill of the writing and tale telling. The zany plots of Saki (H. H. Munro) give the surprise ending a lighthearted twist, such as in his brief but bewitching tale "The Open Window." Each of these three writers takes a plot contrivance but uses it originally, thus making it an integral part of the story. H. E. Bates maintains in *The Modern Short Story* that "by the telling of scores of stories solely for the point, the shock, or the witty surprise of the last line, O. Henry made himself famous and secured for himself a large body of readers."

There are, of course, a variety of other reasons that readers like O. Henry. Perhaps one of the most important is that not all art is meant to appeal primarily to the intellect or the intellectuals. O. Henry's readers wanted to read about regular people. As William Saroyan wrote in the 1960s, "The people of America loved O. Henry... He was a nobody, but he was a nobody who also was a somebody, everybody's somebody." O. Henry's work is popular art, which is specifically created to appeal to the masses, but it is not necessarily a lower form of art.

The engaging nature of "The Gift of the Magi" has no doubt helped O. Henry's reputation throughout the century. This story of a poor married couple who give up their most prized possessions—his watch and her hair—to buy each other Christmas gifts—a watch fob for him and decorative combs for her—has been widely anthologized. It is often taught in high-school English classes because of its accessibility and its usefulness as a tool for discussing the elements of a short story.

"The Gift of the Magi" also is a prime example of O. Henry's talent at presenting situations to which people could, and wanted to, respond. One critic, N. Bryllion Fagin, who finds O. Henry to be at best "a master trickster" in an essay published in Current-Garcia's *O. Henry: A Study of the Short Fiction,* sarcastically details why "The Gift of the Magi" is so popular: "Why is it a masterpiece? Not because it tries to take us into the home of a married couple attempting to exist in our largest city on the husband's income of $20 per week. No, that wouldn't make it famous. Much better stories of poverty have been written, much more faithful and poignant, and the great appreciative public does not even remember them. It is the wizard's mechanics, his stunning invention—that's the thing!" Ironically, Fagin arrives at something utterly crucial to the success of "The Gift of the Magi": that it has everything—an absorbing (if short) narrative drive and a twist ending that makes it wholly original.

The story opens with another of O. Henry's trademarks: a quick, compelling beginning that immediately involves the reader while providing a sense of the background of the narrative drive: "One dollar and eighty-seven cents. That was all. And sixty cents of it was in pennies. Pennies saved one and two at a time by bulldozing the grocer and the vegetable man and the butcher until one's cheeks burned with the silent imputation of parsimony that such close dealing implied." So, even before having knowledge of the impoverished circumstances of the protagonists Della and Jim Dillingham Young, the reader has learned that the main conflict of the story concerns their lack of money. Also foreshadowed in this opening are the sacrifices Della and Jim will make for each other. Della shows herself already acquainted with saving and scrimping, elements of sacrifice; her ability to withstand the reproach of the vendors highlights her ultimate willingness to give up something she values highly—her hair—for that which she values more—her love for her husband.

It is important that readers become involved with the story in the first few lines, for the success of the story, through the surprise ending, truly hinges on its brevity. If readers spend too much time with a story, they may feel they deserve a more complex and "bigger" ending; the story's brevity allows the reader not to feel cheated but, instead, satisfied. The surprise ending really is ideal, for "The Gift of the Magi" never attempts to make a grand statement. In the words of Current-Garcia, it "encapsulates what the world in all its stored-up wisdom knows to be indispensable in ordinary family life": unselfish love, the only thing that has the power to transform. The message itself is so strong that to focus intently on the messengers—the Youngs—would only serve as a deflection.

The message thus can only be effectively delivered in an understated fashion. O. Henry understands this and downplays the theme in his treatment of the Youngs. Despite the rather dour circumstances of their poverty and despite their having fallen from better times, they maintain an air of joy. Della, though having just cut off the hair which could rival the jewels belonging to a queen, still experiences "intoxication" at finding the perfect present for Jim. Jim willingly gives up the watch that would have made King Solomon "pluck at his beard with envy." After they realize that the gifts bought through their mutual sacrifices have no use at the present time, they do not bemoan their fates or even deem their sacrifices unworthy. Della, smiling, asserts, "'My hair grows so fast, Jim!'" Jim, sitting on the couch with his hands behind his head—the posture of a relaxed man—declares, "'let's put our Christmas presents away and keep 'em awhile. They're too nice to use just at present.'" This acceptance also points to his affirming belief that life will improve, that he and Della will not always be poor, and that their lives will be enriched for this sacrifice: instead of having only two possessions "in which they both took a mighty pride," they will have four, after Della's hair grows back and Jim buys another watch.

O. Henry's descriptions of the Youngs and their situation support this viewpoint. Though they wear old clothes, have a "letter-box into which no letter would go, and an electric button from which no mortal finger could coax a ring," and live in an apartment surrounded by "a gray cat walking a gray fence in a gray backyard," they are not shabby, in either sense of the word. Della is akin to a saintlike figure in her capacity for acceptance. She does not regret her lifestyle. "She had a habit of saying little silent prayers about the simplest everyday things," but she does not ask for help for the big ones, such as changing hers and Jim's circumstances. When presented with the combs she reflects how "her heart had simply craved and yearned over them without the least hope of possession." O. Henry clearly approves of her in everything she does. With her short hair, the strong authorial voice notes that she "look[s] wonderfully like a truant schoolboy," while she quite calmly accepts that she now resembles a "Coney Island chorus girl." Yet, she has not lost the respectability necessary to a married woman, for in closing, the authorial voice compares Della and Jim to those holy men who initiated gift giving on Christmas, the three magi.

Certainly elements of the sentimental, the facile, the coincidental—those elements that critics have railed against—can be found in "The Gift of the Magi." To focus on them as faults, however, is to overlook the subtlety through which O. Henry expresses his approval of his characters as well as their growth throughout the few short hours in which the story plays itself out. Such a narrow reading also ignores the overarching message O. Henry wishes to convey: that it is the unselfish sacrifices we make for those we love that are most crucial to the emotional health of the family. This message itself is not sentimental but rather a universal truth, and as such, almost a moral. In presenting this message in the chosen manner, O. Henry avoids preaching, however—certainly one of the most effective ways to distance an audience. In "The Gift of the Magi" O. Henry gives to readers a heroine and hero they can understand and thus learn from. At the same time that the reader is learning about the power of selflessness, so too are Jim and Della learning: that their most precious possessions are not something they will ever own, but each other.

**Source:** Rena Korb, for *Short Stories for Students,* Gale Research, 1997.

## Karen Charmaine Blansfield

*In the following excerpt, Blansfield explores O. Henry's role as a popular artist; she employs the* auteur *theory of criticism, which Blansfield describes as an approach that emphasizes an artist's "entire body of material to discover and analyze structural characteristics and stylistic motifs."*

As a popular artist, [William Sydney] Porter shares company with a host of literary luminaries: Homer, [William] Shakespeare, [Mark] Twain, [Victor] Hugo, [Charles] Dickens, [Herman] Melville, and innumerable others. Like them, he stirred the mass imagination, drawing for material from the world about him, probing the foibles, dilemmas, comedies, and tragedies of human existence, speaking in a voice that could be understood by the multitudes.

This communal kinship lies at the heart of Porter's popularity, as it does for any popular artist.

> There are a variety of reasons that readers like O. Henry. Perhaps one of the most important is that not all art is meant to appeal primarily to the intellect or the intellectuals."

The public could identify with and respond to the people, places, and situations Porter wrote about. His stories offered the escape from daily drudgery so desperately needed by "the four million" and fulfilled the fantasies—if only vicariously—they so often longed for. [In his essay "Oh What A Man Was O. Henry," published in the *Kenyon Review* (November 1967), William Saroyan stated:] "The people of America loved O. Henry.... He was a nobody, but he was a nobody who was also a somebody, everybody's somebody."

Porter, of course, calculated this success to some degree; he knew his audience and gave them what they wanted. "We have got to respect the conventions and delusions of the public to a certain extent," he wrote to his prison comrade Al Jennings. "In order to please John Wanamaker, we will have to assume a virtue that we do not possess." Nevertheless, he perceived his subjects with a compassion and understanding that is unquestionably sincere. He specialized in humanity but did not exploit it. He accepted,

> with a mixture of irony, wit, and sympathy, the distressing fact that a human being can be a clerk, the remarkable fact that a clerk can be a human being....
>
> To O. Henry, ... the clerk is neither abnormal nor subnormal. He writes of him without patronizing him. He realizes the essential and stupendous truth that to himself the clerk is not pitiable.

Besides, Porter spins a good yarn, and he can turn a phrase as few authors ever have, rambling on in an easy, neighborly manner that slaps the reader on the shoulder, bandying an insouciant humor, and displaying a verbal range and precision that is astounding. He is a born raconteur; to listen to him is irresistible.

Above all, he is a master of technique. Even his severest critics acknowledge that as a designer of stories Porter "ranked supreme." His manipulation of elements into a tight literary structure . . . is effective, if mechanical, and were one aspect of Porter's art to be held up as the most important or memorable, it would surely be this one. . . .

All of these characteristics—his empathy for his fellow man, his sharp scrutiny of public demand, and his skill at the narrative craft—contribute to Porter's vast popularity. Furthermore, one other feature essential to popular art—wide-spread distribution—also accelerated Porter's rise to literary fame. . . . [The] superfluity of magazines and the tremendous need for material were propitious conditions for the fledgling author; joined with his talents and the public's desire, they propelled Porter into a position as a popular and widely read writer.

In the decades since, his stories have been anthologized, collected, and reprinted; they have been translated into numerous foreign languages; they have been performed as radio, stage, and television drama, with some also made into films. . . .

Such broad appeal is the domain of the popular artist, be he author, musician, performer, painter, or other creative type. Although he manifests a style distinctly his own and is recognizable by his particular manner, the popular artist conforms to certain expectations, presenting his material in forms familiar to his audiences and mirroring the joys and frustrations, the excitement and ennui of their everyday lives. This direct, personal relationship is one which the popular artist strives for, aiming deliberately to reach and to please his readers or listeners. Unlike "elite" or "high" art, which springs from individual and aesthetic motives, or folk art, which tends to be anonymous and utilitarian, popular art purposely appeals to the masses, while displaying the unmistakable touch of a single creator. . . .

The skills of Porter as popular performer fuse into a style as distinctive and memorable as Charlie Chaplin's or Alfred Hitchcock's, an indelible style which breathes "O. Henryism" into his tales. Two of the most predominant components of this style . . . are plot structures and character types. The most famous and easily recognized plot characteristic is, of course, the surprise ending, a trick which results from clever, careful strategy. Although Porter was certainly not the first writer to employ this device—[Guy] de Maupassant being particularly inclined toward it—he popularized it and staked a peculiar claim upon it, so that it has come to be inextricably linked with him and dubbed "the O. Henry twist." In terms of characters, the most well-known is probably the shopgirl, a type which, again, is invariably associated with the writer.

Other idiosyncrasies also contribute to the "O. Henryism" that generated such enthusiastic response: the folksy narrative voice, confidential asides to the reader, intricate and sometimes outrageous language and dialogue, full-blown metaphors, hyperbole, and copious allusions.

Porter embroiders all these elements together to form a personal style that distinguishes his work from that of other popular writers, even though such writers may employ similar or identical devices. Less skillful popular artists may depend so heavily upon story formula or character stereotypes to accomplish their purposes that individual artistry is obliterated; indeed, a whole slew of nineteenth-century fiction manufacturers churned out material in such quantity and such anonymity that their work "was more or less comparable to the product of machines," and authors were easily interchangeable—names like Horatio Alger, Jr., Laura Jean Libbey, Edward Stratemeyer, and Edward Judson pertain. But a popular artist like Porter is an essential creative force behind his products; his shaping hand is always apparent, and his presence within his work helps to establish the rapport so important to the popular artist. As one critic points out, "To read him is at times almost to feel his physical presence."

This unique style, a compilation of several elements, defines Porter's work internally as well as externally. Besides setting him apart from other popular writers, Porter's style constitutes a kind of formula which recurs within and defines his own body of work. This evolution of a personal, recognizable formula is intrinsic to popular art: "the quality of stylization and convention" that is so important "becomes a kind of stereotyping, a processing of experience, a reliance upon formulae." In other words, the artist employs his selected materials—characters, settings, plots, etc.—over and over again, so that they become familiar aspects within his work, yet he also imbues them with a flavor distinctly his own. . . .

In a sense, because of the personal style that emerges through his recurrent use of specific literary elements, Porter can be considered an *auteur,* and the proposal to examine his body of work in terms of these elements is essentially the approach of *auteur* criticism. Originating in the 1950s as a mode of film criticism, the *auteur* theory offers a worthwhile model for analyzing and interpreting popular culture in general, as John Cawelti suggests in his seminal essay on the subject:

> The art of the *auteur* is that of turning a conventional and generally known and appreciated artistic formula into a medium of personal expression while at the same time giving us a version of the formula which is satisfying because it fulfills our basic expectations. . . .

For a popular artist like Porter, the *auteur* approach, with its emphasis on surveying an entire body of material to discover and analyze structural characteristics and stylistic motifs, seems particularly appropriate and useful. What is distinctive about *auteur* criticism is that it stresses "the whole *corpus*" of material rather than a single work, emphasizing recurring characteristics and themes; it "implies an operation of decipherment" and ultimately defines the *auteur*—the film-maker, the author—in terms of these recurring elements, which come to be recognized as his particular style. "The strong director imposes his own personality on a film," [asserts Andrew Sarris in his *The American Cinema* (1968)], just as a writer can stamp his distinctive seal on his own creations. . . .

[Although not the *entire* body of Porter's work, the] New York stories form a singular portion of his literary output for several reasons: together, they comprise well over a third of his work; they are bound together by their urban characteristics; they were produced during the most significant period of his literary career; and they include most of the stories for which he is so well remembered. Furthermore, the recurring characteristics and themes which are discovered here through "an operation of decipherment" can then serve as models for examining Porter's other stories—of Texas, New Orleans, and South America—which display similar structural and character motifs though in different cultural contexts.

As a popular artist, Porter is similar to the type of filmmaker who emerges in *auteur* criticism, since the latter is essentially a cinematic popular artist. Both the *auteur* and the popular artist utilize formulaic elements of plot and character to create a personal, recognizable style, weaving new variations on old familiar themes. Both, in turn, develop this individual style into a kind of personal formula running through their work. Both are also confronted by similar restrictions—mainly, conventional limitations on characters, setting, and plots, and commercial demands in their given mediums. . . .

So the identities of these two creative types are similar: like the popular artist, the *auteur* is neither

> "A popular artist like Porter is an essential creative force behind his products."

absolutely original nor completely technical; rather, like the popular artist, he is, [as John C. Cawelti claims in *Popular Culture and the Expanding Consciousness* (1973)],

> an individual creator who works within a framework of existing materials, conventional structures created by others, but he is more than a performer because he recreates those conventions to the point that they manifest at least in part the patterns of his own style and vision. . . .

[The patterns] in the plots and characters of Porter's urban stories draw upon conventional situations, reinforce conventional values and expectations, and embody recognizable cultural types. By occurring repeatedly within the body of Porter's work, these plots and characters define it internally; by emulating more universal, archetypal patterns and characters, they achieve a broader recognition and a similarity to other artistic products, while remaining distinctive to Porter's art.

This continual recurrence of specific motifs, so central to Porter's art, to popular art, and to the theory of *auteur* criticism, constitutes the element of formula. For Porter, as for any popular artist, formula provides the fundamental structure for his art, and not surprisingly, it also contributes to his popular appeal. For as a constant and predictable pattern, formula is inherent to the cycle of human existence, and it also characterizes the earliest forms of literature most people learn—myths, fairy tales, songs, etc. Because it is so elemental, formula is familiar and comforting; it is an artistic expression of the subliminal human need for security and certainty in a life that promises just the opposite, and to some extent at least, the presence of formula in popular literature satisfies that need. . . .

The other major element of formula, repetition, involves, like the term "convention," distinctions of degree. Within the context of one author's work—in this case Porter's urban short stories—repetition involves the frequency with which the author employs specific plot patterns and specific cultural elements. It is through such repetition that the works assume a formulaic nature. . . .

Secondly, repetition involves the frequency with which the plot patterns and cultural elements have been employed outside the context of the author's works. This is the universal aspect of repetition and the means by which plot patterns and specific elements become archetypal and serve as models of comparison for specific works. The existence of a universal story pattern, or of a general element such as a character type defined only by human traits, not bounded by cultural details, provides the standard of comparison for an author's works and the framework on which he can, with specific cultural elements, construct a story which will be relevant and meaningful to a certain group of people in a certain place and time.

Elements of repetition are quite apparent in Porter's urban short stories, for he draws recurringly upon a number of basic plot patterns and character types. Variations occur, of course, and not every single story can be neatly categorized according to plot and character; such extremism threatens to squeeze the life out of the literature. Still, in the nearly one hundred stories that deal with the city, recurrent plot patterns and characters do emerge which can be identified and used as a means of classification.

The plots of these stories can be divided into four basic patterns, overlapping to some extent but nevertheless bearing distinguishing characteristics: they are the cross pattern, the habit pattern, the triangular pattern, and the quest pattern. All develop themes familiar to most readers: the cross pattern, for example, builds on the unexpected reunion; the habit pattern provides excitement by an unexpected change in routine; the triangular pattern inserts a new twist in the familiar love triangle, and the quest pattern is Porter's version of the adventure story. . . . Porter repeatedly uses these patterns, or some variation of them, in his stories.

The characters, too, can be divided into six basic types, although because they often play more than one role simultaneously, they are more difficult to classify definitively. These six types [are] the shopgirl, the habitual character, the lover, the aristocrat, the plebeian, and the tramp. . . . Each type is a composite of specific characteristics, such as appearance, lifestyle, and attitude—characteristics which identify the entire group, with little if any attention paid to individual tendencies. Furthermore, each character type responds to conventional expectations: the shopgirl is poor but brave; the habitual character sticks to the ordinary routine of domestic life; the lover places love above self-interest; the aristocrat places money below principle; the plebeian bears the standard marks of poverty; and the tramp sleeps on a park bench.

Thus, Porter draws upon a "conventional system" for structuring his stories. His plot patterns are formulaic within the context of his own works, for he uses a number of patterns repeatedly; they are also formulaic in their relationship to more standard universal models. His characters are formulaic because they appear repeatedly, as types, within the stories and also because they represent, underneath their garb of culture, more universal character types. This recurrence of character type and plot pattern, and the interweaving of specific cultural material with more universal standards, together form the basis of the formulaic art of Porter's urban short stories. . . .

**Source:** Karen Charmaine Blansfield, in her *Cheap Rooms and Restless Hearts: A Study of Formula in the Urban Tales of William Sydney Porter,* Bowling Green State University Popular Press, 1988, 143 p.

## John A. Rea

*In the following essay, Rea traces some of the events and stories that may have led O. Henry to write "The Gift of the Magi," pointing out the differences that make his story superior to its models.*

There are two accounts, differing in significant details, of how O. Henry wrote "The Gift of the Magi," but neither indicates a source for the "gimmick" on which the story rests. Since we intend to suggest such a source, these accounts are worth examining. According to one version, Dan Smith sought out O. Henry, whose Christmas story he was to illustrate for the *World.* O. Henry, who had not yet even an idea for the story, told Smith to proceed with an illustration whose elements he suggested. The author would then fit his story to the picture, a story he later wrote while his friend Lindsey Denison lay on a sofa. In the other version it is William Wash Williams who lay on the couch while O. Henry, who had already given instructions for the illustration, wrote his story to meet a deadline only hours away. The first version surmises that Denison and his wife may have served as models for the couple of the story, although it has also been suggested that the model for the girl may involve memories of O. Henry's first wife Athol.

Both versions cannot be true, since one claims that Denison was present during the writing and the other that Williams was. However, both accounts are rendered suspect by the actual illustration on which they place such emphasis. In Williams' version, O. Henry tells Smith to "draw a picture of a good-looking girl in a flat with a fellow just coming in the door." These scant details are contradicted by the picture itself, which shows the young man, in the middle of the room, leaning on the back of a chair. No door is visible. The other, more detailed account specifies that Smith was to show "a poorly furnished room" with "only a chair or two, a chest of drawers, a bed and a trunk. On the bed a man and a girl are sitting side by side . . . The man has a watch fob in his hand . . . The girl's principal feature is the long beautiful hair that is hanging down her back." But the illustration shows no bed, no chest of drawers, no trunk, and no watch fob. The man and the girl are both standing, and the girl, facing us from the page, wears her hair in a Gibson Girl upsweep. There is a round table strewn with enough objects even to belie the caption. "Della wriggled off the table and went for him."

Williams claims that O. Henry, though at a loss for ideas, would have refused any plot suggestion that might have been offered. Others have also insisted that Porter never borrowed plots, but jotted down ideas "on the cuff" in the streets and taverns of New York. But Davis and Maurice include in their study of the background of O. Henry's stories a flat denial of the notion that he scrupulously avoided borrowing. They examine in this light "The Song and the Sergeant," and "A Retrieved Reformation," which clearly derive from published stories by other authors, including a certain amount of detail beyond the basic plot idea. They discuss similar possibilities for "The Duplicity of Hargreaves," and point out that the idea for "The Last Leaf" is partly based on an episode from the French *Vie de Bohème* by [nineteenth-century French writer Henri] Murger. They delicately conclude that assertions that O. Henry never borrowed plots are "hardly to be accepted as complete." Langford, indeed, finds that O. Henry on occasion even paid others for ideas.

In point of fact, O. Henry seems to have taken the essential plot ingredients for "The Gift of the Magi," as well as many of its circumstantial details, from a French story, as he had previously done in "The Last Leaf." More than sixty years before "The Gift of the Magi," Emile Chevalet, a minor French writer, published a poorly constructed short story named for its heroine, "Dulvina." Chevalet's story opens on its hero, Gilbert, who is "un jeune homme de vingt-deux ans,"—Jim, in the "The Gift of the Magi," we will recall also "was only twenty-two." Gilbert is alone in a "petite chambre ou se trouvaient quelque vieux meubles indispensables,"—like the "poorly furnished room" of the Denison version of the writing of "The Gift of the Magi." Gilbert is in the process of, "considérer attentivement une belle montre d'or qu'il tournait en tous sens, l'ouvrant, examinant le mouvement, la refermant,"—Jim "took a mighty pride" in his gold watch, and even, "Had King Solomon been the janitor, with all his treasures piled up on the basement, Jim would have pulled out his watch every time he passed, just to see him pluck at his beard from envy." Physically Gilbert is described as having a face which, although good looking, is rather "maigre" with a line or two on his forehead, "ouvrage de la pensée,"—Jim too, we recall, "looked thin and very serious."

But our young French couple—like Jim and Della—are having financial difficulties. In a gesture of love, and without telling Dulvina, Gilbert sells his fine gold watch. And then Dulvina, without telling Gilbert, "tout-à-coup" gets the idea of selling her lovely long hair. Going along the streets of Paris she "s'arrêta devant une belle enseigne de coiffeur-parfumeur qui habitait le premier,"—where Della "stopped the sign read: 'Mme. Sofronie. Hair Goods of all Kinds.' One flight up Della ran." When she returns to the flat, Dulvina shows Gilbert her "tête de petit garçon"—after Della sold her hair her "head was covered with tiny close-lying curls that made her look wonderfully like a truant schoolboy." There is a suspicious homeography to the names: DeLla—DuLvinA, JIm—Gilbert.

There is no need to press the point of these and other detailed resemblances, which go well beyond the basic plot business of the hair and the watch, and which are clearly more than sufficient to have allowed O. Henry to give Dan Smith plenty of details for the illustration long before he sat down himself with his needle-sharp pencils and yellow copy paper to remake these ingredients in his own way.

It is instructive to examine differences between the two stories, to see what O. Henry did with this material to make it his own. For example, just as Jim and Della of "The Gift of the Magi" are O. Henry's

> O. Henry seems to have taken the essential plot ingredients for 'The Gift of the Magi,' as well as many of its circumstantial details, from a French story."

watches in horror. Following which, Chevalet cheats his readers, for it turns out that the sale of the hair (but not of the watch) and all that followed was just an "awful dream" of Dulvina's. Gilbert in fact goes on to be one of the most popular authors: which was not, of course, the case with Emile Chevalet, but was indeed with O. Henry, who had the vision to see what could be done with such plot ingredients, and had the skill to bring it all off.

**Source:** John A. Rea, "The Idea for O. Henry's 'Gift of the Magi'," in *Southern Humanities Review,* Vol. VII, No. 3, Summer, 1973, pp. 311–14.

"archetypal husband and wife" (whoever served as immediate model), so Gilbert and Dulvina are the archetypal French young man of good family and his mistress. The change that needs to be made by O. Henry for the Christmas issue of an American Sunday supplement is as clear as the need to replace such "exotic" names as Gilbert and Dulvina by American Jim and Della.

Worse still is the plot structure of "Dulvina," for the selling of the watch and the selling of the hair lack the reciprocal relationship we find in "The Gift of the Magi." In fact, the watch gets sold to pay for Dulvina's cab fare, and the hair is sold to buy food. What O. Henry can do with this is also clear, for the typical O. Henry ending, the ironic twist that the sale of the hair is to buy a chain for the sacrificed watch, and the sale of the watch is to buy combs for the shorn hair, is what makes it possible to say that "in this trite little tale of mutual self-sacrifice, O. Henry crystallized dramatically what the world in all its stored up wisdom knows to be of fundamental value in ordinary family life."

Having missed the motivational possibility offered by sale of the hair and the watch, Chevalet had his heroine sell her hair not to a chilly Mme. Sofronie, but to a fifty-year-old lecher who then attempts to rape her—"Je voulais vendre mes cheveux et non mon corps,"—and who later strangles poor Gilbert with the severed hair while Dulvina

## Further Reading

Bates, H. E. *The Modern Short Story,* Writer, Inc., 1941, 231 p.
Bates surveys the development of short stories in America, France, Russia, and Great Britain from the writers of Edgar Allan Poe's day through the 1940s and explains why O. Henry's short stories are so successful.

Current-Garcia, Eugene. *O. Henry (William Sydney Porter),* Twayne Publishers, Inc., 1965.
This thorough biographical and critical study includes an examination of how O. Henry's regional background influenced his work.

Current-Garcia, Eugene, editor. *O. Henry: A Study of the Short Fiction,* Twayne, 1993, 256 p.
This volume presents Current-Garcia's analyses of the stories of O. Henry and collects articles by various other critics.

Eckley, Wilton. "The Gift of the Magi," in *Reference Guide to Short Fiction,* St. James Press, 1994, pp. 716-17.
After a very short introduction about the writer, Eckley provides a brief general overview of plot and technique in "The Gift of the Magi."

"William Sydney Porter," in *DISCovering Authors Modules* (CD-ROM publication), Gale Research, 1996.
A detailed overview of the author's life, career, and writings, with a number of excerpts from criticism of his works dating from 1917 through 1996.

# Gimpel the Fool

Isaac Bashevis Singer
1953

"Gimpel the Fool," which first appeared in English translation in a 1953 edition of the *Partisan Review,* is considered one of Isaac Bashevis Singer's most notable and representative works of short fiction. Singer wrote the story, as he did most of his early works, in Yiddish, and its Jewish themes of the individual's search for faith and guidance in a cruel world are explored in a parable form with exaggerated details common to folktales. Noted Jewish-American writer Saul Bellow translated the story into English, as he did many of Singer's early works, thus introducing him to a wide audience for the first time, even though Singer had been writing for many years. The character of Gimpel has been praised by critics as an example of the "schlemiel"— a foolish, unlucky man—common to Jewish lore, whose follies are delineated in order to present a moral lesson. Set in the imaginary village of Frampol, the story centers on Gimpel, a baker, who is continuously heckled and tricked by those around him. Since its publication, critical reaction to "Gimpel the Fool" has been positive, with most reviewers praising its blend of tradition, spiritualism, and realism.

## Author Biography

Isaac Bashevis Singer was born on July 14, 1904, in the Polish *shtetl,* or village, of Leoncin, near War-

saw. His parents were devout Jews who wanted their son to become a religious scholar. Singer's interests, however, drew him toward literature, and early in his life he began reading secular, or non-religious, books. His strict religious training often conflicted with his secular interests, and this conflict is explored in his fiction through characters who grapple with faith and skepticism. In 1908 Singer and his family moved to Warsaw, where he spent most of his youth. In 1921, his father made him enroll in the city's rabbinical seminary. Singer remained only one year, and in 1923 he began proofreading for *Literarishe Bletter,* a Yiddish literary magazine. Later he worked as a translator, writing Yiddish versions of popular novels, including Erich Maria Remarque's *All Quiet on the Western Front.*

In 1927 Singer published his first piece of short fiction in *Literarishe Bletter,* and seven years later his first novel, *Satan in Goray,* appeared in serial form in the Yiddish periodical *Globus.* That same year Singer emigrated from Poland to the United States, leaving behind his wife and son. He followed his older brother Israel Joshua, who later achieved prominence as a Yiddish novelist. Singer settled in New York City and began writing reviews and essays for the *Jewish Daily Forward.* In 1940 Singer married his second wife, moved to Manhattan's Upper West Side, and became a regular staff member at the *Forward.*

The death of his brother Israel in 1944 had a profound effect on Singer. While he has acknowledged his brother as "a spiritual father and master," Singer often felt overshadowed by Israel's achievements, which inhibited his own creativity. Thus, he has admitted to feeling both grief and liberation over his brother's death. Throughout the 1940s Singer's fiction was serialized in the *Forward,* and his reputation among Yiddish-speaking readers grew steadily. In 1950 *The Family Moskat* appeared in translation, the first of Singer's novels to be published in English, and in 1953 "Gimpel the Fool" appeared in the *Partisan Review,* as translated by American writer Saul Bellow. Through the efforts of such admirers as Bellow and critic Irving Howe, Singer was introduced to the American public. Singer won numerous literary prizes during his career, including the National Book Award in 1970 and 1974 as well as the Nobel Prize for Literature in 1978. Singer continued to publish new material until his death on July 24, 1991.

## Plot Summary

"Gimpel the Fool," opens with Gimpel, the narrator, announcing that he is called a fool but does not think of himself as one. Others see him as a fool, he says, because he is "easy to take in." He is not a fighter, he reasons, so he tries to ignore them. Even so, he admits that "they take advantage of me," thus demonstrating he understands how others see him and is not as foolish as he seems. Gimpel is an orphan being raised by a grandfather who is "already bent to the grave," so the townspeople turn him over to a baker. In such a public occupation, nearly all the villagers have had the opportunity to fool him at least once.

When Rietze the Candle-dipper tells him his parents have risen from the grave and are looking for him, Gimpel knows full well this cannot be, but he goes outside to look just in case: "What did I stand to lose just by looking?" This incident creates such an uproar that he vows not to believe anything else, but that does not work either. He is confused and turns to the rabbi for advice. The rabbi tells Gimpel, "It is written, better to be a fool all your days than for one hour to be evil. You are not a fool. They are the fools. For he who causes his neighbor to feel shame loses Paradise himself."

Gimpel considers leaving town, but the people will not hear of it. Instead, they decide to fix him up with a wife. He sees several flaws in Elka, his prospective bride, but the townspeople tell him his perceptions are wrong. Elka's "bastard" son is really her little brother, and her limp is "deliberate, from coyness." Furthermore, they threaten to have the rabbi fine him for giving her a bad name.

Elka refuses to let Gimpel into their bed after the wedding, and four months later she gives birth to a boy. Everyone knows that Gimpel is not the father; "the whole House of Prayer rang with laughter." When he confronts Elka about this, she insists that the child is premature and is Gimpel's. He does not believe her, but the next day the schoolmaster assures him that the same thing happened to Adam and Eve. Gimpel begins "to forget his sorrow" because he loves the child. He steals scraps from the pots that women leave in the baker's oven for Elka and begins to love her too.

Gimpel has to sleep at the bakery during the week, but one night he comes home unexpectedly and discovers a man sleeping next to Elka. To avoid waking the child he goes back to the bakery and tries to sleep on the floor. He vows, however, that "there's a limit even to the foolishness of a fool like Gimpel." He goes to the rabbi for advice, and Elka denies everything. The rabbi recommends that Gimpel divorce her, but Gimpel longs for her and the child. Eventually he tells the rabbi that he had made a mistake.

The rabbi reconsiders the case for nine months before telling Gimpel he is free to return home, during which time Elka gives birth to another child. When Gimpel returns, he sees his apprentice in bed beside Elka. She tells him to go outside and check on the goat; when Gimpel returns, the apprentice is gone and Elka denies everything.

Gimpel lives with her for twenty more years, during which time Elka has six more children. He continues to turn a blind eye towards his wife's behavior and professes his belief in everything she says. On her deathbed Elka asks him for forgiveness and confesses that the children are not his. Gimpel imagines that, "dead as she was, she was saying, 'I deceived Gimpel. That was the meaning of my brief life.'"

One night the Spirit of Evil appears to Gimpel, tells him there is no God, and advises him to "deceive the world" as it has deceived him. Gimpel urinates into the bread dough at the bakery, but later Elka appears to him in a dream with a black face and says, "You fool! Because I was false is everything false too? I never deceived anyone but myself. I'm paying for it all, Gimpel." Gimpel awakes, sensing that "everything hung in the balance. A false step now and [he'd] lose Eternal Life." He immediately grabs a shovel and buries the contaminated loaves of bread. Then he divides his belongings among the children and leaves Frampol for good.

Outside Frampol, people suddenly treat him well. He hears "a great deal, many lies and falsehoods," but eventually he comes to understand that "that there were really no lies." Whatever does not really happen is dreamed at night. He begins to "spin yarns—improbable things that could never have happened," and children ask him to tell his stories. In his dreams he still sees Elka, but she is radiant now, and he looks forward to rejoining her in a place "without ridicule, without deception. . . . [where] even Gimpel cannot be deceived."

## Characters

### Devil
*See* The Spirit of Evil

*Isaac Bashevis Singer*

### Elka
Elka, who is known as the town prostitute, marries Gimpel when he agrees to get the town to take up a collection to raise a dowry for her. She is five months pregnant by another man when they are married, but she tells Gimpel the child is his and, when it arrives four months after their marriage, that it is simply premature. Throughout the story Elka commits numerous infidelities and eventually has ten children, none of whom are Gimpel's. On her deathbed she admits her infidelities to her husband and asks him to forgive her.

### The Spirit of Evil
The devil appears to Gimpel the baker and tells him to urinate in the bread intended for the village in order to get revenge for the many injustices the villagers have forced him to endure over the years.

### Gimpel
Gimpel is a baker in the village of Frampol. Although he is constantly teased and tricked by his fellow villagers, he continues to believe in the essential goodness of others and to bear life's burdens. After agreeing to marry Elka, the town

## Media Adaptations

- "Gimpel the Fool" was adapted for the stage by David Schechter and produced by Bakery Theater Cooperative of New York in 1982.

- "Gimpel the Fool" was read by writer Eli Wallach on national public radio station KCRW. Transcripts are available through the National Yiddish Book Society.

- A documentary film called *Isaac Bashevis Singer: Champion of Yiddish Literature* was produced in 1991 by Ergo and is distributed by Ergo Media Inc. In the film, Singer discusses such topics as writing, religion, and Yiddish.

- An Academy Award-nominated documentary, *Isaac Bashevis Singer: Isaac in America* was released in 1994. The film profiles the life of the author and includes readings from Singer's works by actor Judd Hirsch. It is distributed by Monterey Home Video.

---

prostitute, he states, "You can't pass through life unscathed, nor expect to." Gimpel represents the *dos kleine menshele*, or "the common man" of Yiddish literature; his innocence provides humor and conveys a simple goodness that combats evil.

### Rabbi

The rabbi is the spiritual authority in the village of Frampol. Early in the story, Gimpel goes to him for advice after being teased numerous times by the other villagers. The rabbi, who is the only one in the town who recognizes and appreciates Gimpel's goodness, tells him that "it is written, better to be a fool all your days than for one hour to be evil. You are not a fool. They are the fools." Gimpel again goes to the rabbi when he finds Elka in bed with another man. The rabbi tells Gimpel to divorce Elka and to abandon her children. However, when Gimpel tells the rabbi that he loves his wife, the rabbi finds a precedent in the Torah to allow Gimpel to stay with Elka.

## Themes

### Faith

Faith is one of the primary themes in "Gimpel the Fool." Despite being teased and deceived mercilessly by the other villagers as well as by his wife Elka, Gimpel maintains his faith in life, in others, and in God. When Elka continues to nag and bully him, Gimpel simply says, "I'm the type that bears it and says nothing. What's one to do? Shoulders are from God, and burdens too." Gimpel has consciously decided to choose faith over skepticism; through his faith he finds consolation and peace.

### Acceptance and Belonging

Singer also examines the meaning of acceptance in the story. Gimpel is never accepted or appreciated by the villagers for what he is: a kind, compassionate, and honest man. But when he leaves Frampol to become a storyteller, he is considered to be wise and is treated well by those he meets. This suggests that acceptance and belonging is temporal: a person may not be accepted in one environment but is welcomed and respected in another.

Gimpel's acceptance of life, despite his hardships, is also a major theme in the story. He is constantly heckled and mistreated, but he accepts the limitations of and negative qualities in others. He also embraces life, appreciating what he does have: a wife, children, and a successful bakery. Instead of getting angry and vengeful, Gimpel simply states, "One can't pass through life unscathed, nor expect to." While Gimpel does momentarily contemplate revenge on the villagers by urinating in the bread dough, he quickly changes his mind, choosing instead to leave Frampol.

### Knowledge and Ignorance

Although Gimpel is presented as a fool, Singer suggests through his telling of the events of the story that Gimpel actually possesses a special wisdom. It is not that he simply believes the outrageous things the villagers tell him, but rather, that he chooses to do so. For example, when the villagers tell Gimpel that his father and mother "have stood up from the grave," Gimpel states: "To tell the truth, I knew very well that nothing of the sort had happened." Singer also suggests that Gimpel is rather shrewd. He manages to raise a dowry from the villagers for Elka, he becomes a successful baker with his own bakery, and at the end of the story he finds happiness and contentment.

### Honor and Integrity

Although Gimpel is considered a fool, Singer presents him as having much more integrity than others in the village. For example, he takes good care of Elka, treats her ten children as if they were his, and, when he has the opportunity to get revenge on the villagers, he chooses not to. This integrity, Singer suggests, is much more valuable and meaningful than what is typically considered intelligence.

## Style

"Gimpel the Fool" centers on Gimpel, a baker in the village of Frampol. Although he has been heckled and deceived by his fellow villagers since he was a child, he retains his faith in the goodness of others and in life itself.

### Setting

"Gimpel the Fool" is set in an indeterminate time in the fictional Jewish shtetl, or village, of Frampol in Poland. Like many of the settings in Singer's fiction, the shtetl of Frampol is presented as a place where life has a mystical quality, the people are superstitious, survival is difficult, and everyday events and concerns revolve around Jewish faith and traditions.

### Narrative

The story is told exclusively from the viewpoint of Gimpel and is, therefore, an example of first-person narration. Because readers are only given access to Gimpel's thoughts and feelings and not those of the villagers who frequently make fun of him, they are uncertain how reliable Gimpel's account is and are left to wonder if he is truly a fool. Singer also uses a simple storytelling technique in "Gimpel the Fool"; he relates the events of the story sequentially without much explanation and presents the characters without in-depth description.

### Parable

Because "Gimpel the Fool" is intended to teach a moral lesson, it is considered a parable. Parables generally include simple characters who represent abstract ideas. In "Gimpel the Fool," Gimpel represents goodness, innocence, and the common man; the villagers represent malice and deception. Like most parables, the story works on two levels. While it appears to be a simple tale about a town fool, it raises important questions about such universal concerns as the nature of wisdom, faith, and acceptance.

## Topics for Further Study

- Compare Gimpel to the lead character in the 1994 Academy Award-winning movie *Forrest Gump*.
- Research Eastern European shtetls of the late 1800s and early 1900s and discuss similarities between life in the shtetls and in Frampol.
- Gimpel is often described as a "holy fool." Find and describe other examples of the "holy fool" figure in literature. Why do they fit into this category?

### Irony

Singer uses irony, the recognition of a reality different from appearance, throughout "Gimpel the Fool." Irony is apparent at the very beginning of the story, which starts with the words: "I am Gimpel the Fool. I don't think myself a fool. On the contrary. But that's what folks call me." This suggests to the reader that Gimpel may not be the fool he appears to be. In fact, as the story continues, Gimpel tells us that he does not always believe what the villagers tell him even though they think he does. For example, when Elka tells Gimpel that he is the father of the child she bore four months after their marriage, Gimpel seems to accept her explanation, but then admits, "To tell the plain truth, I didn't believe her.... But then, who really knows how such things are?" It is also ironic that when Gimpel leaves Frampol, where he is heckled and mistreated, he becomes a respected and well-liked story teller. Gimpel notes toward the end of the story, "The children run after me, calling 'Grandfather, tell us a story.'"

### Archetype

The character of Gimpel is an archetype, a character type that occurs frequently in literature. He is an example of the "common man" figure that often appears in both Yiddish and Western literature as well as a schlemiel, or "holy fool," a character whose innocence and goodness provides both humor and inspiration.

## Historical Context

### The American Decade

"Gimpel the Fool" was first published in English translation in 1953. The 1950s are sometimes called the "American decade" because European political and military power declined in many areas of the world while the influence of the United States increased. During this time, American economic growth produced an abundance of consumer goods, the population increased by record numbers, and more people became members of the middle class. For example, the population in the United States doubled between 1900 and 1950, with a record 4.3 million births in 1957. During the 1950s the population also shifted from urban areas to suburbs; the urban population only increased 1.5 percent while the suburban population increased 44 percent.

The United States was also at the forefront of technological development. In 1954, Chinese-American An Wang developed and sold the small business calculator; 1955 saw the distribution of the first IBM business computer. Control Data Corporation produced the first commercially successful "super" computer in 1957, and the microchip was developed in 1959.

The spread of communism was a major concern to the United States during these years. The Soviet occupation forces in Germany set up a blockade between Berlin and West Germany and Czechoslovakia was taken over by communists. In 1950, the United States began a three-year involvement in the Korean War, which was fought between the democratic Republic of South Korea and communist-led North Korea. That same year, Senator Joseph McCarthy started a communist "witch hunt" with his House UnAmerican Activities Committee. Many figures in the entertainment industry were accused of having ties to the Communist Party, and the Hollywood Blacklist, which included some 300 writers, directors, and actors, was compiled. Such popular figures as Charlie Chaplin, Lee Grant, and Arthur Miller were accused of being communists or communist sympathizers. Many were driven to social and economic ruin by the accusations.

During the 1950s, the United States began to experiment with atomic energy. The first thermonuclear test took place on the Pacific atoll of Eniwetok in 1951. That same year, atomic bombs were exploded, in the presence of army troops, in the Nevada desert, and the U.S. Atomic Energy Commission opened the first nuclear reactor. The United States conducted another atomic bomb test on the island of Bikini in the Pacific Ocean in 1954 and also launched the *Nautilus,* the first nuclear-powered submarine. In 1955, the Atomic Energy Commission denied that radiation had harmful effects on human health, stating "the scare stories about how dangerous this country's atomic tests are simply not justified." Nevertheless, Americans were also encouraged to build air-raid shelters to protect them from enemy attack in the event of a nuclear war.

## Critical Overview

Critical reaction to "Gimpel the Fool" has been positive ever since the story first appeared in translation in the *Partisan Review* in 1953. It was "Gimpel the Fool," along with the translated novel *The Family Moskat* (1950), that first brought Singer to the attention of American reading audiences. The story has been called a masterpiece of short fiction and has been praised for its depiction of Jewish life; its emphasis on spirituality, faith, and morality; its sympathetic portrayal of ordinary people; and its examination of universal themes. Alfred Kazin, writing in his *Contemporaries,* stated that "it is the integrity of the human imagination that Singer conveys so beautifully," while Paul N. Siegel noted in *The Achievement of Isaac Bashevis Singer* that Gimpel "has become representative of poor, bewildered, suffering humanity." Cynthia Ozick also praised Singer's talents in *The New York Times Book Review:* "[Singer's] tenderness for ordinary folk, their superstitions, their folly, their plainness, their lapses is a classical thread of Yiddish fiction, as well as the tree trunk of Singer's own Hasidic legacy—love and reverence for the down-to-earth."

Critical reaction to Singer's fiction as a whole has also been largely favorable. He was an internationally renowned literary figure who was widely considered the foremost contemporary Yiddish writer. Although he lived in the United States for more than fifty years, Singer wrote almost exclusively in Yiddish. Some critics have faulted Singer for occasional sentimentality and for exploring repetitious

# Compare & Contrast

- **1953:** Americans Ethel and Julius Rosenberg, Jewish members of the Communist Party, are executed for espionage. As civilians, their death sentence sparks controversy.

  **1990s:** Aldrich Ames, a high-ranking CIA official, is convicted of spying for the Soviets during his 31–year career. He receives life in prison, the harshest penalty possible. His wife is also convicted, but she receives only a several years imprisonment.

- **1950s:** Roughly 5 percent of children are born out of wedlock in the United States.

  **Today:** More than 30 percent of children are born out of wedlock in the United States.

- **1956:** Polish workers protest the Communist regime. Over 100 demonstrators are killed.

  **1993:** In the wake of capitalist reforms, Poland suffers a surge of violent crime inflicted by organized mobs.

---

themes, but he is widely admired for his powers of evocation, his talents as a stylist, and his renderings of the Yiddish language. In 1978, Singer was awarded the Nobel Prize in Literature for his "impassioned narrative art which, with roots in a Polish-Jewish cultural tradition, brings universal conditions to life." Singer's reputation rests largely upon his short stories, most notably "Gimpel the Fool."

## Criticism

### Judy Sobeloff

*Judy Sobeloff is a writer and educator who has won several awards for her fiction. In the following essay, she discusses how the character of Gimpel represents the Yiddish archetype of the "schlemiel," the sainted fool, and notes how the structure of the story compares to the biblical story of Hosea.*

"Gimpel the Fool" is widely viewed as Isaac Bashevis Singer's most popular short story. Singer originally wrote the story for a Yiddish newspaper, the *Jewish Daily Forward,* and then Saul Bellow translated it into English for *The Partisan Review* in 1953, bringing "Gimpel" and Singer to the attention of American readers. Gimpel is a kind and loving man who seems to be punished for his generosity. His willingness to believe the people around him—and to suffer as a result of believing them—is a virtue and remains one after everything else falls away. As critic Edward Alexander writes of Singer's wide appeal, "Singer writes almost always as a Jew, to Jews, for Jews, and yet he is heard by everybody."

Many critics see Gimpel as an example of a Yiddish stock character type, *dos kleine menschele* (the little man) or *schlemiel.* Sanford Pinsker, in his *The Schlemiel as Metaphor,* offers the following definitions of this character type: According to the *Universal Jewish Encyclopedia,* a *schlemiel* "handles a situation in the worst possible manner or is dogged by an ill luck that is more or less due to his own ineptness." Pinsker's personal characterization is that when a "*schlimazl*'s bread-and-butter accidentally falls on the floor it always lands butter-side down; with a *schlemiel* it's much the same—except that *he* butters his bread on both sides first."

Pinsker traces the *schlemiel* character back to the mythical town of Chelm, a Jewish community that is the subject of countless "Wise Men of Chelm" stories. Pinsker recounts one such story with a direct parallel to "Gimpel" in which a troubled Chelmite consults his rabbi because his wife has given birth after the couple has been married only three months. The rabbi assists the man with the following calculation: Since the man has lived with his wife three months, and she

## What Do I Read Next?

- I. L. Peretz's short story "Bontsha the Silent" centers on a character who, when offered everything in heaven, asks only for a hot roll with butter for breakfast every morning.

- Sherwood Anderson's short story "I'm a Fool" is told by a first-person narrator, a racehorse groom, who lies to get what he wants.

- The 1989 novel *A Prayer for Owen Meany* by American author John Irving centers on a Christ-like hero and examines the meaning of good and evil.

- Prussian author Fyodor Dostoevsky's 1869 novel *The Idiot* centers on the protagonist's loss of innocence and his experience of sin.

- James Michener's *Poland* (1983) is a fictionalized history of Poland which spans 700 years.

---

has lived with him for three months, and together they have lived three months, then three plus three plus three equals nine months. "'So, what's the problem?'"

In addition to representing the recurrent "wise or sainted fool" of Yiddish literature, Gimpel also represents a "centuries-old archetypal figure of western literature," according to critic Paul Siegel. Siegel traces Gimpel's character type back to the idiot of the Middle Ages and the Renaissance who was regarded as being "under the special protection of God."

The reader knows at some level that Gimpel does not believe the lies the townspeople tell him and that he partially endeavors to believe them out of his goodness, or at least his desire to not make trouble. Siegel writes that in the Yiddish version of the story, this ambiguity is broadcast from the beginning. In Yiddish the epithet used to describe Gimpel in the title and in the opening line of the story is "*chochem*," which means "sage," but which additionally "often has the ironic meaning of 'fool,' the meaning in which the villagers and Gimpel's wife use it." Gimpel's readers are thus lost in a "labyrinth of irony" as they watch him deciding when to believe or not to believe. "His belief, then, was in part the wise acquiescence of the butt who must play his role, knowing that otherwise he will never be free of his wiseacre tormentors."

Like Siegel, Edward Alexander sees Gimpel's "descent from the *schlemiels* of the classical Yiddish writers" and also sees that Gimpel differs from them in several ways, namely that he "*chooses* to be fooled, to be used, to forsake his dignity. This means that not only his creator but he himself is capable of irony about the sacrifices required by faith. Moreover, Gimpel's folly is connected with his credulity, whereas much of the folly of his Yiddish predecessors comes precisely from their unwillingness to credit unusual and extraordinary events, especially if those events portent evil." In other words, Gimpel's literary predecessors were silly optimists, whereas Gimpel would likely believe bad as well as good.

Gimpel's roots extend all the way back to the Bible, according to critic Thomas Hennings who posits that "Gimpel" is based on the Old Testament Book of Hosea. While understanding Singer's Yiddish background is essential to understanding "Gimpel," his Hebraic background is key as well, and the immigrant audience Singer was writing for would be well aware of Biblical allusions. Hennings sees parallels in that both Gimpel and Hosea marry women who are sexually unfaithful and that "Gimpel" follows the four-part structure of the Book of Hosea exactly: first, the marriage; second, the affairs, the birth of the children, and divorce; third, the reconciliation, remarriage, and continued affairs; and fourth, the "social application of it all, that is, the moral and theological implications of the adulterous marriage for the Jewish community." Like Hosea, Gimpel has a reunion with his repentant wife in a dream and progresses from being a foolish baker to a beloved prophet. Hennings sees that Singer, like Hosea, "deliberately chooses to disturb his readers' complacent assumptions about God, about faith, love, wisdom, and folly—and about themselves.... Singer creates a deeply religious story about a man of simple faith who, because of his faith, has a godlike capacity for love, the ideal Jew, if you will."

What sets the Yiddish holy fool apart from fools in British or French or Russian literature (e.g. Dostoevsky's *The Idiot*) is the high value that Jewish culture places on intelligence and learning, says critic Sally Drucker. "The holy fool, a fool who is more than a fool ... both subverts and augments this value." Drucker sees Gimpel as a character who displays "a kind of wisdom that does not have to do with ability to reason—which is closer, perhaps, to the Khassidic religious tradition of the heart, than the Talmudic ideal of the head."

It is also possible to see Gimpel's actions as part of a successful coping strategy. Janet Hadda takes a completely different approach to "Gimpel," applying psychoanalytic theory and asking questions in the way she would conduct a clinical case. She notes that while literary critics tend to emphasize Gimpel's relationship with God, students, on the other hand, tend to view Gimpel as a masochist. Since both views are based on the same evidence, Hadda wonders if perhaps another way of looking at the material might be more to the point. In her view, "Gimpel is not a suffering martyr, although he does experience intense pain.... Gimpel is a successful man whose subjective reality is undaunted by circumstances that would overwhelm a less daring person." She believes that "the central fact" of Gimpel's existence is his orphanhood. When Rietze the Candle-dipper runs into the bakery and tells him that his parents have risen from the dead, Gimpel knows "very well that nothing of the sort had happened," but, writes Hadda, "if there was any chance of seeing a beloved and deeply mourned parent, what small price to serve as the butt of some much less important person's joke."

Indeed, says Hadda, had Gimpel's parents still been alive, they might have been able to protect him from the jokes and pranks. Because of this loss, Gimpel "turns to others in the hope that they will recognize his vulnerable position and therefore treat him with special tenderness—which they certainly do not; quite the contrary." In light of his orphanhood, Hadda believes that Gimpel's seeming masochism can be viewed more as stemming from a "deep need

> "Gimpel's willingness to believe the people around him—and to suffer as a result of believing them—is a virtue and remains one after everything else falls away."

to maintain a bond, no matter at what price." Thus, he maintains his bond with Elka, despite the seemingly high cost, because she gives him "a sense that he is not alone in the world, that he is no longer as abandoned as an orphan, [which] helps him to maintain his equilibrium."

Gimpel asks, "What's the good of *not* believing? Today it's your wife you don't believe; tomorrow it's God Himself you won't take stock in." Of the connection Gimpel makes between faith in one's wife (however unfaithful she herself may be) and faith in God, Alexander points out that "Gimpel never takes the analogy a step further to say that the Jewish people have been far more faithful to their God than [God has been] to them, but in the aftermath of the Holocaust there are few Jewish heads through which that thought will not at least momentarily pass when they read this passage."

A line of *schlemiels* have followed Gimpel in America, according to Sanford Pinsker, most notably in the works of American Jewish authors such as Bernard Malamud, Saul Bellow, Philip Roth, and Woody Allen. But critics such as Alexander and Ruth Wisse note that few *schlemiels* other than Gimpel appear in Yiddish fiction after World War II, possibly because of a disturbing connection between the "schlemiel's innocence or gullibility and the inability or refusal of the majority of Jews 'to face reality' when they were being herded into ghettos, concentration camps, and finally gas chambers." Alexander asks whether it was really the Jews' religious faith that prevented them from seeing the full extent of the threat to their survival, or whether it was their faith in "'mankind' and in the 'world'" that betrayed them. If the latter, then "Gimpel the Fool" can be viewed as a story written "not in spite of, but because of, Singer's awareness of the Holocaust. If worldliness is indeed the gullibility that disbelieves everything, then this is the most intense of all Singer's assaults upon it, for Gimpel is a character who insists on believing everything.... If, Gimpel might say, you disbelieve the nations who threaten to remove the Jewish people from the face of the earth, you will disbelieve anything.''

In the end, after Elka appears to him in a dream saying that her false witness towards him does not mean that everything is false, only that she had deceived herself, Gimpel realizes once and for all that faith is the most important thing. He undergoes a transformation, giving away his worldly possessions and leaving Frampol. What he comes to understand is that ''there were really no lies. Whatever doesn't happen is dreamed at night,'' or it happens to someone else, or ''in a century hence if not next year.''

According to Pinsker, one of the possible derivations of the word *schlemiel* is the Hebrew phrase which means ''sent away from God''; however, another possible translation is ''sent from God,'' as in the sense of being a gift from God. It is often Gimpel's following the dictates of religion which leads him to believe things which at face value are technically untrue. The rabbis reassure Gimpel that to believe is the most important thing. For example, when the townspeople tell him the Messiah has come and his parents have risen from the grave, the rabbi says to Gimpel, ''It is written, better to be a fool all your days than for one hour to be evil.'' When Elka has a child only a few months after the wedding, the schoolmaster tells Gimpel that ''the very same thing had happened to Adam and Eve.'' Gimpel leaves Frampol, continuing to believe even when doing so causes him pain. The longer he lives the more he learns to believe, until even the people around him can see that he is truly wise.

**Source:** Judy Sobeloff, for *Short Stories for Students*, Gale Research, 1997.

## Paul N. Siegel

*Siegel is an American critic who has written extensively on English Renaissance literature and the works of William Shakespeare. In the following excerpt, Siegel views the protagonist and narrator of Singer's short story ''Gimpel the Fool'' as an ironic example of the archetypal wise- or sainted-fool figure in literature.*

''Gimpel the Fool,'' perhaps the most widely acclaimed work of Isaac Bashevis Singer, has its roots deep in the soil of Yiddish literature. It is concerned with two of what Irving Howe and Eliezer Greenberg tell us, in their *Treasury of Yiddish Stories,* are ''the great themes of Yiddish literature,'' ''the virtue of powerlessness'' and ''the sanctity of the insulted and the injured,'' and has as its anti-hero the ''wise or sainted fool'' who is an ''extreme variation'' of ''the central figure of Yiddish literature,'' ''*dos kleine menschele,* the little man.'' The wise or sainted fool is, however, not merely a recurring character in Yiddish fiction; he is a centuries-old archetypal figure of western literature. The manner in which Singer handles this archetypal figure, making use of the ideas associated with it, but in his own distinctive way, makes ''Gimpel the Fool '' the masterpiece of irony that it is....

Gimpel differs from the other representatives of the archetype, the Yiddish ones as well as the others, in that he is the expression of his creator's own idiosyncratic mixture of faith and skepticism. It is this mixture which, as we shall see in analyzing the story, is the source of its pervasive irony. Singer stated in a *Commentary* interview on November, 1963 that it would be foolish to believe the purveyors of fantasies about psychic phenomena—just as it was foolish of Gimpel to believe the fantastic lies he was told—yet the universe *is* mysterious, and there is something of truth after all in these fantasies, at least a revelation concerning the depths of the human psyche from which these fantasies emerged and perhaps something more as well. The need to continue to search for the truth, the realization that this search cannot result in the attainment of the truth, the need to choose belief, the realization that, intellectually speaking, such a choice cannot be defended against the unbeliever—all of this lies behind ''Gimpel the Fool.'' ...

Gimpel is the butt of his village because of his credulity. But is he the fool that the village takes him to be? Telling his story himself, he affirms his own folly in his very first words: ''I am Gimpel the fool.'' In the very next breath, however, he takes it back: ''I don't think myself a fool. On the contrary. But that's what folks call me.'' As he relates the story of his life, this denial of his foolishness seems to be the pitiful defense of his intellect by an evidently weak-witted person who at times tacitly admits that he is a fool, but a steadily deepening ambiguity plays about his narrative. This ambiguity, present from the beginning, is indicated in the title and the opening sentence of the Yiddish, where the epithet used is ''*chochem*'' or ''sage,'' which often has the ironic meaning of "fool," the meaning in which the villagers and Gimpel's wife use it....

His credulity has no limits. Repetition seems to make it easier for him to believe rather than the reverse. We should laugh at this spectacle of the fool continuing in his folly, but we do not, for we have come to wonder if Gimpel, undoubted fool that he has proven himself to be, is not in reality superior to his deceivers. Early in his torments the rabbi had advised him, "It is written, better to be a fool all your days than for one hour to be evil. You are not a fool. They are the fools. For he who causes his neighbor to feel shame loses Paradise himself." The paradox is that Gimpel, born to be a fool all of his days, is not a fool. It is the smart-aleck villagers, devoting their time to playing games upon him, who are fools....

Just as he made a vow before not to believe anything that he was told, a vow which he was unable to keep, so he now makes a vow to believe whatever he is told. "What's the good of *not* believing? Today it's your wife you don't believe; tomorrow it's God Himself you won't take stock in." It is undoubtedly laughable that Gimpel makes faith in the sluttish Elka equivalent to faith in the divine scheme of things. Yet Singer himself, during the *Commentary* interview in November, 1963, in expounding the philosophy of "as if," the doctrine that all of us must lead our lives in accordance with certain assumptions, such as the assumption that we will go on living, even if these assumptions go contrary to the existing evidence, makes use of faith in one's wife as an illustration....

Before Elka dies, she confesses to Gimpel that she has deceived him all of their married life. The Spirit of Evil comes to Gimpel as he is sleeping and, telling him that God and the judgment in the world to come are fables, persuades him to revenge himself against the deceitful world by urinating in the dough so that the "*chachomim*," the sages of the village, may be fooled into eating filth....

After he has baked the unclean bread, however, and lies dozing by the oven, Elka appears in a dream. She calls him "*cho-chem*" —ironically wise man and fool—for believing that because she was false everything else is a lie. She had in reality never deceived anyone but herself, and now she is paying for it in the other world....

The "as if" that Elka is faithful by which Gimpel had lived is now seen by him to give way, after it has sunk under him, to other "as if's." He buries the bread in the ground, divides his wealth among the children—he had earlier casually mentioned in his unworldly way that he had forgotten to say that he had come to be rich—and goes into the world. Before he had regarded his village as the world. Now he finds out that the world has much more in it than he knew. He grows old and gray in his wanderings. He hears many fantastic tales, but the longer he lives the more he comes to realize that there are no lies. Everything, no matter how fantastic, comes to pass sooner or later. The something that was supposed to have happened that he hears and regards as impossible actually happens at a later time. Or even, he says in a sentence omitted in the Bellow translation, a sentence reminiscent of Singer's comment on the magazines devoted to psychic phenomena, if a story is quite imagined, it also has a significance: why does one person dream up one thing and another person an entirely different thing?

Gimpel thus becomes a representative of that other variant of *dos kleine menschele* in Yiddish fiction, "the ecstatic wanderer, hopeless in this world because so profoundly committed to the other," as Greenberg and Howe have put it. He also becomes reminiscent of the Wandering Jew, who according to the legend transmitted through the centuries was punished for having spat into the face of Christ by being deprived of the power to die. Cursed with unwanted life, imbued with the esoteric knowledge he has acquired through having lived through many civilizations, he is generally an evil figure, but he is also sometimes represented as Christ-like in the sustained agony through which he pays for his sin. Longing to join Elka in death, weary from the years of his wandering, Gimpel is transformed by the realization that has come to him from his varied experiences that "the world is entirely an imaginary world," becoming a personification of the ecstatic wisdom that is attained through the agony of suffering.

Yet the wisdom he has attained is the same that he had when, "like a golem," he "believed everyone," reasoning to himself, "Everything is possible, as it is written in the Wisdom of the Fathers, I've forgotten just how." What had seemed to be one of a number of excuses offered by a fool for his gullibility turns out to be indeed wisdom. The outrageously outlandish stories about miraculous births he had accepted really attested to his perception of the miracle of life. The hallucinations which he told himself he had had really attested to his perception that the world is a dream.

> "The outrageously outlandish stories about miraculous births he had accepted really attested to his perception of the miracle of life."

But now he who had listened to stories of marvels is the one who tells them: "Going from place to place, eating at strange tables, it often happens that I spin yarns—improbable things that could never have happened—about devils, magicians, windmills, and the like." Sometimes the children who chase after him tell him the particular story they wish to hear, and he satisfies them with a recital of that tale. For Gimpel, it is implied, has come to understand that each one of us has his own favorite fiction to which he is addicted, his own delusion to which he needs to remain faithful. But a sharp youngster tells him that it is really always the same story that he tells. For all of our delusions derive from the dream that is life in this world. The tales which the aged wanderer relates deal with the folk superstitions to which there have been so many references in "Gimpel the Fool"—the windmills, however, seem to be a reminiscence of the illusions of that glorious madman, Don Quixote—but these superstitions, silly as they are, are glimpses of the truth shadowed forth in the dream of life: "No doubt the world is entirely an imaginary world, but it is only once removed from the true world." ...

**Source:** Paul N. Siegel, "Gimpel and the Archetype of the Wise Fool," in *The Achievement of Isaac Bashevis Singer*, edited by Marcia Allentuck, Southern Illinois University Press, 1969, pp. 159–74.

## Alfred Kazin

*A highly respected American critic, Kazin is best known for his essay collections* The Inmost Leaf *(1955),* Contemporaries *(1962), and* On Native Grounds *(1942), a study of American prose writing since the era of William Dean Howells. In the following excerpt from a review of* Gimpel the Fool, and Other Stories, *Kazin discusses Singer's combination of traditional Jewish and modern literary conventions, focusing on his use of the archetypal fool figure of Jewish literature.*

When I first read "Gimpel the Fool" ... I felt not only that I was reading an extraordinarily beautiful and witty story, but that I was moving through as many historical levels as an archaeologist at work. This is an experience one often gets from the best Jewish writers. The most "advanced" and sophisticated Jewish writers of our time—Babel, Kafka, Bellow—have assimilated, even conquered, the whole tradition of modern literature while reminding us of the unmistakable historic core of the Jewish experience. Equally, a contemporary Yiddish writer like Isaac Bashevis Singer uses all the old Jewish capital of folklore, popular speech and legendry, yet from within this tradition itself is able to duplicate a good deal of the conscious absurdity, the sauciness, the abandon of modern art—without for a moment losing his obvious personal commitment to the immemorial Jewish vision of the world.

Perhaps it is this ability to incarnate all the different periods that Jews have lived through that makes such writers indefinably fascinating to me. They wear whole epochs on their back; they alone record widely separated centuries in dialogue with each other. Yet all these different periods of history, these many *histories,* represent, if not a single point of view, a common historic character. It is the irony with which ancient dogmas are recorded, the imaginative sympathy with which they are translated and transmuted into contemporary terms, that makes the balance that is art.

Gimpel himself is an example of a legendary Jewish type—the saint as *schlemiel*. The mocked, persecuted and wretched people, who nevertheless are the chosen—chosen to bear a certain knowledge through a hostile world—are portrayed again in the town fool, a baker who is married off to a frightful slut without knowing what everyone else in town knows, that she will bear a child in four months. Gimpel is *the* fool of the Jews: a fool because he is endlessly naïve, a fool because, even when he does learn that he has been had, he ignores his own dignity for the sake of others. His wife's unfaithfulness, her shrewishness—these are not the bourgeois concealment, the "cheating" on one's spouse that it would be in another culture, but a massive, hysterical persecution. The child she already has she passes off as her "brother"; Gimpel believes her. When she gives birth to a child four months after the wedding, Gimpel pays for the circumcision honors and rituals, and names the boy after his own father. When he cries out that his wife has deceived him, she deliberately confuses him, as usual, and persuades him that the child is "premature":

> I said, "Isn't he a little too premature?" She said that she had a grandmother who carried just as short a time and she resembled this grandmother of hers as one drop of water does another. She swore to it with such oaths that you would have believed a peasant at the fair if he had used them. To tell the plain truth, I didn't believe her; but when I talked it over next day with the schoolmaster he told me that the very same thing had happened to Adam and Eve. Two they went up to bed, and four they descended.

The humor of this is always very real, for these people are rough old-fashioned village types who know their own. The town boys are always playing tricks on Gimpel, setting him on false trails; he is mocked at his own wedding—some young men carry in a crib as a present. His wife, Elka, is a living nightmare, a shrew of monumental proportions, a Shakespearean harridan. Yet in Gimpel's obstinate attachment to her we recognize, as in his customary meekness, the perfection of a type: what to the great world is folly, in itself may be wisdom; what the world thinks insane may, under the aspect of eternity, be the only sanity....

One night, Gimpel comes home unexpectedly and finds another man in bed with Elka; this time he has had enough, and he separates from her. But the town mischiefs take her side and persecute him, while Gimpel worries whether he *did* see the man:

> Hallucinations do happen. You see a figure or a manikin or something, but when you come up closer it's nothing, there's not a thing there. And if that's so, I'm doing her an injustice. And when I got so far in my thoughts I started to weep. I sobbed so that I wet the floor where I lay. In the morning I went to the rabbi and told him that I had made a mistake.

Elka has another child and "all Frampol refreshed its spirits because of my trouble and grief. However, I resolved that I would always believe what I was told. What's the good of *not* believing? Today it's your wife you don't believe in; tomorrow it's God Himself you won't take stock in."

Even his superstitions—Singer uses local demons and spirits as dramatic motifs—become symbols of his innocent respect for the world. One night, after covering the dough to let it rise, he takes his share of bread and a little sack of flour and starts homeward....

He returns home to find his wife in bed with the apprentice. Characteristically, he suffers rather than storms; characteristically, "the moon went out all at once. It was utterly black, and I trembled"; characteristically, he obeys his wife when she sends him out of the house to see if the goat is well; characteristically, he identifies himself tenderly with the goat, and when he returns home, the apprentice having fled, the wife denies everything, tells him he has been seeing visions, shrieks prodigious curses. Her "brother" beats him with a stick. And Gimpel: "I felt that something about me was deeply wrong, and I said, 'Don't make a scandal. All that's needed now is that people should accuse me of raising spooks and *dybbuks*.'"

So he makes his peace with her, and they live together for twenty years. "All kinds of things happened, but I neither saw nor heard." When his wife dies, she tells him that none of their children is his, and the look on her dead face seems to say to him—"I deceived Gimpel. That was the meaning of my brief life."

Now Gimpel is tempted by the Spirit of Evil himself, who tells him that it is all nothing. "'What,' I said, '*is* there, then?' 'A thick mire.'" And, succumbing to the devil, Gimpel urinates into the risen dough. His dead wife comes to him in a dream—and, when he weeps in shame at his act, "It's all your fault," she cries—"You fool! You fool! Because I was false, is everything false, too?"

When the mourning period for his wife ends, he gives up everything to tramp through the world, often telling stories to children—"about devils, magicians, windmills, and the like." He dreams constantly of his wife, asks when he will be with her; in his dreams, she kisses him and promises him that they will be together soon. "When I awaken I feel her lips and taste the salt of her tears."

The last paragraph of the story, Gimpel's serene meditation before death, is of great beauty. It sums up everything that Jews have ever felt about the divinity that hedges human destiny, and it is indeed one of the most touching avowals of faith that I have ever seen. Yet it is all done with lightness, with wit, with a charming reserve—so that it might almost be read as a tribute to human faithfulness itself....

Singer's story naturally suggests a comparison with I. J. Peretz's famous "Bontsha the Silent," who was offered everything in heaven, and meekly asked for a hot roll with fresh butter every morning for breakfast. One thinks also of Sholem Aleichem's

> "Gimpel's serene meditation before death is of great beauty. It sums up everything that Jews have ever felt about the divinity that hedges human destiny."

Tevye the dairyman, who recited his prayers even as he ran after his runaway horse. But in his technique of ambiguity Singer speaks for our generation far more usefully than the old ritualistic praise of Jewish goodness. While Bontsha and Tevye are entirely folk images, cherished symbols of a tradition, Gimpel—though he and his wife are no less symbols—significantly has to win back his faith, and he wins it in visions, in dreams, that give a background of playfulness and irony to this marvelously subtle story.

This concern with the dream, this everlasting ambiguity in our relations with the divine—this is a condition that our generation has learned to respect, after rejecting the dogmas first of orthodoxy and then of scientific materialism. This delicacy of conception unites Singer to the rest of imaginative humanity today: Man believes even though he knows his belief to be absurd, but what he believes represents a level of imaginative insight which shades off at one end into art, at the other into Gimpel's occasional self-doubt, the thought that he may be "mad."

It is the integrity of the human imagination that Singer conveys so beautifully. He reveals the advantage that an artist can find in his own orthodox training—unlike so many Jews who in the past became mere copyists and mumblers of the holy word. Singer's work *does* stem from the Jewish village, the Jewish seminary, the compact (not closed) Jewish society of Eastern Europe. He does not use the symbols which so many modern writers pass on to each other. For Singer it is not only his materials that are "Jewish"; the world is so. Yet within this world he has found emancipation and universality—through his faith in imagination. . . .

**Source:** Alfred Kazin, "The Saint as Schlemiel," in his *Contemporaries,* Little, Brown, 1962, pp. 283–88.

## Sources

Alexander, Edward. *Isaac Bashevis Singer: A Study of the Short Fiction,* Twayne's Studies in Short Fiction, No. 18, Twayne, 1990.

Drucker, Sally Ann. "I. B. Singer's Two Holy Fools," *Yiddish,* Vol. 8, no. 2, 1992, pp. 35-39.

Hadda, Janet. "Gimpel the Full," *Prooftexts,* Vol. 10, 1990, pp. 283-295.

Hennings, Thomas. "Singer's 'Gimpel the Fool' and *The Book of Hosea*," *The Journal of Narrative Technique,* Vol. 13, no. 1, Winter, 1983, pp. 11-19.

Pinsker, Sanford. "The *Schlemiel* as Metaphor," *Studies in Yiddish and American Jewish Fiction,* Southern Illinois University Press, 1971.

## Further Reading

*Short Story Criticism,* Vol. 3, Gale, 1989.
    Contains previously published criticism on Singer's short fiction.

Siegel, Ben. "Sacred and Profane: Isaac Bashevis Singer's Embattled Spirits," *Critique,* Vol. VI, No. 1 (Spring 1963): 24–47.
    Discusses Singer's blending of Yiddish and Western literary traditions in *Gimpel the Fool* and *The Spinoza of Market Street.*

Singer, Isaac Bashevis, and Burgin, Richard. *Conversations with Isaac Bashevis Singer.* New York: Farrar, Straus, 1986, 190 p.
    Interviews with Singer.

# A Good Man Is Hard to Find

**Flannery O'Connor**

**1955**

Flannery O'Connor's short story "A Good Man Is Hard to Find" first appeared in the author's short story collection by the same name, which was published in 1955. Since then, it has become one of O'Connor's most highly regarded works of short fiction because it exhibits all the characteristics for which she is best known: a contrast of violent action with humorously and carefully drawn characters and a philosophy that underscores her devout Roman Catholic faith. Critics have admired the prose and the way O'Connor infuses the story with her Catholic belief about the role God's grace plays in the lives of ordinary people. The story is disturbing and humorous at the same time—a quality shared by many of O'Connor's other works, including her novels *Wise Blood* and *The Violent Bear It Away*.

Though the story begins innocently enough, O'Connor introduces the character of the Misfit, an escaped murderer who kills the entire family at the end of the story. Through this character, O'Connor explores the Christian concept of "grace"—that a divine pardon from God is available simply for the asking. In the story, it is the Grandmother—a petty, cantankerous, and overbearing individual—who attains grace at the moment of her death, when she reaches out to the Misfit and recognizes him as one of her own children. For O'Connor, God's grace is a force outside the character, something undeserved, an insight or moment of epiphany. Often, however, O'Connor's characters miss moments of opportuni-

ty to make some connection; their spiritual blindness keeps them from seeing truth.

"A Good Man Is Hard to Find" is the title story of O'Connor's first short story collection, and, therefore, often serves as an introduction to the rest of her fiction. The story is enjoyable for its humorous portrayal of a family embarking on a vacation; O'Connor has been unforgiving in her portrayal of these characters—they are not likable. However, in creating characters that elicit little sympathy from readers, O'Connor has carefully set the premise for her main argument: that grace is for everyone, even those who seem loathesome.

## Author Biography

Although she produced relatively few works in her short lifetime of 39 years, Mary Flannery O'Connor is considered one of the most important short story writers of the twentieth century because of her strange but interesting characters, her violent plot elements, and her religious world view. O'Connor was a Roman Catholic writer who knew that most of her audience did not share her strict moral view of the world. She sought, however, to present a message of God's grace and presence in everyday life. Born in the "Bible Belt" Southern city of Savannah, Georgia, on March 25, 1925, O'Connor's region and upbringing influenced her fiction in her depiction of character, of conflict, and in her choice of themes.

O'Connor was the only child of wealthy parents and attended high school in Milledgeville, Georgia. Her father, Edward Francis O'Connor, died when she was sixteen from degenerative lupus, the same disease that later took her life. At the Georgia College for Women, O'Connor majored in social sciences and edited and wrote for school publications. She later received a master's degree in writing from Iowa State University in 1947, using six of her stories as her master's thesis. After completing graduate school, O'Connor attended the prestigious Yaddo writers' colony in upstate New York in 1947-48 where she worked on her first novel *Wise Blood*. Moving to New York and then to Connecticut to live with good friends Sally and Robert Fitzgerald, O'Connor continued to work on her novel until she suffered her first attack of lupus, a chronic, autoimmune disease which causes inflammation of various parts of the body, such as the skin, joints, blood and internal organs. O'Connor then moved back to Milledgeville, where she lived the remainder of her life with her mother.

O'Connor wrote steadily through the 1950s. Her novel *Wise Blood* was published in 1952, and *A Good Man Is Hard to Find*, a short story collection containing the well-known story by the same name, in 1955. A second novel, *The Violent Bear It Away* came out in 1960. The year of her death, 1964, saw the publication of *Three by Flannery O'Connor* and another short story collection, *Everything That Rises Must Converge*. Most of her stories were originally published in periodicals such as *Accent, Mademoiselle, Esquire,* and *Critic*. She won three O. Henry Memorial Awards for her short stories, a Ford Foundation grant, a National Institute of Arts and Letters grant in literature, and two honorary doctor's degrees during her lifetime. After her death, her fiction won a National Book Award, and her collection of letters *The Habit of Being* won an award from the *Library Journal*.

O'Connor's health prevented her from traveling much, so she spent much of her time writing hundreds of letters to friends, family, and strangers. The collection of letters *The Habit of Being* reveals a great deal about O'Connor's compassionate, but often critical, personality. Besides her friendships and her correspondence, O'Connor helped her mother on their Georgia dairy farm Andalusia, painted with oils, and raised peacocks, birds that figure prominently and often symbolically in her fiction. She traveled when she could and presented lectures and speeches. She died on August 3, 1964, at the age of 39, from the effects of her disease and abdominal surgery associated with it; however, her fiction lives on, appearing in anthologies, garnering critical attention, and continuing to astound readers with its depiction of the human condition.

## Plot Summary

O'Connor's story is told by a third person narrator, but the focus is on the Grandmother's perspective of events. Even though she complains that she would rather go to Tennessee than Florida for vacation, she packs herself (and secretly her cat, Pitty Sing) in the car with her son Bailey, his wife, and their children June Star, John Wesley, and the baby. In a comical instance of foreshadowing, she takes pains to dress properly in a dress and hat, so that if she were found dead on the highway everyone would recognize her as a lady.

When the family stops for lunch at Red Sammy Butts' barbecue place, the proprietor, a husky man, is insulted by June Star. Nevertheless, he and the Grandmother discuss the escaped murderer known as the Misfit. Noting that the world is increasingly a more dangerous and unfriendly place, Red Sammy tells the Grandmother that these days "A good man is hard to find." Back on the road, the Grandmother convinces her hen-pecked son to go out of their way so they can visit an old plantation she recalls from her childhood. The children second her suggestion when she mentions that the house contains secret passageways. Soon after Bailey turns down a dirt road "in a swirl of pink dust" with "his jaw as rigid as a horseshoe," the Grandmother realizes that the plantation is not in Georgia, where they are, but in Tennessee. This sudden realization causes her to upset Pitty Sing's basket. The cat leaps out onto Bailey's shoulder, and the surprise causes him to lose control of the car and roll it into a ditch.

No one is seriously hurt, and the children are inclined to view the accident as an adventure. Soon a car happens along the desolate stretch of road and the family believes the driver will stop and help them. As the driver makes his way down the embankment, the Grandmother thinks "his face was as familiar to her as if she had known him all her life but she could not recall who he was." As soon as he starts to speak, however, she recognizes him as the infamous Misfit. He is accompanied by two other men; they are all carrying guns and are dressed in clothes that are clearly not their own. The first thing he wants to know is if the car will still run.

While the Misfit talks with the grandmother, his two accomplices, Hiram and Bobby Lee, take each member of the family off to the woods and shoot them. Soon the Misfit obtains Bailey's bright yellow shirt with blue parrots on it, and he and the Grandmother are alone. She tries to convince him that he is "not a bit common," in an effort to flatter him and spare her life. When it becomes clear that her words are having little effect on him, she becomes speechless for the first time in the story. "She opened and closed her mouth several times before anything came out. Finally she found herself saying, 'Jesus. Jesus,' meaning Jesus will help you, but the way she was saying it, it sounded as if she might be cursing."

The Misfit's explanation for his behavior provides an opportunity for the self-centered Grandmother to reflect on her beliefs in the moments before he shoots her "three times through the

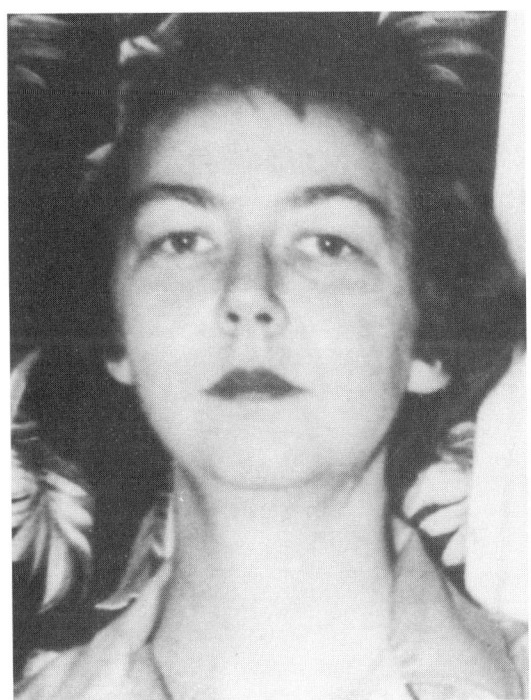

*Flannery O'Connor*

chest." The Misfit explains that "Jesus thown everything off balance." In her final moment, the Grandmother reaches out and touches the Misfit, whispering "You're one of my own children!." The Misfit's final commentary on the Grandmother is that "she would of been a good woman ... if it had been somebody there to shoot her every minute of her life."

## Characters

### Bailey

Bailey is the son of the principal character in the story, the Grandmother, and is the father of June Star and John Wesley. He drives the car as the family embarks on their vacation. Bailey's major importance in the story is his relationship to other people, especially his mother. He allows her to boss him around and to convince him to go out of the way to visit an old house she remembers from her childhood, where the family is killed. Bailey seems unresponsive to his wife and children, allowing them to take advantage of him. Overall, Bailey, who wears a yellow shirt with blue parrots, perhaps symbolizing his cowardice, is a "flat" character.

### Bailey Boy
*See* Bailey

### Red Sammy Butts
Red Sammy Butts owns the barbecue restaurant called the Tower at which the family stops on their car trip. O'Connor describes him as fat with his stomach hanging over his khaki pants "like a sack of meal swaying under his shirt." Signs along the highway advertise his barbecue: "Try Red Sammy's Famous Barbecue. None like Famous Red Sammy's! Red Sam! The Fat Boy with the Happy Laugh. A Veteran! Red Sammy's Your Man!" He orders his wife around and engages in empty chatter with the Grandmother. Red Sammy's statement, "A good man is hard to find," in reference to the proliferation of crime and a nostalgia for the days when people did not have to lock their doors, becomes the title of the story.

### The Grandmother
The Grandmother in "A Good Man Is Hard to Find" is the story's principal character. Her religious epiphany at the story's end provides the philosophical thrust behind the narrative. By giving her no name other than Grandmother and crotchety conversation that provides much of the story's humor, O'Connor paints her as a tragically comic caricature, one that a reader can easily, but wrongly, feel superior to. She is selfish and pushy; in fact, her desire to see a house from her childhood results in the family's death at the end of the story. The story's primary action involves a family car trip on which they encounter an escaped criminal and his gang. If the Grandmother had not insisted they detour to see the old house, which, she realized too late was in Tennessee, not in the part of Georgia where they were, the family would have escaped the disaster. The Grandmother is critical of the children's mother, who is never named, and she dotes on her son Bailey although she treats him like a child. She demonstrates racist behavior by calling a poor Black child "a pickaninny ... Wouldn't that make a picture, now?" and she reveals a superior moral attitude. In her conversation with the murderer, an escaped convict called the Misfit, the Grandmother says that she knows he is from "good people," as she tries to flatter him in order to save her own life. Her last words to him as she reaches out to touch his shoulder, "You're one of my own children," signify that she has experienced a final moment of grace. The Misfit shoots her three times, but her transcendence to grace is underscored by the fact that she died "with her legs crossed under her like a child's and her face smiling up at the cloudless sky." Through her portrait of the Grandmother, O'Connor demonstrates her strong belief in the salvation of religion. Everyone's soul deserves to be saved, she is saying, no matter how impious their actions in life.

### The Misfit
The Misfit is an escaped murderer who kills the family at the end of the story and shoots the Grandmother three times in the chest. Described as wearing tan and white shoes, no socks, no shirt, he is an older man with glasses "that gave him a scholarly look." By his speech, readers can tell that he is rather uneducated. However, he speaks to the grandmother and the others with deliberate politeness. He remains calm throughout the scene as he instructs his two companions, Bobby Lee and Hiram, to take the family to the woods. He says to the Grandmother, "it would have been better for all of you, lady, if you hadn't reckernized me."

In the Misfit's conversation with the Grandmother about Jesus throwing "everything off balance," O'Connor presents a view of a world out of balance. Just as the story's violence does not seem to match its comedy, the Misfit's life of punishment has not fit his crimes. In a long section of dialogue, the Misfit unburdens his soul to the Grandmother about his father's death, his own mistreatment, and his feelings about the world's injustices. He kills her when she calls him one of her "own babies." Although critics have interpreted the actions and words of the Misfit in many ways, one reading is that he brings the Grandmother to a moment of grace in which she makes an unselfish, religious connection with another human being, something she had been incapable of before that time. In his comment, "She would of been a good woman... if it had been somebody there to shoot her every minute of her life," the Misfit seems to understand that her grace required an extreme situation. The Misfit, by helping the Grandmother understand her own mortality and connection with "all God's children," may actually be an unlikely—and evil—messenger from God.

### Red Sam
*See* Red Sammy Butts

### Red Sammy
*See* Red Sammy Butts

### June Star

June Star, the granddaughter of the principal character in the story, is rude, self-centered, and annoying. She argues with her brother John Wesley and seems disappointed when no one is killed in their car accident. When Red Sammy's wife asks her if she would like to live with them, June Star replies, "No I certainly wouldn't.... I wouldn't live in a broken-down place like this for a million bucks!" She, like many of O'Connor's characters, serves as comic relief or as an example of realism.

### John Wesley

John Wesley, the eight-year-old grandson of the principal character of the story, is described as a "stocky child with glasses." He is portrayed as a kid with normal interests and actions. His enthusiasm to see the house his grandmother tells them about, mainly to explore the secret panel she says it contains, influences his father Bailey to make the fateful detour. John Wesley's name is undoubtedly an ironic reference to the English priest who was one of the founders of the Methodist church.

## Themes

In "A Good Man Is Hard to Find" an escaped convict and his companions murder a family because of a series of mishaps on the part of the Grandmother. Thinking that an old house is in Georgia rather than Tennessee, she insists that her son Bailey take a detour that leads them to their deaths. Because she has secretly brought her cat along, her son Bailey drives the car off the road when the cat leaps to his shoulders. Finally, she blurts out the identity of the murderer so that he has no choice but to murder them all. Readers are introduced to a quirky family and what appears to be a typical family car trip, but the story ends on a more philosophical note when the Grandmother attains a state of grace at the moment she realizes that the murderer is "one of her children."

### Prejudice vs. Tolerance

The Grandmother demonstrates racial and class prejudice through her words and actions. She is vain and selfish, and she believes that good character is a result of coming from "good people," an important concept in O'Connor's fiction. When she sees an African-American child without any clothes, she

## Topics for Further Study

- In the 1950s, automobiles became more accessible to many Americans, and people's mobility and freedom reached new proportions. O'Connor often used the automobile as a symbol in her writing. In addition to "A Good Man Is Hard to Find," read "The Life You Save May Be Your Own" and "The Displaced Person" and discuss the importance of the automobile in those narratives.

- Read about the Civil Rights Movement and some of the frustrations African Americans faced in the South during the 1950s and 1960s. Read another story from O'Connor's collection *A Good Man Is Hard to Find* called "The Artificial Nigger." How does a racist lawn statue become a symbol for spiritual searching? What seems to be O'Connor's position on racism?

- Discuss how the tenets of Roman Catholicism are manifest in O'Connor's fiction. How does she interpret her own Catholic faith, and what does she expect her readers to understand about it?

- Compare O'Connor's use of humor to Mark Twain's, especially in *The Adventures of Huckleberry Finn*. How do both of the writers use humor to present the harsh realities of the human condition?

exclaims, "Oh look at the cute little pickaninny!" She continues, "Wouldn't that make a picture, now?" When her granddaughter comments on the child's lack of clothes, the Grandmother says, "He probably didn't have any.... Little niggers in the country don't have things like we do." Believing that she came from a good family and from a time when "People did right," the Grandmother possesses a false sense of self-righteousness. She tells Red Sammy, a restaurant owner, that she believes that the United States' problems can be blamed on Europe. She says "the way Europe acted you would think we were made of money." In her ignorance of others' lifestyles and points of view, the Grandmother is one of O'Connor's numerous characters who flaunt their prejudice. Early in her encounter with the Misfit, she tries to flatter him, telling him that he does not look "common," and therefore could not be a "bad" person. A lifetime of prejudicial attitudes is erased, however, at the end of the story when she realizes her helplessness and the fact that discriminatory views such as hers are related to monstrous behavior like the Mistfit's. This moment is encapsulated in her epiphany: "Why you're one of my babies. You're one of my own children!"

### God and Religion

Most of O'Connor's fiction involves God and religion in some way. She created characters and put them in situations which convey her message that human beings are trapped in their selfish, petty worlds and often overlook opportunities for understanding and connection; they miss out on love. Central to O'Connor's theology is the idea of grace, that God's love and forgiveness are available to people in everyday life. Some have defined grace in O'Connor's fiction as the moment in a human being's life when a power from the outside intervenes in a situation. O'Connor's stories almost always teach by negative example; her characters are often too selfish or unobservant to see the acts of grace in everyday experience. She used violence in her fiction to grab the characters' attention, because she believed that people needed to be coerced into noticing God's presence in the modern world. She shocked readers into understanding that people cannot survive alone in the world. As she said in *Mystery and Manners*, a collection of her nonfiction writing published after her death, grace is "simply a concern with the human reaction to that which, instant by instant, gives life to the soul. It is a concern with a realization that breeds charity and with the charity that breeds action." Charity, in this context, is a synonym for love; certainly, readers have noticed the absence of love in O'Connor's fiction. In "A Good Man Is Hard to Find" all of the characters—most obviously the Grandmother—are concerned only with their own wants and desires. There is no real connection or love between them until they encounter the Misfit and his gang of murderers. When the Grandmother exclaims at the end, "You're one of my children!," she makes the first statement of connection in the story. At this point she receives grace as she understands her place in humanity. All are sinners in O'Connor's fiction, but all are capable of being saved.

### Violence and Cruelty

Much of O'Connor's fiction contains violence, which she claimed was necessary to get readers' attention. Her violence has a purpose, therefore; she claimed that the world in general would not notice God's presence unless something monumental occurred. In "A Good Man Is Hard to Find," the Grandmother must be shocked out of her selfish and judgmental views by the barrel of a gun. Only when her entire family is murdered within earshot of her and when she faces her own death does she make a real connection with another human being. She says to the Misfit, "You're one of my own children!" and recognizes her own mortality, her own sinfulness, and her relationship to other "children of God." O'Connor believed that God's grace often came into people's lives precisely when they are not looking for it. As she said in *Mystery and Manners,* her "subject in fiction is the action of grace in territory held largely by the devil."

## Style

### Symbolism

Symbols, elements in a work of fiction that stand for something more profound or meaningful, allow writers to communicate complicated ideas to readers in a work that appears to be simple. O'Connor includes several symbols in "A Good Man Is Hard to Find." For example, skies and weather are always symbolic to O'Connor, and she often uses such descriptions to reveal a character's state of mind. In another story "The Life You Save May Be Your Own," O'Connor ends the story with a man being "chased" by an ominous thundercloud, because the man is feeling guilty for abandoning his mentally and physically challenged wife at a roadside diner. In "A Good Man Is Hard to Find," the sky at the end of the story is cloudless and clear, indicating that the Grandmother has died with a clear vision of her place in the world. Another symbol in the story is the old house that the Grandmother insists on visiting. It represents the woman's habit of wanting to live in the past, in a time she believes people were more decent and better than they are today. However, the house is not where she thought it was—it was in Tennessee, not Georgia—a realization that symbolizes that one's perception of the past is often distorted. This focus on a distorted past leads the family directly to their ruin; they have been sidetracked by a past that did not exist.

## Point of View

O'Connor was extremely interested in point of view, and she was careful to keep her point of view consistent. "A Good Man Is Hard to Find" is told in third person, which means that it is not told directly by one of the characters involved in the action. The first sentence of the story indicates an "objective" narrator: "The grandmother didn't want to go to Florida." However, the reader is privy to the Grandmother's thoughts and no one else's. This point of view is sometimes called "third person limited," in which the author reveals only one character's emotions and thoughts to the reader. Even the names of characters illustrate the story's point of view; Bailey's wife—the Grandmother's daughter-in-law—is referred to generically as "the children's mother." This reveals that the Grandmother thinks of her only in terms of being her son's wife and her grandchildren's mother. O'Connor is careful, however, not to enter completely into the Grandmother's thoughts; she keeps what is called "authorial distance." O'Connor is often praised for being "detached" in her narration, allowing readers to come to their own conclusions about the characters. Consistent with this idea of detachment is the fact that the Grandmother is never given a name in the story either, a technique that keeps readers from identifying too closely with her, or recognizing her as an individual. She is simply a "type" of person. This tactic allowed O'Connor to present characters who must be judged by their actions, rather than on some criteria that O'Connor would have deemed "less objective."

## Foreshadowing

Instances of foreshadowing, an indication of future events, occur several times in "A Good Man Is Hard to Find." Many writers of short fiction include few superfluous details; every detail contributes to an overall effect that the story intends to produce. Thus, certain descriptive phrases or dialogue in a story that first appear to have no special significance often take on new meaning in retrospect. In the first paragraph of the story, O'Connor introduces the Misfit, the murderer who eventually kills the family. Similarly, as the family prepares to embark on their vacation, the Grandmother plans her outfit with an eye toward tragedy. Dressed in a polka-dot dress trimmed with organdy and decorated by a spray of violets, "anyone seeing her dead on the highway would know at once that she was a lady." Later, as the family drives through the countryside, they pass a cotton field "with five or six graves fenced in the middle of it," a hint of approaching death for the six occupants of the car. Finally, as the Misfit and his gang approach, their car is described as "a big battered hearse-like automobile," a further indication that death will figure into the story.

## Irony

Irony is one of the most difficult elements to identify in a story because it is related to tone and the author's attitude toward the work. Irony is a literary device that is used to impart that things are not what they seem; the simple meanings of the story's words betray an idea that is actually contrary to what has been stated. "Ironic" is not the same as "sarcastic" or "coincidental." Irony can occur in situations in which things happen which are unexpected given the circumstances; an example of this is that a family embarks on a summer vacation and winds up murdered. Or irony can occur through dialogue when a character's words have a meaning other than that intended by the person who utters them. Finally, there is "dramatic irony," in which the reader understands something that the characters do not. In "A Good Man Is Hard to Find" O'Connor uses several kinds of irony to communicate her message about the human condition. At the beginning of the story, the Grandmother says "I wouldn't take my children in any direction with a criminal like that aloose in it. I couldn't answer to my conscience if I did." However, this is exactly what she does when she sidetracks the family to a desolate roadside. Verbal irony occurs after the car accident when June Star announces disappointedly, "But nobody's killed." The story's dramatic irony centers around the family's interaction with the Misfit, when readers understand the gravity of the situation yet the characters do not; Bailey states "we're in a terrible predicament! Nobody realizes what this is."

## Structure

The story is structured to fall into two sections, each with a distinctive tone. The first half of the story, up until the car accident, is humorous and light. After the accident, however, readers understand that a tragedy will occur. The tone turns dark, the subject matter becomes serious, and dialogue becomes more weighted with irony and symbolism. The conversation about religion between the Grandmother and the Misfit is deeply philosophical and in stark contrast to the story's prior petty exchanges about old boyfriends or poor children. The story moves from being a portrait of an unremarkable family to being a dialogue one the themes of death, forgiveness and injustice.

### Tone

In a work of fiction, tone can be discerned from an author's choice of words and action. The tone of "A Good Man Is Hard to Find" combines humor, detachment, irony, and seriousness. Throughout O'Connor's stories, readers confront humorous descriptions or situations, such as in this story when the narrator describes the children's mother as having "a face as broad and innocent as a cabbage... tied around with a green head-kerchief that had two points on the top like rabbit's ears." O'Connor approaches the characters in her story with detachment; in other words, her narrative voice does not help readers to become sympathetic to her characters. She presents them with all their faults and oddities so that readers may judge them honestly. Towards the end of the story, the tone turns more serious and tragic as the Misfit happens upon the family. O'Connor presents a situation in which average people confront a force of pure evil. The dark tone is established when the characters are unable to reason with the evil Misfit and must confront their own mortality.

## Historical Context

### The Civil Rights Movement

Fueled with the speeches of Reverend Martin Luther King, Jr. and with the deaths of several African-American activists, the civil rights movement was at its peak in 1955. Just the year before, the Supreme Court of the United States had struck down legal segregation in schools in a landmark decision. In 1955, Rosa Parks of Montgomery, Alabama, made her heroic and famous decision not to give up her seat on the bus to a white man. This single action engendered a widespread bus boycott which catapulted its organizer, Martin Luther King, Jr., to national attention. Georgia, where O'Connor lived and set the story, was filled with racial tension. The Grandmother's attitudes toward African Americans typify the beliefs of many in the state at the time. When she tells June Star that "Little niggers in the country don't have things like we do," she was expressing a sentiment many people in white society in 1955 held.

### The Era of the Automobile

The 1950s saw a significant increase in the number of cars on American roads, a result of post World War II economic prosperity. In 1955 motorcar sales passed the 7 million mark in the United States, Chevrolet introduced the V-8 engine, and President Eisenhower submitted a 10-year, $101 billion proposal to build a national highway system to Congress. Family vacations by car, like that in "A Good Man Is Hard to Find" became common as Americans took to the highways and embraced the freedom and independence that automobiles provided. Although New York's Long Island Expressway opened in 1955, it was unable to handle the volume of traffic passing over it. As American society became more mobile and independent, the culture changed. Drive-in restaurants and movie theaters proliferated in the 1950s, as did roadside motels and suburban shopping malls. Cars are important to O'Connor's fiction as both an element of realism in her work and as a symbol for a shift in the way Americans think about themselves and their sense of place.

### The Silver Screen, the Small Screen, and Rock 'n' Roll

American popular culture shifted dramatically during the 1950s. The new prosperity allowed increasing numbers of families to buy television sets, and it became a central form of family entertainment. Shows like *Ozzie and Harriet, Leave It to Beaver,* and *Father Knows Best* presented an idealized and skewed picture of American life. Western movies, stories of good guys and bad guys like *The Lone Ranger,* reinforced the country's moral belief that crime does not pay. Many famous movies or musicals also debuted in the 1950s: *Oklahoma!,* Tennessee Williams's *Cat on a Hot Tin Roof, Rebel without a Cause,* and *Blackboard Jungle,* many of which hinted at problems festering just under the surface of American life. Movies often showed a darker side of American life, and many of the movies of the 1950s dealt with the social unrest that would break loose in the next decade. A new form of music, rock'n'roll, debuted in the mid-1950s. Entertainers such as Chuck Berry, Elvis Presley, and Bill Haley enjoyed tremendous popularity as they appealed to young people and often sang about issues that concerned them. Such overwhelming

# Compare & Contrast

- **1955:** Racial tensions run high as the civil rights movement makes real changes in American society. Rosa Parks refuses to go to the back of a bus in Montgomery, Alabama. Two African-American leaders, Lamar D. Smith and George W. Lee, are killed.

   **1996:** Dozens of African-American churches, mostly in the South, burn down during the spring and summer months. Though the cause of some of the blazes is unknown, arson is suspected in many cases.

- **1950:** According to crime statistics, approximately 7,000 murders were committed in the United States during the year.

   **1994:** According to crime statistics, approximately 23,305 murders were committed during the year. Of these, 15,456 involved firearms.

- **1955:** The U.S. census bureau reveals that the American population increased by 2.8 million, the largest 1-year advance on record. The generation born in the years between 1945 and 1960 are dubbed "The Baby Boomers."

   **1990s:** The first Baby Boomers are turning 50, and the United States looks to ways to provide for the health care and social security of such a large number of aging individuals.

---

changes in many facets of American society prompt the Grandmother in "A Good Man is Hard to Find" to feel nostalgia for a lost past.

## Critical Overview

"A Good Man Is Hard to Find," the title selection of O'Connor's 1955 collection, has received a great deal of critical attention. The story serves as an excellent introduction to O'Connor's fiction because it contains all the elements that typify O'Connor's work: a combination of humor and horror, grotesque characters, and an opportunity for characters to accept God's grace. Critics were initially intrigued with O'Connor's use of violence in her stories, uncommon for a writer—not to mention a woman—in the 1950s and 1960s, yet they recognized her ability to draw characters with clarity and detachment. These traits caused critics to categorize O'Connor as a Southern Grotesque writer, similar to William Faulkner, who also wrote critically of his Southern heritage. However, these same critics were confused by her staunch Roman Catholic perspective, which was unusual for a writer in a region that was predominantly Baptist. O'Connor thought of herself as more of an outsider: not a Southern writer because of her Catholicism, and not a Catholic writer because of her Southern roots. Because her point of view is often theological, and because she fails to present a clear, straightforward moral, the message in her stories has often been misinterpreted.

Initial reaction to "A Good Man Is Hard to Find" was positive. Caroline Gordon wrote in *The New York Times Book Review* that the story was "characterized by precision, density and an almost alarming circumscription." Louis D. Rubin, Jr., in an essay entitled "Two Ladies of the South" recognized that O'Connor "is in essence a religious writer. Knowledge of good and evil is at the heart of her stories." In an essay published in *Mystery and Manners,* O'Connor wrote that the Grandmother had been interpreted as being a witch and the Misfit a fallen prophet. She says that "there are perhaps other ways than my own in which ["A Good Man Is Hard to Find"] could be read, but none other by which it could have been written." More recently, Russell Kirk wrote in an essay for *The World* that the Misfit is "the most forlorn and terrifying desperado in all Flannery's tales."

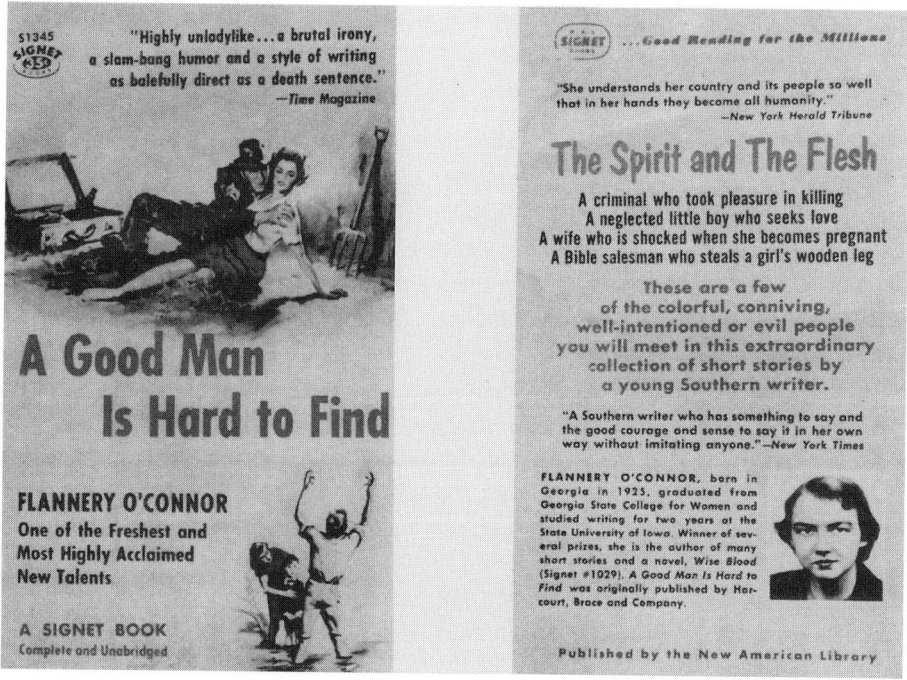

*An early book jacket for O'Connor's* A Good Man Is Hard to Find.

Miles Orvell's *Flannery O'Connor: An Introduction,* written in 1972, is an early introduction and commentary on her fiction. Josephine Hendin, in another work about the author, *The World of Flannery O'Connor,* says that there are two O'Connors: "the perfect daughter who lives in her mother's memory, the uncompromising Catholic O'Connor . . . and the more enigmatic writer of those strange and violent tales." Although some early reviewers were confused by O'Connor's fiction—she seemed to be making fun of religion—the large body of criticism on her work in the past three decades has converged on an accepted interpretation of her work. The New Critics, writers like Cleanth Brooks and John Crowe Ransom who dominated literary criticism in the 1950s promoted O'Connor's fiction, admiring the "intentionality" of her words: every element of the story worked to promote her desired effect. After O'Connor's death, the publication of her many letters in *Mystery and Manners* gave readers added insight through the author's own explanations of her work. In the book, O'Connor emphasizes the form of her stories: writes that the "form of a story gives it a meaning which any other form would change, and unless the student is able, in some degree, to apprehend the form, he will never apprehend anything else about the work."

Today O'Connor's place in the literary world is well established. She is appreciated for her complexity and her contradictions. Anthony DiRenzo's *American Gargoyles: Flannery O'Connor and the Medieval Grotesque* tries to explain some of those contradictions. DiRenzo compares O'Connor's fiction to the medieval cathedrals that were adorned with the grotesque figures of the gargoyle. He says that if one wants to understand O'Connor, one must understand her mixing of the serious and sacred with the comic and the common. The humor in O'Connor keeps readers from crying. Many other studies are available, and the thirty or more years since O'Connor's death have given readers time to appreciate her powerful fiction.

# Criticism

### Elisabeth Piedmont-Marton

*Elisabeth Piedmont-Marton is an educator and the coordinator of the undergraduate writing center at the University of Texas at Austin. In the following essay, she discusses O'Connor's story as a good example of the author's fiction.*

# What Do I Read Next?

- O'Connor's novel *Wise Blood,* published in 1952, deals with religious themes, as does much of her work. The plot revolves around the character of Hazel Motes, a man obsessed with Jesus in ways that the Misfit is. Hazel becomes a preacher for the Church Without Christ. Like "A Good Man Is Hard to Find," *Wise Blood* demonstrates O'Connor's vision of what happens to people who try to live their lives without any kind of spiritual presence.

- *No. 44, The Mysterious Stranger,* by Mark Twain deals with religion in a humorous way.

- *A Curtain of Green,* a collection of stories by Southern writer Eudora Welty. Also characterized as a "Southern Gothic" writer, Welty's fiction often deals with brutal themes as well.

- Carson McCullers has helped to define Southern fiction. *A Member of the Wedding*, *The Ballad of the Sad Cafe,* and *The Heart Is a Lonely Hunter* are three of her most highly regarded novels.

---

"A Good Man Is Hard to Find" is one of the most widely discussed of all Flannery O'Connor's stories. It also provides an excellent introduction to her work because it contains all the major ingredients characteristic of the remarkable literary legacy left by a woman who only lived to be thirty-nine years old and who was too ill to write in her last years. Readers who encounter O'Connor for the first time should be aware that she always identified herself as a Southern writer and as a Catholic writer and that her stories are always informed by these identities and beliefs.

As a Southerner, O'Connor draws on a rich tradition of humor and regional specific detail in her fiction. Beyond the comedic characters and precise rendering of their dialects, however, O'Connor's South is a place rich with myth and history. In two influential essays, "The Fiction Writer and His Country," and "The Regional Writer," now collected in *Mystery and Manners*, O'Connor argued that the best literature is always regional literature because good writing is always rooted in a sense of place, in "a shared past, a sense of alikeness, and the possibility of reading a small history in a universal light." She further claimed that among the regions in the United States, the South has produced the best writing because it has already "had its fall." Southern writers possess special insight, she said, because "we have gone into the modern world with an inburnt knowledge of human limitations and with a sense of mystery which could not have developed in our first state of innocence—as it has not sufficiently developed in the rest of our country."

By the references to the fall and loss of innocence in *Mystery and Manners*, O'Connor meant the Civil War and the crisis of identity, guilt, and shame that accompanied it. Such an experience gave Southerners a richer, more complex sense of who they were and how they were connected to the land than their Northern counterparts had. O'Connor's characters tend to express some degree of confusion and ambivalence toward the South. The Grandmother in "A Good Man Is Hard to Find" is a good example. As James Grimshaw points out, she is a southern stereotype in that she is cautious, devious, indirect, and afraid of the unfamiliar. She is also vain and obsessed with the trappings of class. In O'Connor's own words in a letter to writer John Hawkes, the Grandmother and other "old ladies exactly reflect the banalities of the society and the effect is comical rather than seriously evil."

As an unapologetically religious writer, O'Connor wrote stories informed by the particulars of her Catholic faith. Readers need not share her faith in order to appreciate her fiction, but it helps to be aware of the basic tenets of Catholicism that appear in "A Good Man Is Hard to Find" and her other stories. O'Connor's religious vision was sacramental; that is, she believed that Christ provides outward signs that confer grace on members of the church. In this view, an individual may not earn opportunities for grace by good works, but he or she may turn away, like the Misfit does, from grace when it is offered. In O'Connor's fiction the outward sign of grace often appears as an act of violence. In a letter about "A Good Man Is Hard to Find," O'Connor explained that her use of grace "can be violent or would have to compete with the kind of evil I can make concrete." O'Connor's fiction was always shaped by her beliefs in mystery, grace, redemption, and the devil. In an essay titled "Catholic Novelists," O'Connor explained that the Catholic writer's beliefs make him or her entirely free to observe and that "open and free observation is founded on our ultimate faith that the universe is meaningful, as the Church teaches."

"A Good Man Is Hard to Find" pits the banal and superficial Grandmother against the malevolent Misfit. Although the story starts off as a satire of a typical family vacation, it becomes a tale of cold-blooded murder as the focus narrows to the Misfit and the Grandmother. The story becomes, in O'Connor's words, "a duel of sorts between the Grandmother and her superficial beliefs and the Misfit's more profoundly felt involvement with Christ's action which set the world off balance for him." She also cautions readers that they "should be on the lookout for such things as the action of grace in the Grandmother's soul, and not for the dead bodies." The struggle between the Misfit and the Grandmother is not confined to her efforts to save her own life but also takes the form of an argument about faith and belief. The Grandmother, who has chattered nonstop since the family left home, is gradually rendered mute in the face of the Misfit's assertions about Christ, and when she makes her only sincere gesture of the story, reaching out to touch him, the Misfit is threatened and horrified and shoots her three times through the chest. Before he shoots her, however, the Misfit offers a lengthy explanation for how he ended up where he is and why he believes what he does.

O'Connor uses the Misfit's deeply held and passionate convictions as a foil, or contrast, to the Grandmother's easy platitudes and cliches. The author is critical of the woman's empty reassurances that he is "a good man at heart" and if he would pray "Jesus would help" him. The Misfit, by contrast, devises his own challenging and rational way of looking at the world based on his belief that "Jesus thown everything off balance." The source of his stubborn non-belief is his insistence that everything be explained rationally. Because the Misfit did not see Christ performing any miracles, he cannot believe they ever happened. "The presence of a divine force operating outside the bounds of reason," in the words of Robert Brinkmeyer in an essay published in *The Art and Vision of Flannery O'Connor,* is what upset the balance of the universe. In other words, the Misfit cannot place his faith in something he cannot be rationally certain of, while the Grandmother continues to cling to a faith without an intellectual foundation or certainty of belief. The Misfit is incapable of wrapping himself around the paradox as O'Connor phrased it, "that you must believe in order to understand, not understand in order to believe."

As the paths of these two characters converge in the final moment of the story, they are both given opportunities for grace. When the Grandmother finally runs out of words and is left to mutter "Jesus" over and over, O'Connor is suggesting that she is moving toward a deeper awareness of her faith. Similarly, when the Misfit angrily pounds his fist into the ground and complains, "I wisht I had of been there. It ain't right I wasn't there because if I had been there I would of known," we recognize his frustrated longing for faith. When he confesses, "If I had of been there I would of known and I wouldn't be like I am now," the Grandmother has a moment of clarity and recognizes his twisted humanity as part of her own by calling him one of her children. In O'Connor's words, "The Misfit is touched by the Grace that comes through the old lady when she recognizes him as her child, as she has been touched by the Grace that comes through him in his particular suffering." The Grandmother realizes, O'Connor explained in a later essay, "that she is responsible for the man before her and joined to him by ties of kinship which have their roots deep in the mystery she has been merely prattling about so far."

The Misfit has an opportunity to accept grace but recoils in horror at the Grandmother's gesture. In his parting words, however, he acknowledges how grace had worked through him to strengthen the woman's faith: "She would of been a good woman, if it had been somebody there to shoot her every minute of her life." Brinkmeyer points out that "the Misfit's 'preaching' to the Grandmother 'converts' her to Christ." The Misfit himself seems lost, as his dismissive words to Bobby Lee, "It's no real pleasure in life," indicate. O'Connor, however, had the last word on the Misfit and his future: "I don't want to equate the Misfit with the devil. I prefer to think, however unlikely this may seem, the old lady's gesture, like the mustard-seed, will grow to be a great crow-filled tree in the Misfit's heart, and will be enough of a pain to him there to turn him into the prophet he was meant to become. But that's another story."

**Source:** Elisabeth Piedmont-Marton, for *Short Stories for Students,* Gale Research, 1997.

## Michael Clark

*In the following short essay, Clark discusses the moment of grace in O'Connor's story, when the grandmother reaches out to touch the Misfit. Though O'Connor has repeatedly explained the ending to her story, many critics remain confused about her intentions, particularly those who do not agree with or understand her strict approach to religion.*

"A Good Man Is Hard to Find" is one of Flannery O'Connor's most discussed and most problematic short stories. The major difficulty involves the story's climax. Should the Grandmother's final act—her touching of the Misfit—be taken as a token of true, divine grace and spiritual insight? Or should the story be interpreted strictly as a naturalistic document? Perhaps the Grandmother achieves no spiritual insight. One can find critics on both sides of the argument. Since the issue is central to O'Connor's work at large, it is worth further examination. While this question may ultimately be impossible to resolve with certainty, further light can be shed upon this critical gesture.

In *Mystery and Manners,* O'Connor asserts that the Grandmother's final act is a "moment of grace." Critics, though, have not been convinced. While acknowledging Flannery O'Connor's reading, Madison Jones prefers to stress the "realistic explanation" of grace—a "naturalistic" grace which may be "spelled in lower case letters." Stanley Renner is also uncomfortable with the "religious" explanation and describes "the vague touch" on the Misfit's shoulder as "a parental blessing" or "the ceremonial dubbing of knighthood." Thus the Grandmother's response not so much reflects divine grace as it "touches her almost instinctive springs of sympathy and human kinship." Leon Driskell and Joan Brittain seem to see the Grandmother's final act, not as a transcendent spiritual experience, but as a "gesture of kinship," which comes from one

> "O'Connor's fiction was always shaped by her beliefs in mystery, grace, redemption, and the devil."

whose "revelation, though limited, is adequate." And most recently, Kathleen Ochshorn has entered the fray in a most unequivocal manner, insisting that in "A Good Man Is Hard to Find" "a world of propriety and illusion is laid low by wrath, not redeemed by grace." Rather than seeing the Grandmother's final act as an embodiment of spirituality, Ochshorn asserts that the touch expresses the grandmother's "final hope that her noblesse can alter her fate," an interpretation that renders the grandmother's final gesture as mundane, selfish, and in every sense unredeeming. These critical responses—especially Ochshorn's—are symptomatic of the reluctance to read the story in light of O'Connor's religious beliefs.

Should O'Connor's interpretation of the story be judged as wrong? Critics have an excellent authority for a subversive reading in D.H. Lawrence's well-known dictum: trust the tale, not the teller of the tale. Unless the tale itself can guide us in our interpretation, we are threatened with being like the people in Plato's cave, very inadequate interpreters of shadows on the wall. But there is another piece of evidence in the story which has been overlooked and which strengthens O'Connor's claim that the tale should be read in a theological context.

In an indispensable article several years ago, Hallman Bryant noted that there is no Timothy, Georgia, the setting for the encounter with Red Sammy. He argues persuasively that O'Connor is alluding to "the book in the New Testament which bears the same name"—that is, Paul's Epistle to Timothy. The evidence that Bryant presents leaves no doubt that O'Connor did indeed have the Bible in mind. As Bryant notes, several of Paul's teachings are especially germane to the story: the role of the husband (a negative judgment of Bailey, the Grandmother's son), for example, and strictures against hypocrisy and false religion (which are useful correctives to the family's, especially the Grandmother's, attitudes). However, Bryant glosses

O'Connor's story only with reference to a single book of the Bible, Timothy I. But Timothy II can help explain the crux of the story, the touching of the Misfit; it provides a subtext for the central and problematic episode of O'Connor's story, the grandmother's moment of grace.

In his Second Epistle, Paul stresses to Timothy that true grace is associated with the charismatic tradition of the "laying on of hands":

> I keep the memory of thy tears, and long to see thee again, so as to have my fill of joy when I receive fresh proof of thy sincere faith. That faith dwelt in thy grandmother Lois, and in thy mother, Eunice, before thee; I am fully persuaded that it dwells in thee too. That is why I would remind thee to fan the flame of that special grace which God kindled in thee, when my hands were laid upon thee.

True faith dwelt in Timothy's mother and grandmother and in Timothy too after Paul's hands were laid upon him. When the Grandmother of the story touches the Misfit, she replicates Paul's laying on of hands at the very moment she loses her artificiality and realizes that she and the Misfit are spiritual kin. Both events emphasize the grace which accompanies charismatic physical contact. Those critics who argue for a "realistic" interpretation of the story must ultimately acknowledge and account for O'Connor's biblical allusions. The details of the story, particularly the allusion to Timothy, emphasize that the Grandmother has undergone a personal experience that is significantly different from her normally artificial and spiritually dead self. Aside from whether God exists, such moments are real, and they have *de facto* been defined through history as "religious."

In a newly discovered and just recently published letter, O'Connor (in referring to *The Violent Bear It Away*) states the issue clearly and definitively: The novel "can only be understood in religious terms." The same is true of "A Good Man Is Hard to Find." God's grace is not limited by one's religious orientation. Even the most tough-minded critic will acknowledge that all human beings—even the self-satisfied grandmother—have the potential to experience epiphanies, moments of psychological clarity, that could save them from the sour and life-denying restrictions that human beings may labor under. These are moments (from the clarifying moment of the ordinary life to the trance of the mystic) that historically we have come to define as religious.

In *Mystery and Manners*, O'Connor tells us quite directly that the inescapable threat of death shatters the Grandmother's complaisance and makes her look at the essential: "violence is strangely capable of returning my characters to reality and preparing them to accept their moment of grace." Life is full of such moments—though perhaps rarely on the crucial life-and-death plane of the Grandmother's experience. O'Connor believed that such moments come from God. Theology and art are not mutually exclusive. As O'Connor wrote in *Mystery and Manners*, "In the greatest fiction, the writer's moral sense coincides with his dramatic sense."

**Source:** Michael Clark, "Flannery O'Connor's 'A Good Man Is Hard to Find': The Moment of Grace," in *English Language Notes*, Volume XXIX, No. 2, December, 1991, pp. 66–9.

### Kathleen G. Ochshorn

*In the following essay, Ochshorn attempts to dispel some common misinterpretations of "A Good Man Is Hard to Find"–mainly that the grandmother was evil and the Misfit was misunderstood. Nevertheless, Ochshorn concedes that the grandmother's act of reaching out towards the Misfit was a last-ditch effort to save her own life.*

Flannery O'Connor was often shocked to find how people interpreted her stories. Some readers of "A Good Man is Hard to Find" believed the grandmother was evil, even a witch. Soon O'Connor set out, quite explicitly, in letters and lectures to detail the theology of the story and the importance of the grandmother as an agent of grace. In a letter to John Hawkes, she explained how violence and grace come together:

> More than in the Devil I am interested in the indication of Grace, the moment when you know that Grace has been offered and accepted—such as the moment when the Grandmother realizes the Misfit is one of her own children. These moments are prepared for (by me anyway) by the intensity of the evil circumstances.

When O'Connor speaks of her Catholicism and its expression in her fiction, she is clear-headed, eloquent, and convincing. In *Mystery and Manners*, the posthumous collection of her occasional prose, she claims the assumptions that underlie "A Good Man is Hard to Find" "are those of the central Christian mysteries. These are the assumptions to which a large part of the modern audience takes exception." O'Connor was upset with critics who were determined to count the dead bodies: "And in this story you should be on the lookout for such things as the action of grace in the Grandmother's soul, and not for the dead bodies." For O'Connor, grace is "simply a concern with the human reaction to that which, instant by instant, gives life to the soul. It is a concern with a realization that breeds charity and with the charity that breeds action."

Flannery O'Connor was most sincere in her Catholicism and her view of its expression in her fiction. She was troubled that her readers often identified with the wrong characters or with the right characters for the wrong reasons. She felt readers "had a really sentimental attachment to The Misfit. But then a prophet gone wrong is almost always more interesting than your grandmother, and you have to let people take their pleasures where they find them." When she learned readers were identifying with Hazel Motes' rejection of Christ, O'Connor added a preface to the second edition of *Wise Blood* claiming Motes' integrity lay in his inability to shake the ragged figure of Christ from his mind. Generally O'Connor chalked up all the misreadings and confusion to the spiritual shortcomings of the modern reader: "Today's audience is one in which religious feeling has become, if not atrophied, at least vaporous and sentimental."

But the discrepancies between how O'Connor is often read and how she claimed she should be read cannot simply be explained by her theology of grace or by the lack of religious feeling among readers. Critical opinion over the years has tended to line up behind O'Connor's own explanations; however, O'Connor's analysis of "A Good Man Is Hard to Find" still seems baffling and occasionally a critic has questioned the theology of the fiction. Andre Bleikasten, focusing on O'Connor's novels, claimed that

> the truth of O'Connor's work is the truth of her art, not that of her church. Her fiction does refer to an implicit theology, but if we rely, as we should, on its testimony rather than on the author's comments, we shall have to admit that the Catholic orthodoxy of her work is at least debatable.

And Frederick Asals recalls D. H. Lawrence's advice that a reader should trust the tale and not the teller. Of "A Good Man Is Hard to Find," Asals claims:

> One can easily pass over her [O'Connor's] hope that the grandmother's final gesture to The Misfit might have begun a process which would "turn him into the prophet he was meant to become"; that, as she firmly says, is another story, and it would be a reckless piety indeed which would see it even suggested by the one we have.

Finally, any work of art must speak for itself, and "A Good Man Is Hard to Find" speaks much louder than O'Connor's claims. It depicts evil with a power

> "O'Connor tells us quite directly that the inescapable threat of death shatters the Grandmother's complaisance and makes her look at the essential."

akin to Dostoevsky. Yet Dostoevsky presented holy innocence in characters like Sonia and Alyosha as well as evil in Smerdyakov and Raskolnikov. O'Connor focuses her story on what is sinister in The Misfit and satirical in the grandmother and her family. O'Connor is dark and negative in the modernist tradition, albeit with religious preoccupations. She depicts pure evil in The Misfit as he obliterates the whining grandmother and her clan. This fine story, one of O'Connor's best, derives much of its power from the anger and vengeance it expresses. And that pile of dead bodies cannot be canceled out when the grandmother touches The Misfit.

Yet O'Connor is not diminished by the contradictions between her work and her explanation of her work; she is made richer. The fury that lights up her art keeps "A Good Man Is Hard to Find" from being reduced to a theological exercise. The complexity of this story in part explains its broad appeal to audiences who do not see the story as a parable of grace. Grace is the uneasy cloak O'Connor designed to cover and justify the violence in the story. The grace is a guise, a rationale that is not brought off. O'Connor's naive and deluded mothers and grandmothers are often brought low by a violent encounter that shakes them out of their petty superiorities and their would-be aristocratic and genteel trappings. They are forced to realize their vulnerability, their ridiculous condition.

The character of the grandmother in "A Good Man Is Hard to Find," for several reasons, contradicts any reading of her as an agent of grace. First, the grandmother's judgments of others are totally twisted. She pronounces Red Sammy Butts "a good man" despite the evidence he is a lazy slob who treats his wife like a slave. Throughout the story the grandmother is a full-blown agent of disaster, a

Geiger counter for catastrophe. Her fuzzy fantasies about a southern mansion combined with some assistance from the smuggled cat manage to cause the car wreck. Then her pronouncement "You're The Misfit" seals their fate. The few pleasures in the story involve the grandmother's false sense of superiority. She chuckles over how a "nigger boy" ate the watermelon Mr. Teagarden (E.A.T.) had left for her when they were courting, and she wishes to paint a picture of the "cute little pickaninny" she sees standing, without pants, in the doorway of a shack. Her pleasure and self-esteem increases directly in relation to the degree of superiority she manages to feel. Her limitations are so extreme that it seems impossible to imagine her thinking about anyone but herself, even for a moment.

Then the grandmother deals with The Misfit by appealing to his gentility. She keeps insisting he is a good man, from good people: "You don't look a bit like you have common blood. I know you must come from nice people!" She waves her handkerchief and adjusts the broken brim on her hat, insisting she is a lady and should not be shot. In one of the more bizarre moments in the story, she suggests suburban propriety for what ails The Misfit: "Think how wonderful it would be to settle down and live a comfortable life and not have to think about somebody chasing you all the time." Later, when she asks him to pray, she again appeals to the fact that she is a lady, and she adds, "I'll give you all the money I've got!" The contents of her purse seem an unlikely ransom when the rest of her family has already been shot.

O'Connor does say that the grandmother's head clears before she tells The Misfit "why you're one of my babies. You're one of my own children!" and reaches out to touch him. But by that time he is wearing Bailey's shirt, the yellow one with the blue parrots. And more than extending grace, the grandmother appears to be insisting on what is not real or true, as she has throughout the story. The touch expresses her final hope that her noblesse can alter her fate. But when she wishes upon a Misfit, she is likely to be murdered.

In a sense, O'Connor admitted that the grace she saw in the grandmother's touch could not have run deep. In a letter to John Hawkes, she restated and edited The Misfit's remarks: "She would have been a good woman if he had been there every moment of her life. True enough." Though O'Connor claims the grandmother's limitations do not prevent her from being an agent of Catholic grace, it seems a hard won and shaky grace indeed, dependent, as The Misfit says most precisely, on "somebody there to shoot her every minute of her life." And in death the grandmother smiles up with a child's face, still without comprehension.

Despite their obvious differences, The Misfit and the grandmother are bound by their concern with appearances and superficial respectability. The Misfit reddens when Bailey curses at the grandmother and adds "I don't reckon he meant to talk to you thataway." He admits he would prefer not to shoot a lady. He appears embarrassed when the family huddles in front of him. He apologizes: "I'm sorry I don't have on a shirt before you ladies." The grandmother dresses for accidents; The Misfit, for murders. He gets Bailey's shirt from Bobby Lee.

The power The Misfit has in the story resides not only in his gun and his violent sidekicks. He is energized by his keenness, his experience, his knowledge of evil. Though he claims to be confused about the extent of his own guilt, his view of human nature is certainly more direct than the view of the grandmother and her family. He is the opposite of the children's mother, "whose face was as broad and innocent as a cabbage ...." He has been many different things, including a gospel singer and an undertaker. He has been in a tornado and even says he has seen a woman flogged. He has the same "all or nothing" mentality of Flannery O'Connor herself, who said "I write from the standpoint of Christian orthodoxy." The Misfit says of Christ:

> "If He did what He said, then it's nothing for you to do but throw away everything and follow Him, and if He didn't, then it's nothing for you to do but enjoy the few minutes you got left the best way you can—by killing somebody or burning down his house or doing some other meanness to him. No pleasure but meanness."

While O'Connor clearly feels Christ is all, The Misfit thinks he is managing fine without Him. When The Misfit shoots the grandmother he is recoiling from whatever grace she offers. He is rejecting not just any warmth conveyed in the touch, but also the revolting world she represents and the repulsive notion that he is her child. With good reason, The Misfit is unwilling to be adopted by this grandmother.

Essentially, the story is a stronger indictment of the grandmother and her pathetic view of life than of The Misfit. It is no accident that the grandmother and her entire crew are killed off in the story: this family vacation was doomed from the outset. And it is with no small degree of pleasure that O'Connor finishes off this family. Her fictional world is basically satirical, not theological. She casts a plain and cold eye on a sorry sight, a real world, and renders it mercilessly. A mean pleasure sustains the satire and nourishes the reader. Though The Misfit finally decides "it's no real pleasure in life," there is pleasure in this story.

A personal wrath oozes from "A Good Man Is Hard to Find" and from most of O'Connor's fiction. The wrath is O'Connor's strength and her idealism, her refusal to believe the world around her was all. But apparently her anger left her with guilt enough to cause her to insist on an impossible reading of her own story. In her version a moment of kindness mixed with a plea for mercy would carry the day and push the massacred clan into the background, minimizing the survival of The Misfit.

The story reveals the hidden Flannery O'Connor glimpsed by Katherine Anne Porter. Porter was struck by the discrepancy between O'Connor's appearance and her fiction and suggested that the famous self-portrait with the peacock revealed an inner Flannery:

> Something you might not see on first or even second glance in that tenderly fresh-colored, young, smiling face; something she saw in herself, knew about herself, that she was trying to tell us in a way less personal, yet more vivid than words.
>
> That portrait, I'm trying to say, looked like the girl who wrote those blood-curdling stories about human evil—NOT the living Flannery, whistling to her peacocks, showing off her delightfully freakish breed of chickens.

The force of "A Good Man Is Hard to Find" speaks for an angry outsider, a person without illusions or sentimentality. The grandmother does not go to Florida, and O'Connor has her way. A world of propriety and illusion is laid low by wrath, not redeemed by grace.

**Source:** Kathleen G. Ochshorn, "A Cloak of Grace: Contradictions in 'A Good Man Is Hard to Find'," in *Studies in American Fiction,* Vol. 18, No. 1, Spring, 1990, pp. 113–17.

> "Despite their obvious differences, The Misfit and the grandmother are bound by their concern with appearances and superficial respectability."

## Sources

Brinkmeyer, Jr., Robert H. *The Art and Vision of Flannery O'Connor,* Louisiana State University Press, 1989.

Gordon, Caroline. "With a Glitter of Evil," in *The New York Times Book Review,* June 12, 1955, p. 5.

Hendin, Josephine. *The World of Flannery O'Connor,* Indiana University Press, 1970.

Kirk, Russell. "Flannery O'Connor and the Grotesque Face of God," in *The World and I,* Vol. 2, No. 1, January, 1987, pp. 429–33.

O'Connor, Flannery. *Flannery O'Connor: Mystery and Manners,* edited by Robert Fitzgerald and Sally Fitzgerald, Farrar, Straus and Giroux, 1957.

Orvell, Miles. *An Introduction to Flannery O'Connor,* University Press of Mississippi, 1991.

Rubin, Louis D., Jr. "Two Ladies of the South," in *Critical Essays on Flannery O'Connor,* edited by Melvin J. Friedman and Beverly Lyon Clark, G. K. Hall & Co., 1985, pp. 25–8.

## Further Reading

Asal, Frederick. *Flannery O'Connor: The Imagination of Extremity,* University of Georgia Press, 1982.
  Although the book discusses all her fiction, he devotes a section to "A Good Man Is Hard to Find," a story that "dramatizes a world radically off balance." Posits that the story is a good example of O'Connor's comic treatment to violent material.

Asal, Frederick, editor. *"A Good Man Is Hard to Find": Women Writers, Texts and Contexts,* Rutgers University Press, 1993.
  A useful book for those studying "A Good Man Is Hard to Find." Similar to Norton Critical Editions, this books contains an introduction to the story, the text itself, and many critical essays that explore the story's possible meanings.

Baumgaertner, Jill P. *Flannery O'Connor: A Proper Scaring,* Harold Shaw Publishers, 1988.
  Discusses primarily Flannery O'Connor's use of traditional Roman Catholic emblems in her fiction.

Coles, Robert. *Flannery O'Connor's South,* Louisiana State University Press, 1980.

This is a readable introduction to the author and her fiction, and as the title indicates, it focuses on her ties to her region.

Friedman, Melvin J., and Lewis A. Lawson, editors. *The Added Dimension: The Art and Mind of Flannery O'Connor,* Fordham University Press, 1977.

This volume contains a number of landmark essays by critics and fellow writers about O'Connor's work, as well as an interview, and provides a good summary of the early criticism on O'Connor.

Friedman, Melvin J., and Beverly Lyon Clark, editors. *Critical Essays on Flannery O'Connor.* G.K. Hall Publishing, 1985.

A diverse collection of essays about many aspects of Flannery O'Connor's fiction, from many well-known critics.

Grimshaw, Jr., James A. *The Flannery O'Connor Companion,* Greenwood Press, 1981.

Basic guide to O'Connor's works.

O'Connor, Flannery. *The Habit of Being: Letters of Flannery O'Connor,* edited by Sally and Robert Fitzgerald, Farrar, Straus, and Giroux, 1979.

Award-winning collection of Flannery O'Connor's letters to family, friends, and strangers.

# In the Cemetery Where Al Jolson Is Buried

Amy Hempel

1983

"In the Cemetery Where Al Jolson Is Buried" originally appeared in *TriQuarterly* magazine in 1983. It was reprinted in *Editors' Choice: New American Stories* before being included in Amy Hempel's first published collection of stories, *Reasons to Live,* in 1985. As her most anthologized story to date, "In the Cemetery" reflects Hempel's ability to blend pathos and comedy. In addition, critics praise Hempel for her poetic use of imagery and concise language that creates a short story filled with meaning. Hempel has compressed the narrative until every unnecessary and distracting detail has been squeezed out. This design allows the reader to impose meaning and order on the events rather than having the story control the reader's final response. Critics most often refer to this stylistic technique as "minimalism." For example, the central setting of "In the Cemetery" is presented as if it were a Hollywood movie set—a small detail that takes on great significance. The story was written as an assignment for a fiction workshop Hempel was taking in which she was instructed to write about "the thing you will never live down," she told Jo Sapp of the *Missouri Review.* Hempel's story about betraying a dying friend is dedicated to Jessica Wolfson, a friend who died of a terminal disease.

## Author Biography

Born December 14, 1951, in Chicago, Illinois, Amy Hempel moved to San Francisco as a teenager and attended several California colleges during an academic career that saw frequent interruptions. Deciding to become a writer, she settled in New York City and attended Columbia University where her creative writing instructor was Gordon Lish, a noted novelist, short story writer, and editor. Hempel credits Lish with having had a special influence on her work. She also names other contemporary short story writers such as Mary Robison and Raymond Carver as having affected her style. Hempel says that these writers "re-invent" the language, tell the truth in "shocking ways," and use "a kind of compression and distillation in their work that gets to the heart of things and that gives the reader credit for being able to keep up without having everything explained."

Although Hempel lives and works in New York City, most of her stories resound with the sounds and images of California. Some dramatic events in Hempel's short stories correspond with several of her own unhappy life experiences, which include traumatic car and motorcycle accidents, her mother's suicide, her father's mental illness, and the death of a close friend. In discussing "In the Cemetery Where Al Jolson Is Buried," for example, Hempel told Jo Sapp of the *Missouri Review* that although the dialogue of the story was completely fabricated, it is a true story that accurately reflects her relationship with her dying friend. Her stories have been translated into twelve languages and anthologized in the United States and several other countries. Hempel's literary awards include the Silver Medal from the Commonwealth Club of California for *Reasons to Live* and the *Best American Short Stories* Pushcart Prize. Her work regularly appears in such popular magazines as *Vanity Fair,* the *New York Times Magazine,* and *Vogue.* Hempel is the author of two collections of short stories: *Reasons to Live* which contains her most anthologized short story, "In the Cemetery Where Al Jolson Is Buried," and *At the Gates of the Animal Kingdom.*

## Plot Summary

The story opens with the unnamed narrator visiting her friend, who is also unnamed, in a hospital near Hollywood, California, where the friend is dying, presumably of cancer. The friend asks the narrator to "tell me things I won't mind forgetting." The things the narrator tells her friend are funny and light, items of trivia about the first tape recorder in America and the flying patterns of insects, things which may or may not be true. The friend is interested in hearing about the first chimp that was trained to talk until the narrator warns her that the outcome is sad, at which point the friend commands her to stop the story.

When the friend introduces the narrator to her nurse as "the Best Friend," the narrator is sufficiently attuned to language to note that her use of "the" here rather than "my" implies that in some way the friend views her connection with the nurse as actually being the closer bond now. Feeling guilty, the narrator ponders her reasons for waiting two months to come visit.

The doctor enters the hospital room and the friend flirts with him. Like the nurse, he also seems to have a closer relationship with the friend than does the narrator; he is the "Good Doctor" because he makes jokes about death and disease with her and is "a little in love with her." He suggests that the narrator go to the nearby beach so that he can be alone with her.

At the beach the narrator muses on other forms of danger, recalling a time in college when the two of them thought they could forestall an earthquake by repeating "earthquake, earthquake, earthquake" because "it never happens when you're thinking about it." The verbal repetition, however did nothing to prevent an aftershock during a 1972 earthquake the friends witnessed as college roommates. This thought foreshadows the friend's impending death: she will continue with her joking references to death, attempting to ward it off, until she dies.

The narrator returns from watching teenagers displaying "aggressive health" on the beach to find a second bed in the room, a bed, she realizes, put there so that she can spend the night. She rattles off more trivia for her friend and they watch a movie together lying side by side while eating ice cream. They achieve their former closeness for a moment when the narrator feels sleepy from the injection given to the friend. The two drift off to sleep, but the narrator dreams her friend has decorated her house in festive streamers. When she wakes, her fear overpowers her compassion and she tells her friend, "I have to go home."

Though she feels "weak and small and failed," she also feels "exhilarated" by imagining her escape back to her convertible and visiting trendy Malibu restaurants. The friend throws a fit upon realizing the narrator is leaving, yanking off her protective mask and running out of the room.

The next mention of the friend is when she is "moved to the cemetery, the one where Al Jolson is buried." Although not stated directly, it seems likely that the narrator has never been back to visit. Addressing the death in this fashion allows her to avoid acknowledging that her friend has died: instead her use of language lets her focus on and highlight the fact that Al Jolson is buried in the cemetery in question; he is the one she can accept being dead.

The narrator enrolls in a "Fear of Flying" class that same day. She also finishes the story about the chimpanzee that her friend did not want to hear. The chimp used sign language to communicate with its baby. Even after the baby dies, the chimp attempts to communicate with it, "fluent now in the language of grief."

*Amy Hempel*

## Characters

### Dying Friend

This unnamed woman is the friend whom the narrator visits in the hospital. Her request to the narrator to "tell me things I won't mind forgetting," sets the story in motion. The woman was the narrator's best friend, but her feeling of betrayal is revealed when she introduces the narrator to her nurse as "the Best Friend." The woman is making a concerted effort to deal with her mortality, illustrated by her attempt to engage her friend in a conversation about Elisabeth Kubler-Ross's theory of the psychology of death. Like the narrator, she also uses ironic humor to help defuse the tension of their meeting, like when she wraps a telephone cord around her neck and proclaims it "the end o' the line." However, when her wish that her friend spend the night is rebuffed, the woman is so overwhelmed by the act of abandonment that she tears off her protective face mask and stumbles out of the room. Though the main thrust of the story is the narrator's fear of death, this action—an immense strain on the woman's frail and sickly body—underscores her own psychological pain. Nevertheless, like the earthquake the two roommates hoped to forestall but were unable to prevent, the woman is eventually "moved to the cemetery," a euphemistic way of saying that she has died.

### Narrator

The main character in "In the Cemetery Where Al Jolson Is Buried" is the unnamed narrator who relates the story in first person. While paying a long-overdue visit to a dying friend in the hospital, the narrator muses about her shame and guilt in neglecting a friend in need. Though the narrator seems aware of her fear of death, her fear prevents her from discussing the topic openly. Instead, she seems fixated on grotesque images, like earthquakes and a man who dies of fright after seeing his mutilated arm. Alternately, the narrator uses humor as a form of denial, like when she reads an item from the newspaper about a man who robs a bank with a chicken. Her fears culminate when she realizes her friend wants her to spend the night, it hits her "like an open coffin.... She wants my life." Even after her friend dies, she refuses to confront the situation. She says only that her friend "was moved to the cemetery." In her attempt to confront her fear, she enrolls in a "fear of flying" class, admitting, in part, that she is a fearful person, but still refusing to confront death. The narrator, in her honesty, admits her superficiality by saying that she remembers "only the useless things I hear.... Nothing else seeps through." By the end of the story, however, the narrator returns to the story about a chimpanzee who uses sign language in an attempt to communicate with her dead child. In stating that the animal had become "fluent now in the language of grief," the narrator has confronted a topic that had previously upset her, thereby showing the character's growth. By telling her story anonymously, the narrator is able to relate details that she might otherwise hesitate to reveal. The story is both a confession and a way for her to come to terms with her fear of dying, and the narrator's anonymity allows the reader to identify with her process of catharsis.

## Themes

"In the Cemetery Where Al Jolson Is Buried" begins with the narrator's reluctant visit to a dying friend but evolves into an elegy for the terminally-ill woman and a confession of the narrator's own fear of dying.

### Fear of Death

Readers never know exactly what illness the sick friend dies of or precisely what her symptoms are; therefore, the major focus of the story is on the women's verbal, behavioral, and psychological responses in confronting their own mortality. The one is dying, the other (the narrator) is observing both her friend's behavior and her own reactions to the phenomenon of death.

The dying woman engages in trivial conversation and ghoulish jokes in dealing with her situation. For example, she loops a phone cord around her neck and exclaims "end o' the line." She also wants something specific from the visiting friend when she has a second bed placed in the room. The expectation of spending the night with her dying friend "hit me like an open coffin.... She wants my life."

Conscious of her situation, the dying woman mentions Swiss psychiatrist Elisabeth Kubler-Ross's five stages of accepting death. She wants to know why Kubler-Ross left out Resurrection; "God knows, I want to do it by the book," she says. The narrator, however, remains silent, in the denial stage herself, even though she knows the other stages; she cannot bring herself to speak to her friend directly about death.

Kubler-Ross found that many dying patients are comforted if someone sits and listens to their openly expressed fears and thoughts. She also observed that many dying patients, after the shock of learning their condition, go through five psychological stages: denial, anger, bargaining, grieving, and acceptance. Patients may be assisted in reaching acceptance by the hospital staff's and family's openly talking about death when the patient so desires. In the denial stage, the patient refuses to recognize reality and acts as if the disease does not exist. The patient may then become angry, resenting others who enjoy good health and blaming doctors and relatives for their inability to help. In the bargaining stage the patient tries to "buy time," often in the form of prayers asking for "one more year," in return for being a better person. This psychological stage, which is usually brief, is followed by the first true recognition of reality, and the patient then enters the stage of grief or depression, mourning the loss of his or her own life. In the final stage of acceptance, the patient may still be fearful and angry but is now prepared to die with peace and dignity. This story appears to chart this process both in the dying woman and in her friend who fears death but appears to accept her fear by the end of the story when she relates the sad ending of the chimpanzee's story.

### Friendship

"In the Cemetery" explores the theme of friendship by showing the strain the terminal illness has placed on the women's relationship. The narrator feels guilty when introduced as the generic "Best Friend," a label that indicates the withering of their closeness. "So how come, I'll bet they're wondering, it took me so long to get to such a glamorous place?... Two months, and how long is the drive?" the narrator asks herself, realizing that her absence is a betrayal of their friendship. The implication is that the fearful narrator took too long coming to the side of her dying friend and, once there, will not stay until the end. In its final form, the story also alludes to the friendship between Amy Hempel and the now deceased Jessica Wolfson, whom Hempel promised to write a story about and to whom the story is dedicated.

### Language and Meaning

Inappropriate language is often a symptom of denial. During a time of extreme sadness or danger, people will often tell jokes and talk about trivial things. The dying friend insists on such a dialogue immediately, "Tell me things I won't mind forgetting," she says, in acknowledgment that she will not be around long enough to have to remember anything meaningful. At the end of the story, the narrator's language similarly indicates her denial of her friend's death. Her friend is simply "moved to the cemetery," as if she had simply changed apartments or moved across town. The only fear that she admits to having is a fear of flying. However, her fear of death permeates her actions and thoughts while with her friend. She thinks of a story told to her by a friend who used to work in a mortuary. A man in a car accident was scared to death by the sight of his injured arm. Even though the tale does not pertain directly to her dying friend, it symbolizes how obsessed with death the narrator is.

## Style

### Narrative Voice

"In the Cemetery Where Al Jolson Is Buried" is told in the first-person point of view by an unidentified female narrator. At times the voice telling this story seems to move into a narrative technique known as stream-of-consciousness—the literary attempt to reproduce the pattern of a mind in unchecked thought, simultaneously moving in multiple levels of awareness, issuing an uninterrupted flow of sensations, thoughts, memories, associations, and reflections. This is shown in part by her questions to herself, like "Two months, and how long is the drive."

### Setting

Symbolic in the story's Southern California setting is the idea that the narrator's situation is merely a play or a television show in which she is acting. The hospital, which is near Hollywood, is likened to the one on the television series "Marcus Welby, MD," and a camera guards the sick woman's room. Conscious that she is being filmed, the narrator states "I had my audience," in further recognition of the metaphor. Her tales about insignificant things take on the aura of a performance. "Off camera," she says, further painting a portrait of California, "there is a beach across the street."

### Black Humor

Black humor is comedy of a situational or conversational nature that concentrates on morose

## Topics for Further Study

- What narrative function does the beach scene serve in the story? Does it seem out of place? Why?
- Why does the narrator refuse to stay with her dying friend? What roles do motivation and plot play in the reader's understanding of the narrator's reluctance?
- How does the detail about earthquakes and fear of earthquakes relate to the central concern of the story?
- How does the vignette about the chimpanzee serve as a metaphor for the story as a whole?

themes. In a black comedy, an author will frequently make fun of things of a serious nature, such as illness, death, or disease. In this story, the narrator uses black humor in an effort to ease her fear of death. And the sick woman, ironically, uses it to put her friend at ease, too, like when she wraps the phone cord around her neck or exclaims, "Oh, you're killing me." A further irony in the story is the metaphor of the hospital as a television set, a place for actors. The narrator and her friend assume the role of actors, yet their situation is real.

### Parable

A parable is a story that teaches a lesson. Within "In the Cemetery" is the story about the chimpanzee who learns sign language. In the parable, the mother chimp lies twice when asked "who did it on the desk." This conscious misdirection of language parallels the pattern of distortion found in the trivial dialogue exchanged by the two women. They refuse to confront death, and in effect their idle conversation is a form of "lie" in which they are protecting themselves from pain. At the end of the story, the narrator relates that the chimpanzee's signed request to her dead child is "Baby, come hug, Baby, come hug." The chimp has become "fluent now in the language of grief." By relating this parable, the narrator has also learned to examine her grief, rather than ignore it.

### Catharsis

The process of writing this story and dedicating it to her deceased friend can be said to be a catharsis for the author. In writing about "the thing which you will never live down," Hempel has confronted her feelings of guilt and abandonment at a time when her friend needed her most. The process of expressing such pent-up feelings is known as "catharsis," and is often done to relieve the teller of carrying such a psychological burden.

## Historical Context

### California in the 1980s

Hempel's writing, particularly her stories in *Reasons to Live*, evoke a lifestyle that is Californian in nature. Despite the fact that they were written in New York, most of her stories take place on the West coast, including "In the Cemetery Where Al Jolson Is Buried." Hempel frequently uses cultural references as touchstones for her readers, knowing they will understand what a "Marcus Welby" hospital looks like, or that country singer Tammy Wynette recorded a song called "Stand by Your Man." In doing so, she places her writing firmly in a modern, American context. *Marcus Welby, MD,* a television show starring Robert Young, aired from 1969 to 1976, would be remembered by almost anyone who had been in college during the early 1970s, as the narrator and her friend were. This American setting is further reinforced by her references to California beaches, the narrator's convertible, and a Malibu restaurant that serves "papaya and shrimp and watermelon ice." In the works of contemporary authors Bret Easton Ellis, Joan Didion, and others, a similar California landscape is presented, often with the intention of painting a portrait of a culture that is concerned only with outward appearances and only with the moment—two characteristics that many would say are indicative of American culture in the late twentieth century.

Hempel's vignette regarding the chimpanzee who learned sign language evokes the study regarding Koko, a gorilla who learned sign language in the early 1970s at Stanford University. Koko's ability to communicate in American Sign Language with human beings was not only an important scientific breakthrough during that time, but she also became a sort of folk hero, especially for those who had always suspected that animals possessed intelligence. By placing a similar story within "In the Cemetery," Hempel further plays upon her readers' familiarity with current events.

Other references made by the narrator in the story serve as a type of shorthand. A reader familiar with Elisabeth Kubler-Ross, whose book *On Death and Dying* was published in 1969, will understand the characters' discussion of her stages of grief. Using such a tactic allows the author to accomplish a great deal with few words, effectively relying on the reader's knowledge of contemporary culture. Lastly, by referring to American jazz singer Al Jolson in the title, Hempel helps establish the story's American context even before it begins. In the United States, and particularly in California, places often come to be identified with their connections to the rich and famous. Thus, the cemetery where the narrator's friend is "moved to" is not notable for its name, but for the fact that a famous person, Al Jolson, is buried there.

## Critical Overview

"In the Cemetery Where Al Jolson Is Buried" was frequently cited by critics as one of Hempel's strongest stories in her first collection, *Reasons to Live*. In discussing her sparse, minimalist style, critics often pointed to details in the story like the metaphor of a Hollywood set as the forum for a discussion on death. Discussing the book as a whole, Sybil Steinberg, reviewing the collection for *Publishers Weekly*, described the stories as "debuting a familiar contemporary hard edge, but a surprisingly sentimental and moving interior." Just two years after *Reasons to Live* was published, "In the Cemetery" was included in the prestigious classroom textbook *The Norton Anthology of Short Fiction*.

Though Hempel prefers to call herself a "miniaturist" rather than a minimalist, many critics continue to categorize her as a minimalist. However, since many critics view the minimalist style as outdated, this has put an unfavorable spin on her work. One such critic, Brad Hooper, sees Hempel's stories as "marked by a brevity of exposition and economy of style that verge on the starved." Usually written in the first person and present tense with few details, leaving much of the story's meaning implied, Hempel's prose is, indeed, minimalist in a strict sense of the word. Yet, setting Hempel apart from other practitioners of the form, such as Ernest Hemingway, is her use of humor. Eleanor Wachtel, a noted Canadian radio-journalist, per-

*Al Jolson's gravesite in a California cemetery.*

ceives Hempel's stories as "full of wry scraps of philosophy—more than one-liners, they're ironic twists on one's expectations." Readers who enjoy Hempel's brief stories generally identify her as a frugal writer who manifests a quirky humor and bleak worldview. Most readers see her fictional realm as one of sadness and bittersweet consolation, a world of natural catastrophe, highway accidents, insanity, and death. In 1988, Michael Schumacher began his live interview of Hempel by insisting to his audience that "if you have any intention of understanding the short fiction of Amy Hempel, pain is where you start."

The majority of critical response to Hempel's short fiction appears in the form of book reviews in which the critics praise Hempel's style and stories. Sheila Ballantyne, writing for the *New York Times Book Review,* describes Hempel's fiction as "tough-minded, original and fully felt" with "feelings always contained, never explicit." In a later review for the same publication, Michiko Kakutani notes that Hempel portrays her characters "with charity and understanding." Writing in *New Directions for Women,* Marcia Tager characterizes these brief stories as "snapshots" and "splinters of reality." In effect, critics agree that Hempel's foremost skill is her ability to compress as much into a single sentence as possible.

## Criticism

### Judy Sobeloff

*Judy Sobeloff is a writer and educator who has won several awards for her fiction. In the following essay, she discusses the aspects of minimalism inherent in "In the Cemetery Where Al Jolson Is Buried."*

What is most striking about "In the Cemetery Where Al Jolson Is Buried," widely considered one of Amy Hempel's finest and most moving stories, is its compression and its pain. The writing here is terse; much is left out. The parts left out are what give the story its emotional power. This same minimalist style is apparent in the other stories in Hempel's first collection, *Reasons to Live,* and in her second, *At the Gates of the Animal Kingdom,* as well. "In the Cemetery" weighs in as one of the longest stories in either book, some of which are only a page or two in length. The other stories, too,

## What Do I Read Next?

- *At the Gates of the Animal Kingdom,* Hempel's second collection of short stories, which includes the well-received story about writing stories, "Harvest."

- *Less than Zero,* Bret Easton Ellis's 1985 novel about youth in California, whose unexamined lives have tragic consequences.

- "The Jilting of Granny Weatherall," Katherine Anne Porter's 1929 story about a dying woman troubled by her past; written in first-person, stream-of-consciousness narrative.

- *Will You Please Be Quiet, Please?,* the earliest of Raymond Carver's collection of short stories and the first fiction to which literary critics applied the term "minimalism."

- "Hills Like White Elephants," Ernest Hemingway's minimalist short story about a couple at a crossroads in their relationship. Like "In the Cemetery," their strongest feelings go unspoken.

- *Days,* the initial collection of short stories written by Mary Robison, whose early creative writing efforts were directed by Gordon Lish, and who was a classmate of Hempel's.

- *Coming to Terms with the Short Story,* edited by Susan Lohafer. This collection of essays by renowned short story critics is a treasure of information about the short story as a genre and its role as the "stepchild of literature."

---

focus predominantly on characters struggling with loss and grief.

Minimalism in American literature can be traced back to the early works of Ernest Hemingway, who believed that what is stated overtly in a story should be just the "tip of the iceberg." In his 1964 book, *A Moveable Feast,* he proposed a "new theory that you could omit anything if you knew that you omitted and the omitted parts would strengthen the story and make people feel something more than they understood." In "In the Cemetery," what is omitted is key: The narrator does not discuss her friend's impending death with her then or ever; in fact, after the narrator leaves the hospital, the next mention of the friend is that she was "moved to the cemetery." Discussion of the friend's death, before and after the fact, is completely omitted from the story.

The credo of the contemporary minimalist movement, according to critic Arthur Saltzman, is delineated best by Raymond Carver in his essay "On Writing": "It's possible, in a poem or short story, to write about commonplace things and objects using commonplace but precise language, and to endow those things—a chair, a window curtain, a fork, a stone, a woman's earring—with immense, even startling power."

Certain objects in "In the Cemetery" do carry enormous weight—the friend's leg "you did not want to see," her mask with the bottom strings hanging loose, the second bed—but the real "immense, even startling power" of "In the Cemetery" comes from its use of commonplace language to talk about—or rather, to not talk about—devastating aspects of human experience.

Carver's essay was published in 1983, at the height of minimalism's popularity, the same year "In the Cemetery" first appeared in *TriQuarterly* magazine. A debate over the merits of minimalism eventually ensued, which, using the words of Saltzman, can be framed thus: is minimalism giving us the essence of human experience, "the richness of a glimpse," or does minimalism so boil down the world that it "loses the broth?" Though the style remains controversial, Hempel's critics praise her precision: "Reading Hempel is like reading a heart-stopping telegram," critic Marcia Tager wrote about *Reasons to Live.*

Just as the narrator of "In the Cemetery" abandons her dying friend, many of the other stories in *Reasons to Live* feature characters struggling to cope, characters whose responses to death also seem odd or somehow misguided. In "Nashville Gone to Ashes," the narrator, who has lost both her husband and her dog, realizes that she feels jealous of her pets, that she had to compete with them for her husband's love. The narrator of "San Francisco," a younger sister who had been the one to discover her mother's dead body, now derives satisfaction from tormenting her older sister who wants the mother's watch. In "Going" the narrator has a car accident on flat, dry road that "knocked two days out of [his] head," and "can't even remember all [he's] forgotten"; only in the last paragraph does the reader learn that his mother has died, that somehow the crash and the death are connected.

In "Beg, Sl Tog, Inc, Cont, Rep," the relationship between the two female characters is reminiscent of the relationship between the narrator and her friend in "In the Cemetery," but in "Beg, Sl Tog" the circumstances are reversed; this time the narrator, rather than the friend, is the one directly suffering. The narrator, who has had an abortion, ceases all activity except knitting sweaters for the friend, who is pregnant: "an excess of sweaters—a kind of precaution, a rehearsal against disaster." The narrator in "Beg, Sl Tog" has nightmares, and then accidents—"but the part that hurt was never the part that got hurt." In a sense this narrator seems to be paying penance for the friendship betrayed in "In the Cemetery." Although the immediate situation here (the friend's pregnancy) is ostensibly a joyous one, in this story, too, the narrator fails to support her friend: upon hearing that the friend has given birth, for example, the narrator stops in at the nursery briefly to see that the newborn was there and then "went straight home." Like the narrator in "In the Cemetery" who is able to offer her friend only trivia, this narrator is able to offer her friend only sweaters, many more sweaters than the baby could possibly wear.

Like "In the Cemetery," the other stories in this collection display the classic characteristics of minimalism: plots that play out over a narrow time frame; simple language; short, declarative, present-tense sentences; and first-person narrators. While Hempel's characters are rarely the societal outcasts who populate much of minimalist fiction, their lives do tend to be consistent with another dominant minimalist theme: the rootlessness and shallowness of contemporary American existence. Everyone on

> "Hempel's characters tend to be consistent with another dominant minimalist theme: the rootlessness and shallowness of contemporary American existence."

the beach in "In the Cemetery" is "tranquilized, numb or asleep"; the narrator wants only to jump in her convertible and drive it "too fast down the coast highway," away from her friend and the site of the pain.

The stories in Hempel's second collection display many of these same minimalist characteristics, and again many of the characters struggle to cope with loss. A difference in this collection, though, is the occasional presence of an authorial intrusion, an attribute generally not associated with minimalism. Every now and then the first person narrator makes a comment that sounds more like a reflection from an author looking in on the story than the thoughts of a character looking out. At the end of "And Lead Us Not Into Penn Station," after reeling off a dozen or so anecdotes about the violence and despair of urban existence, the narrator (who sounds like the author speaking) stops: "I don't know what to say about this. *I* am as cut off from meaning and completion as all of these crippled people."

Whether or not the first person narrator in Hempel's second collection is at times Hempel herself, Hempel admits that her work is very autobiographical. What is immediately apparent in comparing "In the Cemetery" to written accounts of Hempel's own life is the distinctive similarities between the two. In an interview with Michael Schumacher, Hempel acknowledges that her best friend died when Hempel was a college student in California; like the narrator in "In the Cemetery," not only did Hempel not attend the funeral, she "barely made it to the hospital."

In fact, it was after the death of her best friend that Hempel left California for New York, enrolled in a writing class with Gordon Lish, and wrote "In the Cemetery," which later became her first published story, in response to Lish's directive to write about an instance of personal failure.

Despite Hempel's move to New York, California remains the natural choice for the setting of her work. The narrator of "In the Cemetery" worries about earthquakes when she goes to the beach. In California, says Hempel, "it's very easy to have your worst fears made tangible in the form of natural disaster." California works well as a setting for other reasons, too. *New York Times* literary critic Michiko Kakutani compares Hempel to Joan Didion for her use of "the tacky, ahistorical landscape of Southern California, with its parking garages, fake Spanish colonial condominiums and fast-food joints." Note the flamingo pink wrought-iron terraces of the Palm Royale, where the narrator of "In the Cemetery" stops for the newspaper and observes graffiti in the lobby which she later quotes to her friend. Hollywood fiction is a genre in itself that can be traced back to America's movement westward, based on a vision of Hollywood born of "external success and inner failure," according to critic Jonas Spatz. Certainly this applies to the narrator of "In the Cemetery," whose need to make everything look all right on the outside despite deep feelings of inner failure, can be seen toward the end of the story when she muses, "It is just possible I will say I stayed the night. And who is there that can say I did not?"

Before she leaves the hospital the narrator sees how she has let language transform their relationship, referring to herself mockingly as "The Best Friend" when she makes her decision to leave. While she felt slighted by her friend's earlier use of the impersonal article "the," now she does not even feel worthy of it. When the friend dies, the narrator shields herself from having to acknowledge this reality by saying only that she was "moved to the cemetery."

"In the Cemetery" is ultimately a story about the limits of language. Like the mother chimp who is trained to sign, the narrator and her friend train themselves to speak only in trivia—like signing, an alternate and artificial form of language—to speak only about things that do not matter. The substitution here of trivia for what is real renders the story the ideal minimalist marriage of form and content: one-liners substitute for authentic communication, and what is omitted, to harken back to Hemingway, becomes most important of all. Like the protective mask that the friend ultimately flings off in rage, this artificial language can shield the characters from—but never prevent—the threat of the friend's imminent death.

Just as the mother chimp continues to sign to her dead baby, the narrator continues her reliance on trivia after the friend dies. This, in fact, becomes all she can do, the only way she can think. She remembers "only the useless things" she hears. After the loss of their loved ones, both the mother chimp and the narrator keep up their ineffectual, meaningless language, unable to stop, "fluent now in the language of grief."

**Source:** Judy Sobeloff, for *Short Stories for Students,* Gale Research, 1997.

### Robert Peltier

*Robert Peltier is an English instructor at Trinity College and has published works of both fiction and nonfiction. In the following essay, he discusses the nature of truth as it is regarded by the characters in this ''postmodern'' story, ultimately stating that the narrator's belief in her ''language of grief'' is a lie.*

Beneath the wisecracking humor and even beneath the despair and fear in Amy Hempel's "In the Cemetery Where Al Jolson Is Buried," there is a deeper bleakness that is both dangerous and forgiving. In fact, the danger springs from forgiving: forgiving oneself for reprehensible behavior because we live in a postmodern world where nothing much matters anyway. There are no truths, there is no meaning to life, there is only death at the end, so what could possibly matter? The danger that springs from this kind of thinking is obvious in this story and, for that matter, in much of the world it reflects. The danger is that we exist in a world that is precarious in its lack of real compassion and fueled by a fear of all that is not material. The danger manifests itself as a detachment from the world of human connection. The narrator in this story has not been able to bring herself to visit her best friend in the hospital for two months; her fear has been stronger than her sense of decency. Judging from the language they use to "communicate" with each other, there has never been much depth in their friendship, and the sick friend should have, and probably did, expect the narrator's lack of emotions except fear and repulsion. The narrator wants only to get away from this dying person and drive fast and go somewhere where there is palpable life.

"Tell me things I won't mind forgetting," the narrator's sick friend says in the opening lines of the story. "Make it useless stuff or skip it." The friend is dying, of course, so why *not* make it "useless stuff?" Yet, if we take the broad view, we are all dying. Thus, using the friend's logic, none of us needs more than "useless stuff." The implications of such a philosophy are much bleaker than a superficial reading of the story would lead one to believe. This line of reasoning leaves no room for commitment to another, for instance. There is no reason to think or feel deeply about anything. And there is no need for the "useless stuff" to be true. Was Bing Crosby the first American to own a tape recorder? Do insects get wet? We don't need to look these "facts" up in an encyclopedia, because Hempel's narrator tell us immediately that they do not matter by telling us something obviously untrue: that the moon is shaped like a banana. It is not so much that lies and truths are mixed in our lives, but that there are no real truths at all. One story is as good as another.

But how does this attitude affect human relationships? If everything is "useless," what is the point of forming relationships? If there is only death, what difference does it make what we do in life? Despairing postmodernism rears up in this story and answers: Do not care about things or people or truths or lies, because it is all going to disappear someday and the caring will make it painful.

Hempel's narrator amplifies this theme when she talks about the chimpanzee who lied: "when they asked her who did it on the desk, she signed back the name of the janitor." By illustrating how nature itself is dishonest, the narrator seems to be rationalizing her own dishonesty. If nature—and by extension, God—is false, then there really is nothing to believe in.

Notice how nervous the narrator gets when she realizes that there is a camera focused on her and her friend. It causes her to stop talking even though there is no microphone to pick up what she is saying. This disturbing intrusion is the one element in the story that suggests that perhaps there is objective truth, that somewhere—even if it is only at the nurse's station—we are held accountable and judged for our actions. But, since the narrator stops only momentarily, the idea is scrapped and the narrator continues telling her "stories." We must assume that the narrator's nervousness is unwarranted, that the camera's observations are as false as any other observer's and worthy of no more consideration.

> "Suntan oil and sand and surgical masks and oxygen tubes exist all in the same world, and part of the maturation process is understanding how this can be so."

---

Even the hospital must somehow be distanced from objective reality, and so the two friends "call this place the Marcus Welby Hospital." Naming it after a television show on which people only pretend to be sick and more rarely only pretend to die, they further distance themselves from the reality of death. Further extending the metaphor, the narrator indicates that the hospital is situated across the street from a beach, a juxtaposition unknown to the television audience because it occurs "off camera." More falsehoods, for who would attempt to explain to television viewers that a beach and a hospital *can* and, in fact, *do* exist in close proximity?

The narrator alludes to the irony in this, but seems incapable of understanding it. Suntan oil and sand and surgical masks and oxygen tubes exist all in the same world, and part of the maturation process is understanding how this can be so. But the narrator does not deepen her understanding. Instead, she and her friend merge the beach and the hospital into the "make believe" hospital that is more suited to their individual needs and their needs as a couple of friends.

The narrator, who is "the Best Friend," has not visited her friend even though she has been in this hospital for two months, and it is her inability to accept this reality that has kept her away. She tells a story of a story that was told to her—a tale now twice removed from reality—about a man who was frightened to death by the grossness of an injury he received in a car wreck. He looked at his injured arm, slashed to the bone, and died of fright. The narrator does not want "to look any closer" at her friend although she considers that she is now doing just that merely by being in the hospital with her. She avoids the close look by making jokes and reciting odd "facts" that may or may not be true, "and hoping that [she] will live through" the visit. She has stayed away from her friend because she is afraid that looking at a reality she normally pretends does not exist will drag her into the abyss. This pathetic weakness has kept her from comforting a person who is dying, a person who is supposedly her closest friend. Now she has overcome that weakness, but only to the degree that she can joke with her friend; a real meaningful connection between them never takes place. Their communication remains superficial; it would be too dangerous otherwise.

They talk about Elisabeth Kubler-Ross, a doctor who has researched death and dying, but as the sick friend says, Kubler-Ross "left out Resurrection." She immediately laughs, however, and the narrator clings "to the sound [of her laughter] the way someone dangling above a ravine holds fast to the thrown rope." If her friend can laugh at death without the hope of resurrection, then death must not really exist. Or, at least, it must not be so hard to face.

When the "good doctor" comes in, the narrator seems to be justifying her detachment by pointing up the doctor's humor *and* her friend's humor. "God didn't give epileptics a fair shake," the doctor says. But the doctor is not "the best friend" and thus is not encouraged to develop a close emotional relationship with his patient. In fact, many doctors purposely distance themselves from their patients not because they are callused or cold, but because of the pain such temporary and ultimately tragic relationships can inflict.

Why not keep it light? Why not joke? There is nothing wrong with humor, but when that humor acts as a curtain behind which deeper feelings are hidden and kept from influencing decent behavior, then that humor can be harmful. When the sick friend says "I feel like hell. I'm about to stop having fun," the narrator becomes almost manic in her attempts to talk about anything but the horror of her friend's situation. She quotes from graffiti and from a newspaper trivia column, and the odd mixture is full of half-truths, exaggerations and outright lies. Eskimos do not need refrigerators to keep their food from freezing; it is childish to believe that all Eskimos live in igloos in a permanently frozen wasteland. And the possibility that "the smell of barbecue sauce" led to the capture of a bank robber is slim (and ludicrous). But the stories have, at least for the moment, done their dirty job: they have signaled the sick friend that she is not to speak of "feeling like hell" again and that her true feelings serve only to push her friend if they are articulated.

But this brush with reality has, apparently, been too much for the narrator. She will not stay the night. She wants to leave, to drive fast to a place where she can drink wine and "shimmer with lust, buzz with heat, vibrate with life, and stay up all night." While one can sympathize with such longings—they are not at all uncommon in the face of death—one cannot condone the narrator's abandonment of her friend, especially when that friend is so traumatized by her friend's rejection that she leaves her isolation room and runs to hide in a supply closet. The narrator, the "best friend," can only watch from the doorway as the nurses rub their patient's back, applying the human touch of which the narrator is incapable.

In the end, after the sick friend has been "moved to the cemetery," the narrator wishes only to remember useless things that she hears. As with the useless things that she once told her friend, she makes no distinction between what is true and what is false, because in a postmodern philosophy (one might say that postmodernism is actually a lack of *any* philosophy) there is no difference and it does not matter. It was not Bob Dylan's mother who invented Wite-Out; it was Monkee Mike Nesmith's mother. The truth of this trivia is not important because truth is merely an irrelevant abstraction in the face of death.

The narrator comforts herself by saying that "it is just possible I will say I stayed the night. And who is there that can say that I did not?" In a world that makes no distinction between truth and lies, she has justified her lack of compassion and decency and—perhaps most disturbing of all—she claims to have gained a knowledge of grief. The most loathsome moment in the story comes at the end when she tells the story of the birth of a baby to that *other* liar, the talking chimp. The baby dies and the mother chimp "signs" to her baby over and over, "fluent now in the language of grief." The parallel between the chimp and the narrator is not just strained, it is entirely false. The narrator has *not* learned the language of grief and will not until she breaks through the barrier of postmodern detachment.

**Source:** Robert Peltier, for *Short Stories for Students,* Gale Research, 1997.

## Amy Hempel with Jo Sapp

*In the following interview, which was conducted in cooperation with the American Prose Library on November 6, 1991, Sapp discusses Hempel's approach to writing fiction, especially the story "In the Cemetery Where Al Jolson Is Buried," which was one of the first stories Hempel ever wrote.*

[Interviewer]: *Many of our readers know your work, but not much about your life. Can you fill us in on your background?*

[Hempel]: I was born in Chicago in 1951, and lived in and around the city till third grade, I think. After that I lived in Denver for eight years, then moved to San Francisco for about twelve years, then to New York where I live now. I was happy to leave California because I was traumatized by the earthquakes. On the positive side, I moved to work in publishing.

*Where did you go to college?*

I had a nonlinear college education. I went to five different colleges and universities in California, where I majored in journalism and took many incompletes. My college time was interrupted by accidents and any number of things going on that took precedence over sitting in class. I went from accident to accident, hospital to hospital; I'd walk out of the house in the morning and half look up to see when the Mosler safe was going to fall out of the sky and smash me into the sidewalk. I used to refer to my twenties as "the lost years," and then I realized it was research. During this time I kept journals, as I had for a long time. My impulse was to note and save things that struck me. It wasn't "Today I did this, today I did that." It was a journal of things people said. When I started writing fiction in my early thirties, I found myself cannibalizing the journals from my twenties. My first book, *Reasons to Live,* came from all of that turmoil. It's no secret that pain teaches. It makes you think, "How can I get myself through this? And this. And this."

*Did you find the same kind of solution that your characters often do? Did you laugh?*

I didn't do a lot of laughing at the time. I looked for small victories. The stories in *Reasons to Live*—my god, what a lofty title—but really, the reasons in many of the stories are pretty small. That's okay. It doesn't have to be any big deal as long as it will pull you through.

*Your narrators and central characters have wonderful defense systems. Quite often they're placed in situations where they're either going ot laugh or cry, and end up doing a little of both.*

Doctors often have the darkest sense of humor. They have to, don't they? I spent a lot of time in hospitals where I picked some of that up. There's a way in which you can make the readers laugh until suddenly they're crying, and they don't know what hit them. It's a very purposeful kind of manipulation. . . .

*Is it true that you wrote all of the stories in* Reasons to Live *as part of [a workshop with writer Gordon Lish]?*

I wrote quite a few of them, not all of them, as workshop "assignments." The only real assignment that he ever gave in the Columbia workshop was to write up our most terrible, despicable secret, "The thing you will never live down." I knew instantly what that was. I'd failed my best friend at the moment when I absolutely couldn't fail her, when she was dying. I wrote that story, my first, called "In the Cemetery Where Al Jolson Is Buried," over the thirteen weeks of the class. There is not a word of dialogue in that story that either one of us ever said, yet it's a true story.

*Would you say that most of your stories are true, in that sense?*

I almost always work from something that actually happened as a point of departure. I resent the notion that observation is something less than imagination, that if you didn't fashion something out of your head it's somehow not art. In this respect, having studied journalism for some time was extremely useful, because I brought that to fiction. The pressure I put on myself from journalistic concerns served my fiction as well; in writing about things that had in fact happened, I reported on them. . . .

*A lot of times what's not reported in your work is more important than what actually appears on the page. Frequently the emotional focus of the story is some underlying event that may not be described or even referred to in the story.*

I don't have any great interest in the sort of dramatic writing that would be necessary to give you the wreck, the murder, the whatever. I come in when the people are sitting around later with their heads in their hands, just looking around the room, saying "Now what?" One of the nicest comments on that point came from William Kennedy, who told me, "You leave out all the right things." Well, yes, I'm trying to leave out those things. What's not there supports what is there.

> **There's a way in which you can make the readers laugh until suddenly they're crying, and they don't know what hit them. It's a very purposeful kind of manipulation.**

---

*What are some of the things that you left out of "In the Cemetery Where Al Jolson Is Buried"?*

I left out some of her anger at me. I was convicting myself. I wanted to be the one who had failed, who had done things wrong, not my dying friend. I didn't want her to appear to be the bitch that she sometimes was, because I wanted to really convict the narrator, myself; it made a better story. There's a late story by Raymond Carver called "Intimacy," in which the narrator returns to visit his ex-wife, and for the length of the story he takes all of her abuse–does not refute a thing she says, does not plead his case–just takes it and takes it and takes it. And at the end before he leaves–is it possible he kisses the hem of her dress? Here's this fellow you've heard the most terrible things about, and he's the one you feel for at the end of the story. You're on much firmer ground, I think, if you're willing to take the blame in a story. If you blame somebody else it sounds like whining. It's just not good form. It's not good manners. . . .

*You've been linked to the minimalists by several reviewers, including* Newsweek, *which labeled you a "minimalist tough cookie," while at least one reviewer prefers to call you a miniaturist. Do you think of yourself in those terms?*

I much prefer the term miniaturist. There's an enormous backlash against whatever minimalism is or was. A lot of the writers called minimalists had nothing to do with each other. It was a catch-all. These days, when you see the *minimalism* in a review, all it tells you is that the reviewer is lazy. Nobody likes to be tagged, but I don't mind miniaturist. Yes, I work small, concise, precise. . . .

*Your stories are deceptively easy to read, fun to read, but my suspicion is that they're not easy to write. Can you talk a little bit about the process? Where does a story begin for you?*

It has always started with an image or a line, something that I thought could support the weight of a story. There's a moment in "The Laundromat"—a one-act play by Marsha Norman, who also wrote "'Night, Mother"—where a recent widow tells another woman that she opened a door to a closet and saw a beach ball, and realized it was filled with her dead husband's breath. That's what I mean by having an image that will support the weight of a play, of a story. It can be an image, it can be a line. "Tell me things I won't mind forgetting." Why? Because I'm dying. . . .

*"In the Cemetery Where Al Jolson Is Buried"; does read like poetry in places. That story, like most of your work, is packed with compelling images, including the chimp who signs her grief over her lost baby at the end. Where did that image come from?*

I heard about one of the early ape language experiments years ago, a chimp fluent in sign language. I logged it mentally, because I thought that someday I'd do something with it. Although the story was done as a homage to my best friend, tactically it was an excuse to get to that image. If you know when you start you have something like that waiting at the finish line, it's a real impetus to get there. . . .

*How does a collection come together for you? Were all of the stories written as separate entities or did you write some things specifically to fill out the collection?*

Reasons to Live *certainly had a thematic wholeness. Those stories belong together. They are aligned. I never wrote anything to fit a collection, or to round out a book, but I did notice that every story I write is about loss of one kind or another. Loss of life, of health, of hope, of a job. After writing thirty stories about loss, the question I put to myself to write the last story in the second collection, "The Rest of God," became "What if there were people who hadn't lost anything? What would they be doing?". They don't lose anything, but of course, they have a close call, so I couldn't entirely get away from it. The work that I've done since that story is very different in feel. It's harder in a way, to write about people who are not faced with any threat. There they are, just having their lives. How do you make a story out of that?. . .

**Source:** Jo Sapp, "An Interview with Amy Hempel," in *The Missouri Review*, Vol. 16, No. 1, 1993, pp. 75–95.

## Dawn Ann Drzal

*In the following review of Hempel's first collection of short stories,* Reasons to Live, *Drzal comments that most of Hempel's stories take place in a limbo-like setting possible only in California.*

The most basic aim of psychoanalysis, Freud said, is "transforming hysterical misery into common unhappiness." While this formulation may seem harsh and hopeless, the characters in [*Reasons to Live*] . . . would be more than willing to settle for it.

Most of the stories in *Reasons to Live* open after a crisis to find the narrator standing, shell-shocked, amidst the rubble of her life. Although the tone of Hempel's spare, first person narratives (the exception is the third person "Today Will Be a Quiet Day") varies from the almost Southern Gothic flavor of "Breathing Jesus" to the silly/surreal "Celia is Back" to the full and touching "In the Cemetery Where Al Jolson Is Buried," they share a veneer of detachment. The alternately wise and wise cracking narrators provide ironic commentary, letting us in on the action and on a store of little-known facts: that Bob Dylan's mother invented White-Out, that insects fly between raindrops, that blue-eyed white cats are usually deaf, and cats that can hear will yawn when you run your finger along the teeth of a comb (this doesn't work; I tried it).

This obsessive collection of facts can be seen as a key to Hempel's sensibility. Her narrators are collectors of small, ironic tidbits, and Hempel seems to put forth the theory that the world is just a random assemblage of these trifles—some poignant, some beautiful, some amusing, but none deriving meaning from their arrangement. . . . Can sanity exist in a senseless world? For Hempel, the answer is obvious.

While it is sometimes witty, the view of the world as absurd deprives the stories of emotional power. Some of them seem merely to be vehicles designed to transport us to the oracular punchline, but fail to lend it resonance along the way. Even at its best, Hempel's prose lacks the neurasthenic charge of Joan Didion's. Didion uses the agglomeration of concrete details to much the same end, but manages to infuse the facts themselves with a simultaneous wonder and irony, to convince the reader that everything she describes, from a hydraulic power plant to a waiter in Zipaquirà, Colombia, is a singular phenomenon with its own body of lore.

Hempel's successes come from another direction. In her one fully-realized, moving story, "In the Cemetery Where Al Jolson Is Buried," and to lesser extent in the fine "Beg, Sl Tog, Inc, Cont, Rep" (knitting instructions), her disaffected tone works to lend depth to her narrator. In the former story, we suffer along with a woman visiting her best friend, who is dying of cancer, in a California hospital room. Only because we suffer with her can we come to understand and pardon the tactics she uses to avoid feeling pain, but we do come to understand. We believe in her fear, her love of life, and her psychological fragility. The cool monologue is revealed for what it is—noise to drown out pain and fear. The stories are less successful when we have to piece together the events from driblets and hints. The trouble with many of Hempel's aimless heroines (and occasional heroes) is that they're too strong to let themselves go and too cynical to believe in strength. If, as in "Beg, Sl Tog, Inc, Cont, Rep," an energizing crisis arrives and anomie slips into madness, the heroine just bobs up again into common unhappiness: she has a psychological air bladder that floats her to the surface but no further. Limbo seems like the only honest place to be in these stories. They take place in earthquake and landslide country, where stability is revealed to be a necessary delusion. To her credit, Ms. Hempel continually strives for, and sometimes manages to find, the poetry and raw humor in meaninglessness. . . .

**Source:** Dawn Ann Drzal, "An Assemblage of Trifles," in *Commonweal*, Vol. CXII, No. 16, September 20, 1985, pp. 505–7.

## Sheila Ballantyne

*In the following review of* Reasons to Live, *Ballantyne mentions the minimalist nature of Hempel's stories, which is the kind that "robs us of nothing" and seems to contain all the information a reader needs.*

Minimalism has its uses, and can achieve surprisingly varied effects: it can allude and expand, as well as leave out and compress. At its most reductive or repetitive, it can induce corresponding states of boredom or trance. There is a kind of writing that masks a lack of substance by itself posing as substance. Rushing to fill that void, a reader must project his own meaning, or assume the presence of some meaning that eludes his grasp. At its worst, minimalism is a kind of fraudulent tic that serves to hide a vacuum or defend against feeling. At its best it can, with economy and restraint, amplify perception and force meaning to leap from the page. In most of the stories that make up this first collection [*Reasons to Live*], Amy Hempel has succeeded in revealing both the substance and intelligence beneath the surface of a spare, elliptical prose.

Some of the one-page pieces in *Reasons to Live* are so truncated and incomplete they are interesting only as snapshots. Sometimes a vignette is just a vignette, a sketch a sketch. There are other misses here and there, gags that fall flat. But at their best these stories are tough-minded, original and fully felt. Some—in particular the wrenching ''In the Cemetery Where Al Jolson Is Buried,'' which describes a friend's dying; and the equally haunting ''Beg, Sl Tog, Inc, Cont, Rep'' (which takes its title from the conventions of knitting instructions), have a kind of effortless, unconscious integrity. They can take your breath away, so in tune are their resolutions with everything that has gone before....

It is tempting to think of this collection as a ''California book'' because many stories seem to spring directly from that soil like native plants: highly colored and direct. The details are perfectly rendered, quintessential California clichés; and yet they are also the truth. They establish the emotional climates in which these characters survive. A peculiarly California kind of drifting is exemplified by the narrator of ''Tonight Is a Favor to Holly'':

> ''Four days a week I drive to La Mirada, to the travel agency where I have a job. It takes me fifty-five minutes to drive one way, and I wish the commute were longer. I like radio personalities, and I like to change lanes. And losing yourself on the freeway is like living at the beach—you're not aware of lapsed time, and suddenly you're there, where it was you were going.''

You can almost hear her gum crack as she speaks. Still, small slips betray a vestigial identity, a wish not to blend, but to stand out: of the beach in the morning, she says, ''I like my prints to be the first of the day.''

True, too, are the details of California overabundance: ''Everything there is the size of something else: strawberries are the size of tomatoes, apples are the size of grapefruits, papayas are the size of watermelons.'' But alongside the particulars that anchor the stories to a place, there are intimations of a growing homogenization of scene....

A subtle universality of feeling infuses the more fully realized stories, transcending the cliché—or forcing it to underscore and serve a greater truth. Waiting helplessly for her friend to die, the narrator of ''In the Cemetery Where Al Jolson Is Buried,'' in a displacement of hallucinatory intensity, envisions a simple beach (''The beach is standing still today. Everyone on it is tranquilized, numb, or asleep'') as the locus of destruction; then transmutes the scene again, observing the way terror can transform itself into desire—the other side of death....

These stories, more than half of which have never been published before, are conspicuously contemporary—both the abbreviated one-page sketches and the more extended pieces of five or six; feeling is always contained, never explicit. Yet this is a kind of minimalism that robs us of nothing, that has room for the largest themes; the best of these stories have a compression that seems to capture it all.

**Source:** Sheila Ballantyne, ''Rancho Libido and Other Hot Spots,'' in *The New York Times Book Review,* April 28, 1985, p. 9.

## Sources

Hemingway, Ernest. *A Moveable Feast,* Macmillan, 1964.

Kakutani, Michiko. ''Uphill Battles,'' *The New York Times,* April 13, 1985, p. 14.

Kubler-Ross, Elisabeth. *On Death and Dying,* Macmillan, 1969.

Saltzman, Arthur M. ''To See a World in a Grain of Sand: Expanding Literary Minimalism,'' *Contemporary Literature,* Vol. XXXI, no. 4, 1990, pp. 423-33.

Schumacher, Michael. ''New Voices in American Fiction,'' *Reasons to Believe,* St. Martin's Press, 1988, pp. 28-45.

Steinberg, Sybil. ''PW Forecasts,'' *Publishers Weekly,* Vol. 227, No. 9, March 1 1985, p. 69.

Tager, Marcia. ''Witty Stories Mask Pain,'' in *New Directions for Women,* Vol. 14, no. 4, July/August 1985, p. 16.

Wachtel, Eleanor, editor. ''Amy Hempel.'' *Writers and Company.* Toronto: Alfred A. Knopf Canada, 1993, pp. 204-214.

## Further Reading

Aldridge, John W. *Talents and Technicians: Literary Chic and the New Assembly-Line Fiction,* Scribner's, 1992.
   Aldridge evaluates the writing styles and creative work of new writers whose fiction has been produced in college and university creative writing centers.

Hallett, Cynthia J. Whitney. "Minimalism—The Short Story." Dissertation, University of South Florida, 1996.
   Contains a full chapter devoted entirely to Hempel in which Hallett addresses Hempel's style and the literary influences that may have contributed to the symptoms of minimalism that pervade the stories.

Hooper, Brad. "Adult Fiction" *Booklist* Vol. 86, No. 13, March 1, 1990, p. 1264.
   A brief yet solid review of Hempel's second collection of short stories, *At the Gates of the Animal Kingdom.*

Jenks, Tom. "How Writers Live Today." *Esquire,* Vol. 104, August, 1985, pp. 123-127.
   A brief statement by Hempel in which she explains the real-life details of her 1979 promise to a dying friend in Los Angles, California, that sparked the totally fictional events and dialogue of "In the Cemetery Where Al Jolson Is Buried."

Winchell, Mark Royden. "What Nothing Means," in *Joan Didion,* edited by Warren French, Twayne, 1980, pp. 121-37.
   Winchell discusses Hollywood fiction, quoting from Jonas Spatz's *Hollywood in Fiction,* and demonstrates the importance of the Hollywood theme to Didion's writing.

# Miss Brill

## Katherine Mansfield
## 1922

"Miss Brill," Katherine Mansfield's short story about a woman's Sunday outing to a park, was published in her 1922 collection of stories entitled *The Garden Party*. The story's enduring popularity is due in part to its use of a stream-of-consciousness narrative in which Miss Brill's character is revealed through her thoughts about others as she watches a crowd from a park bench. Mansfield's talent as a writer is illustrated by the fact that she at no point tells what Miss Brill is thinking about her own life, yet the story draws one of the most succinct, complete character portraits in twentieth-century short fiction. "Miss Brill" has become one of Mansfield's most popular stories, and has been reprinted in numerous anthologies and collections. The story is typical of Mansfield's style; she often employed stream-of-consciousness narration in order to show the psychological complexity of everyday experience in her characters' lives.

## Author Biography

Katherine Mansfield was born Kathleen Mansfield Beauchamp to a wealthy family in Wellington, New Zealand, on October 14, 1888. She was educated in London, deciding early on that she wanted to be a writer. She studied music, wrote for the school newspaper, and gained her intellectual freedom by

studying Oscar Wilde and the other English "decadent" writers of the early twentieth century. Three years later she returned to New Zealand, where her parents expected her to find a suitable husband and lead the life of a well-bred woman. However, Mansfield was rebellious, adventurous, and more enamored of the artistic community than of polite society. She began publishing stories in Australian magazines in 1907, and shortly thereafter returned to London. A brief affair left her pregnant and she consented to marry a man, George Bowden, whom she had known a mere three weeks and who was not the father of her child. She dressed in black for the wedding and left him before the night was over. Upon receiving word of the scandal and fueled by rumors that her daughter had also been involved with several women, Mansfield's mother immediately sailed to London and placed her daughter in a spa in Germany, far away from the Bohemian artists' community of London and her best friend, Ida Baker, whom Mansfield's mother considered a bad influence. During her time in Germany, Mansfield suffered a miscarriage and was cut out of her parents' will. After returning to London, Mansfield moved in with Baker, continuing to write and conduct various love affairs.

In 1911, Mansfield published her first volume of stories, *In a German Pension,* most of which had been written during her stay at the German spa. That same year she met John Middleton Murry, the editor of a literary magazine. Although they lived together on and off for many years, her other affairs continued, most notably with Baker. Together Mansfield and Murry published a small journal, *The Blue Review,* which folded after only three issues. However, the experience gained them entrance into the literary community of the day, and one of their newfound friends was D. H. Lawrence. In 1918, Mansfield was finally granted a divorce from Bowden, and she and Murry married. Stricken with tuberculosis in 1917, Mansfield became increasingly ill. She continued to write, publishing her two most well-known collections, *Bliss and Other Stories* and *The Garden Party and Other Stories* in 1920 and 1922 respectively. The collections received favorable critical attention, and she continued to write even after her health forced her to move to Fontainebleau. Though she was separated from Murray for long periods towards the end of her life, it was he who saw that her literary reputation was established by publishing her last stories and her collections of letters after her death in January, 1923, at the age of thirty-four.

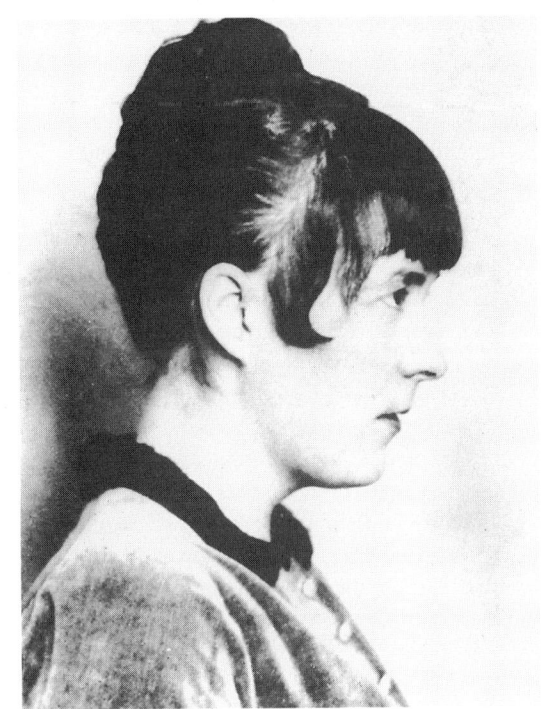

*Katherine Mansfield*

## Plot Summary

The Jardins Publiques (Public Gardens) in a French town on an early autumn Sunday afternoon is the setting for "Miss Brill." The air is still, but there is a "faint chill, like a chill from a glass of iced water before you sip," so Miss Brill is happy to have worn her fur stole. The stole, in accordance to the fashions of the times, was constructed so that its fake eyes and nose could be attached to its tail, securing it around the wearer's neck. It is the first time she has worn it in a while. When preparing for her stroll in the park, she gives it a "good brush," "[rubs] the life back into the dim little eyes," and teasingly calls it her "little rogue."

Miss Brill watches the people in the park with delight. The band sounds "louder and gayer" to her than it has on previous Sundays. She listens to the concert from her "'special' seat" and is disappointed when the other two people seated there do not speak. Her favorite pastime on Sunday afternoon is to eavesdrop on people's conversations.

In one observation, Miss Brill notices that all the people sitting on the benches listening to the band are "odd, silent, nearly all old" and "looked as though they'd just come from dark little rooms or even—even cupboards.'' As Miss Brill listens to the band and watches the children playing, her thoughts drift from the pupils to whom she teaches English, to the old man to whom she reads the newspaper four days a week.

As her exuberance grows, Miss Brill likens her position as that of an actress in a play. As dramas are acted out in the park, Miss Brill realizes that she is a character, too: ''Even she had a part and came every Sunday. No doubt somebody would have noticed if she hadn't been there.'' She delights in the metaphor. The band, which had been taking a break, resumes playing. Miss Brill thinks that the ''whole company'' might begin singing along at any moment. They would sing something ''so beautiful—and moving.'' She feels a vague sense of community with the rest of the people in the park.

A young couple, well-dressed and in love, come and sit near her, and Miss Brill imagines them to be the hero and heroine of the play. She listens to their conversation, but instead of revealing dialogue that fulfills Miss Brill's fantasy of theater, the girl makes fun of Miss Brill's fur collar. The boy, trying to appease his girlfriend, says ''Why does she come here at all—who wants her? Why doesn't she keep her silly old mug at home?'' The girl, snickering, compares the woman's fur to a dead fish, saying that it looks like a ''fried whiting.''

Miss Brill's reaction to the comments are not recorded. Instead, she forgoes her usual stop at the bakery on her way back to her ''little dark room—her room like a cupboard,'' where she sits silently for a long time. Finally, she unclasps her fur quickly without looking at it. As she places it back in the box, she thinks that she hears ''something crying.''

## Characters

### Miss Brill

Miss Brill is a middle-aged, unmarried English woman who lives alone in a small apartment in France. She teaches English to students and reads the newspaper to an elderly man several times a week. One of her prized possessions is a fur necklet that she wears on a Sunday visit to the town's park. The story takes place during one of these Sunday visits in which she eavesdrops on people's conversations and listens to the band. Miss Brill is an astute observer of others, noticing that the other people sitting on the park benches seem ''odd'' as if they had ''just come from dark little rooms.'' She fails, however, to realize that she is one of them. Enchanted by the crisp air and the advent of the Season, Miss Brill compares the park to a stage, and the people—including herself—as actors and actresses in a play. The metaphor takes on the proportions of an epiphany in which she believes that she has finally connected with the community. The realization fills her with joy, and she imagines a young, attractive couple on the bench next to her as the play's hero and heroine. She has made a false connection, though, she realizes when instead of partaking of romantic dialogue, the couple insult her. She has managed to connect with others only in her fantasy. Miss Brill retreats to her apartment without having succeeded in establishing the human contact she desperately wants and has sought. Miss Brill, however, suppresses her sorrow when she imagines that she hears her fur stole crying as she returns it to its box. She is unable to recognize the feeling as her own, just as she has been unable to see herself as others in the park perceive her.

### Fur necklet

Miss Brill's fur necklet, with its ''dim little eyes,'' a nose ''that wasn't at all firm,'' and a mouth that bites ''its tail just by her left ear,'' assumes many human characteristics in the story. It is a friend to Miss Brill, who calls it her ''little rogue,'' and whose eyes ask the question ''What has been happening to me?''—a question that the woman is not able to ask of herself. The fur lives in a box, just as its owner lives in a ''dark little room,'' and together they visit the park on Sunday afternoon. After Miss Brill's day has been spoiled, however, she returns to her apartment and stashes the fur back in its box, ashamed that it has brought her ridicule from people she has admired. The fur, she imagines, is crying—yet another human characteristic Miss Brill ascribes to her fur, which has come to symbolize Miss Brill herself.

### The woman in the ermine toque

The woman in the ermine toque whom Miss Brill observes in the park symbolizes the title character herself, and her rebuff by a man in a gray suit foreshadows Miss Brill's rejection later in the story. Miss Brill notes that the woman's fur hat is ''shabby,'' bought when ''her hair was yellow''; characteristics that could apply to the observer herself, though she fails to realize this. The woman is delighted to see the man in the gray suit, just as Miss

Brill is delighted by the young couple who approach her bench. When he blows smoke in the woman's face, Miss Brill feels the rejection personally by imagining the drum beat of the band calling out "The Brute! The Brute!"

### *The young romantic couple*

The young, romantic couple approach the bench from which Miss Brill is watching the crowd. They are "beautifully dressed" and in love. Immediately, they become the hero and heroine of Miss Brill's imaginary play. However, instead of revealing some sprightly romantic dialogue, the boy and girl are having a quarrel in which the girl insists, "Not here, I can't." In an effort to placate his girlfriend, the "hero" condemns Miss Brill, asking, "who wants her? Why doesn't she keep her silly old mug at home?" In response, the girl giggles that it is the woman's fur that she finds so distracting. Thus, the couple's dialogue, instead of fitting in with Miss Brill's conception of the situation as a stage play in which they are all welcome characters, makes her realize that her presence in the park is not wanted.

## Themes

"Miss Brill" presents an afternoon in the life of a middle-aged spinster. On her usual Sunday visit to the park, she imagines the she and the people in the park are characters in a play. Contributing to her good mood is the fact that she is wearing her prized fur stole. Anticipating the conversation of two strangers who sit down next to her, Miss Brill's vivacious mood is shattered by the couple's ridicule for her and her fur. She returns to her tiny apartment and places the fur back in its box, imagining that she hears it crying.

### *Alienation and Loneliness*

Though Miss Brill does not reveal it in her thoughts, her behavior indicates that she is a lonely woman. She thinks of no family members during her Sunday outing, instead focusing on her few students and the elderly man to whom she reads the newspaper several times a week. Even her name, Miss Brill, suggests an isolating formality; with the absence of a first name, the reader is never introduced to her on a personal level. Her fantasy, in which she imagines the people in the park as characters in a play connected in some psychological and physical way to one another, reveals her loneliness

## Topics for Further Study

- Explain how the narration of the story can be both third-person and stream-of-consciousness. How would the story be different if it had been written in first person? Do you think it would have been as successful?

- If the story was written today, where might it take place and how might Miss Brill be dressed?

- Mansfield stated that "One writes (*one* reason why is) because one does care so passionately that one *must* show it—one must declare one's love." Miss Brill is a character who desperately seeks love, but is incapable of giving or receiving it. What events in the story illustrate this?

in a creative way. Yet, her manufactured sense of connection to these strangers is shattered when she is insulted by the young couple that sit next to her on the bench. When her fantasy of playacting is crushed by the conversation of the romantic couple, she is shown to be alienated from her environment—estranged and apart from the others in the park, to whom she only imagined a connection. Symbolically, this sense of alienation is heightened at the end of the story when Miss Brill returns her fur to its box quickly and without looking at it. This action is in stark contrast to her playful conversation with it earlier in the day, when she called it her "little rogue." The final action of the story completes the characterization of Miss Brill as an alienated and lonely individual when she believes that she hears her beloved fur crying as she returns it to its box, just as she herself has returned to her "room like a cupboard."

### *Appearances and Reality*

Through the stream-of-consciousness narrative in "Miss Brill," Mansfield creates a story in which the stark contrast between appearances and reality are manifest through the thoughts of the main character. At the beginning of the story, Miss Brill is perturbed by the old couple sitting on the bench near her. Their silence makes eavesdropping on their lives difficult. Yet, she does not realize that their behavior echoes her own silent existence. Similarly, Miss Brill notices that the other people sitting on chairs in the park are "odd, silent, nearly all old" and "looked as though they'd just come from dark little rooms or even—even cupboards!" The irony that she is one of these odd people who lives in a cupboard is not recognized. She also notices an old woman wearing a fur hat, which she calls a "shabby ermine," bought when the woman's hair was yellow. When the woman raises her hand to her lips, Miss Brill compares it to a "tiny yellowish paw." While making fun of this woman in her own mind, the comparisons between the "ermine toque" and her own appearance go unnoticed. Later, when Miss Brill's imagination concocts the metaphor of the park visitors as actors in a play, she thinks of them as connected to her in a harmonious way: "we understand, we understand, she thought." Yet, the attractive couple whom she imagines to be the hero and heroine of the play are revealed through their conversation to not be part of this "appearance" of a stage play. In the reality of their cruel comments, they are not "members of the company" who "understand." This strong illusion of playacting Miss Brill has envisioned has been dismantled through the harsh words of the boy and girl. In reality, they think of her not as a fellow actress, but as a "stupid old thing" whose fur resembles a "fried whiting." The play—a metaphor which produced a moment of epiphany for Miss Brill—has taken place only in her mind. Thus, this contrast between appearance and reality in "Miss Brill" further illustrates the story's theme of alienation—the idea that Miss Brill is separated and estranged from her environment.

## Style

"Miss Brill" presents the interior monologue of a woman on a Sunday trip to the park whose pleasant illusions are shattered when reality infringes on her thoughts.

### Setting

"Miss Brill" is set in the "Jardins Publiques," the French term for "public garden," or park. Miss Brill, through her name and the indication that she tutors students in English, is revealed to be a non-native of France, and thus an outsider from the start. These factual references reinforce her emotional isolation, which she attempts to overcome by pretending that she is a cast member in a stage production. The pleasant weather, its crispness perfect for her fur collar, echoes Miss Brill's good mood as she sits in the garden listening to the band and watching the people. When her illusion of understanding with the others in the park is shattered by the comments of the young couple, however, Miss Brill retreats to her "little dark room—her room like a cupboard." This change of setting highlights the main character's abrupt change in mood.

### Symbolism

The primary symbol in "Miss Brill" is the main character's fur stole. It assumes various life-like traits, echoing the traits that characterize Miss Brill herself. She has "taken it out of its box that afternoon" just as Miss Brill has left her "room like a cupboard" for a walk in the park. It is given other human qualities: its nose "wasn't at all firm," and Miss Brill imagines its eyes are asking "What has been happening to me?," and when placed back in its box at the end of the story, she thinks she hears it crying. The boy in the park criticizes Miss Brill's appearance, suggesting that she should "keep her silly old mug at home." Likewise, his girlfriend criticizes the fur, giggling that it looks "exactly like a fried whiting." When Miss Brill takes the fur off at home, she does it "quickly; quickly, without looking," perhaps symbolizing the way she failed to examine her own life or recognize how she appears to others.

### Narration

"Miss Brill" is told in a third-person, stream-of-consciousness narrative, a common device in Mansfield's works which serves to heighten the story's psychological acuity and perceptive characterization. Though the narrative is third-person, the stream-of-consciousness technique allows the reader full access to Miss Brill's thoughts, but nothing more than Miss Brill's thoughts. Thus, the thoughts of others in the story are revealed by dialogue (such as the young couple's), or they are not revealed at all (like the couple seated next to Miss Brill who do not speak). Likewise, the reader is privy to Miss Brill's thoughts about her fur: "Dear little thing! It was nice to feel it again," but is left to intuit much of Miss Brill's character by what she does not realize. The stream-of-consciousness narrative reveals, for example, Miss Brill's perception of the woman wearing an old ermine hat. Miss Brill slightly scorns the woman, calling her hat "shabby" and her hand a "tiny yellowish paw," yet she fails to note that her own appearance is somewhat similar to the woman's. Thus, part of Miss Brill's character is revealed by what her stream-of-consciousness narration fails to address.

## Historical Context

### Europe between the Wars

In the 1920s, Europe was rebuilding after World War I, the most destructive and deadly war in history. As the economy grew, spurred on by the advances in medicine and technology gained during the war, a newfound era of wealth and cultural growth permeated many Western European countries. France, especially, became a haven for expatriate artists and writers from England and the United States drawn to its affordable living conditions. The values of the "Jazz Age" spread to the continent, where the dismantling of strict Victorian protocol resulted in the rise of controversial art like Expressionism and Surrealism and explicit literature from writers like James Joyce.

"Miss Brill" is set during this tumultuous time period, when the sight of an older, single woman wearing an outdated fur stole represented a genteel world forever obliterated by the atrocities of trench warfare, the promise of air travel, and the cynicism generated by the millions of casualties in the war. Like others of her day, Miss Brill is a foreigner living in France, but she is alienated from the thriving community of artists and writers who formed the "moveable feast" in Paris during the 1920s. Instead, Miss Brill has a few students to whom she teaches English and she reads to an elderly gentleman until he falls asleep. Miss Brill's association with this man further represents her alignment with an era now obsolete. The young couple on the bench are of a younger generation, and their comments reveal the attitude towards which young people now regarded their elders.

Mansfield, whose numerous affairs always marked her as a bit of a free spirit, fit into this new social order quite comfortably. However, by the time she wrote "Miss Brill," she was weak from tuberculosis and exerted the bulk of her energy writing stories and letters. In England, the Bloomsbury writers, a loosely-knit group that included Virginia Woolf and whose main literary goal was to eradicate the old social order of the Victorians, were in frequent correspondence with Mansfield.

*Woman wearing fur stole similar to Miss Brill's fur necklet.*

In "Miss Brill," Mansfield created one of her most famous characterizations; one that illustrates the illusions of the old order and how they are shown to be just that: illusions.

## Critical Overview

Mansfield is one of only a few writers to gain critical prominence on the basis of her short stories

# Compare & Contrast

- **1920s:** Few professions other than nursing and teaching are deemed socially acceptable for women who must support themselves.

  **Today:** College graduates are as likely to be female as male, and a majority of women are employed in the workforce and in virtually every profession.

- **1920s:** One's social rank can be determined from one's clothing. Gentlemen wear hats, ladies gloves, and fur denotes a position of some social standing. Women, with few exceptions, always wear dresses or skirts.

  **Today:** Social conventions regarding dress are relaxed. Hats and gloves are uncommon in many circles, and pants are a staple of most women's wardrobes. Many believe fur to be a symbol not of status but rather an indication of cruelty and conspicuous consumption.

- **1920s:** Common forms of recreation include reading, going to the theater, and gathering in public places such as parks or pubs. People often dress up to appear in public.

  **Today:** 98 percent of all households in the United States own televisions. Other forms of mass communication, including the telephone, radio, and the personal computers have infringed on the time spent socializing with others in a public sphere. In suburban areas, the most crowded space is often the shopping mall.

---

alone; she published no novels during her short lifetime. Though published widely while she was still alive, her literary reputation was permanently established after her death with the publication of her collected letters and correspondence. In *The Letters of Katherine Mansfield*, the author gives readers insight into the way in which she constructed "Miss Brill": "I choose the rise and fall of every paragraph to fit her.... After I'd written it I read it aloud—numbers of times—just as one would play over a musical composition—trying to get it nearer and nearer to the expression of Miss Brill—until it fitted her." "Miss Brill" has always been on of Mansfield's most popular stories. Clare Hanson and Andrew Gurr argue in their book *Katherine Mansfield* that Miss Brill is more than a characterization of a lonely spinster: "In Mansfield's view we are all ultimately solitary, and human beings are fundamentally cruel and indifferent to one another except in the rare instances where they love. Without love, and without the comfort of illusions, the reality of life can be grim indeed." They further note that "Miss Brill" has often been regarded as a moral, even as a sentimental story. Echoing the opinion of many critics, Robert L. Hull's essay in *Studies in Short Fiction* states that "[t]he principle theme of Katherine Mansfield's 'Miss Brill' is estrangement."

## Criticism

### Robert Peltier

*Robert Peltier is an English instructor at Trinity College and has published works of both fiction and nonfiction. In the following essay, he provides a general overview of Mansfield's "Miss Brill."*

Katherine Mansfield, born Kathleen Mansfield Beauchamp in 1888 in Wellington, New Zealand, lived a short life, but she established a literary reputation at a young age. Her first published book, *In a German Pension,* was published in 1911, when she was only twenty-two years old. She became friends with some of the great literary figures of her day, including D.H. Lawrence and Virginia Woolf, and married the writer and critic J. Middleton Murry.

Her stories are full of detail and small, albeit significant, incidents in her characters' lives. In an

# What Do I Read Next?

- Mansfield's "Bliss," written in 1918, is another story of a woman's struggle with dissatisfaction and alienation. Bertha is young, married, and a new mother. Her husband is successful, and a nurse helps her with her new baby. A joyous dinner party, with its liveliness and opportunity for interpersonal penetration and imagination, only serves to heighten Bertha's isolation when it ends and she is left once again with a comparatively empty house.

- Katherine Anne Porter's "The Jilting of Granny Weatherall" (1929) concerns a dying woman's final thoughts. Written in the stream-of-consciousness style, Granny Weatherall's interior monologue is notable for what it contains as well as for what is left unspoken.

- A more intimate biography of Katherine Mansfield is provided by LM (Ida Constance Baker) in her 1971 memoir *Katherine Mansfield: The Memories of LM*. LM was Mansfield's close friend and assistant. The book was published in 1971 by Michael Joseph Ltd. and reprinted in 1985 by Virago Press.

- Virginia Woolf's "The Mark on the Wall," first published in 1917, also uses a stream-of-consciousness narrative style like "Miss Brill." A woman contemplates a mark on the wall, imagining what it might be. In the course of her thoughts, her mind wanders over a variety of subjects.

- "Araby" by James Joyce, first published in *Dubliners* (1914), recounts a young narrator's stark realization that the world of romance and religion in which he had immersed himself is a foolish, inaccurate view of reality.

- Heather Murray's *Double Lives: Women in the Stories of Katherine Mansfield* provides a feminist interpretation of Mansfield's work. It was published in 1990 by the University of Otago Press.

---

often-quoted letter published in *The Letters of Katherine Mansfield,* she says of "Miss Brill": "I chose the rise and fall of every paragraph to fit her, and to fit her on that day at that moment." Katherine Fullbrook notes in her biography titled simply *Katherine Mansfield* that "while the surface of her stories often flash with sparkling detail, the underlying tones are sombre, threatening, and register the danger in the most innocent seeming aspects of life."

"Miss Brill," is one of her finest stories, capturing in a moment an event that will forever change the life of the title character. Miss Brill is an older woman of indeterminate age who makes a meager living teaching English to school children and reading newspapers to an "old invalid gentleman." Her joy in life is her visit to the park on Sunday, where she observes all that goes on around her and listens to the conversations of people nearby, as she sits "in on other people's lives." It is when she tries to leave her role as spectator and join the "players" in her little world that she is rebuffed by that world and her fantasy falls apart.

On this particular Sunday, she has taken her fur necklet out of its box, brushed it, cleared its eyes, and put it on. She is glad that she wore it, because the air contains a "faint chill, like a chill from a glass of iced water before you sip." It is a beautiful day, the first Sunday of the Season, so everything seems nicer than usual. Even the band seems to play "louder and gayer."

Miss Brill is somewhat disappointed that there are only two older people near where she is seated. They do not speak, and her observations of the life around her begin in silence. It is clear at this point in the story that she considers herself a spectator, detached from the activities around her. She expects entertainment from the strollers and sitters, but she has been disappointed more than once. Last week, we learn, an Englishman and his wife held a boring conversation which drove Miss Brill to the point of wanting to shake the woman. But she didn't shake her, because that would have meant involving herself in the actions she so quietly observed.

Mansfield's eye for detail and the telling moment exhibits itself here as we, along with Miss Brill, watch the activities in the park: "... couples and groups [parade], [stop] to talk, to greet ... children [run] among them, swooping and laughing." A "high stepping mother" picks up her child who has "suddenly sat down 'flop.'" It is a scene made up of details that we have all, at one time or another, witnessed ourselves. And that is all that Miss Brill does right now: witness the world parading past her.

But then she takes note of the people on the benches. She sees "something funny about nearly all of them." And as she looks at these "odd, silent, nearly all old" people who look as if they have "just come from dark little rooms or even—even cupboards!" she does not see that she is one of them. Mansfield's prose gives us an objective look at the people and events around Miss Brill while at the same time allowing us to see the subjective interpretation Miss Brill makes of that world. We don't know what she thinks of herself, or even if she thinks of herself at all. But if she does, she must not see herself very clearly. She must not believe that she is old or odd or funny.

Now the band strikes up, and the procession continues with young girls and soldiers and peasant women leading donkeys and a nun and a beautiful woman who drops her flowers and, when a little boy picks them up for her, throws them away "as if they'd been poisoned." Miss Brill doesn't know "whether to admire that or not!"

Then an older woman wearing an ermine toque (a hat made of white fur) meets a man. The ermine is "shabby" and bought when "her hair was yellow." Now her hair, as well as her face and "even her eyes" are as white as the fur. She makes superficial, yet somehow strained and desperate conversation but the man walks away after lighting his cigarette and blowing smoke in her face. The band plays more softly as the woman stands there, exposed and alone, but it picks up the tempo and plays even more loudly than before after the woman has pretended to see someone and walks away.

The fur connects them—her toque and Miss Brill's necklet—and we see, as the woman is snubbed by the man, a foreshadowing of what is to happen to Miss Brill later in the story. The woman tried to engage the man in conversation, and Miss Brill will later try to engage with the world.

The pageant resumes with an "old man with long whiskers" nearly being knocked over by "four girls walking abreast." Miss Brill is lost in her fantasy world now, thinking how wonderful it all is. She decides, suddenly, that it is "exactly like a play." The scenery is perfect enough to be a painted backdrop. When a little dog trots on-stage, then off again, she realizes that not only is she—and everyone else—the audience, but they are also the actors. She has her part to play; that is why she comes at the same time each week: so that she will be on time for her performance! This wonderfully romantic idea captures her imagination. It is, she thinks, the reason that she "had quite a queer, shy feeling at telling her English pupils how she spent her Sunday afternoons." (In those days, the theater was not considered a proper or legitimate career and also had dark, often sexual connotations). She imagines telling the old man whom she reads to that, yes, she is an actress, that she "has been an actress for a long time."

She has entered fully now into the world she has previously only observed. She is a part of the play, someone in the cast who would be missed if she were not to come on Sunday afternoons. She delights in this newfound role as the band begins to play again. The music is "warm and sunny," yet there is a "faint chill" to it, echoing the beginning of the story. It makes her want to sing and, as the music gets brighter, she believes that the whole company of actors in her little theater in the park will start singing together at any moment, "and then she, too, and the others on the benches." Having entered the world, she is on the verge of becoming active in it. She feels at one with all the other actors. Her eyes fill with tears and she knows that they understand, although what they understand she is not quite sure.

It is at this moment of epiphany, when she feels a connection to the world, that a young couple arrives and sits on the bench. Miss Brill casts them immediately as the hero and heroine of her drama. She imagines them as just having arrived from his father's yacht and "with that trembling smile," she listens to their dialogue. But the dialogue is not heroic, but vulgar and common. The boy is trying to seduce the girl, and she is playfully, half-heartedly resisting his advances.

In the next few sentences, Miss Brill's illusions are shattered, and she is forced to confront her life as it is. Brutal and direct, the boy asks: "Why does she come here at all—who wants her? Why doesn't she keep her silly old mug at home." And the girl answers: "It's her fu-fur which is so funny.... It's exactly like a fried whiting," comparing the woman's stole to dead fish. Miss Brill has discovered her part in her play, and now she finds that it is a tragedy, not a romance.

She leaves the park and goes home. She does not even stop at the bakery for her Sunday treat. Instead, she goes straight to her "little dark room—her room like a cupboard," which again connects her to the old, odd, silent people on the park benches whom she has imagined as having come from just such rooms. She sits on the bed and puts her fur away in its box, but as she does, she hears something crying. She has now withdrawn so far from the world that has hurt her, that she does not realize that it is she who is crying.

**Source:** Robert Peltier, for *Short Stories for Students,* Gale Research, 1997.

## Clare Hanson and Andrew Gurr

*In the following portion of a chapter from their book* Katherine Mansfield, *Hanson and Gurr recount what is known regarding Mansfield's impetus for writing "Miss Brill" and discuss how Miss Brill manufactures a "false sense of community" that brings about her epiphany.*

...'Miss Brill', written soon after Katherine Mansfield arrived in Menton in November 1920, is structurally related to 'Bliss' as a story in which a shift of feeling in one character is conveyed in a single scene. With unity of action, time and place these shorter stories tend to seem more 'realistic' than episodic pieces like *Prelude* or 'Je ne parle pas français'. However, this smooth narrative texture is in a sense appearance only. As much as in *Prelude* the stories are structured according to the demands of symbolist patterning and almost every detail has a symbolic as well as narrative context. There are also narrative suppressions and ellipses in stories like 'Miss Brill', though they are less obvious than in the longer stories as they are not signalled by formal divisions in the text.

'Miss Brill' has often been regarded as a moral, even as a sentimental story. It drew letters of thanks from solitary readers, and the author herself seems to have rather basked in such attention, writing to Murry after she had received these letters:

> One writes (*one* reason why is) because one does care so passionately that one *must* show it—one must declare one's love.

But in writing the story she adhered to Symbolist principles. Rather than 'declaring her love' she kept her own, or rather the narrator's point of view rigorously out of the story. The events and images function dramatically, the narrator providing only 'objective' description. This is true even of the famous last lines of the story:

> The box that the fur came out of was on the bed. She unclasped the necklet quickly; quickly, without looking, laid it inside. But when she put the lid on she thought she heard something crying.

The narrator provides objective information, then the rapid rhythms of 'quickly; quickly, without looking' shade into the representation of Miss Brill's agitated state. The closing perception of the story is Miss Brill's and not the narrator's and is entirely in accord with her neurotic, fantastic imagination. And it is entirely unsentimental, suggesting very firmly the fear and horror which attend the suppression of any human being.

In 'Miss Brill' all is conveyed obliquely, through concrete imagery and the dramatic device of Miss Brill's inner monologue. Not once is her inner state alluded to or described directly. The story is thus the perfect example of the technique Mansfield described to Murry—oblique, delicately suggestive:

> I might write about a boy eating strawberries or a woman combing her hair on a windy morning and that is the only way I can ever mention [deserts of vast eternity].

The language of the story also reaches a high degree of perfection. She wrote in a well-known letter to Richard Murry that:

> In *Miss Brill* I choose not only the length of every sentence, but even the sound of every sentence. I choose the rise and fall of every paragraph to fit her, and to fit her on that very day at that very moment. After I'd written it I read it aloud—numbers of times—just as one would *play over* a musical composition—trying to get it nearer and nearer the expression of Miss Brill—until it fitted her.

The author's own satisfaction with the style of 'Miss Brill' suggests her success in the story. A poetic intensity and concretion is sustained throughout, the sound of the words and the prose rhythms conveying and enriching meaning. The use of the musical analogy for 'Miss Brill' in the passage quoted above also has more direct relevance. The story is shaped, specifically, as a lament, and something of the quality of a sung lament is deliberately infused into it by the use of para-musical prose rhythms in some sections.

The story is constructed around a series of parallels and contrasts designed to expose with increasing clarity the inner state of the central character. The key themes are the opposition between age and youth, stasis and vitality, solitude and community, illusion and reality.

Miss Brill herself is old, as we realise immediately from the author's handling of her stylised inner monologue. Her speech patterns are those of a nervous, fussy, elderly person. She is associated in the first paragraph of the story with her fur, which acts as a mirror image of the woman herself. The fur, too, is old, with 'dim' eyes, and its nose is 'not at all firm'; 'Never mind—a little dab of black sealing wax when the time came—when it was absolutely necessary ...' The ellipsis signals Miss Brill's reluctance to recognise a time when 'it' will be absolutely necessary, her avoidance of the thought of decay or decomposition.

In the five and a half pages of the story Miss Brill's state is explored through a series of figures who act as parallels for her. At the Jardins Publiques she sits beside an old couple who are as 'still as statues', and she notices the other regular visitors to the park—'There was something funny about nearly all of them. They were odd, silent, nearly all old'—though Miss Brill does not, explicitly, include herself in this company. The most extended view which she has of any other visitor to the park is of a single woman in an ermine toque 'bought when her hair was yellow. Now everything, her hair, her face, even her eyes, was the same colour as the shabby ermine, and her hand, in its cleaned glove, lifted to dab her lips, was a tiny yellowish paw.' The woman in the toque parallels Miss Brill in the efforts which she has made to 'touch up' her shabby appearance before entering the park. The link between the furs—dead animals retaining the appearance of life—and the old people, is insisted on. Miss Brill is linked finally to another elderly man to whom she reads the newspaper:

> She had got quite used to the frail head on the cotton pillow, the hollowed eyes, the open mouth and the high pinched nose. If he'd been dead she mightn't have noticed for weeks; she wouldn't have minded.

He too is a moribund figure, retaining little more than the appearance of life.

The pictures of the old are counterpointed by glimpses Miss Brill has of the younger people in the park, who all seem to be much further away. The old people are solitary and motionless. The younger ones are presented as energetic and vigorous—the conductor of the band flaps his arms, the bandsmen blow out their cheeks. Little children 'swoop' and 'laugh', young mothers 'rush', 'high stepping'. Their vitality distinguishes them, as does the fact that they are all in groups or, more relevantly, in pairs:

> Two young girls in red came by and two young soldiers in blue met them, and they laughed and paired and went off arm in arm.

The theme of solitude against community has already been introduced in the second paragraph where Miss Brill ironically sees herself and the other regular visitors to the park as 'the family', as compared with the 'strangers', the seasonal visitors. (The reverse is of course the case: the regular visitors are all strangers—all alone—whereas the visitors are in family groups.) The theme of false community appears again in the scene with the 'ermine toque'. This woman approaches a 'gentleman' and tries to engage him in conversation. As she chatters, he lights a cigarette and 'while she was still talking and laughing, flicked the match away and walked on'. The 'ermine toque's' pitifully inappropriate behaviour and her imaginary sense of relationship anticipate the central moment of the story. The theme of false community is an integral part of Miss Brill's epiphany, as is the theme of the discrepancy between appearance and reality which is also developed through the story.

From the beginning, the things which Miss Brill sees are described in 'stagey' terms. She herself touches up her fur, that is, her appearance, before she sets out for the park. She sees other elderly people as 'statues'; the running little girls are 'dolls'. Towards the end of the story, her vision flowers into explicit recognition. She realises that everything she sees is like a play:

> How she loved sitting here, watching it all! It was like a play. It was exactly like a play. Who could believe the sky at the back wasn't painted? But it wasn't until a little brown dog trotted on solemnly and then slowly trotted off, like a little 'theatre' dog, a little dog that had been drugged, that Miss Brill discovered what it was that made it so exciting. They were all on the stage. They weren't only the audience, not only looking on; they were acting. Even she had a part and came every Sunday.

When she realises this, Miss Brill looks again at the band, the play within the play. As the music flows out, she has her false epiphany. She feels at one with everyone else, everyone seems united, through the music and also because they are all part of a play and are in this sense a 'company':

... And Miss Brill's eyes filled with tears and she looked smiling at all the other members of the company. Yes, we understand, she thought—though what they understood she didn't know.

The falsity of this sense of community is revealed almost immediately. A young couple replace the silent old couple on the seat beside Miss Brill. They are drawn immediately into her imaginary play— 'The hero and heroine, of course, just arrived from his father's yacht'—only to destroy all its meaning as soon as they actually speak:

> '... Why doesn't she keep her silly old mug at home?'
> 'It's her fu-fur which is so funny ... It's exactly like a fried whiting.'

Thus it is revealed to Miss Brill in the most painful possible way that her play is a play within her mind only. We are made to see the isolation of each individual within their own consciousness, and the all too common discrepancy between on the one hand the appearance which the mind creates through imagination and memory, and on the other hand reality, in the sense of what is generally agreed to be the truth. Miss Brill's most recent sustaining illusion has been that on her Sunday afternoon visits to the Jardins Publiques she has been part of a community of feeling and interest. She has felt that the part which she plays in the Sunday afternoon pageant has mattered to others as theirs had mattered to her. We know that Miss Brill's existence is barely tolerable, but we also know that she transforms her meagre situation, by the power of her imagination, which is creative. She idealises what she sees around her and idealises herself, revealing herself as an artist in this sense.

The young couple tear down the veil of illusion, leaving Miss Brill with nothing. She realises the cruelty of other human beings in the cruelty and indifference of the young couple—whom *she* has idealised. She has hoped that if she were to miss a Sunday afternoon (for reasons not admitted to consciousness) she would in her turn be missed. It is now apparent that this is doubtful, and that certainly no one would care. And Miss Brill realises finally that she does not appear to others as she does to herself (she does not see her face as a 'silly old mug').

Miss Brill's epiphany is too unbearable and her new knowledge cannot be admitted to consciousness at this moment. Hence the ellipsis which follows the speech of the young couple. Miss Brill does not think about what she has just realised, though it may make its way back into consciousness

> "The key themes are the opposition between age and youth, stasis and vitality, solitude and community, illusion and reality."

by degrees. But, we sense, she will then transform this knowledge too by the power of her imagination, the saving grace of her life. This is suggested through the coda of the story as she puts her fur away, thus showing her ability to adjust and construct new appearances.

Miss Brill's situation is extreme and her isolation is intensified because she is a spinster abroad in a foreign country. Yet in Mansfield's view we are all ultimately solitary, and human beings are fundamentally cruel and indifferent to one another except in the rare instances where they love. Without love, and without the comfort of illusions, the reality of life can be grim indeed. 'Miss Brill', for all its brevity, presents a genuinely tragic view of experience. The central character lacks love and has only her capacity of creative imagination between herself and the void. She will go on living and transforming her experience into tolerable forms, but the value and meaning of life on this level is questionable. Without love, what other 'real ideal' can enter Miss Brill's life? The brief descriptions of natural beauty—the sea, the golden leaves, the blue sky— suggest one possibility, but these are the perceptions of the narrator, and are introduced as thematic motifs, rather than being important to Miss Brill. Through a combination of character and circumstance, Miss Brill's life has been reduced to the barest minimum necessary to continued existence. The story is a radical questioning of the meaning of such existence, and of the purpose of the life-force which makes her carry on on these terms. ...

**Source:** Clare Hanson and Andrew Gurr, "The South of France 1918–20," in *Katherine Mansfield*, St. Martin's Press, 1981, pp. 75–82.

## Robert L. Hull

*In the following essay, Hull analyzes the principal theme of "Miss Brill," which he states is*

> "Miss Brill's world is more than lonely; it is also an existential world in which she finds herself in complete solitude estranged from God, man, and, more importantly, from herself."

estrangement from love, and which Mansfield stated was her primary reason for writing the story.

The principal theme of Katherine Mansfield's "Miss Brill" is estrangement. Miss Mansfield gives in this story a significant look, through the eyes of Miss Brill, a look short and startling and at once full of pity, at the world that the lonely woman inhabits. Indeed, Miss Brill's world is more than lonely; it is also an existential world in which she finds herself in complete solitude estranged from God, man, and, more importantly, from herself. Explicators of the story have wholly or partly ignored the theme of estrangement that I feel is the major theme.

Two passages from Miss Mansfield's letters to John Middleton Murry present evidence for her purpose in writing "Miss Brill." "One writes (one reason why is) because one does care so passionately that one must show it—one *must* declare one's love." In another letter she writes: "Last night I walked about and saw the new moon with the old moon in her arms and the lights in the water and the hollow pools full of stars—and lamented there was no God. But I came in and wrote 'Miss Brill' instead; which is my insect Magnificat now and always." The reason for writing and the mood reflected in these two passages point to a clearer definition of purpose in "Miss Brill" than anyone has shown. Lamenting an absence of God and striving to show that one must love, Miss Mansfield created Miss Brill, who strives to show love but is incapable of showing or receiving it. In her solitude she is certainly not protected by any godly benevolence. It is the estrangement from love that alienates Miss Brill.

Some obvious elements of alienation occur in Miss Brill's name and in her residence. Miss Brill's name in French (*briller*) means to shine. The irony is that she does not shine but is indeed a dull spinster without a shining personality or the warming glow of love. In a Swiftian sense, the name further suggests Miss Brill's estrangement from herself. All that she can see and know of herself is that "varnish and tinsel" of the surface. Her fur is the most obvious of the surface fixtures with which she identifies. Secondly, Miss Brill is an alien in France. This fact alone can account for some of her estrangement and inability to communicate freely. However, we can find the less obvious indications of alienation in the paradoxes and comparative events.

The story opens with a thematic paradox. From the description of the atmosphere—"the blue sky powdered with gold and great spots of light like white wine splashed over the Jardins Publiques . . . the air was motionless, but when you opened your mouth there was a faint chill, like a chill from a glass of iced water before you sip, and now and again a leaf came drifting—from nowhere, from the sky"—one immediately can feel the first throes of autumn, that "faint chill" anticipating the colder chill of winter. Yet paradoxically, Miss Brill finds in the chill the feeling of the vibrancy of spring. She takes out her fur piece, renews it for the season, questions its appearance, and then like an awakening "she felt a tingling in her hands and arms, but that came from walking, she supposed. And when she breathed, something light and sad—no, not sad, exactly—something gentle seemed to move in her bosom." This passage certainly parallels the passage beginning what Miss Welty calls Miss Brill's "vision of love." "The Band had been having a rest. Now they started again. And what they played was warm, sunny, yet there was just a faint chill—a something, what was it?—not sadness—no, not sadness—a something that made you want to sing." The "chill" or the "something" points directly yet subtly to Miss Brill's alienation. For her, love—the love of her fur piece, which functions like an unsympathetic mirror into which she cannot see, and the "vision of love," in which she imagines all those gathered in the park singing and thus communicating with one another—is faintly chill because she has been somehow excommunicated from a real experience of love. Thus not knowing love's warmth or having any framework of reference for the experience of love, she can feel or imagine love only in the solitude devoid of warmth, estranged and left cold with absence.

A further suggestion of estrangement is in the meeting of the woman in the ermine toque and the man in the gray suit. The man rejects the woman, whom Miss Brill admires and with whom she identifies. Mansfield drives home the rejection with the man's blowing smoke in the woman's face and with the beat of the bass drum drumming "the Brute, the Brute." Miss Brill in her identification feels that her experiences of rejection are like those experienced by the flirtatious woman. However, as Mr. Thorp points out, the woman is probably a prostitute. Miss Brill, not understanding the nature of the woman, fails to see the significance of her identification. Both women passionately desire to express their love, the woman wearing the toque through the physical contact of sex; Miss Brill through what she imagines. Society rebuffs both expressions. It rejects the one because sex is only one manifestation of love; it rejects the other because of failure to communicate (society cannot read Miss Brill's mind). Katherine Mansfield says in her letter "... one *must* declare one's love." Miss Brill's declaration is unheard and thus, to society, unexpressed.

We can find still further evidence of alienation in the "vision of love," in which Miss Brill is gathered up into an imaginative experience with all the people gathered in the park singing together as a harmonious whole. But even this imaginative attempt at an expression of love fails as Miss Brill thinks: "Yes, we understand, we understand ... though what they understood she didn't know." Even in her most vivid imaginings, Miss Brill can find no understanding or communication. She finds herself completely alone, yet she denies or fails to understand or to confront her position.

The final and most overwhelming evidence of alienation is the tragic scene in which Miss Brill is rebuffed by the young man courting on the seat next to her. The rejection parallels that of the man in the gray suit blowing smoke in the face of the woman in the ermine toque. Both exclusions are crude and brutish. With this confrontation with her solitude, she returns to her "cupboard" with nothing left her but self-pity in her loneliness.

Thus the theme of estrangement has run its course. Miss Brill has made an ever so passionate attempt to express love, to be a part of the whole of society that means so much to her. Her imagination, though sensitive, has failed from lack of experience. She is left, as she began, in her pathetic solitude.

**Source:** Robert L. Hull, "Alienation in 'Miss Brill'," in *Studies in Short Fiction,* Vol. V, No. 1, Fall, 1967, pp. 74–6.

## Sources

*The Letters of Katherine Mansfield,* edited by J. Middleton Murry, Knopf, 1930.

## Further Reading

Fullbrook, Kate. *Katherine Mansfield,* Indiana University Press, 1986.
   Biography of the writer's life.

Kobler, J. F. *Katherine Mansfield: A Study of the Short Fiction,* Twayne, 1990.
   Critical analysis of Mansfield's stories.

Nathan, Rhoda B., *Katherine Mansfield,* Continuum Publishing Company, 1988.
   Biography of the writer's life.

Pilditch, Jan. *The Critical Response to Katherine Mansfield,* Greenwood Press, 1996.
   Collection of reprinted criticism on Mansfield's works.

# The Monkey's Paw

**W. W. Jacobs**

**1902**

"The Monkey's Paw" is W.W. Jacobs' most famous story and is considered to be a classic of horror fiction. It first appeared in *Harper's Monthly* magazine in 1902, and was reprinted in his third collection of short stories, *The Lady of the Barge*, also published in 1902. The story has since been published in many anthologies, adapted for the stage, and made into films. "The Monkey's Paw" was well received when Jacobs first published it; the story garnered rave reviews from some of the most important critics writing at the turn of the century. The story was also very popular with readers.

Like O. Henry, Jacobs was famous during his lifetime for writing a particular type of story rather than for any particular work. Similar to O. Henry's stories, Jacobs' tales are tightly constructed, humorous stories that usually revolve around simple surprise-ending plots. Many of his stories are set on the waterfronts and docks of London, which Jacobs knew from his own childhood.

In addition to humor, Jacobs explored the macabre in several of his tales. "The Monkey's Paw" is probably the best example of this. The story opens with the White family spending a cozy evening together around the hearth. An old friend of Mr. White's comes to visit them. Sergeant-Major Morris, home after more than twenty years in India, entertains his hosts with exotic stories of life abroad. He also sells to Mr. White a mummified monkey's paw, said to have had a spell put on it by a holy man that will grant its owner three wishes. Morris warns the Whites not to wish on it at all—but of course they do, with horrible consequences.

Jacobs uses foreshadowing, imagery and symbolism in this story to explore the consequences of tempting fate. His careful, economical creation of setting and atmosphere add suspense to the tale, while his use of dialogue and slang (another Jacobs trademark) help readers to feel that the characters are genuine.

## Author Biography

W. W. Jacobs was one of the most popular humorists of the early 1900s, although his most famous story, "The Monkey's Paw," is considered a horror classic. William Wymark Jacobs, born September 8, 1863, was the son of a wharf manager and his wife. He grew up in Wapping, a seaport section of London. The docks and wharves of seaport towns later provided the setting for many of his stories.

Jacobs attended private schools and entered the civil service as a clerk in 1879, a job that he hated. When he was about twenty years old, he began writing stories and articles for fun, and by 1885 he began to publish them in magazines. His first collection of stories, *Many Cargoes*, was published in 1896, and the following year, he published two novellas in a single volume—*The Skipper's Wooing/The Brown Man's Servant*. However, Jacobs was a cautious man, and he did not quit his civil service job to devote himself to writing until his third book—another volume of stories, entitled *Sea Urchins*—was published in 1899.

Jacobs married soon after that. His wife, a militant suffragette and socialist, was very different from the conservative Jacobs, and their marriage was not a happy one. This fact may have contributed to the negative depiction of women that runs through most of his fiction.

The writer was very prolific during the early years of his career, producing a book nearly every year until 1911. At that time, the rate at which he wrote new material slowed dramatically, and he wrote very little during the last seventeen years of his life. However, it was in these years that Jacobs enjoyed great popularity with readers and some

*W. W. Jacobs*

fame. Many of his early works were reissued, and he wrote some adaptations of his stories for the stage. He died in 1943.

## Plot Summary

The story opens with Mr. White and his son Herbert playing a game of chess. Mrs. White is knitting by the fire. Mr. White loses the game and becomes agitated and exasperated. Soon, there is a knock at the door and the Sergeant-Major enters. They share a few drinks and the Sergeant-Major tells them some tales about his trips to India, where he obtained a monkey's paw. The paw is magical, allowing three men three wishes each. One man has died and the Sergeant-Major has used up his three wishes. He tosses the paw into the fire, but Mr. White snatches it out and keeps it for himself. The Sergeant-Major tells them that a fakir has put a spell on the paw "to show that fate ruled people's lives." Those who tamper with fate "did so to their sorrow." But Herbert coaxes his father to wish for something modest, like 200 pounds. His father does so, while Herbert plays dramatic chords on the piano in accompaniment. They all go to bed for the night.

In the morning, Herbert leaves for work and tells his parents not to break into the money before he comes home that evening. Mr. and Mrs. White make light-hearted comments about Herbert's return and his reactions to an arrival of the money.

Later, a stranger comes to the door and, after coming into the house, tells the parents that Herbert has been killed at work that morning when he was caught in some machinery. The stranger then gives them compensation from the company: 200 pounds.

Herbert is buried in a nearby cemetery. About a week later, Mr. White is awakened by the sounds of Mrs. White weeping over their son. Suddenly, she remembers the paw and the two wishes that remain. She pleads for Mr. White to get it and to make a wish that Herbert would be alive again. He tries to tell her that since he was mangled in the machinery and had been buried for a week, it would not be a wise wish. But she insists. Despite misgivings about invoking the magic of the paw again, Mr. White wishes for Herbert to be alive again.

They wait. They watch out the window, but nothing happens and no one arrives. They start to bed again when suddenly a slight knock is heard at the door.

Mrs. White then remembers that the cemetery is two miles away and that it would have taken Herbert a while to walk home. The knocking increases, ending in a series of rapid bangings on the door. Mr. White tries to stop her from opening the door. She persists and climbs up on a chair to open the top-most bolt.

Just as she opens the door, Mr. White asks his third wish. The door opens; the street is still and empty. Only a dim streetlight flickers on the roadway.

## Characters

### Father
See Mr. White

### Morris
See Sergeant-Major Morris

### Sergeant-Major Morris
Sergeant-Major Morris is the catalyst for the story: he brings the monkey's paw to the Whites' home. He is "a tall, burly man, beady of eye and rubicund of visage," whose eyes get brighter after his third glass of whiskey at the Whites' hearth. Morris is both familiar and exotic. Morris and Mr. White began their lives in approximately the same way; Mr. White remembers his friend as "a slip of a youth in the warehouse." But in his twenty-one years of travel and soldiering, Morris has seen the world and has brought back tales of "wild scenes and doughty deeds; of wars and plagues and strange peoples." Morris also carries with him the monkey's paw, which changes all the Whites' lives forever.

### Mother
See Mrs. White

### The Other
See The Stranger

### The Stranger
The last character to appear in "The Monkey's Paw" has no name. He is the messenger of death—the company representative sent to tell Herbert's parents about the death of their son in a terrible accident at work. On one level, Jacobs paints a realistic portrait of this man; Mrs. White notes that he is well dressed, and that he seems very nervous, hesitating at their gate, and picking lint from his clothes before he delivers his horrible news. However, on another level, the writer keeps this character anonymous: the man never gives his name, and his face is not described except as "perverted." In this way, the character works as a symbol of death or fate.

### The Visitor
See The Stranger

### Herbert White
Herbert White lives with his elderly parents and gets along with them quite well. He works at a local company called Maw and Meggins. Like his father, he is good-natured and reliable.

Despite this steadiness of character, Herbert is also a little bit silly. He is the first to ask Morris whether the old soldier used three wishes himself, and Morris looks at him "in the way that middle age is wont to regard presumptuous youth." He teases his parents about wishing on the monkey's paw, goading his mother into chasing him around the table, and his father into making the first wish. He remains skeptical and flippant about the paw's powers: "'Well, I don't see the money,' said his son as he picked [the paw] up and placed it on the table, 'and I bet I never shall.'" A bit later in the story, Herbert jokes, "I expect you'll find the cash tied up in a big bag in the middle of your bed."

Like his father's failings, Herbert White's irreverence is perfectly understandable. This quality even contibutes to why Herbert is so likeable. However, when Herbert dies a horrible death, "caught in the machinery" at Maw and Meggins, it is suggested that his death is related to his refusal to take the powers of the monkey's paw more seriously.

### Mr. White

Mr. White is a conservative, satisfied man who enjoys his quiet domestic life. Jacobs shows this in the very first scene in the story, which opens with father and son playing chess in their cozy cottage on a rainy night, while Mrs. White, knitting by the fire, comments on their game. Clearly, the Whites live a contented, if somewhat contained, life. Later in the story, the grandest thing Mr. White can think of to wish for is to clear the mortgage on their little house.

White does have reckless tendencies, though. In the first paragraph of the story, in the chess game with his son, he puts his king "into such sharp and unnecessary perils that it even provoked comment" from his normally docile wife. This recklessness leads him to tempt fate with the monkey's paw, endangering his family as a result.

Mr. White is a kind of "everyman." Happily retired, content with his life and his family, he is nevertheless intrigued by the tales of the exotic that his friend, Sergeant-Major Morris, brings home. His curiosity and his greed (a very minor greed, really) prove to be the undoing of his entire family—but these characteristics are what make him so human.

Although he is influenced by all the other characters, Mr. White is the principal force in the story—the one who makes things happen. Morris brings the monkey's paw, but Mr. White rescues it from the fire and later purchases it from the sergeant-major. Herbert, Mr. White's son, teases him into making the first wish; and it is his wife who forces him to make the second. He makes the third wish by himself, without even a witness to the wish-making. However, as the new owner of the paw, Mr.

## Media Adaptations

- In 1933, *The Monkey's Paw* was made into a 58–minute, black and white film directed by Wesley Ruggles, produced by RKO, and starring C. Aubrey Smith, Ivan Simpson, Bramwell Fletcher, and Louise Carter.

- A British version of *The Monkey's Paw,* produced in 1948, was directed by Norman Lee and produced by Ernest G. Roy. The film is 64 minutes long, black and white, and the cast included Milton Rosmer, Megs Jenkins, Joan Seton and Norman Shelley.

- In 1972 the anthology movie *Tales from the Crypt,* containing five dramatized stories, adapted "The Monkey's Paw" under the title "Wish You Were Here." The film was directed by Freddie Francis and produced by Cinerama. The cast included Sir Ralph Richardson, Joan Collins and Martin Boddey.

- In 1979, the story was adapted as a 19–minute film produced by Martha Moran and now available on video from Phoenix/BFA Films and Video.

- Stillife-Gryphon Films produced a 27–minute version of "The Monkey's Paw" in 1983, available on video from Modern Curriculum Press.

---

White is the person who makes all three wishes. He is the person who truly sets the story in motion, and it can be argued that he is the character who pays the most awful price for wishing on the monkey's paw. For although Herbert loses his life, and Mrs. White loses her central reason for living, Mr. White in effect loses his whole family, and must live with the knowledge that these losses are his own fault.

### Mrs. White

Mrs. White is a calm, reserved woman. In the story's first scene, Jacobs notes that Mr. White's chess moves are so "radical" that they "even provoked comment from the white-haired old lady knitting placidly by the fire''—as if drastic events must take place in order for her to even speak.

Mrs. White enjoys a good relationship with both her husband and her son, Herbert. She jokes with them, and humors them; when Mr. White insists that the monkey's paw moved in his hand when he made the first wish, she replies, soothingly, ''You thought it did.'' She fits the stereotype of the good housewife, common in the time when Jacobs was writing: she keeps the house and sets the supper; her husband and son are the center of her world.

In fact, it is the strength of her maternal instinct that empowers her at the end of the story, after Herbert has died. Overcome by the loss of her beloved son, she forces Mr. White to make the second wish on the monkey's paw: to bring Herbert back. Tragically, neither Mrs. nor Mr. White remembers to request that he come back whole from the grave, and in the moments before the door swings open, Mr. White wishes him gone again, so that his wife need not see the mangled, partly decayed body that both characters believe will be there. Thus, Mrs. White loses her son not once, but twice.

## Themes

### Fate and Chance

In ''The Monkey's Paw,'' Sergeant-Major Morris, an old family friend of the Whites, returns from India with tales of his exotic life and with a strange souvenir—a monkey's paw. This paw has had a spell put on it by a fakir (a holy man), he tells the Whites. Morris goes on to say that the fakir wanted to show that ''fate ruled people's lives, and that those who interfered with it did so to their sorrow. He put a spell on it so that three separate men could each have three wishes from it.''

As the story unfolds, author Jacobs provides many hints that, indeed, the monkey's paw does possess strange powers, and that tempting fate by making the three wishes is a grave mistake. First, the son, Herbert, asks Morris if he has made his three wishes, since he is in possession of the monkey's paw. '''I have,' he said, quietly, and his blotchy face whitened.

'''And did you really have the three wishes granted?' asked Mrs. White.

'''I did,' said the sergeant-major, and his glass tapped against his strong teeth.''

The sergeant major will say nothing else of his own misfortunes, but he does tell the Whites that although he does not know what the first owner of the paw asked for in his first two wishes, ''the third was for death. That's how I got the paw.''

Later that evening, Morris throws the paw on the fire, but Mr. White rescues it. Despite his friend's grave warnings, Mr. White makes a rather modest wish for 200 pounds, so that he may pay off the mortgage on his family's little house. And so, in spite of the original warning of the fakir, the story of the first owner of the monkey's paw, who wished for death at the end, and the warnings of their friend Morris, the Whites attempt to interfere with fate, with terrible consequences.

Morris has also told them that ''the things happened so naturally that you might if you so wished attribute [events] to coincidence.'' This is, in fact, what happens in the story. A strange man appears at the Whites' door the very next morning. He tells them that their son Herbert has been killed in an accident at work, and while the company admits no liability, they would like to settle on the Whites a sum of 200 pounds, as compensation for Herbert's death.

Ten days after the funeral, Mrs. White, almost crazy with grief, forces her husband to make the second wish on the monkey's paw: to bring Herbert back to them. Nothing happens for several hours, but then there is a knock at the door. ''It's my boy! It's Herbert!'' the old lady cries. ''I forgot it was two miles to the cemetery!''

Mr. White imagines his mangled son, risen after ten days in a grave, whose face was barely recognizable after the accident, standing at their door. To spare his wife this horrible sight, he makes the third and final wish on the paw: that Herbert go away.

By tempting fate, and wishing for money, the Whites lose something even more precious: their son, and their happy life as a family.

### Human Condition

It is human nature to want what one cannot have, and to undervalue what one does possess. Another common truth about the human condition is that people's best qualities often turn out to be their worst: the characteristics that can save them on the one hand can be their undoing on the other. The downfall of the White family comes from tendencies within each of the Whites that are only natural.

For example, Mr. White, in his life a reasonable man, is reckless in small ways like in the chess game he plays with his son. He is skeptical about the power of the monkey's paw; he feels foolish wishing on it and discounts the many warnings he hears and sees about the dangers of using it. He does, however, make his wishes. In the end, his "sensible" wish for the mortgage money is his undoing. The fact that he has wished at all is enough to bring on the fakir's curse.

Mrs. White also carries the seed of her destruction in her own character. She is the picture of the ideal housewife at the time the story was written: a good housekeeper, devoted to her husband and son, happy to let the men in the household make the important decisions. In her great love for Herbert, her son—for which she can hardly be faulted—she seizes upon the idea of wishing him back from the dead. Normally quiet and demure, she exhorts Mr. White to wish Herbert back with such force that he cannot deny her, even against his better instincts.

Herbert himself is a good-natured young man, who teases his parents about the power of the monkey's paw. He, too, is skeptical. His joking is not mean; under the circumstances, it seems normal. However, we wonder whether he would have lost his life if he had been more respectful of these mysterious powers.

## Style

### Foreshadowing

Foreshadowing is a technique in which the writer hints at the events to come. Sometimes, authors depict events early in a story that are really microcosms of the plot that is soon to unfold; other times, writers create this effect by developing an atmosphere that projects the tone of what is about to happen. For instance, a rather cliched example would be a stormy night on the eve of a murder. Jacobs uses both types of foreshadowing techniques in "The Monkey's Paw."

The Whites' chess game at the opening of the story, when Mr. White puts his king into "sharp and

## Topics for Further Study

- Research England's occupation and colonization of India. When did it begin? How long did it last? How was England's culture influenced by the information that was brought back from India to the British Isles?

- Research the Industrial Revolution, and locate Jacobs' work within it. How did the Industrial Revolution change life in England? Life in the United States? How did it affect families like the Whites in Jacobs's story?

- What writers and artists were contemporaries of Jacobs? Did they have similar concerns? Did other writers of his day use the literary devices that Jacobs often employed? Were painters and sculptors operating under the same cultural constraints and assumptions, and how did this affect their work?

unnecessary perils''—and soon sees "a fatal mistake after it was too late"—is a kind of mini-drama, one that tells us what is about to happen in the story.

The Whites (and readers) are given plenty of clues that the monkey's paw is dangerous and powerful. When Herbert asks if Morris has had his three wishes, he only replies, "I have," and taps his glass against his teeth. We get the feeling that what happened to him is so terrible that he will not talk about it. Morris also tells the Whites that while he does not know what the first owner of paw wanted in his first two wishes, the man's third wish was for death. Mr. White, despite these warnings, wishes anyway, and feels the monkey's paw move in his hand when he does so.

The atmosphere in the White's little house grows tense and ominous after Mr. White has wished on the paw. The wind rises outside, and "a silence unusual and depressing settled upon all three." Finally, after his parents have gone to bed, Herbert sits alone in the darkness, watching faces in the fire.

*A scene from an early film version of* The Monkey's Paw.

"The last face was so horrible and so simian [monkey-like] that he gazed at it in amazement." The face becomes so vivid that Herbert reaches for a glass of water on the table to throw onto the fire; instead of the water glass, his hand finds the monkey's paw.

These elements of the story, plus the appearance and strange behavior of the "mysterious man" who appears the next morning, prepare readers for the story's first horrible event: Herbert's death.

## Imagery and Symbolism

Two other techniques that Jacobs uses with great skill and subtlety are imagery (the picture created by the story's language) and symbolism (the meaning of an image beyond its literal description). Often, when an image is repeated, it then becomes symbolic. One such image in "The Monkey's Paw" is fire.

At the beginning of the story, fire is a warming, comforting element: with a storm raging outside, the family is grouped around the hearth, with father and son playing chess while mother knits contentedly. After the sergeant-major has arrived and had supper with the Whites, the men again sit in front of the fire, smoking their pipes.

A little later, when Morris tosses the paw onto the flames, the function of the fire changes: its intended role is to consume and purify the evil and destructive force that Morris believes exists in the monkey's paw. At the end of the evening, the same fire becomes ominous (or perhaps, delivers a warning) to Herbert, who sees a horrible, monkey-like face in the flames—one that so disturbs him that he tries to put it out.

In the final scenes of the story, fire fulfills a different purpose—to illuminate, both literally and figuratively. After Mr. White makes the second wish, the candle in the White's room goes out, symbolizing that even more darkness will come into their lives. The father lights a match to show his way to the door, but the match goes out too; frantic, he drops the box of matches in his attempt to light another match. Mr. and Mrs. White are in the dark. Symbolically, this loss of light means that they have lost their direction; that they have lost hope.

The final, sad image in the story is the view the Whites have when they have flung open their front door, where we suppose the dead and mangled Herbert, called forth from the grave, was standing just a moment before. All they see is a quiet and deserted road, illuminated by a flickering street light (street lights, when this story was written, were not powered by electricity and light bulbs, but rather by a gas flame). The Whites' life, without their son, will now be desolate and empty.

## Historical Context

### The British Empire

When Jacobs wrote "The Monkey's Paw" a popular saying was "the sun never sets on the British empire." By the early 1900s, England had conquered and colonized countries all over the world. The saying meant that somewhere in the world it was always daylight, and there a British colony could be found. Sergeant-Major Morris returns from India, a British colony, in "The Monkey's Paw." In colonies like India, Hong Kong, Australia, and South Africa, British military men, explorers, archaeologists, and scientists were learning about ancient cultures and traditions little known in the West. Returning from distant colonies to England, they were firsthand sources of information about other peoples and countries for their countrymen curious about exotic far-off lands. The retired colonel just back from India was a staple character in British popular fiction for many years.

### The Victorian Era

The last decades of the 19th century, and the first decade or so of the 20th century was, culturally, a very structured time, particularly in England. Jacobs grew up and wrote in an era when people lived by rigid, if unspoken, rules. Religious beliefs were strong, the growing middle class honored hard work and social stability. Men were the wage-earners; women were the housekeepers and in charge of raising the children.

### Everyday Life

Over six million people lived in London by 1900. Because of the crowded conditions, several generations of the same family normally lived together in the same house. Housing was too expensive and scarce for most individuals or married couples to live alone. Grandparents, parents, and children often shared the same living quarters. There was no electricity, so all light came from candles or gas lamps. Young people looking for work sometimes turned to colonial service because it paid well and provided some relief from the conditions in England. Those who stayed home often worked in the many industrial factories.

## Critical Overview

Popular with readers and critics alike (P.G. Wodehouse hailed him as a master writer), Jacobs was a prolific writer who published 19 volumes between 1896 and 1926. He wrote short stories, novels, and plays, although critics agree that he was most accomplished at the short story form. Despite the fact that most of his stories were humorous tales of life on the English waterfront at the turn of the century, his most famous story is "The Monkey's Paw," which James Harding in *The Reference Guide to Short Fiction* called "a little masterpiece of horror by an unusually gifted writer."

Jacobs is known for his deft, economical scene-setting and his neat, logical plots, two characteristics which are easily visible in "The Monkey's Paw." His stories show a gradation in humor. Many of them could be considered comedies, but Jacobs also began to experiment with what later became known as "black humor." This vein of writing led him to deal in the macabre, crafting pieces like "The Interruption" (*Sea Whisper*), about a man who murders his wife for her money and is then blackmailed by his housekeeper. He plans to poison the housekeeper but his plans go awry, and he dies instead. Another macabre story, "Jerry Bundler" (*Light Freights*), is a ghost story in which no ghost actually appears—similar to the last scene in "The Monkey's Paw," in which we believe that the mangled, ghost- or zombie-like Herbert is at the door—but never see him.

Jacobs published his first collection of short stories, *Many Cargoes*, in 1896. The book was well received by both readers and critics. G.K. Chesterton, who was regarded as one of England's premier men of letters during the first half of the twentieth century, gave the book a glowing review, favoring Jacobs over Rudyard Kipling: "Mr. Jacobs is in a real sense a classic...compared with Mr. Kipling, Mr. Jacobs is like the Parthenon."

Similar to O. Henry, Jacobs became famous more for the *type* of story that he wrote, rather than any particular work. The action in his stories usually revolves around neat, surprise-ending plots, which were very popular in his day. Sometimes his characters are motivated by money; often they are motivat-

# Compare & Contrast

- **Early 1900s:** England rules over an empire with colonies throughout the world, some of the most important being India and portions of South Africa.

  **Today:** On July 1, 1997, Hong Kong, England's last important colony, is returned to Chinese rule.

- **Early 1900s:** Rickets, a bone disease caused by malnutrition, was common among poor children in England.

  **Today:** Rickets is now a rare disease in England. Other once-common childhood illnesses, such as smallpox and polio, have also been eradicated through advances in medicine.

- **1902:** Popular superstitions, like the curse of Egypt's mummies or the powers of India's shamans, arise from Britain's contact with non-Western cultures.

  **Today:** The popularity of alternative medicine and natural healing remedies stems from society's disenchantment with Western medicine, which is based solely on science.

---

ed by the desire to either be married or to avoid marriage. Nearly all his plots contain trickery or deception.

Jacobs' output slowed considerably, beginning around 1911. However, in the last twenty years or so of his life, his popularity escalated, and many of his earlier works were reissued. In these later years, Jacobs did not produce much new work, but he did write some adaptations of his better-known stories for the stage.

After he died, Jacobs' works fell into obscurity. In the late 1960s, however, interest in his writing was revived, and a number of his works have since been reissued.

## Criticism

### Carl Mowery

*Carl Mowery has a doctorate in rhetoric and composition and has taught at Southern Illinois University and Murray State University. In the following essay, he provides an overview of "The Monkey's Paw" and examines fire imagery in the story.*

The English author W. W. Jacobs did most of his writing in a fifteen-year period around the turn of the twentieth century. Many of his stories were lighthearted tales about life on the English waterfront. But "The Monkey's Paw," first published in 1902 in a collection called *The Lady of the Barge* deals with the ghastly and macabre. According to G. K. Chesterton, it rates very highly "among our modern tales of terror in the fact that [it is] dignified and noble." Chesterton says that Jacobs' "horror is wild, but it is a sane horror." This is in contrast to Edgar Allan Poe's tales of "insane horror."

Even though "The Monkey's Paw" is a short story and does not contain the royal characters or political intrigues of Greek drama, it does contain some elements of Greek tragedy. It begins in happiness and hope, and it closes in grief and despair. Mr. White's desire for easy money (greed) leads him to challenge fate. That violation brings the whole family to grief.

In ancient Greece, there were two types of drama: Comedy and Tragedy. In a Comedy, the action is usually lighthearted and often humorous. The ending is a happy one. In a Tragedy, the action begins with the hero on a high social and/or political level. He or she then descends to a position that is significantly lower in status than where the story began. The hero in a tragedy has a character weakness—the tragic flaw—that causes him or her to make a serious mistake, which causes his fall from the high position. Fate is a major concern in these plays. If the hero interferes with the inevitable, because of his tragic flaw, serious consequences occur. The ending is often intensely dramatic and the hero may die or be killed at the end.

As our tragic little story opens, we are struck by the images of the happy family sitting in the living room, father and son playing chess and mother knitting by the fireplace. This is a typical English family from about the year 1900 and, as such, we know that their lives were highly structured. They lived by a set of strict but unwritten rules. Fathers were the wage earners, and the decision makers in the household. Mothers were homemakers and the family members most responsible for rearing the children. Sons were expected to follow in their father's footsteps, or to go out and earn a living as soon as they were old enough. Daughters were expected to learn how to keep the house and then to marry and rear children.

But even in the most tightly organized situation, events occurred that disturbed the equilibrium. Equilibrium, in a story, is a state of balance among the characters. It is the disruption of equilibrium that creates interest in a story. Mr. and Mrs. White and their son, Herbert, are visited by the Sergeant-Major and things begin to go awry. He comes into the house and entertains the family with stories of his visits to India (a colony in the British Empire at this time). During one trip he has obtained a monkey's paw that has had a magic spell put on it by a fakir (a holy man) "to show that fate ruled people's lives, and those who interfered with it did so to their sorrow." As he describes the paw, "His tones were so grave that a hush fell upon the group." These powers, he explains, should be taken very seriously and should never be trifled with. After the Whites take possession of the paw, the Sergeant-Major tries to convince them not to indulge in its magic, warning them of dire consquences.

Despite the warning of the Sergeant-Major, the family is intent on testing the paw. Mr. White and Herbert are intrigued with the possibilities of gaining wealth by making a single wish. So, heeding the Seargeant-Major's advice "to wish for something sensible," Mr. White makes a wish for just 200 pounds. In one innocent act of greed, Mr. White has set into motion a series of events that are fated to end unhappily. After Herbert is killed in an accident at work, the company sends 200 pounds compensation

## What Do I Read Next?

- *Selected Short Stories,* reprinted in 1975, contains some of Jacobs' best stories.

- The ghost stories of M. R. James are among the finest of the twentieth century. *Ghost Stories of an Antiquary* (1905) is his best known collection.

- An earlier writer of surpernatural tales is Joseph Sheridan Le Fanu, whose *Ghost Stories and Tales of Mystery* (1851) is highly regarded by critics in the genre.

to Mr. and Mrs. White. The wish seems to have come true!

If we accept these events at face value, several questions arise. Did Herbert die because they trifled with fate as the fakir warned? Or is Herbert's death only a happenstance, as suggested by the Sergeant-Major's remark that "things happened so naturally that you might if you wished attribute it to coincidence."

No matter which possibility we choose, Mr. and Mrs. White continue to rely on the paw for assistance, which contributes to their continued descent into despair. Mr. White's flaw, greed, has blinded him to his violation of fate. And after Herbert's death, he succumbs to a deeper greed: to wish his son back from the dead. His failure to learn from his first interference with fate leads him deeper into the magical world.

But his tragic flaw has caused him to fall into a great despair. He ignores the warnings of the Sergeant-Major at the beginning and he ignores his own instincts at the end when, at his wife's urgings, he makes the second wish. His third wish is made, restoring a desolate calm, and this little tragedy has come to an end.

There are two techniques that illuminate the tragedy of the White family. These are imagery (the picture created by the language) and symbolism (the meaning of an image beyond its literal description).

> "Fire is often seen as a source of comfort and warmth. It is also seen as a purifying or a destroying element."

A powerful symbol occurs in the opening scene with father and son playing chess. Here the game is more than just a chess match. It is symbolic of a set of rules, a strict order. As long as the players follow the rules of the game, everything is in order. But if one or the other player violates the rules then chaos will follow. The White family's lives have been governed by a strict set of rules and when we first see them, they are still living within them. But then these rules are violated, and chaos indeed ensues.

Herbert moves from playing chess to playing childish games, taunting his father into making the first wish and then teasing him after the wish is made. Even Mrs. White joins in by chasing Herbert around the table. These childlike games have no rules and are ultimately more dangerous, because they indicate "a carelessness which betokened no great belief in [the paw's] virtues."

Another important image is the fire and flame. Fire is often seen as a source of comfort and warmth. It is also seen as a purifying or a destroying element. As a single flame of a candle or a match, it provides illumination. At first, fire is a part of a warming, comfortable image—mother sitting near the hearth, knitting. Later the two men sit comfortably before the fire and smoke their pipes before going to bed. But this image contains a double meaning. The fire and pipe smoking are both comforting, but they are also destroying something in the process. In both instances there is a reduction of substance, tobacco or fire wood, resulting in darkness, foreshadowing and symbolizing the dying happiness in the life of the family. During the evening, the fire takes on another meaning, when the Sergeant-Major, who is convinced that the paw is evil, tosses it into the fire. Here, fire is a destroying and/or purifying element.

Another important flame image occurs in the final scenes of the story. After Mr. White makes the second wish, the candle in their room goes out before any results come from the wish. Then father lights a match to show his way to the door. But it, too, goes out and he cannot see down the hallway. He drops the box of matches in his frantic attempts to light another match. The symbolism of lost direction and lost hope is seen in the candle and the match going out. The Whites are in the dark, both literally and figuratively. Their passion for the dark power of the paw has clouded their ability to see. But, perhaps, the most poignant fire image in the whole tale is the last, the flickering street light illuminating "a quiet and deserted road." In this final scene, the realization of the loss of their son is all the Whites have.

**Source:** Carl Mowery, for *Short Stories for Students,* Gale Research, 1997.

### Stefan Dziemianowicz

*Stefan Dziemianowicz is the editor of many anthologies of horror and supernatural fiction. In the following essay, he examines the narrative structure of "The Monkey's Paw," which he judges to be "flawlessly crafted."*

W. W. Jacobs' "The Monkey's Paw" is one of the most reprinted tales of horror in the English language. Yet any study of the story's merits as such must take into account that its author was not a horror writer. Although several of his short stories feature macabre elements, Jacobs was best known in his day as a writer of humorous tales, often concerned with the sea and sailors. "The Monkey's Paw" was first published in the general literary magazine *Harper's Monthly* in 1902, and collected that same year in *The Lady of the Barge,* a mixed bag of stories on various themes that differed little in content from Jacobs' previous volumes of short fiction.

"The Monkey's Paw" is a superior work of horror fiction because, first and foremost, it is a flawlessly crafted short story. A deceptively simple tale, it reveals on close inspection Jacobs' meticulous attention to narrative structure and careful handling of foreshadowing, symbolism, and other narrative elements that contribute to its eerie effect.

The story is divided into three parts, a number that Jacobs treats with significance: the monkey's paw grants three wishes, the White family is the third party to benefit from its magic power, and there are three members of the family. As a symbol, the number three can be interpreted to mean many things, including progression and imbalance. In

Jacobs' tale, the universe tolerates neither. The monkey's paw has a spell put on it by a fakir who "wanted to show that fate ruled people's lives, and those who interfered with it did so to their sorrow." Jacobs orchestrates the story's events to show how trying to change one's fate upsets the existing balance and invites a counter-reaction. The futility his characters experience trying to improve their lot with the monkey's paw is mirrored in the structure of the three parts of the story. Each is built around the same central event, a visit to the White household by an outsider. The repetition of this event and the consequences that follow reinforces the tale's lesson concerning the immutability of fate.

The first part of the story lays the foundation on which the other two parts build. Jacobs begins by contrasting the internal and external worlds of his tale: "Without, the night was cold and wet, but in the small corner of Laburnam Villa the blinds were drawn and the fire burned brightly." The world that the Whites know is presented as cozy and bright, and the world beyond their door as inhospitable and dark. Jacobs is setting his scene here, but he is also building the framework for a tale of supernatural horror, which traditionally involves the eruption of dark and hostile forces into the comfortably ordered world of its characters. Indeed, it does not take long for him to evoke this possibility. Although the Whites are at ease with themselves and their surroundings, the "sudden and unlooked-for violence" with which Mr. White responds to losing a chess game suggests that the stability of the household is tenuous and fragile. The first test of its vulnerability is the visiting Sergeant-Major Morris, recently returned from twenty-one years of military duty in India. Morris is a taciturn man whose dourness clashes with the conviviality of the Whites and is clearly related to his experiences abroad. When Mr. White wistfully wishes that he might visit India himself, Morris remarks, "Better where you are," a comment that sounds particularly ominous in light of Mr. White's earlier outburst that "of all the beastly, slushy, out-of-the-way places to live in, this [the family homestead] is the worst." The monkey's paw and the wishes it grants appear to be the root cause of Morris's sullenness. He informs the Whites that he has availed himself of its magic, but is cryptically evasive when asked what he wished for. He does note that its previous owner's third wish was for death, leaving the reader to infer the enormity of what he has suffered from his use of the talisman. This is the first of several instances in which Jacobs evokes horrors indirectly,

> "Jacobs orchestrates the story's events to show how trying to change one's fate upsets the existing balance and invites a counter-reaction."

foreshadowing the final horror which is so terrible that it is enough to suggest it without showing it.

In the first part of the story the monkey's paw is a symbol of the world beyond Laburnam Villa, a souvenir of a distant land but also an embodiment of the dark and foreboding forces that encroach outside the White's happy home. Morris begs the family to wish only for "something sensible," but knows that any wish made with it, no matter how sensible, will exact a devastating price. Mr. White believes "I've got all I want," but is easily goaded by his wife and son Herbert to wish for two hundred pounds. From the moment it is introduced into White's home, the monkey's paw begins disordering its harmony.

The story's second part follows the pattern of the first. When it appears that Mr. White's wish has not come true, everyone makes light of his credulousness. A spirit of "prosaic wholesomeness" prevails in White household until the arrival of the second visitor, this time the representative of Herbert's employer, who informs the mother and father that their son has been killed in a work accident. Jacobs carefully chooses the words that describe Herbert's accident: "He was caught in the machinery" —literally the tools of his trade, but also the mechanism of fate which grinds down those who attempt to resist it.

"The Monkey's Paw" abounds with allusions to a inflexibly ordered universe that is merciless towards those who deviate from its prescribed paths. The first part of the story opens with Mr. White and Herbert playing chess, a game with fixed rules. Mr. White is characterized as someone who "possessed ideas about the game involving radical changes," a trait that puts his king into "sharp and unnecessary perils." By contrast, the man dispatched by Herbert's employers to deliver the news of his death

> "Had White been one merely to accept life, he would have taken the soldier's advice and let the paw burn."

remarks, "I am only their servant and am merely obeying orders." Much of the story's horror derives from its depiction of fate as a mechanism indifferent to human whims and ambitions. In the story's first part, Herbert jokes that his father will find the money he has wished for sitting on his bed, "and something horrible squatting on top of the wardrobe as you pocket your ill-gotten gains." This image, which captures the spirit of much supernatural horror fiction written in Jacobs' time, suggests a world in which good is rewarded, evil is punished, and the moral concerns that govern human behavior matter. "The Monkey's Paw" shows the foolishness of such a world view. When the representative of Herbert's employers informs the family that they "disclaim all responsibility" for his death, he echoes Sergeant-Major Morris's warning "don't blame me for what happens" when Mr. White rescues the paw from the fireplace. There is no arbiter of good and evil working responsibly behind the scenes of Jacobs' story, only a clockwork universe in which the two-hundred pound indemnity paid the Whites amounts to an equal exchange for Herbert's life.

In the third section of the story the stasis one might expect in a universe so rigidly ordered becomes manifest. The Whites have buried their son and though they feel "a state of expectation as though something else was to happen," they are mired in "the hopeless resignation of the old, sometimes miscalled, apathy." A brief boost of hope revives Mrs. White when she realizes that the monkey's paw can still grant two wishes. Once again Mr. White is pressed to make a wish, this time for the return of their son. Thus begins the third and final visit to the White household, a recapitulation of events from the first two parts which the reader knows by now can only lead to despair. When the knocking begins on the downstairs door some time later it appears that Herbert has returned and fate has been contravened. Belatedly, though, Mr. White realizes that in wishing his son back he has neglected to take into account the boy's mutilation and time spent in the grave. A resurrected Herbert would be an abomination, as intolerable to look upon as impossible to exist in the fate-driven universe of the story. In a twist on the events of the first two parts, where outsiders bring misery into the White's home, a family member must now be kept out to prevent even greater misery from occurring. The irony of this turn of events raises the impending sense of horror to an excruciating level at the climax. With his third and final wish, Mr. White cancels out his second, wishing the knocker away. The magic of the monkey's paw is exhausted, and the Whites have gained nothing by it. Jacobs draws the reader's attention to this methodical working out of fate in his final sentence, where Mr. White looks out upon the "deserted road," as empty as it was at the story's beginning.

"The Monkey's Paw" is a model of storytelling economy, whose individual parts reflect and contribute to a tightly integrated whole. Jacobs works out the story's simple premise—the inability to change one's fate—through its plot, but also uses it to organize his narrative. This expertly calculated matching of form to content explains the extraordinary power of Jacobs' tale, and possibly why its numerous imitators have never surpassed its effectiveness as a tale of horror.

**Source:** Stefan Dziemianowicz, for *Short Stories for Students,* Gale Research, 1997.

## Joseph H. Harkey

*In the following brief essay, Harkey explains some instances of foreshadowing in Jacobs's "The Monkey's Paw."*

In the early lines of W. W. Jacobs' "The Monkey's Paw," an altogether chilling story, is embedded the germ of the entire story. Mr. White and his son Herbert were playing chess, the father,

> (*1*) who possessed ideas about the game involving radical changes, (*2*) putting his king into . . . sharp and unnecessary perils. . . . "Hark at the wind," said Mr. White, who, (*3*) having seen a fatal mistake after it was too late, (*4*) was amiably desirous of preventing his son from seeing it.

Contained in this passage are four elements that foreshadow the action of the story, although Jacobs is never heavy-handed in working out the tale as a projection of its opening paragraphs. The obvious parallel to the game of chess, is, of course, the game of life. While Mr. White's choosing a small sum (two hundred pounds) when he made his first wish on the monkey's paw might make him seem less than radical, we must remember that he snatched the paw from the fire when the old soldier tossed it there. Had White been one merely to accept life, he would have taken the soldier's advice and let the paw burn.

The second element, that of putting his king into "sharp and unnecessary peril," comes with the first wish. White had no way of knowing that he was endangering Herbert's life in requesting the £200, but the soldier's demeanor when he told of the magical powers of the paw should have warned a less radical man to let the paw burn. As it turned out, the £200 wished for came as an indemnity for Herbert, who was killed when he fell into some working machinery. While the Gothic tone of the story is not such that one would expect a pun on the "sharp" peril, certainly the peril was *unnecessary*. White planned to use the £200 requested to pay off the mortgage, but there was no urgent need for it to be paid off immediately.

White's seeing a fatal mistake after it was too late was the third element. The fatal mistake here is not the death of his son, however, but something even more terrible—the resurrection of his son with his face still mangled from the machinery. When Mrs. White insisted that White make a second wish—to bring Herbert back—White feared that the wish might bring the son back mutilated. Nevertheless, his fear of his wife caused him to make the second wish. It was only much later, when they heard a noise at the door, that White sensed it was his mutilated son and frantically sought the paw to make a third wish.

This wish—that Herbert be dead again—was an acting out of the fourth element. But it is not the son he is preventing from seeing the fatal mistake this time. It is his wife, who is not aware that the second wish did not include the request that Herbert be restored whole. The third wish prevented the heartstruck mother from seeing the hideous creature outside the door.

Thus in the opening two paragraphs, Jacobs has given us a *micro*-story which contains all the elements of the *macro*-story, if one may use those terms. Still, his symbolic foreshadowing is not heavy-handed. The use of the words "amiably desirous" to describe White's efforts to prevent his son from seeing his mistake, for instance, would seem incongruous were they to describe his effort to prevent his wife from seeing their son. Indeed, despite the symbolic relationship of the chess game to the story proper, Jacobs handled it in such a sophisticated manner that the effect of the game on the reader is suggestive, hinting of the dangers implicit in Mr. White's radical ideas about the game—of life, while at the same time giving us with a few bold strokes a preliminary sketch of the central character in the story.

**Source:** Joseph H. Harkey, "Foreshadowing in 'The Monkey's Paw'," in *Studies in Short Fiction,* Vol. VI, no. 5, Fall, 1969, pp. 653–54.

## Sources

Chesterton, G. K. "W. W. Jacobs," in *A Handful of Authors: Essays on Books and Writers,* edited by Dorothy Collins, Sheed and Ward, 1953, pp. 28-35.

## Further Reading

Adcock, A. St. John. "William Wymark Jacobs," in his *The Glory That Was Grub Street: Impressions of Contemporary Authors,* Musson Book Company, 1928, pp. 147–57.
   Adcock discusses Jacobs's use of humor, horror and sentiment, and praises his stylistic control.

Donaldson, Norman. "W. W. Jacobs," in *Supernatural Fiction Writers, Vol. 1,* edited by E. F. Bleiler, Scribner, 1985, pp. 383-87.
   Donaldson writes a brief description of Jacobs's supernatural tales, including "The Monkey's Paw," which he calls Jacobs's best.

Harding, James. "The Monkey's Paw," in *The Reference Guide to Short Fiction,* edited by Noelle Watson, St. James, 1994, p. 806.
   A short essay on story; book also includes entry on W. W. Jacobs and a bibliography.

Priestley, J. B. "Mr. W. W. Jacobs," in his *Figures in Modern Literature,* Books for Libraries Press, 1970, pp. 103–23.
   Priestley argues that, in his humorous stories, Jacobs created a miniature world of his own where his comedic skills could be best displayed.

Pritchett, V. S. "W. W. Jacobs," in his *Books in General,* Chatto & Windus, 1953, pp. 235–41.
   Pritchett provides an appreciative overview of Jacobs's work as a writer, calling him "one of the supreme craftsmen of the short story."

# An Occurrence at Owl Creek Bridge

**Ambrose Bierce**

**1891**

"An Occurrence at Owl Creek Bridge" is one of the most widely anthologized American short stories and is considered Ambrose Bierce's best work of short fiction. First published in Bierce's short story collection *Tales of Soldiers and Civilians* in 1891, the story centers on Peyton Farquhar, a southern planter who, while not a Confederate Soldier, is about to be hanged by the Union Army for attempting to destroy the railroad bridge at Owl Creek. As Farquhar stands on the bridge with a noose around his neck, Bierce leads the reader to believe that the rope breaks and that Farquhar falls into the water below, only to escape to his farm, where he is reunited with his wife. It is revealed at the end of the story, however, that Farquhar has, in fact, been hanged and that these imaginings took place in the seconds before his death. While "An Occurrence at Owl Creek Bridge" has been occasionally faulted for what some critics consider its gimmicky ending, it has nonetheless been lauded as an example of technical brilliance and innovative narration as well as for its examination of such themes as the nature of time and the complexities of human cognition.

## Author Biography

Ambrose Bierce was born in 1842 in Meigs County, Ohio. His parents were farmers, and he was the tenth of thirteen children, all of whom were given names beginning with "A." In 1846 the family moved to Indiana, where Bierce attended primary and secondary school. He entered the Kentucky Military Institute in 1859 and at the outbreak of the Civil War enlisted in the Union Army, serving in such units as the Ninth Indiana Infantry Regiment and Buell's Army of the Ohio. Bierce fought in numerous military engagements, including the battles of Shiloh and Chickamauga and in Sherman's March to the Sea. After the war, Bierce traveled with a military expedition to San Francisco, where he left the army in 1867.

Bierce's early poetry and prose appeared in the *Californian* magazine. In 1868 he was hired as the editor of the *News Letter,* for which he wrote his famous "Town Crier" column. Bierce became a noted figure in California literary society, establishing friendships with Bret Harte, Mark Twain, and Joaquin Miller. In 1872 Bierce moved to England, where during a three-year stay he wrote for *Fun* and *Figaro* magazines and acquired the nickname "Bitter Bierce." His first three book of sketches, *Nuggets and Dust Panned Out in California* (1872), *The Fiend's Delight* (1873), and *Cobwebs from an Empty Skull* (1874) were published during this period. He returned to San Francisco and worked in a government mint office for one year before becoming associate editor of the *Argonaut.*

Bierce worked for a mining company in South Dakota for two years, but he returned to the city in 1881 to become editor of the weekly *Wasp.* In 1887 Bierce began writing for media mogul William Randolph Hearst's *San Francisco Examiner,* continuing the "Prattler" column he had done for the *Argonaut* and *Wasp.* This provided him with a regular outlet for his essays, epigrams, and many of the short stories subsequently collected in *Tales of Soldiers and Civilians* in 1891 and *Can Such Things Be?* in 1893. A committed opponent of hypocrisy, prejudice, and corruption, Bierce acquired fame as a journalist, becoming an admired but often hated public figure, a man of contradiction and mystery. In 1914 he informed some of his correspondents that he intended to travel to Mexico to join Poncho Villa's forces as an observer during that country's civil war. He was never heard from again, and the circumstances of his death are uncertain.

*Ambrose Bierce*

## Plot Summary

Upon a railroad bridge in Alabama, a man is waiting to be hanged. His hands are tied behind his back, and a rope encircles his neck. He stands upon a platform constructed of loose boards. Members of the Federal Army—the Union Army during the Civil War—are also on the bridge. Some are completing the preparations and some are guarding the bridge. The man about to be hanged, Peyton Farquhar, is a civilian.

On one side of the stream is a forest, on the other a fort. Halfway between the bridge and the fort stand a line of soldiers, all armed. When the soldiers finish their preparations, they move off of the bridge. A sergeant stands at the opposite end of the same board as Farquhar. At the signal from his captain, he will step off the board. The board will tilt down, and Farquhar will fall through the railway ties.

Farquhar closes his eyes to think of his family but he is distracted by a sharp, rhythmic sound. He tries to figure out what it is and how far away it is. He finds he is waiting with impatience and apprehension for the toll, which seems to come less frequently. The sound is so loud that it hurts his ears. What he hears is only the ticking of his watch. Farquhar opens his eyes and looks at the stream. He thinks that if he could free his hands he might be able to dive into the water and swim away from his executioners. He would then flee for home, which is still outside of the territory held by the Union Army. As he is thinking, the sergeant steps off of the board.

The narrative then flashes back to Farquhar and the circumstances that led to his hanging. Though he was a Southern plantation owner, he was unable to serve in combat. Still he longed for the glory of a soldier's service and waited for the chance to prove that he possessed courage. One evening, a Confederate soldier stopped at the plantation, and Farquhar asked for news of the war: The Yankees were pushing forward. The soldier told him that they were repairing the railroads and had built a fort near the Owl Creek bridge. The Yankee commander had issued an order to hang any civilian caught interfering with the railroad. Farquhar asked about the bridge, and the soldier put in his mind how easily the bridge would burn. An hour later, the soldier passed the plantation again, heading north. He was returning to Yankee territory, for he was a scout for the Union Army.

The narrative returns to the present as Peyton Farquhar falls between the railway ties of the bridge, losing consciousness. The sharp pain in his neck and a feeling of suffocation return him to a state of awareness. He is incapable of rational thought. Then he splashes into the stream, and he is again able to think. He knows that the rope has broken. His body sinks toward the bottom of the stream. Without realizing it, he starts to free his hands, which then loosen the rope at his neck. His hands drive him to the surface of the water. After a breath of air, he finds he has an amazing awareness of his surroundings: he can feel each ripple of water, see the colors shining in the dewdrops on the grass, hear the body of a fish parting the water. He also sees the fort and the soldiers, shouting and pointing at him. A bullet strikes the water inches from his face and he hears the orders to fire.

He dives under the water, under a hail of bullets. When he resurfaces, he is further downstream. He knows he must get out of the soldiers' range soon because the officer will give his soldiers the order to fire at will. They even fire a cannonball at him. Fortunately, the water throws him upon the bank opposite from the fort. He runs into the forest and travels all day. At nightfall he stumbles upon a road that leads him in the direction of his home. It is a wide road, yet eerily empty with no one is traveling on it nor fields or homes alongside it.

His throat, his eyes, and his tongue are all swollen. Despite his suffering, he continues walking. He believes he has fallen asleep while walking, for he finds he is at the gate of his own home. His wife is on the veranda to meet him. As he is about to embrace her, he feels a sharp blow on the back of his neck. He sees a bright white light, and then there is blackness. Peyton Farquhar has died. His body, the neck broken, swings beneath the timbers of Owl Creek bridge.

## Characters

### Peyton Farquhar

Peyton Farquhar is a Southern planter of about thirty-five years of age who has been apprehended by the Union Army for attempting to destroy the railroad bridge at Owl Creek. It is this crime for which he is about to be hanged. Farquhar is a prosperous farmer and slave owner from an old and respected Alabama family. While he has been prevented from becoming a Confederate soldier for unknown reasons, it is nonetheless stated that there was "no service too humble for him to perform in aid of the South, no adventure too perilous for him to undertake." Because he dies at the end of the story, Farquhar is sometimes considered a sympathetic and brave character, but many have found him to be callous, foolhardy, and obsessed with honor.

## Themes

"An Occurrence at Owl Creek Bridge" is the story of Peyton Farquhar, a Southern farmer who is about to be hanged by the Union army for trying to destroy the railroad bridge at Owl Creek. While the reader is led to believe he escapes under miraculous circumstances, it is revealed at the end of the story that Farquhar imagined his escape in the split seconds before his death.

### Time

Bierce uses a complex narrative structure to advance the theme of time in "An Occurrence at Owl Creek Bridge." He distorts the reader's sense of time by revealing at the end of the story that Farquhar imagined his escape in the few seconds before he died even though the escape takes up a great portion of the narrative. By doing so, Bierce addresses the ways time can be portrayed and manipulated in fiction, a medium in which the reader is often reliant on the author to represent or create reality. Bierce also stresses that time is subjective and phenomenal, especially during times of mental or emotional duress.

### *Death and Dying*

Bierce also examines the human desire to escape or cheat death and speculates what occurs physically and psychologically at the time of death. Although Farquhar's situation is quite grave—he is standing on a bridge with a noose around his neck as numerous Union soldiers stand guard—a part of him holds out hope that he can escape the situation and, therefore, mortality. By not allowing Farquhar to escape, Bierce emphasizes that death is unavoidable no matter how much people long to avoid it.

Bierce also provides a detailed description of what a person could experience at the moment of death. Farquhar transfers the physical realities of his hanging—the falling from the bridge, the snapping of the neck, the swinging on the rope—to an imagined scenario. In this hallucinatory state, his senses are heightened to such a level that he believes he can hear spiders gliding across the water, see a million blades of grass, and hear the beating of dragon flies' wings. It is unclear, however, if these sensations are a physical or psychological response to death.

### *Deception*

Bierce addresses deception on a variety of levels in the story. Farquhar deceives himself into believing that it is possible to escape hanging, and he imagines that he does so. The reader, wanting to believe that Farquhar has managed to avoid death and achieve the glory he so wanted to attain, ignores clues throughout the narrative that Farquhar is hallucinating. Bierce contributes to this deception by using a complex narrative structure in which the reader is unsure as to who the narrator is and if that narrator is reliable. Bierce, who believed that fiction ought to challenge readers, once wrote that he detested "bad readers—readers who, lacking the habit of analysis, lack also the faculty of discrimination, and take whatever is put before them, with the broad, blind catholicity of a slop-fed conscience or a parlor pig." Finally, Farquhar, who is obsessed with "the opportunity for distinction," allows himself to be tricked by the Union soldier masquerading as a Confederate. The soldier merely has to suggest to Farquhar that the bridge could easily be set on fire for him to attempt the deed. All of these deceptions are caused by people wanting to believe what is impossible or unlikely.

# Media Adaptations

- "An Occurrence at Owl Creek Bridge" was adapted for film in 1962. Produced by Janus, directed by Robert Enrico, and distributed by McGraw-Hill, this thirty-minute black and white film stars Roger Jacquet, Anne Cornaly, and Anker Larsen. It won the Academy Award for Best Live Action Short Film in 1963 and was shown on the television series "The Twilight Zone" that same year.

- The story was also adapted as the film *The Spy* in 1932. It was directed by Charles Vidor and starred Nicholas Bela.

### *Dreams and Reality*

Bierce also comments on the discrepancy between dreams and reality in "An Occurrence at Owl Creek Bridge." In the story, Farquhar, who dreams of being a great war hero for the Confederacy, has a romantic and idealized view of war. When he is confronted with the brutality, deception, and violence of armed conflict, he fantasizes that he escapes and triumphantly returns to his family. Dreams, then, are presented as a way of coping with the harsh realities of life. However, through his telling of the story and his portrayal of Farquhar, Bierce seems to suggest that such fantasies and self-deceptions are cowardly and often have negative consequences.

# Style

"An Occurrence at Owl Creek Bridge" centers on Peyton Farquhar, a southern farmer about to be hanged by the Union army for attempting to destroy the railroad bridge at Owl Creek. As he stands with the noose around his neck, Farquhar imagines that the rope breaks and he escapes. At the end of the story, it is revealed that these imaginings took place in the seconds before his death.

## Topics for Further Study

- Research Realism, Naturalism, and Romanticism in American letters and discuss how "An Occurrence at Owl Creek Bridge" relates to these schools of literary thought.
- Bierce fought on the side of the Union during the Civil War. Discuss how his own experiences during the war may have influenced his telling of "An Occurrence at Owl Creek Bridge."
- Compare and contrast the ending of "An Occurrence at Owl Creek Bridge" to William Wallace's death scene in the 1995 movie *Braveheart*.

### *Structure and Narration*

"An Occurrence at Owl Creek Bridge" is divided into three sections, with each section having its own distinct structure and narrative technique. In the first section, Bierce describes the setting of the execution up to the point the plank beneath Farquhar's feet is removed. It is told from a conventional third-person point of view, with the narrator objectively describing the scene and relating the circumstances from outside the story. The second section provides background information on Farquhar, including how he came to commit the act for which he is about to be hanged. It is revealed that Farquhar was at home with his family when a soldier rode up and told him that the Union Army would soon be advancing across the Owl Creek bridge, which was vulnerable to attack. The soldier then told Farquhar that a great deal of driftwood had piled up against the bridge and that it could easily be set on fire. At the end of the section, the reader is told that the soldier was not a Confederate but rather a Union scout who has tried to provoke Farquhar into attempting to destroy the bridge. This section is also told from the third-person point of view, but it varies somewhat from the narration in the first section because some of Farquhar's perceptions are revealed. The third section picks up where the first section left off; then the rope around Farquhar's neck apparently breaks and he falls into the water. The viewpoint of the story suddenly shifts to a modified first-person point of view, and the reader is given access to Farquhar's thoughts and feelings as he attempts to escape. The narrator describes in great detail what is happening as Farquhar struggles to get out of the river, escape gun shots and cannon fire, and run through the wilderness to his house approximately thirty miles away. At the very end of the section, the story suddenly switches back to the third person and it is revealed that Farquhar is dead. Bierce's shifts in narration create a sense of disorientation in the reader because it is not always clear who is relating the story and if the narrator is reliable. This reflects Farquhar's own disorientation and allows the reader to take part in his hallucinations.

### *Satire*

Bierce treats Farquhar as a satiric object in the story. Satire is a literary technique that uses ridicule, humor, or wit to criticize or provoke change in human nature or institutions. Bierce uses "indirect" satire; he relies on Farquhar's romantic notions of war to emphasize its brutal realities. Farquhar, who for some unknown reason was not allowed to become a Confederate soldier, believes that war is an "opportunity for distinction" and that "all is fair in love and war." He is obsessed with achieving honor and believes that battle would allow "the release of his energies." Because of these beliefs, Farquhar is a prime target for entrapment. The Union soldier merely has to suggest to him that Oak Creek bridge could easily be burned down. Seeing an opportunity for glory, Farquhar rushes off to commit the deed. However, even as he stands with a noose around his neck, he is unable to accept the realities of his impending death. Instead, he imagines an extraordinary series of events during which he, in his mind, emerges a hero.

### *Language*

Bierce uses figurative language—the opposite of literal language, in which every word is truthful, accurate, and free of exaggeration—to enhance the emotional impact of his story. He uses figurative language most extensively in the third section to give clues to the reader that Farquhar is hallucinating and becoming increasingly disoriented. In this section, the narrator's language is often melodramatic. For example, when Farquhar is in the river, fighting to break the rope around his wrists, the narrator declares: "What splendid effort!" and "What superhuman strength!" Additionally, the surroundings are described in the minutest detail, suggesting that Farquhar could not possibly be experiencing what is being described. For example, the narrator states that Farquhar "noted the prismatic colors in all the dew drops upon a million blades of grass," he heard "the beating of the dragon flies' wings," and he heard "the rush of [a fish] parting the water."

Bierce also uses alliteration—the repetition of consonant sounds—to make the language in this section sound unrealistic and hallucinatory: "He was now in full possession of his physical senses," "A piece of dancing driftwood," "His heart. . .had been fluttering faintly." Finally, Bierce uses meter—rhythmic language patterns—to create a singsong, dreamlike effect. For example, he uses iambs, a unit of words consisting of a repeating pattern of an unaccented syllable followed by an accented syllable: "The trees' u-pon' the bank' were gi'-ant gar'-den plants'."

# Historical Context

"An Occurrence at Owl Creek Bridge" was published in 1891, though it is set during the Civil War. This war, which was fought from 1861 to 1865, claimed 525,000 American lives, the most American lives ever lost in a war. (Some 400,000 were lost in World War II.) The Civil War was a bloody conflict that began when the states of the American South withdrew from the Union, arguing that the U.S. Constitution gave them the right to do so if they chose. When President Abraham Lincoln disagreed with their decision and was determined to keep the union together, war broke out between the Northern States, still loyal to a single, united country, and the Southern States, which had formed their own confederacy, a loose association of member states.

Because the South had a much smaller population, and thus had far fewer soldiers, a decision was made in 1861 to organize guerrilla warfare against Union troops. These guerrillas would infiltrate camps behind the battlelines to disrupt the enemy's communications and supplies by blowing up bridges, capturing messengers, and burning stocks of ammunition and food. Civilians were organized into companies of rangers to wage guerrilla warfare against Union troops, while special units of the Confederate Army were created to act as hit-and-run raiders behind Union lines. Besides disrupting Union communications and supply lines, the guerrillas also forced the Union to deploy more troops behind the front, thus easing somewhat the overwhelming manpower advantage the North enjoyed. Among the groups of Southern guerrillas who harassed Union troops was Mosby's Rangers, a civilian force that struck such fear into the Union government that it was common policy each night to remove the planks from all bridges leading to Washington, DC, so that Mosby's Rangers could not enter the city. One of the South's most flamboyant military generals, Nathan Bedford Forrest, became famous for his leadership of behind-the-lines attacks by Confederate cavalry forces in Tennessee and Mississippi during General William Tecumseh Sherman's March to the Sea.

# Critical Overview

Critical reaction to "An Occurrence at Owl Creek Bridge" has been mixed. While it continues to be a popular and frequently anthologized story, it has not received much serious scholarly attention. Some critics have dismissed it for what they consider its contrived ending, blatant sentimentality, reliance on sensationalism, and trivilization of death. Others have criticized Bierce for deceiving and playing with his readers. More recent critics, however, have reexamined the story and have concluded that it has often been misunderstood and misinterpreted and that it is, in fact, complex and innovative. F.J. Logan wrote in *American Literary Realism 1870-1910* that "the story has languished in anthologies, chiefly those used in secondary schools, perhaps because it has been so frequently offered as an action tale of extreme power written by an otherwise unfamiliar Civil War writer." He went on to say: "I am contending that 'Owl Creek Bridge' is not. . .some sort of hysterical gothic horripilator; it is, on the contrary, as tightly controlled and meticulously organized as any story is likely to be." In response to the accusation that Bierce played games with his readers, Harriet Kramer Linkin wrote in 1988 in *The Journal of Narrative Technique* that "Bierce manipulated the reader throughout [the story] but never lies outright. . . . The clues exceptional readers require to share Bierce's perspective are always available." Recent critics have also praised Bierce's focus on psychology and human cognition, particularly hallucinations and dreams.

Bierce's literary reputation is based primarily on his short stories of the Civil War, particularly

# Compare & Contrast

- **1860s:** After the Civil War, the United States officially abolishes slavery in 1865 with the 13th Amendment to the Constitution.

  **1890s:** Jim Crow laws, which permit and encourage racial segregation, are enacted in Alabama, Arkansas, Georgia, and Tennessee in 1891.

  **Today:** While racism still exists in the United States, institutional segregation and racial discrimination are illegal.

- **1860s:** The American Civil War is fought over whether the individual states or the federal government should have paramount political power.

  **1890s:** The Populist Party, a rural protest against the power of the railroads and banks which seeks to radically change the nation's currency system, polls 22 percent of the vote in the 1892 presidential election.

  **Today:** The militia movement in the American West questions the authority and legality of the federal government.

- **1860s:** The Central Pacific Railroad is chartered to build the western section of a transcontinental railroad.

  **1890s:** As of 1890, the United States has 125,000 miles of railroad in operation.

  **Today:** Railroad use in the United States is in decline. Amtrack, the government-run passenger service formed in the early 1970s, loses millions of dollars a year.

---

"Chickamauga," "The Death of Halpin Frayser," and "An Occurrence at Owl Creek Bridge." Bierce's narrative methods have sometimes caused critics to view his works as little more than technical exercises. "Too many of his stories," David Weimer has stated, "lean too heavily on crafty mechanics, on a kind of literary gadgeteering." Yet, according to H.E. Bates, the structure of Bierce's stories is significant because "Bierce began to shorten the short story; he began to bring it to a sharper, more compressed method." While critics have both condemned and praised Bierce's imagination as among the most vicious and morbid in American literature, his works are counted among the most memorable depictions of the precarious, ironic, and futile condition of human existence.

## Criticism

### Rena Korb

*Rena Korb has a master's degree in English literature and creative writing and has written for a wide variety of educational publishers. In the following essay, she sees "An Occurrence at Owl Creek Bridge" as an early example of the portrayal of a character's inner psychology in fiction.*

Ambrose Bierce may very well have been a man out of time. He was a cynical journalist writing at a time when social thought was dominated by optimism. He was the writer who introduced psychological studies in fiction into an American literary scene dominated by realism, naturalism, and regionalism. He was uncompromising in his refusal to bend to the requests of his publishers. Some people have seen his flight to Mexico in 1913 as his deliberate escape from living in that wrong time period. After finishing the preparation of his twelve-volume *Collected Works,* Bierce gave up writing to join with Pancho Villa's revolution as an "observer." He never returned from this last adventure. His disappearance in Mexico has rendered his death as one of the most celebrated among literary people of letters, captivating the imaginations of people throughout the world.

The legend of "Bitter Bierce" grew after his disappearance (his fate was even envisioned in

*A scene from the 1962 film version of* Occurrence at Owl Creek Bridge.

Mexican writer Carlos Fuentes' award-winning novel *The Old Gringo*), leading some to focus more on his adventurous life than on his writings. Many critics do feel that Bierce's work was overlooked and rejected by his contemporaries. One of the reasons for this may lie in Bierce's handling of his own work: he turned down offers of popular magazines to publish his stories because he did not want them to undergo editing; his work was published by small presses in California, not the big East Coast firms, to ensure that Bierce had complete authorial control. While these practices may have preserved his writing in their pristine form, they certainly did nothing to gain Bierce national attention. Despite these obstacles, Bierce did have significant claims to the literary world during his lifetime. Mark Twain numbered among the members of Bierce's California circle of writers, and William Dean Howells referred to him as one of the leading men of letters in America. *In the Midst of Life,* the volume which includes "An Occurrence at Owl Creek Bridge," drew favorable commentary on both sides of the Atlantic upon its publication. Some reviewers even ranked Bierce with such masters of the short story as Edgar Allan Poe and Nathaniel Hawthorne.

## What Do I Read Next?

- Stephen Crane's 1895 Civil War novel *The Red Badge of Courage* realistically depicts the psychological complexities of fear and courage on the battlefield.

- In his essay "The Moon Letters" (1903), Bierce discusses his theories on the responsibilities of readers and writers.

- Edgar Allan Poe's 1842 short story "The Pit and the Pendulum" is told in the first person by a prisoner of the Spanish Inquisition who relates his experiences with imprisonment and torture.

- *The Old Gringo*, a novel by Carlos Fuentes, is an imaginary account of what happened to Bierce after he disappeared in Mexico in 1913.

- In his 1865 poetry collection *Drum-Taps*, which contains such famous poems as "O Captain! My Captain!" and "When Lilacs Last in the Dooryard Bloom'd," American poet Walt Whitman relates his experiences in the Civil War.

- P.M.H. Atwater's 1995 book *Beyond the Light* examines the physical and psychological effects of near-death experiences.

---

In the words of critic Cathy Davidson, Bierce has staked his claim as "the precursor of postmodern fiction." In "An Occurrence at Owl Creek Bridge," his best-known story, Bierce displays many of the literary techniques that show the modernity that was ahead of its time. He was one of the first American writers to hold up the act of war and show it, not humorously or as picturesque, but for what it was: murder. He shortened the short story and made its elements sharper by using compressed methods of description. Most importantly, perhaps, and what would be most influential for twentieth-century writers, he "invented" many literary techniques: the close examination of time; an attention to mental fictions in order to avoid real life; the blending of fantasy and reality. Stories by the Latin American postmodern writers Jorge Luis Borges and Julio Cortazar are clearly indebted to Bierce, both in narration and style. Though fanciful, there is a grain of truth in the reasoning behind one critic's hypothesis that Bierce did not die in 1914, but that he waited in the Andes until the rest of the world caught up with him and then reemerged in South America to write under the name "Jorge Luis Borges"!

In an essay from 1941, H.E. Bates writes, "Bierce is the connecting link between Poe and the American short story of to-day." Bierce carries on this tradition dramatically and skillfully in "An Occurrence at Owl Creek Bridge," in which a Southern gentlemen, Peyton Farquhar, is about to be hanged for sabotaging a Union railroad bridge during the Civil War. Like many of Poe's stories, "An Occurrence at Owl Creek Bridge" has been seen as a work of terror replete with moments of black humor. Other critics have found its early exploration of Farquhar's psychology as a forerunner to the theories of Sigmund Freud. The story has even spawned the fiction of "post-mortem consciousness," in which, at the moment of death, the hero futilely struggles to impose his or her will on the universe, creating another temporary reality and escaping death; Ernest Hemingway, William Golding, Borges, and Cortazar have all written in this genre. More simple yet as important is Stephen Crane's analysis of "An Occurrence at Owl Creek Bridge": "Nothing better exists—the story has everything."

As Bierce may have been a man out of time, so might "An Occurrence at Owl Creek Bridge" have been a story out of time. It is modern in its psychological motif of how a man's consciousness attempts to deal with the fact that he is about to die. Its execution is modern; fifty years after the story was written, and decades before writers like Borges and Cortazar rediscovered Bierce's techniques, H.E. Bates noted that the story was written in a "language much nearer to the prose of our own day than that of Bierce's day." Bierce strives to set the reader firmly and immediately in the story from the opening paragraph: "The man's hands were behind his back, his wrists bound with a cord. A rope closely encircled his neck." Clearly, there is no need for preliminaries. Bierce also shows Farquhar's distortion of time in an effort to fend off death. Farquhar looks down at the "stream racing madly beneath his feet" yet notes only how slowly a piece of driftwood caught in the current seems to move. He becomes aware of a recurring noise that inexplicably slows down so that the "intervals of silence grew progressively longer, the delays became maddening." It is only the ticking of his watch, sounding out "the tolling of a death knell." By the end of the story, Farquhar himself has turned into a timepiece, but one that keeps regular time, as he swings like a pendulum "gently from side to side beneath the timbers of the Owl Creek bridge."

Perhaps the most engaging and provocative technique used in the story is the blending of fantasy and reality, the mixing of the external world of death with Farquhar's internal world, which cries out for life. While some people refer to this lack of distinction as leading to a "trick" ending, most critics (and readers) agree that Farquhar's death is apparent to anyone who pays attention to the clues. The first appears while Farquhar still stands on the railroad bridge. His dream of escape—"I might throw off the noose and spring into the stream. By diving I could evade the bullets and, swimming vigorously, reach the bank, take to the woods and get away home"—is his last conscious thought. Then, he plunges to his death and his mind proceeds to act out this very fantasy, down to the same details of escape. The similarity here is too striking to overlook. That his escape is fantasy is also apparent numerous times throughout its enactment. Farquhar's senses are impossibly keen; he hears ripples in the water as "separate sounds," he is able to see the "individual trees, the leaves and the veining of each leaf...the very insects upon them." If this has not proven the true bent of the story, Bierce next shows Farquhar as inhabiting an unreal environment, one that is unnaturally eerie and devoid of people. He travels on a road "as wide and straight as a city street, yet it seemed untraveled." He can feel that his neck is in pain, his eyes are congested, and his tongue is swollen, yet "he could no longer feel the

> "Perhaps the most engaging and provocative technique used in the story is the blending of fantasy and reality, the mixing of the external world of death with Farquhar's internal world, which cries out for life."

roadway beneath his feet." At this, the end of his life, he finally recognizes that the world is not that secure place where "no adventure was too perilous" but a changing universe in which the very stars have a "secret and malign significance."

This blending of fantasy and reality is also used to show how each of the story's three sections demonstrates a different one of Farquhar's incorrect beliefs. In the first section, Farquhar denies what is about to happen. The use of military terminology and a factual tone convey the clinical and inescapable nature of the hanging—the sergeant "would step aside, the plank would tilt and the condemned man go down between the ties"—yet the "civilian" still delves into fantasy, dreaming of freeing his hands and escaping. The second part of the story, a flashback, shows Farquhar's inability to distinguish military reality with his vision of the glorious, "larger life of the soldier." He clearly has no experience with military tactics and allows himself to be tricked by a Federal spy into burning the railroad bridge. Though he fatally believes that he has the "heart of soldier," when he does not even have the good sense of a soldier, he still embraces this chance at sabotage as his "opportunity for distinction." What Farquhar ultimately finds in war is obscurity; his yearning for a soldier's adventure has led him simply to be "the man who was engaged in being hanged."

If the second and third sections show Farquhar's predisposition for creating fantasy, this third and last part of the story is a sort of "living and breathing" fantasy: that of Farquhar's "escape." The Farquhar seen here is an improved man. He is certainly more knowledgeable than the Farquhar who let himself be tricked by the Yankees; witness his analysis of what kind of shots the troop will fire on him. The language in this last section is luxurious, with the sand of the riverbank "like diamonds, rubies, emeralds" and the forest through which Farquhar travels full of "whispers in an unknown tongue." The descriptions are imaginative as is the journey that Farquhar makes to his home. And even in the moment of death, fantasy does not give way to reality. The noose tightens around his neck, but Farquhar believes he is about to embrace his wife. As the rope tightens, breaking his neck, "he feels a stunning blow upon the back of the neck; a blinding white light blazes all about him with a sound like the shock of a cannon—then all is darkness and silence!" Once Farquhar has entered into his fantasy, nothing can vanquish it except death.

**Source:** Rena Korb, for *Short Stories for Students,* Gale Research, 1997.

## Peter Stoicheff

*In the following essay, Stoicheff analyzes Farquhar's thoughts and actions in terms common to representations of dreams in literature.*

"An Occurrence at Owl Creek Bridge" has received more critical attention than any other single work by Ambrose Bierce. This is probably because it combines into one text the best ingredients distributed among much of Bierce's fiction—satire, irony, manipulation of the reader, the exposure of human self-deception, a surprise ending, and a stylistic compression and tautness. It may also be because something of the story still eludes its commentators, leaving a residual and "uncanny" (to use Bierce's convenient term in the text) sense of revelation hovering just beyond one's grasp. Peyton Farquhar's death at the end is a surprise, so carried away are we by his desire for escape; yet it seems somehow presaged by the very description that keeps it, until the story's last paragraph, obscure and unanticipated. As Stuart C. Woodruff, one of the story's closest analysts, puts it, "[s]omehow the reader is made to participate in the split between imagination and reason, to *feel* that the escape is real while he *knows* it is not" (Woodruff's emphasis). . . .

The premise of the third section of "An Occurrence at Owl Creek Bridge" is that Farquhar imagines his escape in the brief interval between the removal of the plank that supports him and his actual death by hanging. That time is somewhat indeterminate in the story, as it is for at least two reasons in actuality. Some hanging victims die immediately, while others struggle for several seconds—death in these cases becoming a more gruesome and gradual process. More significantly for Bierce's purposes, though, is that "time" itself, when employed to calibrate human experience, seems to become indeterminate at points of maximum emotional disturbance. Though the time it takes for Farquhar to die by hanging is indeterminate, Bierce goes to some length to imply that at the unknowable threshold of death itself time becomes crucially altered and even paradoxical, resistant to commonplace reciprocities of sensation and duration. (The distortion is mirrored in the narrative itself, whose "time" is suspended at the end of the first section and reversed in the second—bold anachrony and analepsis, which are literally impossible and at the same time perfectly acceptable to the reader.) His account in the third section suggests that, within a short time period, sensation does not become effaced, but instead divides itself into infinite units of experience, saturating the mind with stimuli. From this perspective, "time" becomes vertiginous, the span of a second dilating to reveal ever increasing interior units of time, which themselves repeat the process of fractal division. Thus it may take "only" a "split second" for Farquhar to transform from a sensate being to an insensate one (for Farquhar is "as one already dead" within that short time, after all), but that moment itself encounters the threshold of time's erasure, in effect turning time inside out to reveal Blake's eternity in an hour.

The third section corroborates this through a complex association of Farquhar's body, and emotional sensation, with the pendulum. The fact that he "swung through unthinkable arcs of oscillation, like a vast pendulum" suggests the retarded ("What a sluggish stream!") quality of the time units Farquhar experiences once the execution begins, assisted by other details of protracted time ("ages later, it seemed to him"), and of intensified sensation ("pains . . . beat[ing] with an inconceivably rapid periodicity"). Throughout this simultaneously swift and sluggish journey from sensation to its effacement, Farquhar is "conscious of motion," and that consciousness will divide into the minute sensations of physical escape down the creek, as the few seconds for death to "occur" will divide almost infinitesimally into the 24 hours that the escape becomes in his dream. The point that Bierce makes through the "greater infrequency" of Farquhar's watch at the end of section one is not just that time has seemed to slow, as critics argue, but the opposite as well, that sensation has expanded to open time up from the inside as it were, and to prolong it—a transformation necessary for the third section to operate as it does.

Crucial to the principle of the dream that structures this section, however, is the fact that the pendulum is not only a significant metaphor for time and its infinitely divisible (thus "inconceivably rapid" and "unthinkable") periodicity; it is also a most accurate simile for Farquhar's body, which "swung gently from side to side beneath the timbers of the Owl Creek bridge." Farquhar is "conscious of [the] motion . . . of a vast pendulum" because his body literally traces it, and he peripherally senses it, in the last stage in this extended drama of hanging, time, and consciousness. . . .

Similar intrusions of other objective stimuli into Farquhar's experience permeate the third section. The "sharp report" of the firing gun, its slightly later "dulled thunder," and the ostensible "explosion" of the cannon that "was cracking and smashing the branches in the forest beyond" are Farquhar's dreamed revision of the sound of his own neck breaking. Bierce effectively underlines the association, describing the literal event of the breaking neck as occurring "with the sound like the shock of a cannon" at the story's conclusion. Farquhar's sensation of "rising toward the surface" of the water is the dreamer's interpretation of the slight bounce the body describes after reaching the extremity of its flexible rope; the sensation of almost drowning in the creek revises the fact of strangulation itself; the "horribly" aching neck and the "uncomfortably warm" bullet impossibly "lodged between his collar and his neck" under the water reinterpret the pain of hanging; the "counter-swirl" that spins him around in the current recasts the twisting at the end of the rope; the "projecting point which concealed him from his enemies" transforms the bridge (or the plank) now above him; the sensation of his own tongue "thrusting forward from between his teeth into the cold air" registers its grotesque protrusion during strangulation; the inability to "feel the roadway beneath his feet" is a similarly accurate impression, obediently revised into an understandable fatigue, thirst and numbness near the end of his narrative of escape.

The sense of strangulation, the sound of the cannon, and the pendular motion are the three objective stimuli that appear most frequently in various dream distortions in the third section. They trigger Farquhar's narrative of escape, and then are extracted and redistributed across it without regard for their actual external sequence (respectively strangulation, breaking neck, pendular motion) in much the same way that an external stimulus of some duration, such as an alarm clock's ring, will simultaneously generate and become situated within the linear narrative of a dream. Various other details of the "escape" that have been explained merely as examples of Bierce's alerting the reader to its unreality might be accounted for within this dream structure as well. For instance, the ability to hear "the rush of [a fish's] body parting the water" is no doubt impossible, as several readers have concluded, but within Farquhar's suddenly interior world generated by external stimuli it is one conceivable distortion of a final rushing heartbeat sounding amid the "congestion" of the hanged man's head as he dreams of being in the water below. . . .

**Source:** Peter Stoicheff, "'Something Uncanny': The Dream Structure in Ambrose Bierce's 'An Occurrence at Owl Creek Bridge,'" in *Studies in Short Fiction,* Vol. 30, No. 3, Summer, 1993, pp. 349–58.

## George Cheatham and Judy Cheatham

*In the following essay, Cheatham and Cheatham talk about how the name Peyton Farquhar in Bierce's "Occurrence at Owl Creek Bridge" symbolizes the character.*

Peyton Farquhar—no reader of Ambrose Bierce's "An Occurrence at Owl Creek Bridge" fails to note the oddity of the name. Any one having taught the story has no doubt had students find the name humorous. Why then did Bierce, who could have given the character any name, choose the one that he did? Is Peyton Farquhar simply one of those old names, familiar to the nineteenth century, which falls strangely on modern ears, or does its oddness serve some function in the story? A close look at the name suggests the latter point and, further, that Bierce chose the name carefully.

Peyton, first, is a variant spelling of Payton, the Scottish form of Patrick (from the Latin, meaning a patrician, a person of noble descent). Farquhar derives from the Gaelic *Fearachar,* meaning manly or brave, the name of an early Scottish king. Such a pair of names, of course, well suits a "well-to-do planter, of an old and highly respected Alabama family," who is "at heart a soldier."

The name itself, moreover, reinforces the central irony of the story, that Peyton Farquhar is the satiric butt of the story rather than the sympathetic figure he has often been called. Bierce subtly and ironically delineates Farquhar's naively unrealistic view of war, contrasting it with warfare's harsh truths. Bierce reveals Farquhar's past life, for example, through the empty martial abstractions a civilian like Farquhar might use: "gallant army," "inglorious restraint," "larger life of the soldier," "opportunity for distinction," "no adventure too perilous," and so on.

Farquhar's escape also, as he imagines it both before and during the hanging, is the stuff of a civilian's dream of war. Before he begins to drop, noose around his neck, Farquhar outlines his plan:

> "If I could free my hands," he thought, "I might throw off the noose and spring into the stream. By diving I could evade the bullets and, swimming vigorously, reach the bank, take to the woods and get away home."

As he falls, the heroic sketch blossoms into elaborate and precise—yet highly improbable, even impossible—detail. For example:

> The man in the water saw the eye of the man on the bridge gazing into his own through the sights of the rifle. He observed that it was a gray eye and remembered having read that gray eyes were keenest and that all famous marksmen had them. Nevertheless, this one had missed.

Significantly, Peyton Farquhar's martial knowledge derives from books, not experience. A bit later Farquhar dodges not just one shot but a whole volley fired by the Union soldiers. With the "rapidity of lightning," the civilian, rather Walter Mitty-like, reasons militarily:

> The officer will not make the martinet's error a second time. It is as easy to dodge a volley as a single shot. He has probably already given the command to fire at will. God help me, I cannot dodge them all.

But he does dodge them all. Even a Federal cannon cannot impede the hero's flight to home and family:

> ...his wife, looking fresh and cool and sweet, steps down from the veranda to meet him. At the bottom of the steps she stands waiting, with a smile of ineffable joy, an attitude of matchless grace and dignity. Ah, how beautiful she is! He springs forward with extended arms.

This reunion is the epitome of clichéd romance.

To establish the irony systematically, Bierce concludes each of the story's three sections with a flat realistic statement to undercut Farquhar's preceding fantasies or romantic illusions. In section 1, for example, Farquhar's sentimental thought that his "wife and little ones are still beyond the invader's farthest advance" is countered with the narrator's objective statement: "The sergeant stepped aside." The genteely Southern scene of section 2, in which the lady, "with her own white hands," offers water to the "gray-clad soldier," who thanks her "ceremoniously" and bows to her husband, is matched with another objective statement of life's harsh reality: "He was a Federal scout." And in section 3, the narrator's factual intrusion shatters the climactic moment of Farquhar's escape romance: "Peyton Farquhar was dead...." Peyton Farquhar's name itself—not only meaning patrician and manly but also actually sounding somehow aristocratic, genteel—is woven into the texture of the story, heightening the ironic contrast between a civilian's romantic fantasies and the realities of war. The pretensions of his name match those of his dreams, but neither name nor dreams match reality. And the careful selection of so minor a detail as the man's name suggests an artistic thoughtfulness in Bierce's work greater than that allowed by many critics.

**Source:** George Cheatham and Judy Cheatham, "Bierce's 'An Occurrence at Owl Creek Bridge'," in *Explicator,* Vol. 43, No. 1, Fall, 1984, pp. 45-7.

# Sources

Bates, H.E. *The Modern Short Story,* The Writer Inc., 1956, 231 p.

Linkin, Harriet Kramer. "Narrative Technique in 'An Occurrence at Owl Creek Bridge'," *The Journal of Narrative Technique* Vol. 18, no. 2, spring, 1988, pp.137-52.

Logan, F. J. "The Wry Seriousness of 'Owl Creek Bridge'," *American Literary Realism 1870-1910,* Vol. 10, no. 2, spring, 1977, pp. 103-13.

# Further Reading

Ames, Clifford R. "Do I Wake or Sleep? Technique as Content in Ambrose Bierce's's Short Story, 'An Occurrence at Owl Creek Bridge'," *American Literary Realism 1870-1910,* Vol. 19, no. 3, spring, 1987, pp. 52-67.
> Examines how Bierce's concealed manipulation of narrative reliability in the story parallels the story's thematic focus on the confusion between subjective perception and objective events.

Barrett, Gerald R. and Erskine, Thomas L. *From Fiction to Film: Ambrose Bierce's "An Occurrence at Owl Creek Bridge,"* Dickenson Publishing Company, Inc., 1973, 216 pp.

> This volume includes excerpts of several criticisms of the story as well as a scene-by-scene analysis of the film adaptation.

Crane, Kenny. "Crossing the Bar Twice: Post Mortem Consciousness in Bierce, Hemingway, and Golding," in *From Fiction to Film: Ambrose Bierce's "An Occurrence at Owl Creek Bridge,"* edited by Gerald R. Barrett and Thomas L. Erskine, Dickenson Publishing Company, Inc., 1973, pp. 76-80.

> Crane defines the genre of post-mortem consciousness fiction and outlines how Farquhar goes through these stages.

Davidson, Cathy N. *The Experimental Fictions of Ambrose Bierce,* University of Nebraska Press, 1984, 166 p.

> Davidson examines Bierce's work, focusing on the impressionistic, surrealistic, and philosophical elements in his writing. Analyzing the use of literary techniques in "An Occurrence at Owl Creek Bridge," Davidson traces the effect of the story on certain postmodern writers.

Fadiman, Clifton. *In the Midst of Life,* Citadel Press, 1974, pp. 9-17.

> Fadiman's introduction to this collection gives a biographical sketch of Bierce, including an overview of critical reception during his career, and analyzes why he seems to be better received in the decades after his disappearance.

Grenander, M.E. *Ambrose Bierce,* Twayne, Inc., 1971, 193 p.

> Grenander gives detailed biographical information as well as specific analyses of Bierce's writing.

# The Ones Who Walk Away from Omelas

Ursula K. Le Guin

1973

"The Ones Who Walk Away from Omelas" is Ursula K. Le Guin's allegorical tale about a utopian society in which Omelas' happiness is made possible by the sacrifice of one child for the sake of the group. In an allegory, many symbols and images are used in an attempt to illustrate universal truths about life. "Omelas" was first published in the magazine *New Directions* in 1973, and the following year it won Le Guin the prestigious Hugo Award for best short story. It was subsequently printed in her short story collection *The Wind's Twelve Quarters* in 1975. Le Guin is known primarily as a science fiction and fantasy writer, and "The Ones Who Walk Away from Omelas" is notable for being one of the few short stories of the genre to be widely anthologized in collections of general fiction. It is also notable for containing a vagueness uncharacteristic of many short story writers; its narrator leaves it up to the reader to imagine many of the town's details and characters.

The story is subtitled "Variations on a Theme by William James." William James was an early twentieth-century psychologist and the son of the renowned novelist Henry James. Le Guin was intrigued by James's theory of pragmatism, which states that a person's thoughts should guide his or her actions, and that truth is the consequences of a person's belief. Taking this theory to its moral conclusion, she fashioned the land of Omelas.

Readers looking for clues as to where the city of Omelas is located should note that Le Guin devised

the town's name by reading a roadside sign backwards. Thus, "Omelas" is an anagram of Salem, Oregon, a fact that the author has stated is not particularly relevant. Some critics have noted the similarity of the story's ideas with the themes of Russian novelist Fyodor Dostoyevsky, who wrote *Crime and Punishment,* another work concerned with morality. But Le Guin has stated that only in retrospect did the similarities between his work and hers occur to her; it was not a major influence in the writing of the story.

## Author Biography

Ursula K. Le Guin is one of science fiction's most popular writers. She is also one of the genre's most respected. Through her novels, which feature fantastic universes and fictional societies, she explores the idea of dualities. Dualities are concepts that feature two opposing forces, like chaos versus order or harmony versus rebellion. Le Guin stresses the importance of achieving a balance between these forces in order to achieve wholeness in life. Her most famous novels include the *Earthsea* trilogy, *The Left Hand of Darkness,* and *The Lathe of Heaven,* which explore themes common to all her works, including the award-winning "The Ones Who Walk Away from Omelas." Some of these themes are alienation, liberation, and ecological, social, and self awareness. Le Guin has also published poems, children's books, and novels for young adults.

Le Guin was born October 21, 1929, in Berkeley, California, and was encouraged to write from an early age. She is the daughter of an anthropologist and a writer, and her early interests included Celtic and Teutonic (German) myths along with the fantasy tales of Hans Christian Andersen, Lord Dunsany, and J. R. R. Tolkein. After graduating from Radcliffe College and Columbia University, Le Guin married Charles Alfred Le Guin, a historian. Le Guin's first book, *Rocannon's World* was published in 1966. It was about the first human beings who lived on the fictional planet Hain, a race of people who eventually colonized many other planets. The story spans 2,500 years, and concerns a protagonist on a quest to discover his identity and purpose in life. This book, like many of her later works, employs various forms of psychic phenomena, including telepathy (the reading of minds), clairvoyance and precognition (the ability to see things before they happen).

Le Guin has garnered many awards for her writing. In 1970 *The Left Hand of Darkness* won both the Nebula Award and the Hugo Award for best novel. The novel concerns a society of people whose identities have nothing to do with their gender. Through this literary device, Le Guin examines one of her favorite topics: the idea that unity can be achieved through the tension inherent in the duality of male versus female. *The Tombs of Atuan,* one of the Earthsea novels, won a Newbery Award and a National Book Award. *The Dispossessed: An Ambiguous Utopia* won many awards, including a Nebula Award, a Jupiter Award, and a Jules Verne Award. It is another volume in her Hainish cycle, which originated with *Rocannon's World*, that contrasts two planets: one where the inhabitants live responsibly and simply, the other where people are divided by class distinctions and material possessions. In addition to her writing, Le Guin is active in a number of social causes and is a member of the human rights group Amnesty International, as well as the Nature Conservancy and the National Organization for Women.

## Plot Summary

"The Ones Who Walk Away from Omelas" opens as the celebration of the Festival of Summer is getting underway in the city of Omelas. There is an air of genuine excitement about the festival, with its flag-adorned boats, noisy running children, prancing horses, and "great joyous clanging of the bells."

The narrator, who never identifies him or herself, steps back from describing the scene to comment that, "Given a description such as this one tends to make certain assumptions.... Omelas sounds in my words like a city in a fairy tale, long ago and far away, once upon a time."

However, the narrator hastens to add, the people of Omelas "were not barbarians. I do not know the rules and laws of their society, but I suspect they were singularly few." The people of Omelas are happy, and the narrator explains his or her belief that "we" (presumably enlightened, contemporary

*Ursula K. Le Guin*

westerners) have a "bad habit, encouraged by pedants and sophisticates, of considering happiness as something rather stupid."

As the narrator continues to describe the people and the city, he or she stops using the past tense verbs of a traditional narration and switches to the conditional: "I think that there would be no cars or helicopters in and above the streets." The people's happiness is not determined by the external accoutrements of life in Omelas, but rather, whatever is in Omelas "follows from the fact that the people of Omelas are happy people." This happiness is "based on a just discrimination of what is necessary, what is neither necessary nor destructive, and what is destructive." They "could perfectly well" have some of the luxuries belonging to the middle category, but, as the narrator tells the reader, other than the fact that they are happy, what they have or do not have "doesn't matter. As you like it." The narrator has an idea about what life is like there, but the reader is more than welcome to add details of his or her own. If the description given thus far of Omelas strikes the reader as "goody-goody," for example, then the reader is welcome to add an orgy. If there are orgies, though, any resulting offspring will be treated well; in another distinction which makes Omelas seem utopic, "one thing I know there is none of in Omelas is guilt."

Now the horse race is about to begin, and with it the Festival itself officially opens. In case the reader is still skeptical about the nature of Omelas, the narrator will describe "one more thing." At this point the story makes a dramatic shift, turning to what is literally and figuratively beneath the surface of the happy city, the troubling situation at the core of its existence.

In a dirty, dusty, dank, locked room sits a "feeble-minded" child in fear of its surroundings, never directly approached by the townspeople except when they "kick the child to make it stand up ... [or] peer in at it with frightened, disgusted eyes." As with the details of the city itself, the narrator leaves some of the details of the child's existence up to the reader, too: the room is "in a basement under one of the beautiful public buildings of Omelas, or perhaps in the cellar of one of its spacious private homes.... [The child] could be a boy or a girl." But from here, although the reader is given alternatives and choices as to the conditions of the child's existence, the horror of the description proceeds with clarity and certainty.

The adults of Omelas "all know it is there.... Some of them have come to see it, others are content merely to know it is there." All the adults understand that everything that is good and wonderful about their city depends "wholly on this child's abominable misery." People, usually children, who come to see the child for the first time "are always shocked and sickened at the sight." They may ponder the peril of this child "for weeks or years," ultimately realizing that there is nothing they can do. If the child "were cleaned and fed and comforted, that would be a good thing, indeed; but if it were done, in that day and hour all the prosperity and beauty and delight of Omelas would wither and be destroyed. Those are the terms. To exchange all the goodness and grace of every life in Omelas for that single, small improvement: to throw away the happiness of thousands for the chance of the happiness of one: that would be to let guilt within the walls indeed."

Furthermore, says the narrator, the people realize that even if the child were to be released and treated kindly now, it has been degraded for so long already that rescue would come too late; it is unlikely that it would "get much good of its freedom." The tears of the young people "at the bitter injustice dry when they begin to perceive the terrible justice of reality, and to accept it.... Theirs is no vapid, irresponsible happiness. They know that they, like the child, are not free. They know compassion."

The narrator winds up the story by asking the reader if somehow the presence of this suffering, which all the happiness of Omelas is based on, makes the happiness more credible. And then, he or she adds, "There is one more thing to tell, and this is quite incredible." Occasionally one of the adolescents who goes to see the child for the first time, or even one of the older adults who has been pondering the child's situation silently for years, turns away from the town and simply leaves, each one alone, walking "ahead into the darkness, and they do not come back. The place they go towards is a place even less imaginable to most of us than the city of happiness. I cannot describe it at all. It is possible that it does not exist."

## Characters

### The Child

The child, whose existence is revealed toward the end of the story, is abused and mistreated so the other citizens of Omelas can live in prosperity and happiness. Locked in a small room or closet with no windows, the child is dirty, naked, and malnourished. It receives only half a bowl of corn meal and grease a day and often sits in its own excrement. The narrator states that the child "could be boy or a girl. It looks about six, but actually is nearly ten. It is feeble-minded. Perhaps it was born defective, or perhaps it has become imbecile through fear, malnutrition, and neglect." All of the citizens of Omelas know of the child's existence, but they also "know that it has to be there.... [They] all understand that their happiness...[depends] wholly on this child's abominable misery." The child, therefore, is the scapegoat of the story; it is sacrificed for the good of the others in the community.

### The Citizens of Omelas

The citizens of Omelas are described as happy, nonviolent, and intelligent. Everyone is considered equal in Omelas; there are no slaves or rulers. In Omelas, children run about naked, playing; "merry women carry their babies"; and "tall young men wear... flowers in their shining hair." The narrator also stresses that although the citizens are happy, they are not simple or naive; "they were mature, intelligent, passionate adults whose lives were not wretched." All of the citizens know about the child, who is mistreated and locked in a small room, but most accept that their happiness depends on the child's "abominable misery." The ones who are not able to bear the reality of the child's situation leave Omelas forever.

## Themes

"The Ones Who Walk Away from Omelas" is the story of a utopian society whose survival depends on the existence of a child who is locked in a small room and mistreated. Although all of the citizens of Omelas are aware of the child's situation, most of them accept that their happiness is dependent on the child's "abominable misery." Sometimes, however, a few people, after visiting the child and seeing the deplorable conditions under which it lives, leave Omelas forever.

### Morals and Morality

One of the major themes in "The Ones Who Walk Away from Omelas" is morality. Le Guin once wrote in a preface to the story that it is a critique of American moral life. She also explained the story's subtitle, "Variations on a Theme by William James," noting that she was inspired to write the story by something James, an American psychologist and philosopher, stated in his "The Moral Philosopher and the Moral Life": "[If people could be] kept permanently happy on the one simple condition that a certain lost soul on the far-off edge of things should lead a life of lonely torment,...how hideous a thing would be [the enjoyment of this happiness] when deliberately accepted as the fruit of such a bargain." Although James believed people would not accept such a bargain, Le Guin presents in "The Ones Who Walk Away from Omelas" a society that does just that so that she can explore the reasons why people avoid or renounce moral responsibility. In fact, the few people who do choose to leave Omelas after seeing the child are hardly noticed, and their act of protest is not understood by the people or the narrator.

As a political allegory, a story in which characters represent things or ideas to covey a political message, "The Ones Who Walk Away from Omelas" also addresses the morality underlying political systems. The child has been said to repre-

## Topics for Further Study

- Research William James's philosophy of pragmatism, which inspired Le Guin to write "The Ones Who Walk Away from Omelas." Do you think that she agrees with his ideas of happiness in society? Why or why not?

- A kibbutz is a communal farm in Israel. Investigate the style of living and the beliefs of the people who live in a kibbutz. How does this compare with the way the people of Omelas live?

- Give some examples from present-day society in which the well-being of a few must be sacrificed for the good of the whole.

---

sent the underclass in capitalistic Western societies, particularly the United States, as well as the underdeveloped countries of the Third World. In both cases, poor, underprivileged people are often exploited and overlooked by the wealthy and prosperous. Therefore, Le Guin explores the moral accountability of a society where the happiness of the majority rests on the misery of a powerless minority.

Finally, Le Guin examines the moral responsibility of writers and readers by composing a story in which the narrator tries to entice the reader into taking part in the creation of Omelas. Because the reader is told to imagine Omelas "as your fancy bids," the reader is lulled into accepting Omelas and the horrible premise on which it is founded. Therefore, the reader, like the citizens of Omelas, can either accept the society or reject it out of moral indignation.

### Victims and Victimization

Closely related to the theme of morality is the theme of victimization, which is the act of oppressing, harming, or killing an individual or group. In this story, the victim, the child, is a scapegoat—it is sacrificed, the narrator states, so the other citizens of Omelas can live in happiness and peace. However, the narrator gives no good, rational explanation of how this situation came about, who set the terms, or how it is enforced, stating only that "if the child were brought up into the sunlight out of the vile place, if it were cleaned and comforted, that would be a good thing, indeed; but if it were done, in that day and hour all the prosperity and beauty and delight of Omelas would wither and be destroyed. Those are the terms. To exchange all the goodness and grace of every life in Omelas for that single, small improvement." Critics have said this lack of a rational explanation adds to the moral conflict of the story because readers are unable to fully understand why a scapegoat is necessary for Omelas to continue to exist.

### Guilt and Innocence

Le Guin also addresses guilt and innocence in "The Ones Who Walk Away from Omelas." Although the narrator states that there is no guilt in Omelas, the reactions of the citizens to the child's condition seem to suggest otherwise. For example, the narrator says that many people, after going to view the child, are "shocked and sickened at the sight. They feel disgust.... They feel anger, outrage, impotence, despite all the explanations. They would like to do something for the child. But there is nothing they can do." The few people who choose to leave Omelas because they cannot accept the situation on which the society rests also, presumably, feel guilt. But the narrator is unable to fathom such a reaction and merely states, "I cannot describe it at all."

### Happiness

Because "The Ones Who Walk Away from Omelas" is an example of Utopian literature, a type of fiction that depicts seemingly perfect societies, it also examines the meaning and consequences of happiness. Toward the beginning of the story, the narrator tries to explain why people are unable to accept happiness: "The trouble is that we have a bad habit, encouraged by pedants and sophisticates, of considering happiness as something rather stupid. Only pain is intellectual, only evil interesting.... But to praise despair is to condemn delight, to embrace violence is to lose hold of everything else. We have almost lost hold, we can no longer describe a happy man, nor make any celebration of joy." Since there is some truth to such statements, Le Guin causes the reader to wonder if people do, in fact, reject happiness as something "rather stupid" because they are too critical and pessimistic to believe true happiness can exist. This only further entices the reader to accept Omelas and, in turn, the possibility of Utopian societies despite the negative consequences.

## Style

"The Ones Who Walk Away from Omelas" is the story of Omelas, a city where everyone seems to be happy and to live in peace and harmony. Toward the end of the story, however, the narrator reveals that the happiness of Omelas is dependent on the existence of a child who is locked in a small, windowless room and who is abused and mistreated. Although most of the citizens accept the situation, a small number of people leave Omelas forever after seeing the deplorable conditions in which the child lives.

### *Structure*

The story is divided into two fairly distinct sections. In the first section, the narrator attempts to describe Omelas even though he/she notes more than once that the description is inadequate and does not capture the joy and happiness of Omelas. In the second section, the narrator reveals the existence of the child and matter-of-factly describes the awful conditions in which it is forced to live.

### *Narrative*

"The Ones Who Walk Away from Omelas" is told from the point of view of a first-person narrator. The narrator is not an active participant in the story and does not have any special insight into the characters' perceptions. Since the narrator invites the reader to take part in the description of Omelas, he/she is not an objective or reliable observer. For example, toward the beginning of the story, the narrator states: "I wish I could describe [Omelas] better. I wish I could convince you. Omelas sounds in my words like a city in a fairy tale, long ago and far away, once upon a time. Perhaps it would be best if you imagined it as your own fancy bids, assuming it will rise to the occasion, for certainly I cannot suit you all." Since readers are asked to develop their own perceptions of Omelas, they are implicated in the creation of Omelas as well as in the horrible situation on which the society rests.

Le Guin manipulates the narrative, and therefore the reader, by shifting tenses throughout the story. In the first paragraph, the narrator describes the festival in the past tense. As the narrator begins to describe Omelas in more detail, he/she moves to the conditional tense, a verb tense which is subject to or dependent on a condition. In this case, the reality of Omelas is dependent on the involvement of the reader. Finally, after the third paragraph, the narrative shifts to the present tense. Consequently, as Shoshanna Knapp writes in *The Journal of Narrative Technique,* the reader becomes "stuck in the story, to be set free only when a few of the people of Omelas stride out of the land and the story, headed for a country that the narrator cannot describe and that, consequently, may not 'exist.'" The narrator's use of the pronoun "it" to describe the child also adds to the manipulation of the reader because it makes the child seem less than human. Therefore, it is easier for readers to justify the mistreatment and abuse of the child.

### *Allegory*

"The Ones Who Walk Away from Omelas" is considered an allegory, or a tale in which characters representing things or abstract ideas are used to convey a message or teach a lesson. This story has been called both a political allegory and a religious allegory. The child, who is sacrificed for the good of the community, has been said to represent the underclass in capitalistic Western societies as well as the underdeveloped countries of the Third World. In capitalistic societies, particularly the United States, the wealth and privilege of the upper-class is often dependent on the exploitation or denial of the lower-classes. Additionally, some believe the continued prosperity of industrialized Western nations is due in part to the abuse and manipulation of Third World countries. "The Ones Who Walk Away from Omelas" has also been characterized as a religious allegory, with some critics suggesting that the child is a Christ-like figure, or one who is sacrificed so that others may live.

### *Utopia*

The story is also an example of Utopian literature, a form of fiction which describes an imaginary, ideal world where laws, government, and social conditions are perfect. Utopian literature also frequently addresses the impossibility of Utopian societies and examines the negative social, political, and psychological consequences of Utopian worlds. In "The Ones Who Walk Away from Omelas," Le Guin shows that the idealized happiness of Omelas does not come without a price; in order for the society to exist, one child must be terribly abused. By presenting such a dilemma, Le Guin forces the reader to consider which is more important, morality or happiness.

## Historical Context

"The Ones Who Walk Away from Omelas" was first published in 1973 in *New Directions 3*. The late 1960s and early 1970s were a time of enormous political, social, and cultural upheaval in the United States, and most likely the events of this period influenced Le Guin's writing of the story. America's involvement in the Vietnam War, particularly from 1964 to 1973, caused much domestic unrest. Many young people protested the war, and these demonstrations reached their peak in 1969, when 250,000 people marched in Washington D.C. A year later, on May 4, 1970, four students were killed at Kent State University in Ohio by National Guardsmen during a war protest.

The late mid to late 1960s also saw the rise of the "counterculture" in America. A movement that developed largely as a reaction against the war, the counterculture was made up of young people who called themselves hippies or flower children. Believing that it was possible to build a society based on love, happiness, peace, and freedom, the counterculture rejected materialism and traditional middle-class values. They also protested America's involvement in Vietnam, emphasized spirituality, particularly Asian mysticism, called for a sexual revolution, and advocated the use of psychedelic drugs to expand one's consciousness. A popular slogan of the counterculture was "Make love, not war." It was in 1965 that American poet Allen Ginsberg introduced the term "flower power" at an antiwar protest in Berkeley, California. This term was used to describe a strategy of friendly cooperation in confronting what the flower children considered the injustices of the day. That same year, Timothy Leary, a Harvard professor, published *The Psychedelic Reader*, in which he wrote that he had experimented with drugs and advised readers to "turn on, tune in, and drop out." In 1966, the International Society for the Krishna Consciousness, which was founded in India in 1958, was brought to the United States and Canada. The Hare Krishnas rejected materialism and lived communally. In 1968, there were confrontations between the counterculture and the political establishment at the Democratic Party national convention in Chicago. Members of the counterculture held a "Festival of Life," during which they protested the war, attended rock concerts, smoked marijuana, had public sex, held beach nude-ins, and burned their draft cards. Rock 'n' roll was an integral part of the counterculture movement, and in 1967 the first large rock gathering was held in Monterey, California. In 1969, the Woodstock Music and Art Fair, an event attended by 300,000 people, was held on a dairy farm in upstate New York.

During the 1960s, Lyndon Johnson, who became president when John F. Kennedy was assassinated in 1963, attempted top build a "Great Society" by passing numerous laws to advance civil rights, help the poor, and protect the environment. In 1965, the Appalachian Regional Development Act, which provided aid to that economically depressed area, was passed, as was the Housing and Urban Development Act, which established a Cabinet-level department to coordinate federal housing programs. The Medicare bill provided health care to the elderly, and the Higher Education Act provided scholarships for more than 140,000 needy students. Other legislation passed during Johnson's administration liberalized immigrant laws, provided support for the arts, assured truth in packaging, and addressed water and air quality.

This period in U.S. history is also known for the civil rights movement. In March of 1965, Dr. Martin Luther King, Jr. led a march from Selma to Montgomery, Alabama, demanding federal protection of blacks' voting rights; the new Voting Rights Act was signed later that year. It abolished literary tests and other voter restrictions and authorized federal intervention against voter discrimination. Also in 1965, Thurgood Marshall became the first African American to be elected to the U.S. Supreme Court. A couple of years later, in 1968, Martin Luther King, Jr. was assassinated in Memphis, Tennessee.

The feminist movement was also influential during the late 1960s and early 1970s. In the mid-1960s, the birth control pill was introduced in the United States, and in 1973, the U.S. Supreme Court ruled in *Roe vs. Wade* that a state cannot prevent a woman from having an abortion during the first three months of pregnancy. The National Organization for Women (NOW) was founded in 1966. Headed by Betty Friedan, who in 1963 published the book *The Feminine Mystique*, the organiza-

# Compare & Contrast

- **1973:** Many young people involved in the counterculture movement band together to form communes where they attempt to live together without the detriments of modern society. Many settle in California and the Pacific Northwest.

    **1993:** In Waco, Texas, many members of a religious commune known as the Branch Davidians die during a violent standoff with U.S. federal agents.

- **1973:** The infant mortality rate in the United States is 56 per 1,000 live births, among the highest of all industrialized nations.

    **1994:** The infant mortality rate in the United States is 31 per 1,000 births, among the highest of all Western industrialized nations and more than twice the rate of Japan.

- **1973:** Following the Supreme Court's decision on Roe v. Wade, which upholds a woman's right to privacy, abortion is legalized in the United States.

    **1992:** There were 1,359,000 abortions in the United States; a ratio of 23 for every 1,000 live births.

---

tions's membership included many prominent women's rights advocates. NOW devoted most of its early efforts to alleviating discrimination against women in economic, educational, and social arenas. Numerous other women's organizations followed: The National Women's Law Center was founded in 1972 to protect women's rights, and the Women's Campaign fund was founded in 1973 to help fund the political campaigns of women candidates.

Richard Nixon was elected president in 1972. Shortly after, however, it was revealed that members of Nixon's Committee to Re-Elect the President had broken into the Democratic National Committee Headquarters at the Watergate Hotel in June of that year. Nixon's attempt to cover up the scandal led to his resignation from office in August, 1974; he became the only U.S. president to have resigned from office to escape impeachment. The Watergate affair, as well as the Vietnam War, led to an increasing disillusionment with and skepticism of American government and politics.

The period from 1965 to 1975 also saw a great deal of scientific and technological development, particularly in the area of space exploration. In 1965, the world's first commercial communications satellite was launched; later that year Edward White became the first American to walk in space. An unmanned American space probe landed on the moon in 1967, and in 1968 the first manned spacecraft orbited the moon. Neil Armstrong became the first person to step foot on the moon during the Apollo 11 mission of 1969.

## Critical Overview

Although "The Ones Who Walk Away from Omelas" won a Hugo Award for best short story in 1974, it has not received much scholarly attention. The critics who have commented on the story have focused on its complex themes, including scapegoatism, morality, the duality of human nature, and political ideology. For example, Jerre Collins wrote in *Studies in Short Fiction* that "The Ones who Walk Away from Omelas" is "a critique of American moral life," while Shoshana Knapp observed in *The Journal of Narrative Technique* that Le Guin's subject is "the proper morality of art itself." Reviewers have also commented on how Le Guin's narrative technique and symbolism advance the themes of the story. The narrator of the story, for example, tries to convince the reader that Omelas does exist by inviting the reader to take part in its creation: "Perhaps it would be best if you imagined it as your own fancy bids, assuming it will rise to the occasion, for certainly I cannot suit you all." Knapp has noted that because the story's readers "are drafted to be partners in creation, they work together [with the narrator] to construct the hideous moral universe of Omelas."

Critical reaction to Le Guin's career as a whole has been positive. She is a highly respected author of fantasy fiction and has been praised for expanding the scope of the genre by combining conventional elements of science fiction with more traditional literary techniques. Le Guin has also been lauded for working in a wide variety of genres and for incorporating social analysis, reality, and moral conscience into her works.

Le Guin's novel *The Left Hand of Darkness* (1969), for which she received Hugo and Nebula Awards, is generally regarded as among her best works. This book centers on an androgynous alien culture and examines such themes as sexual identity, incest, xenophobia, and fidelity and betrayal. *Dispossessed: An Ambiguous Utopia* (1974), another highly regarded novel, also won Hugo and Nebula Awards and earned praise for its complex characterizations and well-integrated social and political ideas. Le Guin's *Earthsea* cycle, which is comprised of four novels, is considered a major achievement in fantasy literature, comparable in stature to such popular works as J.R.R. Tolkien's *Lord of the Rings*. In addition to her novels, Le Guin has written numerous short stories, many of which are collected in *The Wind's Twelve Quarters* (1975), *Orsinian Tales* (1976), and *The Compass Rose* (1982). *Orsinian Tales* has been acclaimed for the manner in which it weaves elements of European history, specifically references to events in Central Europe prior to the outbreak of World War II, into fantastic narrative. Le Guin has also been praised for her works of children's fiction, including *The Adventures of Cobbler's Rune* (1982) and *Catwings* (1988).

Although Le Guin has experimented with numerous genres, and her works are quite diverse, critics have noted that there are thematic and stylistic similarities running throughout her fiction. Theodore Sturgeon wrote in the *Los Angeles Times* that "there are some notes in her orchestration that come out repeatedly and with power. A cautionary fear of the development of democracy into dictatorship. Celebrations of courage, endurance, risk. Language, not only loved and shaped, but investigated in all its aspects; call that, perhaps, communication. But above all, in almost un-earthly terms, Ursula Le Guin examines, attacks, unbuttons and takes down and exposes our notions of reality."

## Criticism

### Judy Sobeloff

*Judy Sobeloff is a writer and educator who has won several awards for her fiction. In the following essay, she provides a summary of the story's plot and examines its allegorical significance.*

Ursula Le Guin's "The Ones Who Walk Away From Omelas" was first published in 1973 in *New Dimensions 3* and has been published in many anthologies since. When it appeared for the second time in 1975 as part of her short story collection *The Wind's Twelve Quarters,* Le Guin added a two-page preface in which she addresses her subtitle, "Variations on a Theme by William James," and its connection to the story's theme. Le Guin writes in this preface: "The central idea of this psychomyth, the scapegoat, turns up in Dostoevsky's *Brothers Karamozov,* and several people have asked me, rather suspiciously, why I gave the credit to William James." She goes on to say that not having re-read Dostoevsky since she was twenty-five, she had "simply forgotten he used the idea. But when [she] met it in James's 'The Moral Philospher and the Moral Life,' it was with a shock of recognition." Le Guin's preface is friendly and informative in nature: for example, she tells the reader that the name "Omelas" came from her reading the road sign for Salem, Oregon backwards, something she commonly did, reading the word "stop," for example, as "pots." The reference to James and Dostoevsky seems, too, to be merely a helpful, explanatory note from the author, but here the nature of Le Guin's comments can not to be taken for granted. Critic Shoshana Knapp reminds us of D.H. Lawrence's suggestion to "trust the tale instead of the teller": Simply because the author says something does not mean the reader needs to believe it, and perhaps the people who asked Le Guin about Dostoevsky "suspiciously" were right to be suspicious, regardless of her casual dismissal. It matters whether or not one trusts Le Guin's comments about her inspiration for this story.

Since both Dostoevsky and James have written pieces which include some kind of scapegoat which could be a model for the locked-up child of Omelas, looking at these pieces in light of Le Guin's story can be instructive. The passage she cites from James says that if millions of people could be "kept permanently happy on the one simple condition that a certain lost soul on the far-off edge of things should lead a life of lonely torment,... how hideous a thing would be [the enjoyment of this happiness] when deliberately accepted as the fruit of such a bargain.'' James holds the optimistic position that people would not accept this bargain, that a "specifical and independent sort of emotion" would arise which would "immediately make us feel" its hideous nature, "even though an impulse arose within us to clutch at the happiness so offered." In James's view, people would immediately spurn such happiness. The premise of "Omelas" is that the opposite would hold true: in Omelas, walking away is not the norm but happens rarely and is considered, as Knapp points out, "'incredible.' Le Guin's story, then, seems to refute the Jamesian assumption of an innate human decency; in Omelas, the mean and the vulgar are accepted as a necessary part of existence."

Certainly Le Guin's story is aiming for some kind of political interpretation, though exactly what that should be is less clear. Le Guin deals with similar themes in some of her other works, including *The Dispossessed, The Tombs of Atuan,* and *Rocannon's World.* Her story "The Day Before the Revolution," which immediately follows "Omelas" in *The Wind's Twelve Quarters,* is about one of those who walked away, Odo, the female founder of the planet in *The Dispossessed.* Regarding James's encapsulation of the scapegoat, Le Guin writes that "the dilemma of the American conscience can hardly be better stated." As critic Jerre Collins puts it, "the dilemma of the American conscience seems to be twofold: we cannot renounce the exploitation of others that makes possible our high standard of living, nor can we renounce the scapegoat-motif that justifies our comfortable life, [but 'Omelas' challenges] us to renounce both."

For Knapp, there is more to the story than the particular political interpretation Le Guin urges the reader toward, a position which rests on emphasizing the influence of Dostoevsky in addition to James. Knapp sees "Omelas" as being closer to Dostoevsky than to James, because James, in the passage Le Guin cites, discusses an abstract "lost soul" of no particular age, while Dostoevsky gives the reader, in the portrayal of the child Ivan Karamozov, a "painfully concrete picture . . . of isolation, malnutrition, mental torment, and filth," strikingly similar to the child we find in Omelas.

Dostoevsky's Ivan Karamozov walks away from his life condemning the creator (in this case, God); Omelas, writes Knapp, "itself can be seen as a

## What Do I Read Next?

- *The Left Hand of Darkness* (1969) by Ursula K. Le Guin, her science fiction/fantasy novel about a race of androgynous beings.
- *Fahrenheit 451* by Ray Bradbury, published in novel form in 1953. A modern society has banned books and as a result, its unreflective citizens live in a tightly controlled world which they believe has been created for their own good.
- *The Bloody Chamber* (1979) by British writer Angela Carter, a collection of stories that reinterpret classic fairy tales with modern sensibilities.

similar act of dissent, a refusal to write stories that are rotten at the core," to be as guilty as the God in question in *The Brothers Karamozov.* "In the world of Le Guin's fiction, creation, like all acts of freedom and wizardry, entails moral responsibility." Knapp sees Le Guin's subject, then, as not only the moral accountability of a society for which the happiness of the majority rests on the abject misery of a powerless few, but that "her actual subject is the proper morality of art itself."

The Jamesian version of the scapegoat myth is an abstract political idea of oppression, while in Dostoevsky's version, the person who is the scapegoat rails against God, the creator of his situation. In "Omelas," Le Guin sets up the narrator, the reader, and Le Guin herself as creators of the child's situation.

Here there is a further point to be made about trustworthiness. The fact that Le Guin says in her preface to trust her regarding Dostoevsky and James, when the reader may have reason not to, can be viewed as analogous to the narrator saying to trust him or her about the people of Omelas and the legitimacy of their response to their dilemma. According to the narrator, the people of Omelas "would like to do something for the child. But there is nothing they can do. . . . Even if the child could be released, it would not get much good of its free-

> "Not only are the residents of Omelas, those who stay, complicit in the child's misery, but the narrator attempts to draw the reader in and make the reader complicit on some level as well."

dom." Knapp and Collins, however, both criticize the reasons the narrator gives against freeing the child as faulty rationalizations. According to Knapp, the justification "offered by the narrator—that the child makes the inhabitants aware of the 'terrible justice of reality'—is a patent sophistry. To choose between torturing a child and destroying one's society (which includes other children) is a diabolical choice, not a human one." Collins agrees that "the rationalization rings hollow because the narrator has told us earlier that the child had not always been imprisoned in the dark room and 'can remember sunlight and its mother's voice,' and also that it wants out, even pleads to be released. However imbecile it may be, it knows (remembers) an alternative to its present suffering and wants that alternative. The bad faith of the Omelasians' rationalization is implied."

Not only are the residents of Omelas, those who stay, complicit in the child's misery, but the narrator attempts to draw the reader in and make the reader complicit on some level as well. Although the story opens with a well-detailed description of Omelas and its summer festival by a narrator who relates this description with authority, by the third paragraph the narrator goes so far as to say "Perhaps it would be best if you imagined [Omelas] as your own fancy bids, assuming it will rise to the occasion, for certainly I cannot suit you all.... They could perfectly well have central heating ... and all kinds of marvelous devices not yet invented here.... Or they could have none of that: it doesn't matter. As you like it." If the reader accepts this premise, that the details of Omelas are at his or her discretion, then the reader is implicated in the creation of Omelas and thus implicated in the horrible situation on which the society rests.

According to Collins, such "negotiations entice the reader to commit himself or herself to the project of constructing a utopia, a happy world that is intelligible." As the narrator points out, "we have a bad habit ... of considering happiness as something rather stupid"; it is not intelligible to us that a place could simply be happy, so we need a sense of something darker underneath. Because the narrator carries out the process of constructing Omelas with the reader for the good aspects of Omelas as well as for the bad, the reader is lulled into complacency and into accepting the reasonableness of such a world and his/her own role in creating it. As Knapp points out, "sometimes the narrator implies that this society has objective reality, that it is possible to have definite knowledge about it, even if this knowledge is not fully accessible to the narrator or to us," and sometimes not, through doling out to us pieces of information which are "factual" or "optional," a grammar which "traps us more subtly" in the creation of Omelas, as even the verbs change from past tense to present to conditional.

Collins classifies "Omelas" as an example of what she calls "narrative theodicy," a story which, like the necessities of painful labor and of dying in Genesis as "consequences of Adam and Eve's eating the forbidden fruit ... justifies or makes sense of a painful aspect of the status quo." Collins explains that theodicy originally was a way to explain evil and meaningless in the world as somehow being a justified part of God's plan. In "Omelas," the narrator explains that the child suffers so that the rest of the population can live happily, but no logical explanation is given as to why this should be so—and thus, Collins writes, Le Guin is able to make her reader question "a similar failure of Western capitalist theodicy": there is no good reason, despite the "historical, economic, political, racial-genetic-physical, geographical and religious elements" that Western readers may use to explain the "radical inequalities" of "'our' world," as to why certain groups must suffer so that others can have a high standard of living. No justification can be made for capitalism's "[exploitation of] the peoples of the third world, or one's indigenous unprivileged groups (blacks, women, the poor generally)."

Le Guin's ending, in which some individuals leave Omelas for a place "even less imaginable to most of us," points out finally that the dilemma of the scapegoat for the American people has in no way been resolved. The ones who walk away are not thanked for their decency or concern or commitment to social justice, nor does their absence even seem to be noticed. "Omelas" achieves its power through drawing in the reader and then implicating him or her in the highly questionable morality of the Utopia (s)he has participated in describing and thus in creating. Collins thinks that this story has never affected readers to the extent that they would change society because it is too threatening to their world view, that, ironically, the message is too powerful for people to hear.

What is this place, beyond the city of happiness that the narrator can hardly conceive of, much less describe? It would seem to be a place that values morality beyond happiness. We cynical modern Westerners can hardly conceive of a place unburdened by guilt, and it is still harder for us to conceive of a place where people freely renounce happiness which is based on a moral wrong.

**Source:** Judy Sobeloff, for *Short Stories for Students,* Gale Research, 1997.

## Logan Hill

*Logan Hill is a scholar specializing in American literature. In the following essay, he discusses the possible parallels between Omelas and America.*

In her introduction to "The Ones Who Walk Away from Omelas" in *The Wind's Twelve Quarters,* Le Guin writes that her story was inspired by William James formulation of ideals as "the probable cause of experience." Le Guin states that her story was written as a fictive allegory of the scapegoat as the "dilemma of the American conscience." Yet, she never literally states this dilemma. As a fiction writer she illustrates, but never states, the problem. Were she an essayist, she might have written the story as a straightforward question and offered an argument like a newspaper editorialist or a philosophy teacher. She might have asked: If the land you lived in was in every way you could possibly imagine perfect, if it was your own unique, custom-made Utopia and everyone was ecstatically happy because one small child was horribly unhappy and mistreated child, would you give away all of this happiness and leave this land, because you objected? Would you walk away from Omelas?

After setting the question, Le Guin the editorial writer may have related this general question to the unique, particular predicament of American society. As a white woman writing in the contemporary United States, Le Guin may have been painfully aware of the racial discrimination surrounding her. She might have written that, while many white people were living extremely well, rates of African-American poverty, imprisonment and illiteracy were egregiously higher than that of white Americans. Because racist political, legal and educational systems have historically discriminated against African Americans throughout American history, Le Guin might have argued, African Americans have been hindered by more than metal shackles. While America has been a utopian land of plenty for many rich whites, it has been a world of pain for many African Americans who have been murdered, lynched and discriminated against or excluded from middle-class America.

Or, when Le Guin wrote that her story evoked "the dilemma of the American conscience," she might have been thinking particularly of the corporate capitalist class discrimination that allows rich corporate executives to earn hundreds of times more money than most of their employees, an American economic system in which the wealthiest one percent of the population own an extremely disproportionate share of the total wealth of the country, which has often approximated over thirty percent. She might have compared this class to the least wealthy half of the population, which typically shares less than a quarter of the Americans' total wealth, attends poorer schools, dies years earlier than the average upper-class American, has higher rates of infant mortality and imprisonment and is more likely to die as a result of serious illness because of inferior health care.

In spite of Le Guin's admittedly instructive and unabashedly moralistic intentions, she could not simply type such a direct question and such blatant connections as I have sketched out, nor would she desire to do so. Since most readers of fiction resent being force-fed morality or didactically educated in the manner Le Guin proposes, such a didactic argument would not be effective, nor would it carry the emotional or affective force that her fictionalized argument contains. After all, Le Guin is not a teacher or philosopher like William James, whose writing inspired the story. She is a science fiction writer. Because Le Guin incurs an obligation to tell a fantastic, enjoyable story, she cannot allow her instructional intentions to overwhelm this primary responsibility. Her story must educate through this form. She must create a compelling story that will grip her audience, not a didactic treatise that would put many to sleep.

> "Because Le Guin incurs an obligation to tell a fantastic, enjoyable story, she cannot allow her instructional intentions to overwhelm this primary responsibility."

The dilemma that she works through in her story becomes: how to tell a moralistic story to a contemporary fiction audience? Thus, when Le Guin first asks, "How is one to tell about joy?" she is asking, how is one to tell about an ideal? How can one fictionalize an ideal without it sounding false? How can one entertain and educate at the same time?

Le Guin's question, "How is one to tell?" is itself part of her larger answer. By asking the reader such a direct question, she immediately destabilizes the traditional relationship between narrator and reader. Of course, Le Guin's narrative is actually no less structured or solid than a typical short story. Every author neglects some details, but unlike the typical short story narrator, Le Guin's narrator admits the incompletion of the picture, she confesses that she is not sure about the specifics of the religion of this land, the exact effects of "drooze," and so on. Admitting the difficulty and contrived nature of storytelling, the narrator reveals the wizard behind the curtain. Asked, "How is one to tell?" the reader must immediately consider Le Guin's act of writing: the artifice of the fiction. The story presents, not a fully developed fantastic world, but a work-in-progress. From here, the reader's experience becomes a dual experience, following both the plot progression and the story construction. In fact, the plot in this primarily descriptive story becomes the development of whether or not Le Guin's fiction is believable. The conspicuous narrator becomes the main character.

The reader does not follow anyone's specific experience in Omelas, unlike most stories. Instead, in this story the reader consciously follows the narrator's attempt to create a believable world with utopian characteristics. The story can be read as a story about storytelling, a story about the act of creating an alternate, plausible reality. The task and difficulty of writing "The Ones Who Walk Away from Omelas" becomes central to "The Ones Who Walk Away from Omelas" itself, and in the context of Le Guin's attempt to translate William James theoretical formulation of the scapegoat into fiction, her approach has several definite advantages that are particularly effective here.

The question, "How does one tell?" acts first as a disclaimer. It admits that the story sounds unbelievable. Such a humble statement ingratiates the narrator to the reader by asking the reader for help. In opposition to the imperious manner of the typical moralist, Le Guin appears genuine and sympathetic.

Second, the question "How does one tell?" or "How is one to tell?" expands the reader's sense of possibility. Contrary to the typical assumption that a story must proceed according to a single narrative, Le Guin allows and actually requires each reader to envision his or her own narrative, and his or her own personal Utopia.

This is the final and most important advantage to her technique: her questions are not purely rhetorical. When the narrator asks the reader to envision the world as he or she wishes to, it forces the reader to consciously create the story with the narrator. Since the idea of such awesome responsibility is rarely admitted (though it is always the way stories are created), Le Guin softens her request by writing, in relation to technology, "Or they could have none of that: it doesn't matter. As you like it." She eases the readers sense of responsibility while exploiting it and implicating the reader more thoroughly into the act of writing. She proceeds to add her own suggestions, but claims that they are by no means definitive, they are not the only options. She scatters the story with "ifs": "If so, please add an orgy. If an orgy would help, don't hesitate." Her humorous suggestions continue, from a super-drug with the silly name "drooze" to the wild parade and "Festival of Summer." The cumulative effect is that the reader becomes playfully involved in creating this alternate reality thinking that "it doesn't really matter," when it does in a very particular manner.

That the reader consciously collaborates with Le Guin to create this story becomes crucially important. In the context of Le Guin's explicitly instructive intention, the shift in narration actually enhances the sense of urgency and moral responsibility she seeks to stress. Omelas develops as a word created not just by Le Guin, but by Le Guin and the reader. The story offers a space within which each reader may create his or her own Omelas, his or her own Utopia. The reader knowingly becomes an accomplice in the writing of this story and as a responsible creator, must accept the results: The reader has made her bed, now she must decide whether she will sleep in it or not.

Once the reader has imagined her utopian Omelas, Le Guin begins to tighten her narrative. The narrator describes the parade and "The Festival of Summer" and then asks, "Do you believe me? Do you accept the festival, the city, the joy? No? Then let me describe one more thing." With this "let me," the narrator slowly begins to take control of the story. At first, the narrative remains flexible. The child may live "In the basement . . . or perhaps in the cellar." Here, the choice is much more limited than the fanciful daydreaming of the preceding chapters. She continues to describe the child, "It could be a boy or a girl . . . Perhaps it was born defective, or perhaps it has become imbecile through fear." Once again, the choice offered to the reader is strictly limited, and with this final "perhaps," Le Guin ceases to offer options. The story proceeds according to her exact descriptions, from the precise sound of the child's whining to the feelings and thoughts of the child's visitors.

Only in the final paragraph does Le Guin's narrator release the story once again. She writes that some people "leave Omelas" and that "The place they go towards is a place even less imaginable to most of us than the city of happiness. I cannot describe it at all." Crucially, she places the onus of final responsibility back on the reader. Having seen the repulsive underbelly of Omelas, the reader must imagine what this other place must look like. The reader must create her own image for the story's conclusion, another place that does not exploit or oppress anyone. Moreover, the reader's choice becomes imminently important. It is no longer a choice between fantastical worlds, as indicated by the narrator's enigmatic comment, "It is possible that it does not exist." If it were merely a choice between fairy tale lands, this comment would not make sense. Of course, Omelas does not exist, one might argue. There are wild parades, the odd "Festival of Summer" and "drooze!" Why should it matter that an alternate world might not exist?

It matters because Le Guin, by forcing readers to conjure their own Omelas, has forced them to consciously relate the story to their own personal experience. By forcing the reader to create Omelas with her, to co-author our story, she forces us to understand that, while we do not live in ideal worlds, we live with ideals every day of our lives, and that even by not walking away, we support the ideals and the society we live in. That Le Guin cannot imagine a world not based on oppression forces one to face the the oppression of one's own society. Le Guin's "The Ones Who Walk Away from Omelas" is ultimately inspiring because it forces us to examine our own ideals, and to consider both the consequences of those ideals and the means by which we might need to realize them.

**Source:** Logan Hill, for *Short Stories for Students,* Gale Research, 1997.

## Jerre Collins

*In the following essay, Collins analyzes "The Ones Who Walk Away from Omelas" as an allegory of modern American morality.*

Ursula Le Guin's short story "The Ones Who Walk Away From Omelas," subtitled "Variations on a Theme by William James," is a critique of American moral life. At least that is what Ms. Le Guin tells us in the introduction she added when the story was collected in *The Wind's Twelve Quarters* (1975). First she quotes the passage from James's "The Moral Philosopher and the Moral Life" to which the subtitle refers:

> [I]f the hypothesis were offered us of a world in which Messrs. Fourier's and Bellamy's and Morris's utopias should all be outdone, and millions kept permanently happy on the one simple condition that a certain lost soul on the far-off edge of things should lead a life of lonely torment, what except a specifical and independent sort of emotion can it be which would make us immediately feel, even though an impulse arose within us to clutch at the happiness so offered, how hideous a thing would be its enjoyment when deliberately accepted as the fruit of such a bargain?

Le Guin then indicates that her story is to be read politically by adding, "The dilemma of the American conscience can hardly be better stated."

Her story is about a society's use of a scapegoat, a *pharmakos,* to keep the rest of the society happy; and the dilemma of the American conscience seems to be twofold: we cannot renounce the exploitation of others that makes possible our high standard of living, nor can we renounce the scapegoat-motif that justifies our comfortable life. By challenging us to renounce both, "The Ones Who Walk Away From Omelas" takes up what Hans Robert Jauss calls the "*socially formative* function that belongs to literature as it competes with other arts and social forces in the emancipation of mankind from its natural, religious, and social bonds.''

But this story and other stories like it have not so far achieved any notable emancipation; they have not transformed the American conscience. Why not? I propose to take this story as seriously as we are meant to take it, examine how it works as a challenge to our conscience, and then suggest two factors that limit the radicality of that challenge.

As the text begins, the narrator is describing the bustle of preparations for the Festival of Summer in the city of Omelas, whose people are perfectly happy. She makes explicit the reader's complicity in the world-building activity of the story: "Perhaps it would be best if you imagined it as your own fancy bids,... for I certainly cannot suit you all.'' She proceeds to supply examples, and repeatedly asks the reader to change the examples or supply others, as indices of utopian technology, utopian sex, and utopian drugs (among which the narrator playfully includes beer). Her negotiations entice the reader to commit himself or herself to the project of constructing a utopia, a happy world that is intelligible, that forms an intelligible whole.

After more description of the beginning of the Festival of Summer, the narrator pauses to ask, "Do you believe? Do you accept the festival, the city, the joy? No? Then let me describe one more thing,'' and we know that we are now approaching the key that should make the whole intelligible.

Again the narrator insists both on giving particular details and on signaling that the details are mere indices and may be varied, so long as the alternate index has the same signification, carries the same meaning:

> In a basement under one of the beautiful public buildings of Omelas, or perhaps in the cellar of one of its spacious private homes, there is a room. It has one locked door, and no window.... In the room a child is sitting. It could be a boy or a girl. It looks about six, but actually is nearly ten. It is feeble-minded. Perhaps it was born defective, or perhaps it has become imbecile through fear, malnutrition, and neglect.

The child's situation and its misery are described at some length. The passage closes with a physical description of the child, a description familiar to us from the photo-journalism of war, displacement, and famine:

> It is so thin there are no calves to its legs; its belly protrudes; it lives on a half-bowl of corn meal and grease a day. It is naked. Its buttocks and thighs are a mass of festered sores, as it sits in its own excrement continually.

The narrator stresses that all the people of Omelas know about the child, and they all know that there is a connection between the child's unhappiness and their prosperity:

> Some of them understand why, and some do not, but they all understand that their happiness, the beauty of their city, the tenderness of their friendships, the health of their children, the wisdom of their scholars, the skill of their makers, even the abundance of their harvest and the kindly weathers of their skies, depend wholly on this child's abominable misery.

At first the latter items on this list may seem to be excessive and facetious. However, extravagant causality is frequently found in a particular kind of narrative meant to explain or justify the current state of things. For example, the third chapter of Genesis presents the necessity of painful labor (in both senses) and the necessity of dying as consequences of Adam and Eve's eating the forbidden fruit. Let us call this kind of narrative, which justifies or makes sense of a painful aspect of the status quo, a *narrative theodicy*.

"Theodicy'' originally designated a theoretical attempt to explain the problem of evil, to "justify the ways of God to man.'' It takes its place within the larger human project of the creation of an ordered world of experience, a world in which everything "fits'' or has its place—what Benjy bellowed for at the end of *The Sound and the Fury*. Peter Berger calls such an ordered world of experience a "nomos,'' a rule-governed universe. Anything that disorders our world—such as death, sickness, and evil, but also economic and social privations that lead to sickness, suffering, and early death—can cause *anomie*, a loss of nomos. *Anomie* is the chaos into which we fall when our world falls apart. It is a threatening sense of meaninglessness and disorder. We can escape *anomie* only by placing the disorder within a larger pattern of order. This is precisely what theodicies do.

A theodicy need not be religious. Berger notes that "A theodicy may... be established by projecting compensation for the anomic phenomena into a future understood in this-worldly terms,'' and he gives as an example the recurrent millenarianism of the Biblical or Jewish-Christian-Muslim tradition. But the same kind of projection can be seen in secular form. For example, several of Chekhov's plays include a character who speaks, like Vershinin in *Three Sisters,* in secular millenarian terms:

In two or three hundred years, or maybe in a thousand years—it doesn't matter how long exactly—life will be different. It will be happy. Of course, we shan't be able to enjoy that future life, but all the same, what we're living for now is to create it, we work and . . . yes, we suffer in order to create it. That's the goal of our life, and you might say that's the only happiness we shall ever achieve.

Here we see that the suffering of the present, even the perceived lack of meaningfulness of the present, is justified, made meaningful, understood in terms of a humanly satisfying future.

A theodicy can be theoretically articulated (in the type of discourse Barthes calls intellectual), but it can also find expression or be created in the other forms of discourse, including narrative. Perhaps the most powerful, most effective form of theodicy is a narrative: the life of Christ, for instance, or of Socrates, or Marxist apocalyptic history. A good narrative can "make sense" quite compellingly, in a way hard for other forms of discourse to match. And when a culture's narrative theodicy begins to lose its explanatory power, the result can be great *anomie*. It is not surprising, then, that a culture will resist a story that challenges its theodicy.

Let us return to "Omelas." Immediately after describing the suffering child, the narrator adds:

If the child were brought up into the sunlight out of that vile place, if it were cleaned and fed and comforted, that would be a good thing, indeed; but if it were done, in that day and hour all the prosperity and beauty and delight of Omelas would wither and be destroyed. Those are the terms. . . . The terms are strict and absolute; there may not even be a kind word spoken to the child.

The connection between the child's suffering and the people's happiness is stressed, yet while the narrator *says* that the connection can be understood, she advances no details, however hypothetically, as indices of the rationality or intelligibility of the connection. If the child's suffering makes sense, that sense is not demonstrated. But if a theodicy fails to make sense of such a radical inequality of power and privilege, it is a "bad" theodicy; and accepting it implies either stupidity or bad faith. Of course, not accepting it leaves one open to *anomie*.

If the child's suffering is not made rational, the Omelasians' acquiescence *is* rationalized. After describing the child, the narrator explains how those who come to visit the child, mostly young people, come to terms with what they see:

They may brood over it for weeks or years. But as time goes on they begin to realize that even if the child

> "If the child's suffering makes sense, that sense is not demonstrated."

could be released, it would not get much good of its freedom: a little vague pleasure of warmth and food, no doubt, but little more. It is too degraded and imbecile to know any real joy. It has been afraid too long ever to be free of fear. Its habits are too uncouth for it to respond to humane treatment. Indeed, after so long it would probably be wretched without walls about it to protect it, and darkness for its eyes, and its own excrement to sit in. Their tears at the bitter injustice dry when they begin to perceive the terrible justice of reality, and to accept it.

This rationalization has a familiar ring to it. Similar justifications of the status quo sometimes appear in discussions of "first world" relations with the third world or discussions of relations between the prosperous classes and the unprivileged groups of, say, America. In the story, the rationalization rings hollow because the narrator has told us earlier that the child had not always been imprisoned in the dark room and "can remember sunlight and its mother's voice," and also that it wants out, even pleads to be released. However imbecile it may be, it knows (remembers) an alternative to its present suffering and wants that alternative. The bad faith of the Omelasians' rationalization is implied.

The next step in our analysis of how Le Guin's story challenges the American conscience depends on the distinction between story and text. It is often noted that one of the peculiarities of narrative is that different texts can "tell the same story." For example, many see the three synoptic gospels telling the same Christ-story (when compared to the Gospel of John). Moreover, the Christ-story itself can be read as a sequence of functions so that other texts with different events and characters can be said to be telling the Christ-story too (or part of it). We may call this the level of the ur-story. On a higher level of abstraction, the Christ-story and, say, the Oedipus story can be said to be alternate embodiments of the hero-story (see Lord Raglan, *The Hero*). We may call this the level of the ur-ur-story. . . . And so on, as we stutter into infinite regress, onto ever higher levels of abstraction. Note that on each level we may speak meaningfully of variations: variant texts of the same story, variant stories of the same ur-story, and so on.

One way of specifying the relationship among levels is to see the ur-story not as an abstraction from similar stories but as a code or "master plot" by means of which the reader can construct, as he or she reads, innumerable stories in the image of their master. For example, Frederick Jameson, who calls the ur-story the "master code or Ur-narrative," aspires in *The Political Unconscious* to show how all narratives can be seen to be telling (at least a part of) the Marxist Ur-narrative. "Interpretation," he tells us, "is here construed as an essentially allegorical act, which consists in rewriting a given text in terms of a particular interpretive master code."

Whether or not interpretation is "essentially allegorical," Le Guin's story, by conspicuously omitting the explanation that makes the child's suffering understandable, and by conspicuously alluding to elements both of the relations between the economically advanced West and the "backward" countries of the third world, and of the relations between privileged and unprivileged classes within the West, prompts an allegorical reading, a "rewriting" of the given text "in terms of a particular interpretive master code," in this case the Western capitalist ur-story.

But rewriting may be reversible; a flaw in the story may reveal or unveil a flaw in the ur-story. Le Guin's story, by conspicuously failing to enable the reader "to perceive the terrible justice of reality," suggests a similar failure of Western capitalist theodicy. The people of Omelas are able to rationalize to their satisfaction a situation that enables them to continue to enjoy happiness and prosperity. But we are told only one segment of the rationalization, and the weakest segment at that (namely, that the child would be more wretched out of the closet of suffering than in it), the one most strongly suggesting the Omelasians' bad faith. A full rationalization, as we know from "our" world, would include historical, economic, political, racial-genetic-physical, geographical, and religious elements so that such radical inequalities would indeed "make sense." It is because Le Guin's story has by this point become rather obviously an allegory of Western hegemony that the narrator can proceed to say, with a little more bite to her words, "Now do you believe in them [the people of Omelas]? Are they not more credible?" Indeed they are; they look a lot like us.

The story's more radical calling of the reader into question is yet to come, however, in the text's long last paragraph, which the narrator introduces with a monitory "But there is one more thing to tell, and this is quite incredible." Sometimes a boy or girl, man or woman is not persuaded by the Omelasian theodicy nor by the prospect of the good life. For them, neither good faith nor bad faith suffices. Sooner or later, they walk out of the city. And when evening comes, instead of returning they walk on. In a final challenge to our moral imagination, Le Guin has her narrator say:

> They leave Omelas, they walk ahead into the darkness, and they do not come back. The place they go towards is a place even less imaginable to most of us than the city of happiness. I cannot describe it at all. It is possible that it does not exist. But they seem to know where they are going, the ones who walk away from Omelas.

At the very end, then, the story points toward the real utopia, a negative space defined by its difference from Omelas.

Le Guin's authorial comment about "the dilemma of the American conscience," with which we began, ratifies, as it were, the political-economic reading I have outlined here.

The curious fact is that the dilemma, both for the American conscience and for the West's in general, has for a long time remained, and continues to remain, a *dilemma*. The theodicy of Western capitalism is not working well, but neither has it failed altogether. Its continued imperfect success may be attributed partly to bad faith, partly to the extreme difficulty of imagining a genuine alternative and how to get there, but also partly, I suggest, to a third reason.

Le Guin's text can be read in terms of another ur-story besides that of Western capitalism: the religious story of the "suffering servant," the one who suffers to ensure the happiness of the many. A version of this story has been canonized in Christian redemption theology. In this reading, when Le Guin's text fails to explain, to make sense of the child's suffering, that failure suggests that the various reasons advanced in the religious stow also fail finally to make sense.

My point is that the possibility of reading Le Guin's story alternately as a religious allegory and as a politico-economic allegory reveals a narrative-structural similarity in the two ur-stories, and furthermore suggests that some of the difficulty in throwing off Western rationalizations of exploitation is accounted for by a hidden link between redemption-theology and complacency about exploitation. The same ur-story (or ur-ur-story) is involved: exploiting the peoples of the third world, or one's indigenous unprivileged groups (blacks, women, the poor generally) is homologous to being redeemed by the "suffering servant." Rejection of capitalist exploitation-theodicy undermines the redemption-theodicy since they are structurally so similar, and threatens great *anomie*. To walk into the darkness, unable to imagine where one might be going, is very much like walking off the edge of the world. Or rather, in the archetypal imagery of our culture, leaving bright Omelas and walking into the darkness is like going from life into death.

This brings us to one last complication. The Bible, our culture's source of the suffering-servant theodicy, entwines this theodicy with another one, which we may call a "resurrection" theodicy. This theodicy appears already in the Old Testament and is foregrounded in the New. For example, Jesus suffers and dies, only to rise again to a transformed, glorious life in the presence of the Father. A frequently cited "natural" exemplar of this theodicy is the caterpillar that seems to die but instead is transformed into a butterfly.

It is this second theodicy to which Le Guin's story appeals and from which it derives much of its power. If leaving Omelas is like going from life into death, that death (according to the faith of those who leave) leads to a new, transformed life in a place beyond the mountains, a life so different from the present life that it is unimaginable.

But Le Guin's appeal to the resurrection theodicy weakens her attack on the suffering-servant theodicy, since in the Judeo-Christian tradition it is the resurrection theodicy that justifies recourse to the *pharmakos:* it is all right for one person to suffer for the benefit of another, because even the sufferer will end up benefiting—his or her final, transformed state will be vastly better than his or her first state.

Our original question was: Why hasn't Le Guin's story (and others like it) transformed the American conscience? Now we have an answer. On the one hand, the secular, economic version of the suffering-servant theodicy gains power from the religious version, still strong in our culture. Because the economic and religious theodicies are quite similar, a threat to one can easily be seen as a threat to the other. Readers may resist Le Guin's story in order to protect themselves from an increase in *anomie*. On the other hand, the theodicy of resurrection or of renewed, transformed life, cannot function for us as the alternative it might otherwise be, because in our religious culture it is precisely resurrection that gives the suffering-servant theodicy its final justification. So when Le Guin makes sense of a utopian gesture (leaving Omelas) in the imagery of renewed life beyond death, she indirectly buttresses the very scapegoat theodicy she hopes to undermine.

**Source:** Jerre Collins, "Leaving Omelas: Questions of Faith and Understanding," in *Studies in Short Fiction,* Vol. 27, no. 4, Fall, 1990, pp. 525–35.

## Sources

James, William. "The Moral Philosopher and the Moral Life" in *William James: The Essential Writings,* Harper Torchbooks, 1971, pp. 294–308.

Knapp, Shoshana. "The Morality of Creation: Dostoevsky and William James in Le Guin's 'Omelas,'" in *The Journal of Narrative Technique,* Vol. 15, no. 1, Winter, 1985, pp. 75-81.

## Further Reading

DeBolt, Joe, editor. *Ursula K. Le Guin: Voyager to Inner Lands and to Outer Space,* Kennikat Press, 1979.
   A collection of articles examining Le Guin's fictional works.

Slusser, George Edgar. *The Farthest Shores of Ursula K. Le Guin,* Borgo Press, 1976.
   A scholarly overview of Le Guin's career as a writer.

Walker, Paul. "Ursula K. Le Guin" in *Speaking of Science Fiction: The Paul Walker Interviews,* Luna, 1978, pp. 24–36.
   An interview in which Le Guin discusses her works of science fiction and fantasy.

# Paul's Case

**Willa Cather**

**1905**

Willa Cather's story "Paul's Case" was first published in 1905. It was the last of seven stories in her first collection, *The Troll Garden,* which launched Cather's literary career. When the story was printed in *McClure's* in May of the same year, it brought Cather to national attention. In 1920 the story was reprinted by Alfred Knopf in *Youth and the Bright Medusa.*

Like many of the stories in *The Troll Garden,* "Paul's Case" explores the dangers of art and the struggles of artists and artistically inclined youth in a commercial world. Cather once remarked that the events in the story were modeled on an actual incident that occurred while she was teaching English in Pittsburgh, Pennsylvania. Cather's portrayal of a young man who lives for beauty and believes that money can transform his identity influenced F. Scott Fitzgerald, whose novel *The Great Gatsby* explores similar issues.

## Author Biography

Willa Cather was born near Winchester, Virginia, on December 7, 1873. She was the oldest of seven children. When Cather was nine years old, her family moved to Nebraska, where they lived on a farm in rural Webster County and in a nearby town,

Red Cloud. The population of Webster County and Red Cloud represented a diverse array of regions and nations. Cather's neighbors included immigrants from Sweden, France, and Germany, as well as Americans who had moved to Nebraska from large cities in New England and small towns from the South, as the Cathers had.

As a teenager, Cather was a tomboy. At fifteen, she signed her name "William Cather M.D." When she entered the University of Nebraska in Lincoln in 1891, she wore her hair short and dressed in men's clothes. By 1895, when she graduated from college, she had discarded her masculine persona in favor of more conventional dress. While in college, she edited the campus literary magazine and wrote articles and reviews for the *Nebraska State Journal.* These experiences led to her first job as a writer in Pittsburgh, Pennsylvania.

In Pittsburgh, where part of "Paul's Case" is set, Cather edited a woman's magazine called *Home Monthly* and taught high-school English and Latin. She lived and traveled with her friend Isabelle McClung. In 1905 she published her first book of short stories, *The Troll Garden,* which included "Paul's Case."

After *The Troll Garden* was published, Cather moved to New York City, where she became the managing editor of the influential magazine *McClure's.* In 1908 Cather met Sarah Orne Jewett, an author whose work she greatly admired. Jewett read Cather's fiction and advised her to abandon journalism to devote herself to writing fiction full time. "You must find your own quiet center of life," Jewett wrote to Cather: "to work in silence and with all one's heart, that is the writer's lot." Influenced by Jewett's words, Cather resigned her position at *McClure's* and began writing novels. While her first novel, *Alexander's Bridge,* published in 1912, was not a success, she won the Pulitzer Prize for the novel *One of Ours* in 1923. Today, her best known novels are *O Pioneers!* and *My Antonia.* These novels, as with much of her fiction, were inspired by the landscape and people of Nebraska. Cather depicted the struggles of European immigrants in the midwestern prairie states in a realistic yet subtle prose style.

Cather spent the remaining forty years of her life in New York City, where she lived with her friend Edith Lewis. When she died in 1947, she left no diaries, journals, or autobiographies and had prohibited publication or quotation of her personal letters.

## Plot Summary

"Paul's Case" by Willa Cather is, as the subtitle states, "a study in temperament." The story chronicles a few months in the life of Paul, a student at Pittsburgh High School, who would rather be at the opera than in class.

### Part I: Paul in Pittsburgh

The story begins with Paul's faculty hearing one week after he has been suspended from school. Paul is smiling, and his accusers find his appearance—especially the red carnation in his lapel—"not properly significant of the contrite spirit befitting a boy under the ban of suspension." The teachers, full of ill will, list disorder and impertinence as two of the charges against him, but they feel it "scarcely possible to put into words the real cause of the trouble."

Paul is described as "suave," having eyes with "a certain hysterical brilliancy," shuddering from a teacher's casual touch, and having a "contemptuous and irritating" habit of raising his eyebrows. Only his drawing master hints afterward that Paul's behavior may not be what it appears, that perhaps his teachers do not understand the boy. At this point, the teachers share a feeling of dissatisfaction with the meeting and their own behavior, which they liken to that of petty bullies.

Cather introduces the importance of art into Paul's life when he arrives early to Pittsburgh's Carnegie Hall, where he is an usher. First Paul revels in his solitude in the picture gallery. He dons his uniform "excitedly" before entering the hall to become a "gracious and smiling" model usher. Before seeing Paul in the world of art and music, the reader sees him as a twitchy, uncomfortable fellow. At Carnegie Hall Paul reveals a "vivacious and animated" persona freed by his surroundings and music.

After the concert Paul follows the German soloist, a woman with an "indefinable air of achievement," to her hotel. He imagines himself part of her world, entering "an exotic, tropical world of shiny, glistening surfaces and basking ease." Awakened

*Willa Cather*

from his daydream, he heads home to Cordelia Street, a perfectly respectable part of town that he views as ugly and common.

Because it is late, Paul decides not to enter the house and face his father's displeasure. Instead he climbs through a window into the basement, where he sits awake all night fearing rats. He imagines his father mistaking him for a burglar, imagines himself warning his father in time to avoid being shot, and wonders whether his father would ever regret that warning.

On Sunday, the last Sunday in November, Paul and his father and sisters visit on their front steps, according to neighborhood custom. Paul's father talks with a young clerk who works for one of the steel magnates and who he feels is a good model for Paul. Although the man had once needed to "curb his appetites," he has settled down to marriage and a business career; he is "a young man with a future." For Paul, all that really registers is the talk of faraway lands and success stories. That evening he sneaks to the theater under the guise of meeting a friend for help in math.

Paul lives for his weekends at Carnegie Hall and the theater, where he has a young actor friend named Charley Edwards who invites him to rehearsals and generally encourages his dreams. Yet the weekends also reinforce in him the thought that school is "trivial." He has more problems at school, is sent again to the principal, and is removed from school. His father makes him give up his job at Carnegie Hall and begin working in the office of Denny & Carson.

### Part II: Paul in New York

Next the story jumps to January, and Paul is on a train bound for New York City. When he arrives, he buys a new wardrobe and books a room at the Waldorf Hotel. He has planned this escape even before leaving school, Cather notes, and now he has "a curious sense of relief" at being where he feels he belongs. Cather then explains the embezzling that afforded Paul his escape. He has stolen nearly one thousand dollars from a deposit he was to make for Denny & Carson.

As he begins to live the high life of his dreams, Paul shows no remorse for his theft. He sees this life as "what all the struggle was about" and wonders how any honest men exist. Paul lives richly, but inconspicuously, bearing himself with quiet dignity. It is as if he were made for the life he has chosen. He is happy watching the pageant, enjoying his flowers and his sense of power. He is released from "the necessity of petty lying, lying every day" and spends eight happy days before news of his theft appears in the Pittsburgh papers.

Paul learns that his father is coming to New York to find him. After spending a few moments vividly remembering the "gray monotony" of Cordelia Street, he gives the reader a moment of foreshadowing when he realizes that the "glare and glitter about him. . .had again, and for the last time, their old potency." He decides to "finish the thing splendidly." Briefly wondering whether he could have spent the time after his theft any differently, he decides that "he would do the same thing tomorrow" and that "he had lived the sort of life he was meant to live." As he looks at his revolver, it becomes plain that he plans his suicide.

Paul leaves New York on a train and takes a cab west out of Newark, dismissing the driver once they get to the countryside. He walks awhile, noticing that his lapel carnations are "drooping with the cold. . .their red glory all over." His own glory ends in an impact with a train as he remembers all he has not done—"the blue of Adriatic water, the yellow Algerian sands" that he has not seen.

## Characters

### Charley Edwards

Charley is a young actor, the "leading juvenile" of a Pittsburgh stock theater company, and a friend of Paul's. He encourages Paul's interest in the theater, inviting him to the company's Sunday rehearsals and allowing him to hang around. When Paul's school situation worsens and Paul's father puts him to work, Charley "remorsefully" promises not to see Paul again. After Paul leaves home, Cather explains that Charley had helped Paul plan his trip to New York.

### Paul

Paul is the protagonist, or main character, of the story. A "motherless lad," he was born in Colorado, where his mother died of illness in his infancy. He is a thin, pale, dreamy adolescent who feels a need to set himself apart from his conventional surroundings in Pittsburgh. Whereas those around him are concerned about making a living and coming "up in the world," he is attracted to the glamorous world of music, the theater, and art. He desires the beautiful things money can buy, but he disdains the monotonous, cold reality of work and everyday life. After his consistent lying, failure to do schoolwork, and "insolent" attitude lead to his removal from school, Paul steals from his employer and leaves for New York City. There he realizes his dreams of buying expensive clothes, staying at the Waldorf, a grand hotel, attending the opera, and becoming "exactly the kind of boy he had always wanted to be." When his crime is discovered, Paul cannot face returning to the "ugliness and commonness" of Cordelia Street and commits suicide by jumping in front of a moving train. Cather's characterization of Paul is ambivalent, and readers are left to wonder whether Paul freely chose his tragic end or not. While Paul's alienation from his environment is clear, the reader cannot tell whether Paul's is a "case" of environmental determinism or of the folly of youth, of a dreamer who died with "all his lessons unlearned."

### Paul's drawing master

The most sympathetic of Paul's teachers, the drawing master observes that Paul seems somehow haunted and suggests that none of them really understands the boy. He comments on Paul's mother's early death and states that "there is something wrong about the fellow." Through his eyes the reader sees how pale Paul is, with his face "blue-veined" and "drawn and wrinkled like an old man's about the eyes."

### Paul's father

Paul's father, a widower, is the major authority figure in Paul's life, representing the values of hard work and the "American Dream" Paul despises. He works for a railway company and has "a worthy ambition to come up in the world." He hopes Paul might become like one of his neighbors on Cordelia Street, a young man who works as a clerk for one of the "iron kings" of a steel corporation. He is concerned and "perplexed" about his only son: he calls the principal's office after Paul is suspended, pays Denny & Carson the thousand dollars Paul stole from them, and, after Paul runs away, goes to New York to find him. To Paul, though, his father represents oppressive authority and the dreary middle-class life of Cordelia Street. He dreads coming home late to his father, "the figure at the top of the stairs," with his "inquiries and reproaches."

## Media Adaptations

- "Paul's Case" was adapted for television, directed by Lamont Johnson, produced by Ed Lynch, and starring Eric Roberts, Michael Higgins, and Lindsay Crouse, PBS, 1980. Released as part of the "American Short Story Series, Part 2," the 52-minute film is available from Coronet/MTI Film & Video.

- The story was also released as a book-on-tape by HarperCollins in 1981.

- In 1986, Caedmon Audio Cassette released *Paul's Case.*

## Themes

"Paul's Case" is a story about a young man who loves art and beautiful things so much that he steals

## Topics for Further Study

- Research the Age of Steel, particularly in Pittsburgh. How does your knowledge of Pittsburgh during the 1890s and 1900s helps you understand Paul, Paul's father, and the other residents of Cordelia Street?

- Investigate the values and definitions of the "American Dream," and compare your research with your analysis of Paul's values.

- Do you think Paul chose his fate, or do you think environmental or natural laws determined his destiny? Research theories of free will and determinism in philosophy and social science to enhance your analysis.

---

money and goes to New York to live a life of opulence and grandeur. When his crime is discovered, Paul commits suicide rather than return to the dreary, middle-class life he escaped in Pittsburgh. The story's major themes revolve around questions about Paul's character. Was he driven to his fate by the destructive values of America, or is he morally corrupt, responsible for his actions? Is Paul, as his teachers, father, and friends agree, a "bad case," an abnormal personality, or do the others have an overly narrow view of what is "normal"? Do the worlds of business and industry, represented by Cordelia Street, destroy appreciation of culture and aesthetics, or does Paul choose to live in a world of illusion, destroying his grip on reality?

### The American Dream

The American Dream is an underlying theme of the story. Paul's father and the rest of Cordelia Street, a "perfectly respectable" middle-class neighborhood, believe in values of hard work, family and church. During their leisure time, they sit around swapping stories about their bosses, the "captains of industry" who worked themselves up from poverty to lead large corporations and live in luxury. Paul despises the monotonous lives led by Cordelia Street residents, who believe that if they work hard, they too might lead such glamorous lives. But Paul shares their same desire: to become rich and lead a life without worry. He too likes to listen to the "legends of the iron kings." Disdaining the "cash-boy stage," Paul wants the "triumphs of the cash boys who became famous."

Paul does manage to live a life of leisure and beauty, but not through hard work, and only for one week. Through lies and crime, he gains access to what he considers his real home, the New York City high life exemplified by the Waldorf Hotel. There, his "surroundings explained him." In the lap of luxury, Paul realizes that "this was what all the struggle was about" and that "money was everything." Cather prompts her readers to consider whether the American dream of wealth might have corrupted Paul, fostering in him a love of materialism which leads to his ruin.

### Deception

It is through deception that Paul achieves his dream, however briefly, and Cather leaves open the possibility that his achievement is itself a form of self-deception. At home, his lies to his father cover his trips to the theater, and his tall tales at school paint the life he wants to live. In New York, although he feels at peace, freed from "the necessity of petty lying," he is living the biggest lie of his life: that he is a rich boy from Washington awaiting globe-trotting parents. He feels that "this time there would be no awakening," which is either a delusion or a foreshadowing of his suicide.

### Choices and Consequences

Related to the themes of the American Dream and Paul's use of deceit to claim it is the question of free will. Is Paul a sensitive adolescent who is crushed by his environment, or is he a lying thief who refuses to take responsibility for his actions? In the last line of the story, Cather writes that Paul "dropped back into the immense design of things," suggesting that his death was destined to happen. The portrait in Paul's bedroom of theologian John Calvin, well known for his ideas on predestination, lends weight to this possibility. But Paul also seems to choose his fate: for example, he decides that, if he were to choose again, he would do the same thing. It is left to the reader to decide whether Paul had no choice but to escape Pittsburgh and life altogether, or whether his love for illusion and artificiality signals his own weaknesses.

### Beauty

For Paul, beauty is life, and beauty can only be found in illusions: "the natural nearly always wore the guise of ugliness, ... a certain element of artificiality seemed to him necessary in beauty." Paul feels alive and comfortable in art galleries, the theater, the symphony, the opera. Looking at paintings or listening to the opera, Paul "loses himself." His identity dissolves and he merges with his surroundings. Art is a religion for Paul; the narrator describes the theater as his "secret temple." In the story, beauty can be powerful, fascinating Paul and allowing him to feel free. It can be destructive as well, when it makes ordinary life seem "worse than jail."

### Alienation

Caught up in his dreams of beauty and glamor, Paul is estranged from most of humanity. Cather shows his alienation in his discomfort around the people one might expect him to be most comfortable among—his family, neighbors, and fellow students. In the very first sequence, during his faculty hearing, Cather indicates this in the reference to how he shuddered away from his teacher's guiding hand. His own street arouses his "loathing," and when the neighbors gather for friendly chat on a Sunday afternoon, he sits alone on the bottom step, "staring into the street." In class he makes much of his friends at the theater and cannot "bear to have the other pupils think" that he takes school at all seriously. He has only "contempt" for the humdrum world, in which he is convinced he does not belong. Only among strangers, the glittering parade of the wealthy in New York, does he truly feel at home, and even then he has "no especial desire to meet or to know any of these people." Although he is among them, he is not really part of their society.

### Limitations and Opportunities

Paul's alienation grows out of the limitations he perceives as binding him. His father is focused on the business world and disapproves of Paul's desires—"his only reason for allowing Paul to usher was that he thought a boy ought to be earning a little." Paul has to lie to slip away to the theater, suggesting that if his father knew his real errand, he would have kept Paul home. When he reaches the theater, he breathes "like a prisoner set free." Finally he is denied his cultural activities altogether, an event that he regards as an opportunity to escape and live the life he wants. When he learns that his father is coming to New York to bring him back to Pittsburgh, a fate "worse than jail," he decides his only escape from such boundaries now is death.

## Style

### Irony

"Paul's Case" centers on a high school student so taken by the life of wealth and culture that he runs away to New York City on stolen money to live lavishly, if only for a while. When his old middle-class life threatens to reclaim him, Paul commits suicide. The narrator's attitude towards Paul's actions is ironic. The narrator does not endorse Paul's decision to steal in order to live grandly. Nor does the narrator affirm Paul's decision to commit suicide after he realizes that "money was everything." The authorial voice often seems to be talking to the reader, reflecting on what the characters do not realize. For instance, while Paul despises Cordelia Street, it is described as a "perfectly respectable" middle-class neighborhood. Similarly, Paul's starry-eyed response to the world of the arts is directly contrasted to cruder realities: references to a "cracked orchestra" beating out an overture or jerking at a serenade hardly sound sublime, yet Paul's senses are "deliciously, yet delicately fired" nonetheless. Cather's distanced, sparse authorial voice hints at her attitude towards the events she narrates.

### Symbolism

Cather uses symbolism to great effect in this story. Flowers are a continual motif, expressing Paul's character and his views of life. The red carnation Paul wears to meet with his teachers is to them a sign of his outlandish and insolent attitude. It is described as "flippantly red" and "scandalous." Paul also wears violets in his buttonholes and dismisses those who do not do likewise as mundane. At the Waldorf, his grand suite is not complete without flowers, and he notes with awe the artificial beauty of cut flowers in the glass cases of New York flower stands, "against the sides of which the snowflakes stuck and melted." When Paul ventures to the railroad tracks to kill himself, he takes a wilted red carnation from his lapel and buries the flower in the snow. Expensive, extravagant, colorful and ephemeral, flowers represent Paul's desire for beauty in what he sees as a gray world. They also symbolize

*The Waldorf-Astoria Hotel in New York City where Paul flees after stealing money.*

Paul, who, like flowers in winter, is out of place. The flower-killing snow Paul sees on the train to New York and by the railroad tracks at the story's end provide a stark contrast to the bright flowers Paul surrounds himself with.

## *Allusion*

"Paul's Case" is sprinkled with a variety of allusions, or references to cultural figures and works. Some of these deal with disguises and help point out the way Paul's life is woven with deception. A description of Paul's response to the theater, for instance, includes a reference to the opera *Martha*, by Friedrich von Flotow, in which a highborn lady disguises herself as a servant, causing unhappy consequences. At his last dinner in New York, Paul hears music from Ruggiero Leoncavallo's opera *Pagliacci*, which concerns clowns, masks, and the idea of appearance versus reality. Another allusion, to a genie in a bottle, evokes the *Arabian Nights* and vividly describes how trapped Paul feels in the ordinary world and his ordinary life. Cather uses still other allusions to link Paul to the decadence of imperial Rome, as when he wraps himself in a "Roman blanket" after his hot bath, which itself reminds the reader of the decadent Roman baths.

## Historical Context

The years from 1900 to 1910 witnessed great growth in business and industry in America. Fortunes were made producing steel and iron: Andrew Carnegie, Henry Clay Frick, and J. P. Morgan all made vast amounts of money during this period. They were the most famous of the "robber barons," those whose wealth was created by questionable labor practices and whose businesses were favored by the government since they were fundamental in creating the infrastructure necessary for the United States to become a world power. In "Paul's Case" such industrial leaders appear in references to the "iron kings" discussed on Cordelia Street on Sunday afternoons.

With fewer government regulations on business than there are now, industry leaders ruthlessly pursued profit. Their profits allowed them to become voracious consumers of material goods. Thorstein Veblen, in *The Theory of the Leisure Class* (1899), coined the term "conspicuous consumption" to describe such ostentatious display of money and luxury through clothes, travel, cars, and architecture. This use of wealth is most apparent in "Paul's Case" in the section devoted to New

# Compare & Contrast

- **1900s:** Pittsburgh, Pennsylvania, is the center of steel manufacturing in the United States. Many industrialists, including Andrew Carnegie, Henry Clay Frick, and J. P. Morgan, made fortunes producing steel. When the residents of Cordelia Street share their "legends of the iron kings," they most likely are discussing one of these Pittsburgh industrialists.

    **Today:** Steel still ranks among the ten largest industries in America, but by the end of the 1980s, the last of the Pittsburgh steel plants closed.

- **1900s:** Spurred by the country's new-found wealth, grand hotels are built in U.S. cities, attracting wealthy travelers and rivaling European palaces in their glamour. In Pittsburgh, Paul is entranced by glimpses of the Schenley Hotel, and in New York, Paul chooses to stay at the Waldorf, the most luxurious of these luxury hotels.

    **Today:** Urban luxury hotels are less popular. With the arrival of the jet age, more remote areas are now easily accessible, leading rich vacationers to prefer resort areas such as the Caribbean or the French Riviera.

- **1900s:** The Carnegie Foundation for the Advancement of Teaching is founded with a $10 million gift from Andrew Carnegie, the Pittsburgh steel magnate who devoted the last years of his life to philanthropy, donating large sums to establish cultural and educational institutions. Carnegie founded Pittsburgh's Carnegie Music Hall, where Paul works as an usher.

    **Today:** More than 2,500 public libraries owe their existence to Andrew Carnegie. In a time of decreasing public money for education and culture, Carnegie's legacy has a profound effect on the health of American education.

- **1900s:** An important artistic movement is Aestheticism, based on a belief in "art for art's sake." Aestheticists believe in the intense perception of beauty as an end in itself, and they believe art is independent of social, political, or ethical concerns.

    **Today:** While some still hold to Aestheticism, many artists believe that art should comment upon and affect social issues. Multiculturalism, a movement which aims to include non-white, non-Western forms of expression into mainstream America, is one example.

---

York—the Waldorf Hotel, Paul's dress clothes and silk underwear, his champagne and opera. Edith Wharton's novel *The House of Mirth,* published the same year, also deals with the era's high society, focusing on a beautiful and young upper-class woman who seeks to secure her fortunes by marriage but can bring herself to sacrifice neither love nor wealth.

Still, some of the wealthy found ways to spend their surplus in ways that benefited society as a whole. Andrew Carnegie established himself as the country's leading philanthropist by granting money to libraries, foundations, and venues for the arts, including music halls that bear his name in New York City and, as described in "Paul's Case," Pittsburgh.

## Critical Overview

Although "Paul's Case" did not receive much critical attention when it was first published in 1905, it has become Cather's most frequently reprinted and read short story. A Public Broadcasting Corporation (PBS) television adaptation in 1980 revived critical interest in the story.

According to Loretta Wasserman, in "Is Cather's Paul a Case?," one reason the story has historically garnered little notice is because the character of Paul is so unlike Cather's other characters. Whereas most of her fiction takes place in the plains and prairies of the Midwest, "Paul's Case" takes place in smoggy Pittsburgh and glamorous New York. Critics have taken pains to see the story as a fitting end to the short story collection in which it first appeared, *The Troll Garden*. All of the stories in this book concern artists or people of artistic or sensitive temperament who cannot resist the dangerous lure of the gardens of art. James Woodress, in his introduction to *The Troll Garden*, claims that Paul consumes the "forbidden fruit" of art, leading to his tragic end. Susan Rosowski, in *The Voyage Perilous: Willa Cather's Romanticism*, argues that Paul loses himself to the temptations of romantic fantasy.

Unlike other characters in *The Troll Garden*, however, Paul is not an artist at all. Many critics believe he does not even have an artistic temperament. Instead, they argue that Cather is writing a psychiatric "case study." Wasserman argues that Paul is emotionally maladjusted, living in a fantasy world and lacking a firm grip on reality. In her study *Willa Cather's Short Fiction*, Marilyn Arnold argues that Paul is "half-crazy" and cannot describe either reality or art reliably. John A. Weigel, in a *CEA Critic* article, describes how he applied a psychological test to Paul's character and concludes that he is a schizophrenic.

Others ascribe Paul's behavior to social, rather than psychological, causes. David A. Carpenter, in an essay in *American Literature*, sees Paul as a victim of his environment. "The uncreative, superficial and life-destroying values perpetuated in the homes of Pittsburgh" produce in Paul an unhealthy desire for wealth and luxury. In Carpenter's view, the portraits of John Calvin and George Washington that hang above Paul's bed suggest that these are American values. Paul achieves the ends of success without the means, however, and so remains responsible for his actions. He "has consumed himself morally and ethically by living a lie—one purchased through someone else's hard work," according to Carpenter.

Critics ascribing genetic or social causes for Paul's behavior agree that he is "destroyed by his own illusions," as Wasserman puts it. Sharon O'Brien, in *Willa Cather: The Emerging Voice*, considers whether Paul's "probable homosexuality" corresponds to a similar inclination of Cather's. When Cather adopted masculine dress and the name "William Cather, Jr." as an adolescent, she, like Paul who dresses as a dandy, was rejecting the restricting conventions of her day. But Cather's ironic attitude toward Paul signals her belief that there is a difference between loving art and the beautiful places it is found and creating it oneself. Cather both identifies with and distances herself from Paul's selfish, escapist tendencies. Larry Rubin, writing in *Modern Fiction Studies*, and Claude Summers, in *Studies in Short Fiction* consider the possibility of Paul's homosexuality as well. They point to his physical appearance, temperament, and the brief description of his night out in New York with the boy from Yale. But, these critics argue, Paul's thin grasp on reality and his aestheticism, which alienates him from most people, make it impossible for him to recognize and integrate his homosexuality into his life.

## Criticism

### Jennifer Hicks

*Jennifer Hicks is a professor and director of the Academic Support and Writing Assessment program at Massachusetts Bay Community College in Wellesley, MA. In the essay below she explores the question of whether Paul's problem is due to heredity or to environment.*

Are we products of nature or of the way we are nurtured? Do our genes dictate who we will be, or is our environment responsible for that? Are we governed by our own free will, or does destiny mandate what will become of us? These are some of the many questions that plague humanity, the questions that give philosophers, sociologists, scientists, and writers material with which to work. Willa Cather, in her short story "Paul's Case," brings forth these questions with admirable skill but offers no clear resolution, as can be seen by the two primary types of interpretation her critics have given to the story.

According to Loretta Wasserman, in her book *Willa Cather*, the interpretations of "Paul's Case" are divided according to how each individual critic answers the questions. Many see it as a story of a "sensitive, artistically inclined youth crushed by a withering environment, the dreary rigidities of Pittsburgh Presbyterianism and the physical ugliness of

## What Do I Read Next?

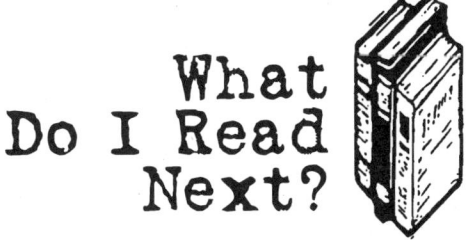

- *My Antonia,* Willa Cather's 1918 novel about the lives of immigrants in the Midwest, is one of her finest and best-known novels.

- F. Scott Fitzgerald's novel *The Great Gatsby,* published in 1925, focuses on Jay Gatsby, a man who lives through romantic dreams. Gatsby defines the American character torn between idealism and materialism.

- *The Andrew Carnegie Reader,* published in 1992 by the University of Pittsburgh Press, contains a selection of Carnegie's writings on business and philanthropy, including "The Age of Steel" and "The Gospel of Wealth According to St. Andrew."

- Oscar Wilde's novel *The Picture of Dorian Gray,* published in 1891, is a key work of the Aestheticist movement. Dorian, vain and rakish, wishes to remain eternally young and handsome. Dorian's portrait ages instead of Dorian, and is kept hidden until the novel's end.

---

Paul's home." Others see it as a study of maladjustment or a pathological state.

It is worthwhile to note here that the time in which Cather lived greatly influenced her writing and her views of life. Born in the middle of the second Industrial Revolution, Cather grew up during a time when new scientific knowledge of physics and chemistry helped build gigantic new industries. The steel industry, in particular, centered in Pittsburgh, used Henry Bessemer's new open-hearth process to create stronger, less expensive steel. His process helped to vastly increase production and profits, which necessitated larger factories, more workers and more machinery. In 1899, Andrew Carnegie created the massive Carnegie Steel Company in Pittsburgh by consolidating many of the local steel works. Only two years later, his company was worth half a billion dollars. However, Carnegie was also involved in the cultural side of life and contributed much money to the arts. He, like Cather, saw that the rapid progress of technology could potentially drown out the more aesthetic side of people, a problem he wished to avoid.

Cather dealt with this technological and aesthetic issue in "Paul's Case," which first appeared in her collection of stories called *The Troll Garden* in 1905. The story is set in Pittsburgh, and the glamorous lives of "iron kings" like Carnegie become a focal point for Paul's aspirations. According to Cather's obituary in the *Pittsburgh Sun-Telegraph,* it was based on the actual suicide of a high-school student in the Pittsburgh area where she lived. The name for the collection was borrowed from a text of Charles Kingsley, who wrote in his book *The Roman and the Teuton* that invading barbarians looked at Rome as "a fairy palace, with a fairy garden" inside which trolls dwelled. The stories in the collection deal with encounters in the art world and according to one critic are "implicitly equated with the compelling but treacherous troll garden." Marilyn Arnold, a professor of English at Brigham Young University, helps explain the relation of the troll garden to "Paul's Case." She writes in an essay in Harold Bloom's anthology *Willa Cather:*

> Paul is obviously the hungry forest child who is utterly helpless before the luscious appeal of the garden, represented for him in the trappings of wealth and in his adolescent perception of the artist's world. For Paul there is no reasoned choice, no weighing of alternatives and consequences, no will to resist; for him there is only ugliness and the garden, and he must have the garden.

Cather later reprinted a revised version of the story in 1920 in another collection called *Youth and the Bright Medusa.* Again Cather focuses on a vision of youth, but to Cather, given the title of this collection, the vision must have been a horrifying one. Medusa, of Greek mythology, is one of three Gorgons, monsters with golden wings, brass claws,

> "We need to remember that Paul is an adolescent. Wanting a life different from the one we are born into is a large part of adolescent longing."

and hair of live snakes who turned to stone those who looked at them. One can assume, then, since Cather created the collections herself, that in her mind, "Paul's Case" dealt with the fairy garden and its treacheries as well as the aspirations of a young man involved in the world of the arts.

In the first part of the story, we meet Paul through the perceptions of his teachers, his behaviors at school, his position as an usher at Carnegie Hall, and his friendship with members of a stock theater company. We learn that at school Paul is perceived as "contemptuous and irritating" and insolent. However, his drawing teacher sees that "there is something wrong" and "sort of haunted" about Paul. His mannerisms at school, from his avoidance of being touched to his "dandy" dressing and his "scandalous red carnation," paint for us a picture of a boy who does not quite fit in to the mold that is expected. In the music hall, again we see that he is not quite the same as the others. He "teased and plagued the boys until, telling him that he was crazy, they put him down on the floor and sat on him." Even with Charley Edwards, Paul's young actor acquaintance, we see that Paul does not fit a mold. Charley allows Paul entrance to the theater in part because he recognizes a "vocation" in him, but also because he cannot afford his own dresser. So here, Paul is perceived as having the theater in his blood, but also as having some use to those who have already toiled to make real what is in their blood.

Cather gives Paul no redeeming quality in these first pages. We see his willingness to tell lies at school and to his father. We see his disdain for his neighborhood and his neighbors; we know he feels that all but him and those in his "garden" world are "stupid and ugly." Yet, with all this, we still find ourselves drawn to Paul. We understand his fervent desire to be part of the "fairy world of a Christmas pantomime" where he "felt a sudden zest of life." We understand that he does not want to feel "destined always to shiver in the black night outside, looking up at it." In fact, we feel compassion when he spends the night in the basement. We can empathize with his fear of rats and understand his desperate loneliness when he wonders whether his father could view Paul as a burglar so as to kill him.

Cather draws us into Paul's fantasy world. When he sits on the "lowest step of his stoop" he listens to another young man speak with his father. They are talking of the young man's boss, apparently one of the "iron kings." The talk of "palaces in Venice, yachts on the Mediterranean, and high play at Monte Carlo appealed to his fancy." We share in the excitement Paul feels as the orchestra tunes up and his feeling of its "being impossible to give up this delicious excitement."

Cather contrasts Paul's two views of his world. He is drawn to "the exotic, tropical world of shiny glistening surfaces" and will, as he later demonstrates, do anything to avoid "the flavorless, colorless mass of everyday existence." Although the narrator explains that Paul lives on "highly respectable" Cordelia street, we are also given Paul's own view of his home. He has a "cold bathroom with [a] grimy zinc tub" and over his bed hang "the pictures of George Washington and John Calvin, and the framed motto, 'Feed my Lambs,' which had been worked...by his mother." Critic David Carpenter suggests that Cather puts these pictures on Paul's wall to emphasize that "the uncreative, superficial and life-destroying values perpetuated in the homes of Pittsburgh are essentially American values." When we look at this view, we might then begin to assume that Cather is siding with the environmental influences on our lives. Wasserman also explains how the embroidered hanging done by Paul's mother "symbolizes his poignant longing for love" that is as absent in his life as his mother is.

There is also a resemblance to Cather's own life in the story that makes the reader aware that such an assumption may have some validity. Edward Brown and Leon Edel write in *Willa Cather: A Critical Biography* that "the dichotomy of Pittsburgh" provided what was to Cather "the breath of life": "out of its ugliness and slums, its industrial smoke and flame sprang the beautiful things." They continue to explain that Cather became enamored of the Pittsburgh stock company, where she forged a lasting relationship with one of the actresses in ways quite like Paul's and Charley's. They further illuminate the similarities when they say Cather painted the neighborhood where Paul lives with the "petty-bourgeois dreariness that Willa Cather had resented during her years of boarding-house living." Professor Dorothy Van Ghent, in an essay included in Bloom's anthology, adds further credence to the assumption that Cather may side with the concept of environmental influence. She writes that Paul is a "young, artistically or merely sensitively gifted person . . . whose inchoate aspiration is offered no imago by the environment, and no direction in which to develop except a blindly accidental one."

However, David A. Carpenter points out in his *American Literature* essay that Cather made great use of irony in the story, and unless a reader is watchful for the irony, the easily drawn assumptions could be erroneous. In literature irony often comes in the form of sarcasm. For instance, in a passage describing Paul's romantic response to the theater, the narrator remarks that "the moment the cracked orchestra beat out the overture . . . or jerked at the serenade . . . all stupid and ugly things slid away from him." Dramatic irony, also evident in "Paul's Case," comes from a character saying something that will have a hidden meaning to the readers, a meaning he himself does not realize. Carpenter uses the scene where Paul sits alone in the Waldorf's dining room to explain this. Paul looks around at the splendor of the room and wonders, "Had he not always been thus, had he not sat here night after night, from as far back as he could remember, looking pensively over just such shimmering textures. . . . He rather thought he had." Clearly, the readers know that Paul has not always lived in the Waldorf. Yet Paul is so entranced in his fairy world that he believes it is where he has always been, and that is why he feels so at peace with himself, because he need tell no more lies. What is very ironic here is that Paul is now living a lie, not just telling one.

However, even as Carpenter vacillates between whether Cather is espousing environment or heredity as deciding factors, Arnold comes down clearly on the side of psychological defect and heredity when she writes:

> Cather portrays in Paul a being who is alienated by more than environment and lack of human contact and understanding. . . [other Cather characters] could all have been saved by altered environmental circumstances and human caring, but not Paul. He thinks an environmental change is all he needs, but he is wrong.

She further states that Cather "makes it clear that not only is Paul not an artist, but his perception of the artist's life and the artist's glittering world is miles from the truth." In the words of the actors, his is "a bad case."

We need to remember, though, that Paul is an adolescent. Wanting a life different from the one we are born into is a large part of adolescent longing. Denying the obvious, such as that it is necessary to work to achieve one's dreams, is a denial we have all made at one time. Believing that all we need to become the real person we are is a change in environment is also a feeling many of us have encountered. So, then, perhaps "Paul's Case" really is a case study—one in which a confused and troubled young man with genes that require excitement actually benefits from a change in environment.

**Source:** Jennifer Hicks, for *Short Stories for Students,* Gale Research, 1997.

## Loretta Wasserman

*In the following essay, Wasserman presents various critical viewpoints to determine whether Paul should be seen as a sympathetic character and whether he has serious mental problems.*

"Paul's Case" is Willa Cather's most popular story—deservedly so, although one of the reasons for its preeminence is that for many years it was the only one Cather would allow reprinted. It remains still the first choice of anthologists, as a glance at any half dozen current collections will show, and it has been dramatized in a popular public television series. Until recently, however, "Paul's Case" received little critical notice. One reason, doubtless, is that Paul's story seems admirably clear-cut: a sensitive adolescent, attracted to music and the theater, is pushed by a callous, commercial society into a desperate theft. Facing discovery, he takes his own life by falling under the wheels of a locomotive, symbol of the iron industrialism and grinding materialism of the age. Certainly that is how students respond to the story, attracted, naturally, by any picture of misunderstood youth and no doubt inclined to sympathize, too, with Paul's aversion to lady high-school teachers, with their shrill voices and "pitiful seriousness about prepositions that govern the dative" (*Troll Garden*).

No doubt a second reason is that "Paul's Case" resists being assimilated to Cather's other work. It seems to lack her stamp. In place of vast prairie horizons or silent cliff dwellings we have a "smoke palled city"—turn-of-the-century Pittsburgh—

and a boy who markedly lacks the vibrancy we expect in Cather's central figures. Paul's specialness is a kind of inarticulate stubbornness: his teachers think of him as a cornered alley cat. Further, as this example suggests, the sweep of imagery and allusion that marks Cather's style elsewhere is missing here—the narrative voice feels cribbed and confined like her hero's actions and purposes. In fact, these actions and purposes are the real trouble. Could the Cather who wrote so frequently against materialism regard with sympathy one who spends stolen money on a week of high living in a New York hotel and who, confronting death, reflects that he knew now "more than ever, that money was everything"? The answer from the critics is no; in fact, the gathering consensus is that her story is bathed in irony.

Serious criticism began by confronting a task that has proved troublesome—fitting the story into the collection where it first appeared, seven stories having to do with art and artists that Cather titled *The Troll Garden,* her first book of fiction, published in 1905. The title and epigraphs suggest certain dangers in art, the work of not-quite-human trolls, fascinating to "forest children" peeking into their garden (the epigraph is from Charles Kingsley's *The Roman and the Teuton*). Cather made these dangers more puzzling and ominous by a second epigraph, from Christina Rossetti's "The Goblin Market": "We must not look at Goblin men, / We must not buy their fruits. . . ." Considerable critical acumen has been expended on this suggested framework. E. K. Brown, Cather's first biographer, asserts rather lamely that "Paul's Case," the last of the seven, makes a "fitting coda." James Woodress, in his Introduction to his definitive edition of *The Troll Garden*, and in his biography, speaks elliptically of a "forest child destroyed by . . . the forbidden fruit," the assumption being, it would seem, that Paul transgresses a moral boundary and that theater and concert hall themselves exude a malevolency.

Other commentators are more explicit or venturesome. Susan Rosowski, in her study of Cather's romanticism, stresses the tempting dangers posed by the troll/goblin artists and the horror of the "bewitched" boy who has "lost his soul" to an "inhuman" fantasy. Marilyn Arnold finds Paul indeed a case, a psychological one, "eccentric, maybe even half-crazy," mistaken even about grimy Cordelia Street where Paul, motherless since birth, lives with his father and two shadowy sisters. Where Paul sees grey ugliness, Arnold sees a respectable neighborhood of white-collar workers, full of children and plans for the future. Paul is equally blind about the world of art, mistaking glitter for real worth. Not unexpectedly, Sharon O'Brien, in her psychobiography, also stresses psychology—Paul's "probable homosexuality" may be a thin disguise for Cather's. Cather/Paul yearns for a dissolution of self, a preoedipal union with the mother—a floating on flowers and music (the New York scenes) ending in the final dissolution of self in death. David Carpenter, in contrast, finds Paul's story a sociological case study of "an extremely bleak and seemingly irremediable type of determinism." Paul is a victim of his society, Pittsburgh Presbyterianism, symbolized by the twin pictures of George Washington and John Calvin over his bed, icons transmuted by business and industry into signifying the "uncreative, superficial and life-destroying values" that dominate American life. Paul is a debased version of these values: the New York scenes are heavily ironic, Carpenter maintains, especially Paul's sense of well-being as he luxuriates in the Waldorf. Nevertheless, Paul remains blameable because he "has consumed himself morally and ethically by living a lie—one purchased through someone else's hard work." We are back with the "half-crazy" boy who "sold his soul," however different the etiology of his pathological condition. In sum, these recent studies all point in the same direction: toward a weak-willed, morally corrupt, or corrupted youth inevitably enmeshed and destroyed by his own illusions.

That these varying analyses of Paul as a case study in psychology or sociology are plausible is proof that Cather has here succeeded in balancing the competing claims of the old arguments between the opposing determinisms of nature and nurture. Part of the fascination of Paul's story must inhere in just this tension. But is this what Cather is telling us about Paul—that he is the sum of forces impinging on him? I think not, and I think we are alerted to a less positivistic perspective through the comments of Paul's teachers, who, after the disciplinary hearing aimed at correcting his vaguely impertinent attitude, feel so baffled: "his drawing master voiced the feeling of them all when he declared there was something about the boy which none of them understood"; "each of his instructors felt that it was scarcely possible to put into words the real cause of the trouble."

One aspect of the story may be agreed upon: it is certainly true, as all the recent commentators stress, that Paul is not a budding artist whose gifts are being wasted. His fascination with art, music, and theater is of a different order. He uses art as a means; the sounds of the orchestra or painted landscapes are avenues. When Paul rushes off from the high-school faculty meeting to his ushering job at Carnegie Hall, he first visits its art gallery where "he sat down before a blue Rico and lost himself." Later, after helping patrons to their seats, he falls into a similar dreamy state as the symphony begins: "he lost himself as he had before the Rico." Cather is explicit that his love of the theater is not based on hidden talent or ambition: "He had no desire to become an actor, any more than he had to become a musician." Nevertheless, Charley Edwards, the stock company juvenile, regrets it when Paul's father forbids Paul to loiter about the dressing rooms because the actor "recognized in Paul something akin to what churchmen term 'vocation'." What is meant by this strange term for Paul's obsession? And how likely is it that this easy-going stock company actor would employ it? It must be that the author is here signaling to her readers over the head of her character. Blanche Gelfant, writing on Cather's poetics, notes her technique of "self-reflexivity," of including hints about how to read her story in the story itself. Casting Paul as one who has heard a summons to spiritual duty must be such a signal. Paul is serving a master who calls—a master who calls him to life: in clinging to music, art, and theater, Paul is keeping alive intimations of "a world elsewhere," a world where he would not be an alien. He is fighting for his life—for the life of his soul. (Cather once wrote in the *Nebraska State Journal:* "'Soul'—it's too bad that we have no word but that to express man's innermost ego.") The life and death nature of his struggle is stressed again and again. When he ushers, he becomes "vivacious and animated," and color comes into his usually pale face, the face that one of his teachers found "drawn and wrinkled like an old man's." The first sound of the orchestra "seemed to free some hilarious spirit within him; something that struggled there like the Genius in the bottle found by the Arab fisherman. He felt a sudden zest of life." His feeling at the concert hall "was all that could be called living at all." "It was at the theatre and at Carnegie Hall that Paul really lived; the rest was but a sleep and a forgetting." Conversely, he thinks of Cordelia Street, where his father in his night clothes stands at the head of the stairs demanding explanations, as threatening death, imaged as suffocation by drowning. ("The moment he turned into Cordelia Street he felt the waters close above his head.") When, in New York, he learns that his

> "Cather has here succeeded in balancing the competing claims of the old arguments between the opposing determinisms of nature and nurture."

father has refunded the stolen money and has come to bring him home, he thinks, "the tepid waters of Cordelia Street were to close over him finally and forever." He can confront suicide with equanimity because, it now seems, "all the world had become Cordelia Street."

Further, Paul's crime, the theft, is treated as an act of self-preservation. When Paul's father placed him as a cash boy in a commercial house and forbade the theater and concert hall, "the whole thing was virtually determined." Paul takes the money instinctively, as a salmon swims upstream. He recalls it merely as "simple" and "astonishingly easy." In fact, he has a sense of relief at his "courage" which, before the theft, he had doubted. . . .

From glitter and stage effects, then, Paul builds a dream world that comforts and sustains. Music and art are merely a means of entrance, a "portal of Romance." Again Cather hints at religious dedication: "Paul had his secret temple . . . his bit of blue-and-white Mediterranean shore." To convey the peculiarly hermetic quality of Paul's "dome in air," Cather alludes through an extended simile to a strange, even lurid, legend that shimmers forth strangely from the usual flat narrative voice: Paul's vision, we are told, "was very like the old stories that used to float about London of fabulously rich Jews, who had subterranean halls there, with palms, and fountains, and soft lamps and richly apparelled women who never saw the disenchanting light of London day." This odd bit of social rumor is vaguely subversive. It hints at Paul's sense of alienation from his world, at his need for refuge, at the security money can buy, at religious apostasy, or paganism: a temple for the senses. Also—an ironic point, which lifts the story above the sentimental—it hints at Paul's limited imagination: this "pleasure dome" seems modeled after the lobby of a first-class hotel—perhaps the Pittsburgh Schenley.

The badge of Paul's fidelity to his dream, his talisman, is the red carnation he wears in the buttonhole of his shabby coat as he confronts his teachers, which they (correctly) interpret as a sign of his unrepentant attitude ("flippantly red"; "the scandalous red carnation.") Cut flowers become a motif: Paul notes that the "prosy" male teachers he despises never wear violets in their button-holes. Arriving in his suite at the Waldorf he orders violets and jonquils. Driving down wintry Fifth Avenue he notes the flower stands, "whole flower gardens blooming under glass cases, against the sides of which the snow flakes stuck and melted; violets, roses, carnations, lilies of the valley." Hot-house flowers, being both artificial (raised by human contrivance under unnatural conditions) and yet also natural (they are *real* flowers) appropriately symbolize the limits of Paul's imagination and his plight. They are expensive. Badges of color in a colorless, gray world, they nurture the inarticulate boy's dim sense of a beauty connected to substance and reality but not available to him. He buys carnations again on his last journey to the snowy hill above the railroad tracks. . . .

With judgment closing in, and death his only out, Paul still has no regrets, and his final thoughts are put in the only terms his circumscribed life has made available. The truth he knows now, "more than ever," is that "money was everything, the wall between all he loathed and all he wanted." In a theatrical, indeed ritualistic, gesture he buries one of his carnations in the snow before launching himself before the train. As he dies, Paul sees the "folly of his haste . . . with merciless clarity": but the "folly" is not his crime, nor his suicide, nor his false moral sense; rather it is his failure to escape further, to more distant lands, to "the blue of Adriatic water, the yellow of Algerian sands." In part Cather is here taking a sly pleasure in balking the sentimental moralists of her day who expect deathbed guilt and remorse. (In this she resembles her admired Mark Twain.) More to the point is Paul's vision of the temple of beauty that blesses his final moments. Surely this is the "epiphanous moment" of the story, confirming his vision as authentic and his fidelity to it justified. The closing line tells us that a compassionate universe receives him: "Then, because the picture making mechanism was crushed . . . . Paul dropped back into the immense design of things." It is a moment of wonder and absolution. . . .

But the immediate appeal of "Paul's Case" does not lie in its relation to the author's personal history or in its relation to other *Troll Garden* stories. It lies, I contend, in our fascination with Paul's transformation of himself, however short-lived, and his discovery, so ultimately wrong, and yet so plausible, so right, "that money was everything." Here is the true accomplishment of the story, the conversion of romantic longing into a devotion to the medium of exchange (of change) itself—currency, the coin of this democratic realm, the glass slipper that can change a sow's ear into a silk purse. It is a very American dream, the romance of money. It was to be given greater and more developed expression a few years after Paul's story in the transformation of James Gatz into Jay Gatsby, who also sought to invent a new self, to find new parents, to create an identity by means of drawers of shirts and opulent surroundings. In fact, there may be a direct line between Paul and Gatsby. In a 1925 letter to Cather, apologizing for what might be seen as plagiarism in the likeness of Daisy Buchanan and Cather's Marian Forrester, Fitzgerald declares himself "one of your greatest admirers" and singles out "Paul's Case," along with her novels, as a favorite.

Although the beauty Paul served was, like Gatsby's, "vast, vulgar and meretricious," and, like Gatsby, he served it criminally, he served it unswervingly. In her note about the Parsifal theme, Cather refers to the Blameless Fool: a nice epitaph for Paul.

**Source:** Loretta Wasserman, "Is Cather's Paul a Case?," in *Modern Fiction Studies,* Vol. 36, No. 1, Spring, 1990 pp. 121-29.

## Joseph S. Salemi

*In the following essay, Salemi investigates Cather's use of specific prose rhythms in "Paul's Case," which he maintains are intentional and an outgrowth of the author's classical education.*

The elements of an individual prose style are elusive of definition. Although we can sometimes describe a writer's characteristic diction, imagery, and idiomatic preferences, most of our comments will be impressionistic and tentative rather than statistically precise. No writer is perpetually true to type, and fine prose, like every other creative manifestation, is often unpredictable in both its methods and effects. Nevertheless, in a well-established literature the rhetorical mannerisms of certain authors are usually distinguishable after long acquaintance. Habits of syntax and predilections in prosody, along with the stylistic resonances they produce, can be as distinctive as a signature in the world of letters.

One minor but useful prosodic device is prose rhythm and cadence. Although sometimes dismissed by plainstyle devotees as a superficial ornament, prose rhythm provides delightful embellishment to a well-constructed sentence by giving it a flow comparable to the measures of verse. These cadences need not follow a fixed pattern; the writer who strives for an auditory effect in prose simply highlights the natural rhythms of his native tongue through the artifice of arrangement and word choice. Certain combinations of stressed and unstressed syllables produce a pleasing, jarring, or otherwise noticeable effect in a sentence, and one which can reinforce the tone of a statement or smooth the flow of a narration. . . .

Most writers who use prose rhythm in English do so in an instinctive rather than a calculated manner. In the case of Willa Cather, however, there are strong indications that her cadences were based on careful training in classical prosody. We know that she received a respectable if not extensive classical education, first from the Englishman William Ducker, who tutored her in Latin and Greek when she was a schoolgirl, and later at preparatory school and the University of Nebraska, where she studied the major ancient authors. As an undergraduate she published creditable translations of Anacreon and Horace in her campus literary magazine. Further, when Cather left home to start out on her career, one of the first positions she held was that of Latin teacher in a Pittsburgh high school. Such a background, certainly more common in Cather's time than it is today, ought to alert us to the possibility of classical influences on her style. And indeed when we look at her prose, we find evidence not just of a professional writer's attention to graceful word arrangement, but also of cadences that are deliberately reminiscent of stately Ciceronian periods. . . .

"Paul's Case" has been widely anthologized, and the story is probably familiar to most teachers of American short fiction. A young Pittsburgh student named Paul, progressively sickened by the numbing routine of his bourgeois family and dreary schoolwork, absconds with a thousand dollars to New York City. There he lives for a week, satisfying all the hunger for luxurious indulgence that had gone unfed in his respectably ordinary existence. At the end of the week, with no money left and his father in town to find him and reclaim him, he chooses to commit suicide rather than return to the leaden monotony of his former life. The story makes extensive use of sensory allusion; colors, odors, textures, tastes, and sounds are lovingly, even morbidly dwelt upon. Paul's drab life in Pittsburgh and his stolen pleasures in New York, the homespun provincial homilies of his town and the frank urbane hedonism of the city, are vividly and effectively counterpoised. Cather's normally solicitous search for *le mot juste* is intensified in the hothouse of sensuous imagery that the development of her theme demands. The story is deliberately tinged with a fascination for the sort of artificiality associated with Nineties Decadents, towards whom the mild irony of the story is probably directed in part.

> "The powerful effect of 'Paul's Case' depends heavily on the hand-in-glove cooperation of sound and sense, on the conscious artistic complicity of diction, rhetoric, syntax, and rhythm."

A good example of deliberate cadence can be found in the last words of a paragraph describing Paul's return to his home on Cordelia Street after a night at the Pittsburgh opera:

> The moment he turned into Cordelia Street he felt the waters close above his head. After each of these orgies of living he experienced all the physical depression which follows a debauch; the loathing of respectable beds, of common food, of a house penetrated by kitchen odors; a shuddering repulsion for the flavorless, colorless mass of everyday existence; a morbid desire for cool things and soft lights and fresh flowers.

The double dactyl of flávŏrlĕss, cólŏrlĕss, with its heavy restraint, leads into a cretic and spondee clausula with a resolved variant:

mass of évĕrÿdăy ĕxístĕnce.

This particular clausula pattern will be familiar to readers of Cicero. They will recall that Cather's évĕrÿdăy ĕxístĕnce is metrically equivalent to *esse videatur,* as illustrated in the *First Catilinarian* 14.5. Now it is possible, of course, that this collocation of stresses in Cather is merely coincidental, but I am not inclined to think so. First of all, this same cretic and spondee pattern is repeated several other times in the story, and second, the pattern always occurs in end position. It would take the credulity of an invincible skepticism to believe that these cadences are purely fortuitous.

In any case, to return to the text, consider how Cather finishes her paragraph after the words "flavorless, colorless mass of everyday existence." The undertow of retarding stresses in these words emphasizes the barren constraint of Paul's life, the prose mirroring, as it were, the chafing repression that holds the boy's libido in check. But Cather completes her sentence with these words:

> a mórbĭd děsírĕ fŏr cóol thíngs and sóft líghts and frésh flówers.

Here, the pent-up energy of the word *desire,* in itself metrically ambiguous, bursts the double dactyl opening of the phrase with a triple spondee. If the passage is read aloud, the effect is unmistakable; the rhythm compels the listener to believe in the power of Paul's desire to break out of his prison.

Another example of the cretic and spondee clausula can be found in a passage that describes Paul's reaction to the ambiance of the theater:

> The moment he inhaled the gassy, painty, dusty odor behind the scenes, he breathed like a prisoner set free, and felt within him the possibility of doing or saying splendid, brilliant, poetic things. The moment the cracked orchestra beat out the overture from *Martha,* or jerked at the serenade from *Rigoletto,* all stupid and ugly things slid from him, and his senses were deliciously, yet delicately fired....

The ultimate proof that Willa Cather was a deliberate creator of prose rhythm lies in a seemingly minor detail of syllabication that a careless reader might easily overlook. One rule of classical poetry is that a terminal and an initial vowel placed next to each other are to be blended into a single quantity. When Vergil writes (*Aen.* 4.54)

> his dictis impenso animum flammavit amore

the words *impenso animum,* although they contain six syllables, constitute only five metric positions, for the *o* and the *a* are blurred in pronunciation into one sound. Such blurring (which also takes place if the second word is aspirated) is called *elision.* If for some reason elision does not occur when it normally should, there is an awkward gap or *hiatus* between the two vowels, and this contingency is almost always avoided in classical metrics. Willa Cather's conscious use of cadence is evident from her careful avoidance of hiatus in end positions. The following paragraph demonstrates how solicitous she could be for perfection in such matters:

> There were a score of cabs about the entrance of his hotel, and his driver had to wait. Boys in livery were running in and out of the awning stretched across the sidewalk, up and down the red velvet carpet laid from the door to the street. Above, about, within it all was the rumble and roar, the hurry and toss of thousands of human beings as hot for pleasure as himself, and on every side of him towered the glaring affirmation of the omnipotence of wealth.

The rhythm of the last words (gláriňg ăffĭrmátĭŏn ŏf the ŏmnípŏtĕnce ŏf weálth) is based on three resolved cretics and a final isolated stress on the word *wealth*. This final stress clinches the key significance of money in the world that Paul has just entered, and the triple cretics hammer the idea into the reader's consciousness. But the rhythm does not work unless the *e* and the *o* of *the omnipotence* are elided. Cather uses a similar elision in another sentence:

> He had only to glance down at his attire to reassure himself that here it would be impossible for anyone to humiliate him....

I anticipate the objection that one can hardly picture Willa Cather or any other great writer slavishly counting syllables and stresses in the heat of literary creation. Even if I were sure of the validity of that objection—which I am not—it would only serve to support my earlier contention that prose rhythm is judged solely by aural criteria; the cadence is there *because we hear it,* as the artist instinctively heard it in the toil of composition. It is not necessary to assume that every good author knows the minutiae of cadence, but what is certain is that fine prose has definite, stable rhythms to which its most masterly practitioners are drawn again and again, as to recurrent patterns of harmony. As one commentator has said, "This kind of artful prose is not so much the product of conscious effort as the overflow of a sensibility thoroughly saturated in a tradition, to the extent that the esthetic unity of form and content has become second nature."

Willa Cather was certainly gifted with such a sensibility, but I am also persuaded that she attempted to carry into her writing the graceful elegance embodied in the periodic and cadenced structure of Ciceronian Latin. The evidence of "Paul's Case" convinces me that she strove not just for excellent prose, but for a prose that registered, acoustically, the very heartbeat of her esthetic impulse. Cather once wrote that "[A great story] must leave in the mind of the sensitive reader an intangible residuum of pleasure; a cadence, a quality of voice that is exclusively the writer's own, individual, unique. A quality that one can remember without the volume at hand, can experience over and over again in the mind but can never absolutely define, as one can experience in memory a melody, or the summer perfume of a garden.'' There is no better description of the achievement of ''Paul's Case'' than these words, which remind us that language, even when silently read, evokes the memory of sound, and the resonance of imagined music.

Once we appreciate the subliminal acoustic capacities of written English as they are revealed in prose rhythm and cadence, we are liberated from the false notion—propagated by too many composition teachers—that prose is simply one more means of communication among a dozen others for getting across some abstractable message. This is a ubiquitous but degraded view of language that is in no small part responsible for the current decline in prose standards. For a master stylist such as Cather, fine prose is the complex product of many intellectual, esthetic, and emotional ingredients, all of them conspiring, as it were, to create a multifaceted mode of expression. The powerful effect of ''Paul's Case'' depends heavily on the hand-in-glove cooperation of sound and sense, on the conscious artistic complicity of diction, rhetoric, syntax, and rhythm. It is precisely this ideal unity of all the available resources of language that the artistry of Willa Cather aspires to attain.

**Source:** Joseph S. Salemi, ''The Measure of the Music: Prose Rhythm in Willa Cather's 'Paul's Case','' in *Classical and Modern Literature,* Vol. 10, No. 4, Summer, 1990, pp. 319-26.

## Sources

''And Death Comes for Willa Cather, Famous Author,'' in *Pittsburgh Sun-Telegraph,* April 25, 1947.

Arnold, Marilyn. *Willa Cather's Short Fiction,* Ohio University Press, 1984.

Bloom, Harold. *Willa Cather,* Chelsea House, 1985, pp. 71-86, 177-83.

Brown, Edward Killoran and Leon Edel. *Willa Cather: A Critical Biography.* Alfred A. Knopf, 1953.

Carpenter, David A. ''Why Willa Cather Revised 'Paul's Case': The Work in Art and Those Sunday Afternoons,'' in *American Literature,* Vol. 59, no. 4, December, 1987, pp. 590–608.

O'Brien, Sharon. *Willa Cather: The Emerging Voice.* Oxford University Press, 1987.

Rosowski, Susan J. *The Voyage Perilous: Willa Cather's Romanticism,* University of Nebraska Press, 1986.

Summers, Claude J. ''A Losing Game in the End: Aestheticism and Homosexuality in Cather's 'Paul's Case','' in *Modern Fiction Studies,* Vol. 36, 1990, pp. 103-19.

Wasserman, Loretta. *Willa Cather,* G.K. Hall, 1991.

Weigel, John A. ''What Kind of Psychology for Students of Literature?,'' in *CEA Critic,* Vol. 20, 1958, pp. 1, 5.

Woodress, James. Introduction to *The Troll Garden,* by Willa Cather, edited by James Woodress, University of Nebraska Press, 1983.

## Further Reading

*DISCovering Authors Modules* (CD-ROM publication), Gale Research, 1996.
  Contains biographical information on Cather's life and works as well as excerpts from a number of critical essays.

*Short Story Criticism,* Vol. 2, Gale Research, 1989, pp. 88-122.
  Contains excerpts from ten critical essays about Cather's works. Carpenter's essay and the introduction deal with ''Paul's Case'' in depth.

# The Red-Headed League

**Arthur Conan Doyle**

**1891**

"The Red-Headed League" first appeared in a popular British magazine, the *Strand,* in August of 1891. It was republished in 1892, along with eleven other Sherlock Holmes stories, in the collection *The Adventures of Sherlock Holmes.* Its style and structure make it a nearly perfect example of the modern detective story, first devised by Edgar Allan Poe fifty years previously. Doyle's ingenious plots and captivating central characters, Holmes and his sidekick Watson, brought the author literary success in his own time. Further, the Sherlock Holmes stories provided later writers with models for their own work. The existence of today's popular detective tales, whether in the form of books, movies, or television shows, are in large part due to Doyle's influence.

Many readers enjoy matching their wits against Sherlock Holmes, trying to see if they can solve the mystery along with him. This is usually a task doomed to failure because of the first-person narrative style, in which the detective's less-intelligent friend Watson tells the story and is as amazed as any reader when the detective reveals his solution. "The Red-Headed League," like Doyle's other detective stories, presents a detailed portrait of turn-of-the-century London and gives readers glimpses of a society undergoing rapid change. Among these changes are alterations in the class structure, Britain's rise as a world economic power, and urban growth—along with a rising crime rate. As he attempts to restore a social order threatened by

criminals like those in "The Red-Headed League," Sherlock Holmes embodies the values of intelligence and individual achievement.

## Author Biography

The elements in Doyle's life that most influenced his Sherlock Holmes' stories were his background as a doctor and his pressing need to earn a living. Born in Scotland in 1859, Doyle entered medical school at the age of seventeen. One of his teachers was Dr. Joseph Bell, whose skill in diagnosing illness had sharpened his powers of observation and reasoning. As a result Bell could, while diagnosing a patient's illness, accurately read clues to his or her background and personality as well. Bell's unusual ability made a lasting impression on Doyle, who modeled some of Holmes' deductive powers on his teacher's example. Doyle served as a ship's surgeon in the early 1880s, traveling to Africa and the Arctic, before returning to England and finishing his degree. At that time, establishing a medical practice was difficult, and Doyle waited in vain for patients to appear.

*Arthur Conan Doyle*

Fortunately, Doyle had another ambition: to become a writer. Several of his early stories, which featured adventure and mystery aboard ship and in Africa, had appeared in magazines while he was still a medical student. The increasing burden of time on his hands—along with a wife and growing family to support—led Doyle to attempt a novel. Doyle turned to his memories of Dr. Bell and his knowledge that detective stories often brought their writers popular success. Relying on the model set by Edgar Allan Poe's stories of the amateur detective Dupin, whose cases are narrated by an admiring and less clever friend, Doyle introduced Holmes and his sidekick Dr. John Watson in *A Study in Scarlet* in 1887.

This novel met with only a lukewarm reception from readers, but an American publisher encouraged Doyle to continue the series with *The Sign of Four* in 1890. Even though Doyle continued to write and publish other kinds of stories, especially science fiction and historical fiction, the need for money kept taking him back to the profitable Sherlock Holmes. He was able to give up his unprofitable medical practice in 1891 when short tales of Holmes' exploits began to command larger and larger payments from the British *Strand* magazine, where they were being published. "The Red-Headed League" was collected in the 1892 volume *The Adventures of Sherlock Holmes,* which Doyle dedicated to Dr. Bell.

Doyle eventually tired of composing detective stories, considering them inferior to his other fiction. He wanted to be best known for his writing on more serious subjects. This led him to kill off Holmes in "The Final Problem," a short story published in 1893. However, so many people complained, and the monetary offers for a change of heart were so tempting, that Doyle was persuaded to bring back his detective in 1902 with *The Hound of the Baskervilles,* a case set during the period before Holmes's death. The resurrection was completed in the next year, when "The Empty House" revealed that Holmes had actually been in hiding during the time he was thought dead. Sherlock Holmes stories continued to appear until 1927, three years before Doyle's death.

The early twentieth century brought Doyle success in other areas as well. In 1902, he was knighted and given the title "Sir" for his volunteer work as a surgeon in South Africa during the Boer War, along with his writings in support of this war. In the period after World War I, he became an authority on spiritualism, the belief that the dead can communicate with the living. He wrote extensively on this subject and lectured throughout Europe, Africa, Australia, and North America. Doyle's historical fiction, science fiction, and nonfiction books about his life, beliefs, and travels are not often read today, but his Sherlock Holmes stories continue to win fans and inspire imitators throughout the world.

## Plot Summary

Dr. Watson drops in on his friend Sherlock Holmes to find him in conversation with a man with fiery red hair, a Mr. Jabez Wilson. Wilson has come to Holmes with a problem concerning an organization for which he was working but that has mysteriously disappeared. Wilson owns a pawnshop but had for the last two months been employed part-time. At Holmes' urging, he tells his story.

Wilson's assistant Vincent Spaulding had pointed out to Wilson a job notice in the newspaper. It was a job sponsored by the Red-Headed League, and only men with red hair need apply. Spaulding convinced Wilson to go to the interview, and because of the bright color of his hair, Wilson was hired. His job was to copy the *Encyclopaedia Britannica* from 10 A.M. until 2 P.M. He was not to leave the room at all, or he would lose his job. Wilson enjoyed the extra money he made but one Saturday, when he showed up at work, he saw a sign that said the League was dissolved. Wilson set out to discover what had happened to the League, and his well-paying job, but could learn nothing. Spaulding advised that he wait until the League got in touch with him, but Wilson came to seek the advice of Sherlock Holmes.

Holmes asks a few questions about Spaulding, finding out that he has been with Wilson for only three months, that he works for half the wages of anyone else, that he develops photographs in the pawnshop's cellar, and that he has a mark upon his forehead. Holmes gets excited at the last bit of information, and it seems that he recognizes Spaulding. Holmes then sends Wilson home, saying he will give him advice in a few days. After reflecting for an hour, Holmes, accompanied by Watson, goes to the square in which Wilson's shop is located. Holmes examines the neighborhood, thumps upon the pavement in front of the shop with his walkingstick, and then knocks on the door. A young man, presumably Spaulding, answers, and Holmes asks directions of him. However, he is most interested in observing the knees of the shop assistant's trousers; he sees there what he had expected to see. The two men then walk around the block to see what shops are behind Wilson's shop. There is a tobacco store, a newspaper store, a restaurant, a carriage-depot, and the City and Suburban Bank.

The two men attend a concert that afternoon. Afterwards, Holmes tells Watson that a serious crime is about to be committed and that he needs Watson's help that evening. Watson returns to Holmes' residence at ten that evening, where police agent Peter Jones, of the Scotland Yard, and Mr. Merryweather, of the City and Suburban Bank, are already gathered. Holmes explains that they are going to meet the master criminal John Clay this evening. The men take carriages to the bank and wait in the vault. Merryweather realizes that Clay is about to attempt to steal a large reserve of gold. The four men then quiet down and wait.

After more than an hour, one of the stones on the floor begins to move. John Clay emerges through the hole in the floor. He pulls his partner, a man with fiery red hair, up after him. Holmes springs out from his hiding place and uses his hunting crop to knock the gun out of Clay's hand. The accomplice has dashed back through the hole, but Holmes had warned Jones to put guards in front of Wilson's house, where the tunnel leads. Jones leads Clay outside to take him to the police station.

In the early hours of the morning, Holmes explains to Watson how he solved the crime. He realized immediately that Wilson's job copying the encyclopedia was simply a ruse to get him out of the pawnshop for several hours a day. Holmes figured that Spaulding, who spent so much time in the pawnshop's cellar, was digging a tunnel leading to a nearby building. By thumping his walkingstick on the pavement, Holmes determined Wilson's cellar stretched behind the house, so he walked around the block to see what businesses were there. When he saw a bank, the tunnel's destination was obvious. Holmes also looked at the knees of Spaulding's trousers to see that they were worn and stained from hours of digging out a tunnel. He knew Spaulding would rob the bank that evening, Saturday, because he would thus have an extra day before the robbery would be discovered and he could make his escape. After solving the problem mentally, Holmes called Jones and Merryweather to help catch the thieves.

Watson openly admires Holmes, but Holmes merely says that solving the case saved him from boredom, a boredom which is already beginning to settle on him again. He says that his life is simply an attempt to "escape from the commonplaces of existence." Watson points out that he helps people as well. Holmes agrees, noting that man himself is nothing, but that his work is everything.

## Characters

### Archie
*See* Duncan Ross

### John Clay
Clay's apparent desire to learn the pawnbroking trade and his hobby of photography, like the assumed name of Spaulding, mask his intent to rob the City and Suburban Bank. Identified as a "murderer, thief, smasher, and forger," he is skilled enough at crime to have eluded the police for years. Holmes seems almost respectful when he identifies Clay as "the fourth smartest man in London" and compliments him on the ingenuity of his scheme. Clay's acid-splashed forehead and pierced ears hint at a colorful past, but the reader learns little about him aside from his royal blood, aristocratic education, and extreme pride. These attributes suggest that Clay was led to crime by the challenge, rather than the need for money. He may even have a Robin Hood-like motive of stealing from the rich to aid the poor, since police agent Jones mentions that Clay "will crack a crib in Scotland one week, and be raising money to build an orphanage in Cornwall the next."

### Sherlock Holmes
Holmes's reputation as a lover of puzzles and solver of crimes leads people with particularly baffling problems, like the one confounding Jabez Wilson, to seek him out. Holmes possesses a nearly superhuman ability to read a person's background by observing small, seemingly-insignificant details, and Watson states that Holmes's powers of reasoning make him appear to be "a man whose knowledge was not that of other mortals." Holmes is aided in his task by a thorough familiarity with previous criminal cases and the inhabitants of London's underworld, along with a scholarly knowledge of such obscure topics as varieties of cigarette ash and kinds of tattoo marks. Possessing a sort of split personality, Holmes swings between moods of thoughtful inactivity and intense action. Even though

## Media Adaptations

- A silent, black and white version of "The Red-Headed League" was filmed in 1921 for a series, *The Adventures of Sherlock Holmes.* This version was produced in Britain by Stoll Picture Productions and stars Eille Norwood as Holmes and Hubert Willis as Watson.

- "The Red-Headed League" was adapted in 1954 for a British television series of Sherlock Holmes's cases, starring Ronald Howard as Holmes. It appears on videotape along with the story "The Deadly Prophecy" from Nostalgia Family Video.

- With Jeremy Brett as Holmes, "The Red-Headed League" appeared in the 1985 PBS series, *The Adventures of Sherlock Holmes* (second series). This adaptation was produced in Britain by Granada Television.

he is happy to help the police catch criminals when a case interests him, Holmes is more concerned with the pleasure he derives from these mental games. As he tells Watson, "My life is spent in one long effort to escape from the commonplaces of existence. These little problems help me to do so."

### Peter Jones
This police officer eagerly accepts Holmes's help in catching John Clay, whom Jones has been unsuccessfully trying to capture for years. Holmes describes Jones as unintelligent and unskilled in his profession, but he does praise the officer's bravery and persistence.

### Mr. Merryweather
The director of the City and Suburban Bank, Merryweather is portrayed as solemn and respectable. He also shows that he is overconfident and has a one-track mind when he seems more concerned about missing his weekly card game than about the possibility that his bank vaults are in danger.

### William Morris
*See* Duncan Ross

### Duncan Ross
When John Clay refers to his red-headed accomplice as Archie in the bank vault, we learn the real name of the manager who supervises Jabez Wilson's employment with the Red-Headed League. He plays the role of businessman well, even convincing the accountant from whom he borrows the office that he is a lawyer.

### Vincent Spaulding
*See* John Clay

### Dr. John Watson
Watson's admiration for his friend Holmes prompts him to chronicle their many adventures together, such as this one. A medical doctor and married man, Watson is willing to drop his own pursuits to follow his friend at a moment's notice. His devotion and trust lead him to accompany Holmes to Wilson's pawnbroking shop and the bank vault, even though he does not understand his friend's motive. Because Watson asks the questions that allow Holmes to reveal his knowledge and his reasoning, Watson serves as a stand-in for the reader. Watson confesses himself "oppressed with a sense of my own stupidity in my dealings with Sherlock Holmes," but he is a careful observer of people and events.

### Jabez Wilson
A red-haired widower and pawnbroker, Wilson seeks out Sherlock Holmes to solve one mystery, only to find out that he is being used as part of an elaborate scheme to rob a bank. Holmes reads clues in Wilson's appearance that reveal his earlier seafaring profession and visit to China, but even Watson can discern Wilson's mental slowness and mediocrity. Wilson's overriding motivation is his love of money, which allows him to be manipulated by Clay and his accomplice.

## Themes

As the story of bank robbers thwarted by a capable investigator, "The Red-Headed League" presents readers with a number of themes related to the classic contest between good and evil. The opposition between detective and criminal tests the warring values each represents. With the detective's victory, the beliefs and qualities he embodies are confirmed as superior.

### Knowledge and Ignorance
Sherlock Holmes's love of mental puzzles leads to his interest in the odd story Jabez Wilson tells him. His knowledge of crime and ability to reason allow him to discern that a serious motive must lie behind Wilson's singular experience with the bizarre Red-Headed League. Guided by this knowledge, and the observations he makes as a result, he stops a bank robbery and the further lawless career of a master criminal. Through Jabez Wilson, whom Holmes disdains as "not over-bright," readers learn that ignorance—especially when it is accompanied by greed—can make people unwitting accomplices to crime.

A keen intellect is not always a force for good, however. Only a brilliant mind like John Clay's could pinpoint Wilson as the ideal target and conceive of the Red-Headed League as the perfect scheme to divert Wilson's attention from his business while a tunnel is being dug in his cellar. This is where the motives and morality guiding the actions of an intelligent mind become important, and where the key differences between the detective and criminal emerge.

### Greed
The bank robber John Clay and his accomplice Archie are motivated by the fabulous sum of money they hope to steal from the City and Suburban Bank. Their greed takes them outside the bounds of law and leads to their capture. Even though the story ends before their trial and punishment, the likely penalty for their history of criminal acts would be execution, demonstrating the fatal consequences of greed.

Jabez Wilson's love of money also promotes crime and makes him an easy target for exploitation. Not only does the promise of money in return for very little work take him away from his shop so John Clay will have free rein; he first becomes vulnerable when he hires Clay as his assistant, thinking he is getting the better bargain because Clay was "willing to come for half wages so as to learn the business." Sherlock Holmes, by contrast, personifies the virtue of unselfishness. After foiling the attempted bank robbery, he tells the manager Mr. Merryweather that he expects no reward beyond the repayment of his expenses.

# Topics for Further Study

- Investigate psychological theories current in the late nineteenth century, and examine ways that Doyle makes use of these theories within his story. You may want to focus on a specific branch of psychology, a related field such as criminology, or the theories of one particular psychologist.

- Research German composers whose music was frequently performed near the end of the nineteenth century. Use this information to speculate on the further knowledge of Sherlock Holmes's character provided by the story's reference to his musical tastes. You might also consider Italian and French music of the same time period, which Holmes dislikes. What does this contrast in Holmes's musical interests reveal about him?

- Examine cultural factors in turn-of-the-century America that could account for the popularity of the Sherlock Holmes stories. You could locate specific developments in American society comparable to the British ones mentioned in this entry. Conversely, you might investigate unique characteristics of American life, thought, or tastes during this time period that would make Doyle's stories appealing to Americans for reasons that differ from those of British readers.

- Research the principles of logic known as induction and deduction. Distinguish between them, and identify the elements of each demonstrated by Sherlock Holmes's reasoning in ''The Red-Headed League.'' You might wish to judge which principle predominates in Holmes's thinking, or which most aids Holmes in solving the mystery.

### Order and Disorder

The orderliness of a society is always threatened by crime. By helping good to triumph over evil, Sherlock Holmes eliminates the threat to his community's stability. Even though Holmes works with the police, and his investigation serves the interests of law and justice, this is not his greatest concern. In fact, Holmes does not appear to recognize that he has accomplished a humanitarian act until Watson reminds him that he is ''a benefactor of the race.''

Instead, the most important type of order restored when the mystery is solved is an economic order. The belief that money received should be directly proportionate to the amount of work accomplished is jeopardized during the course of the story. Not only do the bank robbers desire money they have not earned, but Jabez Wilson twice attempts to get something for nothing: the labor of John Clay as his assistant, and payment from the Red-Headed League based solely on the color of Wilson's hair and ability to copy from the dictionary. Sherlock Holmes correctly perceives that his strongest clue rests in this imbalance between work and payment, and at the story's end, balance is restored.

### Appearance and Reality

Throughout the story, readers are confronted with a series of situations that are not what they first seem. Jabez Wilson simply wishes to learn what has happened to the Red-Headed League and his weekly payment of four pounds, unaware that this odd mystery is a smokescreen for bank robbery. Watson contrasts the ''uncongenial atmosphere'' surrounding Jabez Wilson's pawnshop with the ''fine shops and stately business premises'' that adjoin the City and Suburban Bank, but the two apparently divided locales are connected by an underground tunnel. The criminals themselves do not even appear criminal. Watson describes John Clay, a thief and murderer, as ''a bright-looking, clean-shaven young fellow'' when he first sees Clay at the pawnshop door, later noting his ''white, almost womanly hand'' and ''clean-cut, boyish face'' at the moment of Clay's capture.

Little can be taken at face value in "The Red-Headed League." Because both Wilson and Watson so readily believe that outward appearances reveal truth, we are reminded that this is a common human failing. It is even sometimes appropriate, as readers learn when Jabez Wilson turns out to be exactly the kind of man that both Watson and Holmes guessed him to be. But it is also the detective's job—and a skill readers might imitate—to be suspicious of appearances and suspend judgment until all the evidence has been unearthed.

## Style

### Point of View

"The Red-Headed League" is narrated from the first-person perspective of Dr. Watson, who participates in all aspects of Sherlock Holmes's case. What makes this narrative style especially clever is that Doyle creates a narrator who sees and hears the same information that Holmes does and who can relay the information systematically to readers, but who cannot interpret it. This technique is characteristic of the early detective story, pioneered by Edgar Allan Poe's tales of the sleuth Dupin. It creates suspense, since readers—along with the sidekick narrator—do not have access to the detective's innermost thoughts until he finally chooses to reveal them after the mystery is solved.

### Setting

When Jabez Wilson shows Holmes and Watson the newspaper in which he first learned of the Red-Headed League, we learn that the events of the story take place in 1890, only a year before Doyle wrote the story. Few details allow a reader to picture Holmes's rooms at 221B Baker Street, where he interviews Wilson and where over half the story takes place. However, Doyle gives readers the flavor of late-Victorian London when Holmes and Watson venture outside to examine Wilson's pawnshop and its surroundings. Readers catch glimpses of the bustling commercial district, gas-lit evening streets, and the Underground (subway). The most fully developed setting is the bank vault, where increasing detail draws out the story's climax and increases suspense.

### Structure

The detective story is often seen as one of the purest forms of plot. Not only are the protagonist (the detective) and his antagonist (the criminal) clearly identified by the time the story concludes; in addition, the process of solving a case precisely parallels conventional plot structure. The story begins with exposition, as the case is presented to Holmes. While Holmes investigates the case, forms a theory, and prepares to test this theory, the action rises. The climax comes when Holmes's theory is demonstrated to be correct because a criminal who would have otherwise escaped detection has been apprehended. Holmes's explanation to Watson, which fills in missing information and provides a sense of closure because all loose ends have been tied up, serves as the story's denouement, or falling action.

One additional element often present in detective stories, especially typical of Doyle's Sherlock Holmes tales, is a step in the story's exposition through which Holmes gains his client's—and his reader's—trust. Just as Holmes reads the evidence of Wilson's appearance to reveal his background, he often repeats this action with those who seek him out, sometimes even guessing the nature of their inquiry before they tell him. This establishes Holmes's credibility from the story's outset and gives readers faith that, however impossible a solution may seem at times, one will finally emerge if the reader perseveres until the story's final paragraphs.

### Symbols

The movement and meaning of a detective story most often come through the mental and physical operations of the detective, rather than through intricate structures of symbols and images. However, the detective himself can be seen as a concrete symbol of abstract traits the author values, such as intelligence, imagination, curiosity, and unselfishness. Giving humanity to the abstraction are Sherlock Holmes' character quirks, such as his sense of humor, pipe-smoking (along with a cocaine habit, mentioned in several other stories), musical tastes, and fluctuation between the poetic and energetic poles of his "dual nature."

Critics have also suggested that Doyle's settings carry symbolic meanings. In Rosemary Jann's judgment, the tunnel that connects the seedy world of Jabez Wilson's pawnshop to the more refined business district of the City and Suburban bank symbolizes the insecurity and vulnerability of middle- and upper-class life.

## Doppelganger

Even though they act on different sides of the law, it is curious that the character most resembling Sherlock Holmes in "The Red-Headed League" is the bank robber, John Clay. Both are intelligent and imaginative, and Clay's pride in his royal background mirrors Holmes' pride in his mental powers and detecting success. In Clay, Holmes recognizes a formidable mind that nearly matches his own. As police agent Jones suggests, Clay even has a charitable impulse to complement Holmes's.

It is understandable that a detective must think like a criminal to understand his thought processes and predict his behavior, accentuating in the detective those qualities most comparable to his quarry. However, detective stories like Doyle's often emphasize innate similarities between these two figures. Critics such as Ian Ousby trace this doubling to nineteenth-century distrust of the police, through which even an amateur detective bears traces of the negative qualities frequently attributed to early police forces. On a broader level, similarities between the detective and his doppelganger, or mirrored reflection, demonstrate that both good and evil can spring from the same sources. Only individual choice determines whether talents and skills are used positively or negatively.

# Historical Context

## Turn-of-the-Century Readers

The detective stories Doyle published in the *Strand* magazine during the 1890s, including "The Red-Headed League," are credited with doubling subscribers to the magazine. During the Victorian Age, which stretched from the beginning of Queen Victoria's reign in 1837 to her death in 1901, major writers such as Charles Dickens, George Eliot, and Thomas Hardy often published novels serially, in weekly or monthly parts. Doyle, however, was the first to write short stories using a similar method, relying upon interest in a central character rather than an ongoing plot to keep readers coming back for more. The factors that led to this amazing popularity reveal the interests and make-up of the reading public in Doyle's day.

England increasingly became a nation of readers in the decades before Sherlock Holmes first appeared, since the Education Act of 1870 and legislation to limit child labor made it possible for a wider segment of the population to attend school. In

# What Do I Read Next?

- "The Murders in the Rue Morgue," "The Purloined Letter," and "The Mystery of Marie Roget" are Edgar Allan Poe's pioneering detective stories. Poe's Dupin character and the unnamed friend who narrates the stories present parallels to Holmes and Watson.

- *Dr. Jekyll and Mr. Hyde,* the 1886 novel by Robert Louis Stevenson, is, like Doyle's Sherlock Holmes stories, concerned with human psychology and the role of science in society.

- Oscar Wilde's controversial 1891 novel, *The Picture of Dorian Gray,* is often seen as the bible of the late-Victorian aesthetic and decadent philosophy.

- Bram Stoker's 1897 *Dracula,* although concerned more with supernatural rather than rational phenomena, portrays in its characters' hunt for the vampire Dracula detective work that rivals Holmes's own.

- *The Hound of the Baskervilles,* Doyle's short Holmes novel published in 1902, in which Holmes, with the help of the devoted Watson, investigates an unexplained death, a family curse, and a ghostly dog on the moors surrounding ancient Baskerville Hall.

- *The Maltese Falcon* by Dashiell Hammett introduced readers to the hard-boiled, rough-edged detective Sam Spade.

1880, all children were guaranteed schooling through the age of ten. Since recreational reading among this newly literate class was often done in short spans of time—while riding the train or subway, for instance—forms of writing flourished that could be quickly consumed, like articles or short stories in newspapers and magazines. Similarly, true or fictional accounts of action, adventure, and crime captivated the attention of lower- and middle-class readers who worked hard for a living and whose lives often contained little of the excitement they

# Compare & Contrast

- **1890s:** A middle-class gentleman could support his family, including several servants, on an annual income of 500 pounds. The maximum pay for a police constable was just under 2 pounds a week.

  **Today:** The average annual household income in the United Kingdom in the early 1990s was 15,800 pounds, or approximately $25,900 in U.S. dollars.

- **1890:** The world's first electrically operated underground subway system opens in London.

  **Today:** Over 270 miles of electrically powered subway lines—the second-longest system in the world behind New York's—snake beneath the London metropolitan area.

- **1890s:** The ninth edition of the *Encyclopaedia Britannica*, its 24 volumes appearing between 1875 and 1889, runs to a total of 21,572 pages.

  **Today:** With its 32 volumes and 31,729 pages, the fifteenth edition of the *Encyclopaedia Britannica* was completed in 1991.

---

sought in literature. Doyle wrote for such readers, often reinforcing through his stories beliefs that his readers would be likely to hold.

### The Police

Even though a British police force had been established in 1829, the institution was not held in universal high esteem. Early police had often been seen as paid spies, and cases of bribery, corruption, and incompetence made the public skeptical of police honesty and expertise. Due in part to low wages, the police were often drawn from the lowest ranks of society, leading many people who considered themselves socially superior to question their authority and skill. Doyle's portrayal of police agent Jones and Holmes's attitude toward him repeat these stereotypes. In other Sherlock Holmes stories, too, the police are depicted as earnest in their desire to promote justice but unable to accomplish this without Holmes's aid.

### Class and Urbanization in British Society

Changes in class structure and living conditions of British society are also reflected in Doyle's stories. London became a world center of industry and commerce during the nineteenth century, its population rising from approximately 850,000 in 1810 to almost 5 million by the end of the century. Many were drawn to the city by dreams of financial success. In this environment of progress, skill and intelligence became keys to social advancement and prosperity, rather than the prominence of one's family. Sherlock Holmes represents this new ideal of the gentleman, someone who achieves distinction and respect through his own merit and talents.

The average British citizen also began to question why the upper class should be considered naturally superior. On numerous occasions, members of the British aristocracy, even of the royal family, had been involved in well-publicized sexual, marital, and economic scandals. Such behavior was little in keeping with the moral standards the middle class was proud to uphold. John Clay in ''The Red-Headed League'' confirms widespread suspicions of aristocratic corruption. He has turned to crime when his background and education would have opened the doors of more honorable professions to him. His pride in his social rank appears ridiculous, since he has given up all claims to true respectability.

### Scientific Advances

The middle and late decades of the nineteenth century also represented an explosion in scientific thought. This flowering of the sciences came in the wake of Charles Darwin's theory of natural selection, announced in his 1859 *The Origin of Species*

*Clive Brooks as Sherlock Holmes.*

and 1871 *The Descent of Man.* Darwin had proposed that each element of the natural world was not only part of an ongoing and orderly process of evolution but also carried physical signs of these evolutionary stages. His concept, and later theories indebted to it, led to increasing belief that all phenomenon could be explained using the skills of observation and reasoning. Sherlock Holmes is seen by many critics as an embodiment of this new faith in scientific reasoning as a way of giving order and meaning to the world.

But because science also threatened previous systems of belief, especially deeply held religious beliefs, Sherlock Holmes also presents a reassuring example of the usefulness of the scientist to society. Even though Holmes spends much of his time amassing information that might seem little more than academic or even humorous to the average reader—such as the study of tattoo marks mentioned in ''The Red-Headed League''—the same methods of thinking that promote these academic studies prove vital to achieving the goals of justice and social order.

Just as advances in scientific thought spread worldwide, the social changes and attitudes discussed above were not unique to England. Growing literacy, urbanization, changes in class structure, and the questioning of police authority and competence typical of British society had especially strong parallels in American culture. This might explain why Sherlock Holmes quickly became as familiar and appealing to American readers as to those in the country where his adventures were first published.

## Critical Overview

Detective fiction has often been categorized as pure entertainment. For this reason, much critical opinion of "The Red-Headed League" and Doyle's other Sherlock Holmes stories is influenced by a particular critic's viewpoint on the value of this literary niche. In recent decades, criticism has begun to shift toward a more serious consideration of these tales. Doyle's detective stories are seen as fascinating clues to the culture in which they were written and as explorations of the attitudes characteristic of late-Victorian life.

Most early book reviewers had favorable opinions of *The Adventures of Sherlock Holmes*, in which "The Red-Headed League" appeared. Typical is the judgment voiced by one anonymous critic in a British periodical, *The Athenaeum,* who said of the collection, "Of its kind it is excellent; there is little literary pretension about it, and there is hardly any waste of time about subtle character-drawing; but incident succeeds incident with the most businesslike rapidity, and the unexpected always occurs with appropriate regularity." Another reviewer, William Morton Payne, singled out "The Red-Headed League" for particular note in an American journal, *The Dial,* remarking that the story "is a striking illustration of the author's originality." Years later, Doyle cited the same reason for ranking "The Red-Headed League" as his second favorite Holmes story (with "The Speckled Band" first). In 1959, a poll among readers of the *Baker Street Journal,* a magazine for Sherlock Holmes fans, concurred with Doyle.

The largest body of criticism on the Sherlock Holmes stories comes from groups of enthusiasts who call themselves "Sherlockians" or "Holmesians." In over 50 journals and newsletters published worldwide, the most prominent being the American *Baker Street Journal* and British *Sherlock Holmes Journal,* writers attempt to resolve inconsistencies in the stories or deduce aspects of Holmes's and Watson's lives from clues given in the stories. The central premise shared by these writers, from which much of the fun of their essays arises, is that Holmes was an actual person who solved real mysteries. As a result, writers on "The Red-Headed League" have produced wonderfully logical articles attempting to establish the true location of Saxe-Coburg Square, since no place by this name exists in London, or arguing that the Red-Headed League might really have existed.

Such articles must obviously be read from the same tongue-in-cheek perspective in which they were written. However, they often provide worthwhile information on the historical background of Doyle's stories and testify to the mystique Sherlock Holmes still holds today. One of the best examples of criticism in this "Sherlockian" vein is Gordon L. Iseminger's essay on Holmes as a Victorian archetype, since it demonstrates ways in which Holmes was a product of the culture from which he emerged.

A similar appreciative tone marks much critical writing on Doyle during the early and middle decades of the twentieth century. Writers occasionally disparage the form in which Doyle chose to write, but they nevertheless praise his clever plots. One exception was the poet T.S. Eliot, who enjoyed the character of Sherlock Holmes but complained, in a 1929 review of the complete collection of the Holmes stories, that the solution to "The Red-Headed League" was "perfectly obvious from the beginning." Critics then, as now, frequently marvel at the level of popularity Holmes had achieved and speculate on the reasons for this phenomenon.

More recent criticism has often focused on Doyle's life as an influence upon his detective stories. Links are often drawn between the characterization of Holmes and Doyle's own scientific interests and political convictions, including his patriotism, contradictory views on women's rights, and skepticism toward the British judicial system. By these critics' reasoning, Holmes becomes an extension of Doyle himself, perhaps even Doyle's vision of an ideal self. A central problem for these biographical critics is Doyle's intense interest in spiritualism, especially during his later life, because it appears to deny the spirit of rationalism that infuses the Holmes stories.

The work of most contemporary scholars builds from the assumption that the popular literature of any time period provides special insight into that period. Attitudes regarding class status, gender, and race are of special interest to these critics. Along with the qualities in Holmes that are a debt to his times, the types of crimes he encounters are often seen as symptoms of the anxieties that plagued late-Victorian readers—and for which only a superhuman figure like Holmes could find a solution. For these reasons, "The Red-Headed League" has attracted critical attention because of contrasts between the class positions of Jabez Wilson, Holmes, and John Clay. In her discussion of the story, for instance, critic Rosemary Jann demonstrates that both Wilson and Clay, as poles on the spectrum of class status, represent threats to the middle class and its strongly ingrained work ethic. She also argues that Doyle may use Clay, with his "white, almost womanly hand," pierced ears, and partnership with another man, to play upon and then relieve through Clay's eventual capture another set of late-Victorian fears regarding homosexuality.

Along with their interest in the social issues that play a role in Doyle's stories, critics are also exploring literary trends current in the nineteenth century that may have influenced his writing. The aesthetic or decadent movement in late-Victorian literature is often perceived as one such influence. This movement prized the mental and sensory experiences of art over the mundane details of everyday existence, and the artificial over the natural. Even though Doyle writes in a realistic style, the character of Sherlock Holmes, with his artistic interests and habit of uttering witty statements, or epigrams, is indebted to the aesthetic movement.

Growing attention to both popular fiction as a category and Doyle as a writer has led critics and readers alike to reexamine Doyle's other writing, such as his science fiction and historical novels. This nearly forgotten body of work is proving to be of interest in its own right, along with its value in illuminating relationships between different types of popular fiction and parallels to the immortal Holmes stories.

## Criticism

### Rena Korb

*Rena Korb has a master's degree in English literature and creative writing and has written for a wide variety of educational publishers. In the following essay she provides an overview of the continuing popularity of the Sherlock Holmes' saga and examines the elements that make up "The Red-Headed League."*

> "Watson, although a bright man and a medical doctor, plays the slow-witted counterpart to Holmes' quick deductive reasoning."

Sherlock Holmes is one of the most legendary literary figures, not only among lovers of detective fiction. Stories of Holmes' adventures—and there are only 56 short stories and 4 novels—have been translated throughout the world and made into plays, films, and television programs. There are more than 50 magazines devoted to the discussion of Sherlock Holmes and countless societies formed by people to celebrate him. When Arthur Conan Doyle sold all rights to *A Study in Scarlet* in 1886 for a mere 25 pounds, he could not possibly have imagined what a star he, Holmes' assistant Dr. Watson, and the detective himself would become.

Why is Sherlock Holmes so popular? Even his dedicated readers admit that his plots are sometimes rather thin and that the details do not always add up. For instance, "The Red-Headed League" has inspired several articles pointing out its inconsistencies; notes from a Sherlock Holmes' society meeting discussing the same matter have even been published. Yet enjoyment in the story has never abated. It seems that Doyle has succeeded at something far more important than fabricating complicated mysteries: he has recreated the world of London in the 1880s; he has supplied rich detail and compelling characters; most important, he has invented Sherlock Holmes, one of modern literature's most enduring characters.

"The Red-Headed League" is one of the earliest Holmes stories. It shows Holmes foiling a bank robbery attempted by a master criminal. The affair is brought to Holmes' attention by a pawnbroker, upset at having lost his job with a group called the Red-Headed League of copying the *Encyclopaedia Britannica*. Holmes is rightly suspicious, and after doing a bit of investigating, figures out when and where a robbery will take place. He then arrives at the scene first, accompanied by an agent from Scotland Yard, to arrest the criminals.

Michael Atkinson sees in this story "a symbolic commentary on the nature of plot itself"; it shows the reader how the plot of the story can be used to get underneath the plot to show deeper connections between characters and action. This is highlighted by Holmes' movements and thoughts mirroring the physical action of the story. As Holmes physically moves from Baker Street to Saxe-Coburg Square to the concert hall and back to Baker Street again, his mental process proceeds from logical guess to confirmation, reflection, and finally, to the formulation of a plan. The aptly named John Clay is the anti-Holmes. His scarred forehead, symbolizing "reason disfigured," provides a contrast to Holmes, whose reason is straight and sure. Clay insists on his nobility while Holmes brushes aside any idea of nobility as playing a part in his foiling of the crime. The two men even react to their knowledge of each other in a similar fashion. When he recognizes the description of Clay, "Holmes sat up in his chair in considerable excitement" but then lapsed into his usual calm demeanor; Clay exclaims "Great Scott!" when he sees Holmes but then composes himself "with the utmost coolness." According to Atkinson, these correspondences serve to show "an abyss which is always in the neighborhood of a Holmes story, the chasm which separates thought from moral feeling here, the terrible gulf between the powers of reason and the health of the soul."

Other readers appoint themselves critics in enumerating the inconsistencies and the flawed logic of the plot. Vernon Goslin actually copied pages out of the *Encyclopaedia Britannica* in order to make the discovery that "Wilson had just achieved the incredible feat of writing, with a quill pen, *over one million words in longhand,* in precisely 224 hours!" Other issues abound. Where did the criminals put the dirt they dug out of the ground to make the tunnel? If Wilson applied for the job in late April, "[j]ust two months ago," how could the League have closed its doors in mid-October? More irking, perhaps, is the fact that Holmes and Clay are clearly acquainted, for Holmes "had one or two little scores of [his] own to settle with Mr. Clay." Clay, aka Vincent Spaulding, therefore, must have recognized Holmes at the pawnshop—why then did this criminal "at the head of his profession" and, according to Holmes' estimation, "the fourth smartest man in London," continue with the plan that could only deliver him into the hands of the arch sleuth? For other readers of "The Red-Headed League," the story is best appreciated through the sheer enjoyment of the reading. As with other Holmes' stories, the humor, plot-enriching details, and characters are certainly enough to make the story successful.

Humor is perhaps the most apparent aspect of the story. The very plot itself centers around comedy. Jabez Wilson seems not to understand the incongruity of the tale he relates, though his narrative abounds with ludicrous details: Spaulding's unprefaced declaration that "I wish to the Lord, Mr. Wilson, that I was a red-headed man"; Wilson's description of the London street as men came out in answer to the advertisement—"From north, south, east, and west every man who had a shade of red in his hair had tramped into the city...Fleet Street was choked with red-headed folk, and Pope's Court looked like a coster's orange barrow"; the criminals' insistence that Wilson provide his own pen and paper, all while paying him the generous-for-the-time sum of four pounds a week to copy the encyclopedia; and, of course, the image of Wilson himself, laboring over his longhand and hoping to "get on to the B's before very long," who never realizes that such a foolish task must be a ruse to get him out of his shop. Surely one can overlook a few inaccurate dates for the sake of such an imaginative tale.

The details of character and those of the London surroundings work in conjunction with the unraveling and meaning of the plot. Very little in "The Red-Headed League" is superfluous—everything has significance. Names play an important role. John Clay is so named because he travels underneath the earth. Perhaps less apparent is the implication of the name of Jabez Wilson, though certainly many readers may note its uniqueness. The name *Jabez,* however, belonged to a Biblical scribe who belonged to the tribe of Judah. Compare these two men then, one who recorded the words of an important tribe in the development of the Judeo-Christian religion, the other who blindly records the dry words of an encyclopedia. On the other hand, Merryweather's name does not have such strong implications but simply provides another spot of humor; he is "sad-faced" and "solemn," speaks "gloomily" and bemoans that he is missing his bridge game to save his bank. The descriptions of London, too, highlight the unraveling of the plot. Holmes and Watson, along their journey through the maze of lies, "rattled through an endless labyrinth of gas-lit streets until [they] emerged into Farrington Street." "We are close there," Holmes then says, "there" being the physical destination as well as the solution to the puzzle.

Much has been said about the characters, Sherlock Holmes and Dr. John Watson, as an integral part of Doyle's success. Indeed, the two men work off each other, but in a complementary fashion as opposed to the adversarial relationship between Holmes and Clay. Watson, although a bright man and a medical doctor, plays the slow-witted counterpart to Holmes' quick deductive reasoning. When presented with the same clues, Watson never sees things through Holmes' eyes. Indeed in "The Red-Headed League" Watson "thought over it all, from the extraordinary story of the red-headed copier of the Encyclopaedia down to the visit to Saxe-Coburg Square," yet has no inkling as to what the details he has observed and heard mean; "I tried to puzzle it out," Watson says, "but gave up in despair." The reader, on the other hand, can put together at least a shadow plot of the mystery. That Wilson's shop abuts a bank is a clear indicator. When Holmes explains the solving of the crime to Watson, it is clear that Watson—and the reader—has been privy to almost all the same information as the detective. Exceptions include what Holmes saw on Spaulding's trousers (they were "worn, wrinkled, and stained") and what he determined from tapping the pavement with his walking stick (the cellar extended underneath the building to the rear). Holmes certainly is privy to greater knowledge about European criminals and their tendencies, yet it is not necessary to know that one "John Clay, the murderer, thief, smasher, and forger" seeks to rob the City bank to know that the bank will be robbed.

Some critics find that the Holmes character is presented to the reader as a nearly perfect crime solver. Others, however, find that much of the appeal in Doyle's Sherlock Holmes stories lies in the reader's being allowed to practice his or her own deductive powers along with Holmes. These two ideas are not contrary. All readers can reason out some of the mysteries as does Holmes. But Holmes is far different from the average reader of his cases. Not all readers have Holmes' keen perceptive ability or his firsthand knowledge of the criminal. Most importantly, readers do not share Holmes' ennui, a boredom with life so great that he is driven to solve crimes in "one long effort to escape from the commonplaces of existence." Doyle has said, "Sherlock is utterly inhuman, no heart, but with a beautiful logical intellect." Truly, Holmes does not interact with the world around him except to step in, briefly, and make it right again. Chances are that the reader does not share these commonalties with Holmes. Thus the stories about this singular character's exploits provide a bit of adventure and challenge in the reader's own existence.

**Source:** Rena Korb, for *Short Stories for Students*, Gale Research, 1997.

## *Michael Atkinson*

*In the following essay, Atkinson discusses "The Red-Headed League" as a supreme example of the nature of plot, in which a "sequence of events" becomes "a structure of revelation."*

Most Sherlock Holmes stories begin with someone coming to visit the famous detective. The master sleuth listens judiciously as the hapless visitor spells out the details of his story, a confusing sequence of events uninformed by a clear meaning, a chain of mysterious occurrences of which the visitor feels himself somehow to be the victim, and thus now turns to the renowned intellect in the hope he can illuminate the puzzle—in short, the kind of encounter familiar to any English teacher who has ever held office hours the day before a major essay came due.

But this moment in which a relationship between fact and meaning, event and pattern, occurrence and revelation is about to be created has higher purposes than the elucidation of the archetypal roots of the essay conference. In particular, Sherlock Holmes stories can help us explain to our students the difference between a plot and a story—a distinction that is crucial to understanding the process of fiction itself. In the Introduction to Literary Study course taught to prepare majors for the further serious study of literature, I use "The Red Headed League" (conveniently included in Lynn Altenbernd's standard *Anthology*) to introduce and demonstrate the process by which a story (a sequence of events) becomes plot (a structure of revelation)—not only because this tale embodies this concept of plot paradigmatically, as many Holmes stories do, but because among these stories "The Red-Headed League" is so clearly *a symbolic commentary on the nature of plot itself*. Students love it, and learn, in a way they like to remember, an understanding of plot which, if not elementary, is at least fundamental.

The story itself is easy to summarize. Watson stumbles in on Holmes who is listening to the tale of Jabez Wilson, a red-headed pawnbroker who, two months before, had been alerted to the existence of the Red-Headed League by his assistant, one Vincent Spaulding, a man so eager to learn the pawnbroker's trade that he had hired on for half wages,

> "Perhaps the first point to be made about any plot—of a tale by Borges, a novel by Dickens, a play by Shakespeare, or a legend set down by Ovid—is that as the action unfolds, the meaning of each action changes."

his only personal quirk being a penchant for photography which frequently took him to the basement where he developed things. Spaulding showed Wilson an advertisement offering a sinecure to the right red-headed man, even guided him to the League's office, where Wilson was selected from a horde of carrot-tops, for the singular duty of copying the *Encyclopaedia Britannica* daily from ten to two for four pounds a week. This he proceeded to do for eight weeks, only to arrive at the office one day to find a notice proclaiming the dissolution of the League. Unable to trace his former red-headed patron (one "William Morris," under whose tutelage he has copied out articles on Abbots, Armour, Archery, Architecture, and Attica!), and too disturbed to take the advice of his assistant to wait and see what developed, the porcine Jabez Wilson, ruing the loss of his extra income, has come to consult Holmes.

Holmes starts involuntarily at the description of Wilson's assistant, a small, stout man with a white splash of acid on his forehead, and satisfies himself and us that he knows the man when Wilson confirms Holmes' guess that Spaulding's ears are pierced. Holmes dismisses Wilson for the duration (the man is so thick Doyle puts him to sleep during the climactic action) and what began as the pawnbroker's story becomes the detective's. Holmes predicts this will be a three-pipe problem; but before retiring to smoke it out, he invites Watson to join him for an afternoon concert later in the day. On their way to the hall, the pair stop off in Saxe-Coburg Square, and as they stand before Wilson's shop, Holmes thumps the pavement with his walking stick, then knocks on the door and feigns to inquire directions of the assistant, his actual purpose being a surreptitious glance at the man's knees. Then Holmes and Watson go around to "explore the parts which lie behind" the shabby-genteel square and observe, among the sequence of buildings along the busy thoroughfare, a bank. Once at the concert, Holmes ponders mightily while Watson reflects upon his friend's genius, sure (and assuring the reader) that it is at work. The concert over, they agree to meet at ten; Watson is to pack a revolver against potential danger—and for heightened suspense.

At ten, Watson reaches Baker Street to find Holmes with the fundamentally stupid but tenacious Inspector Jones and a phlegmatic Mr. Merryweather, who sporadically whines about missing his rubber of bridge for this caper (he is chairman of the bank whose back abuts the pawnshop). Holmes' announced mission is to deliver into Jones' hands one nefarious criminal, John Clay (a.k.a. Vincent Spaulding) and to keep in the hands of Merryweather some 30,000 napoleons of French gold. The foursome proceed to the cellar of the bank where Merryweather proclaims the soundness of the vault, for emphasis tapping its floor with his cane. The floor rings as hollow as his boast, and confirmed in the knowledge the bank's security is undermined, the four shut the lantern and sit down in the dark to await the arrival of the felons. In just over an hour's time, John Clay chips his way through the floor to carry out the theft and is apprehended by Holmes. Clay's companion flees to the tunnel's other end and into the arms of the law. Holmes and Clay swap compliments about the crime and the capture respectively. But as Jones handcuffs him, Clay disdainfully insists on being addressed as nobility, a whim Jones indulges as he leads him off to jail. Accepting Merryweather's thanks, Holmes confesses he had old scores to settle with Clay, and is glad too to have heard the story of the Red-Headed League.

To Watson, Holmes explains what was obvious to him from the first—that the League was a ruse to clear Wilson from his shop and that the assistant who worked for half wages was behind it. His frequent visits to the cellar meant tunneling, confirmed by the worn knees on his trousers, and the solid tap on the sidewalk in front of the shop meant the cellar tunnel went behind it, confirmed by the presence of the bank on the thoroughfare. When the tunnel was fully opened, the League was closed, and the robbery promised to take place on Saturday night, leaving all Sunday for undetected escape. Hence Holmes could know the crime, the place, the time. Watson praises Holmes' virtue as benefactor to mankind, but Holmes graciously avers it was but an escape from ennui for him—as it has certainly been for us.

What a fiction like this can highlight for students of literature is the conversion of story into significance. Perhaps the first point to be made about any plot—of a tale by Borges, a novel by Dickens, a play by Shakespeare, or a legend set down by Ovid—is that as the action unfolds, the meaning of each action changes. Insignificant actions become significant in light of later revelations, one person's story becomes another's, the casual becomes the causal, the immoral becomes the principled, the irrational is revealed to be reason itself. In the tale of ratiocination, this element of retrospective re-patterning is especially pronounced, because the characters (not just the readers) are engaged in the process. Events become clues, and clues solve the mystery, explaining the puzzle of events we began with. This retrospective patterning is what turns a story (sequence of events) into a plot (generator of meaning, structure of revelation).

In the typical Holmes story, this process is formalized by splitting the narrative into three stages, the narration of each stage governed by a different character (though all are filtered through Watson). The first stage is the truly puzzling relation of events by the perplexed client (Wilson's inability to connect fact to meaning is symbolized by his being given an encyclopaedia to copy); Holmes' actions—responses to the facts and simultaneously investigations of them—narrated by Watson, who misses most of the clues we pick up, comprise the second stage (here meaning is not absent or present, but palpably potential); and, of course, the third stage is the final full revelation of meaning by Holmes. At each stage, there is an increase of significance, which is why our marks in the margins of this or any other story get denser as the tale goes on. Beneath this sequence of events is another, invisible to us for the most part, but reflected in the events we witness and powerfully affecting our interest in those events. As Holmes moves from Baker Street to Saxe-Coburg Square to the concert hall and back, he also moves from educated guess, to confirmation, reflection, and articulation of a plan (in the twin sense of diagram and directive). His movement is the quickening movement of meaning itself in the narrative.

The second point to be made about the emergence of event into meaning is that in art as in life all meaning emerges through correspondence. A scientific theory is meaningful when the several terms of its mathematical formulae prove adequate metaphors for the observed data. A proverb has meaning for us when its "if" and "then" correspond to and illuminate the perceived sequences of our acts and feelings. A story gains meaning as we perceive its life corresponding metaphorically to our own—but also as we perceive one part corresponding to another, internally. Daisy's green dock light, her green cards for kisses, Gatsby's car's green upholstery, and the fresh green breast of the new world; Huck's faked death and new way of living on the river; the blinding of Gloucester, the blindness of Lear; Holden's feelings for sister, for nuns, for a young prostitute; Robin Molineaux's response to this man, to that man, to his kinsman in the cart. Meaning emerges through correspondence.

So we move from the fact that Holmes' theories correspond to and thus explain the strange facts of the case, to a deeper level of correspondence. "The Red-Headed League" is typical of Holmes stories and typical of fiction in general because such correspondences abound. But it is unusual in that the correspondences not only are fictional—giving us the sense of something made—but are also symbolic of fiction, plot making and plot realization.

Probably the most noticeable correspondence in the story is the one between the taps of Holmes' stick on the pavement and the tap of Merryweather's cane on the vault floor. It takes no Hermes Trismegistus to see that with the echo of this second tap resonating with the first we have dramatically been admitted to the realm of "as above, so below." Suddenly we have been given access to Holmes' thoughts, which have been running silently beneath the events all along, like an underground stream ready to burst up in a spring—or, to put a very fine point on it, like a tunnel connecting two buildings, structures, which face in different directions but have secret connections, like the structure of events in Wilson's tale and the peripatetics of Holmes—both his strolling and explaining.

And this leads us straight to the symbolic plot, for what goes on in "The Red-Headed League" is not just what goes on behind the façade—here the façades of the pawnshop and bank as well as the duplicitous façade of the League. A plot is an action, but as we know from county and cemetery maps, it is also a piece of ground. And this is a tale about providing (constructing) a mental plat-map (that is, a plot map, a land diagram) to survey the shape of things beneath the Square. The story points to the truth behind this and all stories; the plot is there so that we can find out what goes on *beneath* the plot. Like Holmes, good readers infer the existence of secret tunnels which link the trivial to the treasured, pawnshops to banks, enabling us to pull off "raids on the inarticulate." And to do so we must go down into the basement to see what develops—or (at the other end of the tunnel) be willing to sit "in the dark" for a spell and wait for meaning and confirmation to burst through intuitively before we can apprehend and illuminate it.

Of course, other correspondences at both ends of the tunnel connect Holmes to the Clay he finds under the earth. For beneath this plot do we not find a radical correspondence?—the common Clay, his forehead symbolically scarred, reflecting reason disfigured, yet insisting on his nobility; while Holmes' lofty brow remains unwrinkled as he insists on the absence of noble motives, claiming to have solved the crime to settle an old score and drive off ennui (a point Doyle underscores by making all those who benefit from Holmes' action either ridiculous or repellent). No wonder Holmes is content to put his hands on the Clay that worked beneath his feet and has no inclination to curse or mock him. And except for Clay's being startled, which corresponds with Holmes' jumping when he recognizes Clay's description, Clay is as cool as Holmes. The two men even exchange compliments, a tacit acknowledgement of their complementary natures.

The face-to-face meeting between Holmes and Clay opens beneath us an abyss which is always in the neighborhood of a Holmes story, the chasm which separates thought from moral feeling here, the terrible gulf between the powers of reason and the health of the soul—linked only by quirk and chance in Holmes' alignment with, rather than against, humane sentiments and their encodement into law.

Using plot to get beneath plot is always a sobering as well as a delightful experience, one which makes us more reserved in our judgments as it increases the catholicity of our appreciation. A study of a Sherlock Holmes story such as "The Red-Headed League" can lead to some absolutely fundamental insights about plot—and it can also help us understand that such a tale of ratiocination lies beneath literature, not in being inferior or a subspecies, but in being a root, a radical paradigm for fiction, as charm and riddle are for poetry.

**Source:** Michael Atkinson, "Sherlock Holmes and 'The Red-Headed League': A Symbolic Paradigm for the Teaching of Plot," in *College Literature,* Vol. VII, No. 2, Spring, 1980, pp. 153–57.

### Gordon L. Iseminger

*In the following essay, Iseminger explains how the character of Sherlock Holmes epitomizes the British Victorian man in terms of attitude, behavior, and beliefs.*

The typical nineteenth-century Englishman of the upper or middle classes considered himself a citizen of the greatest nation in the world. The foremost beneficiary of the industrial revolution, he shared with Lord Macaulay an unshakable belief in progress and took material prosperity in stride. He took it for granted that enterprise and invention would produce more and more convenience and abundance. He was a Thomas Gradgrind, a man of realities, a man of facts and calculations. He may have been aware of his rights under the constitution, but he emphasized more the duty of which Charles Kingsley wrote in his famous novel *Westward Ho!.* He taught by example and did not sympathize with the Robert Owenses who believed they could engineer a positive change in human behaviour. Victorian to his fingertips, this typical Englishman may have been vigorously disliked around the world, but he set the moral tone for the age and in many ways was the most successful and the most representative being in the nineteenth century.

Victorians believed firmly in the doctrine of *laissez-faire,* which in its most naked form allowed the utmost of competition and individualism. The classical school of economics was seemingly in the interests of the businessman, but the best interests of all society would be served when each individual sought his own interests. What was good for business was good for Britain, and businessmen were accorded status and respectability in a society whose greatest rewards and honours had traditionally been bestowed upon military figures, statesmen, and members of the nobility. By competing with their fellows and producing ever-greater profits, entrepreneurs were serving and benefiting all of society....

The English historian David Thomson once wrote that it was perhaps natural that an England as prosperous and proud as she was at the mid-point of the nineteenth century would find a suitable historian to reinterpret English history. Lord Macaulay was that historian. Inevitably a figure would be found who typified the character traits associated with Victorianism. That man was Sherlock Holmes, the world's first consulting detective. Englishmen needed someone who could unravel the mysteries of a hostile world and ensure a highly personal justice. This person could function in a mechanistic universe whose rules for operation could be laid bare by a logical mind. For every confusing effect this person could supply the logical cause. The reading public turned eagerly to Dr. Watson's accounts of the great detective's adventures.

The stories often opened in much the same way, and the introductions provide the first insight into the Victorianism manifested in the adventures. Holmes was usually in his sitting room waiting for business to come to him, the dream of the aggressive Victorian entrepreneur who had to seek out his customers and create his own business opportunities. Holmes was often performing chemical experiments, which was typical of the mechanistic Victorian approach to the riddle of the universe. There was a pull on the bell and the sound of someone mounting the seventeen steps of the stairs. The prospective client was shown in, often by the long-suffering but properly deferential housekeeper. Mrs. Hudson knew her place in society and did not presume to rise above it. Holmes thereupon proceeded to unsettle the client with what observation and deduction revealed about that client's background and profession. Then the client unburdened himself of his problem and Holmes set to work.

The great detective's Baker Street address provides another insight into the Victorianism depicted in the adventures. Baker Street was more *bon-ton* in the nineteenth century than it is today. It was on the outskirts of London proper, boasted a railway station leading to the suburbs, and was in close proximity to the London Zoo and to Madame Tussaud's Wax Museum. The famous 221B was also close enough to the theatrical and business centres of London and to the museums, universities, and hospitals to be quite convenient. Yet Baker Street was sufficiently far removed for an inhabitant, if he wished, to consider himself ''in'' London without being ''of'' London.

But Holmes's London never got mixed up with the real London. Victorians did not question society and averted their eyes from what they did not wish to see. In the great detective's day a third of the

> "Like many Victorians, Holmes accepted without question that he was extraordinary."

British people were housed in wretched slums, and were undernourished and underpaid. Very few of this third of the population figured in the stories. The humanitarian work of William Ewart Gladstone and the Earl of Shaftesbury document that there were large numbers of prostitutes in the nation's capital, but Holmes's female clients were respectable women—gainfully employed or dutifully married. Holmes and Watson were abroad on London's streets and alleys in all seasons and at all hours. Never once were they accosted by a woman of the night. . . .

Victorian society was male-dominated and -oriented and Holmes did not question this arrangement. Nearly all his cases centered upon a male figure. With rare exceptions, women were not credited with having been endowed with intuitive powers or possessing any shrewdness. Women needed to be protected. Holmes declared that if Violet Hunter were his sister, he would never have allowed her to take the position of governess at the Copper Beeches. The women in Holmes's cases were quite often shallow, dominated, retiring, and emotional. Victorian wives were expected to be subordinate, unassuming, uncomplaining, and useful. So much was this accepted behaviour that Holmes deduced from examining Henry Baker's hat (in ''Blue Carbuncle'') that Baker's wife no longer loved him: the hat had not been brushed for weeks. Holmes's advice to Watson on women in [''The Sign of Four''] reflected a generally held Victorian attitude. Said the misogynous Holmes, ''I would not tell them too much, women are never to be entirely trusted—not the best of them.''

An emphasis on science was another dominant characteristic of Victorian society and Holmes was a scientist, a scientist of crime. Like his colleagues in the laboratory, he was willing to risk his life in the service of his calling but he took no chances and was careful to an extreme. In ''A Case of Identity'' he scrutinised two typewritten notes with his ever-present glass and concluded from his comparison that they had been typed on the same machine and by the same person. He examined dust and minute soil particles found at the sites of crimes to establish the identity and home territory of criminals. Readers learned in "Boscombe Valley" that Holmes could identify 140 types of tobacco ash. Also like his fellow scientists, Holmes wrote papers summarizing his studies and experiments. He composed monographs on cyphers, on perfumes, and on the influence of a trade upon the form of the hand. He had two short monographs on what could be learned from the distinctive features of the human ear. . . .

Holding himself above the ordinary in typical Victorian fashion, Holmes often did not deign to discuss money matters, such as fees for his services. Even he on occasion showed his susceptibility, however. When what later proved to be a royal client drew up to the kerb at 221B in ["A Scandal in Bohemia"], Holmes (as he so often did) speculated on the visitor's profession and purpose while observing him from the window. After appraising the fine carriage and magnificent team of horses, he gave a whistle of amazement and to Watson exclaimed in what could only have been gleeful anticipation, "A nice little brougham and a pair of beauties. A hundred and fifty guineas apiece. There's money in this case, Watson, if there is nothing else." Nineteenth-century aesthetes may have believed in art for art's sake, but Holmes, like his fellow Victorians, preferred material rewards. They knew and respected the power of money.

For all their unseemly devotion to mammon, Victorians found room in their hearts for yet another object of worship. Many revered Queen Victoria, and Sherlock Holmes was among them. No matter how preoccupied he was with his chemical analyses or with his investigations, he left everything to serve the crown. "The Adventure of the Bruce-Partington Plans" drew him away from work on the polyphonic motets of Lassus. In this celebrated case Holmes performed a valuable service for his country by recovering plans for the highly secret Bruce-Partington submarine, an invention that would completely alter naval warfare. But Holmes brushed aside his brother Mycroft's suggestion that if he liked his name could be on the next Honours List. Holmes insisted that he played the game for the game's own sake. At the successful conclusion of the case, however, he spent a memorable day at Windsor and returned with a remarkably fine emerald tie pin. When asked by Watson whether he had purchased it, Holmes replied that it was a gift from a certain gracious lady in whose interests he had been able to carry out a small commission.

Holmes also shared the Victorians' views on law and lawbreakers. There was certainty here. Crime was crime and criminals were criminals. Victorians did not question society, nor did Holmes. He did not believe that environment, social conditions, or disadvantage motivated a person to commit crimes. Nor were crimes committed out of passion; the murder in "A Study in Scarlet" was one exception. Crimes were carefully planned by men with motives. Victorians held every man responsible for his actions, and Holmes was certain that a man became a criminal of his own volition. Charles Augustus Milverton the blackmailer and Professor Moriarty, the Napoleon of crime, were the best examples. Both men came from respectable backgrounds, both were afforded every opportunity and both possessed outstanding abilities. Yet both opted for a life of crime. . . .

Holmes had only one serious vice, but it was fittingly and excusably aristocratic. He was addicted at least for a time to cocaine—to the famous seven-per-cent solution. He was not addicted to the alcohol of the ordinary man nor to the opium of the decadent wastrel. Only cocaine would suffice to drive away the ordinariness of life and allow the free play of his great intelligence.

The usually impeccable Holmes committed at least one sin, an unpardonable breach of decency and good manners. Victorians often treated the love affairs of their domestic servants as something comic, as matters not to be taken seriously. And in "Charles Augustus Milverton" Holmes displayed an unattractive side of his Victorian character by trifling with the affections of Agatha, a maid in the blackmailer's household. Needing to secure information and to familiarise himself with the interior of the house, the great detective posed as a plumber, paid court to Agatha, and proposed marriage. . . .

Like many Victorians, Holmes accepted without question that he was extraordinary. His great mind, unexcelled abilities, and position as the world's greatest detective allowed him prerogatives denied to others, and placed him, when circumstances warranted, above the law. He burgled Charles Augustus Milverton's house and emptied the blackmailer's files of incriminating material, into the fire. Holmes told Watson that the action was morally justifiable because there were some crimes which the law could not deal with and which therefore allowed private revenge. In ["Five Orange Pips"] Holmes bluntly informed Watson that he would be his own police, and he often dispensed justice himself, unhindered by legal considerations. He allowed Ryder to go free in ["Blue Carbuncle"] and advised the king of Bohemia to steal, lie, and commit perjury in order to spare himself from being blackmailed. When Watson suggested obtaining a search warrant in ["The Adventure of the Bruce-Partington Plans"], the impatient Holmes insisted that one should not stick at trifles. "Think of Mycroft's note," he said, "of the Admiralty, the Cabinet, the exalted person who awaits the news." Thus convinced, Watson aided Holmes in rifling the house of Mr. Hugo Oberstein to find materials with which to incriminate him. Like the nation in which he lived, Holmes was responsible only to himself.

As vehicles to convey accurate historical information, Holmes's adventures as reported have some limitations, but they provide an insight into Victorianism. The insight is the more valuable because it is presented unpretentiously and unconsciously. Conan Doyle's observations on Victorian society were candid and unassuming. He presented underlying social assumptions, unexamined attitudes, and unguarded comments. In the great detective's cases, the Victorians can be observed without their being aware that they are being observed. They appear at their best and at their worst, naturally and unembarrassed. And the archetypical Victorian Sherlock Holmes wears his Victorianism as comfortably and as unaffectedly as he wears his familiar mouse-coloured dressing gown.

**Source:** Gordon L. Iseminger, "Sherlock Holmes: Victorian Archetype," in *The Baker Street Journal*, Vol. 29, No. 3, September, 1979, pp. 156–66.

## Sources

Eliot, T. S. "Books of the Quarter: *The Complete Sherlock Holmes Short Stories*," in *The Criterion*, Vol. 8, no. 32, April, 1929, pp. 553-56.

Goslin, Vernon, "The Extraordinary Story of the Red-Headed Copier," in *The Sherlock Holmes Journal*, Vol. 10, no. 3, Winter, 1971, pp. 77-78.

Jann, Rosemary. *The Adventures of Sherlock Holmes: Detecting Social Order*, Twayne Publishers, 1995.

Payne, William Morton. "Recent English and Canadian Fiction: *The Adventures of Sherlock Holmes*," in *The Dial*, Vol. 13, no. 154, November 16, 1892, p. 311.

Review of *The Adventures of Sherlock Holmes*, in *The Athenaeum*, November 5, 1892, p. 626.

## Further Reading

Barolsky, Paul. "The Case of the Domesticated Aesthete," in *Virginia Quarterly Review*, Vol. 60, no. 3, Summer, 1984, pp. 438-52.
   Gives examples from Doyle's stories to demonstrate Holmes's artistic interests.

Clausen, Christopher. "Sherlock Holmes, Order, and the Late-Victorian Mind," in *Georgia Review*, Vol. 38, no. 1, Spring, 1984, pp. 104-23.
   Early portions of this article discuss the relationship between Sherlock Holmes and nineteenth-century interests in science and rationality. Clausen argues that Doyle prizes social order above all other values and that his later stories are less interesting than the earlier ones.

Hoffman, Banesh, "Red Faces and 'The Red-Headed League," in *Beyond Baker Street*, edited by Michael Harrison, Bobbs-Merrill, 1976, pp. 175-85.
   This essay examines some deliberate lies told by Holmes while solving the mystery, reasons why Clay continues with his plot after being exposed to Holmes, and puts forth a mathematical solution to the issue of where the criminals put the dirt from the tunnel.

Moorman, Charles, "The Appeal of Sherlock Holmes," in *The Southern Quarterly*, Vol. 14, 1976, pp. 71-82.
   Through an examination of several different Holmes works, Moorman explicates the detective's wide appeal.

Orel, Harold, introduction to *Critical Essays on Sir Arthur Conan Doyle*, G. K. Hall, 1992, pp. 1-24.
   The introduction provides a broad overview to the work of Doyle and its reception by the reading public.

Ousby, Ian. *The Bloodhounds of Heaven: The Detective in English Fiction from Godwin to Doyle*, Harvard University Press, 1976.
   Ousby explores the social factors that influenced the development of the fictional detective, focusing especially on the growth of police forces and public attitudes toward them.

Scholefield, C. E., "Red-Headed Clients' Conundrums," in *Sherlock Holmes Journal*, Vol. 10, no. 3, Winter, 1971, pp. 74-76.
   Scholefield raises several of the seeming flaws of logic and unexplained details in "The Red-Headed League" and poses some answers.

Wertheim, Mary, "Sherlock Holmes: The Detective as Hero," in *Columbia Library Columns*, Vol. 35, no. 2, February, 1986, pp. 12-24.
   Wertheim discusses both Holmes and Watson in their roles as detectives and with regard to each other.

# The Rocking-Horse Winner

**D. H. Lawrence**

**1926**

D. H. Lawrence's "The Rocking-Horse Winner" was first published in 1926 in *Harper's Bazaar* magazine. It was published again that same year in a collection that was put together by Lady Cynthia Asquith, a friend of Lawrence's. Some critics have argued that the characters in the story are modeled after Asquith and her autistic son. Lawrence's works are known for their explorations of human nature through frank discussions of sex, psychology and religion. Lawrence's later short stories, such as "The Rocking-Horse Winner," display a movement toward fabulation and satire as opposed to his earlier short fiction, which reflected more the traditional nineteenth-century English short story—anecdotal, or tales of adventure. "The Rocking-Horse Winner" is a sardonic tale employing devices of the fairy tale and a mockingly detached tone to moralize on the value of love and the dangers of money. In "The Rocking-Horse Winner" and other later stories, Lawrence moved beyond the strictures of realism and encompassed a broader range of styles and subjects than in his earlier work. Critics view "The Rocking-Horse Winner" as an example of Lawrence's most accomplished writing. Lawrence is considered a modernist, a member of a literary school opposed to the literary conventions of nineteenth-century morality, taste, and tradition. Evident in "The Rocking-Horse Winner" is Lawrence's distain for conspicuous consumption, crass materialism, and an emotionally distant style of parenting popularly thought to exist in England during the late nineteenth and early twentieth centuries. Thus, the story is considered by many to be an example of modernist prose.

## Author Biography

David Herbert Lawrence was born September 11, 1885. His father was Arthur John Lawrence, an illiterate coal miner in the Nottinghamshire area of England; his mother was Lydia Beardsall Lawrence, a teacher. The fact that his mother had more education than his father caused friction in the Lawrence household. From boyhood, Lawrence was very close to his mother and, following his mother's encouragement, he studied at Nottingham University College, where he began writing short stories. In 1908, he moved to Croyden, just south of London, and began teaching. He never returned to his childhood home.

Lawrence began to publish poetry and, because he had developed tuberculosis, decided to quit teaching and write full time in 1911. That same year he published his first novel, *The White Peacock*, which was well received by critics. When he was twenty-seven years old, Lawrence eloped to Germany with Frieda von Richthofen Weekly, the wife of one of his college professors, and they were married in 1914. He and Frieda returned to England just before the beginning of World War I, but they endured continual harassment from the English government due to Lawrence's objections to the war and Frieda's German ancestry.

Lawrence's next novel, *The Rainbow*, was judged obscene and was banned in England; many of his subsequent works incited similar controversy. This experience left Lawrence bitter and more convinced than ever that the forces of modern civilization were oppressive and unhealthy. After the war, the Lawrences lived an itinerant life in Germany, Austria, Italy, Sicily, England, France, Australia, and Mexico, before finally settling in Taos, New Mexico. All this travelling provided the settings for many of the stories and novels that Lawrence wrote in the 1920s and also inspired four books of travel sketches. In 1930, Lawrence entered a hospital in France in an attempt to cure the tuberculosis that had plagued him most of his life, but he died that same year. Although he was originally buried in Vence, France, his remains were later moved to Taos, New Mexico, and buried at Kiowa Ranch.

Although Lawrence's most famous work is his novel *Lady Chatterley's Lover*, many critics agree that his short stories, including "The Rocking-Horse Winner" (1926) are better than his novels. His thematic focus on relationships between men and women, the destruction of relationships by the desire for wealth, and his explorations of psychological motivation in human behavior earned him an international reputation as an important twentieth-century author.

## Plot Summary

"The Rocking-Horse Winner" is the story of a boy's gift for picking the winners in horse races. An omniscient narrator relates the tale of a boy whose family is always short of money. His mother is incapable of showing love and is obsessed with the status that material wealth can provide. Her son is acutely aware of his mother's desire for money, and he is motivated to take action. He wants to help her, but he also wants to silence the voice that haunts him, the voice of the house itself whispering, "There must be more money! There must be more money!"

Paul questions his mother about the family's circumstances. When he asks her why they do not have a car and why they are the "poor members of the family," she responds "it's because your father has no luck." Dissatisfied with her answer, the boy presses her for an explanation of what makes one person lucky and another unlucky. Finally, he declares that he knows himself to be lucky because God told him so. With the help of Basset the gardener and his mother's brother Oscar, Paul sets out to prove his brazen assertion true by picking the winners in horse races. While riding on his rocking horse, Paul envisions the winners.

Paul proves to be unnaturally talented at divining the winners of the races, and before too long he has saved a considerable sum of money. When his uncle asks him what he plans to do with the money he reveals that he wants to give it to his mother. He hopes that his contribution will bring her luck and make the house stop whispering. Because Paul wants to keep his success at betting a secret, Paul arranges through his uncle to give his mother a anonymous gift of a thousand pounds each year for five years. His gift does not have the intended effect, however. Instead of being delighted when she opens the envelope on her birthday, Paul's mother is indifferent, "her voice cold and absent." Desperate

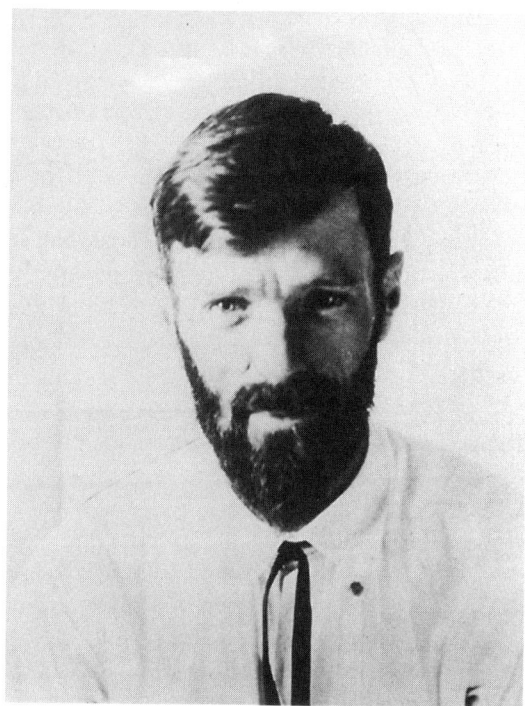

*D. H. Lawrence*

to please her, the boy agrees to let his mother have the whole five thousand at once.

Instead of quieting the voices in house, Paul's generous gift causes the voices to go "mad, like a chorus of frogs on a spring evening." Although his mother finally can afford some of the fine things she has been craving, like fresh flowers and private school for Paul, the voices just "trilled and screamed in a sort of ecstasy." The more Paul gives, the more his mother and the voices in the house demand. Though his uncle tries to calm him, Paul becomes obsessed with picking the winner of the upcoming Derby, "his blue eyes blazing with a sort of madness" as he rides his rocking horse. The mother feels uncharacteristically sympathetic toward her son and urges him to join the family at seaside, but Paul insists on staying until after the Derby.

The reason that Paul needs to stay in the house until the Derby is that his "secret of secrets" is his childhood rocking horse. The secret that he has never revealed to Basset or Uncle Oscar is that he is able to ride the rocking horse, which he has long since outgrown, until the wooden horse reveals to him the name of the winner in the next race. With so much riding on the Derby and the house whispering more insistently than ever, Paul knows he must be prepared for the ride of his young life. In fact, Paul is so anxious that even his mother feels the tension and suffers "sudden strange seizures of anxiety about him." Nevertheless, she decides to attend a big party two nights before the Derby, leaving Paul at home.

Throughout the evening the mother is distracted by worry about her son's well-being. When she and her husband come home around one o'clock, she rushes immediately to Paul's room. Standing outside his door, the mother is frozen in her tracks by a "strange, heavy, and yet not loud noise" coming from inside the room. When she finally gathers the courage to enter the room she sees her son "in his green pajamas, madly urging on the rocking-horse." She has arrived just in time to here him cry out "'It's Malabar!' ... in a powerful, strange voice." Then, "his eyes blazed at her for one strange and senseless second" and he crashes to the floor unconscious.

Neither the mother nor the father understand the significance of the word, but Uncle Oscar knows that it is one of the horses racing in the Derby. Oscar, "in spite of himself," places a bet on Malabar and passes on the tip to Basset. By the third day, the day of the Derby, the boy has still not regained consciousness and his condition appears to be worsening. Desperate for anything that might help her son, the mother allows Basset a short visit with Paul. Paul does regain consciousness, but just long enough to learn that Malabar had been the winner and that he has made over eighty thousand pounds for his mother. His mother still does not acknowledge that her son had been lucky or that she truly loves him. At the moment of Paul's death, Oscar chides his sister: "My God, Hester, you're eighty-odd thousand pounds the to good, and a poor devil of a son to the bad."

## Characters

### *Bassett*

Bassett is the family gardener who helps Paul place bets on horses. He used to work around horses and racing and he talks about racing all the time, so it seems reasonable that Paul would seek his advice. He takes the boy seriously and follows all the boy's instructions in placing the bets. He also keeps Paul's money safely hidden away, at least until Uncle Oscar gets involved. He is the only adult who treats Paul with a serious respect. It is Bassett's seriousness that convinces Uncle Oscar that Paul's gift for picking winners is real. He is trustworthy and kind, but he is also a servant, so once Uncle Oscar takes over, he respectfully withdraws from the action.

### *Oscar Cresswell*

Oscar Cresswell is Paul's uncle and Hester's brother. He is in a better financial position than Hester, since he owns his own car and a place in Hampshire. This is because he inherited the entire family fortune, leaving Hester to depend on her husband for support. It is Uncle Oscar who stumbles upon Paul's secret of earning money through gambling, but he does not at first believe in Paul's gift. He thinks that Paul is not serious and treats the boy as if he were merely playing a game. After Oscar realizes that Paul's tips are dependable, he encourages the gambling. Oscar arranges for a lawyer to funnel money to Hester. He also bets his own money, using Paul's tips for his own profit.

Although Uncle Oscar seems harmless at first, the reader becomes aware that he is using Paul for his own benefit. He makes no effort to teach Paul about being careful with money or the dangers of gambling. Oscar does nothing to help Hester and her family, neither by giving money nor by helping Hester budget what money she does have. Because Oscar only uses Paul for his own financial gain, he is revealed to be shallow and selfish.

### *Hester*

Hester is Paul's mother, who is incapable of loving others. She is not only obsessed with money, but she is also irresponsible with the money she does get. When Paul arranges through his attorney to give her a thousand pounds a month from his winnings, she immediately begs the attorney for the entire amount. However, instead of paying her debts, she spends the money on new things for the house. This results in an even greater need for more money. She also does not express any thanks for this sudden windfall, depriving Paul of the joy of providing the much-needed income for his family.

Although at the end of the story Hester becomes increasingly concerned about Paul's deteriorating health, she still does not love him, even when he dies. At the beginning of the story, it is stated that "at the center of her heart was a hard little place that could not feel love, no, not for anybody." This image is repeated at the end of the story, when Hester sits by her son's bedside "feeling her heart had gone, turned actually into a stone." Before he

# Media Adaptations

- *The Rocking-Horse Winner* was filmed in 1950 by Two Cities Films and stars John Mills and Valerie Hobson. The adaptation was written and directed by Anthony Pelessier.
- *The Rocking-Horse Winner* was filmed in 1977 starring Kenneth More, directed by Peter Medak, adapted by Julian Bond, distributed by Learning Corp.

dies Paul asks "Mother, did I ever tell you? I'm lucky," she responds, "No, you never did." However, the reader remembers that Paul did, indeed, tell her that he was lucky earlier in the story. Since she pays little attention to him, she does not remember this.

When Hester finally receives the financial fortune she has always wanted but loses her son in the process, the reader realizes that Hester will probably not feel the loss of her son and will probably waste all that money in record time. All of these details show Hester to be cold, unfeeling, wasteful, and shallow.

### *Uncle Oscar*

*See* Oscar Cresswell

### *Paul*

Paul is the young boy in the story who tries desperately to find a way to have "luck," meaning money, for his mother. He begins to ride his rocking horse furiously, even though he has outgrown it, because when he does so, he somehow is given the name of the horse that will win the next race. He makes an astounding amount of money this way with the help of the gardener Bassett (who places his bets for him), and later with the help also of his Uncle Oscar. For the final big race, the Derby, he rides himself into a feverish delirium, but he is sure of the winner. His uncle places a large bet for him.

Just as his uncle arrives to tell him of the fortune he has made, he dies from the fever. Paul dies for the sake of making money for the family, particularly his mother, even though her "heart was a stone."

Paul seems completely unaware that he has overtaken responsibilities that are rightly his parents'. He seems only concerned with relieving the anxiety he perceives in the house caused by a lack of money. He tries to understand why there is not enough money by asking his mother, but she only says that his father "has no luck." He directly associates luck with money, so the gambling seems like a natural solution to the problem. He is so innocent in his enthusiasm for the game he begins playing with Bassett that even when his uncle discovers that he has been gambling, he does not stop Paul from gambling further. Even though Paul is still a child, all of the adults, Bassett, Uncle Oscar, and Paul's mother, seem to treat him like an adult. No one anticipates that Paul will pay a huge price for playing this game. No one even questions Paul's ability to pick the winners of the horse races, or wonders how in the world Paul is able to pick winners so accurately.

Throughout the story Paul remains innocent, as well as desperate, to help his mother, who seems oblivious to Paul's concerns. Although it is clear to the reader that Paul is very intelligent and sensitive, no one in the story seems to notice or appreciate Paul's gifts until it is too late.

## Themes

In "The Rocking-Horse Winner," a young boy, Paul, perceives that there is never enough money in his family, he sets out to find a way to get money through luck. He discovers that if he rides his rocking-horse fast enough, he will somehow "know" the name of the winning horse in the next race. He begins to make money and secretly funnel this money to his mother, but the desire for more money only grows more intense instead of going away. He finally rides his rocking-horse so furiously in order to discover the winner of the Derby that he falls into illness and dies, just as the winning horse earns his family an enormous fortune.

### Responsibility

The obsession with wealth and material items is pitted against the responsibilities of parenting in "The Rocking-Horse Winner." It is the responsibility of the parents to provide for the children in a family. It is also the responsibility of the parents to spend money wisely and budget carefully, so that the bills are paid and no one goes without food, clothing, or shelter. However, in this story, Lawrence turns this on its ear, making the parents complete failures at financial dealings and their son Paul incredibly gifted at making money, albeit by gambling.

The parents in the story drift from one thing to another, never really finding anything they can do to provide for the family. The mother "tried this thing and the other, but could not find anything successful." The father, whose main talents are having expensive tastes and being handsome, "seemed as if he would never be able to do anything worth doing." When Paul gives his mother 5,000 pounds from his winnings, rather than paying off debts and saving for the future, she spends all of it on material things, causing an even more urgent need for more money.

### Generosity and Greed

The disparity between Paul's generosity and his mother's greed is another theme of "The Rocking-Horse Winner." Paul generously offers all his winnings to the family, in order to relieve the family's dire need for money. He seems to have no needs of his own and is motivated solely by the desire to help his mother. Paul's unselfish generosity is contrasted starkly with the mother's greed and selfishness. When the mother first receives the news from the lawyer that she has "inherited" 5,000 pounds from a long-lost relative which will be paid out to her in yearly increments of 1,000 pounds (a scheme dreamed up by Paul), she does not inform the family of their good fortune. Instead, she goes immediately to the lawyer and asks to receive the entire amount right away. Paul agrees, and the money is spent foolishly on more material things for the house. Instead of relieving the family's need for money, Paul's plan backfires and thus there is a need for even more money.

Paul and his mother are complete opposites. Paul, in his childish innocence, gives and gives to the family, without any desire for thanks and without any desire to keep any of the money for himself. He ultimately gives the most precious gift of all: his life. Hester, Paul's mother, has no idea where all this money is coming from and does not seem to care. Hester has become so obsessed with wealth that her heart turns completely to stone; she cannot even feel sad when her son dies.

### *Oedipus Complex*

Paul's desire to earn money for the family can be said to be an unconscious desire to take his father's place, a concept that psychoanalyst Sigmund Freud termed the "Oedipus complex." This is a reference to the story from ancient Greece in which Oedipus, who was raised away from his parents, accidently kills his father and marries his mother. Freud suggested that all boys go through a stage where they want to take their father's place. Paul's desire to take care of the family's needs is Oedipal. Since the main way of earning this money—the rocking horse—is also bound up in sexual imagery, it seems clear that Lawrence intentionally characterizes Paul this way.

## Style

### *Style*

The opening paragraphs of "The Rocking-Horse Winner" are written in a style similar to that of a fairy tale. Instead of "once upon a time," though, Lawrence begins with "There was a woman who was beautiful, who started with all the advantages, yet she had no luck." This is a conscious attempt on the part of the author to use the traditional oral storytelling technique. This story also combines the supernatural elements of a fable, mainly Paul's ability to "know" the winners just by riding his rocking horse, with the serious themes of an unhappy marriage and an unhealthy desire for wealth at all costs. The story begins with fable-like simplicity but ends with a serious message about wasted lives.

### *Symbolism*

The symbolism in this story is very sexually oriented. The rocking horse represents both Paul's desire to make money for his mother and his own sexuality. The rocking horse is his "mount" which is "forced" onwards in a "furious ride" towards "frenzy." These descriptions are very suggestive of sexual activity. However, this is disturbing because Paul is very young and he is participating in

## Topics for Further Study

- Although the children's father is mentioned in "The Rocking-Horse Winner," he never actually appears. Why do you think the mother's brother, Uncle Oscar, has a larger role to play in this story? What do you think Lawrence was trying to say about the role of men in the raising of their sons?

- How does "The Rocking-Horse Winner" portray the desire for material wealth?

- What were women's career options during the 1920s? How might this reality figure into the mother's lack of love for children? Explain your answer.

this act for the sake of his mother. The rocking horse can also represent the fact that the overwhelming desire for money is a road that leads to nowhere, since this is a rocking horse that does not actually travel anywhere. Also, the desire for wealth can be said to be extremely unhealthy as well, since it results in Hester's unhappiness and Paul's death.

## Historical Context

### *The Modern Era*

Lawrence was writing during the early part of the twentieth century, and he, like most writers of the day, was significantly influenced by World War I. He had read and loved the novels of nineteenth-century writers George Eliot, author of *Silas Marner,* and Thomas Hardy, author of *Tess of the D'Urbervilles,* but grew dissatisfied with the predictability of such characters. After the war, many people began to question the old ways of looking at the world. Lawrence joined in the questioning by making his characters less sure of themselves, less bound by the rules of polite society that dominated nineteeth-century fiction.

# Compare & Contrast

- **Then:** The financial circumstances experienced by the family in "The Rocking-Horse Winner" are shared by many upper-class people in the years surrounding World War I. Great emphasis is placed on possessions and the appearance of wealth among the privileged, particularly in London.

  **Now:** In 1996, Princess Diana officially divorces Prince Charles, receiving an estimated $26 million dollars to insure that her lifestyle remains secure.

- **Then:** The English family undergoes a transformation with married couples having fewer children than previous generations. Of couples married in 1925, 16 percent have no children, 25 percent have one child, 25 percent have two, and only 14 percent have three or more children.

  **Now:** From 1970–1995, the average number of children per family worldwide falls from six to three. The average size of a family in a developing country is 3.9.

- **Then:** By 1928 in England, all women eighteen years or older can vote. Increasing numbers of women begin to seek out intellectual and economic opportunities for themselves.

  **Now:** Opportunities for women are largely equal to those for men. In 1990, Margaret Thatcher steps down after 11 years as Great Britain's prime minister.

---

Lawrence became interested in the psychological motivations for why people do the things they do. Psychology as a science was in its infancy at this time. Sigmund Freud, the "father" of modern psychology, was formulating his theories regarding the unconscious through observing his patients at his practice in Vienna. Lawrence was also convinced that the modern way of life, long hours at cruel jobs for little pay, was dehumanizing. His characters were often failures in relationships who felt aliented in their misery. Furthermore, his writing was frequently embellished with themes about greed, materialism, and degrading work, which were issues of increasing concern to people at the time.

## Critical Overview

Many critics consider Lawrence's short stories his most artistically accomplished writing and have attributed much of their success to the constraints of the form, which forced Lawrence to deny himself the elaborations, diversions, and repetitions that are integral aspects of his longer works. Critics view "The Rocking-Horse Winner" in this light, as an example of economical style and structure in Lawrence's short fiction. Lawrence's early short stories were written in a manner similar to that of Robert Louis Stevenson or Rudyard Kipling, whose anecdotes and tales of adventure epitomized the traditional nineteenth-century English short story. His later short stories, such as "The Rocking-Horse Winner," emphasize abstraction and argument. Critics argue that this story is an example of Lawrence moving away from realism and encompassing a broader range of styles and subjects. They view "The Rocking-Horse Winner" as an example of Lawrence's later period, in which his keen insight and sturdy craft are the result of many years of experience.

Many of Lawrence's works were considered controversial, and "The Rocking-Horse Winner" is no exception. The story has generated a large amount of scholarly debate and has been compared to a wide variety of other works, including classic myths, parables, and the writings of Charles Dickens, among others. Some critics focus on the socio-economic, religious, and sexual aspects of the story.

Other critics have highlighted the Freudian aspects of the work or have interpreted it in terms of economic theories and spiritual allusions. "The Rocking-Horse Winner" has been criticized for its didactic qualities; that is, some critics feel the story is too focused on teaching a lesson. Though the story continues to stimulate debate, most critics agree that the plot, description, dialogue, and symbolism of the story are presented with great skill.

# Criticism

## Elisabeth Piedmont-Marton

*Piedmont-Marton is the coordinator of the Undergraduate Writing Center at the University of Texas at Austin. In the following essay, she discusses various aspects of "The Rocking-Horse Winner."*

"The Rocking-Horse Winner" belongs to the group of stories D. H. Lawrence wrote in the last years of his life. During this period, critics have noted, he abandoned the realism that characterizes his mid-career work, and turned toward a style of short story that more closely resembles the fable or folktale. In the words of Janice Hubbard Harris, in *The Short Fiction of D. H. Lawrence*, "The Rocking-Horse Winner" and other stories of the period, represent the "desire of a fierce and dying man to prophesy, sum up, *assess* the world he is leaving rather than *present* or imitate it." The story also presents several themes that held Lawrence's attention throughout his career.

The style and tone of "The Rocking-Horse Winner" reveal immediately that this story comes from the world of fable and legend. The distant, solemn tone of the narrator: "There was a woman who was beautiful," signals us that this is an old story. Quickly it becomes apparent that this is a quest narrative of some sort. The boy hero will try to win the love of the distant queen/mother. The object of the quest is to gain access to "the centre of her heart [that] was a hard place that could not feel love, no, not for anybody." The hero rides off, captures the treasure, and returns home to present the riches to his love. But the opening of the story is also foreboding, because "undercutting this fairy tale, however, is another, which forms a grotesque shadow, a nightmare counter to the wish-fulfillment narrative," in Harris's words. The quest is hopeless, Harris points out, because the mother can never be satisfied and "every success brings a new and greater trial."

Given the stylized characterization and the symbolic landscape that Lawrence creates in "The Rocking-Horse Winner," we can read the meaning of the story on several levels. In the first place, Lawrence seems to be offering a broad satire on rising consumerism in English culture. In particular, this story criticizes those who equate love with money, luck with happiness. The mother with her insatiable desire for material possessions believes that money will make her happy despite the obvious fact that so far it has not. For Lawrence she represents the futility of the new consumer culture in which *luck* and *lucre* mean the same thing. Paul, who learns from his mother to associate love with money, represents the desperate search for values in a cash culture. The force of Lawrence's satire is directed at a society that is dominated by a quest for cash, and at those who buy into the deadly equation of love equals money.

This fable about a boy's doomed attempts to satisfy his mother's desires and win her love also provides Lawrence the opportunity to work out one of the themes that dominate his entire body of work, the relationship between mothers and sons. Lawrence's theory, which is the central concern of one of his most famous novels, *Sons and Lovers*, is that mothers mold their sons into men who are the opposites of their undesirable husbands. Since mothers know that they cannot change their husbands, they throw all their passion into creating desirable sons, whom, of course, they cannot possess. In "The Rocking-Horse Winner," the husband's inadequacy is explicit. The narrator describes him as "one who was always very handsome and expensive in his tastes, [and] seemed as if he never *would* be able to do anything worth doing." Making her feelings very clear to her young son, the mother "bitterly" characterizes her husband as "very unlucky." When she confides in her son that she is dissatisfied with her husband, the mother sets in motion the boys futile quest to please her, to be the man she wants him/her husband to be. After this, the father is hardly mentioned in the story, let alone seen. The mother's desire to make and possess her son constitutes another dark counter-narrative to the story's wish-fulfillment theme.

Both Paul's desire to win his mother's love as well as her desire to make him into the image of an

## What Do I Read Next?

- *The Collected Short Stories of D. H. Lawrence* (1974) is the complete collection of Lawrence's short stories.
- *Lorenzo in Taos* (1932) by Mabel Dodge Luhan, describes the time that Lawrence spent in Taos, New Mexico.
- "King of the Bingo Game" by Ralph Ellison is a story that explores the role of fate in a black man's life at a moment he is in particular need of money to save his dying wife.
- "Araby" by James Joyce, a contemporary of Lawrence, is a story about a boy's epiphany regarding his schoolboy crush on a playmate's sister.

---

ideal husband are doomed to futility. This kind of misdirected and frustrated sexuality is a persistent theme in Lawrence's fiction and nonfiction writing, and the fable-like quality of "The Rocking-Horse Winner" gives Lawrence an opportunity to dramatize some of theories about sexuality on a symbolic level. The course of Lawrence's career demonstrates the evolution of his theories on sexuality and gender. By the end of his life, when "The Rocking-Horse Winner" was written, Lawrence's ideas had evolved into his theory of polarity, which is based on the premise that maleness and femaleness are absolute opposites and that men and women cannot have any attributes of the opposite sex. The theory of polarity, which is derived in part from Lawrence's acquaintance with Freudian psychology, asserts that an individual achieves wholeness by balancing his or her energy against another individual's. For Lawrence, this balance is achieved by a flow of energy, like an electric current, which is usually rendered as sexual desire in his fiction.

Critics have noted the connections between Lawrence's published ideas about sexuality, particularly in the essay "Pornography and Obscenity," and in "The Rocking-Horse Winner." In "A Rocking-Horse: The Symbol, the Pattern, the Way to Live," an influential article written in 1958, W. D. Snodgrass analyzed the psychosexual dimensions of the story through the lens of Lawrence's published writings. Snodgrass summarizes Lawrence's thesis as the argument that pornography is "art which contrives to make sex ugly . . . and so leads the observer away from sexual intercourse and toward masturbation." Paul's rocking horse riding, then, represents masturbation, "the child's imitation of the sex act, for the riding which goes nowhere." Lawrence's point, however, is not that Paul's "secret of secrets" kills him. What is unnatural from Lawrence's point of view is that Paul and his mother are locked into a pattern of mutually frustrated desire. Neither one of them is directing their energy at an appropriate "polarity." Significantly, however, they do not share equal responsibility for their situation. Lawrence, through his narrator, places all the blame on the mother and martyrs the boy in one final self-sacrificing ride.

**Source:** Elisabeth Piedmont-Marton, for *Short Stories for Students,* Gale Research, 1997.

### Rosemary Reeves Davies

*In the following essay, Davies presents information about some of the possible real-life subjects for Lawrence's story "The Rocking-Horse Winner," particularly Paul and his mother, who were patterned after friends of Lawrence's.*

D. H. Lawrence's habit of making identifiable use of his friends and acquaintances in his novels and short stories has been well documented, as has his lack of concern for the possible distress such portraits might cause. Lady Ottoline Morrell and Philip Heseltine were outraged by their appearance in *Women in Love* as Hermione and Halliday, and although Lawrence tried to assure his friend Mark

Gertler that he was not the model for the rat-like Loerke in the same novel, it is generally agreed that he was. John Middleton Murry, despite his admiration for Lawrence, was never able to forgive him for the group of short stories in which Murry is made to look ridiculous, and Compton Mackenzie was annoyed at finding himself the protagonist in "The Man Who Loved Islands." "England, My England," with its satiric portraits of Percy Lucas and the Meynell family, was published shortly before Lucas' death in France, and has been called Lawrence's "cruelest story à clef." To these and other stories can be added another based upon a real-life situation, "The Rocking-Horse Winner."

This story was first published in the fall of 1926 in a collection called *The Ghost Book* assembled by Lawrence's longtime friend, Lady Cynthia Asquith. As I hope to show, the story was probably suggested by the tragic illness of Lady Cynthia's oldest son John and by the Asquith marriage itself. Although it is unlikely that Lady Cynthia recognized herself in the character Hester, or connected her son's tragedy—at its height almost ten years before the story was written—with Paul, biographical materials demonstrate that Lawrence found in the Asquith household the ingredients for his story on destructive materialism.

That Lawrence used these materials as he did is surprising because it is generally agreed that Lady Cynthia occupied a rather special place in his life. His biographer, Harry T. Moore, remarks that "Lawrence felt a respectful affection, if not love for her," and her *Diaries* show that she held the novelist in considerable esteem. In her memoir, written many years after Lawrence's death, she speaks very warmly of him, stressing his electric aliveness and gentleness. In other stories in which she is the model for the heroine, she is treated with tact and affection. An early sketch, "The Thimble," was intended as a "word-picture" of her, and was sent to her for her criticism. She was uneasy about its probable contents; having read *The Rainbow* in manuscript, she feared a "minute 'belly' analysis" of herself. But she was pleased by the story and found it "extremely well-written .... I think some of his character hints are damnably good." Two later stories, *The Ladybird* and "Glad Ghosts," are also considered to contain heroines modeled on Lady Cynthia, both attractive figures.

Not only is Lady Cynthia pleasantly presented, but most stories in which she was the model for the

> "The force of Lawrence's satire is directed at a society that is dominated by a quest for cash, and at those who buy into the deadly equation of love equals money."

heroine do not end unhappily. In "The Thimble" the couple is re-born, and becomes capable of growing into full maturity and love as a result. In *The Ladybird*, Lady Daphne, unfulfilled by her adoring husband, reaches unity of being through her love affair with Count Dionys. In "Glad Ghosts" Carlotta's husband, stimulated by the advice of a Lawrence-like house guest, suddenly gains insight into the importance of the body. His marriage is revitalized, his bad luck overcome, and Carlotta gives birth to a charming blond boy "like a little crocus" nine months later. (Lawrence had nicknamed Lady Cynthia's son "Jonquil.") Rather ambiguously, the guest is visited at night by a feminine ghost, and he is uncertain in the morning whether it was a ghost or a living woman. It has been suggested that Lawrence decided against sending this story to Lady Cynthia because of the implications of its conclusion, and after considering it, submitted "The Rocking-Horse Winner" instead.

Biographical materials will show the striking similarities between the Asquith family and the family in the story. Lady Cynthia, like Carlotta and Hester, was visited by very bad luck indeed in her firstborn son. In his infancy he seemed normal, and his charm and sweet temper delighted everyone. Lawrence in letters written in 1913 inquired about "the fat and smiling John," and asked, "How is the jonquil with the golden smile." But by the time the boy was four years old, it had become obvious that something was seriously wrong with him. The editor of the *Diaries* labels his condition autism, a disorder still not well understood. And the Lawrences' close association with the Asquiths began just as the mother's fears were beginning to crystalize.

The Lawrences visited Lady Cynthia in Brighton in May 1915, and John had tea with them. She reports in her diary that "the Lawrences were

> "'The Rocking-Horse Winner' was probably suggested by the tragic illness of Lady Cynthia's oldest son John and by the Asquith marriage itself."

riveted by the freakishness of John, about whom they showed extraordinary interest and sympathy ... he was in a wild, monkey mood—very challenging, just doing things for the sake of being told not to—impishly defiant and still his peculiar, indescribable detachment.'' The next day Lawrence and Lady Cynthia strolled to the cliffs overlooking Brighton and discussed John's condition for several hours. The mother, who elsewhere expresses her admiration for Lawrence's deep insight into character, received a long and depressing analysis. She was upset to learn that her friend believed she was responsible for her son's condition, that the boy was reacting to her scepticism and cynicism, to her lack of positive belief that made her appear, on the surface, charmingly tolerant and kind. Later he told her that her spirit was ''hard and stoical,'' a judgment which she rejected, but which is parallel to Hester who ''knew that at the center of her heart was a hard little place that could not feel love. . . .''

A few days later Lawrence wrote a long letter about John in which he argued that she and her husband lacked a living belief in anything, that the world in which she lived had stunted her soul, and she had not resisted. ''Your own soul knew ... that it was itself bound in like a tree that grows under a low roof and can never break through, and which must be deformed, unfulfilled. Herbert Asquith must have known the same thing, in his soul.'' John had been born from the womb and loins of unbelief, distorted from his conception: ''. . . the soul of John acts from your soul, even from the start: because he knows that you are Unbelief, and he reacts from your affirmation of belief always with hostility.'' He cautions her against trying to force her son's love: ''That you fight is only a sign that you are wanting in yourself. The child knows that. Your own soul is deficient, so it fights for the love of the child.''

A recent article on ''The Rocking-Horse Winner'' reaches conclusions on the story itself that are very similar to Lawrence's analysis. Commenting on the wildness of Paul's obsession, Charles Koban says,''It is as if an alien spirit inhabited and drove him ... and the spirit is of course the spirit of the mother, the spirit of greed.'' It is Paul's ''mystical openness to her that leaves him vulnerable to the terrible forces she unleashes in her own household.'' It must be made clear that there is little to suggest that Lady Cynthia or her husband were as obsessed with money and material things as the couple in the story. But from Lawrence's perspective, the Asquiths could not avoid obsessive concern for possessions, given their chosen style of life. Lady Cynthia describes Lawrence strolling about their living room after tea, and suddenly noticing a small Louis XV table. After he stared at it for a moment, '''Come away!' he shrilled out, looking at me as if I stood in immediate deadly peril. 'Come away. Free yourself at once, or before you know where you are, your furniture will be on top instead of under you.' This admonition gave me a nightmare in which I was trampled to death by the legs of my own tables and chairs.'' A harmless antique table became an instant symbol of the money-lie. Despite Lawrence's fondness for this couple, the link between possessions and the failure of human relationships seems clearly established.

Another letter concerned with Herbert Asquith also prefigures the story, as Lawrence tries to persuade Lady Cynthia not to push her husband into the money-making trap. The Asquiths were not rich, and lack of money was a constant concern. That Lawrence was well aware of this is shown in ''The Thimble'' where the heroine, left alone when her husband goes to war, cannot maintain the family town house, and takes a small flat which she furnishes with second-hand furniture bought from friends. Lady Cynthia herself spent the war years ''cuckooing,'' that is, living with friends and family to avoid the expense of her own establishment. She worked for some years as a secretary for Sir James Barrie, wrote and published books, and like Hester, once received a summons for debt, a ''wretched fourteen-shillings bill.'' Like the couple in the story, the Asquiths were poor relations compared to the social set to which they belonged by birth. Lawrence, who was tortured by the money-hunger he saw everywhere, urged his friend to realize the connection between money-lust and war:

> It doesn't matter whether you *need* money or not. You *do* need it. But the fact that you would ask him to

*John Howard Davies as Paul in Universal International's production of "The Rocking-Horse Winner."*

work, put his soul into getting it, makes him love better war and pure destruction. The thing is painfully irrational. How can a man be so developed to be able to devote himself to making money, and at the same time keep himself in utter antagonism to the whole system of money....

The defeated, inarticulate husband in "The Rocking-Horse Winner," who goes "into town to some office," is foreshadowed here and in other letters. In one written in 1915, when the Lawrences were planning to leave England, he urged Lady Cynthia to consider leaving also. It was her duty, he felt, to remove her children from "this slow flux of destruction," and to seek a truer existence: "Your husband should have left this decomposing life. There was nowhere to go. Perhaps now he is beaten. Perhaps now the true living is defeated in him. But it is not defeated in you.... So don't give John to this decline and fall. Give him to the *future*...."

The Lawrences did not leave England, however, until 1919, and during these years Lady Cynthia records her growing distress at her son's condition. She speaks of his "eerie Puck faces," of his sitting "silent and absorbed in his own thoughts" at a lively family tea party, and of the "strange completeness about him as he is. . . .'' After a dedicated governess managed to teach him to read and write, the mother comments sadly that his performance "gives you the impression of a *tour de force* like a performing animal." Her growing inability to believe that the boy would ever be normal was becoming strong just as the Lawrences again entered her orbit. In April 1917 Lawrence visited her, and again insisted that the boy's condition was spiritual, not psychological. His mother had submitted to an unreal existence, "the result being that John is quite off the plane I have violated myself in order to remain on." Almost a year later, Lawrence again discussed John, still certain that he could be helped by "proper psychic influence," and offered to take him for a time to see if association with him and Frieda would help.

And finally Lady Cynthia lost her capacity to love her son, although she struggled not to do so. In a diary entry two days after the Lawrences had come to tea, she speaks of "the John tragedy," which blackened her life for her. It was a nightmare for her to be in the same room with him, and she was violently reproached by his governess for her apparent callousness. Her growing horror of the boy increased, no doubt because his affliction grew steadily more disturbing as he grew older, and in her diary she speaks of a visit to him as "an ordeal behind me." Since the Lawrences were seeing Lady Cynthia during this time period, it is quite likely that he at least was aware of the mother who could not love her son, and of the strong guilt feelings she experienced in consequence.

It is to be regretted that the editor of the *Diaries* felt it necessary to remove much of the material concerning John, since some of the omitted passages might have provided additional links with the story. But the descriptions of him that remain suggest Paul's behavior in the story: his wildness, his self-absorption, his uncanny faces, his non-human quality, and the sense of his isolation from other members of the household. And it is a matter of common knowledge that a behavior trait among children afflicted with autism is a forward-backward rocking motion of their bodies. It is likely that John would have had a rocking horse, and that he would have used it long after he outgrew it, given his condition. But about these possible, even probable, clues we can only speculate.

A small but significant hint in the story itself suggests that Lawrence had the Asquiths in mind, particularly since the phrasing seems to be a minor slip of the pen. Hester "was at a big party in town, when one of her rushes of anxiety about her boy, her first-born, gripped her heart until she could hardly speak." Not only does the sudden rush of concern describe what Lady Cynthia unquestionably must have experienced on many occasions, but the stipulation "first-born" is interesting. Earlier in the story we are told that Paul has an *elder* sister. Lawrence seems to have deliberately rearranged the ages and sexes of the children—Lady Cynthia had in fact three children, all boys—but unconsciously returned, as he wrote of the mother's anguish, to the original model for his character.

It would seem that in the Asquiths and in their eldest son Lawrence found ample background material for his story. Lady Cynthia was personally a charming and lovable woman, quite unlike the cold and selfish Hester. And yet Lawrence believed that basic deficiencies in her character had worked against her son's health and happiness. Her marriage had begun as a love match, opposed by her father because neither family could provide an adequate income for the couple. But Lawrence implied his belief that her relationship with her husband could not be satisfactory both in his direct comments in his letters and in the fact that he arranges a better marital relationship, a rebirth, for the heroines in three of his Asquith-inspired stories. The Asquiths' social position, well-connected but comparatively poor, parallels the one described in "The Rocking-Horse Winner." And concerning what was apparently his last visit to her in October 1925, a visit during which she probably asked him to write something for her anthology, he reported laconically to a friend, "Went to Cynthia Asquith's—more sense of failure." It was this sense of failure in her life, as well as in the lives of other friends and acquaintances whom Lawrence visited during his brief stay in England, that produced the bitterness and discouragement of "The Rocking-Horse Winner."

**Source:** Rosemary Reeves Davies, "Lawrence, Lady Cynthia Asquith, and 'The Rocking-Horse Winner,'" in *Studies in Short Fiction,* Vol. 20, No. 2–3, Spring-Summer, 1983, pp. 121–6.

## Donald Junkins

*Junkins is an American poet, educator, and critic. In the following short essay, Junkins theorizes that "The Rocking-Horse Winner" exhibits many attributes of a myth through its style and symbolism.*

A recent critical exchange has re-focused attention on the controversial "Rocking-Horse Winner" by D. H. Lawrence. Except for that of W. R. Martin, the general critical evaluation of the story has been unfavorable, and for the specific reason that critics have failed to perceive the story's essentially mythical quality. The story does precisely what Burroughs and other Lawrence critics (Leavis, Hough, Gordon, and Tate) feel that it fails to do: it presents life. Because of its mythical nature, Burroughs' criticism that the story "is limited by application of Lawrence's hackneyed didacticism to a pathetic plot of fantasy" is not relevant. It is a story of meaning, not morality, and the meaning depends precisely upon the organic relationship between the fantastic and the real.

"The Rocking-Horse Winner" dramatizes modern man's unsuccessful attempt to act out and emerge from his oedipal conflict with the woman-mother. Lawrence states here the same theme as that of the earlier *Sons and Lovers*. Here the boy Paul, whose name is also the same as that of the central character in *Sons and Lovers*, takes upon himself the intolerable burden of attempting to solve the mother's "problem," which is demonstrated in the unspoken overtones of the lack of money in the household. The mother attributes this to her lack of "luck"; therefore Paul summons all his energies in order to obtain this luck for his mother. His private incantations assume the form of frenzied riding of his hobbyhorse, which, as Paul points out to his Uncle Oscar, has no name. The fact that when the boy successfully divines in advance the winners of real horse races, and by doing so wins a great deal of "lucky" money which fails to make his mother happy, demonstrates that money is not the mother's central need. The money does not bring her "luck." The growing anguish and tormented frustration that Paul experiences come to a climax at the end of the story with his death as a result of riding his hobbyhorse too long and too hard in the dark of his room at night. He literally sacrifices himself, and the agent of his death is his hobbyhorse. Death is his only way out of his dilemma; Uncle Oscar says at the end of the story, "My God, Hester, you're eighty-odd thousand to the good and a poor devil of a son to the bad. But, poor, devil, poor devil, he's best gone out of a life where he rides his rocking-horse to find a winner."

The story is couched in the symbols of the ancient myths. The mother is the poor, unsatisfied fairy princess who yearns for happiness; Paul is the gallant knight on horseback who rides to her rescue. But Paul's stallion, the traditional symbol of the self, or potency or masculinity, is only a wooden rocking horse. As such it denotes Paul's impotency, his pre-pubertal innocence, his unrealized manhood. He consequently has no self—the horse is both wooden and anonymous—because he has not emerged as a man. What prevents him from this emergence before death is the insatiable needs of the unsatisfied woman-mother. Although Hester, the mother, disguises her feminine needs of self-realization and fulfillment (in the largest sense of the meaning of sexuality), and although Paul responds directly to the disguise, he is indirectly and unconsciously responding to her indirect and unconscious needs. For him as a self-less and unrealized man-boy, the task he sets for himself is impossible. He dies as a result of his quest; it is the relentlessly unsatisfied woman-mother which kills him. The ancient myth of the man-devouring woman is re-created in modern terms.

The mythical aspect of the story is evident in the style and the symbols. The opening lines, "There was a woman who was beautiful, who started with all the advantages, yet she had no luck," contains both the ancient and the modern. The first seven words have a fable-like quality reminiscent of any number of fairy princess tales, yet the word *advantages* locates us in the atmosphere of the modern world; so does the word *luck*. The same juxtaposition of the mythical and the modern continues through the story; the same combination of the anonymous and the personal is repeated. Passages like the following demonstrate this juxtaposition of myth and modernity:

> There were a boy and two little girls. They lived in a pleasant house, with a garden, and they had discreet servants and felt themselves superior to any one in the neighborhood. Although they lived in style, they felt always an anxiety in the house....The child had never been to a race-meeting before, and his eyes were blue fire. He pursed his mouth tight, and watched. A Frenchman just in front had put his money on Lancelot. Wild with excitement, he flayed his arms up and down, yelling "Lancelot! Lancelot!" in his French accent....

The father in the story has no identity; he goes "into town to some office" and his "prospects never materialized." The central conflict is between the mother and the son, not between the man and his wife, even though the husband-man is responsible for the mother's plight. Where the man-husband fails, the son-boy tries to compensate; because it is the nature of the mother's needs that the boy cannot satisfy them, the boy is doomed from the beginning. The bizarre scene in which the bedeviled boy rides himself to death dramatizes Lawrence's idea that modern man is terrorized and finally engulfed by his incapacities to overcome his oedipal confrontation with the devouring woman-mother.

**Source:** Donald Junkins, "'The Rocking-Horse Winner': A Modern Myth," in *Studies in Short Fiction,* Vol. II, No. 1, Fall, 1964, pp. 87–9.

## Sources

Harris, Janice Hubbard. *The Short Fiction of D. H. Lawrence,* Rutgers University Press, 1984, pp. 1-11, 224-27.

Snodgrass, W. D., "A Rocking-Horse: The Symbol, The Patterns, The Way to Live," in *D. H. Lawrence: A Collection of Critical Essays,* edited by Mark Spilka, G. K. Hall, 1990, pp. 117-27.

## Further Reading

Blanchard, Lydia. "D. H. Lawrence," in *Magill's Critical Survey of Short Fiction,* edited by Frank N. Magill, Salem Press, 1981, pp. 1788–94.
    Provides an analysis of Lawrence's short stories.

Spilka, Mark. An introduction to *D. H. Lawrence: A Collection of Critical Essays,* Prentice-Hall, 1963, pp. 1-14.
    Spilka gives an overview of Lawrence's career and works.

# Sonny's Blues

**James Baldwin
1957**

Frequently anthologized, James Baldwin's "Sonny's Blues" tells the story of two brothers who come to understand each other. More specifically, it highlights, through its two main characters, the two sides of the African-American experience. The narrator has assimilated into white society as much as possible but still feels the pain of institutional racism and the limits placed upon his opportunity. Conversely, Sonny has never tried assimilate and must find an outlet for the deep pain and suffering that his status as permanent outsider confers upon him. Sonny channels his suffering into music, especially bebop jazz and the blues, forms developed by African-American musicians. "Sonny's Blues" was first published in 1957 and was collected in Baldwin's 1965 book, *Going to Meet the Man*.

The story also has biblical implications. Baldwin became a street preacher early in his life, and religious themes appear throughout his writings. In "Sonny's Blues," Baldwin uses the image from the book of Isaiah of the "cup of trembling" to symbolize the suffering and trouble that Sonny has experienced in his life. At the end of the story, while Sonny is playing the piano, Sonny's brother watches a barmaid bring a glass of Scotch and milk to the piano, which "glowed and shook above my brother's head like the very cup of trembling." As Sonny plays, the cup reminds his brother of all of the suffering that both he and Sonny have endured. His brother finally understands that it is through music

that Sonny is able to turn his suffering into something worthwhile.

## Author Biography

Born in New York City in 1924, James Baldwin grew up in the city's Harlem section, which was then the center of black intellectual and cultural life in America. By 1938, while attending DeWitt Clinton High School in the Bronx, he began to preach at the Fireside Pentecostal Assembly. His early theological training echoes in the religious themes and allusions that appear in his work. By 1944, however, he had renounced the ministry and moved to Greenwich Village, where he met Richard Wright and many other important writers and artists of the time.

It was also at this time that he began to write seriously. As the beneficiary of numerous fellowships during the late 1940s, he was able to move to Paris, France, and apply himself to his writing. In 1953 his novel *Go Tell It on the Mountain* appeared. Over the next few years he produced a number of plays, novels, and essays, including *The Amen Corner, Giovanni's Room,* and *Notes of a Native Son.*

Critics have seen his move to Paris as crucial to his development as a writer. Baldwin himself said that after moving to France, "I could see where I came from very clearly, and I could see that I carried myself, which is my home, with me. You can never escape that. I am the grandson of a slave, and I am a writer. I must deal with both." Also in Europe, Baldwin came to accept his homosexuality.

In the 1960s, Baldwin became involved in the civil rights movement in America. At this time, however, the movement was splintering into several factions. Baldwin found himself at odds with one, the "Black Arts Movement," led by writer LeRoi Jones, who later changed his name to Amiri Baraka. Baldwin refused to call himself a "black writer," feeling that a more fitting label for himself was "American writer." He felt that his position as an artist was to speak for the entire human race. For this stance, Baldwin earned the enmity of, among others, the influential writer Eldridge Cleaver, who accused Baldwin of having a "shameful, fanatical fawning" love of white people.

In the 1970s and 1980s Baldwin continued to write best-selling books, but critics began to feel that his powers were declining. His attention remained fixed on the relations between blacks and whites in America. In one of his last works, *The Evidence of Things Not Seen* (1985), he took on the subject of the Atlanta child murders of 1979-81. Baldwin died of stomach cancer in 1987. Eulogizing Baldwin, his one-time adversary Amiri Baraka said that he "reported, criticized, made beautiful, analyzed, cajoled, lyricized, attacked, sang, made us think, made us better, made us consciously human."

## Plot Summary

"Sonny's Blues" opens as the narrator learns from a newspaper that his younger brother, Sonny, has been arrested for dealing heroin. The narrator is taking the subway to his high-school teaching job. At the end of the school day, the "insular and mocking" laughter of his students reminds him that as youths he and Sonny had been filled with rage and had known "two darknesses"—the one of their lives and the one of the movies that made them momentarily forget about their lives. Leaving the school, the narrator comes across an old friend of Sonny's in the school yard.

While Sonny's friend and the narrator talk about Sonny's arrest, they tell each other some of their fears. In front of a bar that blasts "black and bouncy" music, the friend, who is not given a name, says that he "can't much help old Sonny no more." This angers the narrator because it reminds him that he himself had given up trying to help his brother because he had not known how; indeed, he had not even seen Sonny in a year. It disturbs the narrator to see his situation shared by someone who is not even related to Sonny. The friend mentions that he thought Sonny was too smart to get caught in a drug bust. In anger, the narrator criticizes the friend, sarcastically implying that the friend must have been smarter since he had not been arrested himself. The friend pauses and replies that he would have killed himself a long time ago if he were really smart, implying that he believes death is better than addiction. He then begins to explain to the older brother how he feels responsible for turning Sonny onto drugs, but the narrator breaks in and asks what will happen to Sonny next. The friend says that Sonny will be sent to a place where they will try and cure him and then he will be let loose to start his habit again. When the narrator questions why nothing else will occur, the friend's response shows how separate Sonny and his brother are. The narrator asks why Sonny wants to die and is told that "don't nobody want to die ever." The two men part after the narrator gives the friend five dollars when the friend asks for change.

The narrator does not get in touch with his brother for a long time. After his daughter dies, he realizes he had begun to wonder about him. The narrator wonders if the seven-year age difference between himself and Sonny can ever be bridged. He meets with Sonny after Sonny gets out of prison. At Sonny's request, they take a long cab ride around the elegant city before heading to the "vivid, killing streets" of their childhood where they each remember leaving part of themselves behind. The narrator begins to flashback to the childhood he and Sonny shared. The reader sees the family on a typical Sunday evening. As the skies darken, the adults sit quietly with faces darkening like the sky. The children are somewhat frightened as they witness this, and one hopes that the "hand which strokes his forehead will never stop."

Immediately following this scene readers see the narrator and his mother in conversation. The narrator learns for the first time that his father had a brother who was killed by a car full of drunk white men. The narrator's mother tells the story to let him know how important he and his brother are to each other and how he, as the older, more stable one, needs to let Sonny know he is "there" for Sonny. The narrator experiences a pang of guilt as he reflects on not having done as his mother asked, but he also remembers that Sonny's choice of being a jazz musician instead of a classical one "seemed— beneath him, somehow." The narrator relates the time when he asked Sonny to play like Louis Armstrong did, and Sonny told him that Charlie Parker was his model instead. This emphasizes the different lives the brothers are leading.

The narrator witnesses a revival scene from his window that sets him on the road to understanding his brother. Sonny watches the same scene from the sidewalk, and both are struck by the fact that the women in the meeting "addressed each other as Sister." This leads to a conversation between the brothers where, for the first time, the narrator tries to understand his brother's point of view. When Sonny

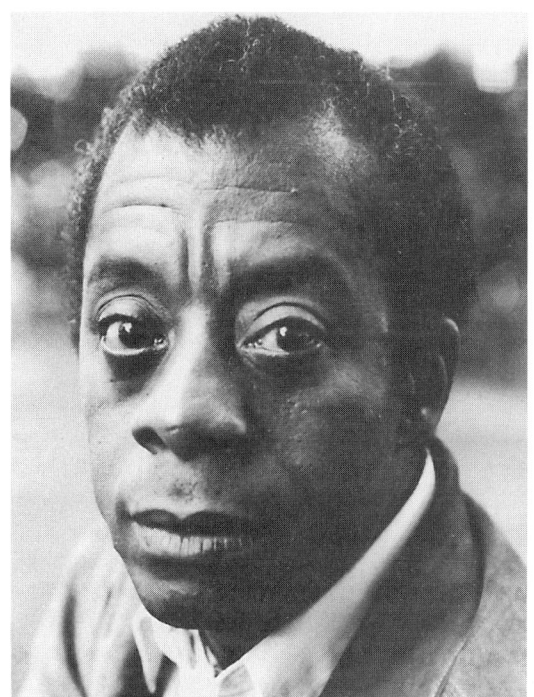

*James Baldwin*

tells him that the revival meeting reminded him of how in control he felt with heroin, the narrator realizes that Sonny is actually speaking of something much greater. Here it is learned that Sonny uses drugs to "keep from drowning in" the suffering all humans have to go through. He explains that in order to gain anything or learn anything from the suffering, there needs to be a way to make it your own. For Sonny, heroin accomplishes this, as does jazz.

The narrator goes with Sonny to a jazz club. Sonny is going to play and everyone there greets him with expectation. The club is dark, except for a spotlight on the musicians. While Sonny plays, the narrator defines the blues as something "personal and private." Sonny plays a set that the narrator understands is not the best he can do; he watches the older musician give Sonny room to take the lead but Sonny ignores it until later in the next set. As he begins to play "Am I Blue," Sonny takes control of the music, and becomes "part of a family again." At the end of the set, the narrator realizes that the music has helped Sonny to stay free and avoid drowning in his suffering. Furthermore, the narrator recognizes that the blues can help everyone be true to what and who they are.

# Characters

### Creole

Creole is a bass player who leads the band that Sonny plays in at the end of the story. He functions as a kind of father figure for Sonny; he believes it is his purpose to guide Sonny through his blues and teach him how to turn them into music. He also attempts to show Sonny's brother how to understand Sonny.

### Sonny

Although the story is narrated by Sonny's unnamed older brother, Sonny is the most important character. Sonny is described in a common stereotype of the time, a stereotype that his own brother holds until the end of the story: the heroin-addicted jazz musician. Sonny has just been arrested for "peddling and using heroin" and must do time in a prison upstate.

As the story progresses, however, the reader learns more about Sonny's life before the arrest. He was the "apple of his father's eye," but in his youth he always had a tendency to stray from what his family thought would be the safe route. He decides that he wants to be a jazz musician, a choice that his brother finds regrettable. Sonny takes his music very seriously, and for a time he lives with his sister-in-law's family while his brother is in the army. He takes his music so seriously that the family finds him strange—"it wasn't like living with a person at all, it was like living with sound."

Sonny and his brother fight periodically and are utterly unable to understand each other until Sonny returns from prison and his brother finally goes to Greenwich Village to hear Sonny play. A man named Creole leads the band, and Sonny admires his control of the music they play. As Sonny plays the piano in the jazz club, his brother begins to understand the deep suffering and the blues that have always preoccupied Sonny.

### Sonny's Brother

The experiences of Sonny are shown through the eyes of the story's narrator, Sonny's brother. The unnamed narrator is a high school algebra teacher who grew up in Harlem but has made an attempt to escape its cruel streets by getting a good job and integrating himself, as best he can, into white society. In subtle ways, however, he has internalized many of the prejudices of that society. When Sonny tells him that he wants to be a musician, his brother immediately assumes that this means a classical musician. After it becomes clear that Sonny wants to play jazz—a traditionally black genre—his brother thinks that "it seemed—beneath him, somehow."

While Sonny has allowed his blues to dominate his life, his brother has internalized his own blues; only rarely do they make it to the surface. He is married to a woman named Isabel and seems happy, although one of their children dies while Sonny is in jail. He looks upon the streets of Harlem as a place he has left behind, but he is still comfortable there. He feels the blues that possess Sonny, but his moderate success has allowed him to keep them deep down inside himself.

### Sonny's Father

Sonny's father dies "during a drunken weekend in the middle of the war" when Sonny is fifteen. Little is revealed about him except that he was very strict with Sonny because his younger son was "the apple of his eye." The father's own brother was killed by a drunken group of white men long ago in the South. After that point, the mother tells Sonny's brother, "he weren't sure but that every white man he saw was the man that killed his brother."

### Sonny's Mother

Sonny's mother dies while Sonny is in school and his brother is still in the army, but she had already charged Sonny's brother with Sonny's care. "You got to hold on to your brother," she tells him in their last moments together, "and don't let him fall, no matter what it looks like is happening to him and no matter how evil you gets with him." Sonny's brother accepts her request until Sonny begins to spend time downtown with jazz musicians.

# Themes

In "Sonny's Blues," a man finally comes to understand the darkness and suffering that consumes his brother, and he begins to appreciate the music that his brother uses to calm those blues.

### Suffering

The main theme of "Sonny's Blues" is suffering, particularly the sufferings of black people in America. Although Baldwin presents only one example of overt racism in the story—the death of Sonny's uncle under the wheels of a car driven by a group of drunken whites—the repercussions of the treatment received by black people is omnipresent. Sonny's father is tormented by the memory of his brother's death and suffers from a hatred of white people as a result. This hatred, Baldwin suggests, warps his soul. Sonny's mother also suffers from the harshness of life in Harlem and from her knowledge that her younger son feels this suffering more strongly than most.

Sonny's brother, the narrator of the story, also suffers. Although he tries to block them out, the blues become apparent in the darkness that he sees everywhere, even in his students. He imagines them using heroin in the bathroom between classes and says that "their laughter ... was not the joyous laughter which—God knows why—one associates with children." For him, childhood has no joy.

His neighborhood, too, is "filled with a hidden menace" that the new housing project in which he and his wife live cannot hide. "It looks like a parody of the good, clean, faceless life—God knows the people who live in it do their best to make it a parody.... The minute Sonny and I started into the house I had the feeling that I was simply bringing him back into the danger he had almost died trying to escape."

Baldwin makes Sonny's blues the focus of the story. Sonny has not experienced anything significantly more traumatic than his brother has, but he feels it more intensely. Sonny always "moved ... in a distant stillness," his brother says. For that reason, his mother urges his brother to watch out for him. "You may not be able to stop nothing from happening. But you got to let him know you's *there*."

For Sonny, heroin is a seductive outlet for his blues, but he knows that in the end it will kill him. Sonny is looking for a way to conceal the blues within him but admits in a letter to his brother that "trouble is the one thing that never does get stopped." Music promises freedom from these blues, though, and during Sonny's solo at the end of the story his brother sees this: "he could help us to be free if we would just listen, that he would never be free until we did. I heard what he had gone through, and would continue to go through until he came to rest in earth."

### *Race and Racism*
The fact that race is only a contributing factor in Sonny's blues is characteristic of Baldwin's beliefs. For him, the fact that he was black formed only part of his identity but did not ultimately define him.

## Topics for Further Study

- Read about the development of bebop jazz music in the 1940s. Who were some of the important figures? How was bebop different from traditional jazz? Why was it controversial?

- How were black people treated in Northern cities in the 1940s and 1950s? How did daily life in the North differ from daily life in the South for a working-class black family? Was Sonny's brother, with his middle-class life, an exception?

- Investigate the role of the church in Harlem today. What services does the church provide? How do the roles of religious institutions in neighborhoods like Harlem differ from their roles in other parts of the city?

---

Similarly, Sonny's blues result in large part from the circumstances of his race—his upbringing in Harlem, the temptations of the streets, and the limits on his economic opportunity—but they also result from the natural human obligation to suffer. Additionally, the biblical reference at the end of the story serves to universalize Sonny's troubles.

The history of oppression that blacks in America have suffered, however, certainly informs Sonny's blues. This history is made distinctly personal when Sonny's brother hears how his uncle died—run over by drunk white men in the South. Sonny's brother also reminds readers of the circumstances of black people in the city when he details the poverty and neglect in his Harlem neighborhood.

### *Art and Expression*
Baldwin believed in the power of art to save people from suffering, or at least to minimize their suffering. Correspondingly, Sonny uses blues and jazz as an outlet for his feelings, an outlet which his brother at first does not understand. Once Sonny's brother visits the jazz club and hears Sonny play, however, he begins to comprehend the power and importance of music in Sonny's life.

## Style

### Narration and Point of View

"Sonny's Blues" chronicles the relationship between two brothers at various points in their lives. Baldwin arranges the story's events to show the building of an understanding between the two brothers. Sonny's brother, who is never named in the story, narrates "Sonny's Blues." Although the story focuses on the events of Sonny's life, the fact that readers hear his brother's reactions to and feelings about Sonny's actions broadens the scope of the story to include the brother's life as well. Baldwin uses this double focus to bring out one of his most important themes: the growing understanding between estranged brothers.

### Setting

The story is set in New York City, although at one point Sonny speaks in a letter from his prison cell upstate. Baldwin varies the time in which the story is set. By blending the time periods together with little separation or even clear notice, Baldwin establishes a sense of duration. Sonny's brother narrates the important events of Sonny's life as if they had happened at the same time. The fact that the events all share a sense of suffering or hardship or alienation hammers home the realization—which Sonny's brother finally arrives at in the jazz club—that suffering has been the dominant mode of Sonny's life. Baldwin arranges the story's events thematically—as opposed to arranging them chronologically—to emphasize their content, instead of their sequence or causality.

### Catharsis

In literature "catharsis" refers to the outlet given the audience's emotions at the end of a story. In "Sonny's Blues," the cathartic moment occurs in the jazz club, when both Sonny's brother and the reader watch Sonny overcome, for a moment, the troubles of the world through his music. The growing tension in the story is the reader's and the narrator's gradual understanding of Sonny and the burden he bears. The catharsis Baldwin grants both the reader and the narrator is seeing Sonny find a way to defuse his suffering. In this catharsis, the reader also watches Sonny's own catharsis, as he uses his music as an outlet for his blues.

## Historical Context

### Bebop

In the late 1930s and early 1940s, a new form of jazz music was being developed. The style, called "bebop," "bop," or later, "hard bop," centered on a very complex and abstract type of soloing during familiar tunes. Often in the solo, only the chords of the original melody would remain the same, and the tune would bear no resemblance to more traditional versions. The soloist would also play at blistering speeds. The earliest bebop musicians were trumpet players Dizzy Gillespie and Miles Davis, pianist Thelonious Monk, and saxophonist Charlie Parker. Parker is often credited as the originator of the genre.

Bebop became very controversial at a time when jazz was gaining respectability, and many of the traditional jazz musicians opposed it. Where traditional jazz music and its more popular subform, swing, encouraged audiences to dance and enjoy themselves, bebop focused attention on the soloist and on his technical virtuosity. In this way, it was akin to other forms of modernist art, which exalted difficulty and formal experimentation. The English poet Philip Larkin expressed this association between bebop and modernist art when he condemned what he considered the three main figures of modernism, "Picasso, Pound and Parker," referring to artist Pablo Picasso, poet Ezra Pound, and musician Charlie Parker. Bebop was intellectualized where jazz and swing were pleasant and sensual, and the emotions that bebop expressed were often dark and brooding.

Contributing to bebop's somewhat dangerous and seamy reputation were the highly publicized drug problems of many of bebop's central figures. Charlie Parker, Art Pepper, Miles Davis, John Coltrane, and many other important bebop innovators suffered from addictions to drugs; heroin was the most common drug in the jazz world. Most of bebop's important figures lived in New York City by the late 1940s, playing clubs in Greenwich Village and on 52nd Street where heroin was easy to find. By the 1950s, bebop and heroin were virtually synonymous.

In Baldwin's story, the character of Sonny represents bebop in both its positive and negative aspects. The brother thinks of jazz as "clowning around on bandstands," while for Sonny music is deadly serious, life itself. When the brother finally

# Compare & Contrast

- **1950s:** Jazz innovators, such as Charlie Parker, Thelonious Monk, Charles Mingus, Miles Davis, Max Roach, and Bud Powell either live in or spend a great deal of time playing in New York City. Clubs such as the Village Vanguard and Birdland are world-famous for their revolutionary jazz offerings.

  **Today:** After a long period of drought, bebop-influenced jazz (now viewed as "traditional") is again popular in New York City. Players such as Joshua Redman and Roy Ayres, known as "Young Lions," bring the old sounds back to the old clubs like the Vanguard and the Blue Note, while jazzman Wynton Marsalis has an office at Lincoln Center, the epitome of musical classicism.

- **1950s:** Heroin is an underground drug, synonymous with jazzmen, beatniks and lowlifes. Although many artists, musicians, and urban dwellers are addicted to the drug, the general population is primarily unaware of its existence.

  **Today:** Heroin use is surging among young people after decades of unpopularity. Musician Kurt Cobain of the group Nirvana kills himself in 1994 after battling unsuccessfully with a heroin addiction.

- **1957:** In Little Rock, Arkansas, federal troops are needed to integrate Central High School after Arkansas governor Orval Faubus refuses to let black children enter the building.

  **1997:** President and former Arkansas governor Bill Clinton seeks to integrate his White House Cabinet, hoping to make his closest group of advisers "look more like America."

---

does go to see Sonny play, he begins to understand what bebop is all about. The "clowning" that he previously felt was the essence of jazz is nowhere to be found, and in its place there is the blues. The deep emotional expression of the song Sonny plays—"Am I Blue"—connects with Sonny's brother. "He hit something in me, myself."

### Race in New York City

James Baldwin grew up in New York City and therefore was spared the brutal racial oppression of the South in the 1930s and 1940s. Baldwin's neighborhood, Harlem, had by the 1920s become a haven for blacks coming north from Florida, Georgia, the Carolinas, and Virginia. Although the North did not have the racist Jim Crow laws that characterized the South, it was by no means a land of equality. Blacks in the North suffered from limited educational and economic opportunities. They were the "last hired and the first fired" for most jobs. Harlem was often a rude shock to poor blacks fleeing the South. Expecting a friendly reception from a proudly black city, they were often greeted by crime, poverty, and the infamous New York attitude that disdains newcomers and country people.

However difficult life was in Harlem, though, it was better than life in the South. For that reason many of the leading lights of African-American culture congregated there, and in the 1920s the neighborhood enjoyed a cultural high point called the "Harlem Renaissance." Writers such as Langston Hughes and Zora Neale Hurston, musicians such as Duke Ellington and Louis Armstrong, and many other artistic and intellectual figures made Harlem and New York City a haven for culture.

Baldwin was born into this world, where extreme poverty and deprivation were often overshadowed by the achievements of a few of the neighborhood's inhabitants. "You see, there were two Harlems," Baldwin said in 1969. "There were those who lived in Sugar Hill and there was the Hollow, where we lived. There was a great divide between the black people on the hill and us. I was just a raggedy, funky black shoeshine boy and was

*The Apollo Theater in Harlem, the epicenter of jazz music in the 1950s.*

afraid of the people on the Hill, who, for their part, didn't want to have anything to do with me.''

Although New York was often difficult and daunting, throughout his life Baldwin continued to feel most at home in Harlem. The city of New York, with its extremes, retained a central importance in Baldwin's work until his death. In Harlem, he said in 1989, "people know what I know, and we can talk and laugh, and it would never occur to anybody to say what we all know."

## Critical Overview

Though Baldwin published "Sonny's Blues" as part of his only story collection, *Going to Meet the Man,* in 1965, the story had appeared in a periodical several years before. While stories in periodicals are generally not reviewed, the magazine in which "Sonny's Blues" appeared does give some indication of Baldwin's place in the literary world at that time. "Sonny's Blues" led off the summer, 1957, issue of *Partisan Review,* which at the time was of America's leading journals of culture and politics. Baldwin's story was longer than most stories and was given the prestigious first position in the magazine, demonstrating the respect that the magazine's editors felt Baldwin deserved.

Baldwin had long been a figure in New York's intellectual community. He had moved to Greenwich Village from Harlem in 1944, where he met Richard Wright, then America's most important black writer. Baldwin wrote for the *Nation* and the *New Leader* while in the Village, before moving to Paris in 1948. During the 1940s and early 1950s, he received fellowships and grants from important cultural organizations and wrote for major American magazines while producing important works of drama, fiction, and nonfiction.

Baldwin's work was almost immediately lauded by the critics. His 1953 novel *Go Tell It on the Mountain* announced the presence of a major American writer. Another book of the same time, *Notes of a Native Son,* was a collection of essays primarily concentrating on questions of race in America. Baldwin claimed Wright's mantle as the most important black writer in America. His next novel, however, went in a direction that critics were not expecting and reviews were negative. *Giovanni's Room* tells the story of a love affair between a white

American student in Paris and an Italian bartender. Its frank depiction of homosexuality signaled Baldwin's acceptance of his own sexual orientation but alienated many readers and critics. Baldwin continued to write about life as a gay man throughout his career. By the late 1950s it had almost become a "critical commonplace," according to John M. Reilly in *James Baldwin: A Critical Evaluation,* that Baldwin's nonfiction was of superior quality to his fiction and the plays that he wrote.

In 1965, Baldwin published *Going to Meet the Man,* and critics began to write about "Sonny's Blues." The story, like Baldwin's career itself, was viewed from opposing perspectives: critics either reviewed it as a story specifically about the black experience in America or about suffering's role in the human condition. Whichever side of this debate a critic came down on, though, almost all critics agreed that "Sonny's Blues" was a major accomplishment in the short story form. "Nearly every word, every gesture in it, adds up toward the meeting of form, theme and meaning," Stanley Macebuh held in *James Baldwin: A Critical Study.* Macebuh went on to state that "the meaning of the story is to be found in its structure.... of a blues song," in which there are no "profundities of thought" or "events that are in themselves of cataclysmic import," but simply a "ritualistic repetition of feeling, emotion and mood."

Louis H. Pratt took the opposite viewpoint, believing that "Sonny's Blues" is specifically a black story. He asserted in *James Baldwin* that the stories in *Going to Meet the Man* all deal with the "insurmountable fears—conscious and unconscious—which grow out of the experience of being black in a white-oriented society." To overcome these fears, Pratt believed, Baldwin's characters must "open a line of communication with the past." "This channel can be opened only though personal suffering," Pratt concluded. Where Sonny already has this channel open and is using the blues to overcome his fears and his suffering, Sonny's brother must experience the death of his daughter first in order to open himself up to the blues.

Reilly, in *James Baldwin: A Critical Evaluation,* believed that the story "not only states dramatically the motive for Baldwin's famous polemics in the cause of Black freedom, but it also provides an esthetic linking his work, in all genres, with the cultures of the Black ghetto." For Reilly, as for Pratt, Baldwin's story is essentially an African-American one.

More recent critics have taken different approaches to the story. Patricia R. Robertson, in *The University of Mississippi Studies in English,* examined the religious grounding of the story, while Suzy Bernstein Goldman, in *Negro American Literature Forum,* discussed jazz and blues parallels. In the last few years, the most popular approach to Baldwin's work has been an examination of his themes of homosexuality, but few of those articles deal with "Sonny's Blues." In general, the critics agree that "Sonny's Blues" is a masterpiece of the short story form, one in which Baldwin demonstrates his ability to illustrate the relationship between seemingly "black" literature and American literature.

## Criticism

### Jennifer Hicks

*Jennifer Hicks is a professor and director of the Academic Support and Writing Assessment program at Massachusetts Bay Community College in Wellesley, MA. In the following essay, she discusses the racial issues that serve as a backdrop in "Sonny's Blues."*

Each of us wants to live a life where we feel fulfilled and joyous. A few of us accomplish this with seemingly little effort; others struggle on their journey through periods of self doubt, rejection, depression, or the blues. James Baldwin was no different; yet while he struggled toward his own individual fulfillment, he began to feel a driving need to tie the idea of individual effort and fulfillment to the black race. In fact, according to C.W.E. Bigsby, editor of *The Black American Writer,* the central point of conflict in much of Baldwin's writing is to show that "the job of ethnic renewal [lies] in individual fulfillment rather than racial separatism or political revolution."

Putting emphasis on the individual is also a way to portray blacks as unique "members of a community with its own traditions and values," according to Irving Howe in *Dissent.* In part, this emphasis stems from racial bias against blacks. It also stems, however, from the realization that with the Harlem Renaissance, the black "writer has come to appreciate the relevance of his own experience to a nation searching for its own sense of identity and purpose," according to Bigsby. For these reasons, the times and community in which Baldwin grew up

## What Do I Read Next?

- *Go Tell It on the Mountain,* Baldwin's landmark novel about the condition of African Americans in the United States.
- *Notes of a Native Son,* Baldwin's highly regarded collection of essays which discuss race issues.
- *Invisible Man* by Ralph Ellison is another landmark novel about the position of blacks in American society.
- *Mexico City Blues* (1959) by Jack Kerouac is a song-like novel written in the style of jazz compositions. Kerouac was a leader of the Beat Movement in literature, a group of New York City writers in the 1940s and 1950s who were influenced by the milieu of Harlem, be-bop jazz music, blues, and drugs.

---

become important. They contributed to his need to find how "the specialness of [his] experience could be made to connect [him] to other people instead of dividing [him] from them."

Baldwin's early experiences became integral to his writings. The eldest of nine children, he was born in 1924 in Harlem to a preacher and his wife. At that time, Harlem was the country's largest black community. It was home to many blacks who had come North to escape the severe repression of the Jim Crow laws in the South. According to Baldwin, Harlem was a "dreadful place . . . a kind of concentration camp," where at the age of ten he was beaten by two police officers because of the color of his skin. It was also the place where his mother said no child would ever be safe. At the age of 24, Baldwin needed to get away from "the dehumanizing society of New York" to avoid becoming engulfed by "the fury of the color problem." He accepted a literary prize that included a monetary stipend in 1948 and went to France to write.

Apparently the escape was worthwhile. Baldwin worked at finding the individual within himself after he had a breakdown and spent some recuperative time listening to the blues music of Bessie Smith. Within the next few years he produced the critically-acclaimed *Go Tell It on the Mountain* in 1953 and the controversial *Giovanni's Room* in 1956. Although one of the reasons Baldwin had escaped to Europe was to avoid being categorized as a "Negro writer," events occurring at this time in the United States made him think the time had come to accept the label. He saw the U.S. Supreme Court rule that segregation was illegal in the case of Brown vs. The Board of Education in 1954, and he also saw Rosa Parks arrested for not moving to the back of a bus a year after that. Then in 1957, he heard of the race riot in Arkansas that occurred after nine black students began attending an all-white school. As a member of an ethnic and cultural community that was experiencing rapid change, Baldwin felt obligated to return to the United States.

Baldwin published "Sonny's Blues" the year he returned. The story contains evidence of the conflict Baldwin faced: between following an individual path and maintaining or renewing ethnic ties. According to John Reilly in *James Baldwin: A Collection of Critical Essays,* "the discovery of identity is nowhere presented more successfully than in the short story of 'Sonny's Blues'." The story concerns two estranged brothers and their quest to find fulfillment. Their relationship undergoes change as they tentatively reach an understanding and begin to talk with one another again.

"Sonny's Blues" powerfully shows the growth of Sonny's older brother, the narrator, who had responded to his racial status by fitting in with the status quo. The narrator is an algebra teacher in a New York high school. His success in assimilating into the white-dominated society separates him from his brother and a world that "filled everything, the people, the houses, the music, the dark, quicksilver barmaid, with the menace [that] was their reality."

On the other hand, his younger brother Sonny lives outside of the accepted white society. Sonny is initially portrayed as the family failure, the kind of character that Baldwin so easily criticized in his early essay "The Protest Novel." Rather than fulfilling himself by assimilating into the mainstream culture and following the American Dream, he chooses to immerse himself in the blues world and become a heroin addict. It is within this portrayal of how individuals react to and deal with their circumstances that we see Baldwin looking both at individual importance and ethnic renewal.

Baldwin weaves images and concepts from his past into the story. He writes of a neighborhood quite reminiscent of his own. The students in the story are "smothering in these houses, [coming] down into the streets for light and air and [finding] themselves encircled by danger." The brothers' parents consider their environment unsafe, but then too the father says, "Ain't no place safe for kids, nor anybody." Like Sonny, he also uses the blues—an African-American folk music genre that originated in the South—as a key metaphor. (Metaphors are devices used in writing to show how something totally unlike something else may in fact share similar characteristics.) In "Sonny's Blues," the blues become the instrument that, as one critic says, helps rebuild relationships, either of the self or with others. The relationship being repaired belongs to Sonny and the narrator. In Baldwin's own life the blues were his mainstay during his breakdown. The music helped connect him to who he was. Thus, Baldwin uses the blues in this story to show us an individual's road to fulfillment. As Howe says, however, it is also used to depict the "living culture of men and women . . . who share in the emotion and desires of common humanity . . . as evidence of [Black] worth . . . moral tenacity, and right to self-acceptance." The music becomes, therefore, a device to explain individual fulfillment and extend it to identify a culture.

When Baldwin writes of the narrator's students "living as we'd been living then, . . . growing up with a rush and their heads bumped abruptly against the low ceiling of their actual possibilities," he reminds readers of the realities for American blacks in the 1950s. When he describes in detail the revival scene on the sidewalk, he demonstrates a tradition with value in that same community. At the end of the story, when both brothers are in the nightclub and Creole steps aside to let Sonny solo, the narrator overcomes his isolationist position and feels a sense of empathy and community with his brother. He allows himself re-entrance into his culture while he listens to what Sonny plays: "He began to make it his. It was very beautiful because it wasn't hurried and it was no longer a lament. I seemed to hear with what burning he had made it his, with what burning we had yet to make it ours, how we could cease lamenting. Freedom lurked around us and I understood, at last, that he could help us to be free if we would listen, that he would never be free until we did."

**Source:** Jennifer Hicks, for *Short Stories for Students,* Gale Research, 1997.

> "It is within this portrayal of how individuals react to and deal with their circumstances that we see Baldwin looking both at individual importance and ethnic renewal."

### Patricia R. Robertson

*In the following essay, Robertson explores the theme of the scapegoat in "Sonny's Blues," which she says is developed through the images of music and the street revival.*

In James Baldwin's only book of short stories, *Going to Meet the Man,* "Sonny's Blues" stands out as the best, most memorable. This story is both realistic and symbolic, part autobiography and part fiction. So memorable is "Sonny's Blues" that a student once put it at the top of a list of thirty stories read for a course in fiction. She commented, "The story haunts you; its beauty continues in your mind long after the original reading and discussion." The story's haunting beauty comes from our participation in the scapegoat metaphor that creates the intricate tracery which holds the story together, forming a graceful spiral, a pattern of correspondences which informs and entices as it helps us to be free.

The scapegoat metaphor is developed through several images, the most important of which is music, with its links to suffering and brotherhood. But we are only dimly aware of this scapegoat pattern until we see the final, startling biblical image of the scotch and milk drink, "the very cup of trembling," which follows Sonny's playing of the blues and which clarifies the story's meaning. This "cup of trembling," then, is at once the Old Testament cup of justice and the New Testament cup of Gethsemane, or mercy. The Old Testament allusion to the "cup of trembling" leads directly to the scapegoat metaphor and the idea of pain and suffering of a people. The New Testament story of hope is carried in Sonny's name which suggests Christ symbolism and leads to the New Testament message of the 'cup of trembling' as the cup of Gethsemane which Christ drank, symbolizing the removal of sins for all who believe and hope for eternal life through belief in him. Sonny's name echoes this special relationship. Sonny, the scapegoat, is the hope of his particular world.

The power of guilt and suffering is revealed in Sonny's tenuous relationship with his own brother and in his immediate empathy with the revivalists; it has been foreshadowed in the anguish of the young friend who still feels a connection with Sonny. Through these people's responses we come to understand that brothers—literal or metaphorical—rescue, redeem, bring righteous anger, and act as scapegoats to open up the world of suffering; the friend begins this for Sonny's brother, the revivalists for Sonny, and Sonny for his brother and for us.

Further, the scapegoat metaphor is strengthened and enriched by the metaphor of shared suffering carried through music—either by a young boy's whistle, by the revivalist's hymns, or finally and most significantly by Sonny's hot piano on which he plays the blues. The blues metaphor also involves suffering and the sharing of suffering that supercedes race and time and cements us all together within our shared humanity. Sonny's music—the blues—has power to transform both his and our pain; through his sharing, Sonny becomes the ultimate scapegoat.

The term 'scapegoat' means 'sharing of pain'; it implies a true understanding of another's suffering. According to *Webster's New World Dictionary,* the scapegoat, the *caper emissarius,* or azazel, was originally ''a goat over the heads of which the high priest of the ancient Jews confessed the sins of the people on the Day of Atonement, after which it was allowed to escape.'' More secularly and popularly, the scapegoat is ''a person, group, or thing upon whom the blame for the mistakes or crimes of others is thrust.''

Baldwin, himself, defines for us the scapegoat metaphor when he asserts ''That all mankind is united by virtue of their humanity.'' He writes elsewhere, '''It is a terrible, an inexorable, law that one cannot deny the humanity of another without diminishing one's own: in the face of one's victim, one sees oneself.''' In another context, Jack Matthews, in *Archetypal Themes in the Modern Story,* asks ''When is a person not himself?'' He answers, ''When he reminds you of someone else and you can't see the living presence because of the remembered image. Or when, through accident or muddled design, he begins to embody our own secret fears. In psychology, this is termed projection; in a story or folktale, it is a celebration of the Scapegoat theme.'' Thus the literary scapegoat, through his own personal suffering or by his metaphorical sharing of his own sorrow, may allow us to see into life and into ourselves and thus vicariously transfer our guilt and pain through him and his suffering.

In this story music is the thread that accompanies and develops the brotherhood/scapegoat metaphor. For in his music Sonny reveals both his suffering and his understanding of others' pain. His music becomes a mystical, spiritual medium, an open-ended metaphor simultaneously comforting the player and the listener and releasing their guilt and pain. No words *could* have expressed so well what Sonny's music conveyed effortlessly. For, according to Cirlot [in *A Dictionary of Symbols*], ''Music represents an intermediate zone between the differentiated or material world and the undifferentiated realm of the 'pure will' of [German philosopher Arthur] Schopenhauer.'' The power of this emotional transfer is seen in the brother's response. For through Sonny's music his brother comes to understand his own life, his parents' experience, his daughter's death, and his wife's grief. The brother recapitulates his own, Sonny's, and the family's suffering here at the end of the story. But as [Danish philosopher Soren] Kierkegaard says, in *Repetition,* ''repetition'' replaces ''the more traditional Platonic term anamnesis or recollection.'' This is ''not the simple repeating of an experience, but the recreating of it which redeems or awakens it to life, the end of the process...being the apocalyptic promise: 'Behold, I make all things new.''' Sonny's awakening is done through his blues, and its effect is revealed through the brother's sudden understanding, conveyed in the final image of the Scotch and milk drink, ''the very cup of trembling.'' This central biblical image reverberates with life and reinforces the scapegoat metaphor. This recreation of life is also what the blues are all about. We come full circle.

The scapegoat metaphor is first presented very quietly when Sonny's childhood friend offers to become a scapegoat, insisting upon his symbolic action when he tells Sonny's brother, ''Funny thing, ... when I saw the papers this morning, the first thing I asked myself was if I had anything to do with [Sonny's arrest for using and selling heroin]. I felt sort of responsible.'' The young man offers to take the blame for Sonny's fall, but his hesitant plea is offensive to the brother who, like us, does not understand the symbolic significance of the act. For, instead of accepting and sharing the man's guilt, the brother becomes angry at the friend's panhandling. He feels superior to him and rejects his offer and his sympathy.

Just prior to this meeting with the old friend a boy's whistle echoes through the school yard. The whistle is "at once very complicated and very simple; it seemed to be pouring out of him as though he were a bird, and it sounded very cool and moving through all that harsh, bright air, only just holding its own through all those other sounds." But this music creates a central abstract image, a tone poem carrying the sadness and guilt of the brother, a simple yet complicated sounding of pain.

This first subtle pairing of music with guilt and pain sets the tone for the story. This young man, this emotional 'brother,' cannot comfort Sonny's brother, but paradoxically his sincere concern increases the brother's understanding of Sonny's problems. Further, this sad young man illustrates the community's desperate need for a savior as well as setting up the scapegoat metaphor. For the brother sees in the friend as in a mirror the great sadness and courage of Sonny. He says "All at once something inside gave and threatened to come pouring out of me. I didn't hate him [the friend] any more. I felt that in another moment I'd start crying like a child." This emotional release is the first step toward understanding and the first presentation of the Old Testament scapegoat motif so delicately interwoven in this story.

The scapegoat metaphor is next presented and perfectly symbolized by the street revival. The street people are a paradigm of life, a kind of representative cross-section of humanity. All sorts of people watch and listen to the street revivalists—working people, children, older folks, street women, Sonny, and Sonny's brother who watches from above at the window. At this "old fashioned revival meeting" there are "three sisters in black, and a brother. All they [have are] their voices and their Bibles and a tambourine." These people sing "'Tis the old ship of Zion'. . . .it has rescued many a thousand!"

The listeners hear nothing new, only the old pain and suffering and the offer of relief from three sisters and a brother, mortals like themselves; yet these four make suffering real. Their music acts as a mirror for the watchers whose response illustrates the scapegoat metaphor in action: "As the singing

> "In this story music is the thread that accompanies and develops the brotherhood/scapegoat metaphor."

filled the air the watching, listening faces underwent a change, the eyes focusing on something within; the music seemed to soothe a poison out of them; and time seemed, nearly, to fall away from the sullen, belligerent, battered faces, as though they were fleeing back to their first condition, while dreaming of their last." These spirituals are an amalgam of joy and the blues, touching everyone who listens and helping them share the guilt and pain of the human condition.

The revival, central to the brother's awareness since it incorporates music, religion, and suffering, helps Sonny to articulate the relationship between suffering and human understanding. Also, for Sonny, the woman revivalist serves as a scapegoat; she helps him to understand his own suffering just as she had helped those who listened and contributed to her cause. For Sonny, this insight into the woman's suffering makes his own pain bearable, makes it possible to reach out to his brother. For Sonny understands this scene. Touched by their pain, he alone articulates its universal meaning—suffering. New Testament echoes of brother and savior are palpable in his response: "It's *repulsive* to think you have to suffer that much." But ironically, the biblical scapegoat metaphor suggests group suffering as well as individual suffering.

Sonny's own pain has been personal and private. He had tried to tell his brother about his suffering in the letter from prison, but he was almost inarticulate. His suffering went beyond words. Now, after the brothers have experienced the revival, Sonny tries again to communicate with his brother by explaining his relationship with music: "you finally try to get with it and play it, [and] you realize *nobody's* listening. So *you've* got to listen. You got to find a way to listen," to distance the pain, to look at despair and deal with guilt in order to live. To play this way requires brutal honesty and empathy with the suffering of others. Sonny says, I "can't forget—where I've been. I don't mean just the physical place I've been, I mean where I've *been*. And *what* I've been....I've been something I didn't recognize, didn't know I could be. Didn't know anybody could be." But the painful rendition of the revivalists shows him musically that others have been there too.

Significantly, Sonny invites his brother to hear him play right after the street revival when they talk for almost the first time. Sonny understands his own need and his brother's suffering because someone else's suffering mirrors his own, effectively causing his confession and his sharing of his own pain through his music, mirror of man's soul. Music is able to heal wounds, for when Sonny is in perfect harmony with himself and with his environment, when he understands, he plays the piano effortlessly. Now Sonny's confession of failure also prepares for the final scene where Sonny plays the blues, an appropriate musical form based on folk music and characterized by minor harmonies, slow tempo, and melancholy words. The blues, like the tuneless whistle and the melancholy spirituals sung by the revivalists, reinforce the idea of human suffering carried by the scapegoat metaphor. For the blues, sad and melancholy jazz, are a mood, a feeling, a means of escape and entertainment; the blues, especially, are a way of sharing suffering, a way of strengthening the idea of community. The blues, the tune without the words in this instance, help the inarticulate young pianist to communicate with his brother and with the world. Thus he enriches the central metaphor for the story. For according to C. W. Sylvander, "Art can be a means for release from the 'previous condition' when it is heard, listened to, understood."

The linkage between the scapegoat motif and the music is clearly revealed when Creole has the group play the blues and signifies that this particular rendition is 'Sonny's blues.' L. H. Pratt notes that "Once the narrator draws near to listen, the blues becomes the means by which Sonny is able to lead his brother, through a confrontation with the meaning of life, into a discovery of self." Through the blues the brothers can communicate. The blues become the last and greatest reinforcer of the scapegoat metaphor. For through the music something magical happens.

The narrator comes to understand that "not many people ever hear [music]. [But]...When something opens within, and the music enters, what we mainly hear, or hear corroborated, are personal, private, vanishing evocations." The same thing is true of our suffering and our alienation from others. Until we understand another's pain, we cannot understand our own. We must be transformed as the musician is. The musician, a kind of scapegoat, removes the pain of existence and helps us understand our suffering.

Sonny—the name echoes his strong New Testament scapegoat position—takes the pain away for all those who listen when he plays the blues. But as Baldwin says, Sonny cannot be free unless we listen and we will not be free either until he removes our pain—or until we believe in his ability to remove that suffering; Sonny thus serves to free those who listen as the cup of Gethsemane serves to free those who believe. Sonny's name echoes this special relationship and speaks of him as the ultimate scapegoat.

The brother, then, represents us also as he vividly illustrates our human response to the scapegoat offer. We accept, as understanding and insight come through the music; we change, for the function of the scapegoat is vicarious death. The ancient scapegoat was presented *alive* and allowed to escape; but metaphorically he represented the death of sin and pain for those covered by his action. Metaphysically what happens when we hear, as Sonny knows, is a death of our old understanding or the old ways and a recreation of a new way of being. So finally, at the end, in the image of the Scotch and milk drink, an image so unprepared for as to be startling, we see Sonny's symbolic value as the scapegoat. The transformation occurs as the music plays, because for the musician "What is evoked ... is of another order, more terrible because it has no words, and triumphant, too, for that same reason. And his triumph, when he triumphs, is ours."

Only in music can Sonny truly tell all and fulfill his function as a scapegoat. Only in music can he reach our hearts and minds. Thus the last and clearest presentation of the scapegoat metaphor comes at the end of the story. Here "Sonny's fingers filled the air with life, his life. But that life contained so many others.... It was no longer a lament." This is a clear expression of the scapegoat metaphor. For Sonny's sharing through music transforms the pain. As the narrator says, "Freedom lurked around us and I understood at last that he could help us be free if we would listen, that he would never be free until we did." This freedom is the Black's escape, the reader's escape, Sonny's escape. It is the scapegoat metaphor in action, a release for Sonny's brother and for us too. For

Sonny "was giving it back, as everything must be given back, so that, passing through death, it can live forever."

The reversal of the situation at the end is important. The blues which Creole guides Sonny to play are central. For to play the blues one must first have suffered; then one creates the form to hold the pain, a fluid changing style where, according to John Reilly, "One uses the skill one has achieved by practice and experience in order to reach toward others." The narrator expresses it best: "For, while the tale of how we suffer, and how we are delighted, and how we may triumph is never new, it always must be heard. There isn't any other tale to tell, it's the only light we've got in all this darkness."

Sonny's brother indicates that he both understands and symbolically shares Sonny's pain and guilt by sending the Scotch and milk drink. He affirms the religious connection with his comment, "For me, then, as they began to play again [the cup of Scotch and milk] glowed and shook above my brother's head like the very cup of trembling." The drink of Scotch and milk develops the image of Sonny as sinner and savior, the God/man, the scapegoat, the unlikely mixture which saves. This image conveys Sonny's complex purpose and suggests, on an earthly level, that Sonny's pain will continue, but his pain is shared and understood by his brother. On the second level it suggests that as God took away the pain for Israel, and as Christ takes away the pain and sin of the world for the believer, so does Sonny, the scapegoat, take away pain and guilt for his brother, for the listeners, and for us. As Keith Byerman said [in *Studies in Short Fiction*], "The drink itself, Scotch and milk, is an emblem of simultaneous destruction and nurture to the system; it cannot be reduced to one or the other. Sonny's acceptance of it indicates that his life will continue on the edge between the poison of his addiction and the nourishment of his music." But Sonny *has* drunk the cup of pain before; now the brother joins in, empathizes, understands. Sonny drinks the Scotch and milk and continues to suffer, but part of his suffering is removed by his brother's understanding. For the brother, the action itself suggests increased understanding and a sharing of Sonny's pain.

The brother's final comment about the 'cup of trembling' emphasizes the narrator's understanding and reinterprets the image, making Sonny a true scapegoat for the reader and enlarging our vision as well. Only with the last image do we reflect on the biblical imagery, seeing Sonny's linkage to Aaron and to Christ. Then we concentrate on Sonny's name; he is transformed before our very eyes and we see in his ceremonial acceptance of the drink his function as a scapegoat, a substitute for all.

**Source:** Patricia R. Robertson, "Baldwin's 'Sonny's Blues': The Scapegoat Metaphor," in *The University of Mississippi Studies in English,* Vol. IX, 1991, pp. 189-96.

## Suzy Bernstein Goldman

*In the following essay, Goldman discusses the musicality of "Sonny's Blues," particularly the influence of jazz music, and how the form of the story echoes that of a longer musical work.*

In "Sonny's Blues" theme, form, and image blend into perfect harmony and rise to a thundering crescendo. The story, written in 1957 but carrying a vital social message for us today, tells of two black brothers' struggle to understand one another. The older brother, a straight-laced Harlem algebra teacher, is the unnamed narrator who represents, in his anonymity, everyman's brother; the younger man is Sonny, a jazz pianist who, when the story opens, has just been arrested for peddling and using heroin. As in so much of Baldwin's fiction, chronological time is upset. Instead the subject creates its own form. Musical terms along with words like "hear" and "listen" give the title a double meaning. This story about communication between people then reaches its climax when the narrator finally hears his brother's sorrow in his music, hears, that is, Sonny's blues.

The story begins when the narrator learns of Sonny's arrest in a most impersonal manner—by reading the newspaper. Yet this rude discovery sounds the initial note in these two brothers' growing closeness. The shock of recognition forces the narrator to confront his past refusal to accept the miserable truths around him. For too long, he admits, he had been "talking about algebra to a lot of boys who might, every one of them . . . be popping off needles every time they went to the head." He completes his own first lesson in understanding and takes his first step towards Sonny when he begins to hear his own students:

> I listened to the boys outside. . . . Their laughter struck me for perhaps the first time. It was not the joyous laughter which . . . one associates with children. It was mocking and insular, its intent to denigrate. It was disenchanted, and in this, also, lay the authority of their curses. Perhaps I was listening to them because I was thinking about my brother and in them I heard my brother. And myself.

> "In this story of a musician, four time sequences mark four movements while the leitmotifs of this symphonic lesson in communication are provided by the images of sound."

> One boy was whistling a tune, at once very complicated and very simple, it seemed to be pouring out of him as though he were a bird, and it sounded very cool and moving through that harsh, bright air, only just holding its own through all those other sounds.

This last boy particularly suggests Sonny, the young man who makes himself heard and transcends the disenchantment, the darkness, with his song. Then immediately the narrator encounters another surrogate brother in Sonny's old friend who has come to the school to bring the news. Conversation between the two is guarded and hostile until the narrator, although he has never liked his brother's friend, begins to hear the boy and to feel guilty for never having heard him before, "for never having supposed that the poor bastard had a story of his own, much less a sad one." Standing together outside a bar while a juke box sounds from within, the friend confesses that he first described to Sonny the effects of heroin. Again the narrator psychologically retreats. Fearful of learning about heroin and too anxious himself to help Sonny, he timidly asks what the arrest means. The friend's reply is telling. "Listen," he shouts. "They'll let him out and then it'll just start all over again. That's what I mean." The two part after the friend, pretending to have left all his money home, plays upon the narrator's guilt and basic kindness to the tune of five dollars. Thus the first movement ends.

The second movement opens with the narrator's first letter to Sonny. Sonny's answer, equating drug addiction with prison and both with Harlem, shows his need to reach his brother. Finally the two men have begun to communicate with one another. The letters continue until Sonny's return to New York when the narrator, who has started at last "to wonder about Sonny, about the life that Sonny lived inside," takes him home. The narrator is awkward here, wanting only to hear that Sonny is safe and refusing to accept the fact that he might not be. He is still unwilling to see Sonny on Sonny's terms; like an overly anxious parent he must make Sonny conform to his own concepts of respectability.

The word "safe" is the note that takes us into the third movement, to time past when Sonny's father claimed there was "no place safe." In the flashbacks the narrator recalls events that fuse past, present, and future. Parallels are drawn between the father and Sonny, between the Harlem of one generation and the Harlem of the other. Images of darkness mingle with those of sound. For each generation, however, the tragedy is new, for the older people are reluctant to inform the young ones of the condition of the Black race. The old folks who sit in the dark quit talking, because if the child "knows too much about what's happened to *them*, he'll know too much too soon about what's going to happen to him." Thus even in the past, silence was preferable to expression.

We learn also of another pair of brothers, Sonny's father and uncle. The uncle, like Sonny, was a musician, but he got killed one night when some drunk white men ran him over in their car. The narrator's mother tells her older son this story to make him look after his brother, but her death, occurring shortly after this conversation, only shows the immeasurable gulf between the two boys. The narrator, recently married, thinks he is taking care of Sonny by forcing him to live with his wife's family, but Sonny, already on drugs though unable to admit it, could not want anything less. Their failure to communicate is at its peak. When Sonny announces his ambition "to play jazz," the appalled narrator is totally unresponsive. The most he can promise is to buy Charlie Parker's records, although Sonny insists he doesn't care what his brother listens to. Certainly he doesn't listen to Sonny, urging him only to be respectable and stay in school:

> "You only got another year. . . . Just try to put up with it till I come back. Will you please do that? For me?"
>
> He didn't answer and he wouldn't look at me.
>
> "Sonny, you hear me?"
>
> He pulled away. "I hear you. But you never hear anything I say."

The narrator, though he didn't know what to say to that, reminds Sonny of the piano at his in-laws, and Sonny gives in. Later we learn of Sonny's obsession with the piano. Because he has no one to communicate with, the piano becomes his only source of expression:

> As soon as he came in ..., until suppertime. And, after supper, he went back to that piano and stayed there until everybody went to bed. He was at the piano all day Saturday and all day Sunday....
>
> Isabel finally confessed that it wasn't like living with a person at all, it was like living with sound. And the sound didn't make any sense to her, didn't make any sense to any of them—naturally.... He moved in an atmosphere which wasn't like theirs at all.... There wasn't any way to reach him....
>
> They dimly sensed, as I sensed, ... that Sonny was at that piano playing for his life.

They succeed in reaching him, however, when they discover he has not been in school but in a white girl's Greenwich Village apartment playing music. After that Sonny enlists. When he returns, a man, although the narrator "wasn't willing to see it," the brothers fight, for to the narrator Sonny's "music seemed to be merely an excuse for the life he led. It sounded just that weird and disordered." At this point they cut off all contact.

The fourth movement begins by recapitulating and developing the first. "I read about Sonny's troubles in the spring. Little Grace died in the fall." We move through time easily now, perceiving the connection between the narrator's first letter to Sonny and his daughter's death: "My trouble made his real." He has begun, finally, to sympathize, to understand.

The last movement then begins its own theme, the new relationship between the brothers. A subtly presented but major change in this relationship occurs when they watch a street revival meeting:

> The revival was being carried on by three sisters in black, and a brother. All they had were their voices and their Bibles and a tambourine....
>
> *"Tis the old ship of Zion,"* they sang.... Not a soul under the sound of their voices was hearing this song for the first time, not one of them had been rescued.... The woman with the tambourine, whose voice dominated the air, whose face was bright with joy, was divided by very little from the woman who stood watching her, a cigarette between her heavy, chapped lips, her hair a cuckoo's nest, her face scarred and swollen from many beatings, and her black eyes glittering like coal. Perhaps they both knew this, which was why, when, as rarely, they addressed each other, they addressed each other as Sister.

There is a greater brotherhood among people than mere kinship. Moreover, the narrator realizes that their music saves them, for it "seemed to soothe a poison out of them." The narrator's simultaneous recognition of the meaning of brotherhood and the power of music leads directly to Sonny's invitation. He asks his brother to listen, that night, to his own music. That street song is thus a prelude to the brothers' first honest talk and carries us to the finale when Sonny plays for the narrator.

Sonny now tells his brother that the woman's voice reminded him "of what heroin feels like." This equation of music and drugs, recalling the narrator's discussion with Sonny's friend outside a bar, explains why the one could be a positive alternative to the other. We better understand Sonny's desperate commitment to the piano. Sonny is "doing his best to talk," and the narrator knows that he should "listen." He realizes the profundity of Sonny's suffering now and sees also his own part in it: "There stood between us, forever, beyond the power of time or forgiveness, the fact that I had held silence—so long!—when he had needed human speech to help him."

The narrator's epiphany allows Sonny to continue, and he makes explicit now the connection between music and his own need to be heard:

> There's not really a living ass to talk to, ... and there's no way of getting it out—that storm inside. You can't talk it and you can't make love with it, and when you finally try to get with it and play it, you realize *nobody's* listening. So *you've* got to listen. You got to find a way to listen.

Playing his own song, Sonny finds a way to listen, though he confesses that heroin sometimes helped him release the storm. Now he wants his brother to hear the storm too.

And he finally does. When Sonny, his voice barely audible, says of heroin "It can come again," the brother replies, "All right ... so it can come again. All right." For that first true acceptance of himself, Sonny tells the narrator, "You're my brother."

The finale brings our two themes of interpersonal communication and music together. Baldwin arranges a discussion between the musicians and their instruments using the language of ordinary conversation. Creole, the leader of the group, is guiding Sonny as they begin to play. "He was listening to Sonny. He was having a dialogue with Sonny." Then they work towards the climax:

> The dry, low, black man said something awful on the drums, Creole answered, and the drums talked back. Then the horn insisted, ... and Creole listened, commenting now and then.... Then they all came together again, and Sonny was part of the family again....
>
> Creole began to tell us what the blues were all about.... He and his boys up there were keeping it new, at the risk of ruin, destruction, madness, and death, in order to find new ways to make us listen. For,

while the tale of how we suffer, and how we are delighted, and how we may triumph is never new, it always must be heard. There isn't any other tale to tell, it's the only light we've got in all this darkness.

Finally Creole steps back to let Sonny speak for himself:

> Listen, Creole seemed to be saying, listen. Now these are Sonny's blues....
>
> Sonny's fingers filled the air with life, his life.... Sonny ... really began with the spare, flat statement of the opening phrase of the song.... I understood, at last, that he could help us to be free if we would listen, that he would never be free until we did.

Sonny's music stirs special memories in the brothers' lives, but these blues belong to all of us, for they symbolize the darkness which surrounds all those who fail to listen to and remain unheard by their fellow men.

**Source:** Suzy Bernstein Goldman, "James Baldwin's 'Sonny's Blues': A Message in Music," in *Negro American Literature Forum,* Vol. 8, no. 3, Fall, 1974, pp. 231-3.

## Sources

Bigsby, C.W.E. Introduction to *The Black American Writer,* Vol. 1, Everett/Edwards, Inc., 1969.

Howe, Irving. "Black Boys and Native Sons," in *Dissent,* Autumn, 1963.

Macebuh, Stanley. *James Baldwin: A Critical Study,* Third Press, 1973.

Pratt, Louis H. *Twayne's U.S. Authors Series: James Baldwin,* G.K. Hall & Co., 1978.

Reilly, John M. "'Sonny's Blues': James Baldwin's Image of Black Community," in *James Baldwin: A Collection of Critical Essays,* edited by Keith Kinnamon, Prentice-Hall, 1974.

## Further Reading

Albert, Richard N. "The Jazz-Blues Motif in Baldwin's 'Sonny's Blues'," in *College Literature,* Spring, 1984, pp. 178-85.
> This article discusses the use that Baldwin makes of music in "Sonny's Blues," and explains the role that jazz and blues play in the African-American tradition.

Bone, Robert A. *The Negro Novel in America* Yale University Press, 1958.
> A classic, if somewhat dated, historical evaluation of the place of the novel in the African-American literary tradition and the place of African-American novels in American literary history. A "Postscript" concentrates specifically on James Baldwin.

Hakutani, Yoshinobu, and Robert Butler. *The City in African-American Literature,* Farleigh Dickinson University Press, 1995.
> Containing two essays specifically about James Baldwin, this collection traces the use of the image of the city in African-American literature from Frederick Douglass to the present day. One of the Baldwin essays, by Fred L. Standley, holds that Baldwin viewed the city as far superior to the countryside, and discusses Baldwin's trips to the South.

O'Daniel, Therman B., editor. *James Baldwin: A Critical Evaluation,* Howard University Press, 1977.
> O'Daniel has compiled the works of others that provide an assessment of Baldwin as an essayist, playwright, and fiction writer. It deals extensively with Baldwin's principal works and less with his short stories.

# The Story of an Hour

**Kate Chopin**
**1894**

Although Kate Chopin is regarded as an important writer today, her reputation has not always been so strong. Known primarily as a Southern regionalist writer, or "local colorist" during her lifetime, Chopin's stories and novels shocked many of her nineteenth-century readers. In the 1960s, with the rise of the feminist movement, critics rediscovered Chopin. "The Story of an Hour," first published in 1894 in *Vogue* magazine, is one of Chopin's briefest and most widely read stories. Louise Mallard's response to the news that her husband has been killed and her demise upon his appearance, exemplifies Chopin's beliefs regarding women's roles in marriage and feminine identity. The story was initially rejected by *Century* magazine, and by *Vogue* as well, and it was published only after Chopin's collection *Bayou Folk* garnered critical acclaim.

## Author Biography

Kate Chopin was born in St. Louis in 1851. Her parents, Thomas and Eliza O'Flaherty, were wealthy, slave-owning Catholics who held a prominent position in their community. When Chopin was four, her father died in a train accident, and she was raised by her French-Creole mother and great-grandmother. At seventeen, she graduated from the Academy of the Sacred Heart. Two years later, in 1870, she married Oscar Chopin, a Louisiana busi-

nessman of French-Creole descent. In New Orleans, where she and her husband lived until 1879, Chopin was at the center of Southern aristocratic social life. During this period, she bore six children. In 1879, when Oscar's business failed, the family moved to Cloutierville, where Oscar's family owned a farm and a plantation store. When Oscar died in 1882, Chopin was left with six children and meager financial resources. The family moved back to St. Louis in 1884.

At the age of thirty-nine, Chopin began writing poetry and fiction. Her early short stories were published in magazines in St. Louis and New Orleans, and were influenced by writers such as Guy de Maupassant and Moliere. Most of her stories are set in Louisiana, and they portray characters as diverse as Southern belles, Arcadians and Creoles, mulattos and blacks. The stories center around the themes of class relations, relationships between men and women, and feminine sexuality. In the 1890s, Chopin began receiving national attention for her fiction. She published *Bayou Folk* in 1894, and *A Night in Acadie,* which contains her often anthologized short story "The Story of an Hour," in 1897. The success of these two collections made Chopin financially independent and nationally known as a major author. In 1899, Chopin published *The Awakening,* now regarded as her masterpiece. The novel's frank treatment of an independent woman who, after an extramarital affair and a sexual "awakening," commits suicide rather than conform to society's mores, provoked outrage among readers and critics. The novel was banned in St. Louis and elsewhere. As a result of the hostile reception to the novel and difficulties with publishers, Chopin wrote very little at the end of her life. Five years after the publication of *The Awakening,* Chopin died of a stroke in St. Louis on August 22, 1904.

## Plot Summary

Chopin's "The Story of an Hour" is the story of an hour in the life of Mrs. Louise Mallard, a young woman whose wrinkles portray "repression" and "strength." As the story begins, the narrator reveals that Mrs. Mallard has "heart trouble." Her sister Josephine and her husband's friend Richards have come to her after hearing of a railroad disaster that has resulted in the death of Mr. Mallard. Both are concerned that the news will make Mrs. Mallard ill and Josephine takes great care to tell her the news as cautiously as she is able.

Mrs. Mallard reacts to the news with "sudden, wild abandonment" and locks herself in her bedroom. In the solitude of her room Mrs. Mallard understands the fundamental change taking place in her life. She sits in a chair, no longer crying, looking out the window at the "new spring life." She "suspend[s] intelligent thought" and fearfully waits for a "subtle and elusive" idea to "possess her." She begins to comprehend that she is joyful that her husband is dead, but she attempts to suppress the thought.

Once Mrs. Mallard accepts the feeling, even though she knows that her husband had really loved her, she is ecstatic that she will never have to bend her will to his again. Now that her husband is dead, she will be free to assert herself in ways she never before dreamed while he was alive. She recognizes that she had loved her husband sometimes, but that now she would be "Free! Body and soul free!" She begins to look forward to the rest of her life when just the day before she shuddered at the thought of it.

Mrs. Mallard leaves her room and rejoins her sister who has been outside the door worrying. She carries herself "like a goddess of Victory" as she joins her sister to return downstairs where Richards still waits. On their way down the stairs, they hear the front door open and see Mr. Mallard walk in. He had been no where near the accident scene. The short story ends with the abrupt death of Mrs. Mallard, whose heart gives out. Her doctors explain that she died "of joy that kills."

## Characters

### Josephine

Josephine is Mrs. Mallard's sister. It is Josephine who tells Mrs. Mallard of her husband's death and who implores Louise to let her into the room after she has shut herself inside. Josephine, a woman who embodies the feminine ideal, assumes that Louise is suffering terribly from the news, not knowing that her sister is actually overjoyed with the prospect of being a widow.

### Louise

*See* Mrs. Mallard

### Brently Mallard

Brently Mallard, Mrs. Mallard's husband, is assumed dead after a railroad disaster. When he reappears at the front door, the shock causes Mrs. Mallard's death.

### Mrs. Mallard

In the beginning of the story Mrs. Mallard is known simply by her married name. A wife who suffers from "heart trouble," she is described as "young, with a fair, calm face, whose lines bespoke repression and even a certain strength." When Mrs. Mallard learns of her husband's death, she becomes "Louise," a woman aware of her own desires, enjoying the prospect of being freed from the confines of marriage. Louise dies of a "joy that kills" when her husband reappears. Her character represents feminine individuality; she is a strong-willed, independent woman excited by the prospect of beginning her life again after the reported demise of her husband.

*Kate Chopin*

## Themes

### Identity and Selfhood

Chopin deals with the issues of female self-discovery and identity in "The Story of an Hour." After Mrs. Mallard learns of her husband's death, she is initially overcome with grief. But quickly she begins to feel a previously unknown sense of freedom and relief. At first, she is frightened of her own awakening: "There was something coming to her and she was waiting for it, fearfully." Her own feelings come upon her, possessing her. When she first utters the words "free, free, free!" she is described as having "abandoned herself." But after she speaks these words, she relaxes and gains more control over herself. As she imagines life without her husband, she embraces visions of the future. She realizes that whether or not she had loved him was less important than "this possession of self-assertion" she now feels. The happiness Louise gains by this recognition of selfhood is so strong that, when she realizes that her husband is in fact alive, she immediately collapses. Chopin suggests that Louise could not bear to abandon her newfound freedom and return to life with her husband, where she would be required to bend her will to his.

### Role of Women in Marriage

Intimately connected with the theme of identity and selfhood is the theme of the role of women in marriage. Mrs. Mallard is known in the beginning of the story only as a wife; very little is revealed concerning Mr. and Mrs. Mallard's relationship. Even Louise is unsure whether or not they had been happily married: "And yet she had loved him—sometimes. Often she had not. What did it matter!" Thus, the specifics of the relationship matter less than the conventions of marriage in general. Louise is ecstatic when she realizes that "there would be no powerful will bending hers in that blind persistence with which men and women believe they have a right to impose a private will upon a fellow-creature." Whether one is acting out of love or not,

## Media Adaptations

- "The Story of an Hour," was adapted in 1985 into a 56-minute long video, *Kate Chopin: The Joy That Kills,* available through Films for the Humanities & Sciences.
- An audio cassette of "The Story of an Hour," is available through Books in Motion (1992).

Chopin seems to be making a comment on nineteenth-century marriages, which granted one person—the man—right to own and dominate another—the woman. This theme, unpopular in an era when women were not even allowed to vote, is examined in many of Chopin's other works, most notably *The Awakening*.

## Style

The action of "The Story of an Hour" is simple: Mrs. Mallard, who suffers from "a heart trouble," is informed about her husband's demise in a train accident. At first she is beset by grief, but then she begins to feel a sense of freedom. When she leaves her room and descends the stairs, her husband appears at the front door. Upon seeing her husband alive, Louise Mallard's heart gives out and she dies.

### Point of View

The story is told from a detached, third-person limited point of view. The reader identifies with Louise, the only character whose thoughts are accessible. At the beginning of the story, Louise is incapable of reflecting on her own experience. As Louise becomes conscious of her situation and emotions, the reader gains access to her thinking which reveals her character. When she goes back downstairs, the reader is quickly cut off from her thoughts. Thus Chopin skillfully manipulates the narrative point of view to underscore the story's theme.

### Setting

The setting of "The Story of an Hour" is unspecified. It takes place in the Mallard's house, but Chopin does not offer many clues as to where or when the action takes place. This generic setting is consistent with the story's thematic focus on the general, commonly accepted views of the appropriate roles for women in society. Given Chopin's other works and the concerns she expresses about women's role in marriage in this story and in other writings, the reader can assume that the story takes place during Chopin's lifetime, the late nineteenth century. However, Chopin was known for being a local colorist, a writer who focuses on a particular people in a particular locale. In Chopin's case, her stories are usually set among the Cajun and Creole societies in Louisiana. For this reason, "The Story of an Hour" is usually assumed to take place in Louisiana.

### Irony

Chopin uses irony, a technique that reveals the distance between what appears to be true and what is actually true, to conclude her story. In "The Story of an Hour," there is incongruity between what is understood to be true by the characters within the drama and what is understood by the reader. What killed Mrs. Mallard? While Brently Mallard, Richards, Josephine, and the doctors might believe her weak heart gave out upon such sudden happiness, readers are led to suspect that sudden grief killed her. At the story's conclusion, the story's first line, "Knowing that Mrs. Mallard was afflicted with a heart trouble," becomes ironic—referring to Mrs. Mallard's spiritual condition and not to a medical condition. The story's concluding line, she died "from the joy that kills," is also ironic.

### Symbolism

The story is set during spring, and Louise's "awakening" is symbolized by the rebirth of nature. Through her bedroom window, Louise sees nature, like herself, "all acquiver with the new spring life." The internal changes taking place within Louise are mirrored by what she views—when she is distraught with grief, rain falls, and when she realizes her freedom, the skies clear up. What occurs outside the window parallels what is occurring to Louise.

## Historical Context

### The Woman Question

"The Story of an Hour" was published in 1894, an era in which many social and cultural questions occupied Americans' minds. One of these, referred to as the "Woman Question," involved which roles were acceptable for women to assume in society. Charles Darwin's *The Origin of Species* (1892) had further incited this controversy. Darwin's theory of evolution was used by both sides of the issue; some argued the theory supported female self-assertion and independence, others felt the theory proved that motherhood should be the primary role of a woman in society.

Although women were not granted the right to vote until 1920, the struggle for their enfranchisement began in 1848 with the Seneca Falls Convention in New York state. The passage of the 15th Amendment to the United States Constitution, granting enfranchisement to black men, was passed in 1869. Several prominent feminists, including Elizabeth Cady Stanton and Susan B. Anthony, refused to support the amendment because it denied women the vote. Other suffragists argued that the enfranchisement of women would soon follow black enfranchisement. In 1890, these two factions united in the National American Woman Suffrage Association (NAWSA). That year, Wyoming became the first state to grant women the vote. While the suffrage movement sought reform, mainstream Victorian culture regarded the self-sacrificing wife, dependent on her husband and devoted to her children, as the ideal of femininity.

## Critical Overview

A popular writer during her lifetime, Chopin is best known today for her psychological novel *The Awak-*

## Topics for Further Study

- Research marriage law in the 1890s and compare this to contemporary marriage laws. How has the institution of marriage changed in the last one-hundred years?

- Discuss Mrs. Mallard as a sympathetic character or as a cruel and selfish character. How might your own gender, age, class or ethnicity influence your response?

- Do you think Chopin's critique of the institution of marriage, as expressed by Louise, is applicable today?

- Research the suffrage movement of the late nineteenth century. How do Louise's reflections of her situation in society reflect the concerns of this movement? Which concerns are still issues today?

*ening*. Chopin's depiction of female self-assertion was regarded as immoral. When Chopin submitted "The Story of an Hour" to *Century* magazine, it was rejected. After Chopin's collection of short stories, *Bayou Folk* garnered critical acclaim, *Vogue* published the story. According to Barbara C. Ewell in her book, *Kate Chopin,* the editor of *Century,* R. W. Gilder, rejected the manuscript because of its feminist message. The magazine had been publishing anti-suffragist articles during this period and upheld a vision of women as selfless wives and mothers.

Since the 1960s, with the rise of the feminist movement, Chopin's fiction, including "The Story of an Hour," has been rediscovered and is now acclaimed for precisely the reasons it was denounced during her lifetime. Per Seyersted, in *Kate Chopin: A Critical Biography,* extols the story's "theme of self-assertion." Burt Bender, in his essay "Kate Chopin's Lyrical Short Stories," argues that the story is a "shockingly unorthodox" expression of the inequities of marriage. Other critics, while agreeing that the story is bold and unconventional, quali-

*New Orleans courtyard typical of the era and area in which Chopin lived and many of her stories took place.*

fy the view that Louise becomes an independent, assertive woman during the hour in which the story takes place. In *Verging on the Abyss: The Social Fiction of Kate Chopin and Edith Wharton,* Mary E. Papke considers the darker aspects of Chopin's vision of feminine identity. For Papke, the ending of the story implies that should a woman glimpse herself as an individual and then be denied the chance to live freely, the result will be death, or the dissolution of that new identity. Unless the world changes, Papke argues, Chopin suggests that there is no hope for independent, unconventional women to survive in society.

In addition to her treatment of social issues, "The Story of an Hour" has been heralded for its formal strengths. Chopin's use of irony and ambiguity have been extolled by many critics. Other critics find fault in some of the formal aspects of the story. In an essay published in the *The Markham Review,* Madonne M. Miner analyzes how readers respond to the organization of words in the story. Focusing on Chopin's use of the passive voice, Miner argues that the story's themes of autonomy and identity are undermined by its grammatical structure. For instance, Miner points out that Louise does not possess but is "possessed by" her impulses. Many of the story's key sentences, including the first one, are written in the passive voice. For Miner, although the reader may wish to identify with Louise's possession of self, the language of the story keeps the reader distanced.

## Criticism

### Jennifer Hicks

*Jennifer Hicks is director of the Academic Support and Writing Assessment program at Massachusetts Bay Community College. In the following essay, she discusses the theme of female self-assertion as it relates to "The Story of an Hour."*

In Donald F. Larsson's entry on Kate Chopin in *Critical Survey of Short Fiction,* we learn that "consistently . . . strong-willed, independent heroines . . . [who] cast a skeptical eye on the institution of marriage" are very characteristic of her stories. In "The Story of an Hour," we do not so much see as intuit Mrs. Mallard's skeptical eye. Certainly, we are told of the joy she feels with the freedom she finds in her husband's death, but we are not specifically told that she is skeptical of marriage in general. Indeed, if we take the last line of the story literally, we would understand that Mrs. Mallard was so enamored of her marriage to her husband that she died from the excitement of knowing he was still alive. Yet, obviously, Chopin is engaging in some heavy handed irony. Mrs. Mallard, the young "repressed" woman who began to look at her widowhood as a rebirth, similar to the "new spring" outside her window, did not die from such excitement. She expired from "a heart problem"—an instantaneous knowledge that her momentary glimpse into a "life she would live for herself," a "life that might be long," was not to be.

Some of Chopin's short stories were rejected for publication on moral grounds, for editors perceived in them an unseemly interest in female self-assertion and sexual liberation. Per Seyersted, Chopin's biographer, writes in his introduction to *The Complete Works of Kate Chopin,* Volume 1, that the "reason why editors turned down a number of her stories was very likely that her women became more passionate and emancipated." Given that "The Story of an Hour" was published in 1894, several

# Compare & Contrast

- **1890s:** The suffragist movement unites in the National American Woman Suffrage Association (NAWSA). Wyoming becomes the first state to grant women the vote.

  **Today:** Although efforts to add an Equal Rights Amendment to the United States Constitution failed in 1982, women continue to gain political and cultural independence. As of 1988, over 56 percent of women in the country hold jobs.

- **1890s:** Though there are more women than men attending high school by 1890, higher education is largely closed to women. Employment opportunities for women include housekeeping, nursing, and elementary education.

  **Today:** Opportunities in both education and employment are virtually equal for men and women, although many issues regarding equality remain.

- **1890s:** Though a few women writers have achieved some degree of success, it is still considered improper for a woman to be a writer. Louisa May Alcott and Sarah Orne Jewett are two women writers who gain success and popularity.

  **Today:** Many women writers of the late nineteenth century are being rediscovered, including Chopin, who gained popularity during the women's movement of the 1960s.

---

years after it was written, we can comprehend the importance of moral grounds as a basis for rejection. Marriage was considered a sacred institution. Divorce was quite rare in the 1800s and if one was to occur, men were automatically given legal control of all property and children. Even the constitutional amendments of 1868 and 1870, granting rights of citizenship and voting, gave these rights to African-Americans not women. Women were not granted the right to vote in political elections until 1920. Obviously then, a female writer who wrote of women wanting independence would not be received very highly, especially one who wrote of a woman rejoicing in the death of her husband. The fact that she pays for her elation with her life at the end of the story is not enough to redeem either the character or the author.

Although "The Story of an Hour" is brief, Chopin demonstrates her skills as a writer in several ways. Fred Lewis Pattee says in *A History of American Literature Since 1870,* that the strength of Chopin's work comes from "what may be described as a native aptitude for narration amounting almost to genius." Larsson notes her remarkable ability to "convey character and setting simply yet completely." All of these qualities are evidenced in "The Story of an Hour."

The story opens with the narrator telling us that Mrs. Mallard has "a heart trouble." A quick reading of the phrase might mislead the reader into thinking that Mrs. Mallard, therefore, has heart disease. Yet Chopin chose her phrase with care. She wants her readers to know that Mrs. Mallard has a very specific condition that interferes with the workings of her heart. Later, when we see Mrs. Mallard "warmed and relaxed," we realize that the problem with her heart is that her marriage has not allowed her to "live for herself."

Another instance of Chopin's gift of narration enables the reader to understand that what is being told is more than a tale. This illustration involves Mrs. Mallard's reaction to the news of her husband's death: "She did not hear the story as many women would have heard the same, with a paralyzed inability to accept its significance." If a reader had paused at this sentence, he or she might have wondered what there was in the marriage that would keep Mrs. Mallard from becoming prostrate with grief. The reader might have questioned why

## What Do I Read Next?

- *The Awakening,* Kate Chopin's 1899 novel, tells of Edna Pointellier, a traditional wife and mother who becomes "awakened" to sexual and spiritual independence after an extramarital affair.

- "The Yellow Wallpaper" (1892) by Charlotte Perkins Gilman is the story of a woman who lacks an outlet for her creativity and descends into madness.

- To learn about the suffragette movement and the struggle for women's rights in the late-nineteenth and early-twentieth century, see *Eighty Years and More: Reminiscences* (1992), by the pioneering feminist, Elizabeth Cady Stanton.

- Adrienne Rich's poetry, particularly her collection, *Diving Into the Wreck* (1973), explores feminism, female sexuality and women's roles in society.

---

Mrs. Mallard was not consumed with wondering how she would go on with her life without her husband. Yet, in the very next line we see that she is assuredly grieving as she cries with "wild abandonment." We find ourselves a bit surprised at this point. Surely a woman in a troubled marriage would not carry on in such a manner. In this instant, Chopin has hinted that a problem exists, but also that Mrs. Mallard is not "paralyzed" by the significance that she is alone. Chopin elaborates upon this when the narrator says that Mrs. Mallard "would have no one follow her." While the implication is that she would have no one follow her to her room, the reader wonders in hindsight whether Mrs. Mallard might have meant also that she would have no one interfere with her life again.

It is also easy to come to the same conclusion as Larsson does, that the setting is simple but definitely complete. The breaking of the news takes place in an unspecified room within the Mallard's house. The revelation of freedom occurs in the bedroom, and Mrs. Mallard's demise occurs on the stairway leading to the front door that her husband opened. Chopin gives us no details about the stairway or the room in which we first meet Mrs. Mallard. Although news of death and death itself occur in these areas and are certainly among a few of life's most tragic and momentous events, the setting could be anywhere. Conversely, we are inundated, or overwhelmed, with details in the bedroom where Mrs. Mallard becomes her own person. We see the "comfortable, roomy armchair" in which she sits with "her head thrown back upon the cushion." We see the "tops of trees . . . aquiver with new spring life" that we can hear and smell from her window.

Some critics argue that Chopin wisely tempers the emotional elements inherent in Mrs. Mallard's situation. Although the emotion in Mrs. Mallard's bedroom is indisputable, the "suspension of intelligent thought" removes from the reader the need to share in the widow's grief and instead allows him or her to remain an onlooker, as eager as Mrs. Mallard to see "what was approaching to possess her." Other critics credit Chopin's readings of Charles Darwin and other scientists who prescribed to the "survival of the fittest" theory as the impetus, or driving force, behind her questioning of contemporary mores and the constraints placed upon women. In "The Story of an Hour" Chopin implicitly questions the institution of marriage, perhaps as a by-product or her scientific questioning of mores, but she does so in a cleverly tempered way.

Chopin, fatherless at four, was certainly a product of her Creole heritage, and was strongly influenced by her mother and her maternal grandmother. Perhaps it is because she grew up in a female-dominated environment that she was not a stereotypical product of her times and so could not conform to socially acceptable themes in her writing. Chopin even went so far as to assume the managerial role of her husband's business after he died in 1883. This behavior, in addition to her fascination with scientific principles, her upbringing, and her penchant for feminist characters would seem to indicate that individuality, freedom, and joy were as important to Chopin as they are to the characters in her stories. Yet it appears to be as difficult for critics to agree on Chopin's view of her own life as it is for them to accept the heroines of her stories. Per Seyersted believes that Chopin enjoyed "living alone as an independent writer," but other critics have argued that Chopin was happily married and bore little resemblance to the characters in her stories.

Perhaps Larsson's analysis of Chopin in *Critical Survey of Short Fiction* best sums up the importance of Chopin to present-day readers. He writes: "Her concern with women's place in society and in marriage, her refusal to mix guilt with sexuality, and her narrative stance of sympathetic detachment make her as relevant to modern readers as her marked ability to convey character and setting." It can be inspiring to know that more than a century ago, women were not necessarily so different from what they are today. Certainly, woman have experienced and benefited from many newer technologies and changing attitudes, but, for a woman, finding her way in life can still present temporary difficulties. Chopin's "The Story of an Hour" illustrates many of these issues.

**Source:** Jennifer Hicks, for *Short Stories for Students,* Gale Research, 1997.

## Mary E. Papke

*In the following portion of a chapter from a longer work, Papke interprets "The Story of an Hour" as a story that warns against the consequences of what happens when "the individual changes and not the world."*

.... "The Story of an Hour," for instance, details a very ordinary reality and conscientiously analyzes that moment in a woman's life when the boundaries of the accepted everyday world are suddenly shattered and the process of self-consciousness begins. Louise Mallard, dutiful wife and true woman, is gently told that her husband has been killed in a train accident. Her response is atypical, however, and that is the subject of the story: what Louise thinks and feels as she finds herself thrust into solitude and self-contemplation for the first time.

Louise appears in the opening as the frail, genteel, devoted wife of a prosperous businessman;

> Chopin wants her readers to know that Mrs. Mallard has a very specific condition that interferes with the workings of her heart. Later, when we see Mrs. Mallard 'warmed and relaxed,' we realize that the problem with her heart is that her marriage has not allowed her to 'live for herself.'"

she is at first only named as such: Mrs. Mallard. However, her first response to the tragedy indicates a second Louise nestling within that social shell: "she did not hear the story as many women have heard the same, with a paralyzed inability to accept its significance. She wept at once, with sudden, wild abandonment, in her sister's arms." Chopin thus implies that perhaps some part of Louise readily accepts the news. She also intimates that since Louise unconsciously chooses to enfold herself in a female embrace and not in the arms of the male friend who tells her of Mallard's death, Louise has already turned to a female world, one in which she is central. It is in the mid-section of the story, set in Louise's room, that Louise and Chopin's reader explore and come to understand reaction and potential action, social self—Mrs. Mallard—and private, female self—Louise.

Louise sits before an open window at first thinking nothing but merely letting impressions of the outer and inner worlds wash over her. She is physically and spiritually depleted but is still sensuously receptive. She sees the "new spring life" in budding trees, smells rain, hears human and animal songs as well as a man "crying his wares." She is like both a tired child dreaming a sad dream and a young woman self-restrained but with hidden strengths. She is yet Mrs. Mallard.

As she sits in "a suspension of intelligent thought," she feels something unnameable coming to her through her senses. It is frightening because it is not of her true womanhood world; it reaches to her from the larger world outside and would "possess her." the unnameable is, of course, her self-consciousness that is embraced once she names her experience as emancipation and not destitution: "she said it over and over under her breath: 'free, free, free!' . . . Her pulses beat fast, and the coursing blood warmed and relaxed every inch of her body." It is at this point that she begins to think, the point at which she is reborn through and in her body, an experience analogous to that of Edna Pontellier in *The Awakening*.

Louise then immediately recognizes her two selves and comprehends how each will co-exist, the old finally giving way to the one new self. Mrs. Mallard will grieve for the husband who had loved her, but Louise will eventually revel in the "monstrous joy" of self-fulfillment, beyond ideological strictures and the repressive effects of love:

> she would live for herself. There would be no powerful will bending hers in that blind persistence with which men and women believe they have a right to impose a private will upon a fellow-creature. A kind intention or a cruel intention made the act seem no less a crime as she looked upon it in that brief moment of illumination.
>
> And yet she had loved him—sometimes. Often she had not. What did it matter! What could love, the unsolved mystery, count for in face of this possession of self-assertion which she suddenly recognized as the strongest impulse of her being!

It is only after Louise embraces this new consciousness, her sense of personal and spiritual freedom in a new world, that she is named as female self by her sister. This is no doubt ironic since her sister only unconsciously recognizes her; she can have little idea of the revolution that has taken place in Louise's own room. Yet Chopin does not allow simple utopian endings, and Louise's sister's intrusion into Louise's world also prefigures the abrupt end to her "drinking in a very elixir of life through that open window."

Louise leaves her room and descends again into her past world. Though she carries herself "like a goddess of Victory" and has transcended the boundaries of her past self, she is not armed for the lethal intrusion of the past world through her front door. Brently Mallard unlocks his door and enters unharmed. His return from the dead kills Louise, and Chopin's conclusion is the critical and caustic remark that all believed "she had died of heart disease—of joy that kills."

It is easy for the reader to be overwhelmed by the pathos of the story, a natural response since the reader comes to consciousness of the text just as Louise awakens to self-consciousness. Chopin offers the reader only that one point of identification—Louise, whose powers of reflection have been repressed, suddenly shocked into being, and then brutally cut off. It is a disorienting reading experience to be cut off as well after being awakened to Louise's new self-possibilities. It is also beyond irony to be left at the conclusion with the knowledge that only Louise and the reader perceived the earlier "death" of the true woman Mrs. Mallard; and that what murdered her was, indeed, a monstrous joy, the birth of individual self, and the erasure of that joy when her husband and, necessarily, her old self returned. Far from being a melodramatic ending, the conclusion both informs and warns: should a woman see the real world and her individual self within it only to be denied the right to live out that vision, then in her way lies non-sense, self-division, and dissolution. Chopin's analysis of womanhood ideology and quest for self here takes on a darker hue. Her earlier stories examined the destruction of women who lived within traditional society; this piece offers no escape for those who live outside that world but who do so only in a private world in themselves. Either way, Chopin seems to be saying, there lies self-oblivion if only the individual changes and not the world. . . .

**Source:** Mary E. Papke, "Kate Chopin's Social Fiction," in *Verging on the Abyss,* Greenwood Press, 1990, pp. 62–4.

### Barbara C. Ewell

*In the following excerpt, Ewell analyzes "The Story of an Hour," noting in particular the dramatic tension caused by the shift in point of view towards the end of the story.*

. . . . "The Story of an Hour" recounts Louise Mallard's unexpected response to the reported death of her husband, Brently, in a train accident. Grieving alone in her room, she slowly recognizes that she has lost only chains: "'Free! Body and soul free!' she kept whispering." Then when her husband suddenly reappears, the report of his death a mistake, she drops dead at the sight of him—of "heart disease," the doctors announce, "of joy that kills."

Chopin's handling of details illustrates how subtly she manages this controversial material. Louise Mallard's heart disease, for example, the key to the final ironies and ambiguities, is introduced in the first sentence, like the loaded gun of melodrama.

But her illness gradually deepens in significance from a physical detail—a symptom of delicacy and a reason to break the bad news gently—to a deeply spiritual problem. The more we learn about Brently Mallard's overbearing nature and the greater his wife's relief grows, the better we understand her "heart trouble." Indeed, that "trouble" vanishes with Brently's death and returns—fatally—only when he reappears.

But Chopin also exposes Louise's complicity in Mallard's subtle oppression. Her submission to his "blind persistence" has been the guise of Love, that self-sacrificing Victorian ideal. Glorified in fiction Chopin had often decried, this love has been, for Louise and others, the primary purpose of life. But through her new perspective, she comprehends that "love, the unsolved mystery" counts for very little "in face of this possession of self-assertion which she suddenly recognized as the strongest impulse of her being!" As Chopin often insists, love is not a substitute for selfhood; indeed, selfhood is love's pre-condition. Such a strong and unconventional assertion of feminine independence likely explains *Century's* rejection. Its editor, R. W. Gilder, had zealously guarded the feminine ideal of self-denying love, and was that very summer publishing editorials against women's suffrage as a threat to family and home.

The setting, too, reflecting Chopin's local-color lessons, buttresses her themes. Louise stares through an "open window" at a scene which is "all aquiver with the new spring life." A renewing rain accompanies her "storm of grief," followed by "patches of blue sky." Then, explicitly "through the sounds, the scents, the color that filled the air," "it" comes "creeping out of the sky" upon her. Louise at first dutifully resists and then helplessly succumbs. The sense of physical, even sexual, release that accompanies her acquiescence to this nameless "thing" underpins a vision of freedom that Chopin characteristically affirms as a human right—as natural as generation, spring, or even death.

The transforming power of that insight is echoed in Louise's altered view of the future, whose length "only yesterday" she had dreaded, but to which she now "opened and spread her arms ... in welcome." But it is a false vision. The habit of repression has so weakened Louise that her glimpse of freedom—her birthright—does not empower her, but leaves her unable to cope with the everyday reality to which she is abruptly restored. In her conventional marriage, the vision is truly illusory.

> It is only after Louise embraces this new consciousness, her sense of personal and spiritual freedom in a new world, that she is named as female self by her sister. This is no doubt ironic since her sister only unconsciously recognizes her; she can have little idea of the revolution that has taken place in Louise's own room."

Chopin skillfully manipulates the point of view to intensify the final revelation and the shifting perspectives on Louise's life. "Mrs. Mallard" appears to us at first from a distance; but the focus gradually internalizes, until we are confined within her thoughts, struggling with "Louise" toward insight. As she leaves the private room of her inner self, our point of view retreats; we see her "like a goddess of Victory" as she descends the stairs, and then, as the door opens, we are identified with the unsuspecting Brently, sharing his amazement at his sister-in-law's outcry and his friend's futile effort to block his wife's view. The final sentence, giving the doctors' clinical interpretation of her death, is still more distant. That distance—and the shift it represents—is crucial. To outsiders, Louise Mallard's demise is as misunderstood as is her reaction to Brently's death. That even the respected medical profession misinterprets her collapse indicts the conventional view of female devotion and suggests that Louise Mallard is not the only woman whose behavior has been misread. . . .

**Source:** Barbara C. Ewell, "'A Night in Acadie': The Confidence of Success," in *Kate Chopin,* Ungar Publishing, 1986, pp. 88–91.

## Madonne M. Miner

*In the following scholarly essay, Miner interprets "The Story of an Hour" from the viewpoint of*

> "'Mrs. Mallard' appears to us at first from a distance; but the focus gradually internalizes, until we are confined within her thoughts, struggling with 'Louise' toward insight."

*an affective stylist—one who is concerned with the specific meanings and pairings of words for effect.*

.... "The Story of an Hour" is built around the "expression of a woman's shockingly unorthodox feelings about her marriage"; so says Bert Bender, in an essay devoted to Chopin's short fiction. Similarly, Per Seyersted calls the story "an extreme example of the theme of self-assertion." Although both critics display considerable perception and insight, neither adequately accounts for the actual effect of the story. As we move through this short story, one element in our experience certainly points to self-assertion, encouraging us to hope for it in ourselves and Louise Mallard both. But the text also undermines, with its qualifications and negatives, all possibility for the fulfillment of this hope. In contrast to the thematic movement toward self-assertion, affective stylistics reveals a more subtle movement, in the reader, toward doubt. Chopin stimulates a sense that something, a vague something, is askew. Upon close analysis, word-by-word and sentence-by-sentence, a reader finds that Chopin denies her reader information about those figures who instigate or are responsible for action in the story. Further, as she manipulates grammatical structures and conventions, Chopin thwarts the reader's expectations and confidence.

The plot of "The Story of an Hour" may be summarized quite simply. After hearing of her husband's death, Louise Mallard leaves her sister Josephine and her husband's friend Richards for the solitude of her upstairs bedroom. Josephine and Richards allow her to go, assuming that she needs time alone to vent her grief. As Louise contemplates the fact of Brently Mallard's death, however, her grief gives way to a far more powerful feeling—a feeling of joy in her own freedom. Louise realizes that she will feel sad when she sees Brently's "kind, tender hands folded in death," but she also realizes that for the first time in years she actually wants to live. While Louise is intoxicated with this new-found joy, Josephine, who fears that Louise might harm herself in her anguish over Brently's death, implores her to leave the locked room and come downstairs. As the two women descend the staircase, Brently Mallard walks in the front door. Chopin comments, "he had been far from the scene of accident, and did not even know there had been one." Upon seeing her husband, Louise suffers a heart attack and dies. This simple surface action belies the complexities of the prose style.

The first sentence of "The Story of an Hour" reads: "Knowing that Mrs. Mallard was afflicted with a heart trouble, great care was taken to break to her as gently as possible the news of her husband's death." If we approach this sentence merely as factual communique, we might say that it conveys three messages: Mrs. Mallard suffers from a heart trouble; Mrs. Mallard's husband has died; someone has taken great care to inform Mrs. Mallard of her husband's death. If, however, we analyze the way in which we proceed through the sentence, we discover a more complex layer of meaning. The first word of the sentence, *knowing,* introduces a participial phrase. A reader expects, and grammatical usage requires, that a primary position participle modify the subject of the subsequent independent clause. Chopin violates our expectations. As we move through the participial phrase and into the independent clause, we expect to be told *who* knows that Mrs. Mallard suffers from a heart condition, but Chopin's passive construction—"great care was taken"—denies us this knowledge. The agent remains unidentified. This denial is the first and perhaps most powerful instance of Chopin's manipulation of sentence structure in order to withhold information about an agent. In this instance, although we know what the sentence says, we cannot be positive about what it means. We must wonder why the author refuses to divulge the agent of an action after she has structured her sentence to anticipate this information.

The reader's experience of the first sentence actually opposes the surface communication of its main clause: "great care was taken to break the news to Mrs. Mallard." This clause suggests that the situation is under control, but Chopin's ungrammatical construction hints at just the opposite: our experience generates a very vague feeling that despite "great care," something is amiss. We are as ignorant about the source of our feeling as we are about the agent of the first sentence, and our ignorance fosters a skepticism that further colors our reading. As a result, we may question yet another small deviation from common usage within the first sentence: why does Chopin choose to modify Mrs. Mallard's heart trouble with the indefinite article *a*? The more usual construction would be simply, "Mrs. Mallard was afflicted with heart trouble." The indefinite article implies that Mrs. Mallard suffers from a particular kind of heart trouble, and yet, because we are not told *which* kind, our desire for more knowledge is frustrated at the same time that we learn that this information does exist. The prose style thus withholds information and undermines our confidence as readers, and so we enter Chopin's story with some hesitation, some trepidation.

The second paragraph opens by identifying the agent who eluded us in the first: "It was her sister Josephine who told her, in broken sentences, veiled hints that revealed in half concealing." This identification is qualified, however, by Chopin's cool reportorial tone and the construction "it was," a topicalized construction that simultaneously focuses upon the agent and *objectifies* her. As focus of the sentence, Josephine *should* be its grammatical subject; instead, she suffers relegation to the subordinate clause. Thus, although we are told who instigated an action, this agent's power diminishes. The meaningless "it was" assumes priority. Chopin chose not to use the simpler "Josephine told her," apparently because this more direct construction does not hint at the uncertainty that the more distanced phrasing allows. In her description of Josephine's broken sentences, Chopin pinpoints the source of the uncertainty that the reader experiences while progressing through the story: "veiled hints that revealed in half concealing." We are meant to infer that Josephine intentionally obscures the details of Brently's death in order to spare Louise pain, but another inference is possible: Josephine's hints are "veiled" and "half concealing" because, without knowing it herself, Josephine delivers information that is not wholly true. Although Chopin identifies the agent in this sentence ("It was Josephine") the sentence as a whole undermines the competence of that agent. Thus, within the first two paragraphs of "The Story of an Hour," we are confronted with two instances in which matter and manner conflict. Neither of these instances is blatant, but a reader informed by affective stylistics cannot help but feel that he experiences something unusual here, and something that bodes ill.

The next two sentences in the second paragraph do nothing to alleviate these sensations. "Her husband's friend Richards was there, too, near her. It was he who had been in the newspaper office when intelligence of the railroad disaster was received, with Brently Mallard's name leading the list of 'killed'." This sentence also appears straightforward: we are told *who* Richards is ("her husband's friend") as well as *where* he is ("there near her"); and these simple statements of fact reassure the reader. The reassurance is, however, only momentary. The next sentence opens with "it was," which has the same effect here as earlier: it focuses, then subordinates, thereby reducing the power associated with a fully realized agent-verb construction. Three other aspects of this sentence also diminish or deny our sense of agent. First, through the passive verb in the adverbial clause "when intelligence of the railroad disaster was received," Chopin refuses to provide any information about who sent the news. Second, she tells us that Brently Mallard's *name* leads the list of killed. Although it is not unusual to relay information of a man's death by stating that his "name" (only a part of the man) leads a list, this synecdoche distances a reader, if ever so slightly, from the death of the whole man. Finally, Chopin encloses *killed* in quotation marks; again, this may be idiomatic, but within the context of the first three sentences of this story, even idioms become suspect. . . .

Louise responds immediately to the news of Brently's death: "She wept at once, with a sudden, wild abandonment, in her sister's arms. When the storm of grief had spent itself she went away to her room alone." Chopin presents us with a pattern of assertion and negation; we read one sentence in which Louise appears to act only to learn in the next that she is *subjected to* something that *acts upon* her. Louise weeps, but she has abandoned herself to "the storm of grief" that must spend itself before Louise is free to go to her room. Repetition of this pattern increases its effectiveness. Only two sentences after the sentences above we come upon the following: "Into this armchair she sank, pressed down by a physical exhaustion that haunted her body and seemed to reach into her soul." We cannot even credit Louise with responsibility for her own sinking; "a physical exhaustion" *presses* her down. But the most forceful example of this pattern occurs a few paragraphs later. Louise sits in a chair near the window, observing the "signs of new spring life":

> "Chopin presents us with a pattern of assertion and negation; we read one sentence in which Louise appears to act only to learn in the next that she is <u>subjected to</u> something that <u>acts upon</u> her."

"She sat with her head thrown back upon the cushion of the chair, quite motionless, except when a sob came up into her throat and shook her." Louise obviously has far less control than does this sob, which shakes her and which, curiously, appears to act independently of the woman in whose throat it arises....

At this point we want to applaud Louise's action; we want to encourage her independence. But our experience with ambiguity requires us to hesitate before approving Louise's surrender to an unknown "something"; schooled by the text, we sense the danger here. Words describing this surrender do nothing to mitigate our fear. We read a series of sentences that focus on parts instead of wholes (her eyes "stayed keen and bright. Her pulses beat fast, and the coursing blood warmed and relaxed every inch of her body"), and then we are told: "She did not stop to ask if it were or were not a monstrous joy that held her. A clear and exalted perception enabled her to dismiss the suggestion as trivial." Louise may not pause to question the possibly monstrous quality of her joy, but *we* do. After all, the joy is only vaguely specified (it may be monstrous, but we do not know precisely), but it is "holding" Louise. Then, too, we might question the adjectives "clear and exalted" as modifiers for "perception." To this point, nothing within our experience has been clear and exalted; having been exposed to one ambiguity after the next, we feel skeptical about the flat assertion of clarity.

We follow Louise's mental and physical movements during her "brief moment of illumination." She remembers the "kind, tender hands" of her husband and realizes that she will weep anew when she views the corpse. But looking yet further into the future, she knows that she will delight in her solitude; she opens her arms to the long procession of years "that would belong to her absolutely." Given Louise's history of powerlessness, however, we suspect her ability to commandeer these years. Chopin substantiates this suspicion a few sentences later, in a statement of Louise's feelings about love and self-assertion: "What could love, the unsolved mystery, count for in face of this possession of self-assertion which she suddenly recognized as the strongest impulse of her being." The sentence itself seems to imply that Louise possesses this impulse, but all description up to this point suggests that Louise *is possessed by* the impulse. Because of Chopin's phrasing, both active and passive possibilities exist simultaneously; Louise is both subject and object....

Josephine, afraid that Louise will make herself ill (ironically, Josephine's perception of Louise's illness differs both from that of the reader and of Louise) calls to her from outside the locked door. Louise opens the door and the two women descend the staircase. After the momentous occurrence in the preceding paragraphs—Louise's decision to live for herself—the rhythm of the sentences here appears too easy. A fault lies beneath this smooth surface. Then: "Some one was opening the front door with a latchkey. It was Brently Mallard who entered." Within the space of two sentences, our unspoken questions, our unconscious suspicions, all stemming from Chopin's refusal to supply us with expected information, fall into place. The first sentence, "Some one was opening," prompts us to recall the description of Louise's joy: "There was something coming to her . . . What was it? She did not know; it was too subtle and elusive to name." The sentences merge; in both instances, we feel thwarted by insufficient information. In the second instance, however, Chopin grants us a full report: no longer "subtle and elusive," the agent is realized in the shape of Brently Mallard. Although couched in the reportorial "it was" construction, this emphatic identification is stunning. We sensed throughout the story that something is wrong, but the verification is terribly frustrating. We do not want the story to end this way: against all evidence, we hope that we are wrong and that our suspicions are misplaced. But the story ends. Louise sees her husband. "When the doctors came they said she had died of heart disease—of joy that kills."

An almost inevitable response to reading this story for this first time is to read it again. Multiple readings reveal even more clearly the cumulative effect of Chopin's subtle textual manipulations. If we review the story as a whole, we realize that the disquieting effect of the first sentence is heightened as we confront instances of agent disjunction and pronominalization, ambiguity, and diminution. Our positive feelings about Louise's self-assertion are qualified word by word. Although Louise struggles with a few moments of fearful anticipation, her progression toward self-assertion is predicated on "news" and "veiled hints," and she gives herself up to an undefined "something" without stopping to ask if it is or is not a "monstrous joy." As much as we would like to follow her, the route is closed to us. The cumulative experience of the text does not allow such simple complicity.

**Source:** Madonne M. Miner, "Veiled Hints: An Affective Stylist's Reading of Kate Chopin's 'Story of an Hour'," in *The Markham Review,* Vol. 11, Winter, 1982, pp. 29–32.

## Sources

Bender, Bert. "Kate Chopin's Lyrical Short Stories," *Studies in Short Fiction,* Vol. XI, no. 3, Summer, 1974, pp. 257–66.

Ewell, Barbara C. *Kate Chopin,* Ungar Publishing Company, 1986.

Larsson, Donald F. "Kate Chopin," in *Magill's Critical Survey of Short Fiction,* edited by Frank N. Magill, Salem Press, 1981, pp. 1131–36.

Pattee, Fred Lewis. "The Triumph of the Short Story," in his *A History of American Literature Since 1870,* Cooper Square Publishers, 1968, pp. 355–84.

Seyersted, Per. *Kate Chopin: A Critical Biography,* Louisiana State University Press, 1969.

## Further Reading

*Twentieth-Century Literature Criticism,* Vol. 14, Gale Research, 1984.
   Contains a useful introduction and previously published criticism of Chopin's work, both positive and negative.

# The Swimmer

## John Cheever

## 1964

John Cheever's "The Swimmer" was published in 1964 in the short story collection *The Brigadier and the Golf Widow*. Cheever once stated this story was originally meant to be part of a novel and was pared down from over 150 pages of notes. He also stated that he originally intended to write a story that paralleled the tale of Narcissus, a character in Greek mythology who died while staring at his reflection in a pool of water. However, the author eventually found the retelling of this myth too restrictive. As published, this critically acclaimed story takes place in the affluent suburbs of Westchester County, New York, and focuses on Neddy Merrill. Though no longer a young man, Neddy wants to retain his youth and believes that he is a vibrant individual and something of a hero. In an attempt to blaze new trails, he decides to find a new way home. When the story opens, Neddy is at a cocktail party and realizes that by following the chain of private and public pools in his affluent community, he can literally swim home. Praised for its blend of realism and surrealism, the story is respected for its dreamlike and nightmarish aspects, as well as its thematic exploration of suburban America and the life cycle. Critics admire Cheever's commentary on affluence, hypocrisy, and the relationship between wealth and happiness in "The Swimmer," along with his use of myth and symbolism.

## Author Biography

John Cheever was born in Quincy, Massachusetts, on May 27, 1912. He attended the private Thayer Academy but was expelled before graduating, an experience that became the basis for his first story, "Expelled," in 1930. Cheever subsequently pursued a writing career, contributing work to various publications, including *The Atlantic, The Yale Review,* and *The New Yorker.* During this period, he supported himself with odd jobs, including writing book synopses for the Metro-Goldwyn-Mayer film studio. In 1941 he married Mary M. Winternitz, with whom he eventually had three children.

Cheever served for two years in the army during World War II, and it was during this time that he had his first book of fiction, *The Way Some People Live* published. After the war, Cheever found work as a scriptwriter, producing scripts for television series including *Life with Father.* Cheever also began teaching after the war, and during the course of his lifetime he taught at such institutions as the University of Iowa, Boston University, Barnard College, and Sing Sing Prison. Cheever published his second work of fiction, *The Enormous Radio and Other Stories,* in 1953 to critical acclaim. Cheever's 1978 collection *The Stories of John Cheever* received the Pulitzer Prize, the National Book Award, and the National Book Critics Circle Award, and prompted serious scholarly interest in his works. Other collections of short fiction by Cheever include *The Housebreaker of Shady Hill and Other Stories, Some People, Places and Things That Will Not Appear in My Next Novel, The Brigadier and the Golf Widow,* (which contains his story "The Swimmer"), and *Thirteen Uncollected Stories by John Cheever.* Cheever died of cancer June 18, 1982.

## Plot Summary

"The Swimmer" opens on a humorous note: it "was one of those midsummer Sundays when everyone sits around saying, 'I *drank* too much last night,'" the narrator says. It is a beautiful summer day, and a large white cloud "like a city seen from a distance" is on the horizon. Neddy Merrill, a slender and young-looking man, sits beside the pool with a glass of gin. He decides that he could "reach his home . . . eight miles to the south . . . by water." He can swim home via the pools of the inhabitants

*John Cheever*

of the suburbs where he lives. He names the string of pools the "Lucinda River" after his wife Lucinda.

This is not such a strange idea for him to have, the narrator reveals, because "he was . . . determinedly original and had a vague and modest idea of himself as a legendary figure." Beginning at the Westerhazys' pool, he embarks upon his journey. The next pool he reaches is the Grahams', where Mrs. Graham gives him a drink. He remains there until some friends of the Grahams arrive from Connecticut, at which time he slips away. Arriving at the Hammer house, he swims through their pool undisturbed, as he does at the Lears'. The Howlands and Crosscups are away, and he swims their pools easily.

At the Bunkers' house, he runs into his first obstacle: a party with a caterer and "caterer's men in white coats." Detained there for time enough to have a drink, he then proceeds to the Tomlinsons' and crosses their pool. The next house, belonging to the Levys, has been the scene of another party— though no one is currently around—and Neddy pours himself another drink after crossing their pool. He feels "tired, clean, and pleased."

As he sits at the Levys' house, a storm breaks. He sits in their gazebo and waits it out. After the storm, he crosses the Lindleys' riding ring to the Welcher house and the next pool. The pool is empty, however, and "this breach in the chain of water disappointed him absurdly." The Welchers seem to have gone away; indeed there is a FOR SALE sign on a tree out front. His bad luck continues when he crosses Route 424, cold and wet, and the cars will not stop to let him by. After he finally gets across, he arrives at Lancaster's Recreation Center, where he must cross the crowded pool. The water there is much less pleasant than in his friends' pools, and he has to wash his feet "in a bitter and cloudy solution." When it is discovered that Neddy does not have proper identification, the lifeguards throw him out of the pool.

Ducking through the fence, he escapes to the Halloran estate. He tells the Hallorans about his quest. Mrs. Halloran responds: "We've been *terribly* sorry about all your misfortunes." Neddy asks what she means and she continues: "we heard that you'd sold the house and that your poor children...." Neddy insists that everything is fine and continues on. At the Hallorans' daughter's house he is unable to get a drink because they have given up alcohol. Moving on, he arrives at the Biswangers'. They are having a party but treat him as a gate crasher because he has snubbed them in the past. He has a drink and leaves. The next house belongs to "his old mistress, Shirley Adams." She refuses to lend him any money, although he does not ask, and he swims her pool and leaves.

On the last leg of his journey, Neddy begins to feel intensely cold and tired. He cries because he cannot understand why the people on the last half of his journey have been so rude to him. He swims the last two pools and finally arrives home exhausted. However, his house is dark and locked and he does not have the key. His wife, whom he was expecting to be home, is not there, and the story ends with Neddy pounding on the door of his own house and shouting, only to find that the place is empty.

## Characters

### Shirley Adams
Shirley Adams is Neddy's former mistress. When Neddy arrives at her home, she is shocked by his presence and warns him that she will not lend him any money. She is with a younger man.

### Grace Biswanger
Grace Biswanger is hosting a party when Neddy arrives and is angered by his presence, calling him a gate-crasher. Grace regularly invites Neddy and his wife to her parties, but they consistently decline. Neddy and his wife consider the Biswangers socially inferior. Grace reveals that Neddy is broke and has attempted to borrow money from her and her husband.

### Enid Bunker
Enid Bunker is an acquaintance of Neddy's and Lucinda's. She and her husband are hosting a pool party that Neddy interrupts on his swim home. Neddy and his wife were invited to the party but decided not to attend it. Enid is subsequently surprised and happy to see Neddy there, and she detains Neddy on his journey by giving him a drink, assuming that he has come to join the festivities.

### Mrs. Halloran
Mrs. Halloran is the mother of Helen Sachs and is one of Neddy Merrill's friends whom he encounters on his swim home while she sits next to her pool reading *The New York Times*. She and her husband are elderly and rich. They are also something of nonconformists. They prefer to swim in the nude and are rumored to be communists. Mrs. Halloran is the first character in the story to mention Neddy's recent misfortunes, all of which Neddy denies.

### Lucinda Merrill
Lucinda Merrill is Neddy Merrill's wife. It is after her that Neddy names the stream of pools that he has "discovered." She, like Neddy, is active in their neighborhood's social circle. Because of her relationship with the Biswangers, it is implied that she and Neddy are somewhat snobbish and unwilling to associate with the "wrong" sort of people. When the story opens, she speaks her only line: "We all *drank* too much."

### Neddy Merrill
The protagonist of "The Swimmer," Neddy Merrill, has a young, active, and playful spirit. He is described as having slid down the bannister earlier in the day even though he is approaching middle age. He is also likened "to a summer's day, particularly the last hours of one, and . . . the impression [he made] was definitely one of youth, sport, and clement weather." He sees himself as something of a heroic figure and explorer and decides to swim home through the chain of pools in his suburban

neighborhood. His wife is named Lucinda, and he has four daughters. He and his wife are active in their neighborhood's social circle and attend numerous parties. They have also declined to attend several functions, which has offended some of their acquaintances and resulted in their gaining a snobbish reputation. As this surreal tale unfolds, however, Neddy is additionally described or portrayed as lonely, miserable, fatigued, and either forgetful, senile, or disoriented. He is also in financial trouble and has had extramarital affairs. His status as a hero is considered ironic.

### Eric Sachs

Eric Sachs is the husband of Helen Sachs and a friend of Neddy's. Eric has given up drinking due to an operation he had three years earlier. He still has scars on his stomach from this operation.

### Helen Sachs

Helen Sachs is the daughter of Mr. and Mrs. Halloran and the wife of Eric Sachs, a friend of Neddy's. She is unable to give Neddy the drink that he requests; Eric had an operation three years ago, after which they both stopped drinking. Helen's comments mystify Neddy, who does not remember that her husband had an operation. Neddy subsequently begins to doubt his memory. Kind and hospitable, Helen directs Neddy to a party at a nearby neighbor's house where he can get a drink.

## Themes

Cheever's allegorical story of a man swimming across his town presents several themes common to twentieth-century fiction.

### Affluence

Set in an affluent county in suburban New York, "The Swimmer" comments on the wealth associated with the upper classes of American society. The beginning of the tale opens with Neddy Merrill at a cocktail party on a pleasant midsummer afternoon. He has a drink in one hand and is dangling his other hand in a backyard swimming pool. Although pools are frequently considered a luxury by most people, in this community they are commonplace. In fact, pools are so prevalent in his neighborhood that Neddy can make the eight-mile journey home by swimming. The wealth of Neddy and his neighbors is reinforced by the fact that one

## Media Adaptations

- A film version of "The Swimmer" was released in 1968 by Columbia Pictures. It was directed by Frank Perry (and Sydney Pollack, uncredited), adapted by Eleanor Perry, and starred Burt Lancaster.

of them even has a riding range that Neddy must cross on his journey home. The affluence of the upper class is also reflected in Neddy's and his friends' predilection for—and ability to afford—parties. At the story's beginning, Neddy's wife and friends are complaining about the previous night's party at which they had too much to drink. Furthermore, on his journey home, Neddy attends other parties, all of which are catered. In an ironic reversal, however, by the tale's end it is revealed that Neddy is in financial trouble.

### Appearance vs. Reality

Despite the financial well-being of Neddy's circle of friends, their situations are not necessarily happy or hopeful. Critics have noted that their parties represent the emptiness of contemporary American society and the meaningless and hypocrisy of the middle and upper classes. For example, Neddy tries to gain a sense of accomplishment and to recapture his youth by swimming home—an act that he considers meaningful, but one that is bizarre and of no real importance. The happiness supposedly associated with wealth is also elusive. Friends continue to offer their sympathies about Neddy's recent financial misfortunes, and the domesticity associated with suburbia is shattered when it is revealed that despite his happy marriage to Lucinda, Neddy has had an affair with one of his neighbors, Shirley Adams. The hypocrisy suggested by Neddy's affair is also reflected in his relationship with the Biswangers. Although repeatedly invited, Neddy and his wife refused to attend the Biswangers' parties because they associated with the wrong sort of people. These people include real estate agents, veterinarians, and eye doctors; although all these

## Topics for Further Study

- Research the idea of the mythic hero. How does Neddy Merrill resemble the mythic hero? In what ways does he not represent a hero?

- Discuss the social and political climate of America in the 1960s. Compare this to the picture of American life presented in ''The Swimmer.''

- Research Sigmund Freud's theories concerning dream interpretation. Based on your findings, examine the importance of various events and items that appear in ''The Swimmer.''

- Analyze the importance of water imagery in ''The Swimmer'' and other works of literature, for example, John Steinbeck's *The Grapes of Wrath* and Saul Bellow's *Seize the Day*. What different kinds of things does water represent in these works?

individuals are trained and respected members of the community, they do not fit into the Merrills' social group.

### Alienation and Loneliness

Neddy's affair and the circumstances surrounding his arrival home reveal an ultimate loneliness and alienation that are considered major themes of ''The Swimmer.'' Other details in the story also reflect this thematic emphasis. Neddy, for example, is snubbed and treated as a gate-crasher at the Biswangers' party. Of the homes he encounters on his journey, several are locked up, and one house is even vacant and for sale. Also, at the story's conclusion, Neddy arrives home, but instead of finding his wife and daughters, he discovers that his house is dark, locked, and empty.

### The Life Cycle

The life cycle and the passage of time are also prominent themes of ''The Swimmer.'' When the story begins, Neddy, who is described as being near the prime of his life, decides to affirm his vitality by swimming home. At first his journey goes smoothly. He does, however, run into various obstacles, represented by physical challenges (hedges, gravel paths, highways, and the like) as well as by people, the various friends and neighbors he encounters. As he progresses on his journey, he grows more fatigued and is struck by the loneliness of his situation. Cold and miserable (and a little drunk), he even considers giving up the journey. During the course of his trip, Neddy also becomes less and less sure of his abilities and memories. Friends offer their consolations about his recent misfortunes, but he denies that there is anything wrong. It is, however, unclear whether Neddy is merely denying that something is wrong or whether his memory has failed him. Appearing cold, tired, miserable, and alone at the end of the story, Neddy stands in sharp contrast to the vibrant man who began the swim home at the story's onset. The passage of time is also reflected in the story in a surreal way in its focus on the seasons. When Neddy's begins his swim, it is a beautiful and warm summer day. By the end of the story, he has encountered a terrible storm and the temperature has dropped drastically. Furthermore, the leaves have started to turn and are beginning to fall in preparation for winter.

## Style

### Allegory

''The Swimmer'' is often considered an allegory about decline, the aging process, and the life cycle. An allegory is a symbolic representation through characters or events of truths or generalizations about human existence. In allegories, people, places, and events often have more than one meaning—that is, they can stand for more than one thing. As such, allegories relate a surface story and a ''hidden'' story that focuses on other issues. The surface story of ''The Swimmer'' concerns the protagonist's swim home. The hidden, allegorical meaning of ''The Swimmer'' has to do with aging, physical decline, the life cycle, and the hypocrisy of the upper classes. Parables and fables are often considered types of allegories.

### Point of View

The point of view of ''The Swimmer'' is one of the most intriguing aspects of story. Because it is told completely in the third person (''I'' constructions are not used), the reader is never able to get inside Neddy Merrill's mind. This adds to the confusion of the story. For example, when friends try to console Neddy about his recent misfortunes, he denies that anything bad has happened. As a result of this narrative strategy, the reader is unable to decide whether Neddy is telling the truth, lying, deluding himself, or if he is simply disoriented.

### Hero/Heroine

The concept of the hero is another important aspect of "The Swimmer." In a certain sense, Neddy, as the protagonist of the story, is the hero of the story. He even views himself as something of a hero or a legendary figure. This view of himself as larger than life accounts, in part, for his desire to find a new way home. Swimming home is something that has not been done before, and his success will only add to his worth as a hero. "The Swimmer" also draws parallels between Neddy and characters appearing in other works of fiction. Many critics note that Neddy's journey shares many similarities with the journey of the hero as depicted in classical mythology, particularly with Odysseus in Homer's *The Odyssey*.

### Irony

Irony is another important aspect of the "The Swimmer." Irony is a literary technique that attempts to highlight the opposite meaning of a situation. Cheever's portrait of the hero, for example, is ironic. Instead of being vibrant, successful, and young—qualities often associated with heroes— Neddy is eventually portrayed as old, fatigued, weak, miserable, confused, lonely, and disoriented. He has been snubbed by acquaintances and seems to have forgotten various details about his life. Swimming through a series of pools is also not the great undertaking Neddy assumes it is. His homecoming is also considered ironic; homecomings for heroes are typically joyous occasions. Neddy's return to his home, which is empty, dark, and locked, is disheartening.

### Dream Vision

Neddy's tale is often considered a modification of the dream vision, or a story in which the main character falls asleep and dreams the events in the story. Dream visions are often filled with surreal, fantastic, and illogical events that make it difficult for the reader to discern what really is happening. Washington Irving's tale about Rip Van Winkle is an example of a dream vision. In Irving's story, Rip falls asleep for several years and, upon waking, learns that things have changed drastically. In Cheever's version of the dream vision, Neddy is not said to have fallen asleep, but he similarly ages considerably during his surreal journey. Within the span of an afternoon, Neddy grows older, can no longer trust his memory, and finds that the seasons have changed. As in dreams, time does not have meaning and events seem illogical for Neddy.

### Names

The meanings of the names mentioned in "The Swimmer" are considered significant. The name of Levy, for example, brings to mind the word levee, a word associated with water. Likewise, the Welchers' pool is empty; as welshers, they have disappointed Neddy by not having water in their pool and living up to their "word." Neddy's desire to get home to his wife and warm home is reflected in his wife's name, Lucinda, which means light. Several other names given in the story are related to water. For example, Merrill means "sea-bright"; Lear means "dweller by the sea"; the Clyde is a river in Scotland; and Halloran means "stranger from beyond the sea." The name Lear also brings to mind the Shakespearean king who lapsed into madness and lost his belongings and family. Critics have noted that names like Hammers, Bunkers, and Crosscups foreshadow violence, and that the owners of the pools that Neddy encounters in the first half of the tale are largely of Anglo-Saxon descent, much like Neddy. The names that are mentioned in the second half of the story, during which Neddy becomes more and more alienated, are more ethnically diverse.

## Historical Context

"The Swimmer" was published in 1964, at a time of great prosperity for middle- and upper-class Americans. Having survived World War II, which ended in 1945, and the Korean War, which took place in the 1950s, many Americans—at least white Americans—were enjoying the wealth and affluence of the postwar era. It was during this time that the American suburbs, the setting of "The Swimmer," grew at a rapid pace. This world of the upper classes is the world of Neddy Merrill as he appears at the beginning of "The Swimmer."

Neddy Merrill's world was in no way, however, one to which most Americans had access. The

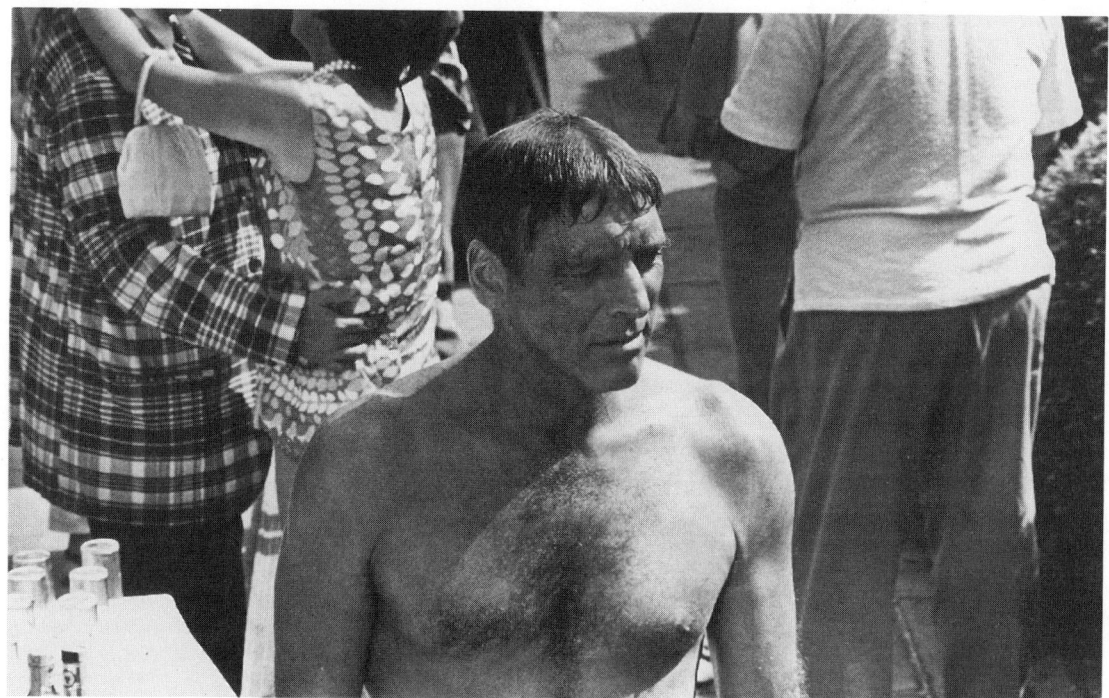

*Burt Lancaster as Neddy Merrill in the film version of* The Swimmer.

civil rights movement was active, and basic liberties were still an issue of great concern for many Americans. Although slaves had been freed as outlined in the Emancipation Proclamation in 1863 and slavery was abolished in 1865 with the enactment of the Thirteenth Amendment, many African Americans continued to be denied their civil rights. The civil rights act issued in June 1964 was intended to end this discrimination. Despite the progress that the passage of this bill symbolized, the problems faced by women and many minorities were not immediately resolved. Various other "rights" movements were also active in the early 1960s. The environmental movement gained much momentum in 1962 with the publication of Rachel Carson's *Silent Spring*. Betty Friedan's *The Feminine Mystique* (1963) shed much light on the problems faced by American women.

## Critical Overview

"The Swimmer" is recognized as one of Cheever's best short stories and explores themes that are considered typical of his fiction as a whole. In this story, which is set in an affluent community, Cheever chronicles the morals, rituals, and hypocrisy of the upper class through his focus on Neddy Merrill, who is, at the beginning of the tale, a vibrant man with a home, a wife, and four beautiful daughters. The story opens with the protagonist Neddy, his wife, and some friends sitting around a pool complaining that they had too much to drink the previous night. Furthermore, when the protagonist tries to do something new—something heroic and legendary—all he can come up with is to swim home through a chain of 16 pools. The hypocrisy of Neddy's situation becomes more evident as the tale unfolds. It is revealed that Neddy and his wife are something of snobs; they only associate with the "right" kind of people. Additionally, the illusion of Neddy's wealth and happy domestic life is shown to be fleeting and illusory. If the events that Cheever describes are to be taken at face value and accepted as true, it is revealed, at the story's end, that Neddy's marriage has been shattered by adultery, that he is financially broke, and that he has lost his home and children. In this manner, this American Chekhov of the suburbs has been recognized as providing yet more insight into the upper strata of American society, proving the adage that money and power can't buy you happiness. Indeed, for Neddy, privi-

# Compare & Contrast

- **1960s:** Affluent Americans have more money than ever before. The gross national product, the value of goods produced by the national workforce, increases almost 36 percent during the first half of the decade. Salaries increase about 20 percent during this same period.

   **Today:** The United States uses about one-third of the world's raw materials consumed each year. This is five times the average consumption for 1/15th of the earth's population.

- **1960s:** Many cities continue to experience a rise in suburban development which began in the 1950s. Many middle-class whites flee from cities to the suburbs, resulting in an increasing disparity between the quality of life in the city versus the surrounding area.

   **Today:** The federal government institutes a number of programs designed to rejuvenate America's cities, among which is the designation of "empowerment zones." The program is designed to spark growth in these areas by offering incentives to businesses located within the zone.

- **1960:** Some 400,000 marriages are dissolved by the courts.

   **Today:** In 1994, 1.2 million marriages were dissolved by the courts. Experts estimate that 50 percent of all marriages will end in divorce.

---

lege breeds unhappiness and empty actions. Furthermore, Neddy is so wrapped up in his own life, heroism, and desire to keep up with—and surpass—the proverbial Joneses that he cannot even admit to himself and to others that he is having a string of bad luck.

"The Swimmer" has also been praised by critics as a dream vision and a thematic exploration of decline and the life cycle. When the story begins, Neddy is a young(ish) and vibrant man who desires to do something legendary—though he hopes to accomplish this through the meaningless act of swimming home. As the story progresses, he becomes more fatigued. Critics note that this is reflected in the story on a textual level; Neddy completes the first part of the journey in record time, but the crossing of a busy highway—at which point he is feeling and looking horrible—is revealed through numerous lines of text. (In other words, the pace of the story slows as Neddy's energy level does.) Similarly, the reader learns that friends that are Neddy's age, notably Eric Sachs, are no longer the images of good health that they once were. Eric, for example, has had to give up drinking for health reasons. Neddy's denial of his problems—and confusion about his friends' statements and behavior—can also be seen as signs of senility. Even Neddy's surroundings reflect this deterioration. When the story begins, it is a temperate, sunny day in early summer. During the course of Neddy's journey, which supposedly takes places in a matter of hours, the weather turns cold, storms take place, flowers associated with the autumn are seen, and the summer constellations disappear. It must be noted, however, that although this tale succeeds as an allegory about one man's physical decline, its surreal qualities contribute to the story being interpreted as a dream (or nightmare). The seasons cannot logically change within the course of day, nor can a man age in the course of one afternoon. Critics note that Cheever's blending of realistic and surrealistic detail and use of the third-person narrative enhance the reader's experience of the tale and the story's ability to work on various levels.

The symbolism and irony of the tale have also been praised by critics. Many critics note that one of the story's strongest points is its use of mythology and focus on the hero. Like Homer's Odysseus, Neddy undertakes a voyage by water to get home. Neddy's obstacles, however, pale in comparison to those of Odysseus; Neddy only has to deal with gravel paths, drunken friends, a busy highway,

## What Do I Read Next?

- John Updike's "Rabbit" series—*Rabbit, Run* (1960), *Rabbit Redux* (1971), *Rabbit Is Rich* (1981), and *Rabbit at Rest* (1990)—offers commentary on American society in the last part of the twentieth century, by focusing on the life of suburban, upper-class protagonist, Harry "Rabbit" Angstrom.

- In Washington Irving's "Rip Van Winkle" (1819), the title character falls asleep and awakens years later to discover that much has changed during his "nap." Rip's entire experience, like Neddy Merrill's, has been interpreted as a dream.

- Cheever's *The Brigadier and the Golf Widow* (1964) examines the themes of American affluence and suburbia.

- J. D. Salinger's classic, *Catcher in the Rye* (1951), is the story of one young man's coming of age and search for truth in a world full of "phonies."

---

empty pools. Other characters in the story also find their counterparts in Odysseus's tale: his wife, Lucinda, can be seen as Penelope; Shirley Adams as Circe; the Bunkers as the Sirens; and the various party-goers as the lotus-eaters who try to dissuade the hero from his objective. The highway and public pool that Neddy must cross have similarly been likened to the rivers Lethe and Styx. Critics have also noted similarities between other classical heroes, including the character Dante in *La divina commedia* (c. 1300; *The Divine Comedy*), and other myths, including those of the Fisher King and the Holy Grail. Neddy's journey is, however, told ironically. His quest is of relatively no importance, and his homecoming is presented as less than hospitable. Critics note that the closer that Neddy gets to home, the more alienated and troubled he becomes. The trivialness of Neddy's quest is often interpreted as further commentary on the meaningless lives of the American upper-class.

## Criticism

### Greg Barnhisel

*Greg Barnhisel is an assistant instructor and assistant director of the Undergraduate Writing Program at the University of Texas at Austin. In the following essay, Barnhisel discusses the major themes of "The Swimmer."*

On a literal level, "The Swimmer" is the story of one man's initially fanciful, ultimately quite serious adventure swimming through every pool in the county on his way home. On a deeper level, though, the story alludes to some of Western literature's most enduring themes. Neddy Merrill, Cheever's hero, is Odysseus, Dante, the Fisher King, a knight of King Arthur. Through his story of a man's exhausting journey home, Cheever examines themes of dissociation, alienation, and the loss of purpose.

"The Swimmer" examines the plight of a character familiar to readers of Cheever's fiction. Along with John Updike and J. D. Salinger, Cheever is one of the famous trio of "*New Yorker* authors" of the 1940s through the 1960s (Cheever published a total of 121 stories in the *New Yorker* magazine), and he quickly became well-known for chronicling the lives of New York professionals and surburbanites. "The Swimmer" appeared during a period in which Cheever's own alcoholism was bringing a dark tone to his writing.

Neddy Merrill, the story's hero, is "far from young" but not yet middle-aged—"he might have been compared to a summer's day, particularly the last hours of one." Incipient darkness and age is everywhere in the story, haunting the apparently idyllic summer day on which the story takes place. The setting is the well-to-do Westchester County suburbs of New York City, where the towns and villages divide themselves up along very strict lines of class, religion and national origin. The weekend parties and barbecues, and their carefully delineated guest lists, are the social milieu in which these divisions play out, and Neddy seems quite at home there.

When the story begins, we see Neddy in the middle of the most desirable party, the Westerhazy's. He feels comfortable in his surroundings—"his life was not confining," the narrator tells us—but he has "a vague and modest idea of himself as a legendary figure." To accomplish what he sees as his modest contribution to the tradition of mythical figures, he decides to make the eight-mile journey home from the Westerhazy's not by car, as would be customary, but by water. He will swim "that stream of swimming pools, that quasi-subterranean stream that curved across the county." He names the stream "Lucinda" after his wife and departs.

The gently humorous irony of Neddy's quest draws attention to one of Cheever's enduring concerns: the lack of transcendent meaning, or even of base importance, in the lives of the privileged in the middle of the American century. Cheever's men are troubled by their lack of purpose, and often channel this frustration into alcohol (and Neddy drinks at least five times during his trip home). On first reading, it seems to the reader that it is a slightly drunken fancy that leads Neddy to embark upon his quest.

Neddy's project is, though, quite serious. Cheever originally intended Neddy to call to mind the Greek mythological figure of Narcissus, the beautiful youth who saw his reflection in a pool and kills himself trying to unite with his image. "When I began," Cheever is quoted as explaining in Patrick Meanor's *John Cheever Revisited,* "the story was to have been a simple one about Narcissus.... Then swimming every day as I do, I thought, it's absurd to limit him to the tight mythological plot—being trapped in his own image, in a single pool."

Perhaps the strongest parallel Cheever's story has is to Dante's *Divine Comedy,* in which the poet travels into the depths of Hell in order to learn more about the purpose of human existence. Like Dante, as Neddy journeys on he reaches ever more perilous reaches of the county. The trip begins at the

> "Cheever originally intended Neddy to call to mind the Greek mythological figure of Narcissus, the beautiful youth who saw his reflection in a pool and kills himself trying to unite with his image."

Westerhazys, then continues on through the friendly estates of the Grahams, the Hammers, the Lears, the Howlands and the Crosscups. Neddy's first trial is at the Bunker house, where a party is in full force. Greeted warmly by the hostess and many of the guests, Neddy is forced to delay his voyage. He moves on to the Tomlinson place and then to the eerily deserted Levy house, where rain stops him for a time.

The next house, the Welchers', presents him with a disappointment: their pool has been drained, and the house is for sale, although Neddy cannot remember hearing any such thing about them. Neddy feels the first pains of his voyage—"was his memory failing?"—but then reaches his next test: the highway, where shivering he withstands insults and a flung beer can from passing motorists. "He seemed pitiful.... Why was he determined to complete his journey even if it meant putting his life in danger?" Finally across the highway, he then reaches the most difficult test: the public pool. The water is foul-smelling and acrid and murky, and the pool is crowded. The lifeguards demand he leave the pool, and he escapes.

Just as Dante survived the horror of the Inferno only to be confronted by the tests of Purgatory, Neddy still has to endure a few more hardships before arriving home. The Halloran pool is welcoming, but for the first time we hear about Neddy's own problems: "We've been *terribly* sorry to hear about your misfortunes," Mrs. Halloran sympathizes. He then stops at the Biswanger house, where he is regarded as a gate-crasher because of his own repeated social snubs of them, and finally at the house of Shirley Adams, "his old mistress." She, too, makes reference to Neddy's recent difficulties. Once Neddy makes it through the Inferno, therefore, the perils become less external and more internal. Not only is he now cold and tired, but the people he encounters allude to his own unspecified troubles.

Unfortunately for Neddy, the end does not bring a glimpse of Beatrice and the sacred rose. His arrival home does not bring him to the light (the name Lucinda is derived from the Latin for "light"): "the place was dark." All of the unidentified troubles now confront the traveller, and he can no longer escape them. The Dantean equivalence also is complicated by Neddy's inward-directed focus during the story. Where Dante eagerly questions the inhabitants of the various levels of Hell, Neddy is either unaware of or uninterested in the people he meets along the way.

Another appealing parallel for Neddy is the Homeric hero Odysseus. Like Odysseus, Neddy takes a leisurely, roundabout trip home, stopping his journey in places. Many of the characters in "The Swimmer" then fall into the Homeric structure: Lucinda is Penelope, Shirley is Circe, Mrs. Bunker represents the Sirens, her party symbolizes the Lotus-eaters, and the Biswangers stand for the Cyclops. And like Odysseus, Neddy also faces another trial once he actually returns home before he can be reunited with Lucinda.

Critics have also compared Neddy to Washington Irving's Rip Van Winkle and Neddy's journey to that of the knights of the round table. Rip's twenty-year sleep is a counterpart to Neddy's journey, and Neddy's repression of his problems during his swim reminds us of Rip's status, upon waking, as a "man out of time." Both men confront their final fates uncomprehendingly. Neddy can also be seen as Jesus, the pools as his Stations of the Cross. Shirley's comment to him reinforces this interpretation: "Good Christ. Will you ever grow up?" However, perhaps the most apt parallel for "The Swimmer" is the King Arthur Holy Grail myth. Enduring numerous perils, the knights (and Neddy) are questing for something they don't fully understand. Even the name of one of the pools Neddy traverses, the Crosscups, alludes to the holy chalice of Jesus.

The image of the drinking-cup refers back, in turn, to the constant drinking in which Neddy and his friends engage. Although critics seem most eager to trace out the story's mythical allusions, it would be irresponsible not to grant that Neddy's confusion at the end of the book could simply be the result of an alcoholic's denial and memory loss. Neddy's vision of himself as "a legendary figure" could also result from his drinking, as could the strange pattern of time-passage in Neddy's mind. In his book *John Cheever Revisited,* Patrick Meanor holds that "Cheever's time warp in 'The Swimmer' is explainable as a symptom of the serious physical, mental, and spiritual disintegration caused by prolonged alcoholic drinking."

Whether Neddy is our century's equivalent of a hero, trying to carve out a mythical legacy in a banal environment, or whether he is simply a delusional alcoholic trying to make his life seem more exciting, conclusions can only be drawn ultimately from Neddy's own perceptions. The narration is strict third-person limited—the narrator is not Neddy himself, but refers to Neddy as "he" and does not have access to all of Neddy's thoughts and feelings. Some critics have seen this limitation as a problem. Ultimately, the reader does not get to know Neddy very thoroughly and since the precise nature of Neddy's "misfortunes" is unclear, it is difficult for us to judge his actions.

However, Cheever achieves a greater complexity in his story by this self-imposed limitation. When Neddy arrives home and the house is not only empty but in disrepair, the reader is confused: is Lucinda just late? Do the Merrills still live there? Are the Merrills even still married? If we see Neddy's quest as a drunken one, then perhaps he only imagined Lucinda's presence at the Westerhazys' party. In this view, his "troubles" could be with his marriage—it is known that Neddy had a mistress. Drunk, he thinks he is still married, and only when he arrives home does cold, dark, wet, sober reality confront him. By not revealing the actuality of the situation, Cheever creates in his readers the confusion of the alcoholic. Read on a mythical or a literal level, "The Swimmer" is a powerful evocation of the loss of a sense of purpose among America's privileged class in particular and among twentieth-century people in general.

**Source:** Greg Barnhisel, for *Short Stories for Students,* Gale Research, 1997.

## Loren C. Bell

*In the following essay, Bell compares Cheever's "The Swimmer" to Shakespeare's* A Midsummer

Night's Dream *and analyzes some of the story's dream imagery.*

The opening paragraph of John Cheever's "The Swimmer" establishes the common malady lingering poolside at the Westerhazys' that midsummer Sunday. "We all *drank* too much," said Lucinda Merrill. While the others talk about their hangovers, Neddy Merrill sits "by the green water, one hand in it, one around a glass of gin." Apparently instead of talking, Neddy "had been swimming and now he was breathing deeply, stertorously as if he could gulp into his lungs the components of that moment, the heat of the sun, the intenseness of his pleasure." Debilitated by his hangover and his swim, warmed by the hot sun and cold gin, his deep breathing resonant with heavy snoring sounds, Neddy slips into the most natural condition given the circumstances: he falls asleep. His pleasure invents a dream of heroic exploration which ends with a desolate vision within a midsummer's nightmare.

The invitation to transform *A Midsummer Night's Dream* into "a midsummer's nightmare" is tempting, first, because Cheever's references to midsummer seem insistent. The story begins, "It was one of those midsummer Sundays. . . ." About the midpoint, after the wind has stripped the Levys' maple tree of its autumnal leaves, Neddy reasons that "since it was midsummer the tree must be blighted. . . ." Near his journey's end, under a winter sky, Neddy wonders, "What had become of the constellations of midsummer?." A further link to the play is the mystifying confusion of the seasons:

> The spring, the summer,
> The childing autumn, angry winter, change
> Their wonted liveries; and the mazed world,
> By their increase, now knows not which is which. (II.i.111–14)

The transformation seems more than ironic wordplay when we consider another connection to Shakespeare: Cheever's observation that Neddy "might have been compared to a summer's day, particularly the last hours of one. . . ." Despite his impression of "youth, sport, and clement weather," Neddy is not a likely subject for a sonnet, at least not for Sonnet 18: "Shall I compare thee to a summer's day? / Thou art more lovely and more temperate." Alcoholic, snobbish, adulterous, self-indulgent— Neddy is by no means mild or temperate, yet he is linked to the sonnet. He is the other subject of the poem, the inevitability of decline. Thus, he is compared to the last hours of a summer's day because,

> "The ambiguity of the word passing is effective. Neddy's 'passing affection' may be only transitory; his nightmare will show that what he holds dear is indeed fleeting."

like the season, Neddy's "lease hath all too short a date." As "every fair from fair sometime declines, / By chance or nature's changing course untrimmed," so Neddy's "eternal summer"—his illusory youthful vigor and, more important, his illusion of success, his share in the tenuous American dream— will also fade. Whether or not he has actually lost his money and status, his house and family, in the context of his dream he seems to have lost "possession of that fair [he] owest." As his pilgrimage to that realization ends, we sense that Neddy has indeed wandered through the valley of the shadow.

The dream motif (and its direction) having thus been suggested, Neddy snores beside the pool; "the components of that moment . . . seemed to flow into his chest." Here the narrative becomes internalized in Neddy. The dream itself begins and, with it, the "implied progression from day to night, summer to winter, vigorous manhood to old age."

The surrealistic quality of dreams insinuates itself throughout Neddy's journey. With his "discovery" of the Lucinda River, we see that superior point of view of the dreamer, suspended, detached, not quite real: "He seemed to see, with a cartographer's eye, that string of swimming pools, that quasi-subterranean stream that curved across the county." Removing "a sweater that was hung over his shoulders" (had it been hung there by someone else?), he plunges into the stream of his subconscious. "To be embraced and sustained by the light green water . . . seemed," to Neddy, to be "the resumption of a natural condition"; the dreamer floats on waves of sleep like the swimmer buoyed by light green water.

When Neddy hears the Bunkers' distant poolside party, "the water refracted the sound of voices and laughter and seemed to suspend it in midair,'' distant, disembodied voices made nearer by the trick of water and physics. It is one of those phenomena of reality that make us recall the dream distortion of sound as well as place and time. When he leaves the Bunkers', ''the brilliant, watery sound of voices fade[s],'' as if he leaves some bright sanctuary to pursue his darkening journey. Near the Lancaster public pool, ''the effect of the water on voices, the illusion of brilliance and suspense, was the same ... but the sounds here were louder, harsher, and more shrill. ...'' The distortion will recur at the Biswangers' with even harsher effects.

Another illustration of the dream motif is Neddy's sense of separation and detachment. As he surveys the scene at the Bunkers' pool, including the red de Haviland trainer ''circling around and around and around in the sky with something like the glee of a child in a swing,'' he ''felt a passing affection for the scene, a tenderness for the gathering, as if it was something he might touch.'' The ambiguity of the word *passing* is effective. Neddy's ''passing affection'' may be only transitory; his nightmare will show that what he holds dear is indeed fleeting. But given the tenderness with which he regards his own life and this scene of ''prosperous men and women,'' *passing* suggests rather convincingly its archaic sense of ''great'' or ''surpassing.'' For the moment he is held outside that circle rather like Hawthorne's Robin Molineux when the boy views his family gathered for vespers under the spreading tree in their dooryard. But the door will not be shut in Neddy's face—not just yet, for he enters this scene as a welcome guest and greets his fellow players (or playfellows) in a dizzying round of kisses and handshakes, even though the thunder has sounded.

''I had the *strangest* dream last night I was standing on the shoulder of Route 424, waiting to cross, and I was *naked*. ...'' So Neddy, on some other day, waking from some other dream, might well have recounted that common dream image. But his vulnerability and exposure in this afternoon's dream will probably not be another amusing anecdote told at breakfast. When he reaches the highway, he is ''close to naked,'' naked enough to be ''exposed to all kinds of ridicule,'' but perhaps not naked enough to perceive any truths beyond his discomfort and his perplexing inability to turn back. He is genuinely naked when he steps out of his trunks and through the Hallorans' yellowed beech hedge to encounter something closer to the naked truth when Mrs. Halloran says,

''We've been *terribly* sorry to hear about all your misfortunes, Neddy.''

''My misfortunes?'' Ned asked. ''I don't know what you mean.''

''Why, we heard that you'd sold the house and that your poor children. ...''

''I don't recall having sold the house,'' Ned said, ''and the girls are at home.''

Neddy's first response seems natural enough, yet when Mrs. Halloran begins to tell him precisely what she does mean, he interrupts her. Like unsettling, bright pinpoints of truth abruptly piercing an alcoholic black-out, her explanation hints at sharp truths that must ultimately be faced. Neddy's reply seems more an evasion than an answer, the suppression of a dark truth's glimmering. It also suggests the illogical, if not absurd, utterances of dreams.

To discern truth from within or without a dream is difficult enough, but to discern the dream itself from within is more difficult. For Neddy, it is impossible. Unprepared for the humiliation along Route 424, he is bewildered, but ''he could not go back, he could not even recall with any clearness the green water at the Westerhazys', the sense of inhaling the day's components, the friendly and relaxed voices saying that they had *drunk* too much.'' Caught powerless and unaware in a nightmare that now controls him, he can only swim with its current. At the Sachses' pool, he still feels obliged to swim, ''that he had no freedom of choice about his means of travel.'' Just two pools from his own house, obligation has become compulsion: ''While he could have cut directly across the road to his home he went on to the Gilmartins' pool'' and then ''staggered with fatigue on his way to the Clydes'.''

It is in dreams that apple blossoms and roses are replaced with the ''stubborn autumnal fragrance'' of chrysanthemums or marigolds. It is in dreams that midsummer constellations become the stars of a winter sky, and slender, youngish Neddy Merrill goes ''stooped'' and ''stupified'' to whatever truth, whatever self-discovery, his nightmare has led him. ''He had been immersed too long, and his nose and throat were sore from the water,'' a swimmer's complaint that might be shared by an afternoon sleeper whose snoring has been too long and loud, and whose dream is too frightening.

In *A Midsummer Night's Dream*, we are told that ''the course of true love never did run smooth.'' Neddy's encounters with love would seem to bear witness. The easy familiarity with which he greeted his bronze Aphrodite that morning is rebuffed by Shirley Adams, his former mistress with "hair the color of brass." Despite Neddy's "passing affection," the course of his real love—his pursuit of the American dream of success and suburban happiness—runs no more smoothly. Perhaps it too is besieged,

> Making it momentary as a sound,
> Swift as a shadow, short as any dream;
> Brief as the lightning in the collied night,
> That, in a spleen, unfolds both heaven and earth,
> And ere a man hath power to say "Behold!"
> The jaws of darkness do devour it up.
> So quick bright things come to confusion. (I.i.143–49)

In the nightmarish ruin of the "quick bright things" in Neddy's life, he has been led to the vision that his dream of wealth, status, and happiness is transitory, illusory, and fraught with perils. If our dreams are empty, what then are we? The use of that discovery, whether for reform or despair, is left to Neddy and to us. Perhaps he will mend his ways, or (as Prufrock fears) Neddy Merrill may awake from his watery dream only to drown—in one way or another.

**Source:** Loren C. Bell, "'The Swimmer': A Midsummer's Nightmare," in *Studies in Short Fiction,* Vol. 24, No. 4, Fall, 1987, pp. 433–6.

## Michael D. Byrne

*In the following brief article, Byrne discusses the symbolism of names in "The Swimmer."*

Like modern writers as diverse as Joyce, Fitzgerald, and Barthelme, John Cheever found an artistic delight in lists, specifically a list of names: "It's perfectly beautiful. You can use an invitation list as a lyrical poem. A sort of evocation. I believe I've used it once or twice." One of Cheever's most anthologized stories, "The Swimmer," includes a list of names representing ports of call on Neddy Merrill's Sunday odyssey: "The only maps and charts he had to go by were remembered or imaginary but these were clear enough. First there were the Grahams, the Hammers, the Lears, the Howlands, and the Crosscups. He would cross Ditmar Street to the Bunkers and come, after a short portage, to the Levys, the Welchers, and the public pool in Lancaster. Then there were the Hallorans, the Sachses, the Biswangers, Shirley Adams, the Gilmartins and the Clydes." Like the famous litany of guests at Gatsby's parties, Cheever's list is a carefully crafted

> Even the most cursory attention to the names suggests that they were not selected randomly from the Ossining telephone directory."

narrative device, yet none of the critical commentaries on "The Swimmer" have scrutinized it. We do know that Cheever began the story as a novel and that, at one point, he had accumulated 150 pages of manuscript. Obviously, the finished work underwent a radical condensation of material. The list of names was one way Cheever provided concise symbolic resonance to the action. In fact, the list stands for Neddy's dilemma, writ small.

Even the most cursory attention to the names suggests that they were not selected randomly from the Ossining telephone directory. At the Westerhazys, where everyone is trying to shake off the mental fog of a hangover, Neddy decides to travel to his home in Bullet Park "by taking a dogleg to the southwest." But he will confront social and psychological violence and conflict, as "Hammers," "Crosscups" and "Bunkers" foreshadow. Like Lear, he will wander dispossessed across a landscape once friendly, now hostile, partly because he has been a "Welcher" socially, romantically and financially.

Cheever intensifies the theme of ostracism through his ethnic arrangement of the names. On the first half of the trek, Neddy Merrill (whose ancestry is English) finds full pools and hospitable neighbors (whose ancestry, English, German and one Scot speaks of long-established social position). One of them, Howland, can even claim to be a *Mayflower* descendant. At the Levys' (the halfway mark of the swim), however, the ethnic note changes, as does Neddy's reception. In this second lap, Neddy calls on two Jewish and two Irish neighbors; of these, the two neighbors who are home genuinely care for and welcome him. Playing on the second string socially, they understand nonconformity and exclusion (the Hallorans, weekend nudists, are thought to be Communists). Of the English or German neighbors in this part of the story, two have no pools and two rebuff Neddy for his casual arrogance in dropping by. The Englishman turns into Wandering Jew.

Cheever slyly links this theme of social ostracism with aquatic nomadism through the meaning of some of these surnames. Merrill is "a descendant of Muriel ('sea-bright')." Welch means "the stranger"; Lear, "the dweller by the sea." Halloran (an Irish name) is "the stranger from beyond the sea." Neddy's penultimate stop is the Clydes, whose name is shared by a long, winding river in Scotland.

The swim finished, Neddy "climbed up the ladder and wondered if he had the strength to get home. He had done what he wanted, he had swum the country, but he was so stupified with exhaustion that his triumph seemed vague." In one of his short masterworks, Cheever's triumph was anything but vague, as his river of names makes clear.

**Source:** Michael D. Byrne, "The River of Names in 'The Swimmer'," in *Studies in Short Fiction,* Vol. 23, No. 3, Summer, 1986, pp. 326–7.

## Cortland P. Auser

*In the following essay, Auser talks about the mythical aspects of "The Swimmer," and compares the story to the* Odyssey, *a legendary Greek tale.*

Many critics and reviewers have long praised John Cheever as one of the most devoted craftsmen of the short story. Others have also noted his artful employment of myth, or mythic elements, to develop structure, character, or theme within his stories. In his anthology *The Brigadier and the Golf Widow*, the group of short short stories entitled "Metamorphoses" offers a good illustration of his use of mythic elements. It is in a separate story, "The Swimmer," however, that he has created an imaginative and vital myth of time and modern man.

If a reader employs the criteria of Professor Henry A. Murray in identifying modern myth creation, Cheever has been successful on all counts. His work is mythic for it is a "sensible symbolic representation of an imagined series of events." Cheever has not only used a contemporary suburban environment as a "mythic referent," but the story in its "emotive" and "convictional functions" creates indelible impressions on a reader and leaves him a "parable of wisdom."

Cheever uses the age-old themes of quest, journey, initiation, and discovery as he makes the story a commentary upon the times. Professor Frederick Bracher has perceptively noted how the tale combines the patterns of the *Odyssey* and "Rip Van Winkle." Ned Merrill, the central character, is a modern Ulysses of sorts, but he is a man who does not accept (by his refusal to confront) the harsh truth of time's passage. The story's concentrated and subdued drama and its significant theme inevitably recall Irving's narrative. It is peculiarly appropriate that this modern myth has its locale in the general Westchester area associated with Irving. And the apt epithet of "Ovid in Ossining" for Cheever in a *Time* cover story is justified as we read the story, for Ned undergoes a severe metamorphosis.

At one level, the story begins significantly on a midsummer Sunday when bibulous suburbanites are shaking off the effects of the previous night's drinking. It is a fuzzy world of hangover in which many utter regrets about having drunk too much. Ned Merrill, although not young, prides himself on both his youthful appearance and exuberance; he sits hugging a glass of gin by the poolside of a friend. Seeing himself in his illusions as something of a legendary figure, Ned decides to do something devotional to celebrate the beauty of the day and his own youthfulness. He reflects that his own home lies only eight miles distant and imagines that by stringing together a series of swimming pools of his neighbors and acquaintances, he might swim home by such a "river." In his whimsy he christens this stream "Lucinda" after his wife. Having committed himself to the test, he hurls himself into this suburban Alpheus to begin the journey home.

Cheever's description of the Westchester setting is distinctly credible, for he has an eye for selective details in just the right amount to maintain the "reality" and suggest the "fantasy." Simultaneously, Cheever unobtrusively interweaves his pattern of myth. We feel the waters of the Lucinda River becoming symbolic of time's passage.

As Ned proceeds, he feels there is no greater reward than to accomplish the goal he has set for himself. In his intense quest, he feels like "a pilgrim, an explorer a man with a destiny." He feels too, that he moves in a beneficent world one made for his pleasure. But Ned does not proceed directly to his goal without interruption. Hospitality is offered by "friends" along the route; he rationalizes the temporary delays. As he continues to indulge his fancy, he buoys himself up by a recurring sense of conviviality—a drink at the Grahams and more drinks at the Bunkers, and so on. He still feels affection for the scenes through which he passes, even as thunder ominously sounds in the distance.

Reality sounds sharply when Ned hears the whistle of a train bringing him back at one point to ponder about what time it is. The autumnal coloring of the leaves against the darkness of a storm attracts his attention, but only momentarily. By such means Cheever adroitly expands and compresses time credibly.

With the progression of the journey from one pool to another, Ned finds his memory is obviously unclear; he merely "seems" to remember events. As he meets acquaintances along his route of travel and converses with them, he begins questioning his sense of truth—whether he has been unable to face unpleasantnesses along the "way."

The crossing of a main highway forces him to sense how ludicrous his position is. It is at this juncture in time that he reflects about returning. His early jauntiness has worn off; there is no feeling of the "legendary" any more, for the journey has become deadly serious. He still nurtures the picture of himself as explorer. His passage through the property of the Hallorans and his meeting them *deshabillés* symbolically reveal to him the unadorned truth, for they allude sympathetically to misfortunes which he cannot recall experiencing. His sense of time and his recollections are completely confused.

Ned physically now feels the concomitants of age—the heaviness of fatigue, a loss of weight and a coldness within the bones. He assures himself that whiskey will see him through the journey; but the way he is now treated by people at the last pools he has to swim makes him feel that he has undergone somehow a loss of social esteem. He is only tolerated. There is no longer any feeling of conviviality. As he passes through the property of his onetime mistress, she chides him scornfully about his inability to grow up.

When he finally emerges from the last pool, he is miserable and exhausted. Literally and figuratively, Ned knows he has been "in the swim" too long. His own home is dark; the locks on the doors are rusty. As he peers through the windows of the house, he discovers that it is empty.

> With the progression of the journey from one pool to another, Ned finds his memory is obviously unclear; he merely 'seems' to remember events."

As mythopoeist, Cheever has employed the river and water to represent the flowing of time, the passage through phases of life. The sun's setting and the seasonal changes bring Ned the wayfarer closer to age and death. His final initiation brings self-knowledge too late. The autumn of life, as it were, has brought no emancipation, no release, no renewal, only what we might identify as bitter isolation.

Cheever's commentary through his imaginative merger of fantasy and reality in this myth, I think, is clear enough. Ned as a typical modern man has indulged himself and his whims; he has immersed himself in the pleasures of drink and sex to the degree that he is not aware of what is happening to him. Immaturity and irresponsibility prevent him from seeing what he has done with his life. Repeatedly, he has fallen back upon the illusion that he is controlling his life and its direction. He has rationalized and accepted any bypaths of pleasure. He has the gift for the concealment of *pain;* it cannot happen to him. At times, he finally glimpses the absurdity of continuing the direction he has chosen, but at such points he "creates" his own "reality." Because he refuses to face the actualities of time's passage, his illusion of his own youthfulness makes him appear increasingly pathetic and pitiful at the end of the journey. His compulsion to go on and his blindness have continued even after the pleasures have been lost. Ned's final peering through the windows of his house is symbolic of his "seeing" the emptiness within himself.

"The Swimmer," then, is a myth of time and man as it is also a modern myth of metamorphosis. Coincidentally, Cheever as story teller recalls the figure of the philosopher in Ovid's masterpiece, one who has the faculty of seeing "with clarity of mind and heart," of telling the story of "men who seem born to die and chilled by death." Two lines from the fifteenth book of *The Metamorphoses* adequately sum up the author's story, for Cheever has imaginatively created a significant myth about

> . . . sky, wind, earth and time forever changing Time like a river in its ceaseless motion.

**Source:** Cortland P. Auser, "John Cheever's Myth of Man and Time: 'The Swimmer'," in *CEA Critic,* Vol. XXIX, No. 6, March, 1967, p. 18–9.

## Sources

Meanor, Patrick. *John Cheever Revisited,* Twayne Publishers, 1995.

## Further Reading

Cheever, John. *The Journals of John Cheever,* Alfred A. Knopf, 1991.
　Contains journal excerpts covering a period from the late 1940s until 1982 in which Cheever comments on his homosexuality, his alcoholism, and his processes of composition.

Riley, Kathryn. "John Cheever and the Limitations of Fantasy," in *CEA Critic,* Vol. 45, nos. 3-4, March-May, 1983, pp. 21-26.
　Riley provides a brief thematic overview of "The Swimmer" and other stories by Cheever.

Slabey, Robert M. "John Cheever: The 'Swimming' of America," in *Critical Essays on John Cheever,* edited by R. G. Collins, G. K. Hall, 1982.
　A close reading of the story, concentrating on mythological parallels and sources for Cheever's character names.

# The Train from Rhodesia

Nadine Gordimer
1952

"The Train from Rhodesia" is one of Nadine Gordimer's earliest stories, first published in 1952 in her collection *The Soft Voice of the Serpent and Other Stories*. The short piece about a train's brief stop in an impoverished African village exhibits the concise complexity that marks much of Gordimer's other work. As a native South African of European heritage, Gordimer has focused much of her writing on the injustice of apartheid as practiced in the country. Though not an overtly political story, "The Train from Rhodesia" depicts the prejudicial attitudes that caused apartheid and reinforced it once racial segregation became law. Critics have praised the story for its unflinching yet subtle social commentary, a tactic that allowed Gordimer to publish it in South Africa without it being censored. By presenting characters of both races who are degraded by their belief in racial inequality, the author shows how both black and white South Africans are harmed by apartheid. While readers debate the merits of her detached, unemotional style, many find themselves compelled by her passion. The story has been published in several of Gordimer's collections as well as in other general short story anthologies.

## Author Biography

Nadine Gordimer was born in Springs, South Africa, a gold mining town near Johannesburg, in 1923.

Her parents were Jewish emigrants from London. She began writing at age nine when a heart condition limited her activity. She credits her isolation and her powers of observation for her success as a writer—traits that were evident to her even at this early age. At the private schools she attended, she was confronted with the omnipresence of racial discrimination. Even amidst the Catholic church, blacks were not afforded any semblance of status or respect, and the young intellectual wondered why. Gordimer began publishing stories at age fifteen which were generally concerned with racism and generally published in liberal magazines. With the assistance of Afrikaner poet Uys Krige and Sydney Saterstein, her agent, she soon began to publish in major literary magazines and American literary journals like *The Yale Review, Harper's, Atlantic* and the *New Yorker*. This international recognition gained her a supportive audience during the times in which her own community sought to suppress her. Gordimer attended the University of Witwatersrand in Johannesburg, and was married to Gerald Gavronsky in 1949. The couple had one child and divorced three years later. In 1954 she married Reinhold Cassirer, the owner of an art gallery, and subsequently they had a son. In the mid-1950s when she was barely thirty years old, Gordimer had published two highly respected collections of short stories and her first novel *The Lying Days*.

Much of Gordimer's work is concerned with how South Africa's volatile political situation negatively affects the lives of whites. Consistently, she has argued that apartheid hurts everyone, a belief that prompted the South African government to censor books like *A World of Strangers* and *The Late Bourgeois World*. The latter was banned for twelve years for portraying a friendship that illustrates what Gordimer called the "cruelty and idiocy of apartheid and the dangers of daily life for blacks." Aside from the political implications of her fiction, Gordimer is also known for her detached style, in which the narration appears very objective and scenes of great outward emotion are related with a sense of distance from the characters. In recognition for her talent as a writer, Gordimer has won many literary prizes, including the James Tait Black Memorial Prize in 1970 for *A Guest of Honour*, the book many call her best, and the 1991 Nobel Prize for Literature. Gordimer often lectures and teaches abroad, but she continues to live in Johannesburg.

## Plot Summary

A train is heading toward a small, rural station in Southern Africa. The area around the station is impoverished, as are the people who live there. In the station, the stationmaster, the venders, and the children prepare for the train's arrival.

The train, from the white, considerably more wealthy area of Rhodesia, approaches the station. A young white woman stretches out of the train's window to look at a carved lion that an old African man has to sell. The poor villagers flock to the windows of the train, selling items or begging for handouts from the other passengers. Children ask for pennies. Dogs and hens surround the dining car waiting for scraps. One girl throws out chocolates—"the hard kind, that no one liked"—but the hens get them before the dogs do.

The young woman decides the lion is too expensive: three shillings and sixpence. Her husband thinks the price is preposterous also, but his wife urges him to stop bargaining with the old man. She withdraws from the window to sit in the compartment across the train's corridor. She thinks about the lion she has not purchased and all the other similar carvings she has already bought: bucks, hippos, and elephants. She wonders how these items, which have come to represent the unreality of her honeymoon trip, will fit in at home and what meaning they will take on in her everyday life. She realizes that she has been subconsciously thinking that her new husband was part of this unreality, as if he would vanish as soon as the honeymoon ends.

The bell rings in the station, and the stationmaster prepares the train to leave. As the train starts moving on the track, the old man with the lion runs alongside it, offering the carving for "one-and-six"—only a fraction of what he had asked for before. The husband tosses the money out the window and the old man throws the lion to him. As the train leaves the station, the old man is standing, holding the shilling and sixpence he has picked up from the ground.

The young man enters the compartment where his wife sits, pleased with having obtained the lion figure for so little, and hands it to her. Though she admires its finely crafted features and the ruff of fur around its neck, she holds it away from her. She is dismayed at this purchase because it represents the humiliation her husband has forced upon the old African. She demands to know why he did not pay a fair price for it. He protests that she herself had said it was too expensive. The young woman throws the lion onto the seat in frustration.

A sense of shame engulfs her as she thinks of the price. She feels an emptiness inside herself. She has felt this way before but mistakenly thought it came from being alone too much; now she knows that is not true. The empty feeling is tied up with her new husband and their differing value systems. Her husband is sprawled out on the seat and she remains with her back toward him. The abandoned lion has fallen into a corner.

## Characters

### Old man

The old man initially tries to sell his carved lion for three shillings and sixpence to the young couple, but fails. Later, he shouts to the young man already on the train that he will sell it for one-and-six. His acceptance of such a low price and his breath, visible "between his ribs," indicate that he is desperate and probably very poor. His polite manners, his "smiling, not from the heart, but at the customer," indicate both his dire circumstances and his dependence on tourists like the young couple. Gordimer offers little description, but indicates that he is very old, a man who murmurs, "as old people repeat things to themselves." Gordimer refers twice to his feet in the sand, thus showing the old man's connection with the land, which contrasts with the young couple who are enclosed in the train.

### Stationmaster

The stationmaster appears briefly in the story. As the train approaches, he comes "out of his little brick station with its pointed chalet roof, feeling the creases in his serge uniform." His discomfort in the suit represents his attempt to fit in an unnatural role imposed on him by his job. The presence of his barefoot children and wife emphasize the poverty of the small town. When his children collect "their mother's two loaves of bread," the stationmaster's dependence on the benevolence of the train from white, European-dominated Rhodesia is emphasized.

### Young man

The young man accompanies the young woman on the train. He is surprised when she declines to buy the lion from the native at the train station. Despite the woman's decision, he bargains with the

*Nadine Gordimer*

old man "for fun" and then "automatically" accepts the old man's low offer of one-and-six. He throws the money to the old man and catches the lion as it is thrown to him. Whereas the young woman's conscience is torn, the young man simply seems to be enjoying his trip. Thus, with "laughter and triumph" he presents the lion to the young woman and is "shocked by the dismay of her face." He is finally depicted, "sitting, with his hands drooping between his sprawled legs." His silence implies an inability to understand the young woman.

### Young woman

The young woman is the central character of the story, since it is her thoughts upon which the pathos of the story depends. Upon arriving at the train station, she admires a carved lion but declines to buy it, saying that the old man selling it wants too much money. When she retreats into the train, though, it is revealed that she already owns several similar items and does not know what she will do with them once she is home. The woman becomes upset after her husband buys the lion for a few cents. "If you wanted it, why didn't you pay for it?" she asks, "Why didn't you take it decently, when he offered?" This outburst indicates that the woman feels guilty over the patronizing and demeaning way her husband has treated the old man. As the train pulls out of the station, her shame overwhelms her, and they sit in an angry silence. Their relationship has been affected by the racial injustice her husband defines as "fun, bargaining."

Gordimer reveals the thoughts of only the young woman, thereby focusing the exchange in the train station on the human toll exacted by apartheid. The woman is wealthy enough to travel in style; as a white, she is a beneficiary of the government's system of racial discrimination. Nevertheless, even as she participates willingly in an unjust society, she tries to appreciate the natives—especially for their fine artistry. When unsettling feelings overcome her, she blames them on "being alone and belonging too much" to herself. The incident on the train, however, makes her realize that she is upset by larger social issues. The starving man was made to beg for a few coins in return for an elaborately and skillfully carved animal. Yet, she remains with her back towards her husband, indicating that she is still unable to discuss the topic; she is too bound by her complicity in society.

## Themes

In "The Train from Rhodesia," a train's short stop in a poor African village highlights the racial and class barriers that typify South African life in the 1950s. Though only a few pages long, Gordimer's story encompasses several themes besides racial inequality, including greed, poverty, and conscience.

### Race and Racism

In South Africa, apartheid, the legal separation of races, became law in 1947. It is not necessary for Gordimer to mention the race of the characters in the story. Readers in the 1950s understood that the "old native" was black and the rich tourists were white. In a society so harshly divided, Gordimer writes of an instance in which the two races interact, thus revealing the patronizing attitudes of whites towards blacks and the blacks' virtual enslavement and dependency on the whites. The whites, moreover, are not native to the country; just as the train passengers are merely "tourists" in the village that exists frozen in time before and after the train leaves. The villagers are shown as belonging to the land: "the sand became the sea, and closed over the children's black feet softly and without imprint." In contrast, the white tourists are removed from nature and from the land: in their compartments with "caged faces, boxed in, cut off after the contact of outside," they are indifferent to those on the outside. The beer drinkers "looked out, as if they could not see beyond" the windows of the train. Some passengers throw scraps of food to the dogs that hover near the train, just as others throw pennies to the children. In this image, Gordimer emphasizes the effect of the whites' superior attitudes on the natives: it forces them to act like animals. That the young couple has collected tribal art on their vacation further represents their patronizing attitude towards the country's natives. The tribal objects, which have great symbolic meaning to those who make them, become nothing more than decorations in the houses of the upper, ruling class. The woman wonders "How will they look at home.... Away from the unreality of the last few weeks?" To her, a honeymoon journey through Africa seems "unreal," but to the people who live there, like the barefoot children who live in mud huts, it is very "real" indeed.

### Wealth and Poverty

Enmeshed in the law of apartheid is the sharp division between wealth and poverty. While the inhabitants of the small village are so poor that they cannot afford shoes, the woman and man return to the city with bags of souvenirs that they do not know what they will do with. After picking up the coins thrown to him by the man on the train, the old man's "breath [blows] out the skin between his ribs," indicating the hunger and malnutrition prevalent in South Africa's rural areas. The stationmaster's children are depicted "clutching" a mere two loaves of bread. Meanwhile, the train passengers sit comfortably in their cabins—one woman actually gives her excess food to the dogs, ignoring the children begging at the train's windows. Desperate to make money, the merchants are reduced to acting "like performing animals, the better to exhibit the fantasy held toward the faces on the train."

### Greed

The man selling the lion initially asks for "three-and-six." Though probably a fair price, the man on the train balks in an effort to get it for less. Since he and his wife already have several items like it, this bargaining is just a game to him. Thus, the impoverished seller is at the man's mercy. He needs the money more than the man needs the lion; this discrepancy becomes a prime opportunity for the young man to exhibit his greed. In waiting until the last possible moment—when the train is leaving the station—the man obtains the lion for just a fraction of its original price. He has made the poor man beg for the few coins, and he has received a finely crafted artwork for his wife. He does not recognize his greed: "I was arguing with him for fun, bargaining," he tells his wife, oblivious to the fact that his "fun" reduced the native to "gasping, his skinny toes splaying in the sand."

### Conscience

The young woman wrestles with her conscience over her appreciation for the lion and her outrage at her husband's greed in obtaining it. She represents those who are not entirely comfortable with apartheid but benefit from it anyhow. Her initial reaction to the seller's offer is "No, leave it." Though she says it is too expensive, it seems likely that she is troubled by the dichotomy of wealth and poverty the train trip has presented to her. She retreats inside the train rather than deal with the poor natives. This action represents many whites' preference for going along with the travesty of apartheid rather than deal openly with the painful issues of inequality it presents. She feels shameful and sick for exploiting the native Africans, but refuses to explain these feelings to her husband. Previously, she had attributed such feelings to being single and alone. She argues with her husband and they both end up feeling hurt and disconnected from one another. Thus, her conscience has divided them; this event illustrates how apartheid can drive a wedge between all people and even divide families. In the end, the woman rejects both her husband and the lion, which had "fallen on its side in the corner."

## Style

### Narrative

"The Train from Rhodesia" begins and ends with the symbol of the train. Gordimer structures her story around this metaphor and uses limited third-person narration to tell it. The narrator reveals only the thoughts of the young woman, thus focusing the story around her perspective, even though the stationmaster and his family are introduced to the reader before the train arrives. The woman's thoughts are conveyed through interruptions in Gordimer's detailed narrative. These interruptions reveal her moral questions about her husband's bargaining for the carving: "Everything was turning around inside her. One-and-six. One-and-

## Topics for Further Study

- How would "The Train from Rhodesia" be different if told from the perspective of the old man? The young man?

- Investigate how contemporary South Africa differs from the apartheid South Africa of 1952. Could a situation like that in "The Train from Rhodesia" take place there today?

- Research the art of the indigenous Africans. What were the carved figures like those in the story used for? What were some features common to them and what did they symbolize?

six." That no one else's thoughts are revealed by the narrator further emphasizes the psychological distance between the woman and the other characters in the story.

### Symbolism and Imagery

In a story so short, images and symbols must be chosen carefully and used efficiently if the story's themes are to be presented clearly. In "The Train from Rhodesia," the train itself is the most overt symbol. The train comes from Rhodesia, a privileged British colony in South Africa, and thus symbolizes British colonialism. "Creaking, jerking, jostling, gasping, the train filled the station," Gordimer describes it, thus imparting a view that British domination resembles a huge, mechanical, unhealthy, and overbearing beast. The train only stops briefly and few people get on or off, further symbolizing the indifference and lack of understanding inherent in British imperialism. The train moves along "the single, straight track," emphasizing the "tunnel vision" of the dominant power. The old man and his impoverished neighbors are incidental; the train is merely passing through on its way to another British outpost. As it leaves, it "cast the station like a skin," an image that imparts the idea that the village was something to be rid of, unwanted and unneeded.

In contrast to the mechanical, manufactured symbol of the train to represent the whites, the

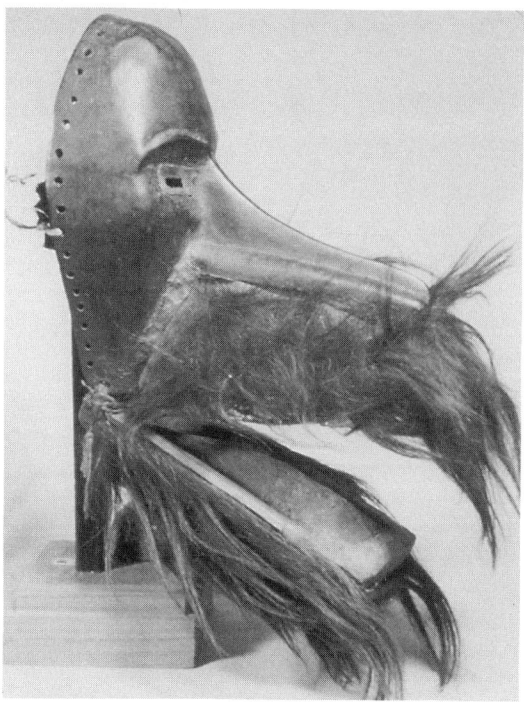

*An African tribal mask, a typical souvenir item for Western travelers through the region.*

Africans of the small village are identified with images of nature. The villagers are surrounded by "sand, that lapped all around, from sky to sky, cast little rhythmical cups of shadow," and which closes over the barefoot children's feet. Furthermore, the stationmaster's wife is identified with a sheep's carcass that is hanging over the veranda. This, also, is a symbol of nature, even though it negatively connotes their position in society as nothing more than pieces of meat. Nevertheless, these images reveal that the villagers are an organic part of the environment. When Gordimer describes the old man's feet "splaying the sand," she brings to mind a tradition in African art in which exaggeratedly large feet symbolize a connection with the land and the generations of those who have cultivated it. She contrasts this organic connection with the sterile, compartmentalized separation of the British who sit "behind glass, drinking beer, two by two, on either side of a uniform railway vase with its pale dead flower." Sand connects the old man, the stationmaster and his children to each other, but the British have no symbol to connect themselves to one another beyond the loud, lumbering train that "heaved and bumped back against itself." When sand is used as an image for the young woman, however, it symbolizes the shame she feels, which "sounded in her ears like the sound of sand, pouring."

## Historical Context

### Legal Separation of the Races

When Gordimer published "The Train from Rhodesia" in 1952, South African society was legally divided along racial lines by apartheid. The all-white National Party won control of the government in 1948 and dominated South African politics for much of the next two decades. Black Africans and other non-whites, including those of mixed-race heritage, were denied the most basic human rights and forced to live apart from whites in substandard living conditions. They were allowed only disproportionately small representation in government, and by 1960 they were denied all representation. This political exclusion insured a monumental divide in the respective standards of living between whites and non-whites. While whites enjoyed excellent hygiene, health care, food, education and transportation, non-whites, like the old man and the stationmaster's family in the story, suffered from malnutrition, disease, and severe poverty. In accordance with the Population Registration Act of 1950, all South Africans were divided by their race and treated accordingly. Members of each of the four established ethnic groups (Asian, African White and Coloured, or mixed-race) were strictly segregated in all aspects of their lives. Interracial sex and marriage were prohibited and the Group Areas Act of 1950 divided all cities and towns into segregated districts of both residential and business property.

In order to effect this total division, thousands of Coloureds and Indians were forced out of white areas by the government so that each district would be racially homogenous. Strict laws prohibited non-whites from sharing the same trains, buses, taxis, or even hearses as whites. For these reasons, none of the black Africans boarded the train to Rhodesia in the story. While the white population prospered in wealthy urban areas like Rhodesia, the non-white population suffered economic and political exploitation in the rest of the country, such as the rural area Gordimer describes. Non-whites were only allowed in the all-white districts to work and were required to return directly to their districts afterwards. While white children learned to read at very

# Compare & Contrast

- **1950s:** Black South Africans cannot vote, represent themselves in government, or live in the same areas as white South Africans.

  **1990s:** Black South Africans participate in the South African government, vote, and maintain the same legal rights as white South Africans, though vast ghetto areas like Soweto still exist.

- **1964:** Nelson Mandela is arrested by the South African government and imprisoned for treason after nearly two decades of work for the African National Congress.

  **1996:** South African President Nelson Mandela and the African National Congress-dominated parliament approve a new, more egalitarian constitution for South Africa, with former president Frederick W. de Klerk acting as Mandela's deputy. The new constitution outlaws the death penalty, grants protection to striking workers, and provides greater access to public documents.

- **1953:** James Baldwin publishes *Go Tell It on the Mountain*, and Ralph Ellison publishes *The Invisible Man*, both seminal works on the theme of racial prejudice.

  **1997:** The popularity of Oprah Winfrey's book club results in the skyrocketing sales of Toni Morrison's books.

---

early ages, most black South Africans remained illiterate. In 1953, the white South African government even outlawed missionary schools so that it could control native Africans' educations.

However, by 1950, resistance to apartheid was growing. At this time, the African National Congress gained members under the leadership of President Albert Lutuli and his companions, Oliver Tambo, and Nelson Mandela. While the white-controlled government sought to crush such resistance movements through violence, surveillance, and sometimes assassination, the African National Congress continued to exist even after it was outlawed and its leaders, including Mandela, were imprisoned. The Suppression of Communism Act of 1950 allowed the police to arrest anyone without the right to a lawyer, a trial, or an appeal. These laws were used to punish demonstrators in 1952, when they protested laws that even the South African Supreme Court had declared racist. Leaders of the resistance vowed that the illegal political protests would continue until all of the country's jails were overcrowded. In response to this, the South African Parliament extended dictatorial powers to Prime Minister Daniel F. Malan in 1953. The resulting police state took the lives of many bright young political leaders and caused guerrilla warfare that characterized South African politics until the early 1990s, when apartheid was dismantled.

## Critical Overview

When Gordimer published "The Train from Rhodesia" in 1952, overt criticism of South Africa's political system by writers often resulted in censorship of their works. Thus, the story was Gordimer's subtle attempt to illustrate the insidious ramifications of racial discrimination. While she had already published many short stories in literary magazines, her readership was limited to a small audience of liberal, white South Africans. Internationally, her condemnation of apartheid gained her respect, but her second novel, *A World of Strangers,* was banned by the South African government. Yet even as her critics attacked her politics, others praised her technical mastery of language, her fluid imagery, and natural characterizations. "The Train from Rhodesia" itself, however, received little attention from critics upon its publication.

The volatile racial tensions in South Africa have continued to affect the reception of Gordimer's literature throughout her career. Many critics have attempted to categorize Gordimer as a political writer, though she has resisted this label. She has always maintained that her writing is first about people and that she seeks to speak honestly and creatively about people's lives, not politics. Though admitting that writing can have radical effects on people's lives, Gordimer argues that one should focus on the writing itself when writing, and not think of one's audience. Intentionally writing propaganda, she says, would destroy the aesthetic merit of her work. Many critics apparently concur, since Gordimer received the Nobel Prize for Literature in 1991, for "her magnificent epic writing [which] has been of very great benefit to humanity." A few critics steadfastly maintain that downplaying the politics of her stories is an evasion of her political responsibility. The South African government, however, disagrees; her 1966 novel *The Late Bourgeois World* was banned for twelve years.

Contemporary scholars respect the strategy of Gordimer's fiction. According to scholars like John Cooke, who wrote *The Novels of Nadine Gordimer: Private Lives, Public Landscapes,* and Stephen Clingman, who wrote *History from the Inside: The Novels of Nadine Gordimer,* Gordimer's fiction tells the stories of vast social change through the everyday experiences of individuals. Because Gordimer has chosen to write about the small moments in people's lives, like those in "The Train from Rhodesia," her writing receives almost a universal warm welcome today. This is in contrast with the 1950s and 1960s, when such "small moments" were sometimes criticized as both didactic and unpolitical. In the 1950s and 1960s, many critics and readers preferred stories that stressed national politicians and prominent leaders over the dailiness of life. Today, in light of the trend towards minimalism in fiction, "small moments" are almost universally acknowledged to be suitable topics for literature. Reviewing *A Soldier's Embrace,* Edith Milton writes, "Gordimer is no reformer; she looks beyond political and social outrage to the sad contradiction of the human spirit."

## Criticism

### Rena Korb

*Rena Korb has a master's degree in English literature and creative writing and has written for a wide variety of educational publishers. In the following essay, she discusses the representative characteristics of Gordimer's writing that are apparent in "The Train from Rhodesia."*

Nadine Gordimer has been called South Africa's "First Lady of Letters," and she is perhaps that country's most distinguished living fiction writer. The author of many volumes of collected short stories and novels, in addition to numerous lectures, essays, and other works of nonfiction, Gordimer was awarded the Nobel Prize for Literature in 1991. This international recognition of Gordimer's work not only confirmed her reputation as an artist, but it also stressed the importance of writing about the effects of apartheid on the people of South Africa. The length of Gordimer's career—she published her first story when she was thirteen, her first book at twenty-six—has allowed her to document the changes in South African society over the course of several generations.

Throughout her career, Gordimer has insisted that because politics affect all aspects of life, her writing always deals either directly or indirectly with political matters. Moreover, she believes that only the truth can help a good cause. More directly, she believes that her writing deals with the truth, thus she makes no attempt to espouse specific political views regarding South Africa. Taking this view, Gordimer often sees herself as isolated between the external world of politics and the internal world of the individual. Her work reflects this sense of detachment, and Gordimer has been admires by some and criticized by others for it. Likewise, some critics feel that Gordimer does not take a strong enough stand against racism, and others feel that she goes too far. The South African government, for example, has banned several of her works, and sometimes prevents others from being published in paperback, which is the only way many black South Africans could afford her novels.

Gordimer's fiction has been the subject of much commentary in South Africa over the years. One review of *A World of Strangers,* Gordimer's second novel, complains that she writes of "the wider and more dangerous pastures of the sociological novel." A reviewer of her next novel, *Occasion for Loving,* which concerns an affair between a white English woman and a black South African man, insists that "the theme and incidents of the story will seem less important than those stretches of interior writing in which the author's still, small

# What Do I Read Next?

- *A Guest of Honor* (1990) by Nadine Gordimer. An idealistic colonel's discovery of corruption among the leaders of a newly independent African nation results in his assassination.

- "Children of the Sea," (1993) by Edwidge Danticat. A young couple are separated by a dictatorial regime in Haiti, forcing the young man to make a dangerous boat crossing to the United States.

- "Vengeful Creditor" (1971) by Chinua Achebe. A story about a wealthy Nigerian's brush with free public education, which makes it difficult for her to find suitable servants to care for her children.

- "Blues Ain't No Mocking Bird" (1972) by Toni Cade Bambara. A poor, African-American family is approached by a crew of filmmakers who want to shoot footage of their modest home for their project on the government food stamp program.

- "Everyday Use" (1973) by Alice Walker. An African-American family's successful, college-educated daughter wants possession of the family crazy quilt so she can hang it over her sofa as an example of American folk art.

- *Fools and Other Stories* (1983) by Njabulo Ndebele, a former leader of the Congress of South African Writers. A collection of stories that explores the lives of South African children growing up in the 1960s.

- *Cry, the Beloved Country* (1948) by South African writer Alan Paton, a classic novel that follows Reverend Steven Kamalo through the black ghettos of Johannesburg on a search for his lost son.

- *Biko* by Donald Woods recounts the dynamic life of Stephen Biko, South African Black Consciousness Movement leader, who was battered to death while under police interrogation in 1977.

---

voice is heard above the sounds of ordinary living and the common day." It is not surprising that the most passionate analysis of Gordimer's work and the most hostile reactions generally come from other South Africans or ex-Africans. Gordimer's position, that of the white South African opposing apartheid—a minority within a minority—has led to strong emotions and occasional suppression.

The *Atlantic Monthly* has called Gordimer "one of the most gifted practitioners of the short story anywhere in English," and it was her short stories that first led critics to consider her a major writer. Her talent for short fiction has been compared to that of the poet, particularly for her interweaving of event, meaning, and symbol in a short amount of space. Martin Trump also points out that Gordimer depicts how women as well as Africans have suffered from the inequality present in South African society. Racial inequality, since it permeates all facets of life, is always present in her stories, despite the race and social class of her characters.

"The Train from Rhodesia," one of Gordimer's early stories, concerns a young couple on a train stopped at a rural station. The young woman is interested in a carved lion an old black man has to sell but claims the price is too high. Her husband bargains with the vendor and obtains the carving for an unfairly low price, causing his wife to feel humiliated and isolated from him. At first, this story may not seem to deal with the racial problems specific to South Africa—after all, oppressed and impoverished people are taken advantage of the world over. But the inequality that permeates South African society is depicted in the shared humiliation of the old black man and the young white woman. Gordimer explained this relationship in an interview: the young woman "suffered from seeing her husband or lover demean himself by falling into this

> "Gordimer has insisted that because politics affect all aspects of life, her writing always deals either directly or indirectly with political matters."

black-white cliche of beating down the African. . . . She suffered really from seeing herself demeaned through her lover."

The woman identifies with the black carver and thus rejects, at least for the moment, the typical white world of South Africa. Gordimer achieves this emotional connection in part through symbolism. While she draws distinctions between the white world of the train and the black world of the station, she implies that the black world is more honest. The whites live in a fragile world of their own construction symbolized by the train. Before they buy the blacks' wares, the whites require them to act "like performing animals, the better to exhibit the fantasy held towards the faces on the train." Though the black world is filled with "mud huts," "barefoot children," and "a garden in which nothing grew," it is still shown as a place of community. This is in contrast this with the passengers on the train with their "caged faces" and who are "boxed in." They are willing to donate items to the poor children outside but only those they do not value, such as the chocolate that "wasn't very nice."

Such an incident illustrates the unfruitful match between the young man and woman on the train. The couple, presumably on their honeymoon, have been caught up in "the unreality of the last few weeks." They have bought many animal carvings during their travels, and the young woman wonders how they will fit in at home. The buck, hippos, and elephants (and later, the lion), all ferocious or frightening animals, stand in opposition to the refined world she and her husband inhabit. But after seeing her husband act in such an insensitive, exploitative manner toward the old black man, she knows that nothing she has recently acquired is in harmony with her life and values. Her husband, however, confronted with the dichotomy of the white and black worlds of South African has no problem accepting it.

The emptiness she feels at this realization of the differences between them fills her with a "weariness" and "tastelessness." The woman has felt this way before, but she has mistakenly thought "it was something to do with singleness, with being alone and belonging too much to oneself." The incident at the train station makes her painfully aware that this "void" has been caused by her alliance with her husband, who argues with an impoverished old vendor "for fun." Yet she does not voice these frustrations to him. Though the woman does not want to have anything to associate with this emptiness, so that "no object, word or sight. . .might recur and so recall the feeling," it will clearly not be possible to ignore their basic incompatibility in the future. The man's failure to understand his wife's unspoken signals reveals their fundamental inability to communicate. Thus, he misses "the occasion for loving."

In addition to developing the theme of sterile love through her characters' actions towards one another, Gordimer also uses sexual imagery and symbolism. As the story begins, the train entering the station represents the potential for a healthy relationship. The train represents the man; it "[flares] out. . . . Creaking, jerking . . . gasping, the train fills the station." The woman is the station, whose tracks "[flare] out to let it in." But, like the doubts that have been lurking in the back of the young woman's mind, there are hints of the impending division: the train behind the engine is a "dwindling body"; the train calls out "I'm coming" but receives "no answer." The sexual promise of the relationship is snuffed out by the husband's purchase of the lion. As the train leaves the station, the young woman then feels the "impotence of anger," and the "heat of shame [mounts] through her legs." Finally, the train casts "the station like a skin." Once again it calls "I'm coming," and receives no reply. Thus, through this metaphor, Gordimer indicates the young couple's emotional estrangement.

Gordimer's reputation as a descriptive writer rests not on her portrayal of details such as eye color or hair color but in the layering of telling details. In the 1980s, Gordimer and photographer David Goldblatt collaborated on two books in which selections from her fiction were accompanied by his pictures. Andrew Vogel Ettin finds these artists to be well matched in their interest of social and physical environments. Goldblatt does not illustrate Gordimer's words per se but shows the backdrop against which her stories take place. Ettın draws particular attention to the final image of the couple in "The Train from Rhodesia" as an example of the "expressive power of the physical": "Smuts blew in grittily, settled on her hands. Her back remained at exactly the same angle, turned against the young man sitting with his hands drooping between his sprawled legs, and the lion, fallen on its side in the corner." This "caught moment" deserves its place as the pinnacle of the story. It includes many elements central to Gordimer's fiction: the intrusion of the white world of the train in the black world of the station, the separation of man and woman, and the chance for love destroyed by the racial problems of South Africa.

**Source:** Rena Korb, for *Short Stories for Students,* Gale Research, 1997.

## David Kippen

*David Kippen is an educator and specialist on British colonial literature and twentieth-century South African fiction. In the following essay, he discusses the symbolism of location and geography in "The Train from Rhodesia" and how it underscores the silence and symmetry of the narrative.*

In one of the more insightful recent discussions of Nadine Gordimer's "The Train from Rhodesia," South African critic Robert Green writes in *The Novels of Nadine Gordimer* that the story "map[s] out the silence and asymmetry between black and white." There is much to recommend using these ideas of "silence" and "asymmetry" as points of departure into Gordimer's story. The building blocks Gordimer selects for her setting—the station, the train, and her principal characters—provide context essential to the story's action. If the silence between the domains of black and white is most evident in the unfolding of Gordimer's plot, it is in the construction of setting that the asymmetry Green remarks upon can be most clearly seen. Since the asymmetry between these domains generates the silence which mark their boundaries, it is here, with setting, that I shall begin.

Though it is impossible to date the story's action with certainty, it is reasonable to assume that it is set sometime between the closing years of the nineteenth century, when the first major train lines linking South Africa with countries to the north

> "Where the station is a study in degrees of poverty, the train is a demonstration of the world's opulence."

were built, and 1953. However, given the political events of the late 1940s and early 1950s, a later date seems more likely. The exact location of the station cannot be established with any certainty, but Gordimer's descriptions of the hot, arid, desert-like conditions suggest a setting on either the Little or Great Karoo (Khoisan for "desert") in the Cape Colony. Gordimer could, of course, have chosen to be more specific about the location and date if she had wished, but it is precisely the approximate nature of these details that gives her story the sense of an endlessly recurring cycle. It is worth observing that, although her other works generally provide very detailed scenes, here she furnishes only a few details about the station and the train. From Gordimer's description one might take away the impression that all of South Africa is similarly arid and empty, but this is not so. Though the country's interior is largely arid, the Eastern and Southern coast are as fertile, well-watered, pleasant and densely populated as the United States' Gulf Coast. Why, then, does she pick this location? Her decision to place the story's action in the Karoo is most probably both a strategic move and a practical necessity, for it is in locations such as this one that the disparity between the worlds of black and white are visible in their simplest, most direct relief. This is not to say that there is no disparity in coastal South Africa—the opposite was, and remains, the case—but rather, that the Karoo setting provides an ideal territory for a study in miniature of three tiers of South African society.

In this hierarchy, the polished, well-to-do English-speaking people appear both on top economically and as social transients on the landscape ("settler," with its implication of transience, is a term of insult to many South African whites). Their presence on the train therefore provides a setting which is both entirely plausible and a wonderfully ironic commentary on their presence on this landscape. Where the station is a study in degrees of poverty, the train is a demonstration of the world's opulence elsewhere, a caravan of delights from which the stationmaster's family is in exile, and from which the station's blacks are permanently excluded. This fact is mirrored spatially as well, with the passengers up high, reaching down to toss money or examine artifacts.

In a letter of November 5, 1899, a young Winston Churchill, on his way to report on the Boer War (1899-1902) wrote that "railway traveling in South Africa is more expensive but just as comfortable as in India. Lying-down accommodation is provided for all. . . . The sun is warm, and the air is keen and delicious. But the scenery would depress the most buoyant spirits. . . . with the daylight the train was in the middle of the Great Karoo. Wherefore was this miserable land of stone and scrub created?" Churchill's comments underscore the dichotomy between the harsh, unpleasant conditions outside on one hand, and the train's self-contained opulence on the other. From the perspective of the station, the train's call of "I'm coming" represents an unanswerable, false promise. At the story's end the train removes from the barren station everything it brought. Shedding the station like a snake sheds its used-up skin, it leaves behind only some bread, some pocket-change, an orange and some candies that are "not very nice."

Gordimer provides little detail about the newly married couple beyond suggesting that they are honeymooning and that they are not themselves from southern Africa. The young wife's comments about "the unreality of the last few weeks," the difficulty of finding places "at home" to put the carvings and baskets they have thus far bought on their trip, and the changing meaning of these things "away from the places [she] found them" suggest that the honeymooners are not themselves Rhodesian, but are touring Africa and, like Churchill, will return to Britain when their honeymoon is over. (Rhodesia, which lies directly north of South Africa, was a British colony until November 12th, 1965. The name change to Zimbabwe took place in 1980.)

On the next rung down from the transients on the train is a somewhat cliched depiction of the stalwart Afrikaner family, carving out a niche from the unforgiving country. Like the principal characters the stationmaster remains nameless, but his social rank is nonetheless clearly identified. His uniform is rumpled and creased. His house is made of tin. A sheep carcass hangs in the verandah. His children wander around barefoot. His garden grows nothing. Taken together, these points mean to demonstrate that the stationmaster and his family are from the poorest part of South Africa's white working class, not coincidentally, the group in the most direct competition with blacks for unskilled positions. (David Harrison writes in *The White Tribe of Africa* that "between 1924 and 1933 the proportion of unskilled white workers on the railways rose from 9.5. . .to 39.9 % while the proportion of blacks fell from 75. . .to 48.9 %.")

At this early stage in her career Gordimer fails to get much closer to the station's black inhabitants than her heroine does. However, the details she provides from a distance demonstrate that their lives of unpleasant, undignified dependency are in as sharp a contrast to the relative well-being of the stationmaster and his family as they are to the idealized, mythical Africa they sell—the Africa of woven baskets, of carved buck, of "lions. . .grappling with strange, thin, elongated warriors who clutched spears and showed no fear." This is, in the protagonist's words, "the fantasy" of a world in balance, a world in which blacks live dignified lives in harmony with the world they inhabit, a world in which there is no asymmetry between hunter and hunted or between black and white. But beyond the fantasy they sell is a very different reality, one in which the black majority accommodate themselves however they can while they mourn, mythologize, and commercialize their heritage for British consumption. The station, then, is a self-contained economic world, consisting only of the stationmaster's house, a goods store, and an adjacent *kraal*. (Similar to "corral," the Afrikaans *kraal* also describes a small group of huts within the wall).

Together, these locations suggest an entirely artificial micro-economy, subject to the passing trains for continuance. The stationmaster and his wife buy goods to sell to the blacks living in the adjacent kraal. The blacks, in turn, have no recourse but to carve and weave artifacts to sell to train passengers in order to buy goods from the stationmaster's store. Until the arrival of this particular train, the system remains asymmetrical, static, timeless. This imbalance of power is the principal asymmetry from which all others arise. There is, without truly representative government, no mechanism to allow the blacks at the base of the economic pyramid to invert the structures of power and race, nor is there any incentive for the white minority to let go of their franchise and make the government representative.

The story's plot sets this stasis in motion. It details how an artfully carved lion reaches across the barriers of race, class and silence that separate the domains, of white and black South Africans—a disarmingly simple theme. However, this simple theme supports a complex and nuanced rising awareness on the part of the female protagonist. Ultimately, her rejection of her new husband powerfully demonstrates the impossibility of living "outside" incompatible ideologies. Though the young woman is certainly not intentionally looking for opportunities to mingle with the natives, the old man smiles "not from the heart, but at the customer." His carving "speaks" to her in a different language, uncomfortably bridging the chasm of silence between the domains of black and white South Africa. Its mane "tell[s] you. . . that the artist had delight in the lion." It is this "delight," by the story's conclusion, that makes the young woman unable to quell her awareness of the humanity that she and the woodcarver share. The protagonist senses that a moral wrong has been done, but she is certainly unwilling, perhaps even unable, to understand the origin of her disquiet. In a pointed, ironic commentary on the relativity of values aesthetic systems, the woman is outraged, not because her husband meanly cheated another man out of a ridiculously small amount of change, but that he did so for a lion that was pretty, suggesting that the real victim is the undervalued artwork, not the old man standing by the railroad panting. (The lion's price, whether three-or one-and six shillings is ridiculously low by any standard. Gordimer underscores this by withholding the key word "shilling" until nearly the end of the story, inviting the reader to substitute the basic South African currency unit "rand" in its place.) So threatening are the possibilities in every direction—on one hand, that the carver is as human as she is; on the other, that she can no longer respect her husband—that the protagonist is gradually squeezed into a state of emotional paralysis. Handled by a ham-fisted author this approach would have led the protagonist to buy the lion, make more contact with the man, and reach back across the divide in sudden, blinding self-awareness. But Gordimer avoids such sentimentality, instead following her protagonist from the stasis of the external setting to the paralysis of limited self-awareness while leading the reader along the contours of race, class, and culture that defined South Africa at the outset of *apartheid,* and, to some measure, continue to define it today.

**Source:** David Kippen, for *Short Stories for Students,* Gale Research, 1997.

## Nadine Gordimer

*In the following essay, originally written as a foreword to her collection,* Selected Stories, *Gordimer outlines her philosophy of short story writing. "The Train from Rhodesia" is included in the collection.*

> After I had selected and arranged these stories, the present publisher asked me to provide some kind of introduction to them. If they were now making their first appearance I might have recoiled from this invitation, but they have all been printed and some reprinted, and have therefore been through a period of probation. Whatever I may say about them now cannot alter what has been said by others, and can hardly increase or lessen the likelihood of their being read—that must depend on the stories themselves.

The words are William Plomer's, but the attitude comes so close to my own that I do not hesitate to fly his declaration at the masthead of this book. William Plomer not only wrote some stories that have become classic, he also had a special interest in and fascination with the short story as a form used in widely diverse ways by others. His code holds good for me; for all of us. I take it further; if the story itself does not succeed in conveying all the writer meant it should, no matter when he wrote it, neither explication nor afterthought can change this. Conversely, if the story has been *achieved,* the patronizing backward glance its writer might cast upon it, as something he could now do with one hand tied behind his back but no longer would care to do at all, will not detract from it.

I wrote these stories [in *Selected Stories*] over thirty years. I have attempted now to influence any reader's judgment of or pleasure in them only to the extent implied by the fact that I have chosen some and excluded others. In this sense, I suppose, I have 'rewritten': imposed a certain form, shaped by retrospect, upon the collection as an entity. For everything one writes is part of the whole story, so far as any individual writer attempts to build the pattern of his own perception out of chaos. To make sense of life: that story, in which everything, novels, stories, the false starts, the half-completed, the abandoned, has its meaningful place, will be complete with the last sentence written before one dies or imagination atrophies. As for retrospect as a valid critique, I realize it has no fixed existence but represents my own constantly changing effort to teach myself how to make out of words a total form for whatever content I seize upon. This I understood only too clearly when I was obliged to read through my five existing collections of stories and saw how there are some stories I have gone on writing, again and again, all my life, not so much because the themes are obsessional but because I found other ways to take hold of them; because I hoped to make the revelation of new perceptions through the different techniques these demanded. I felt for the touch that would release the spring that shuts off appearance from reality. If I were to make a choice of my stories in five years' time, I might choose a different selection, in the light of what I might have learnt about these things by then. My 'retrospect' would be based upon which stories approached most nearly what I happened to have most recently taught myself. That is inevitable.

Why write short stories?

The question implies the larger one: what makes one write? Both have brought answers from experts who study writers as a psychological and social phenomenon. It is easier and more comforting to be explained than to try and explain oneself. Both have also brought answers of a kind from many writers; devious answers; as mine may be. (If one found out exactly how one walks the tightrope, would one fall immediately?) Some have lived—or died—to contradict their own theories; Ernest Hemingway said we write out our sicknesses in books, and shot himself. Of course I find I agree with those writers whose theories coincide at least in part with mine. What is experienced as solitude (and too quickly dubbed alienation) is pretty generally agreed to be a common condition conducive to becoming a writer. Octavio Paz speaks of the 'double solitude', as an intellectual and a woman, of the famous early Spanish-American writer, Sor Juana Inès de la Cruz. Growing up in a gold-mining town in South Africa as a member of a white minority, to begin with, my particular solitude as an intellectual-by-inclination was so complete I did not even know I was one: the concept 'intellectual', gathered from reading, belonged as categorically to the Northern Hemisphere as a snowy Christmas. Certainly there must have been other people who were intellectuals, but they no doubt accepted their isolation too philosophically to give a signal they scarcely hoped would be answered, let alone attract an acolyte. As for the specific solitude of the woman-as-intellectual, I must say truthfully that my femininity has never constituted any special kind of solitude, for me. Indeed, in that small town, walled up among the mine dumps, born exiled from the European world of ideas, ignorant that such a world existed among Africans, my only genuine and innocent connection with the social life of the town (in the sense that I was not pretending to be what I was not, forever hiding the activities of mind and imagination which must be suspect, must be concealed) was through my femaleness. As an adolescent, at least I felt and followed sexual attraction in common with others; that was a form of communion I could share. Rapunzel's hair is the right metaphor for this femininity: by means of it, I was able to let myself out and live in the body, with others, as well as—alone—in the mind. To be young and in the sun; my experience of this was similar to that of Camus, although I did not enter into it as fully as he did, I did not play football. . . .

In any case, I question the existence of the specific solitude of woman-as-intellectual when that woman is a writer, because when it comes to their essential faculty as writers, all writers are androgynous beings.

The difference between alienation and solitude should be clear enough. Writers' needs in this respect are less clear, and certainly less well and honestly understood, even by themselves. Some form of solitude (there are writers who are said to find it in a crowded cafe, or less romantically among the cockroaches in a night-time family kitchen, others who must have a cabin in the woods) is the condition of creation. The less serious—shall we say professional?—form of alienation follows inevitably. It is very different from the kind of serious psychic rupture between the writer and his society that has occurred in the Soviet Union and in South Africa, for example, and that I shall not discuss here, since it requires a study in itself.

I believe—I *know* (there are not many things I should care to dogmatize about, on the subject of writing) that writers need solitude, and seek alienation of a kind every day of their working lives. (And remember, they are not even aware when and when not they are working. . .) Powers of observation heightened beyond the normal imply extraordinary disinvolvement; or rather the double process, excessive preoccupation and identification with the lives of others, and at the same time a monstrous detachment. For identification brings the superficial loyalties (that is, to the self) of concealment and privacy, while detachment brings the harsher fidelities (to the truth about the self) of revealment and exposure. The tension between standing apart and being fully involved; that is what makes a writer. That is where we begin. The validity of this dialectic is the synthesis of revelation; our achievement of, or even attempt at this is the moral, the human justification for what we do.

Here I am referring to an accusation that every writer meets, that we 'use' people, or rather other people's lives. Of course we do. As unconscious eternal eavesdroppers and observers, snoopers, nothing that is human is alien to the imagination and the particular intuition to which it is a trance-like state of entry. I have written *from the starting-point* of other people's 'real' lives; what I have written represents alternatives to the development of a life as it was formed before I encountered it and as it will continue, out of my sight. A writer sees in your life what you do not. That is why people who think they recognize themselves as 'models' for this character or that in a story will protest triumphantly, 'it wasn't that way at all'. They think they know better; but perhaps it is the novelist or short story writer who does? Fiction is a way of exploring possibilities present but undreamt of in the living of a single life.

There is also the assumption, sometimes prurient or deliciously scandalized, that writers write only about themselves. I know that I have used my own life much the same way as I have that of others: events (emotions are events, too, of the spirit) mark exits and entrances in a warren where many burrows lead off into the same darkness but this one might debouch far distant from that. What emerges most often is an alternative fate, the predisposition to which exists in what 'actually' happened.

How can the eavesdropper, observer, snooper ever be the prototype? The stories in this book were written between the ages of twenty and fifty. Where am I, in them? I search for myself. At most, reading them over for the first time in many years, I see my own shadow dancing on a wall behind and over certain stories. I can make a guess at remembering what significatory event it was that casts it there. The story's 'truth' or lack of it is not attached to or dependent upon that lost event.

But part of these stories' 'truth' does depend upon faithfulness to another series of lost events—the shifts in social attitudes as evidenced in the characters and situations. I had wanted to arrange the selection in sequence from the earliest story collection to the latest simply because when reading story collections I myself enjoy following the development of a writer. Then I found that this order had another logic to which my first was complementary. The chronological order turns out to be an historical one. The change in social attitudes unconsciously reflected in the stories represents both that of the people in my society—that is to say, history—and my apprehension of it; in the writing, I am acting upon my society, and in the manner of my apprehension, all the time history is acting upon me....

What I am saying is that I see that many of these stories *could not have been written* later or earlier than they were. If I could have juggled them around in the contents list of this collection without that being evident, they would have been false in some way important to me as a writer.

What I am also saying, then, is that in a certain sense a writer is 'selected' by his subject—his subject being *the consciousness* of his own era. How he deals with this is, to me, the fundament of commitment, although 'commitment' is usually understood as the reverse process: a writer's selection of a subject in conformity with the rationalization of his own ideological and/or political beliefs.

My time and place have been twentieth-century Africa. Emerging from it, immersed in it, the first form in which I wrote was the short story. I write fewer and fewer stories, now, and more novels, but I don't think I shall ever stop writing stories. What makes a writer turn from one to the other? How do they differ?

Nobody has ever succeeded in defining a short story in a manner to satisfy all who write or read them, and I shall not, here. I sometimes wonder if one shouldn't simply state flatly: a short story is a piece of fiction short enough to be read at one sitting? No, that will satisfy no one, least myself. But for me certainly there is a clue, there, to the choice of the short story by writers, as a form: whether or not it has a narrative in the external or internal sense, whether it sprawls or neatly bites its own tail, a short story is a concept that the writer can

> "Growing up in a gold-mining town in South Africa as a member of a white minority, to begin with, my particular solitude as an intellectual-by-inclination was so complete I did not even know I was one."

'hold', fully realized, in his imagination, at one time. A novel is, by comparison, staked out, and must be taken possession of stage by stage; it is impossible to contain, all at once, the proliferation of concepts it ultimately may use. For this reason I cannot understand how people can suppose one makes a conscious choice, *after* knowing what one wants to write about, between writing a novel or a short story. A short story *occurs,* in the imaginative sense. To write one is to express from a situation in the exterior or interior world the life-giving drop—sweat, tear, semen, saliva—that will spread an intensity on the page; burn a hole in it.

**Source:** Nadine Gordimer, an introduction to *Selected Stories,* 1975. Reprint by the Viking Press, 1976, pp. 9–14.

## Thomas H. Gullason

*In the following essay, Gullason discusses the categorization of the short story as a second-class citizen of literature, but offers evidence that as a form it is deserving of much more. By way of example, he discusses Gordimer's "The Train from Rhodesia."*

...What must we do so that the short story can receive the kind of consideration it deserves? We can try to rid the genre of the prejudices that have conspired against it. We can come to it as though it were a fresh discovery. We can settle on one term for the medium, like "short fiction" or "short story." References to names like "anecdote," "tale," "narrative," "sketch," though convenient, merely add to the confusion and suggest indecision and a possible inferiority complex. Too many names attached to the short story have made it seem almost nameless. Even the provincial attitude of teachers and anthologists has not helped. Most often students are fed on a strict diet of British and American short-story writers. But the short story is not solely a British and American product; it is an international art form, and Continental as well as Oriental, and other authors should be more fully represented in any educational program. As Maurice Beebe reminds us, "Once translated, Zola, Mann, Proust, Kafka become authors in English and American literature...." Once this philosophy is accepted, the short story will automatically increase in vitality and stature....

A more modern illustration . . . is South Africa's Nadine Gordimer in her 2400-word story "The Train from Rhodesia" (1949). What one discovers with this example is that even extreme brevity cannot stifle the short story. "The Train from Rhodesia" is a puzzling story, for Miss Gordimer is trying to say far more than she reveals on the surface. One sees that she is in a world of censorship, the possible loss of a passport, and possible imprisonment and therefore sends cryptic notes from underground. Miss Gordimer's art is the poetic art of ellipsis—much has been omitted; the reader must fill in.

What Miss Gordimer has done is to take a brief space of time and lives and make it suggest a large panorama of feelings and attitudes. For in the story we see the separateness of black and white, and white and white, the world of primitivism (suggested by the hunk of sheep's carcass dangling in a current of air) and civilization (suggested by the train and its inhabitants), and hunger (suggested by the piccanins and the animals) versus sloth (suggested by occupants of the train, who throw out chocolates). The train expands these various threads. For one, the train is from Rhodesia and is to be burdened with white and native problems. In the opening of the story we hear: the "train came out of the red horizon and bore down toward them...." Before the train stops in the station, it "called out, along the sky; but there was no answer; and the cry hung on: "I'm coming . . . I'm coming...." The last paragraph of the story returns to the train and extends its meaning: "The train had cast the station like a skin. It called out to the sky, I'm coming, I'm coming, I'm coming; and again, there was no answer."

The specific actions lead us to the generalizations made above. The pitiful natives smile not "from the heart, but at the customer." Their primitive art, like the carved lion, is "majestic," but they as vendors are bent "like performing animals." The old vendor who sells his art work to the young husband for one-and-six has his opened palm "held in the attitude of receiving." The crisis of husband and wife at the story's end is not resolved; it merges with the tempo—gnarled, fierce, disconnected—of the humanized train which expands and heightens the various estrangements. In one place, the wife reflects: "How will they [the native goods] look at home? Where will you put them? What will they mean away from the places you found them? Away from the unreality of the last few weeks? The man outside. But he is not part of the unreality; he is for good now. Odd . . . somewhere there was an idea that he, that living with him, was part of the holiday, the strange places." This private reflection becomes a public estrangement with her husband: "If you wanted the thing [the carved lion] . . . why didn't you buy it in the first place? If you wanted it, why didn't you pay for it? Why didn't you take it decently, when he offered it? Why did you have to wait for him to run after the train with it, and give him one-and-six? One-and-six!'' The wife returns to her private world: "She had thought it was something to do with singleness, with being alone and belonging too much to oneself." The train's choric chant at the end—"I'm coming, I'm coming; and again, there was no answer''—helps to magnify a world of loneliness, separation, and discord.

... [This] story defies the rules: Its action is small; its meanings are large. It is a poetic story—even more important, an impressionistic painting, for Miss Gordimer wants us to *see* and to *feel* the world of Africa through this one incident. The incident is not closed; there are the after effects, nothing is finished off, the problem still exists....

The novelist has been called the "long-distance runner," and he is not lonely. The short-story writer has been called a "sprinter," and he is lonely. Carlos Baker's reading of Hemingway's short stories is penetrating, as he uses Hemingway's own statement to explain the depths of the form. "The dignity of movement of an iceberg," Hemingway once said, "is due to only one-eighth of it being above water." Many of our great modern short-story writers write in shorthand; and one word, a phrase, can raise the short story to a new level of meaning. There is dignity and hidden depth in the short story. It has been in a deep freeze too long. One looks forward to a thawing out period.

**Source:** Thomas H. Gullason, "The Short Story: An Underrated Art," in *Studies in Short Fiction,* Vol. 2, No. 1, Fall, 1964, pp. 13–31.

## Sources

Clingman, Stephen R. *The Novels of Nadine Gordimer: History from the Inside,* Allen & Unwin, 1988.

Cooke, John. *The Novels of Nadine Gordimer: Private Lives/Public Landscapes,* Louisiana State University Press, 1985, 235 p.

Ettin, Andrew Vogel. *Betrayals of the Body Politic,* University Press of Virginia, 1992, 150 p.

Harrison, David. *The White Tribe of Africa,* University of California Press, 1981.

Trump, Martin. "The Short Fiction of Nadine Gordimer," in *Research in African Literatures,* Vol. 17, No. 3, Fall, 1986, pp. 341-66.

## Further Reading

Haugh, Robert F. *Nadine Gordimer,* Twayne, 1974, 174 p.
Haugh discusses the body of Gordimer's work and her talents as a writer.

Herbert, Michael. "The Train from Rhodesia," in *Reference Guide to Short Fiction,* edited by Noelle Watson, St. James Press, 1994, p. 937–38.
Includes essays on both Gordimer and "The Train from Rhodesia," concentrating on their literary significance.

Huggan, Graham. "Echoes from Elsewhere: Gordimer's Short Fiction as Social Critique," in *Research in African Literature* Spring, 1994.
Huggan discusses Gordimer's works of self-criticism and her conviction that the short story is a particularly relevant and effective genre. This essay focuses on several stories, including "Six Feet of the Country," "A Company of Old Laughing Faces," "Livingstone's Companions" and "Keeping Fit."

Smith, Rowland. Introduction to *Critical Essays on Nadine Gordimer,* from the Critical Essays on World Literature Series, G.K. Hall, 1990, pp. 1-22.
Smith presents a detailed overview of South African and international responses to the work of Nadine Gordimer, and chronicles how they have changed in the decades she has been writing.

Terkel, Studs. "Conversations with Nadine Gordimer," in *Perspective on Ideals and the Arts,* Vol. 12, No. 3, May 1963, pp. 42-49.
An interview with Gordimer in which the author discusses the viewpoint of the young woman in "The Train From Rhodesia."

Wade, Michael. *Nadine Gordimer,* Evans, 1976.
Wade examines novels like *The Lying Days, A Occasion for Loving* and *The Conservationist* thoroughly, and refers briefly to her short stories.

# *A Worn Path*

**Eudora Welty**

**1941**

Eudora Welty's "A Worn Path," first published in *Atlantic Monthly* in February, 1941, is the tale of Phoenix Jackson's journey through the woods of Mississippi to the town of Natchez. The story won an O. Henry Prize the year it was published and later appeared in Welty's collection *The Wide Net*. Since then, it has been frequently anthologized. At first the story appears simple, but its mythic undertones and ambiguity gives a depth and richness that has been praised by critics. Welty has said that she was inspired to write the story after seeing an old African-American woman walking alone across the southern landscape. In "A Worn Path," the woman's trek is spurred by the need to obtain medicine for her ill grandson. Along the way, Phoenix encounters several obstacles and the story becomes a quest for her to overcome the trials she faces, which mirror her plight in society at large. The story is one of the best examples of Welty's writing, which is known for its realistic portrayal of the American South, particularly during the depression.

## Author Biography

Eudora Welty was born on April 13, 1909, in Jackson, Mississippi, to Christian Webb and Chestina Andrews Welty. Her father was an insurance company president. She attended Mississippi State College for Women for a year and graduated from the

University of Wisconsin in 1929 with a major in English literature. She also attended the Columbia University Graduate School of Business where she studied advertising. After graduation, the Great Depression hampered her ability to find a job in her chosen field, so she worked as a part-time journalist and copywriter at newspapers and radio stations near her home in Mississippi. She also acquired a job as a Works Progress Administration (WPA) photographer, a job that took her on assignments throughout Mississippi. The experience of traveling throughout the South in order to observe people gave her the impetus to begin writing stories. Her first published story, "Death of a Traveling Salesman," was accepted in the journal *Manuscript,* and within two years her work was being accepted in many publications, including the *Atlantic* and the *Southern Review.*

Welty has never married, and despite stints in Wisconsin in college and New York City as a member of the *New York Times Book Review* staff, Welty has lived on Pinehurst Street in Jackson most of her life. Her fiction reveals these deep ties to the South, and though often set in Mississippi, her stories reveal truths about the human condition that transcend region. Welty has published several collections of short stories, six novels, and has tried her hand at plays, poems, and children's books. Welty's published photographs also reveal an artist with a sharp eye for detail and compassionate treatment of her subjects. Winner of the 1972 Pulitzer Prize for her novel *The Optimist's Daughter,* several O. Henry Awards, two American Book Awards, and numerous others, Eudora Welty has established herself as one of the most admired fiction writers of the twentieth century.

## Plot Summary

The story opens on a chilly December morning. An elderly African-American woman named Phoenix Jackson is making her way, slowly but surely, through the woods, tapping an umbrella on the ground in front of her as she walks. Her shoes are untied. While she taps along, she talks to the animals in the woods, telling them to keep out of her way. As the path goes up a hill, she complains about how difficult walking becomes. It becomes evident that she has made this journey many times before; she is familiar with all the twists and turns in the trail. She talks aimlessly to herself. Her eyesight is poor, and she catches her skirt in the thorns on a bush.

After walking across a log to traverse a stream, she rests. She imagines a boy bringing her a slice of cake but opens her eyes to find her hand in the air, grasping nothing. The terrain becomes more difficult, and at a certain point she thinks she sees a ghost, but it is only a scarecrow. Blaming the confusion on her age and the fact that her "senses is gone," she moves on. She meets a black dog with a "lolling tongue." She hits the dog lightly with her cane, and the effort knocks her off balance and she falls into a ditch.

The dog's owner, a white hunter, happens by and helps her out of the ditch. When he hears that she is attempting to make it into town, he says it is too far and tells her to go home. But Phoenix is determined, and the hunter laughs, saying "I know you old colored people! Wouldn't miss going to town to see Santa Claus." While he is laughing, a nickel falls out of his pocket. While he momentarily turns his attention to his dogs, she snatches the nickel from the ground. When he returns, he points the gun at her and asks if it scares her. After she tells him that it does not, he leaves her and she continues walking. Finally she reaches Natchez, where the Christmas bells are ringing and the town is festooned with decorations. She asks a white woman to tie her shoe, and the woman obliges.

Arriving at her destination, the woman climbs a set of stairs and enters a doctor's office. The attendant assumes Phoenix is a charity case. The nurse replies that it is "just old Aunt Phoenix" who has come to get medicine for her grandson. Phoenix remains silent as the nurse asks her questions. The nurse eventually loses patience and urges the old woman to "tell us quickly about your grandson, and get it over." Phoenix snaps out of her daze when a "flame of comprehension" comes to her. She explains what the nurse already knows, that her grandson swallowed lye and now needs medicine periodically to soothe his throat. The nurse offers Phoenix a few pennies, to which she responds "Five pennies is a nickel." After the nurse gives her the nickel, she lays her two nickels side by side in her hand and then leaves the office to buy her grandson a paper windmill.

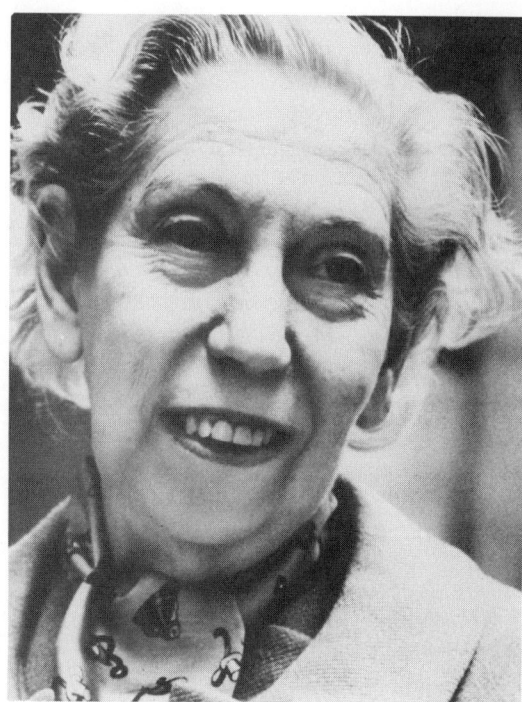

*Eudora Welty*

## Characters

### The Grandson

Phoenix's grandson does not appear in the story, but his medical condition is the reason for the old woman's journey. Having swallowed lye (a strong alkaline substance used in making soap) several years ago, the boy's throat is permanently damaged. His grandmother is the only relative he has left, and she makes the trip to town to receive medicine that soothes the pain. There has been no change in his condition, Phoenix tells the nurse, he sits with his "mouth open like a little bird." She also says that though he suffers, he has "a sweet look." Though Phoenix says he is not dead, some critics have theorized that he is.

### The Hunter

The hunter encounters Phoenix after she has fallen into a ditch, the unfortunate result of an encounter with one of his dogs. He helps her up, demonstrating his willingness to assist a person in need. But his subsequent conversation with her reveals his disrespect for her and biased attitudes towards African Americans in general. When he learns that she intends to walk to town, he assumes Phoenix is not able to make the long journey and he tells her to go home; he has no qualms about issuing the order. But when she persists, he relents, assuming that the only reason "old colored people" would embark on such a long trail would be to see Santa Claus. In a second instance of disrespect, he tells Phoenix that he would give her a dime if he had one, unaware that Phoenix has already picked up the nickel that fell out of his pocket. In a third example, he points a gun at her face and asks if it scares her. He is amused by the fact that it does not, further emphasizing his insensitivity. Throughout the conversation, he refers to her as "Granny," as the other characters do, all of whom are unwilling to look beyond Phoenix's age and see her as an individual.

### Phoenix Jackson

Old Phoenix Jackson is the protagonist of the story. She is described in vivid colors, suggesting her lively nature: she wears a red rag in her hair and her skin is described as "yellow," "golden" and "copper." Her age is indicated by the way she moves—slowly, in small steps, with the assistance of a cane—and by the wrinkles on her face, which form "a pattern all its own . . . as though a whole little tree stood in the middle of her forehead." Because of her frailty, her determination to continue on her journey highlights her resilience and perseverance. Old Phoenix sees the Natchez Trace as an obstacle course, one that she tolerates with a fair sense of humor, despite her lapses into senility. She tells the animals to stay out of her way. Her dress gets caught in a thorny bush, and she tells the thorns "you doing your appointed work. Never want to let folks pass, no sir." When a dog causes her to fall into a ditch she cannot climb out of, she simply awaits help—her sense of determination never succumbs to defeat.

When Phoenix is finally rescued by the white hunter, she suffers his indignations with stoic resolve. He tells her to go home and finally assumes that the purpose of her long journey is to see Santa Claus. Phoenix does not feel the need to ingratiate herself to him by explaining the purpose for her trip, however. Yet her willingness to take advantage of him for her own gain is demonstrated by her quick response to the nickel falling out of his pocket. However, her conscience bothers her: "God watching me the whole time. I come to stealing." Ultimately, the hunter displays his disregard for her by pointing his hunting rifle at her. Phoenix remains unflustered. But she is not beyond asking for help. When she gets to town she asks a woman to tie her shoes for her. ''I doesn't mind asking a nice lady to tie up my shoe,'' she says, indicating that her pride does not interfere with her humility. Still, Phoenix suffers insults: the woman calls her ''Grandma,'' and the nurse at the doctor's office tells her ''You mustn't take up our time this way.''

In addition to remaining undaunted by the demeaning comments of others, Phoenix perseveres in the face of senility as well. During her trek, she imagines a boy bringing her a slice of cake and is startled back to reality by the sight of her arm grasping the air. At the doctor's office, the nurse speaks to her at first to no avail: ''It was my memory had left me'' she says finally, ''There I sat and forgot why I made my long trip.'' When her mission is revealed—to get medicine for her grandson—Phoenix's determination is immediately apparent. She has made the journey selflessly, for someone else's sake. ''We is the only two left in the world,'' she says, revealing her strong commitment to her family and her sacrificing nature.

Phoenix's name is symbolic of the mythological bird who rises from its own ashes to begin another cycle of life. The old woman's name thus suggests her timelessness and the fact that she can never be suppressed, even by those who would try to break her spirit.

### The Nurse

The nurse reveals information about Phoenix Jackson that the reader does not know during the course of her journey. Thus, her conversation with Phoenix is the climax of the story. The nurse, who represents society's general attitudes, displays some sensitivity towards the woman, assuring the attendant that ''Old Aunt Phoenix... doesn't come for herself—she has a little grandson.'' Even so, the nurse treats the old woman with the same sense of belittlement that other characters in the story have. ''You mustn't take up our time this way,'' she says, exasperated when the woman lapses into a spell of forgetfulness, ''Tell us quickly about your grandson, and get it over.'' Like the other people on Phoenix's obstacle-course journey, the nurse prefers not to give Phoenix too much respect since she is old, African American, and a woman. Thus, in the nurse's eyes, Phoenix is not entitled to all the respect granted others in society.

## Media Adaptations

- ''A Worn Path'' was adapted into a into a 20-minute film produced by Worn Path Productions and distributed by Pyramid Film and Video. The film includes a ten-minute interview with Eudora Welty, conducted by Pulitzer Prize–winning playwright Beth Henley.

- ''Eudora Welty Reads 'Why I Live at the P.O.' and ''A Worn Path''' was produced by Caedmon Audio Cassettes in 1992.

## Themes

''A Worn Path'' is Eudora Welty's story of an old African-American woman's ritual journey. Its themes are elicited from the symbol of the journey as well as the encounters the old woman has on her journey. Critics have praised Welty's use of language, myth, and symbol in this deceptively simple story.

### Race and Racism

Issues of race often inform Welty's fiction for the fact that so much of her fiction is set in Mississippi during the 1940s and 1950s. Phoenix's brief encounters on her journey typify the views of many Southern whites during the era. A white hunter helps her out of a ditch but patronizes her and trivializes her journey: ''I know you old colored people! Wouldn't miss going to town to see Santa Claus!'' He also taunts her by pointing his loaded gun at her and asking, ''Doesn't the gun scare you?'' Through these exchanges, Welty shows how some whites regarded blacks. He also calls her ''Granny,'' a term common for older African-American women. Often whites would call older blacks ''Aunt,'' ''Granny,'' or ''Uncle'' as a way of denying them their dignity and individuality. In another example of this, the nurse calls her ''aunt Phoenix'' instead of the more formal ''Mrs. Jackson.'' Although no one in the story is actually rude or discriminatory towards Phoenix, Welty demonstrates

## Topics for Further Study

- Research the history of the Natchez Trace in Mississippi and the surrounding area. How has the trail been important to various groups throughout history, and why is this an appropriate setting for Welty's story of Phoenix Jackson?

- Find out about race relations in the United States, especially in Mississippi, during the early 1940s. Are these the same attitudes Welty depicts in "A Worn Path"?

- The journey has been a literary device since ancient Greek times when Homer wrote *The Odyssey*. How is Phoenix Jackson's walk through the woods similar to Odysseus's seven-year journey home after the Trojan War?

---

the subtle persecutions that blacks suffer in a white world.

### Duty and Responsibility

Phoenix Jackson is mobilized by her sense of duty to her grandson. Because she is the only person her grandson has to rely on—"We is the only two left in the world," she tells the nurse—she is determined to make it to town to obtain the medicine that will soothe his injured throat. Her sense of responsibility dominates her personality, overcoming her encroaching senility, her poor eyesight, and her difficulty in walking. Phoenix relates her determination with a sense of urgency to the hunter: she tells the hunter: "I bound to go to town, mister. . . . The time come around." In the character of Phoenix, Welty relates the virtue in doing selfless things for others.

The nurse also has a duty and a responsibility to keep giving Phoenix the medicine as long as she keeps coming to get it. She says that "the doctor said as long as you came to get it, you could have it. . . . But it's an obstinate case." The attendant gives Phoenix a nickel to spend, but she seems to do it out of a sense of duty because it is Christmas time. Even the hunter, who helps Phoenix out of the ditch, and the young woman on the street, who ties her shoes, seem to act out of duty, not out of compassion or love. Only Phoenix's actions—making the arduous journey into town for her grandson—transcend responsibility and are motivated by a sense of true love.

### Guilt

A minor theme in "A Worn Path" concerns guilt and innocence. Phoenix feels guilty when she picks up the nickel that falls from the pocket of the white hunter. She indicates in her words to the hunter that she believes that she deserves to be shot for the offense: "I seen plenty go off closer by, in my day, and for less than what I done." Even though the hunter has lied to her, claiming that he does not have any money, she knows it is not right to retaliate through artifice on her own part. However, other actions that should inspire guilt—the hunter aiming a loaded gun at her face, for instance—do not. The attendant at the doctor's office, perhaps feeling guilty for her impatient comment, "Are you deaf?" may be offering amends when she gives Phoenix the nickel. The symbol of innocence in the story is surely the grandson, a helpless young boy who is unable to care for himself and whose throat periodically closes up, causing him to gasp for breath. His innocence is protected by the caring and love his grandmother provides. Readers wonder, knowing how old and frail Phoenix is, what will become of him once she dies and he is left without anyone to care for him.

### Resurrection

Phoenix's name points to the theme of resurrection in "A Worn Path." The phoenix was the bird in ancient mythology that rose from its own ashes every 500 years to begin a new life cycle. Phoenix Jackson, whose statement that she was "too old at the Surrender" to go to school—1865—hints that she is probably over eighty at the time the story takes place, but she refuses to die or give up. Phoenix's ritual journey into town symbolizes the continual rising-up of the old woman, like the bird she is allied with. Her description given at the beginning of the story also seems to suggest fire and life: "a golden color ran underneath, and the two knobs of her cheeks were illumined by a yellow burning under the dark. Under the red rag her hair came down on her neck in the frailest of ringlets, still black, and with an odor like copper."

# Style

## Point of View

"A Worn Path" is told from a third-person limited point of view. This allows the reader to empathize with Phoenix, because her thoughts and actions are shown. Yet, in third-person, the reader is allowed to view Phoenix from a distance, and thereby see her as others see her.

## Symbolism

The most obvious symbol in the story is Phoenix Jackson's comparison to the mythological bird, the phoenix. Dressed in vivid colors, Phoenix's resilience is underscored by her comparison with a bird that rises from the ashes every 500 years. Additionally, Phoenix's grandson is described by the woman as "[wearing] a little patch quilt and peep out holding his mouth open like a little bird."

## Similes

Welty has been praised from early on for her use of language. In using similes, she makes vivid comparisons that help the reader form a mind's eye picture of the action. Similes are direct comparisons that use words such as "like" or "as" to link the two ideas. One such simile in this story occurs in the description of Phoenix Jackson's face: "Her skin had a pattern all its own of numberless branching wrinkles and as though a whole little tree stood in the middle of her forehead...." The narrator describes her cane as being "limber as a buggy whip." As Phoenix walks across the log, she looks "like a festival figure in some parade." She encounters big dead trees "like black men with one arm." Other similes in the story appeal to various senses, such as smell: "she gave off perfume like the red roses in the summer." In touching the scarecrow, Phoenix finds "a coat and inside that an emptiness, cold as ice."

## Setting

Setting is crucial to the purpose of this story because Welty conceived the idea for the tale of Phoenix Jackson as she sat with a painter friend out on the Old Natchez Trace. The Trace is an old highway that runs from Nashville, Tennessee, to Natchez, Mississippi. By 1800 it was the busiest in the American South. Phoenix lives "away back off the Old Natchez Trace," as the nurse in the doctor's office says. This indicates that Phoenix lives fairly far from Natchez, which means that the journey—compounded by the fact that it is December—is difficult for her. In the rural area, she encounters animals, thorny bushes, ditches, streams to be crossed by logs, barbed-wire fences, and even people. These obstacles underscore how deeply she cares and sacrifices for her grandson. When the narrator tells us at the end of the story that "her slow step began on the stairs, going down," it indicates that she is faced with a return journey as arduous as the one she just completed. Time is also important in the story: Phoenix says that she was "too old at the Surrender" to go to school. If the story takes place in the time it was written, 1941, Phoenix would be anywhere from 80 to 100 years old. This further magnifies the intensity of her journey and the tragic situation of her grandson's dependence on her.

## Conflict

Every work of fiction has some kind of conflict, and most obvious one in "A Worn Path" is Phoenix's struggle against nature and the landscape. The determination Phoenix shows when faced with various hardships on her path help define her character for the reader. Other outward conflicts in the story result from her encounters with the hunter and with the attendant in the doctor's office. The hunter teases her and points a gun at her; Phoenix remains calm and steady, causing the hunter to exclaim "Well, Granny... you must be a hundred years old, and scared of nothing." The conflict with the office attendant serves to show another side of Phoenix, her dignity in the face of racial and age discrimination. She refuses to speak to the condescending woman until the nurse comes in and explains who she is. When the attendant, possibly out of guilt, offers to give Phoenix a few pennies from her purse, Phoenix "stiffly" says, "Five pennies is a nickel." Through the use of the conflicts, which seem ordinary, Welty shows how daily life can be a struggle for someone like Phoenix.

# Historical Context

## War and Poverty

Welty's "A Worn Path" was published in 1941, the same year the United States entered World War II. Europe had already been involved in the conflict for several years since Adolph Hitler began enlarging Germany's empire. Germany declared war on the United States in December, after the Japanese bombing of Pearl Harbor and the U.S.'s declaration of war against Japan. Set against the brewing global conflict, Welty's tale of rural life

## Compare & Contrast

- **1941:** *Native Son*, a stage adaptation of James Baldwin's novel, opens at the St. James Theater in New York City.

  **1997:** Tiger Woods becomes the youngest person to win golf's Master's Tournament, as well as the first person of color to do so.

- **1941:** African-American doctor Charles Richard Drew opens the first blood bank in New York. Segregation laws prevent him from donating his own blood.

  **1997:** The White House issues an official policy to the survivors and families of the Tuskegee Syphilis experiment which began in the 1940s. Hundreds of infected black men were denied treatment in order to study the effects of the disease over time.

- **1941:** *Negro Digest* begins publishing in Chicago with an initial circulation of 3,000.

  **1997:** African-American filmmaker Spike Lee forms an advertising company to make television commercials geared towards black and urban consumers.

---

in the South may seem out of context for the times. Phoenix Jackson's world is much smaller than the global world of international warfare. Her world revolves around her home, her grandson, and the rural life of Natchez, Mississippi.

The story was inspired in part by the work Welty was doing in the early 1940s for the Works Progress Administration (WPA). The WPA was established by President Franklin Roosevelt in 1934 as a way to put many unemployed people to work building necessary infrastructure—bridges, dams, power plants—to make the country a modern and efficient world power. Welty was a photographer for the WPA, which also included many arts programs, and as she observed an elderly black woman laboriously crossing a field, the idea for "A Worn Path" emerged. Poverty during these years was a reality for many, particularly for blacks and particularly for rural Southerners. Phoenix Jackson was both of these. Quite possibly, Phoenix was old enough to have been born into slavery, or at the very least into the era of sharecropping that followed. Most tobacco and cotton plantations—two of the primary industries of the South at the turn of the century—were owned by wealthy whites who allowed the blacks to work for them in return for an overpriced room and board of meagre proportions. For her generation, their economic situation was grim, and it was only exacerbated by the Great Depression. Phoenix wears red rags in her hair and an apron of sugar sacks. At the clinic, the nurse writes "charity" next to her name. The two nickels Phoenix acquires in the story seem may have seemed like a small fortune to her, and the paper windmill she wants to buy for her grandson is most likely a luxury and quite possibly the only store-bought toy he would have received that year.

## Critical Overview

Since its publication, Welty's story "A Worn Path" has found a responsive audience. One of the most widely anthologized stories of any American writer, the story of Phoenix Jackson's trip into town for her grandson's medicine has been praised both for its simplicity and for its depth. Although the story is brief and simple—the tale of an elderly black woman who travels into town—it contains a level of ambiguity that has fascinated readers for sixty years. Readers have wondered whether the grandson for whom Phoenix Jackson travels along the Natchez Trace is already dead when the story begins. Evidence within the story could support either interpretation, and Welty has said herself only that at least Phoenix believes that he is alive. She says

## What Do I Read Next?

- "Why I Live at the P.O.," a critically acclaimed story by Welty, in which a young woman's difficult relationship with her parents is exposed with humor.

- Carson McCullers also writes of the Southern experience although from a different point of view. Her novels *The Heart Is a Lonely Hunter* and *Reflections in a Golden Eye* were written in the same era as Welty's first stories.

- "A Rose for Emily," a short story by fellow Southerner William Faulkner is also about an older single woman.

- Toni Morrison's Pulitzer Prize-winning novel *Beloved* examines the aftermath of slavery in rural Ohio in the late nineteenth-century.

- *The Optimist's Daughter*, Welty's semi-autobiographical novel about the strained ties between a parent and child won the Pulitzer Prize in 1972.

---

that Phoenix must believe that her journey is in pursuit of life, not death.

Welty's stories are set in the South, and thus her characters' region is often distinguished by their speech and habits; however, Welty's themes transcend regional boundaries and have universal appeal. Critics responded to her first collection, *A Curtain of Green*, favorably and predicted that she would continue to write engaging fiction. With her second collection of stories, *The Wide Net and Other Stories*, critics such as Diana Trilling and Robert Penn Warren noticed that Welty's fiction was becoming richer in theme and allusion. Critics began to call her style impressionistic since she often uses metaphor and symbol to convey her meaning. Warren said that "the items of fiction (scene, action, character, etc.) are presented not as document but as comment, not as report but as a thing made, not as history but as idea."

Through the 1940s Welty continued to refine her vision for her work, and her third collection *The Golden Apples* won many critics over with its highly symbolic complexity, quite different from the simple regional stories with which she began. In the 1950s she published another collection of short stories, *The Bride of Innisfallen,* and won the William Dean Howells Medal of the Academy of Arts and Letters for her novella *The Ponder Heart*. Welty wrote little during the 1960s, but after a period of traveling and lecturing, she returned to writing with two novels, *Losing Battles* and *The Optimist's Daughter*, for which she won the Pulitzer Prize for fiction. Although her last stories were written in 1955, the publication in 1980 of the *Collected Stories of Eudora Welty* verifies her standing as one of the most popular story writers of her era.

Robert Penn Warren, in an important essay in 1944, wrote that Welty writes her stories as if "the author cannot be quite sure what did happen, cannot quite undertake to resolve the meaning of the recorded event, cannot, in fact, be too sure of recording all of the event." In other words, Welty presents an ambiguous situation in her stories and is not concerned about answering all the questions she raised. Using point of view carefully so as not to reveal too much, Welty has been praised for her ability to convey a strong sense of her character's emotions and experience at specific moments in time. Critics have responded well to her use of symbolism and allusion to communicate sensory impressions. In her fiction, Welty merges the everyday with the universal, and readers have been able to enter her world and feel at home.

Other elements of Welty's fiction that critics have praised include her skillful use of language and her diversity in content, form, and tone. While one would not call Welty an experimental writer like her fellow Mississippian William Faulkner, her fiction

> **Welty's critics still wrestle over whether she grants blacks sufficient human diversity, or whether, like her fellow Mississippian Faulkner, she treats them too much as simple symbols of endurance.**

does contain a wide array of moods, subjects, and voices. While some of her stories are light, humorous, or even outright hilarious, such as "Why I Live at the P.O.," others are tragic and serious, such as "Clytie." Some critics have not responded well to Welty's use of the grotesque or absurd, as in the story "The Petrified Man," and some critics have questioned her approach to race issues, but most agree that her stories contain truth, as Eunice Glenn says, "making everyday life appear as it often does, without the use of a magnifying glass."

## Criticism

### Greg Barnhisel

*Greg Barnhisel is an English literature scholar, educator, and writer. In the following essay, he discusses the implications of race in "A Worn Path."*

Eudora Welty's "A Worn Path," written in 1940, is one of the author's most frequently anthologized stories, but this by no means indicates that it is her easiest. There is a depth of ambiguity in it. Twentieth-century critics have chosen, for the most part, to examine the role race plays in the story and through that to either condemn Welty or exalt her for her views. But race is certainly not the story's only concern. Questions of age, service, dedication, and myth also inform the story.

However, it is with race that any discussion of Welty's story must begin. Welty comes from Mississippi, in many ways the most notoriously troubled of Southern states. Born there in 1909 (to Northern parents), she grew up and has spent most of her life in Jackson. She grew up in an era where the Civil War and Reconstruction were still remembered by many of her neighbors, and she herself has lived through the civil rights struggles of the 1950s and 1960s and the Southern renaissance of the 1980s and 1990s. However, politics very rarely enters her work directly. Her stories deal with race relations on a personal level.

Welty has discussed the genesis of "A Worn Path" in numerous interviews. The inspiration for Phoenix Jackson was an ancient black woman whom Welty saw walking across the countryside as Welty was sitting under a tree near the Natchez Trace with a painter friend. "I watched her cross that landscape in the half-distance," she explains, "and when I got home I wrote that story that she had made me think of." In another interview, she added that "I knew she was going somewhere. I knew she was bent on an errand, even at that distance. It was not anything casual. It was a purposeful, measured journey she was making—you wouldn't go on an errand like that—unless it were for someone else, you know. Unless it were an emergency."

"A Worn Path" traces the journey of an ancient black woman who walks to Natchez, Mississippi, in order to obtain medicine for her grandson, who permanently injured himself by swallowing lye. On this, most of her critics agree, but that is as far as they go. One group holds that Welty's portrayal of the black race through her main character, Phoenix Jackson, is eminently sympathetic; another feels that Welty shares with many other Southern writers a tendency to portray blacks as long-suffering and enduring, and in doing so robs them of their true complexity as human beings.

Crucial to any assessment of this question is whether Phoenix Jackson is intended to stand as a representative of her race. Certainly, she plays into one stereotypical Southern image of blacks: the ancient, plodding, superstitious grandmother who talks to herself. Welty seems to undercut this image by introducing the hunter, who treats Jackson as precisely that kind of a stereotype. "I know you old colored people!" he tells her. "Wouldn't miss going to town to see Santa Claus!" He seems like a buffoon here, but when he drops his nickel and she picks it up, critics see the action as either indicative of another pejorative stereotype of blacks (craftiness and dishonesty) or as illustrative of her superiority over him. Similarly, critics disagree on the significance of the white woman in Natchez tying Jackson's shoe. Is this an indication, as one critic holds, of "courtesy warranted by virtue of her age and her 'fealty' to the white race," or is it a comical representation of black helplessness?

The position that Welty's characterization of Jackson relies heavily on stereotypes is quite convincing. There is a long tradition of white Southern writers exalting the primitiveness of blacks: a move that, while not racist in intent (their primitiveness is used to teach more "sophisticated" whites about the virtues of simplicity), is somewhat demeaning in effect. If Jackson is meant to represent blacks as a whole, what are we to make of her "naivete and helplessness"? If her great age is in one respect an asset, does it not also suggest that blacks are changeless and eternal? The final words in William Faulkner's *The Sound and the Fury*, "They endure," is his summary assessment of the state of blacks in the South. Certainly, he has respect for their "endurance," but is it not also patronizing to confer only this compliment upon an entire race of people? Welty's critics still wrestle over whether she grants blacks sufficient human diversity, or whether, like her fellow Mississippian Faulkner, she treats them too much as simple symbols of endurance.

Welty herself, in 1965, anticipated this conflict, and argued that it was off the mark. In her essay "Must the Novelist Crusade?" she shifts the question, saying that the relationship between the races cannot be separated from other relationships between people. "There are relationships of blood, of the passions and affections, of thought and spirit and deed. This is the relationship between the races. How can one kind of relationship be set apart from the others? Like a great root system of an old and long-established growing plant, they are all tangled up together; to separate them you would have to cleave the plant itself from top to bottom." The very nature of her metaphor of the "long-established plant," though, seems to many critics to subtly defend a slow pace of change in the South: this situation is very old, she seems to be saying, and we cannot rush things.

The other primary approach to this story has been to examine its mythological underpinnings. Phoenix Jackson's name is a reference to the mythological "phoenix"—a mythical bird that lives in the desert for 500-600 years and then sets itself on fire, only to rise again from its own ashes, and is a popular symbol for immortality. Certainly, age plays a significant part in the story. If we accept that the story is set in Welty's present, i.e. at the time when

> "The story is suggestive of a religious pilgrimage, while the conclusion implies that the return trip will be like the journey of the Magi."

she wrote the story, then the "present" is 1940. Jackson tells the scarecrow: "My senses is gone. I too old. I the oldest people I ever know." When the hunter asks her how old she is, she replies, "There is no telling, mister." However, if what she tells the nurse is true—that she was too old to go to school when Lee surrendered in 1865—then she must be nearly a hundred years old. Yet, like the phoenix, she rises to makes periodic trips to Natchez to get medicine for her grandson.

The season in which the story takes place—Christmas time—reinforces the theme of rebirth. If we see the story as a Christian allegory, then the marble cake that Jackson dreams of suggests the Communion wafers and her crossing of the cornfield suggests the parting of the Red Sea. Also, the soothing medicine which she gives to her permanently sick grandson can be seen as God's grace, and Jackson herself as a Christ figure. In addition, the difficulties which Jackson endures on her way to Natchez can either represent the temptations of Christ in the desert or the stations of the cross.

A number of critics have questioned whether or not Jackson's grandson is even alive. The story is especially affecting if we know that he is already dead, Roland Bartel proposes, and Jackson's apparent bout of forgetfulness and senility in the doctor's office could be her nagging realization that her grandson is, in fact, dead. Welty responded personally to this question in a 1974 essay, acknowledging the possibility that Jackson's grandson is no longer alive, but insisting that she "must assume that the boy is alive" and admonishing readers that "it is the journey—that is the story." Given that, we must return to the story's mythological resonances. In addition to the aforementioned Christian parallels, the story also suggests Dante, the Italian author of the epic *Divine Comedy*. The dog, the hunter, and even the descent down the stairs at the end of the story parallel incidents in Dante's *Inferno*.

> "I had not meant to mystify readers by withholding any fact; it is not a writer's business to tease."

"A Worn Path" is finally a simple story, though. Welty's short tale of an old woman's journey to get medicine for her grandson is valuable simply as that, and the starkness of its simplicity is too often undervalued. That very simplicity gives it the ability to support so many political and mythological interpretations. Welty even suggests another, far more personal analogy for Phoenix's journey: her own journey towards the creation of "great fiction." "Like Phoenix, you work all your life to find your way, through all the obstructions and the false appearances and the upsets you may have brought on yourself, to reach a meaning—And finally too, like Phoenix, you have to assume that what your are working in aid of is life, not death."

**Source:** Greg Barnhisel, for *Short Stories for Students,* Gale Research, 1997.

## Neil D. Isaacs

*In the following essay, which originally appeared in the* Sewanee Review *in 1963, Isaacs shows how the deceptively "simple" story "A Worn Path" employs a number of meanings that make it more "densely complex" than it first appears.*

The first four sentences of "A Worn Path" contain simple declarative statements using the simple past of the verb "to be": "It was December...," "... there was an old Negro woman...," "Her name was Phoenix Jackson," "She was very old and small...." The note of simplicity thus struck is the keynote of Eudora Welty's artistic design in the story. For it is a simple story (a common reaction is "simply beautiful"). But it is also a story which employs many of the devices which can make of the modern short story an intricate and densely complex form. It uses them, however, in such a way that it demonstrates how a single meaning may be enriched through the use of various techniques. Thus, instead of various levels of meaning, we have here a single meaning reinforced on several levels of perception. Moreover, there is no muddying of levels and techniques; they are neatly arranged, straightforwardly presented, and simply perceived.

The plot-line follows Phoenix Jackson, who is graphically described in the second paragraph, on her long walk into Natchez where she has to get medicine for her grandson. The trek is especially difficult because of her age, and in the process of struggling on she forgets the reason for the struggle. At the end she has remembered, received the medicine, and decided to buy the child a Christmas present with the ten cents she has acquired during the day.

What makes this a story? It barely appears to fulfill even Sidney Cox's generous criterion of "turning a corner or at least a hair." But it does belong to a specific story-teller's genre familiar from Homer to [Henry] Fielding to [Jack] Kerouac—"road" literature. This form provides a ready-made plot pattern with some inherent weaknesses. The story concerns the struggle to achieve a goal, the completion of the journey; and the story's beginning, middle, and end are the same as those of the road. The primary weakness of this structure is its susceptibility to too much middle.

A traditional concept of road literature, whether the mythical journey of the sun across the heavens or a boy's trip down the Mississippi or any other variation, is its implicit equation with life: the road of life, life's journey, ups and downs, the straight and narrow, and a host of other clichés reflect the universality of this primitive metaphor. "A Worn Path" makes explicit, beginning with the very title, Eudora Welty's acceptance of the traditional equation as a basic aspect of the story. In fact, the whole meaning of "A Worn Path" will rely on an immediate recognition of the equation—the worn path equals the path of life—which is probably why it is so explicit. But we needn't start with a concept which is metaphorical or perhaps primitively allegorical. It will probably be best for us to begin with the other literal elements in the story: they will lead us back to the sub- or supra-literal eventually anyway.

An important part of the setting is the time element, that is, the specific time of the year. We learn immediately that it is "a bright frozen day" in December, and there are several subsequent, direct statements which mark it more precisely as Christmas time. The hunter talks about Santa Claus and the attendant at the hospital says that "It's Christmas time," echoing what the author has said earlier. There are several other references and images forming a pattern to underline the idea of Christmas time, such as "Up above her was a tree in a pearly cloud of *mistletoe.*" [Italics in this paragraph all mine.] Notice especially the elaborate color pattern of red, green, and silver, the traditional colors of Christmas. It begins with Phoenix's head "in a *red* rag, coming along a path through the pinewoods" (which are green as well as Christmas trees). Later she sees "a wagon track, where the *silver grass* blew between the *red* ruts" and "little strings of trees *silver* in their dead leaves" (reddish brown?). This pattern comes to a climax in the description of the city and the lady's packages, which also serves to make explicit its purpose, return it to the literal: "There were red and green electric lights strung and crisscrossed everywhere....... an armful of red-, green-, and silver-wrapped presents."

From the plot-line alone the idea of Christmas doesn't seem to be more than incidental, but it is obvious from the persistent references that Christmas is going to play an important part in the total effect of the story. Besides the direct statements already mentioned, there proliferates around the pattern throughout the story a dense cluster of allusions to and suggestions of the Christmas myth at large and to the *meanings* of Christmas in particular. For instance, as Phoenix rests under a tree, she has a vision of a little boy offering her a slice of marble-cake on a little plate, and she says, "That would be acceptable." The allusion here is to Communion and Church ritual. Later, when a bird flies by, Phoenix says, "God watching me the whole time." Then there are references to the Eden story (the ordering of the species, the snake in summer to be avoided), to the parting of the Red Sea (Phoenix walking through the field of corn), to a sequence of temptations, to the River Jordan and the City of Heaven (when Phoenix gets to the river, sees the city shining, and hears the bells ringing; then there is the angel who waits on her, tying her shoes), to the Christ-child in the manger (Phoenix describing her grandson as "all wrapped up" in "a little patch quilt... like a little bird" with "a sweet look"). In addition, the whole story is suggestive of a religious pilgrimage, while the conclusion implies that the return trip will be like the journey of the Magi, with Phoenix following a star (the marvelous windmill) to bring a gift to the child (medicine, also windmill). Moreover, there's the hunter who is, in part, a Santa Claus figure himself (he carries a big sack over his shoulder, he is always laughing, he brings Phoenix a gift of nickel).

> Old Phoenix is not a stereotype but a symbol of immortality."

The richness of all this evocation of a Christianity-Christmas frame of a reference heightens the specific points about the meanings of Christmas. The Christmas spirit, of course, is the Christian ethic in its simplest terms: giving, doing for others, charity. This concept is made explicit when the nurse says of Phoenix, "She doesn't come for herself." But it had already been presented in a brilliant piece of ironic juxtaposition [Italics mine]:

> She entered a door, and there she saw *nailed up on the wall* the document that had been stamped with the *gold seal* and framed in the *gold frame* which *matched the dream that was hung up in her head.*
>
> *"Here I be,"* she said. There was a *fixed and ceremonial stiffness* over her body. "A *charity* case, I suppose," said an attendant....

Amid the Christmas season and the dense Christmas imagery, Phoenix, with an abiding intuitive faith, arrives at the shrine of her pilgrimage, beholds a symbolic crucifixion, presents herself as a celebrant in the faith, and is recognized as an embodiment of the message of the faith. This entire scene, however, with its gold trimming and the attitude of the attendant, is turned ironically to suggest greed, corruption, cynicism—the very opposite of the word used, charity. Yet the episode, which is Phoenix's final and most severe trial, also results in her final emergence as a redeemer and might be called her Calvary.

Perhaps a better way to get at the meaning of Christmas and the meaning of "A Worn Path" is to talk about life and death. In a sense, the meaning of Christmas and that of Easter are the same—a celebration of life out of death. (Notice that Phoenix refers to herself as a *June* bug and that the woman with the packages "gave off perfume like the *red roses in hot summer.*") [Italics mine.] Christ is born in the death of the year and in a near-dead nature-society situation in order to rejuvenate life itself, naturally and spiritually. He dies in order that the life of others may be saved. He is reborn out of death, and so are nature, love, and the spirit of man. All this is the potent Christian explanation of the central irony of human existence, that life means death and death is life. One might state the meaning of "A Worn Path" in similar terms, where Phoenix endures a long, agonizing dying in order to redeem her grandson's life. So the medicine, which the nurse calls charity as she makes a check in her book, is a symbol of love and life. The windmill represents the same duality, but lighter sides of both aspects. If the path is the path of life, then its end is death and the purpose of that death is new life.

It would be misleading, however, to suggest that the story is merely a paralleling of the Christian nature-myth. It is, rather, a miniature nature-myth of its own which uses elements of many traditions. The most obvious example is the name Phoenix from the mythological Egyptian bird, symbol of immortality and resurrection, which dies so that a new Phoenix may emerge from its ashes. There is a reference to the Daedalus labyrinth myth when Phoenix walks through the corn field and Miss Welty puns: "'Though the maze now,' she said, for there was no path." That ambivalent figure of the hunter comes into play here as both a death figure (killer, bag full of slain quail) and a life figure (unconscious giver of life with the nickel, banisher of Cerberus-like black dog who is attacking Phoenix), but in any case a folk-legend figure who can fill "the whole landscape" with his laugh. And there are several references to the course of the sun across the sky which gives a new dimension to the life-road equation; e.g., "Sun so high!... The time getting all gone here."

The most impressive extra-Christian elements are the patterns that identify Phoenix as a creature of nature herself and as a ritual-magic figure. Thus, Phoenix makes a sound "like the chirping of a solitary little bird," her hair has "an odor like copper," and at one point "with [her] mouth drawn down, [she] shook her head once or twice in a little strutting way." Even more remarkable is the "fixed and ceremonial stiffness" of her body, which moves "like a festival figure in some parade." The cane she carries, made from an umbrella, is tapped on the ground like a magic wand, and she uses it to "switch at the brush as if to rouse up any hiding things." At the same time she utters little spells:

> Out of my way, all you foxes, owls, beetles, jack rabbits, coons, and wild animals!... Keep out from under these feet, little bob-whites.... Keep the big wild hogs out of my path. Don't let none of those come running my direction.... Ghost, ... who be you the ghost of? ... Sweetgum makes the water sweet.... Nobody know who made this well for it was here when I was born.... Sleep on, alligators, and blow your bubbles.

Other suggestions of magic appear in the whirling of cornhusks in streamers about her skirts, when she parts "her way from side to side with the cane, through the whispering field," when the quail seem "unseen," and when the cabins are "all like old women under a spell sitting there." Finally, ironically, when Phoenix swings at the black dog, she goes over "in the ditch, like a little puff of mile-weed."

More or less remote, more or less direct, all these allusions are used for the same effect as are the references to Christianity, to reinforce a statement of the meaning of life. This brings us back to the basic life-road equation of the story, and there are numerous indications that the path is life and that the end of the road is death and renewal of life. These suggestions are of three types; statements which relate the road, the trip, or Phoenix to time: Phoenix walks "with the balanced heaviness and lightness of a pendulum in a grandfather clock"; she tells the hunter, "I bound to go.... The time come around"; and the nurse says "She makes these trips just as regular as clockwork." Second (the most frequent type), there are descriptions of the road or episodes along the way which are suggestive of life, usually in a simple metaphorical way: "I got a long way" (ambiguously referring to past and future); "I in the thorny bush"; "up through pines.... Now down through oaks"; "This the easy place. This the easy going." Third, there are direct references to death, age, and life: Phoenix says to a buzzard, "Who you watching?" and to a scarecrow, "Who be you the ghost of? For I have heard of nary death close by"; then she performs a little dance of death with the scarecrow after she says, "My senses is gone. I too old. I the oldest people I ever know."

This brings us full circle in an examination of the design of the story, and it should be possible now to say something about the total meaning of "A Worn Path." The path is the path of life, and the story is an attempt to probe the meaning of life in its simplest, most elementary terms. Through the story we arrive at a definition of life, albeit a teleological one. When the hunter tells Phoenix to "take my advice and stay home, and nothing will happen to you," the irony is obvious and so is the metaphor: don't live and you can't die. When Phoenix forgets why she has made the arduous trek to Natchez, we understand that it is only a rare person who knows the meaning of his life, that living does not imply knowing. When Phoenix describes the Christ-like child waiting for her and says, "I not going to forget him again, no, the whole enduring time. I could tell him from all the others in creation," we understand several things about it: her life is almost over, she sees clearly the meaning of life, she has an abiding faith in that meaning, and she will share with her grandson this great revelation just as together they embody its significance. And when Phoenix's "slow step began on the stairs, going down," as she starts back to bring the boy the medicine and the windmill, we see a composite symbol of life itself, dying so that life may continue. Life is a journey toward death, because one must die in order that life may go on.

**Source:** Neil D. Isaacs, "Life for Phoenix," in *The Critical Response to Eudora Welty's Fiction,* edited by Laura Champion, Greenwood Press, 1994, pp. 37–42.

## Eudora Welty

*In the following essay, Welty talks about her inspiration to write "A Worn Path" and answers those who have asked her if Phoenix's grandson is really dead at the time of her trek in to town.*

A story writer is more than happy to be read by students; the fact that these serious readers think and feel something in response to his work he finds life-giving. At the same time, he may not always be able to reply to their specific questions in kind. I wondered if it might clarify something, for both the questioners and myself, if I set down a general reply to the question that comes to me most often in the mail, from both students and their teachers, after some classroom discussion. The unrivaled favorite is this: "Is Phoenix Jackson's grandson really *dead?*"

It refers to a short story I wrote years ago called "A Worn Path," which tells of a day's journey an old woman makes on foot from deep in the country into town and into a doctor's office on behalf of her little grandson; he is at home, periodically ill, and periodically she comes for his medicine; they give it to her as usual, she receives it and starts the journey back.

I had not meant to mystify readers by withholding any fact; it is not a writer's business to tease. The story is told through Phoenix's mind as she undertakes her errand. As the author at one with the character as I tell it, I must assume that the boy is alive. As the reader, you are free to think as you like, of course: the story invites you to believe that no matter what happens, Phoenix, for as long as she is able to walk and can hold to her purpose, will make her journey. The *possibility* that she would keep on even if he were dead is there in her devotion and its single-minded, single-track errand. Certainly the *artistic* truth, which should be good enough for the fact, lies in Phoenix's own answer to that question. When the nurse asks, "He isn't dead, is he?" she speaks for herself: "He still the same. He going to last."

The grandchild is the incentive. But it is the journey, the going of the errand, that is the story, and the question is not whether the grandchild is in reality alive or dead. It doesn't affect the outcome of the story or its meaning from start to finish. But it is not the question itself that has struck me as much as the idea, almost without exception implied in the asking, that for Phoenix's grandson to be dead would somehow make the story "better."

It's *all right,* I want to say to the students who write to me, for things to be what they appear to be, for words to mean what they say. It's all right too for words and appearances to mean more than one thing—ambiguity is a fact of life. But it is not all right, not in good faith, for things *not* to mean what they say. A fiction writer's responsibility covers not only what he presents as the facts of a given story but what he chooses to stir up as their implications. In the end, these implications too become facts, in the larger, fictional sense.

The grandson's plight was real and it made the truth of the story, which is the story of an errand of love carried out. If the child no longer lived, the truth would persist in the "wornness" of the path. But his being dead can't increase the truth of the story, can't affect it one way or the other. I think I signal this, because the end of the story has been reached before old Phoenix gets home again: she simply starts back. To the question "Is the grandson really dead?" I could reply that it doesn't make any difference. I could also say that I did not make him up in order to let him play a trick on Phoenix. But my best answer would be: "*Phoenix is alive.*"

The origin of a story is sometimes a trustworthy clue to the author—or can provide him with the clue—to its key image; maybe in this case it will do the same for the reader. One day I saw a solitary old woman like Phoenix. She was walking; I saw her, at middle distance, in a winter country landscape, and watched her slowly make her way across my line of vision. That sight of her made me write the story. I invented an errand for her, but that only seemed a living part of the figure she was herself: what errand other than for someone else could be making her go? And her going was the first thing, her persisting in her landscape was the real thing, and the first and the real were what I wanted and worked to keep. I brought her up close enough, by imagination, to describe her face, make her present to the eyes, but the full-length figure moving across the winter fields was the indelible one and the image to keep, and the perspective extending into the vanishing distance the true one to hold in mind.

I invented for my character, as I wrote, some passing adventures—some dreams and harassments and a small triumph or two, some jolts to her pride, some flights of fancy to console her, one or two encounters to scare her, a moment that gave her cause to feel ashamed, a moment to dance and preen—for it had to be a *journey*, and all these things belonged to that, parts of life's uncertainty.

A narrative line is in its deeper sense, of course, the tracing out of a meaning, and the real continuity of a story lies in this probing forward. The real dramatic force of a story depends on the strength of the emotion that has set it going. The emotional value is the measure of the reach of the story. What gives any such content to "A Worn Path" is not its circumstances but its *subject*: the deep-grained habit of love.

What I hoped would come clear was that in the whole surround of this story, the world it threads through, the only certain thing at all is the worn path. The habit of love cuts through confusion and stumbles or contrives its way out of difficulty, it remembers the way even when it forgets, for a dumbfounded moment, its reason for being. The path is the thing that matters.

*Her* victory—old Phoenix's—is when she sees the diploma in the doctor's office, when she finds "nailed up on the wall the document that had been stamped with the gold seal and framed in the gold frame, which matched the dream that was hung up in her head." The return with the medicine is just a matter of retracing her own footsteps. It is the part of the journey, and of the story, that can now go without saying.

In the matter of function, old Phoenix's way might even do as a sort of parallel to your way of work if you are a writer of stories. The way to get there is the all-important, all-absorbing problem, and this problem is your reason for undertaking the story. Your only guide, too, is your sureness about your subject, about what this subject is. Like Phoenix, you work all your life to find your way, through all the obstructions and the false appearances and the upsets you may have brought on yourself, to reach a meaning—using inventions of your imagination, perhaps helped out by your dreams and bits of good luck. And finally, too, like Phoenix, you have to assume that what you are working in aid of is life, not death.

But you would make the trip anyway, wouldn't you?—just on hope.

**Source:** Eudora Welty, "Is Phoenix Jackson's Grandson Really Dead?," in *Critical Inquiry,* Vol. 1, No. 1, September, 1974, pp. 219–21.

## Dan Donlan

*In the following short essay, Donlan argues that Phoenix Jackson, far from being a stereotyped African-American character, is actually a symbol of immortality.*

On the surface Eudora Welty's short story "A Worn Path" is an account of an old black woman's journey from Old Natchez Trace to Natchez. In fact, some readers may perceive Old Phoenix as a negative black stereotype. However, a second level of interpretation indicates a powerful statement of man's immortality. This paper will be concerned with three elements that substantiate the theme of immortality: references to death, references to time, and references to the Phoenix myth from Egyptian mythology. In this way, Old Phoenix is not a stereotype but a symbol of immortality.

Old Phoenix' journey has significance. The title of the story—"A Worn Path"—suggests the journey to be ritualistic, an idea supported by the phrase "festival figure" used to describe Old Phoenix. During her journey Old Phoenix is surrounded by death. The season is winter. The earth is frozen. The woods are still, and the dove mourns. She encounters "big dead trees," a hunter carrying dead birds, dead weeds. She even dances with a scarecrow. Though she is "in death," Old Phoenix does not die. In fact, she survives splendidly. She appears indestructible, even immortal.

Her immortality is suggested by Welty's references to time. A time image is used to describe Old Phoenix' walk: "the balanced heaviness and lightness of a pendulum in a grandfather clock." Her appearance is "blue with age." When the hunter encounters Old Phoenix, he says "You must be a hundred years old." Even Phoenix says of herself, "I the oldest people I ever saw."

The idea that Old Phoenix is immortal is given additional support by frequent reference to the Phoenix myth in Egyptian mythology. The Phoenix—also known by the terms *bennu* and *Roc*—is a large bird that retains immortality by restoring itself every five hundred years (scholars differ as to the precise period of time) by setting fire to its nest and immolating itself by fanning the fire with its wings. From the ashes a new Phoenix arises. It collects the ashes into an egg and flies to Heliopolis, a religious city in Egypt, and deposits the egg at the Temple of the Sun. Some scholars have linked the death and rebirth of the Phoenix with the rising and setting of the sun.

Although "A Worn Path" is not an exact retelling of the Phoenix myth, certain parallels merit discussion. First, Old Phoenix resembles the mythical bird in personal appearance. The bennu is known for its brilliant scarlet and gold plumage. Welty describes Old Phoenix in this way: "A golden color ran underneath and the two knobs of her cheeks were illuminated by a yellow burning under the dark. Under the red rag, her hair came down on her neck. . . ." When Old Phoenix walks, she resembles a giant bird: "She wore a dark striped dress reaching down to her shoe tops, and an equally long apron of bleached sugar sacks. . . . Every time she took a step she might have fallen over her unlaced shoes." Even the bennu's ceremonial song finds its parallel: "A grave and persistent noise in the still air, that seemed meditative like the chirping of a little bird."

Second, parallels exist in the two journeys. Both are made ritually. The nurse at the hospital comments that Old Phoenix "makes these trips as regular as clockwork." The destinations in both cases are large cities: Heliopolis and Natchez. Enroute to the city, both travellers stop ceremonially to restore themselves. The Phoenix burns itself on the nest, only to rise from the ashes, fresh and young. When Old Phoenix sits down to rest, she gives the appearance of nesting: "She spread her skirts on the bank around her and folded her hands over her knees." Then Welty describes the rejuvenated Phoenix: "There she had to creep and crawl, spreading her knees and stretching her fingers like a baby trying to climb the steps." Further youth images substantiate her rejuvenation: Old Phoenix' request that a lady lace up her shoe, the flame of comprehension at the doctor's office, and the paper windmill. The frequent references to birds also help in constructing the mythological basis for the story.

Two further mythological references are worth considering. The shiny nickel which Old Phoenix retrieves "With the grace and care . . . in lifting an egg from under a setting hen" has its parallel in the egg of myrrh taken by the Phoenix to the Temple of the Sun. Second, the two visitations—the imagined encounter with the small boy and the real encounter with the hunter—parallel the manifestations of the sun god Ra, who would assume human form—young in the morning, old in the evening, to correlate with the rising and setting of the sun. This parallel is supported by the many references to sun and light throughout the story.

"A Worn Path," read as a simple narrative, communicates a human experience, both logically and memorably. However, the symbolic level of interpretation, revealing the theme of immortality, gives the story texture and power.

**Source:** Dan Donlan, "'A Worn Path': Immortality of Stereotype," in *English Journal*, Vol. 62, No. 4, April, 1973, pp. 549–50.

## Sources

Glenn, Eunice. "Fantasy in the Fiction of Eudora Welty," in *Critiques and Essays on Modern Fiction: Representing the Achievement of Modern America and British Critics, 1920–1951*, edited by John W. Aldridge, The Ronald Press Company, 1952, pp. 506–17.

Warren, Robert Penn. "The Love and the Separateness of Miss Welty," in *Kenyon Review*, Volume 6, 1944, pp. 246-259.

Welty, Eudora. *The Eye of the Story: Selected Essays and Reviews*, Vintage Books/Random House, 1979.

## Further Reading

Butterworth, Nancy K. "From Civil War to Civil Rights: Race Relations in 'A Worn Path,'" in *Eudora Welty: Eye of the Storyteller*, edited by Dawn Trouard, Kent State University Press, 1989.
    Butterworth discusses the racial politics of the story.

*Conversations with Eudora Welty*, edited by Peggy Whitman Prenshaw, University Press of Mississippi, 1984.
    Collected here are many interviews and personal conversations various people have had with Eudora

Welty. A valuable resource for those interested in the author herself, her work, her life, and her concerns.

*Eudora Welty,* edited by Harold Bloom, Chelsea House Publishers, 1986.
This collection of thirteen essays about Eudora Welty's fiction provides an excellent introduction to her work. These essays are written by some very well-known critics and writers, such as Katherine Anne Porter, Joyce Carol Oates, and Robert Penn Warren.

Schmidt, Peter. *The Heart of the Story: Eudora Welty's Short Fiction,* University Press of Mississippi, 1991.
An analysis of Welty's short stories in the contexts of Southern writing and women's writing.

Welty, Eudora. *One Writer's Beginnings,* Harvard University Press, 1984.
This autobiography of sorts is a more recent publication by Welty. The sections "Listening," "Learning to See," and "Finding a Voice" may provide inspiration to those who wish to become writers.

Westling, Louise. *Eudora Welty,* Barnes and Noble Books, 1989.
This book comes from the "Women Writers" series, and, therefore, it has a somewhat gender-based approach. The chapters deal with ways that women appear in the work of Welty, a writer who is sometimes uncomfortable with the ideas of feminism.

# *Glossary of Literary Terms*

## A

**Aestheticism:** A literary and artistic movement of the nineteenth century. Followers of the movement believed that art should not be mixed with social, political, or moral teaching. The statement "art for art's sake" is a good summary of aestheticism. The movement had its roots in France, but it gained widespread importance in England in the last half of the nineteenth century, where it helped change the Victorian practice of including moral lessons in literature. Edgar Allan Poe is one of the best-known American "aesthetes."

**Allegory:** A narrative technique in which characters representing things or abstract ideas are used to convey a message or teach a lesson. Allegory is typically used to teach moral, ethical, or religious lessons but is sometimes used for satiric or political purposes. Many fairy tales are allegories.

**Allusion:** A reference to a familiar literary or historical person or event, used to make an idea more easily understood. Joyce Carol Oates's story "Where Are You Going, Where Have You Been?" exhibits several allusions to popular music.

**Analogy:** A comparison of two things made to explain something unfamiliar through its similarities to something familiar, or to prove one point based on the acceptance of another. Similes and metaphors are types of analogies.

**Antagonist:** The major character in a narrative or drama who works against the hero or protagonist. The Misfit in Flannery O'Connor's story "A Good Man Is Hard to Find" serves as the antagonist for the Grandmother.

**Anthology:** A collection of similar works of literature, art, or music. Zora Neale Hurston's "The Eatonville Anthology" is a collection of stories that take place in the same town.

**Anthropomorphism:** The presentation of animals or objects in human shape or with human characteristics. The term is derived from the Greek word for "human form." The fur necklet in Katherine Mansfield's story "Miss Brill" has anthropomorphic characteristics.

**Anti-hero:** A central character in a work of literature who lacks traditional heroic qualities such as courage, physical prowess, and fortitude. Anti-heroes typically distrust conventional values and are unable to commit themselves to any ideals. They generally feel helpless in a world over which they have no control. Anti-heroes usually accept, and often celebrate, their positions as social outcasts. A well-known anti-hero is Walter Mitty in James Thurber's story "The Secret Life of Walter Mitty."

**Archetype:** The word archetype is commonly used to describe an original pattern or model from which all other things of the same kind are made. Archetypes are the literary images that grow out of the "collective unconscious," a theory proposed by psychologist Carl Jung. They appear in literature as incidents and plots that repeat basic patterns of life. They may also appear as stereotyped characters. The "schlemiel" of Yiddish literature is an archetype.

**Autobiography:** A narrative in which an individual tells his or her life story. Examples include Benjamin Franklin's *Autobiography* and Amy Hempel's story "In the Cemetery Where Al Jolson Is Buried," which has autobiographical characteristics even though it is a work of fiction.

*Avant-garde*: A literary term that describes new writing that rejects traditional approaches to literature in favor of innovations in style or content. Twentieth-century examples of the literary *avant-garde* include the modernists and the minimalists.

*Belles-lettres*: A French term meaning "fine letters" or "beautiful writing." It is often used as a synonym for literature, typically referring to imaginative and artistic rather than scientific or expository writing. Current usage sometimes restricts the meaning to light or humorous writing and appreciative essays about literature. Lewis Carroll's *Alice in Wonderland* epitomizes the realm of *belles-lettres*.

*Bildungsroman*: A German word meaning "novel of development." The *bildungsroman* is a study of the maturation of a youthful character, typically brought about through a series of social or sexual encounters that lead to self-awareness. J. D. Salinger's *Catcher in the Rye* is a *bildungsroman*, and Doris Lessing's story "Through the Tunnel" exhibits characteristics of a *bildungsroman* as well.

# B

**Black Aesthetic Movement:** A period of artistic and literary development among African Americans in the 1960s and early 1970s. This was the first major African-American artistic movement since the Harlem Renaissance and was closely paralleled by the civil rights and black power movements. The black aesthetic writers attempted to produce works of art that would be meaningful to the black masses. Key figures in black aesthetics included one of its founders, poet and playwright Amiri Baraka, formerly known as LeRoi Jones; poet and essayist Haki R. Madhubuti, formerly Don L. Lee; poet and playwright Sonia Sanchez; and dramatist Ed Bullins. Works representative of the Black Aesthetic Movement include Amiri Baraka's play *Dutchman*, a 1964 Obie award-winner.

**Black Humor:** Writing that places grotesque elements side by side with humorous ones in an attempt to shock the reader, forcing him or her to laugh at the horrifying reality of a disordered world. Joseph Heller's novel *Catch-22* is considered a superb example of the use of black humor. Flannery O'Connor often used black humor in her stories, including the characterizations in "A Good Man Is Hard to Find."

# C

**Catharsis:** The release or purging of unwanted emotions—specifically fear and pity—brought about by exposure to art. The term was first used by the Greek philosopher Aristotle in his *Poetics* to refer to the desired effect of tragedy on spectators.

**Character:** Broadly speaking, a person in a literary work. The actions of characters are what constitute the plot of a story, novel, or poem. There are numerous types of characters, ranging from simple, stereotypical figures to intricate, multifaceted ones. "Characterization" is the process by which an author creates vivid, believable characters in a work of art. This may be done in a variety of ways, including (1) direct description of the character by the narrator; (2) the direct presentation of the speech, thoughts, or actions of the character; and (3) the responses of other characters to the character. The term "character" also refers to a form originated by the ancient Greek writer Theophrastus that later became popular in the seventeenth and eighteenth centuries. It is a short essay or sketch of a person who prominently displays a specific attribute or quality, such as miserliness or ambition. "Miss Brill," a story by Katherine Mansfield, is an example of a character sketch.

**Classical:** In its strictest definition in literary criticism, classicism refers to works of ancient Greek or Roman literature. The term may also be used to describe a literary work of recognized importance (a "classic") from any time period or literature that exhibits the traits of classicism. Examples of later works and authors now described as classical include French literature of the seventeenth century, Western novels of the nineteenth century, and American fiction of the mid-nineteenth century such as that written by James Fenimore Cooper and Mark Twain.

**Climax:** The turning point in a narrative, the moment when the conflict is at its most intense. Typically, the structure of stories, novels, and plays is one of rising action, in which tension builds to the climax, followed by falling action, in which tension lessens as the story moves to its conclusion.

**Comedy:** One of two major types of drama, the other being tragedy. Its aim is to amuse, and it typically ends happily. Comedy assumes many forms, such as farce and burlesque, and uses a variety of techniques, from parody to satire. In a restricted sense the term comedy refers only to dramatic presentations, but in general usage it is commonly applied to nondramatic works as well.

**Comic Relief:** The use of humor to lighten the mood of a serious or tragic story, especially in plays. The technique is very common in Elizabethan works, and can be an integral part of the plot or simply a brief event designed to break the tension of the scene.

**Conflict:** The conflict in a work of fiction is the issue to be resolved in the story. It usually occurs between two characters, the protagonist and the antagonist, or between the protagonist and society or the protagonist and himself or herself. The conflict in Washington Irving's story ''The Devil and Tom Walker'' is that the Devil wants Tom Walker's soul but Tom does not want to go to hell.

**Criticism:** The systematic study and evaluation of literary works, usually based on a specific method or set of principles. An important part of literary studies since ancient times, the practice of criticism has given rise to numerous theories, methods, and ''schools,'' sometimes producing conflicting, even contradictory, interpretations of literature in general as well as of individual works. Even such basic issues as what constitutes a poem or a novel have been the subject of much criticism over the centuries. Seminal texts of literary criticism include Plato's *Republic,* Aristotle's *Poetics,* Sir Philip Sidney's *The Defence of Poesie,* and John Dryden's *Of Dramatic Poesie.* Contemporary schools of criticism include deconstruction, feminist, psychoanalytic, poststructuralist, new historicist, postcolonialist, and reader-response.

# D

**Deconstruction:** A method of literary criticism characterized by multiple conflicting interpretations of a given work. Deconstructionists consider the impact of the language of a work and suggest that the true meaning of the work is not necessarily the meaning that the author intended.

**Deduction:** The process of reaching a conclusion through reasoning from general premises to a specific premise. Arthur Conan Doyle's character Sherlock Holmes often used deductive reasoning to solve mysteries.

**Denotation:** The definition of a word, apart from the impressions or feelings it creates in the reader. The word ''apartheid'' denotes a political and economic policy of segregation by race, but its connotations—oppression, slavery, inequality—are numerous.

*Denouement*: A French word meaning ''the unknotting.'' In literature, it denotes the resolution of conflict in fiction or drama. The *denouement* follows the climax and provides an outcome to the primary plot situation as well as an explanation of secondary plot complications. A well-known example of *denouement* is the last scene of the play *As You Like It* by William Shakespeare, in which couples are married, an evildoer repents, the identities of two disguised characters are revealed, and a ruler is restored to power. Also known as ''falling action.''

**Detective Story:** A narrative about the solution of a mystery or the identification of a criminal. The conventions of the detective story include the detective's scrupulous use of logic in solving the mystery; incompetent or ineffectual police; a suspect who appears guilty at first but is later proved innocent; and the detective's friend or confidant—often the narrator—whose slowness in interpreting clues emphasizes by contrast the detective's brilliance. Edgar Allan Poe's ''Murders in the Rue Morgue'' is commonly regarded as the earliest example of this type of story. Other practitioners are Arthur Conan Doyle, Dashiell Hammett, and Agatha Christie.

**Dialogue:** Dialogue is conversation between people in a literary work. In its most restricted sense, it refers specifically to the speech of characters in a drama. As a specific literary genre, a ''dialogue'' is a composition in which characters debate an issue or idea.

**Didactic:** A term used to describe works of literature that aim to teach a moral, religious, political, or practical lesson. Although didactic elements are often found in artistically pleasing works, the term ''didactic'' usually refers to literature in which the message is more important than the form. The term may also be used to criticize a work that the critic finds ''overly didactic,'' that is, heavy-handed in its delivery of a lesson. An example of didactic literature is John Bunyan's *Pilgrim's Progress.*

**Dramatic Irony:** Occurs when the reader of a work of literature knows something that a character in the work itself does not know. The irony is in the contrast between the intended meaning of the statements or actions of a character and the additional information understood by the audience.

**Dystopia:** An imaginary place in a work of fiction where the characters lead dehumanized, fearful lives. George Orwell's *Nineteen Eighty-four,* and Margaret Atwood's *The Handmaid's Tale* portray versions of dystopia.

# E

**Edwardian:** Describes cultural conventions identified with the period of the reign of Edward VII of England (1901-1910). Writers of the Edwardian Age typically displayed a strong reaction against the propriety and conservatism of the Victorian Age. Their work often exhibits distrust of authority in religion, politics, and art and expresses strong doubts about the soundness of conventional values. Writers of this era include E. M. Forster, H. G. Wells, and Joseph Conrad.

**Empathy:** A sense of shared experience, including emotional and physical feelings, with someone or something other than oneself. Empathy is often used to describe the response of a reader to a literary character.

**Epilogue:** A concluding statement or section of a literary work. In dramas, particularly those of the seventeenth and eighteenth centuries, the epilogue is a closing speech, often in verse, delivered by an actor at the end of a play and spoken directly to the audience.

**Epiphany:** A sudden revelation of truth inspired by a seemingly trivial incident. The term was widely used by James Joyce in his critical writings, and the stories in Joyce's *Dubliners* are commonly called "epiphanies."

**Epistolary Novel:** A novel in the form of letters. The form was particularly popular in the eighteenth century. The form can also be applied to short stories, as in Edwidge Danticat's "Children of the Sea."

**Epithet:** A word or phrase, often disparaging or abusive, that expresses a character trait of someone or something. "The Napoleon of crime" is an epithet applied to Professor Moriarty, arch-rival of Sherlock Holmes in Arthur Conan Doyle's series of detective stories.

**Existentialism:** A predominantly twentieth-century philosophy concerned with the nature and perception of human existence. There are two major strains of existentialist thought: atheistic and Christian. Followers of atheistic existentialism believe that the individual is alone in a godless universe and that the basic human condition is one of suffering and loneliness. Nevertheless, because there are no fixed values, individuals can create their own characters—indeed, they can shape themselves—through the exercise of free will. The atheistic strain culminates in and is popularly associated with the works of Jean-Paul Sartre. The Christian existentialists, on the other hand, believe that only in God may people find freedom from life's anguish. The two strains hold certain beliefs in common: that existence cannot be fully understood or described through empirical effort; that anguish is a universal element of life; that individuals must bear responsibility for their actions; and that there is no common standard of behavior or perception for religious and ethical matters. Existentialist thought figures prominently in the works of such authors as Franz Kafka, Fyodor Dostoyevsky, and Albert Camus.

**Expatriatism:** The practice of leaving one's country to live for an extended period in another country. Literary expatriates include Irish author James Joyce who moved to Italy and France, American writers James Baldwin, Ernest Hemingway, Gertrude Stein, and F. Scott Fitzgerald who lived and wrote in Paris, and Polish novelist Joseph Conrad in England.

**Exposition:** Writing intended to explain the nature of an idea, thing, or theme. Expository writing is often combined with description, narration, or argument.

**Expressionism:** An indistinct literary term, originally used to describe an early twentieth-century school of German painting. The term applies to almost any mode of unconventional, highly subjective writing that distorts reality in some way. Advocates of Expressionism include Federico Garcia Lorca, Eugene O'Neill, Franz Kafka, and James Joyce.

# F

**Fable:** A prose or verse narrative intended to convey a moral. Animals or inanimate objects with human characteristics often serve as characters in fables. A famous fable is Aesop's "The Tortoise and the Hare."

**Fantasy:** A literary form related to mythology and folklore. Fantasy literature is typically set in nonexistent realms and features supernatural beings. Notable examples of literature with elements of fantasy are Gabriel Garcia Marquez's story "The Handsomest Drowned Man in the World" and Ursula K. LeGuin's "The Ones Who Walk Away from Omelas."

**Farce:** A type of comedy characterized by broad humor, outlandish incidents, and often vulgar subject matter. Much of the "comedy" in film and television could more accurately be described as farce.

**Fiction:** Any story that is the product of imagination rather than a documentation of fact. Characters and events in such narratives may be based in real life but their ultimate form and configuration is a creation of the author.

**Figurative Language:** A technique in which an author uses figures of speech such as hyperbole, irony, metaphor, or simile for a particular effect. Figurative language is the opposite of literal language, in which every word is truthful, accurate, and free of exaggeration or embellishment.

**Flashback:** A device used in literature to present action that occurred before the beginning of the story. Flashbacks are often introduced as the dreams or recollections of one or more characters.

**Foil:** A character in a work of literature whose physical or psychological qualities contrast strongly with, and therefore highlight, the corresponding qualities of another character. In his Sherlock Holmes stories, Arthur Conan Doyle portrayed Dr. Watson as a man of normal habits and intelligence, making him a foil for the eccentric and unusually perceptive Sherlock Holmes.

**Folklore:** Traditions and myths preserved in a culture or group of people. Typically, these are passed on by word of mouth in various forms—such as legends, songs, and proverbs—or preserved in customs and ceremonies. Washington Irving, in "The Devil and Tom Walker" and many of his other stories, incorporates many elements of the folklore of New England and Germany.

**Folktale:** A story originating in oral tradition. Folktales fall into a variety of categories, including legends, ghost stories, fairy tales, fables, and anecdotes based on historical figures and events.

**Foreshadowing:** A device used in literature to create expectation or to set up an explanation of later developments. Edgar Allan Poe uses foreshadowing to create suspense in "The Fall of the House of Usher" when the narrator comments on the crumbling state of disrepair in which he finds the house.

# G

**Genre:** A category of literary work. Genre may refer to both the content of a given work—tragedy, comedy, horror, science fiction—and to its form, such as poetry, novel, or drama.

**Gilded Age:** A period in American history during the 1870s and after characterized by political corruption and materialism. A number of important novels of social and political criticism were written during this time. Henry James and Kate Chopin are two writers who were prominent during the Gilded Age.

**Gothicism:** In literature, works characterized by a taste for medieval or morbid characters and situations. A gothic novel prominently features elements of horror, the supernatural, gloom, and violence: clanking chains, terror, ghosts, medieval castles, and unexplained phenomena. The term "gothic novel" is also applied to novels that lack elements of the traditional Gothic setting but that create a similar atmosphere of terror or dread. The term can also be applied to stories, plays, and poems. Mary Shelley's *Frankenstein* and Joyce Carol Oates's *Bellefleur* are both gothic novels.

**Grotesque:** In literature, a work that is characterized by exaggeration, deformity, freakishness, and disorder. The grotesque often includes an element of comic absurdity. Examples of the grotesque can be found in the works of Edgar Allan Poe, Flannery O'Connor, Joseph Heller, and Shirley Jackson.

# H

**Harlem Renaissance:** The Harlem Renaissance of the 1920s is generally considered the first significant movement of black writers and artists in the United States. During this period, new and established black writers, many of whom lived in the region of New York City known as Harlem, published more fiction and poetry than ever before, the first influential black literary journals were established, and black authors and artists received their first widespread recognition and serious critical appraisal. Among the major writers associated with this period are Countee Cullen, Langston Hughes, Arna Bontemps, and Zora Neale Hurston.

**Hero/Heroine:** The principal sympathetic character in a literary work. Heroes and heroines typically exhibit admirable traits: idealism, courage, and integrity, for example. Famous heroes and heroines of literature include Charles Dickens's Oliver Twist, Margaret Mitchell's Scarlett O'Hara, and the anonymous narrator in Ralph Ellison's *Invisible Man*.

**Hyperbole:** Deliberate exaggeration used to achieve an effect. In William Shakespeare's *Macbeth*, Lady Macbeth hyperbolizes when she says, "All the perfumes of Arabia could not sweeten this little hand."

# I

**Image:** A concrete representation of an object or sensory experience. Typically, such a representation helps evoke the feelings associated with the object or experience itself. Images are either "literal" or "figurative." Literal images are especially concrete and involve little or no extension of the obvious meaning of the words used to express them. Figurative images do not follow the literal meaning of the words exactly. Images in literature are usually visual, but the term "image" can also refer to the representation of any sensory experience.

**Imagery:** The array of images in a literary work. Also used to convey the author's overall use of figurative language in a work.

***In medias res***: A Latin term meaning "in the middle of things." It refers to the technique of beginning a story at its midpoint and then using various flashback devices to reveal previous action. This technique originated in such epics as Virgil's *Aeneid*.

**Interior Monologue:** A narrative technique in which characters' thoughts are revealed in a way that appears to be uncontrolled by the author. The interior monologue typically aims to reveal the inner self of a character. It portrays emotional experiences as they occur at both a conscious and unconscious level. One of the best-known interior monologues in English is the Molly Bloom section at the close of James Joyce's *Ulysses*. Katherine Anne Porter's "The Jilting of Granny Weatherall" is also told in the form of an interior monologue.

**Irony:** In literary criticism, the effect of language in which the intended meaning is the opposite of what is stated. The title of Jonathan Swift's "A Modest Proposal" is ironic because what Swift proposes in this essay is cannibalism—hardly "modest."

# J

**Jargon:** Language that is used or understood only by a select group of people. Jargon may refer to terminology used in a certain profession, such as computer jargon, or it may refer to any nonsensical language that is not understood by most people. Anthony Burgess's *A Clockwork Orange* and James Thurber's "The Secret Life of Walter Mitty" both use jargon.

# K

**Knickerbocker Group:** An indistinct group of New York writers of the first half of the nineteenth century. Members of the group were linked only by location and a common theme: New York life. Two famous members of the Knickerbocker Group were Washington Irving and William Cullen Bryant. The group's name derives from Irving's *Knickerbocker's History of New York*.

# L

**Literal Language:** An author uses literal language when he or she writes without exaggerating or embellishing the subject matter and without any tools of figurative language. To say "He ran very quickly down the street" is to use literal language, whereas to say "He ran like a hare down the street" would be using figurative language.

**Literature:** Literature is broadly defined as any written or spoken material, but the term most often refers to creative works. Literature includes poetry, drama, fiction, and many kinds of nonfiction writing, as well as oral, dramatic, and broadcast compositions not necessarily preserved in a written format, such as films and television programs.

**Lost Generation:** A term first used by Gertrude Stein to describe the post-World War I generation of American writers: men and women haunted by a sense of betrayal and emptiness brought about by the destructiveness of the war. The term is commonly applied to Hart Crane, Ernest Hemingway, F. Scott Fitzgerald, and others.

# M

**Magic Realism:** A form of literature that incorporates fantasy elements or supernatural occurrences into the narrative and accepts them as truth. Gabriel Garcia Marquez and Laura Esquivel are two writers known for their works of magic realism.

**Metaphor:** A figure of speech that expresses an idea through the image of another object. Metaphors suggest the essence of the first object by identifying it with certain qualities of the second object. An example is "But soft, what light through yonder window breaks?/ It is the east, and Juliet is the sun" in William Shakespeare's *Romeo and Juliet*. Here, Juliet, the first object, is identified with qualities of the second object, the sun.

**Minimalism:** A literary style characterized by spare, simple prose with few elaborations. In minimalism, the main theme of the work is often never discussed directly. Amy Hempel and Ernest Hemingway are two writers known for their works of minimalism.

**Modernism:** Modern literary practices. Also, the principles of a literary school that lasted from roughly the beginning of the twentieth century until the end of World War II. Modernism is defined by its rejection of the literary conventions of the nineteenth century and by its opposition to conventional morality, taste, traditions, and economic values. Many writers are associated with the concepts of modernism, including Albert Camus, D. H. Lawrence, Ernest Hemingway, William Faulkner, Eugene O'Neill, and James Joyce.

**Monologue:** A composition, written or oral, by a single individual. More specifically, a speech given by a single individual in a drama or other public entertainment. It has no set length, although it is usually several or more lines long. "I Stand Here Ironing" by Tillie Olsen is an example of a story written in the form of a monologue.

**Mood:** The prevailing emotions of a work or of the author in his or her creation of the work. The mood of a work is not always what might be expected based on its subject matter.

**Motif:** A theme, character type, image, metaphor, or other verbal element that recurs throughout a single work of literature or occurs in a number of different works over a period of time. For example, the color white in Herman Melville's *Moby Dick* is a "specific" motif, while the trials of star-crossed lovers is a "conventional" motif from the literature of all periods.

# N

**Narration:** The telling of a series of events, real or invented. A narration may be either a simple narrative, in which the events are recounted chronologically, or a narrative with a plot, in which the account is given in a style reflecting the author's artistic concept of the story. Narration is sometimes used as a synonym for "storyline."

**Narrative:** A verse or prose accounting of an event or sequence of events, real or invented. The term is also used as an adjective in the sense "method of narration." For example, in literary criticism, the expression "narrative technique" usually refers to the way the author structures and presents his or her story. Different narrative forms include diaries, travelogues, novels, ballads, epics, short stories, and other fictional forms.

**Narrator:** The teller of a story. The narrator may be the author or a character in the story through whom the author speaks. Huckleberry Finn is the narrator of Mark Twain's *The Adventures of Huckleberry Finn*.

**Novella:** An Italian term meaning "story." This term has been especially used to describe fourteenth-century Italian tales, but it also refers to modern short novels. Modern novellas include Leo Tolstoy's *The Death of Ivan Ilych,* Fyodor Dostoyevsky's *Notes from the Underground,* and Joseph Conrad's *Heart of Darkness*.

# O

**Oedipus Complex:** A son's romantic obsession with his mother. The phrase is derived from the story of the ancient Theban hero Oedipus, who unknowingly killed his father and married his mother, and was popularized by Sigmund Freud's theory of psychoanalysis. Literary occurrences of the Oedipus complex include Sophocles' *Oedipus Rex* and D. H. Lawrence's "The Rocking-Horse Winner."

**Onomatopoeia:** The use of words whose sounds express or suggest their meaning. In its simplest sense, onomatopoeia may be represented by words that mimic the sounds they denote such as "hiss" or "meow." At a more subtle level, the pattern and rhythm of sounds and rhymes of a line or poem may be onomatopoeic.

**Oral Tradition:** A process by which songs, ballads, folklore, and other material are transmitted by word of mouth. The tradition of oral transmission predates the written record systems of literate society.

Oral transmission preserves material sometimes over generations, although often with variations. Memory plays a large part in the recitation and preservation of orally transmitted material. Native American myths and legends, and African folktales told by plantation slaves are examples of orally transmitted literature.

# P

**Parable:** A story intended to teach a moral lesson or answer an ethical question. Examples of parables are the stories told by Jesus Christ in the New Testament, notably "The Prodigal Son," but parables also are used in Sufism, rabbinic literature, Hasidism, and Zen Buddhism. Isaac Bashevis Singer's story "Gimpel the Fool" exhibits characteristics of a parable.

**Paradox:** A statement that appears illogical or contradictory at first, but may actually point to an underlying truth. A literary example of a paradox is George Orwell's statement "All animals are equal, but some animals are more equal than others" in *Animal Farm*.

**Parody:** In literature, this term refers to an imitation of a serious literary work or the signature style of a particular author in a ridiculous manner. A typical parody adopts the style of the original and applies it to an inappropriate subject for humorous effect. Parody is a form of satire and could be considered the literary equivalent of a caricature or cartoon. Henry Fielding's *Shamela* is a parody of Samuel Richardson's *Pamela*.

**Persona**: A Latin term meaning "mask." Personae are the characters in a fictional work of literature. The persona generally functions as a mask through which the author tells a story in a voice other than his or her own. A persona is usually either a character in a story who acts as a narrator or an "implied author," a voice created by the author to act as the narrator for himself or herself. The persona in Charlotte Perkins Gilman's story "The Yellow Wallpaper" is the unnamed young mother experiencing a mental breakdown.

**Personification:** A figure of speech that gives human qualities to abstract ideas, animals, and inanimate objects. To say that "the sun is smiling" is to personify the sun.

**Plot:** The pattern of events in a narrative or drama. In its simplest sense, the plot guides the author in composing the work and helps the reader follow the work. Typically, plots exhibit causality and unity and have a beginning, a middle, and an end. Sometimes, however, a plot may consist of a series of disconnected events, in which case it is known as an "episodic plot."

**Poetic Justice:** An outcome in a literary work, not necessarily a poem, in which the good are rewarded and the evil are punished, especially in ways that particularly fit their virtues or crimes. For example, a murderer may himself be murdered, or a thief will find himself penniless.

**Poetic License:** Distortions of fact and literary convention made by a writer—not always a poet—for the sake of the effect gained. Poetic license is closely related to the concept of "artistic freedom." An author exercises poetic license by saying that a pile of money "reaches as high as a mountain" when the pile is actually only a foot or two high.

**Point of View:** The narrative perspective from which a literary work is presented to the reader. There are four traditional points of view. The "third person omniscient" gives the reader a "godlike" perspective, unrestricted by time or place, from which to see actions and look into the minds of characters. This allows the author to comment openly on characters and events in the work. The "third person" point of view presents the events of the story from outside of any single character's perception, much like the omniscient point of view, but the reader must understand the action as it takes place and without any special insight into characters' minds or motivations. The "first person" or "personal" point of view relates events as they are perceived by a single character. The main character "tells" the story and may offer opinions about the action and characters which differ from those of the author. Much less common than omniscient, third person, and first person is the "second person" point of view, wherein the author tells the story as if it is happening to the reader. James Thurber employs the omniscient point of view in his short story "The Secret Life of Walter Mitty." Ernest Hemingway's "A Clean, Well-Lighted Place" is a short story told from the third person point of view. Mark Twain's novel *Huckleberry Finn* is presented from the first person viewpoint. Jay McInerney's *Bright Lights, Big City* is an example of a novel which uses the second person point of view.

**Pornography:** Writing intended to provoke feelings of lust in the reader. Such works are often condemned by critics and teachers, but those which can be shown to have literary value are viewed less harshly. Literary works that have been described as pornographic include D. H. Lawrence's *Lady Chatterley's Lover* and James Joyce's *Ulysses.*

**Post-Aesthetic Movement:** An artistic response made by African Americans to the black aesthetic movement of the 1960s and early 1970s. Writers since that time have adopted a somewhat different tone in their work, with less emphasis placed on the disparity between black and white in the United States. In the words of post-aesthetic authors such as Toni Morrison, John Edgar Wideman, and Kristin Hunter, African Americans are portrayed as looking inward for answers to their own questions, rather than always looking to the outside world. Two well-known examples of works produced as part of the post-aesthetic movement are the Pulitzer Prize-winning novels *The Color Purple* by Alice Walker and *Beloved* by Toni Morrison.

**Postmodernism:** Writing from the 1960s onward characterized by experimentation and application of modernist elements, which include existentialism and alienation. Postmodernists have gone a step further in the rejection of tradition begun with the modernists by also rejecting traditional forms, preferring the anti-novel over the novel and the anti-hero over the hero. Postmodern writers include Thomas Pynchon, Margaret Drabble, and Gabriel Garcia Marquez.

**Prologue:** An introductory section of a literary work. It often contains information establishing the situation of the characters or presents information about the setting, time period, or action. In drama, the prologue is spoken by a chorus or by one of the principal characters.

**Prose:** A literary medium that attempts to mirror the language of everyday speech. It is distinguished from poetry by its use of unmetered, unrhymed language consisting of logically related sentences. Prose is usually grouped into paragraphs that form a cohesive whole such as an essay or a novel. The term is sometimes used to mean an author's general writing.

**Protagonist:** The central character of a story who serves as a focus for its themes and incidents and as the principal rationale for its development. The protagonist is sometimes referred to in discussions of modern literature as the hero or anti-hero. Well-known protagonists are Hamlet in William Shakespeare's *Hamlet* and Jay Gatsby in F. Scott Fitzgerald's *The Great Gatsby.*

# R

**Realism:** A nineteenth-century European literary movement that sought to portray familiar characters, situations, and settings in a realistic manner. This was done primarily by using an objective narrative point of view and through the buildup of accurate detail. The standard for success of any realistic work depends on how faithfully it transfers common experience into fictional forms. The realistic method may be altered or extended, as in stream of consciousness writing, to record highly subjective experience. Contemporary authors who often write in a realistic way include Nadine Gordimer and Grace Paley.

**Resolution:** The portion of a story following the climax, in which the conflict is resolved. The resolution of Jane Austen's *Northanger Abbey* is neatly summed up in the following sentence: "Henry and Catherine were married, the bells rang and every body smiled."

**Rising Action:** The part of a drama where the plot becomes increasingly complicated. Rising action leads up to the climax, or turning point, of a drama. The final "chase scene" of an action film is generally the rising action which culminates in the film's climax.

***Roman a clef***: A French phrase meaning "novel with a key." It refers to a narrative in which real persons are portrayed under fictitious names. Jack Kerouac, for example, portrayed various his friends under fictitious names in the novel *On the Road.* D. H. Lawrence based "The Rocking-Horse Winner" on a family he knew.

**Romanticism:** This term has two widely accepted meanings. In historical criticism, it refers to a European intellectual and artistic movement of the late eighteenth and early nineteenth centuries that sought greater freedom of personal expression than that allowed by the strict rules of literary form and logic of the eighteenth-century neoclassicists. The Romantics preferred emotional and imaginative expression to rational analysis. They considered the individual to be at the center of all experience and so placed him or her at the center of their art. The Romantics believed that the creative imagination reveals nobler truths—unique feelings and attitudes—than those that could be discovered by logic or by scientific examination. "Romanticism" is also used as a general term to refer to a type of sensibility found in all periods of literary history and usually considered to be in opposition to the principles of classicism. In this sense, Romanticism signifies any work or philosophy in which the exotic or dreamlike figure strongly, or that is devoted to individualistic expression, self-analysis, or a pursuit of a higher realm of knowledge than can be discovered by human reason. Prominent Romantics include Jean-Jacques Rousseau, William Wordsworth, John Keats, Lord Byron, and Johann Wolfgang von Goethe.

# S

**Satire:** A work that uses ridicule, humor, and wit to criticize and provoke change in human nature and institutions. Voltaire's novella *Candide* and Jonathan Swift's essay "A Modest Proposal" are both satires. Flannery O'Connor's portrayal of the family in "A Good Man Is Hard to Find" is a satire of a modern, Southern, American family.

**Science Fiction:** A type of narrative based upon real or imagined scientific theories and technology. Science fiction is often peopled with alien creatures and set on other planets or in different dimensions. Popular writers of science fiction are Isaac Asimov, Karel Capek, Ray Bradbury, and Ursula K. Le Guin.

**Setting:** The time, place, and culture in which the action of a narrative takes place. The elements of setting may include geographic location, characters' physical and mental environments, prevailing cultural attitudes, or the historical time in which the action takes place.

**Short Story:** A fictional prose narrative shorter and more focused than a novella. The short story usually deals with a single episode and often a single character. The "tone," the author's attitude toward his or her subject and audience, is uniform throughout. The short story frequently also lacks *denouement*, ending instead at its climax.

**Signifying Monkey:** A popular trickster figure in black folklore, with hundreds of tales about this character documented since the 19th century. Henry Louis Gates Jr. examines the history of the signifying monkey in *The Signifying Monkey: Towards a Theory of Afro-American Literary Criticism,* published in 1988.

**Simile:** A comparison, usually using "like" or "as", of two essentially dissimilar things, as in "coffee as cold as ice" or "He sounded like a broken record." The title of Ernest Hemingway's "Hills Like White Elephants" contains a simile.

**Socialist Realism:** The Socialist Realism school of literary theory was proposed by Maxim Gorky and established as a dogma by the first Soviet Congress of Writers. It demanded adherence to a communist worldview in works of literature. Its doctrines required an objective viewpoint comprehensible to the working classes and themes of social struggle featuring strong proletarian heroes. Gabriel Garcia Marquez's stories exhibit some characteristics of Socialist Realism.

**Stereotype:** A stereotype was originally the name for a duplication made during the printing process; this led to its modern definition as a person or thing that is (or is assumed to be) the same as all others of its type. Common stereotypical characters include the absent-minded professor, the nagging wife, the troublemaking teenager, and the kindhearted grandmother.

**Stream of Consciousness:** A narrative technique for rendering the inward experience of a character. This technique is designed to give the impression of an ever-changing series of thoughts, emotions, images, and memories in the spontaneous and seemingly illogical order that they occur in life. The textbook example of stream of consciousness is the last section of James Joyce's *Ulysses.*

**Structure:** The form taken by a piece of literature. The structure may be made obvious for ease of understanding, as in nonfiction works, or may obscured for artistic purposes, as in some poetry or seemingly "unstructured" prose.

**Style:** A writer's distinctive manner of arranging words to suit his or her ideas and purpose in writing. The unique imprint of the author's personality upon his or her writing, style is the product of an author's way of arranging ideas and his or her use of diction, different sentence structures, rhythm, figures of speech, rhetorical principles, and other elements of composition.

**Suspense:** A literary device in which the author maintains the audience's attention through the build-up of events, the outcome of which will soon be revealed. Suspense in William Shakespeare's *Hamlet* is sustained throughout by the question of whether or not the Prince will achieve what he has been instructed to do and of what he intends to do.

**Symbol:** Something that suggests or stands for something else without losing its original identity. In literature, symbols combine their literal meaning with the suggestion of an abstract concept. Literary symbols are of two types: those that carry complex associations of meaning no matter what their contexts, and those that derive their suggestive meaning from their functions in specific literary works. Examples of symbols are sunshine suggesting happiness, rain suggesting sorrow, and storm clouds suggesting despair.

# T

**Tale:** A story told by a narrator with a simple plot and little character development. Tales are usually relatively short and often carry a simple message. Examples of tales can be found in the works of Saki, Anton Chekhov, Guy de Maupassant, and O. Henry.

**Tall Tale:** A humorous tale told in a straightforward, credible tone but relating absolutely impossible events or feats of the characters. Such tales were commonly told of frontier adventures during the settlement of the West in the United States. Literary use of tall tales can be found in Washington Irving's *History of New York,* Mark Twain's *Life on the Mississippi,* and in R. F. Raspe's *Baron Munchausen's Narratives of His Marvellous Travels and Campaigns in Russia.*

**Theme:** The main point of a work of literature. The term is used interchangeably with thesis. Many works have multiple themes. One of the themes of Nathaniel Hawthorne's "Young Goodman Brown" is loss of faith.

**Tone:** The author's attitude toward his or her audience may be deduced from the tone of the work. A formal tone may create distance or convey politeness, while an informal tone may encourage a friendly, intimate, or intrusive feeling in the reader. The author's attitude toward his or her subject matter may also be deduced from the tone of the words he or she uses in discussing it. The tone of John F. Kennedy's speech which included the appeal to "ask not what your country can do for you" was intended to instill feelings of camaraderie and national pride in listeners.

**Tragedy:** A drama in prose or poetry about a noble, courageous hero of excellent character who, because of some tragic character flaw, brings ruin upon him- or herself. Tragedy treats its subjects in a dignified and serious manner, using poetic language to help evoke pity and fear and bring about catharsis, a purging of these emotions. The tragic form was practiced extensively by the ancient Greeks. The classical form of tragedy was revived in the sixteenth century; it flourished especially on the Elizabethan stage. In modern times, dramatists have attempted to adapt the form to the needs of modern society by drawing their heroes from the ranks of ordinary men and women and defining the nobility of these heroes in terms of spirit rather than exalted social standing. Some contemporary works that are thought of as tragedies include *The Great Gatsby* by F. Scott Fitzgerald, and *The Sound and the Fury* by William Faulkner.

**Tragic Flaw:** In a tragedy, the quality within the hero or heroine which leads to his or her downfall. Examples of the tragic flaw include Othello's jealousy and Hamlet's indecisiveness, although most great tragedies defy such simple interpretation.

# U

**Utopia:** A fictional perfect place, such as "paradise" or "heaven." An early literary utopia was described in Plato's *Republic,* and in modern literature, Ursula K. Le Guin depicts a utopia in "The Ones Who Walk Away from Omelas."

# V

**Victorian:** Refers broadly to the reign of Queen Victoria of England (1837-1901) and to anything with qualities typical of that era. For example, the qualities of smug narrow-mindedness, bourgeois materialism, faith in social progress, and priggish morality are often considered Victorian. In literature, the Victorian Period was the great age of the English novel, and the latter part of the era saw the rise of movements such as decadence and symbolism.

# Cumulative Author/Title Index

## A
*Araby* (Joyce): V1

## B
Baldwin, James
    *Sonny's Blues:* V2
*The Bear* (Faulkner): V2
Bierce, Ambrose
    *An Occurrence at Owl Creek Bridge:* V2
Bradbury, Ray
    *There Will Come Soft Rains:* V1

## C
Capote, Truman
    *A Christmas Memory:* V2
Cather, Willa
    *Paul's Case:* V2
*The Celebrated Jumping Frog of Calaveras County* (Twain): V1
Cheever, John
    *The Swimmer:* V2
*Children of the Sea* (Danticat): V1
Chopin, Kate
    *The Story of an Hour:* V2
*A Christmas Memory* (Capote): V2
Connell, Richard
    *The Most Dangerous Game:* V1
Conrad, Joseph
    *The Secret Sharer:* V1

## D
Danticat, Edwidge
    *Children of the Sea:* V1
*The Devil and Tom Walker* (Irving): V1
Doyle, Arthur Conan
    *The Red-Headed League:* V2

## E
*The Eatonville Anthology* (Hurston): V1
Ellison, Ralph
    *King of the Bingo Game:* V1
*Everyday Use* (Walker): V2

## F
*The Fall of the House of Usher* (Poe): V2
Faulkner, William
    *The Bear:* V2

## G
*The Gift of the Magi* (Henry): V2
Gilman, Charlotte Perkins
    *The Yellow Wallpaper:* V1
*Gimpel the Fool* (Singer): V2
*A Good Man Is Hard to Find* (O'Connor): V2
Gordimer, Nadine
    *The Train from Rhodesia:* V2

## H
*The Handsomest Drowned Man in the World* (Marquez): V1
Hawthorne, Nathaniel
    *Young Goodman Brown:* V1
Hemingway, Ernest
    *The Short Happy Life of Francis Macomber:* V1
Hempel, Amy
    *In the Cemetery Where Al Jolson Is Buried:* V2
Henry, O.
    *The Gift of the Magi:* V2
Hurston, Zora Neale
    *The Eatonville Anthology:* V1

## I
*In the Cemetery Where Al Jolson Is Buried* (Hempel): V2
Irving, Washington
    *The Devil and Tom Walker:* V1
*I Stand Here Ironing* (Olsen): V1

## J
Jackson, Shirley
    *The Lottery:* V1
Jacobs, W. W.
    *The Monkey's Paw:* V2
*The Jilting of Granny Weatherall* (Porter): V1
Joyce, James
    *Araby:* V1

## K

*King of the Bingo Game* (Ellison): V1

## L

Lawrence, D. H.
  *The Rocking-Horse Winner:* V2
Le Guin, Ursula K.
  *The Ones Who Walk Away from Omelas:* V2
Lessing, Doris
  *Through the Tunnel:* V1
*The Lottery* (Jackson): V1

## M

Mansfield, Katherine
  *Miss Brill:* V2
Marquez, Gabriel Garcia
  *The Handsomest Drowned Man in the World:* V1
*Miss Brill* (Mansfield): V2
*The Monkey's Paw* (Jacobs): V2
*The Most Dangerous Game* (Connell): V1

## O

Oates, Joyce Carol
  *Where Are You Going, Where Have You Been?:* V1
*An Occurrence at Owl Creek Bridge* (Bierce): V2
O'Connor, Flannery
  *A Good Man Is Hard to Find:* V2
Olsen, Tillie
  *I Stand Here Ironing:* V1
*The Ones Who Walk Away from Omelas* (Le Guin): V2
*The Open Window* (Saki): V1

## P

*Paul's Case* (Cather): V2
Poe, Edgar Allan
  *The Fall of the House of Usher:* V2
Porter, Katherine Anne
  *The Jilting of Granny Weatherall:* V1

## R

*The Red-Headed League* (Doyle): V2
*The Rocking-Horse Winner* (Lawrence): V2

## S

Saki
  *The Open Window:* V1
*The Secret Life of Walter Mitty* (Thurber): V1
*The Secret Sharer* (Conrad): V1
*The Short, Happy Life of Francis Macomber* (Hemingway): V1
Singer, Isaac Bashevis
  *Gimpel the Fool:* V2
*Sonny's Blues* (Baldwin): V2
*The Story of an Hour* (Chopin): V2
*The Swimmer* (Cheever): V2

## T

*There Will Come Soft Rains* (Bradbury): V1
*Through the Tunnel* (Lessing): V1
Thurber, James
  *The Secret Life of Walter Mitty:* V1
*The Train from Rhodesia* (Gordimer): V2
Twain, Mark
  *The Celebrated Jumping Frog of Calaveras County:* V1

## W

*Where Are You Going, Where Have You Been?* (Oates): V1
*A Worn Path* (Welty): V2
Walker, Alice
  *Everyday Use:* V2
Welty, Eudora
  *A Worn Path:* V2

## Y

*The Yellow Wallpaper* (Gilman): V1
*Young Goodman Brown* (Hawthorne): V1

# Nationality/Ethnicity Index

## African American
Baldwin, James
   *Sonny's Blues:* V2
Ellison, Ralph
   *King of the Bingo Game:* V1
Hurston, Zora Neale
   *The Eatonville Anthology:* V1
Walker, Alice
   *Everyday Use:* V2

## American
Baldwin, James
   *Sonny's Blues:* V2
Bierce, Ambrose
   *An Occurrence at Owl Creek Bridge:* V2
Bradbury, Ray
   *There Will Come Soft Rains:* V1
Capote, Truman
   *A Christmas Memory:* V2
Cather, Willa
   *Paul's Case:* V2
Cheever, John
   *The Swimmer:* V2
Chopin, Kate
   *The Story of an Hour:* V2
Connell, Richard
   *The Most Dangerous Game:* V1
Ellison, Ralph
   *King of the Bingo Game:* V1
Faulkner, William
   *The Bear:* V2
Gilman, Charlotte Perkins
   *The Yellow Wallpaper:* V1
Hawthorne, Nathaniel
   *Young Goodman Brown:* V1
Hemingway, Ernest
   *The Short Happy Life of Francis Macomber:* V1
Hempel, Amy
   *In the Cemetery Where Al Jolson Is Buried:* V2
Henry, O.
   *The Gift of the Magi:* V2
Hurston, Zora Neale
   *The Eatonville Anthology:* V1
Irving, Washington
   *The Devil and Tom Walker:* V1
Jackson, Shirley
   *The Lottery:* V1
Le Guin, Ursula K.
   *The Ones Who Walk Away from Omelas:* V2
Oates, Joyce Carol
   *Where Are You Going, Where Have You Been?:* V1
O'Connor, Flannery
   *A Good Man Is Hard to Find:* V2
Olsen, Tillie
   *I Stand Here Ironing:* V1
Poe, Edgar Allan
   *The Fall of the House of Usher:* V2
Porter, Katherine Anne
   *The Jilting of Granny Weatherall:* V1
Singer, Isaac Bashevis
   *Gimpel the Fool:* V2
Thurber, James
   *The Secret Life of Walter Mitty:* V1
Twain, Mark
   *The Celebrated Jumping Frog of Calaveras County:* V1
Walker, Alice
   *Everyday Use:* V2
Welty, Eudora
   *A Worn Path:* V2

## British
Conrad, Joseph
   *The Secret Sharer:* V1
Jacobs, W. W.
   *The Monkey's Paw:* V2
Lawrence, D. H.
   *The Rocking-Horse Winner:* V2
Lessing, Doris
   *Through the Tunnel:* V1
Saki
   *The Open Window:* V1

## Colombian
Marquez, Gabriel Garcia
   *The Handsomest Drowned Man in the World:* V1

## Haitian
Danticat, Edwidge
   *Children of the Sea:* V1

## Irish
Joyce, James
   *Araby:* V1

### New Zealander
Mansfield, Katherine
*Miss Brill:* V2

### Polish
Conrad, Joseph
*The Secret Sharer:* V1
Singer, Isaac Bashevis
*Gimpel the Fool:* V2

### Scottish
Doyle, Arthur Conan
*The Red-Headed League:* V2

### South African
Gordimer, Nadine
*The Train from Rhodesia:* V2

# Subject/Theme Index

*Boldface terms appear as subheads in Themes section.

## A

Abandonment
   *The Story of an Hour:* 264-265
**Acceptance and Belonging**
   *Gimpel the Fool:* 86
Adulthood
   *A Christmas Memory:* 20, 24-26
Adventure and Exploration
   *An Occurrence at Owl Creek Bridge:* 166-169
   *A Worn Path:* 322-324
**Affluence**
   *The Swimmer:* 281
Africa
   *The Train from Rhodesia:* 295-296, 299, 301-307
Alcoholism, Drugs, and Drug Addiction
   *The Ones Who Walk Away from Omelas:* 180
   *Sonny's Blues:* 246-247, 250-251, 260-261
   *The Swimmer:* 288
**Alienation**
   *Paul's Case:* 197
**Alienation and Loneliness**
   *Miss Brill:* 135-138, 145
   *The Swimmer:* 282
Allegory
   *Gimpel the Fool:* 83, 87
   *The Ones Who Walk Away from Omelas:* 174, 177, 179, 187, 190
   *The Swimmer:* 281-282
**American Dream**
   *Paul's Case:* 196
American Northeast
   *Paul's Case:* 192, 194, 196-200
   *Sonny's Blues:* 251-252
American South
   *The Bear:* 1, 3, 7, 9-11
   *A Christmas Memory:* 21
   *A Good Man Is Hard to Find:* 98-99, 102-105
   *An Occurrence at Owl Creek Bridge:* 165-166
   *Sonny's Blues:* 253
   *A Worn Path:* 312-313, 317-318
American Southwest
   *In the Cemetery Where Al Jolson Is Buried:* 116, 119-121, 124, 131
Apartheid
   *The Train from Rhodesia:* 295, 298-301
Apathy
   *A Good Man Is Hard to Find:* 103-105
**Appearance and Reality**
   *Miss Brill:* 135
   *The Red-Headed League:* 215
   *The Swimmer:* 281
**Art and Expression**
   *Sonny's Blues:* 249
Atonement
   *The Bear:* 14-15
   *The Ones Who Walk Away from Omelas:* 190-191
   *Sonny's Blues:* 258

## B

**Beauty**
   *Paul's Case:* 192, 195-197, 200
Bildungsroman
   *A Christmas Memory:* 25-27
Black Arts Movement
   *Everyday Use:* 36-37, 42-43

## C

Capitalism
   *The Ones Who Walk Away from Omelas:* 190-191
Catharsis
   *Sonny's Blues:* 250
Charity
   *A Worn Path:* 322-324
Childhood
   *A Christmas Memory:* 20, 24-25
**Choices and Consequences**
   *Paul's Case:* 196
Christianity
   *Everyday Use:* 43-45
   *A Worn Path:* 324
City Life
   *The Gift of the Magi:* 79-80
Classicism
   *Paul's Case:* 206-208
**Coming of Age**
   *A Christmas Memory:* 25

# Subject/Theme Index

**Community vs. Isolation**
  *Everyday Use:* 40
**Conscience**
  *The Train from Rhodesia:* 299
Crime and Criminals
  *A Good Man Is Hard to Find:* 103-105
  *Paul's Case:* 195-198, 204-206
  *The Red-Headed League:* 211-218, 222-224, 227-229
Cruelty
  *A Good Man Is Hard to Find:* 97, 102, 105-106

## D

Death
  *The Bear:* 3, 6-8, 13, 16-18
  *The Fall of the House of Usher:* 54-57, 63-66
  *A Good Man Is Hard to Find:* 98, 102-104
  *In the Cemetery Where Al Jolson Is Buried:* 115-128
  *The Monkey's Paw:* 147-148, 151-154
  *An Occurrence at Owl Creek Bridge:* 162-166, 169-171
  *The Story of an Hour:* 264-266, 274-276
  *A Worn Path:* 325
**Death and Dying**
  *An Occurrence at Owl Creek Bridge:* 163
Deceit
  *The Swimmer:* 278, 281-282
**Deception**
  *An Occurrence at Owl Creek Bridge:* 163
  *Paul's Case:* 196
Depression and Melancholy
  *The Fall of the House of Usher:* 53-55
  *Sonny's Blues:* 257-258
Detective Fiction
  *The Red-Headed League:* 210, 214, 216-217, 227-229
Drama
  *The Monkey's Paw:* 154
  *Paul's Case:* 194, 196-198, 204-205
**Dreams and Reality**
  *An Occurrence at Owl Creek Bridge:* 163
Dreams and Visions
  *The Fall of the House of Usher:* 65-66
  *Gimpel the Fool:* 95-96
  *An Occurrence at Owl Creek Bridge:* 171
  *The Swimmer:* 278, 283, 285, 289-291

**Duty and Responsibility**
  *A Worn Path:* 316
Duty and Responsibility
  *The Ones Who Walk Away from Omelas:* 185-187

## E

Europe
  *Gimpel the Fool:* 87-89
  *Miss Brill:* 133, 136-137
  *The Monkey's Paw:* 153-154
  *The Red-Headed League:* 216-222, 227
  *The Rocking-Horse Winner:* 230-231, 236
  *Sonny's Blues:* 246
Evil
  *The Fall of the House of Usher:* 54-55
Evil
  *The Bear:* 6, 11, 15
  *A Good Man Is Hard to Find:* 102, 104-105, 111-113
  *The Ones Who Walk Away from Omelas:* 178, 184, 188-189
  *The Red-Headed League:* 215, 217

## F

**Faith**
  *Gimpel the Fool:* 86
Farm and Rural Life
  *A Christmas Memory:* 21-22, 26
  *Everyday Use:* 36, 40-43
**Fate and Chance**
  *The Monkey's Paw:* 147, 150, 154-155, 158
Fate and Chance
  *The Rocking-Horse Winner:* 231, 234-235
Fear and Terror
  *The Fall of the House of Usher:* 51, 53, 55-58, 64, 66
  *In the Cemetery Where Al Jolson Is Buried:* 116-119, 125-126
  *The Monkey's Paw:* 157-158
**Fear of Death**
  *In the Cemetery Where Al Jolson Is Buried:* 118
Film
  *A Christmas Memory:* 20, 22, 26, 28
Folklore
  *The Rocking-Horse Winner:* 243
  *The Swimmer:* 282
**Friendship**
  *A Christmas Memory:* 24
  *In the Cemetery Where Al Jolson Is Buried:* 118

## G

**Generosity**
  *The Gift of the Magi:* 70
**Generosity and Greed**
  *The Rocking-Horse Winner:* 234
Ghost
  *Gimpel the Fool:* 95-96
  *A Worn Path:* 324
God
  *Gimpel the Fool:* 90-92
  *A Good Man Is Hard to Find:* 102, 105
  *The Ones Who Walk Away from Omelas:* 183
**God and Religion**
  *A Good Man Is Hard to Find:* 102
Gothicism
  *The Fall of the House of Usher:* 51, 56, 66
Great Depression
  *A Christmas Memory:* 26, 28
**Greed**
  *The Red-Headed League:* 214
  *The Train from Rhodesia:* 298-299
Greed
  *The Monkey's Paw:* 154-155
  *The Rocking-Horse Winner:* 234, 236
Grief and Sorrow
  *The Bear:* 15-16
  *In the Cemetery Where Al Jolson Is Buried:* 118-120
  *The Story of an Hour:* 275
Grotesque
  *A Good Man Is Hard to Find:* 105-106
**Guilt**
  *A Worn Path:* 316-317
Guilt
  *The Ones Who Walk Away from Omelas:* 176, 178-179, 183-185
  *Sonny's Blues:* 257, 259
**Guilt and Innocence**
  *The Ones Who Walk Away from Omelas:* 178

## H

**Happiness**
  *The Ones Who Walk Away from Omelas:* 178
Happiness and Gaiety
  *The Ones Who Walk Away from Omelas:* 174-180, 183-190
  *The Story of an Hour:* 265-266, 276-278
  *The Swimmer:* 283-284
Hatred
  *The Bear:* 3, 8

**Heritage**
*Everyday Use:* 39
Heritage and Ancestry
*Everyday Use:* 36-45
Heroism
*Miss Brill:* 134-136
*The Monkey's Paw:* 155
*The Rocking-Horse Winner:* 239-240
*The Swimmer:* 278, 283, 285-286
History
*The Bear:* 1, 3, 6
*Everyday Use:* 37-38
*A Worn Path:* 319
**Honor and Integrity**
*Gimpel the Fool:* 87
**Human Condition**
*The Monkey's Paw:* 150
Humor
*A Christmas Memory:* 31-32
*The Gift of the Magi:* 71, 73
*Gimpel the Fool:* 91
*A Good Man Is Hard to Find:* 97-98, 104-106
*In the Cemetery Where Al Jolson Is Buried:* 116, 118-121, 125-126

## I

**Identity and Selfhood**
*The Story of an Hour:* 265
Imagery and Symbolism
*The Bear:* 3, 7, 17-18
*Everyday Use:* 41
*The Fall of the House of Usher:* 51, 56, 58, 66
*In the Cemetery Where Al Jolson Is Buried:* 115, 119
*Miss Brill:* 141
*The Monkey's Paw:* 147, 152, 154-156
*Paul's Case:* 206
*The Red-Headed League:* 223, 225-226
*Sonny's Blues:* 256-259
*The Swimmer:* 293
*The Train from Rhodesia:* 298-301
Imagination
*Everyday Use:* 48-49
*Miss Brill:* 143
*An Occurrence at Owl Creek Bridge:* 168-170
Impatience
*The Fall of the House of Usher:* 53, 55
Insanity
*The Fall of the House of Usher:* 51, 54-56, 61-63
Irony
*The Bear:* 15
*Gimpel the Fool:* 87, 90, 92-93
*A Good Man Is Hard to Find:* 104
*In the Cemetery Where Al Jolson Is Buried:* 129
*An Occurrence at Owl Creek Bridge:* 171-172
*Paul's Case:* 204-205
*The Story of an Hour:* 268, 272-273
*The Swimmer:* 283, 285
*A Worn Path:* 323-324
Islamism
*Everyday Use:* 41

## J

Judaism
*Gimpel the Fool:* 83, 87-92, 96

## K

Killers and Killing
*The Bear:* 2-3, 7, 15-16
*A Good Man Is Hard to Find:* 103, 105
Knowledge
*The Red-Headed League:* 214, 229
**Knowledge and Ignorance**
*Gimpel the Fool:* 86
*The Red-Headed League:* 214

## L

Landscape
*The Bear:* 1-3, 7-11, 15-19
*An Occurrence at Owl Creek Bridge:* 162, 164-165
*A Worn Path:* 312-313, 318, 323-324
**Language and Meaning**
*In the Cemetery Where Al Jolson Is Buried:* 118
Law and Order
*The Ones Who Walk Away from Omelas:* 175-176, 180-181
*The Red-Headed League:* 212, 214-215, 218-220, 224, 226-229
*The Train from Rhodesia:* 298, 300-301
**Life Cycle**
*The Swimmer:* 282
**Limitations and Opportunities**
*Paul's Case:* 197
Literary Criticism
*Gimpel the Fool:* 91
Loneliness
*A Christmas Memory:* 20, 27
*Miss Brill:* 135-136, 143-145
*The Train from Rhodesia:* 311
Love
*The Gift of the Magi:* 70
Love and Passion
*The Bear:* 15-16
*The Gift of the Magi:* 70-71
*Gimpel the Fool:* 91
*A Good Man Is Hard to Find:* 102, 104
*Miss Brill:* 141, 143-145
*The Rocking-Horse Winner:* 239-242
*The Swimmer:* 289-291
*The Train from Rhodesia:* 304-305

## M

**Madness and Insanity**
*The Fall of the House of Usher:* 55
Magic
*The Fall of the House of Usher:* 64-65
*The Monkey's Paw:* 147-148, 151, 155-158
Marriage
*Gimpel the Fool:* 90, 92
*The Rocking-Horse Winner:* 239-240
*The Story of an Hour:* 263, 265-271
**Materialism**
*Everyday Use:* 39
**Memory and Reminiscence**
*A Christmas Memory:* 20, 22, 24-26
Mental Instability
*The Fall of the House of Usher:* 59, 62
Middle East
*The Monkey's Paw:* 146-147, 153-154
Modernism
*The Bear:* 8, 10
*Sonny's Blues:* 250
Money and Economics
*The Bear:* 3, 8-10
*A Christmas Memory:* 22, 24, 26, 28
*The Gift of the Magi:* 68, 72
*The Ones Who Walk Away from Omelas:* 179-181
*Paul's Case:* 194, 196-199, 204-206
*The Red-Headed League:* 212, 214-218
*The Rocking-Horse Winner:* 231, 234-237
*The Swimmer:* 280, 284-285
*The Train from Rhodesia:* 298, 300, 305-306

# Subject/Theme Index

**Morals and Morality**
  *The Ones Who Walk Away from Omelas:* 177
Morals and Morality
  *The Bear:* 1, 10, 16
  *The Fall of the House of Usher:* 51
  *A Good Man Is Hard to Find:* 103-105
  *The Ones Who Walk Away from Omelas:* 174-175, 178, 180-183, 187-191
  *The Red-Headed League:* 214, 216, 218, 229
  *Sonny's Blues:* 256
Murder
  *A Good Man Is Hard to Find:* 97, 99, 101-103
Music
  *Everyday Use:* 49
  *The Fall of the House of Usher:* 53, 55-56
  *Miss Brill:* 142
  *Paul's Case:* 193, 197-199, 204-205
  *Sonny's Blues:* 246-262
Mystery and Intrigue
  *The Red-Headed League:* 210, 212, 215-216, 220, 229
Myths and Legends
  *The Bear:* 6, 8-9
  *The Fall of the House of Usher:* 62-65
  *Paul's Case:* 202-205
  *The Rocking-Horse Winner:* 243
  *The Swimmer:* 278-279, 284-288, 293-294
  *A Worn Path:* 313-327

## N

Nation of Islam
  *Everyday Use:* 41-42
Nature
  *The Bear:* 3, 6-7, 13-14, 18
  *A Christmas Memory:* 24-25
  *The Fall of the House of Usher:* 53-54, 64
  *An Occurrence at Owl Creek Bridge:* 160, 164
  *Paul's Case:* 204-205
  *The Train from Rhodesia:* 300, 305
  *A Worn Path:* 317, 323-324
Nightmare
  *The Fall of the House of Usher:* 65-66
  *The Swimmer:* 290
1950s
  *A Good Man Is Hard to Find:* 104-106
  *Sonny's Blues:* 251-253
  *The Train from Rhodesia:* 301-302
1970s
  *Everyday Use:* 41-43
1960s
  *The Ones Who Walk Away from Omelas:* 180
1930s
  *A Christmas Memory:* 21, 26, 28
1920s
  *Miss Brill:* 137-138

## O

**Oedipus Complex**
  *The Rocking-Horse Winner:* 235
Old Age
  *A Christmas Memory:* 21-22, 27-30
  *The Train from Rhodesia:* 298-300
  *A Worn Path:* 315-316
**Order and Disorder**
  *The Red-Headed League:* 215

## P

Painting
  *The Fall of the House of Usher:* 53, 55-56, 65-66
Permanence
  *A Worn Path:* 320-321
Persecution
  *Gimpel the Fool:* 94-95
Perseverance
  *A Worn Path:* 320-321
Personal Identity
  *Sonny's Blues:* 253-254
  *The Story of an Hour:* 265, 268
Philosophical Ideas
  *The Ones Who Walk Away from Omelas:* 177
Plants
  *Paul's Case:* 194, 197-199
Poetry
  *The Fall of the House of Usher:* 53, 57-58
Politics
  *An Occurrence at Owl Creek Bridge:* 161, 165-166
  *The Train from Rhodesia:* 300-302
Postmodernism
  *In the Cemetery Where Al Jolson Is Buried:* 124-126
Poverty
  *The Train from Rhodesia:* 295-296, 299-300
**Prejudice vs. Tolerance**
  *A Good Man Is Hard to Find:* 101
Pride
  *The Bear:* 14-16
Psychology and the Human Mind
  *The Fall of the House of Usher:* 51, 55, 57-58, 66
  *Paul's Case:* 204
  *The Story of an Hour:* 267

## R

Race
  *The Bear:* 6, 8-9, 19
  *Everyday Use:* 36, 39-43
  *A Good Man Is Hard to Find:* 104-105
  *The Monkey's Paw:* 150-153
  *Sonny's Blues:* 245, 249, 251-255
  *The Train from Rhodesia:* 295, 298-301, 304-307
  *A Worn Path:* 313, 315-318, 321, 327
**Race and Racism**
  *Sonny's Blues:* 249
  *The Train from Rhodesia:* 298
  *A Worn Path:* 315
**Race and Slavery**
  *The Bear:* 6
Racism and Prejudice
  *The Train from Rhodesia:* 295, 300-301
Religion and Religious Thought
  *Everyday Use:* 41
  *Gimpel the Fool:* 91-92
  *A Good Man Is Hard to Find:* 103, 105-111
  *The Ones Who Walk Away from Omelas:* 190-191
  *Sonny's Blues:* 259
  *A Worn Path:* 321, 323
**Responsibility**
  *The Rocking-Horse Winner:* 234
**Resurrection**
  *A Worn Path:* 316
Revenge
  *Gimpel the Fool:* 86-87
**Rites of Passage**
  *The Bear:* 6
**Role of Women in Marriage**
  *The Story of an Hour:* 265
Roman Catholicism
  *A Good Man Is Hard to Find:* 97, 105-106

## S

Satire
  *A Good Man Is Hard to Find:* 111, 113
  *An Occurrence at Owl Creek Bridge:* 164

# Subject/Theme Index

*The Rocking-Horse Winner:* 237, 239
Science and Technology
  *Paul's Case:* 201
  *The Red-Headed League:* 218-221
Self-realization
  *Sonny's Blues:* 253-255
Sex and Sexuality
  *The Rocking-Horse Winner:* 238
Sickness
  *In the Cemetery Where Al Jolson Is Buried:* 118-119
Sin
  *The Bear:* 10-11, 19
  *The Monkey's Paw:* 156
  *The Ones Who Walk Away from Omelas:* 189
  *The Red-Headed League:* 218
  *Sonny's Blues:* 256, 258-259
Slavery
  *The Bear:* 3, 6-14
Social Order
  *The Red-Headed League:* 210, 219, 229
Solitude
  *Miss Brill:* 141-145
  *The Train from Rhodesia:* 309
Spiritual Leaders
  *Gimpel the Fool:* 84-86
Spirituality
  *Gimpel the Fool:* 83-84, 87-88, 91-92
  *A Good Man Is Hard to Find:* 108
  *The Ones Who Walk Away from Omelas:* 189-191
Sports and the Sporting Life
  *The Bear:* 1-3, 7-16

Storms and Weather Conditions
  *The Swimmer:* 279-280, 285
Stream of Consciousness
  *Miss Brill:* 132, 135-137
Suburban Life
  *The Swimmer:* 278-279, 283-285
**Suffering**
  *Sonny's Blues:* 248
Suicide
  *Paul's Case:* 194, 196-197
Supernatural
  *The Fall of the House of Usher:* 51, 55-56, 63-64

# T

**Time**
  *An Occurrence at Owl Creek Bridge:* 162
Time and Change
  *The Fall of the House of Usher:* 51, 55-57
Tragedy
  *The Monkey's Paw:* 154-155
Tragic Flaw
  *The Monkey's Paw:* 155
Trust
  *The Ones Who Walk Away from Omelas:* 182-183

# U

Understanding
  *Gimpel the Fool:* 90
  *Sonny's Blues:* 256-259

Upper Class
  *The Red-Headed League:* 217-218
Utopianism
  *The Ones Who Walk Away from Omelas:* 174, 176-179, 186-188, 191

# V

**Victims and Victimization**
  *The Ones Who Walk Away from Omelas:* 178
**Violence and Cruelty**
  *A Good Man Is Hard to Find:* 102

# W

War, the Military, and Soldier Life
  *The Monkey's Paw:* 155-156
  *An Occurrence at Owl Creek Bridge:* 161-166, 169, 171-172
Wealth
  *The Gift of the Magi:* 70-72
  *Paul's Case:* 197-200
  *The Swimmer:* 281, 283-285
**Wealth and Poverty**
  *The Gift of the Magi:* 71
  *The Train from Rhodesia:* 298
Wildlife
  *The Bear:* 2-3, 7-11, 18-19
  *A Worn Path:* 316-318
Wisdom
  *The Gift of the Magi:* 67-71
  *Gimpel the Fool:* 90-93

HERNANDO COUNTY
PUBLIC LIBRARY SYSTEM

MAR 2000

238 HOWELL AVENUE
BROOKSVILLE FL 34601

DISCARD